# GERMAN RESISTANCE
# AGAINST HITLER

# GERMAN RESISTANCE AGAINST HITLER

## The Search for Allies Abroad, 1938–1945

KLEMENS VON KLEMPERER

CLARENDON PRESS · OXFORD
1992

Oxford University Press, Walton Street, Oxford OX2 6DP
Oxford New York Toronto
Delhi Bombay Calcutta Madras Karachi
Petaling Jaya Singapore Hong Kong Tokyo
Nairobi Dar es Salaam Cape Town
Melbourne Auckland
and associated companies in
Berlin Ibadan

Oxford is a trade mark of Oxford University Press

Published in the United States
by Oxford University Press, New York

British Library Cataloguing in Publication Data

Data available

Library of Congress Cataloging in Publication Data

Von Klemperer, Klemens, 1916–
German resistance against Hitler: the search for allies abroad,
1938–1945/Klemens von Klemperer.
p.    cm.
Includes bibliographical references and index.
1. Anti-Nazi movement—Germany. 2. Germany—Foreign
relations—1933–1945. 3. World War, 1939–1945—Diplomatic history.
I. Title.
DD256.3.V673  1992     943.086—dc20     91–34961
ISBN 0–19–821940–7

Typeset by Butler & Tanner Ltd, Frome and London
Printed and bound in
Great Britain by Bookcraft Ltd,
Midsomer Norton, Bath

TO THE MEMORY OF

GEORGE BELL

*Bishop of Chichester*

and

WILLEM A. VISSER'T HOOFT

*General Secretary of the World
Council of Churches in Process of Formation*

# PREFACE

EVERYTHING I have written in the past has been dictated by more than purely antiquarian curiosity. In each case the choice of my subject was guided by a personal concern and involvement in the problem I took up. This is especially the case with this book. All along my preoccupation in my writing has been with the crisis era, the 1920s to the 1940s, and with the crisis zone of Europe, Central Europe, and especially with the darkest chapter of German history—the Nazi period. Over the past two decades I have been ever more drawn to those who took it upon themselves to keep burning the flame of human decency and freedom. I have always been aware of the duty to face this task responsibly and to keep my own concerns in check by a dispassionate, critical approach to my topic.

By now a large literature has sprung up concerning the German Resistance. I must single out first of all Peter Hoffmann's magisterial work and also the encyclopaedic volume edited by Jürgen Schmädeke and Peter Steinbach covering the transactions in Berlin of July 1984 of the International Conference on the *Widerstand*. Concerning my specific topic, the foreign relations of the German Resistance, a great deal of work has also been done which has found its way into a number of monographs and biographies as well as chapters of books and articles. But there has been no comprehensive work covering the whole subject. I have set out to perform this task in this book.

It has taken me a long time to finish this manuscript, not only because I write slowly, but also because I found that the canvas before me was enormous and that the surreptitious diplomacy which the conspirators against Hitler were forced to pursue had many facets. Because of my personal involvement in my chosen topic I had always to remind myself that my first duty was not to prejudge the case, and not to let my passions run away with me, but to follow the wisdom of the Masters of history: to put the full evidence before the readers[1] *sine ira et studio* and to tell the story 'wie es eigentlich gewesen'. In this way the readers may then be able to judge for themselves just as I, for myself, am in the end at liberty to draw my own conclusions. Only in this way could I hope to do justice to the subject for which I care so much.

Virtually each chapter or sub-chapter of this book deserves a monograph of its own. In so far as such treatises exist, I have fallen back on them. Thus I have greatly benefited from the work of those who have laboured before

---

[1] I hope, however, to be forgiven for having omitted some distinctly marginal foreign connections of the German Resistance.

me in my vineyard, and I have given due credit to their work wherever called for.[2]

While working on this book over the years, my commitment to it has never faltered, not even for a moment. My encounter with the way of life and death of men such as Dietrich Bonhoeffer, Carl Goerdeler, Hans-Bernd von Haeften, Helmuth James von Moltke, Adam von Trott zu Solz, and, last but not least, Claus Schenk Graf von Stauffenberg has been a constant encouragement to me and has sustained my sense of duty to see my task through to the end. It was my privilege to meet some of the few survivors of the *Widerstand*, namely Axel von dem Bussche, Hasso von Etzdorf, Eugen Gerstenmaier, Otto John, Richard Löwenthal, Josef Müller, Marie-Luise Sarre, Fabian von Schlabrendorff, and Eduard Waetjen. I owe a great debt, moreover, to the families and friends of the resisters who have given me the benefit of their memories and often of their hospitality, and who put their documents at my disposal. Invariably they have respected the fact that the historian's perspective is not always identical with that of the kin or friend. This volume relies heavily on their assistance and advice, and I feel honour bound to mention in this connection David Astor, Eberhard and Renate Bethge, Christabel Bielenberg, Alexander Böker, Barbara von Haeften, Alfred von Hofacker, David and Diana Hopkinson, Inga Kempe, Karl-Albrecht von Kessel, Lore Kordt, Sabine Leibholz-Bonhoeffer, Gerhard Leibholz, Marianne Meyer-Krahmer, Freya von Moltke, Mariane von Nostitz, Achim Oster, Shiela Sokolov Grant, Clarita von Trott zu Solz, Ingrid Warburg-Spinelli, and Hans Wilbrandt.

Moreover, I should like to acknowledge with gratitude the assistance I have obtained from the staffs of the archives and libraries listed in the Bibliography, which I have been able to consult, and I should also mention the people who have given me help with their advice or with documents: Sidney Aster, Mary Bancroft, Philip F. T. Bankwitz, Richard Breitman, Michael Dawson, Michael Ermarth, A. E. Fontenay, Leonidas E. Hill, Sir Francis Harry Hinsley, Peter Hoffmann, Walter A. Jackson, Hans-Adolf Jacobsen, George O. Kent, Michael Krüger-Charlé, Richard Lamb, Hsi-Huey Liang, Peter Ludlow, Nancy Lukens, Henry O. Malone, Claire Nix, Ger van Roon, Beate Ruhm von Oppen, Bradley F. Smith, Margiana Stinnes, Jochanan Wijnhoven, Igor Zelljadt, Ruth Zerner.

My extensive archival trips have been generously supported by The American Philosophical Society and the American Council of Learned Societies. I have also had the privilege of being a fellow at Churchill College (Cambridge), Trinity College (Oxford), and the Wissenschaftskolleg zu Berlin. These insti-

---

[2] I am thinking in particular of the contributions to my subject by Michael Balfour, Harold C. Deutsch, Ingeborg Fleischhauer, Hermann Graml, Klaus Hildebrand, Walter Lipgens, Peter W. Ludlow, Henry O. Malone, Christian Müller, Klaus-Jürgen Müller, Gerhard Ritter, Hans Rothfels, Ger van Roon, and Graf von Thun-Hohenstein.

tutions have been a great source of encouragement and inspiration to me.

If my English style is in any way up to what it should be, I owe it to Allison Lockwood who has gone over every single page I have written. Finally, I owe a debt to Bill Fivel and Laurie Looney for saving me from the worst hazards of the computer age, and to John G. Graiff, interlibrary loan samaritan.

This book, then, is a co-operative effort in what I believe to be an important cause. I alone, however, am responsible for any judgements expressed and for any error in the text that the readers might detect.

As the readers make their way through this volume, they will understand why it is dedicated to the memory of Bishop George Bell of Chichester and Willem A. Visser't Hooft.

K.v.K.

# CONTENTS

# LIST OF ILLUSTRATIONS

*Between pp. 240–241*

1. Overseas patrons of the Widerstand: (a) Willem A. Visser't Hooft, General Secretary of the World Council of Churches in Process of Formation. (b) George Kennedy Allen Bell, Bishop of Chichester.

2. The horizon of European diplomacy: (a) Theo Kordt, German Chargé in London and Prime Minister Neville Chamberlain in London, 1938. (b) Sir Robert Vansittart, Chief Diplomatic Adviser to the Foreign Secretary.

3. The Men of the Widerstand (I): (a) Colonel General Ludwig Beck. (b) Carl Goerdeler. (c) Ulrich von Hassell. (d) Major General Hans Oster.

4. The Men of the Widerstand (II): (a) Helmuth James von Moltke. (b) Adam von Trott zu Solz. (c) Dietrich Bonhoeffer. (d) Albrecht Haushofer.

5. The Men of the Widerstand (III): (a) Josef Müller. (b) Otto John. (c) Claus Schenk, Count von Stauffenberg. (d) Julius Leber.

6. Intelligence chiefs: (a) 'C', Major General Sir Stewart Menzies, Chief of the British Secret Intelligence Service (MI6). (b) Major General William J. Donovan, Director of the OSS. (c) Admiral Wilhelm Canaris, Chief of the Abwehr. (d) Allen W. Dulles, Chief of the OSS in Berne, and his assistant Gero von Schulze Gaevernitz.

7. From the Nazi People's Court: (a) Roland Freisler, President of the People's Court. (b) Carl Goerdeler facing the People's Court.

8. Documents: (a) Telegram from Carl Goerdeler to the British Foreign Office, 30 August 1939. (b) Farewell letter from Adam von Trott (pseudonym F. Adams) to Dr. Harry Johansson of the Nordic Ecumenical Institute in Sigtuna, Sweden, 26 September 1942.

# ABBREVIATIONS

| | |
|---|---|
| AA/PA | Auswärtiges Amt, Politisches Archiv |
| ADAP | Akten zur deutschen auswärtigen Politik |
| BA/K | Bundesarchiv/Koblenz |
| BA/M | Bundesarchiv/Militärarchiv, Freiburg i. Br. |
| BDO | Bund Deutscher Offiziere (League of German Officers) |
| Bonhoeffer, *GS* | Dietrich Bonhoeffer, *Gesammelte Schriften*, vols. i (*Ökumene, Briefe, Aufsätze, Dokumente 1928–1942*), ii (*Kirchenkampf und Finkenwalde. Resolutionen, Aufsätze, Rundbriefe 1933–1943*), vi (*Tagebücher, Briefe, Dokumente 1923–1945*), ed. Eberhard Bethge (Munich, 1965, 1965, 1974) |
| CAB | (PRO) Cabinet Papers |
| CHRS | Christie Papers, Churchill College, Cambridge |
| *DBFP* | *Documents on British Foreign Policy 1919–1939*, 2nd ser., vol. xvii; 3rd ser., vols. i, ii, v–vii (London, 1979, 1949, 1949, 1952, 1953) |
| Deutsch, *The Conspiracy* | Harold C. Deutsch, *The Conspiracy against Hitler in the Twilight War* (Minneapolis, 1968) |
| *DGFP* | *Documents on German Foreign Policy 1918–1945*, ser. D, vols. ii, vi, vii, xi (Washington, DC, 1949, 1956, 1956, 1964) |
| DNVP | Deutschnationale Volkspartei (German National People's Party) |
| FBI | Federal Bureau of Investigation |
| FDR Library | Franklin Delano Roosevelt Library, Hyde Park, NY |
| FO | Foreign Office: (PRO) Foreign Office Papers |
| *FRUS* | *Foreign Relations of the United States: Diplomatic Papers*, 1939, vol. i; 1940, vol. i; 1944, vol. i, The Conferences at Cairo and Tehran 1943 (Washington, DC, 1956, 1959, 1966, 1961) |
| *Die Hassell-Tagebücher* | Ulrich von Hassell, *Die Hassell-Tagebücher 1938–1944, Aufzeichnungen vom anderen Deutschland*, ed. Friedrich Freiherr von Gaertringen (Berlin, 1988) |
| Hoffmann, *History* | Peter Hoffmann, *The History of the German Resistance 1933–1945* (Cambridge, Mass., 1979) |
| IfZ | Institut für Zeitgeschichte, Munich |
| JIC | Joint Intelligence Subcommittee of Chiefs of Staff |
| von Kessel 'Verborgene Saat' | Albrecht von Kessel, 'Verborgene Saat. Das "Andere" Deutschland', bound typescript No. 40. Written in Rome late 1944 to early 1945 |
| MI6 | Military Intelligence Department, UK (also SIS) |

| | |
|---|---|
| von Moltke, *Briefe an Freya* | Helmuth James von Moltke, *Briefe an Freya 1939–1945*, ed. Beate Ruhm von Oppen (Munich, 1988) |
| NA | National Archives, Washington, DC |
| NKFD | Nationalkomitee 'Freies Deutschland' (National Committee for a Free Germany) |
| OKH | Oberkommando des Heeres (Supreme Command of the Army) |
| OKW | Oberkommando der Wehrmacht (Supreme Command of the Armed Forces) |
| OSS | Office of Strategic Services |
| PREM | (PRO) Papers of the Prime Minister's Office |
| PRO | Public Record Office |
| PWE | Political Warfare Executive |
| Ritter, *Carl Goerdeler* | Gerhard Ritter, *Carl Goerdeler und die deutsche Widerstandsbewegung* (Stuttgart, 1955) |
| van Roon, *Neuordnung* | *Neuordnung im Widerstand. Der Kreisauer Kreis innerhalb der deutschen Widerstandsbewegung* (Munich, 1967) |
| RSHA | Reichssicherheitshauptamt (Chief Reich Security Office) |
| SD | Sicherheitsdienst (Security Service) |
| SIS | Secret Intelligence Service |
| SOE | Special Operations Executive |
| SS | Schutzstaffel (Hitler's Élite Guard) |
| Clarita von Trott, 'Adam von Trott' | Clarita von Trott zu Solz, 'Adam von Trott zu Solz. Eine erste Materialsammlung. Sichtung und Zusammenstellung', bound typescript (Reinbek near Hamburg, 1957, 1958) |
| *VfZ* | *Vierteljahrshefte für Zeitgeschichte* |
| WCC (ipof) | World Council of Churches (in Process of Formation) |
| *Die Weizsäcker-Papiere* | *Die Weizsäcker-Papiere 1933–1950*, ed. Leonidas E. Hill (Frankfurt/M., 1974) |
| WM | (PRO) War Cabinet Conclusions |
| WO | (PRO) War Office document |
| WP | (PRO) War Cabinet Memorandum |

# Introduction

I N the course of the decades since the Second World War, historians have been sorting out the various factors which contributed to the defeat of Hitler's Germany: statesmanship, strategic planning, military operations, intelligence work, and superior economic and industrial strength of the Allies together with Hitler's miscalculations—and, last but not least, internal resistance within Germany itself to Nazism. This book will deal with the German *Widerstand*, that is the German Resistance against Hitler and its role in the struggle against Nazi tyranny and world dominion. It should be anticipated here and now, however, that the mystique of the European Resistance movements, for which the French word *Résistance* has become the general designation, as having been widely engaged in a common fight to free their countries from occupation and to reinstate some form of national integrity and human rights, has been somewhat scaled down since the end of the war. Resistance everywhere came late; it was a matter of the few rather than the many. Alas, even the gulf between resistance and collaboration was not as wide as the stereotypes prevalent immediately after the war would have us believe. Furthermore the prevailing opinion among historians now is that the impact of the European Resistance movements upon winning the war was actually minute. The case of the Russians and the Yugoslav Partisans serves as the exception which proves the rule. General de Gaulle was perhaps quoted correctly as having said, in an uncharacteristic moment of candour and self-humour: 'Resistance was a bluff that came off.'[1] What matters, of course, is that in the wake of the massive effort of the Allied armies it did come off. And even if the *Résistance* was not effective strategically, if its impact was 'puny', as has been exaggeratedly claimed,[2] it gave back pride to the people, and hope to all men threatened by total dominion.

If the impact of the *Résistance* upon the war effort was limited, what then can be said of the *Widerstand* in this respect? To begin with, the German Resistance must be assessed, as it has by its leading chronicler, to have been a 'failure' and 'tragic'.[3] As a matter of fact, the designation *Widerstand* was not even current among those who resisted Hitler.[4] One of the interviews I have conducted with the few survivors was with one of the most fearless members of the conspiracy to free Germany from the tyrant. She said to me insistently: 'Don't talk about "*Widerstand*". We did not think of ourselves as being part of a *Widerstand*. We merely thought somehow to survive in dignity.'[5] Just as there was no common nomenclature, there was no common resistance movement in Germany, unlike in most other countries under the Fascist yoke. No popular movement backed the German Resistance. The grip on Germany of the Nazi dictatorship certainly had a decisive bearing upon the formation of resistance. It is worth recalling the often overlooked fact that dictatorship in Germany was, as Richard Löwenthal put it, 'native';[6] it came closer than elsewhere to the model of total control: control through mass manipulation backed up by terror. The consensual quality of Nazi control is one of its most vexing paradoxes. It made oppression all the more humiliating and rendered the task of resisting all the more difficult. In Germany, resistance had to be staged without the 'social support'[7] which was available, at least latently, to the Resistance in other countries.

Since there was, and could be, no popular resistance movement, German resistance was thus all the more many-faceted and fragmented. Under the prevailing circumstances in Germany, the spectrum of attitudes, refusals, and deeds that could qualify as dissent was indeed all the wider.[8] Even the failure or refusal to give the Nazi salute in public signified an act of defiance. Joining the army could serve the function of seeking immunity from Party control, though of course it constituted a much less drastic act than did conscientious objection, which meant the risk of death.[9] Labour slow-downs and sabotage also had their place in the whole scheme of things as did the betrayal of state secrets. Elaborate memoranda and plans for a regenerated Germany were to serve the same purpose as assassination attempts, and solitary actions coincided with conspiracy. And what started as 'social refusal'[10] on the part of individuals, interest groups, and institutions, in defence of their integrity, as it was encroached upon by the oppressor, culminated eventually in political and principled resistance.[11]

In the German case in particular, it follows that much of the burden to identify what was resistance falls upon the historian. He must pull together all the different manifestations of resistance, passive and active, direct and indirect, inside Germany as well as among those Germans in exile. There has hitherto been a tendency among historians to focus all too readily on the centres of resistance which promised an effective overthrow of the Nazi regime and particularly on the pre-history of the 20 July 1944 attempt at assassination of Hitler which, however unsuccessful, constituted historically the most visible expression of German resistance.[12] Certainly the workers' resistance, long neglected in the literature, deserves the kind of close scrutiny which it has been getting in recent years. The two major groups of the German Left, after all, the Communists and the Social Democrats, however hostile to each other, were the first to feel the full impact of Nazi terror; and even though they were effectively neutralized in the first years of the Third Reich, they were able eventually to reorganize under the direction of their respective exiled leaders. While the workers' resistance at no time constituted a real threat to the Nazi regime, it nevertheless served to hold together the stalwarts and enabled them to resume underground activity of a more restricted kind. Actually the best prepared for illegality were the smaller groups to the Left of the Social Democrats, such as the ISK (Internationaler Sozialistischer Kampfbund) and Neu Beginnen, both of which had formed during the Weimar days in efforts to revitalize the Party. Their dilemma, however, was that their conspiratorial effectiveness depended upon their forgoing an expansion of their organizations.[13]

Considering the oppression prevailing in Nazi Germany, many opponents of the regime had to opt for exile, and in exile they continued their political activities. Political exile became a way of fighting against Hitler's Germany from without and of supporting the efforts in Germany to undermine Nazi rule. It was Otto Wels, the one-time head of the Social Democratic Party, who, from his Parisian exile, emphasized that he kept his 'face towards Germany'.[14] In this respect also, the historian of the Resistance in Germany is faced by the challenge of where to set the limits to the task. He need not go all the way and equate 'resistance in illegality' with 'resistance in exile'.[15] Resistance is, after all, resistance; and exile is exile. Their identity of aim should not blind us to the differences between the two in the experience, the means of operation, and the hardships and hazards involved. But while they do not really constitute a unit, they certainly are closely interconnected, and a history of the German Resistance can no longer be written without close attention to the workings of those who went into exile.

Nevertheless, there is no way of getting around the fact that in the 'vast gaol',[16] as a Socialist member of the Resistance, Wilhelm Leuschner, described Nazi Germany, the only potentially effective resistance could be resistance from within the system. It is for this reason that the traditional establishments—the Churches, the public service, and the army—emerged as the most promising nuclei of opposition. This meant that much of the resistance was, and, in fact, had to be, 'resistance without the "people"', as Hans Mommsen put it.[17] In Germany in particular, then, the convergence of resistance and compliance was almost imperative. In many instances continued service to the Nazi state seemed justified by the calculation that it might be effective in causing obstruction and averting the worst excesses of the regime. In many cases, staying in office served as a necessary cover for conspiracy. Most of those who resisted did so, indeed had to do so, from within the old establishments and thus had to take upon themselves the burden of a split existence which is the law of conspiracy. But, alas, by virtue of their tradition, these very groups were little predisposed to rebellion against state and authority. They had in the past displayed a marked indifference if not hostility to the Weimar Republic and towards democracy in general. All too long they had been satisfied with fending off the new regime's intrusions into their own respective spheres rather than facing up to the comprehensive threat of Nazism to the nation as a whole. The Churches might have become the wardens of the Christian conscience in the fight against persecution, arbitrariness, and brutality. The public service, resorting to 'opposition in service',[18] could have served as an effective cover for conspiracy. Likewise the army, once removed from Party control, could have become an effective instrument of insurrection in the hands of anti-Nazi commanders. However, none of these groups went into resistance *en bloc*, and each, as might have been expected of almost any collective under those circumstances, had its share of the courageous, the cunning, the cowardly, and also, alas, of the dedicated party-liners.

In any case, resistance, as we have learned from the experience of the Second World War, is primarily a matter of individuals and not groups. 'Character, not ... class origin,' observed M. R. D. Foot quite correctly, 'made people into resisters,'[19] and he might have added 'not political, social, or religious grouping'. Hitherto in the histories of the Resistance, German and non-German, too much deference has been paid to the 'representational theory of resistance'[20] which insists upon correlating resistance with specific groups. This certainly cannot tell the whole story. In the German case, the groups in question tended not to go much beyond the point of 'social refusal' inasmuch as they primarily sought to fend off intrusion into their respective realms. But genuine resistance is above all a matter of personal decision to stand fast and to fight evil, a matter of 'self-discovery' and 'self-renewal', as Richard Cobb has rightly put it.[21] Eventually many individuals did reconnect with new–old groupings like that of the Communists, rejuvenated after their initial virtual destruction, or the various left-wing splinter groups. Others were brought together in new formations in the form of improvised circles of like-minded people or friends such as the group around General Ludwig Beck and Carl Goerdeler; the group in the Armed Forces Intelligence (OKW/Amt Ausland/Abwehr); the so-called *Freundeskreis* in the Foreign Office (Auswärtiges Amt); the Kreisau Circle around Helmuth James von Moltke; and youth groups such as the 'Edelweiss-Pirates' and the 'White Rose' conspiracy centred in Munich.

In Germany, therefore, unlike in occupied countries, the formation of a unified resistance movement never came about; the burden of resistance fell primarily on individuals relying on their own consciences and on small, informal groups. The isolation of the Germans was urgently conveyed by Helmuth von Moltke in a letter of March 1943, which he sent via a Swedish ecumenical connection to his old friend Lionel Curtis in England. 'People outside Germany do not realize the following handicaps under which we labour and which distinguish the position in Germany from that of any other of the occupied countries: lack of unity, lack of men, lack of communications'. He added: 'In the other countries suppressed by Hitler's tyranny even the ordinary criminal has a chance of being classified as martyr. With us it is different: even the martyr is certain to be classed as an ordinary criminal

...'.[22] Nevertheless, the Resistance kept planning, scheming, and conspiring. Indeed it proceeded from plot to plot—haltingly at first, headlong towards the end—and culminated in Colonel Claus Schenk Graf von Stauffenberg's valiant but unsuccessful attempt on Hitler's life on 20 July 1944, after which the Concentration Camp Universe celebrated its last macabre triumphs only to be cut short by the occupation of the Reich by the conquering Allied armies.

As for the impact of the *Widerstand* upon the conduct of Allied diplomacy and the war, it must be stated at the outset that it was for all practical purposes minimal in spite of unceasing efforts on the part of the Germans to establish ties with the 'other side'. Actually, throughout the whole period of Nazi domination, especially from 1938 to 1945, a stream of emissaries kept going abroad, to London especially and also to Washington, and after the outbreak of war, to neutral capitals and the capitals of occupied countries. They went in order to explore reactions to Nazi policies, to inform, to warn of impending war, to press for definition of peace terms, to negotiate with the 'enemy' on conditions for facilitating a coup and on territorial terms to be offered to a post-Nazi Germany, to help prisoners of war as well as deportees and Jews, to establish ties with Resistance movements abroad, and last but not least to say to the world: 'we are here'.

If official German agencies like the Auswärtiges Amt and the Abwehr were involved in this traffic, it was for the purpose of placing their men abroad or providing for others the proper pretext and the necessary papers to leave the country. As for the rest, the 'strange field of unofficial oppositional diplomacy', as David Astor has fittingly called it,[23] was left to 'oppositional' German individuals or groups attempting to reach the Powers directly before the war began, and then across the battle lines, to enlist foreign offices, political friends abroad, journalists, businessmen, the Churches and churchmen, indeed secret services and not infrequently busybodies in order to put their message over. They did not enjoy the benefit of official legitimization and the protection of being accredited. Their 'diplomacy' was altogether surreptitious, hazardous, and prone to be misunderstood and distrusted even by those whom it was designed to reach.

The reasons for the failure of communication between the German resisters and the Allies are complex. In any case, an American professional in foreign affairs, no less a personage than George Kennan, reminds us that any attempt by one nation at direct talking to another about the latter's political affairs is 'a questionable procedure, replete with possibilities for misunderstanding and resentment'.[24] Was it not understandable that the German overtures should have been dismissed as nuisances and embarrassments that might interfere in the business of the Foreign Office professionals and detract first from their efforts to maintain a workable relation with the German government and thereafter from the pursuit of the war? Indeed, why should these overtures not have been distrusted, in particular when coming from those who had stayed in office? 'Are the stories which reach us of dissident groups in Germany genuine,' asked a typical British Foreign Office document, 'or inspired by the German Secret Service?'[25] The truth of the matter is that in many instances they were both, since the German (Armed Forces) Secret Service (the Abwehr) was deeply involved in the conspiracy against Hitler. Indeed Colonel Hans Oster of the Abwehr, having kept the Dutch Military Attaché abreast of the dates of the German offensive in the west, was promptly dismissed by Holland's Commander-in-Chief, General Winkelmann, as a 'miserable fellow' ('erbärmlicher Kerl').[26] Like his confrères in the Resistance, Oster served, indeed had to serve, a regime which they disclaimed to a point of committing treason; they conspired with the potential and actual enemy in order to secure peace. In turn those to whom they reached out were not disposed to trust them.

There is no doubt but that, on balance, the foreign ventures of the German Resistance added up to a failure. To start with, Great Britain, the primary target of the German opposition before the war, had other concerns than just Germany, especially with regard to her imperial interests in the Far East and in the Mediterranean.[27] She therefore could not afford to pay attention to the German problem to the exclusion of these others. With the outbreak of war, moreover, the commitment to France was a further deterrent for Britain against closer involvement with Germans of any kind. And certainly after the Twilight War the fury of the war itself assumed its relentless momentum. The policy of 'absolute silence' towards all overtures from the other side, as adopted by His Majesty's Government in January 1941, the entry of the United States into the war in December 1941, the Grand Alliance with Russia and in turn Franklin Delano Roosevelt's Casablanca formula of 'unconditional surrender' in January 1943, together pushed the war to its final denouement, leaving the German emissaries and their plans by the wayside.

A perceptive, but I daresay sometimes wrong-headed, friend of mine recently said to me that I was working on a 'non-problem'. The rudimentary argumentation which I have presented thus far seems to support this discouraging verdict. Indeed, the literature on the subject overwhelmingly reflects this condition. It has been given either to perplexity and lamentation over the marginality of the German overtures to the calculations of the Allies and to the outcome of the war, or to the all too ready dismissal of them as irrelevant. Criticism of the Allies for their rebuff of the German Resistance, as voiced primarily by the older generation of West German historians,[28] gave way to the harsh scrutiny of the *Widerstand*, still predominant at present among the younger West German historians, for its failure to co-ordinate its approaches to the outside world and also for its nationalistic war-aims policy which seems to have coincided with that of the Nazis whom it supposedly sought to displace.[29] Furthermore, some of the more recent studies, in an attempt to correlate the efforts of the German Resistance with the grid system of high diplomacy and strategy, have emerged with the verdict that the *Widerstand* in no way came to terms with the 'foreign political realities' of the times and that its alternatives were altogether 'unrealistic'.[30] Thus they have thought to close the books on any further discussion of the foreign relations of the German Resistance.[31]

This book, then, is the story of a failure. But need it be stressed that failure, just as much as success and triumph, is part of the tapestry of history? Success in itself is not the outcome of manifest destiny. Those forces that did not prevail, and which some historians would argue thus did not become 'real', are part of history none the less. Even if only by virtue of a Hegelian 'cunning of reason', they too have had their impact upon history. They belong to a vast reserve army of historical alternatives which has played its part in the drama of history and which, if neglected by the historian, would deprive his discipline of its wealth and its human quality. Indeed, given a different turn of events, this reserve army might have been activated and thus have come closer to overt 'victory'.

These general considerations, then, lead me to reopen the case of the German Resistance. Indeed a second look at its plight, and in particular at its foreign relations, moves the German Resistance from a somewhat marginal position right into the centre of the European experience of the era since the First World War. That war witnessed the culmination of the nation state with its almost absolute claims to the allegiance of its citizens and, at the same time, the loosening of that hold by broader currents activated by the American entry into the war and by the Russian Revolution. Both Bolshevism and Wilsonianism were bearers of a universal message that transcended national loyalties. In fact both stood oddly at the crossing point between the nation and a new universalism. They appeared early in 1918 as the proponents of the 'New Diplomacy' that promised to transcend national antagonisms and thus to launch a new deal to peoples as against governments. Both Woodrow Wilson and Lenin preached self-determination and, at the same time, by means of their divergent messianic visions, an overcoming of the nation-state concept. Fascism and National Socialism, both derivative from the war, betrayed a similar ambiguity inasmuch as they both represented extreme manifestations of modern nationalism and ideological positions which cut across lines of nationality and competed with liberal democracy and Communism for the minds of all Europeans. Thus it appeared, at least during the first half of our century, as though Europe was experiencing a 'crisis of the nation state' and as though the old Continent had entered a 'century of ideologies'.[32]

In this setting the German *Widerstand* occupied a particular place. The

Resistance movements in France, Holland, and Norway were directed against occupation and oppression by a foreign power. Their struggle for liberation was a clear and unequivocal assertion of national interests as well as of human rights. But the German Resistance against Hitler was clearly out of step with the national effort, indeed with the waging of the war, and was subversive, at least of what appeared as the national interest. For the success of the plot might have meant defeat for the fatherland.

The German Resistance, then, was involved in a situation virtually paradigmatic of the era following the First World War. It was singularly entangled in a conflict of loyalties which reflected the ambiguities of what Margret Boveri has called the 'landscape of treason' of the 1930s and 1940s, when national loyalties were challenged by broader loyalties and alignments in which conventional meanings of loyalty and treason burst.[33] If the German Resistance broke the code of loyalty, it was in terms of a literal reading of it which demanded unquestioning, slavish obedience to authority; and if it came close to the realm of treason it was, again, in terms of the most literal understanding of treason.[34] Before staging the coup of 20 July 1944, Stauffenberg said explicitly: 'It is time now that something was done. But he who has the courage to do something must do so in the knowledge that he will go down in German history as a traitor ... '.[35] Treason was justified, he believed, in an extreme situation in which the state had turned into a tyranny, when, as Friedrich Schiller's Stauffacher said, 'justice is denied to the oppressed, when the burden becomes insupportable'. It was at this point that resistance was freed from the stigma of illegality, as was treason from the stigma of disloyalty, and that resistance could lay claim to supra-legality and the act of treason to supra-loyalty.

Their ventures abroad, it must be noted, led the German Resistance into the most exposed position in the conflict of loyalties. In criticism of the German resisters who so insistently sought contacts abroad, it has been argued that 'successful revolutions are not, as a matter of historical observation, preceded by an elaborate search for foreign support'.[36] The issue of support, however, was not actually a primary one. At no point was there any hope of obtaining material help of the sort which the Allied intelligence agencies, the British SOE and the American OSS, extended to the *Résistance*. The main item on the agenda of the Germans in this respect was, as already mentioned, to negotiate conditions for facilitating a coup and territorial terms to be offered to a post-Nazi Germany. It must be understood first and foremost that it was precisely the extreme situation in which the *Widerstand* found itself, deriving from the conflict of loyalties, which made it turn abroad. Unlike the *Widerstand*, the European Resistance movements had their governments-in-exile as legitimate intermediaries and also the direct support of the Allied intelligence services. And even though relations between them were not always easy, they were all acknowledged to be serving the interests of the peoples under foreign occupation. It might thus be said that the *Résistance* needed no foreign policy. The *Widerstand*, by contrast, in its particular predicament of witnessing its own nation degraded at home, and having to turn against its own government, had reason to detect in the war the dimension of a 'world civil war'[37] in which it could make common cause and discuss 'common plans'[38] with the powers fighting its own country. The same thought was also poignantly expressed in a statement by a Socialist exile: 'The front goes through all nations.'[39] It was this perspective on the war which impelled the 'other Germany' to seek the 'connection with the greater world'[40] and thus to attest to the 'solidarity', as Adam von Trott expressed it, 'in thoughts and in deeds'.[41] It was the German Resistance alone, therefore, which needed to resort to what we might call resistance foreign policy. Following the tradition of the 'New Diplomacy' of the earlier part of the century, it thus opened up a new chapter in the history of foreign relations.

Resistance foreign policy, then, is the effort of a disaffected resistance group, bypassing official channels, to establish contact with the outside world, often a foreign government, with the objective of dialogue and co-operation based upon common principles and interests. Clearly the groups and individuals who worked out of Germany itself were the main agents of this effort. Their first purpose was to correlate their foreign ventures with the domestic effort and to make them serve the strategy of conspiracy and insurrection. They belonged largely to the 'conservative' *Widerstand*, that is, to the Resistance which emanated from the opposition groups close to the centres of power. It is for this reason that the focus in this book is primarily on the conservative resistance—on resistance groups within the army, the Foreign Office and the Churches, on circles such as the Kreisau Circle and on individuals such as Carl Goerdeler, Ulrich von Hassell, Helmuth von Moltke, Adam von Trott, and Dietrich Bonhoeffer.[42] But the activities of exile groups, of individual exiles, or of the Social Democrats and the Communists abroad cannot be ignored. In many instances exiles linked up with emissaries of the *Widerstand.* As for the Socialists and the Communists, there may be an irony connected with the fact that these two international groups were less prepared than was the conservative sector to launch a resistance foreign policy. The Social Democratic Party in exile (Sopade) was able to maintain only the most tenuous contact with its fellow SPD members in Germany. Much of the Communist activity abroad was also essentially exile-based and in turn steered by Moscow. Nevertheless the left Resistance, like the conservative one, was part of the 'landscape of treason'. The effort of the Socialist exiles in London to obtain recognition from the British government as the voice of the 'other Germany' placed them in the very state of tension between national and supra-national loyalties that was characteristic of that 'landscape'. The Communists, the 'Red Orchestra' (*Rote Kapelle*), as the Communist intelligence organization in Germany was dubbed by the Gestapo, we must acknowledge,

was more than a mere espionage ring. In the summer of 1943, after the battle
of Stalingrad, when the Russians launched first the 'National Committee for
a Free Germany', and then the 'League of German Officers' (designed to
enlist officers and soldiers of the defeated German Sixth Army), Soviet Russia,
by its seeming deference to German national pride and interests, appeared
to take the lead in speaking to and encouraging the forces of resistance in
Germany. Also, the smaller German socialist groups in between the Social
Democrats and the Communists must be kept in view. Neu Beginnen
especially actively established connections abroad which somewhere along
the road linked up with Adam von Trott on his American journey in the
winter of 1939/40. While, then, the focus of this study must remain necessarily
narrow and specific, its canvas is by necessity broad, even vast.

The evidence before us is clearly more than episodic. The foreign relations
of the German Resistance constitute an intricate network of efforts attesting
to the determination of the German opponents of Hitler to break out of the
grip of the Leviathan. Their efforts will be recorded and evaluated in the
following chapters. Granted, there were differences in motivation, emphasis
and outlook. What are we to make of them? Most of the men of the
older generation, and especially those who belonged to the so-called Beck–
Goerdeler–von Hassell group, were beyond doubt deeply committed to the
Prussian ethos as well as the German imperial tradition and were tied to
German hegemonial thinking. Yet even in their case we might anticipate that
the Nazi dictatorship and resistance against it elicited in them, as seen
especially in Carl Goerdeler, an educational experience that led to a broader
European outlook. Also it should be said here and now that the members of
the younger generation, such as Trott and Moltke, had freed themselves of
the traditional assumptions of the older group and envisioned a European
federalism amounting to an altogether new beginning. But whatever the basic
positions were in the wide spectrum of the *Widerstand* concerning a post-
Hitlerian order, we can assume that all were at one in their attempt to
burst the narrow confines of obedience, statism, and nationalism. All sought
alternatives to Nazi dominion by addressing themselves to the conscience of
the world. All, in fact, contributed to bring about a new balance in their
country's troubled history between *Weltbürgertum* and *Nationalstaat*.

Just as the foreign ventures of the *Widerstand* should not be dismissed as
mere episodes, so should the war in its origins and course not be seen as a
*marche générale* that of necessity had to bypass the Germans of the Resistance. The 'what if' question, that is, what if the Allies had been more
responsive to the German opposition initiatives, is no less justified than any
question dealing with reasonable political alternatives; it is of the essence of
the historical-political argument. The peace plans emanating from the
German Resistance before the outbreak of the war were by no means designed
in a vacuum. The formula 'peace without appeasement', which came from

the *Widerstand*, can be considered to have constituted a reasonable political alternative to the course which events actually took and must therefore be considered a legitimate field of investigation. There is no doubt about the willingness on the part of both the British and the German Resistance to come to terms during the period of the Twilight War. The question to be answered is, why did these negotiations fail? And why, then, did the messages and messengers keep coming? If anything, the plotters redoubled their efforts. Were they foolhardy and quixotic? Had not the Allies decided that the war was to be fought, come what may, 'to the bitter end'?[43] Nevertheless, the historian might be able to register that, even though shunned and ignored, the Germans after all scored in some notable ways.

Inasmuch as some of the continuing traffic was routed through the intelligence community, especially that of the Americans, the question is in order whether this was done on the Allied side for the mere purpose of obtaining information from the Germans or whether there was beyond that a disposition to give a hearing to the German argument. In any case, what started as a curious shadow-boxing across the frontiers before and during the war, ended up as a dialogue in the deepest sense of the word, the ecumenical dialogue of men like Trott, Moltke, and Bonhoeffer with leaders of the Ecumenical Movement abroad, in Switzerland and Sweden and even in Britain and the USA. George Bell, Bishop of Chichester, became in the course of the war one of the most vociferous advocates of the German Resistance.[44] He went on record loudly and persistently that the war was essentially 'a war between rival philosophies of life' and ideological in nature.[45] Much to the discomfort of many in the House of Lords Bell insisted that the 'other Germany' existed and urged that it be engaged in the struggle against the 'common enemy'.[46] Like his fellow ecumenists, Bell was clearly a churchman without much political weight. The British Foreign Office dismissed him patronizingly as 'our good German bishop' and Anthony Eden impatiently chided him as 'this pestilent priest'.[47] Nevertheless, even though the ecumenical connection was wholly out of step with the immediate imperatives of the Grand Alliance, it suggests that at the time there were thoughtful spiritual leaders outside Germany who did not dismiss the German emissaries as suspect meddlers and crypto-Nazis, but who indeed recognized them as suppliants and valiant combatants for a cause that, transcending national interest and even politics itself, involved human rights[48] and bordered on the religious realm. The ecumenical argument thus brought out clearly the features of the 'landscape of treason'.

It was, in fact, Willem A. Visser't Hooft, the Dutch General Secretary of the provisional World Council of Churches, a man who from his strategic position in Geneva had ties with the Resistance all over Europe, who remarked that 'imaginative statesmanship'[49] could have found a way of encouraging the German Opposition without giving up the principles underlying the Allied policy. What if the outlines of the Allied war and peace aims could at least have been defined or if the distinction between Germans and Nazis could have been consistently adhered to in public statements on the Allied side? What if some encouragement had been spelled out to the Germans in case of a successful uprising? What if some tangible liaison had been established and maintained by the Allies with the socialist exiles in London? What if some informal contact in a neutral country with a representative of the *Widerstand*, as repeatedly suggested by the Germans, had been established? Could the Americans and the British, taking a leaf from the Soviets, not then have pursued a two-tier foreign policy—official and unofficial, formal and informal—which would have benefited them and the *Widerstand* short of affecting the alliance with Russia? It is now, of course, sheer speculation as to whether a more flexible statesmanship would have furthered the uprising in Germany and thus made an earlier end to the war, prevented the Russian penetration into East Central Europe, and thus have resulted in a very different Europe. Such, however, were certainly the conjectures of the German emissaries and also of their friends abroad.

But, notwithstanding the obvious failure of communications between the Allies and the German opposition, we ought to go further afield and examine the contacts between *Widerstand* and *Résistance*, and especially their more conservative groups. The rejection of the German Resistance was not an isolated phenomenon; it was paralleled by the rift which developed in the later phases of the war, in particular after the Tehran Conference of November 1943, between the Allied governments and the *Résistance*. At this point in the policies of the Allied governments, annexation took precedence over European order; and this new policy left the *Résistance* out in the cold. Scanty as the contacts were between *Widerstand* and *Résistance*, they nevertheless yielded a convergence of ideas and a rudimentary co-ordination of efforts, to the extent that we can talk of a legacy of the European Resistance which, though it did not find realization in 1945, fed into the tradition of the European movement of the post-war era.

One last consideration may help to put our deliberations into a perspective of enduring significance. Transcending, as it did, national interest in the name of human rights, the foreign policy of resistance may stand as a model for the human-rights policy which has evolved since the Second World War in a world still plagued by dictatorships. The 'landscape of treason' has not exactly contracted in the post-war era, and today's dissenters and resisters are in a position similar to that of the Germans of the *Widerstand*.[50] And the more that our present-day statesmanship perceives their plight as a universal responsibility, the more we may be able to assume that the overtures of the Germans of the Resistance were not altogether in vain.

## INTRODUCTION

1. M. R. D. Foot, *Resistance: An Analysis of European Resistance to Nazism 1940-1945* (London, 1976), 319.
2. Ibid.
3. Hoffmann, *History*, p. xi.
4. The usage of the word *Widerstand* was not common. Among the few incidences are the following: in January 1940 Adam von Trott zu Solz, on his return trip to the United States via the Far East and Siberia, met up in Hawaii with an old acquaintance, Klaus Mehnert, and is quoted to have said that his American stay, and especially his participation at the Conference of the Institute of Pacific Relations in November/December 1939, had served the purpose of acquainting leading Americans with the thoughts of the German *Widerstand* (Klaus Mehnert, *Ein Deutscher in der Welt: Erinnerungen 1906–1981*, Stuttgart, 1981, 235). The leaflets of the Munich University group, the so-called 'White Rose', used the term *passiver Widerstand* and called for the support of the *Widerstandsbewegung* (Inge Scholl, *Die weisse Rose*, Frankfurt/M., 1955, 135, 138, 150). But considering the limited range of the White Rose group, the latter designation hardly reflects the reality.
5. Interview with Mrs Marie-Luise Sarre, 8 Mar. 1978.
6. Richard Löwenthal, 'Widerstand im totalen Staat', in Richard Löwenthal and Patrick von zur Mühlen (eds.), *Widerstand und Verweigerung in Deutschland 1933 bis 1945* (Berlin, 1982), 12.
7. For the importance of 'social support' in oppressive situations see Barrington Moore, Jr., *Injustice: The Social Bases of Obedience and Revolt* (New York, 1978), 97. M. R. D. Foot writes about the importance of the 'feeling of participation'; Foot, *Resistance*, 4.
8. See in particular Ian Kershaw, '"Widerstand ohne Volk?" Dissens und Widerstand im Dritten Reich', in Jürgen Schmädeke and Peter Steinbach (eds.), *Der Widerstand gegen den Nationalsozialismus. Die deutsche Gesellschaft und der Widerstand gegen Hitler* (Munich, 1985), 779-98.
9. See e.g. the case of the Austrian peasant Franz Jägerstätter; Gordon C. Zahn, *Er folgte seinem Gewissen. Das einsame Zeugnis des Franz Jägerstätter* (Graz, 1979), trans. as *In Solitary Witness: The Life and Death of Franz Jägerstätter* (New York, 1965); also Georg Bergmann, *Franz Jägerstätter: Ein Leben vom Gewissen entschieden* (Stein am Rhein, 1980); Ernst T. Mader and Jakob Knab, *Das Lächeln des Esels: Das Leben und die Hinrichtung des Allgäuer Bauernsohnes Michael Lerpscher (1905–1940)* (Blöcktach, 1987).
10. *Gesellschaftliche Verweigerung*; Richard Löwenthal, 'Widerstand im totalen Staat', in Löwenthal and von zur Mühlen (eds.), *Widerstand*. A distinction similar to this one made by Löwenthal between *Widerstand* and *gesellschaftliche Verweigerung* has been made earlier by Martin Broszat between *Widerstand* and *Resistenz*; Martin Broszat, 'Resistenz und Widerstand', in Martin Broszat *et al.* (eds.), *Bayern in der NS-Zeit*, vol. iv: *Herrschaft und Gesellschaft im Konflikt*, pt. C (Munich, 1981), 691-709. The concept *Resistenz* has become widely accepted and used by historians in recent years. Apart from the fact that, in a comparative treatment of the problems of resistance, it is linguistically misleading, the excessive emphasis on the incidence of *Resistenz* as a predominantly value-free concept has had the unfortunate effect of detracting from our understanding of the Nazi claims for near-total control of power as it has also tended to detract from the dignity of the ethical decision involved in resistance itself.
11. In this work I propose to use for the *Widerstand*, as is the general practice, the designations 'Opposition' and 'Resistance' interchangeably. In the context of total rule there is, unlike in open societies, clearly no place for legal or loyal opposition. Any opposition therefore becomes, in effect, resistance. Within the broad category of 'Opposition' or 'Resistance', however, there were of course shadings and differences pertaining to motivation, intensity of principled commitment, method, and objectives. These will become evident as the story of the *Widerstand* will unfold in the following chapters of this book.
12. See in particular the magisterial work by Peter Hoffmann, *Widerstand, Staatsstreich, Attentat: Der Kampf der Opposition gegen Hitler* (Munich, 1969), trans. as *The History of the German Resistance 1933–1945* (Cambridge, Mass., 1977). For a plea to broaden the study of the *Widerstand* see Leonidas E. Hill, 'Towards a New History of the German Resistance to Hitler', *Central European History*, 14 (Dec. 1981), 369-99.

13. The literature on resistance from the left is now extensive. See, in particular, the good summaries by Hans J. Reichhardt, 'Möglichkeiten und Grenzen des Widerstandes der Arbeiterbewegung', in Walter Schmitthenner and Hans Buchheim (eds.), *Der deutsche Widerstand gegen Hitler* (Cologne, 1966), 169–213; and the corresponding chapters in Christoph Klessmann and Falk Pingel (eds.), *Gegner des Nationalsozialismus: Wissenschaftler und Widerstandskämpfer auf der Suche nach historischer Wirklichkeit* (Frankfurt/M., 1980); Löwenthal and von zur Mühlen (eds.), *Widerstand*; and Klaus-Jürgen Müller (ed.), *Der deutsche Widerstand 1933–1945* (Paderborn, 1986). A pioneering work which will always remain a classic is Günther Weisenborn (ed.), *Der lautlose Aufstand* (Hamburg, 1962); for more recent summary treatments see *Widerstand und Exil der deutschen Arbeiterbewegung 1933–1945*, ed. Friedrich Ebert-Stiftung (Bonn, 1982); and Klaus Mammach, *Widerstand 1933–1939: Geschichte der deutschen antifaschistischen Widerstandsbewegung im Inland und in der Emigration* (East Berlin, 1984); idem, *Widerstand 1939–1945 . . .* (East Berlin, 1987). Otherwise, a great many local studies have been written in recent years, such as Barbara Mausbach-Bromberger's *Arbeiterwiderstand in Frankfurt am Main gegen den Faschismus, 1933–1945* (Frankfurt/M., 1976); and Detlev Peukert, *Ruhrarbeiter gegen den Faschismus: Dokumentation über den Widerstand im Ruhrgebiet 1933–1945* (Frankfurt/M., 1976).

14. 'Mit dem Gesicht nach Deutschland'; *Mit dem Gesicht nach Deutschland. Eine Dokumentation über die sozialdemokratische Emigration. Aus dem Nachlass von Friedrich Stampfer*, ed. Erich Matthias (Düsseldorf, 1968), 7.

15. This equation has recently been suggested by Werner Röder, 'Deutscher Widerstand im Ausland: Zur Geschichte des politischen Exils 1933–1945', 'Aus Politik und Zeitgeschichte', B 31/80, *Das Parlament*, 2 Aug. 1980, 7. For a close correlation between resistance and exile see also *Widerstand und Exil*, ed. Friedrich-Ebert-Stiftung, *passim*.

16. 'Wir sind gefangen in einem grossen Zuchthaus', quoted in Eberhard Zeller, *Geist der Freiheit: Der zwanzigste Juli* (Munich, 1963), 95.

17. '*Widerstand ohne "Volk"*', Hans Mommsen, 'Gesellschaftsbild und Verfassungspläne des deutschen Widerstandes', in Schmitthenner and Buchheim (eds.), *Der deutsche Widerstand*, 76.

18. See Herbert von Borch, 'Obrigkeit und Widerstand', *Vierteljahrshefte für Zeitgeschichte* (*VfZ*), 3 (July 1955), 297–310.

19. Foot, *Resistance*, 11.

20. 'Repräsentationstheorie des Widerstandes'; Peter Hüttenberger, 'Vorüberlegungen zum "Widerstandsbegriff"', in Jürgen Kocka (ed.), *Theorien in der Praxis des Historikers* (Göttingen, 1977), 118.

21. Richard Cobb, 'A Personal State of War', *Times Literary Supplement*, 10 Mar. 1978, 270.

22. Letter from Helmuth von Moltke to Lionel Curtis, Stockholm, 25 Mar. 1943, in Michael Balfour and Julian Frisby, *Helmuth von Moltke: A Leader against Hitler* (London, 1972), 216, 220.

23. David Astor, 'Why the Revolt against Hitler was Ignored', *Encounter*, 32 (June 1969), 7.

24. George F. Kennan, 'America and the Russian Future', *Foreign Affairs*, 29 (Apr. 1951), 369.

25. 'German "Dissident" Groups', 8 June 1944; PRO, London, FO 371/39087/C 8865/180/18.

26. IfZ, ZS G.J. Sas 1626, 16.

27. On this subject see esp. the paper delivered by David Dilks, 'Britain and Germany, 1937–1939: A Context for British Reactions to the German Resistance', at the Anglo-German Conference on the German Resistance and Great Britain in Leeds, England, 6–9 May 1986.

28. See esp. Gerhard Ritter, 'The Foreign Relations of the Anti-Hitler Plot in Germany' in 'Record of General Meeting Held at Chatham House' (London, 31 Oct. 1949); also Gerhard Ritter, 'Die aussenpolitischen Hoffnungen der Verschwörer des 20. Juli 1944', *Merkur*, 3 (Nov. 1949), 1121–38 and Gerhard Ritter, 'The German Opposition to Hitler', *Contemporary Review*, 177 (June 1950), 339–45; Hans Rothfels, 'The German Resistance in its International Aspects', in 'Record of General Meeting Held at Chatham House' (London, 14 Mar. 1958); also Hans Rothfels, 'The German Resistance in its International Aspects', *International Affairs*, 34 (Oct. 1958), 477–89. Hans Rothfels expressed what he

called the 'bitter irony of history' which willed 'that the Western Powers virtually co-operated not with the German Resistance, but with Hitler', ibid. 488.

29. See esp. George K. Romoser, 'The Politics of Uncertainty: The German Resistance Movement', *Social Research*, 31 (spring 1964), 73–93; Lothar Kettenacker, 'Die britische Haltung zum deutschen Widerstand während des Zweiten Weltkriegs', in Lothar Kettenacker (ed.), *Das 'Andere Deutschland' im Zweiten Weltkrieg: Emigation und Widerstand in internationaler Perspektive* (Stuttgart, 1977), 49–76; Klaus-Jürgen Müller, 'The German Military Opposition before the Second World War', in Wolfgang J. Mommsen and Lothar Kettenacker (eds.), *The Fascist Challenge and the Policy of Appeasement* (London, 1983), 61–75. At the International Conference on the German Resistance in Berlin, 2–6 July 1984 this position was vigorously expressed by Klaus-Jürgen Müller (Hamburg), Hedva Ben-Israel (Israel), and Bernd Martin (Freiburg i. Br.); see Schmädeke and Steinbach (eds.), *Der Widerstand*, 329–44, 732–50, 1037–60. It might be added that the harshest criticism, as can be expected, of the foreign policy objectives of the German *Widerstand* has come from the apologist Nazi literature (see esp. Annelies von Ribbentrop, *Die Kriegsschuld des Widerstandes: Aus britischen Geheimdokumenten 1938/39*, Leoni am Starnbergersee, 1974) and from the historiography of the German Democratic Republic (see Walter Bartel, 'Die deutsche Widerstandsbewegung und die Alliierten zur Zeit des zweiten Weltkrieges', *Zeitschrift für Geschichtswissenschaft*, 5 (1961), 993–1013). The former indicts the conspirators against Hitler for their alleged decisive part in precipitating the British declaration of war; the latter condemned them for having aimed at preserving German imperialism, the army, indeed the Fascist state apparatus even though without its offensive leadership; it was finally, so the argument goes, the German Opposition's attempt to split up the anti-Hitler coalition which condemned its plans to failure (see Wilhelm Ersil, 'Das aussenpolitische Programm der militärischen Verschwörung vom 20. Juli 1944', *Deutsche Aussenpolitik*, 7, 1959, 743–58). In recent years, however, the East German historiography has made a point of distinguishing between the reactionary forces in the *Widerstand*, especially the group around Goerdeler, and the men of the Kreisau Circle as well as Stauffenberg himself. The latter, so the argument goes, were not averse to establishing contacts with the Soviet government and represented an opposition within the ruling class (see Kurt Finker, *Graf Moltke und der Kreisauer Kreis*, East Berlin, 1978, esp. 198; Kurt Finker, *Stauffenberg und der 20. Juli 1944*, East Berlin, 1977, esp. 237 ff.).

30. Kettenacker, 'Die britische Haltung', in Kettenacker (ed.), *Das 'Andere Deutschland'*, 49 ff.; Bernd Martin, *Friedensinitiativen und Machtpolitik im Zweiten Weltkrieg (1939–1942)* (Düsseldorf, 1974), 520; see also Romoser, 'The Politics of Uncertainty', *Social Research*, 79.

31. For summary treatments of the foreign relations of the German Resistance see Helmut Krausnick and Hermann Graml, 'Der deutsche Widerstand und die Alliierten', 'Aus Politik und Zeitgeschichte', *Das Parlament*, 19 July 1961; Hermann Graml, 'Die aussenpolitischen Vorstellungen des deutschen Widerstandes', in Schmitthenner and Buchheim (eds.), *Der deutsche Widerstand*, 15–167. These treatises, while exemplary and balanced as historical analyses, were as yet restricted to the conservative Resistance and could not avail themselves of the wealth of documentation which has since opened up. See also D. C. Watt, 'Les Alliés et la Résistance Allemande (1939–1944)', *Revue d'Histoire de la Deuxième Guerre Mondiale* (Oct. 1959), 65–86; Peter Hoffmann, 'Peace through Coup d'État: The Foreign Contacts of the German Resistance 1933–1944', *Central European History*, 19 (Mar. 1986), 3–44; Klaus-Jürgen Müller, *Der deutsche Widerstand und das Ausland*, Beiträge zum Widerstand 1933–1945 (Berlin, 1986); and Klemens von Klemperer, Die 'Verbindung mit der grossen Welt': *Aussenbeziehungen des deutschen Widerstands 1938–1945*, Beiträge zum Widerstand 1933–1945 (Berlin, 1990).

32. See esp. Hans Rothfels, 'Zur Krise des Nationalstaats', *VfZ*, 1 (Apr. 1953), 138–52; Karl Dietrich Bracher, *Zeit der Ideologien: Eine Geschichte politischen Denkens im 20. Jahrhundert* (Stuttgart, 1982).

33. Margret Boveri, *Treason in the Twentieth Century* (London, 1956), 19 ff.

34. The German criminal code which was valid until the defeat of the Third Reich made a distinction between *Hochverrat* (high treason) and *Landesverrat* (betrayal of the country). *Hochverrat* is an act committed against the inner foundations of the state, its constitution,

and territory. *Landesverrat* is the greater crime including all acts affecting the external security of the state and especially national defence; see *Strafgesetzbuch für das Deutsche Reich mit Nebengesetzen*, ed. Eduard Kohlrausch (Berlin, 1930), para. 80–98. For a systematic treatment of *Hochverrat* and *Landesverrat* and the modifications in the codification since 1933 see Walter Wagner, *Der Volksgerichtshof im nationalsozialistischen Staat* (Stuttgart, 1974), 50–8.

35. Joachim Kramarz, *Stauffenberg: The Architect of the Famous July 20th Conspiracy to Assassinate Hitler* (New York, 1967), 185.

36. Christopher Sykes, 'Heroes and Suspects: The German Resistance in Perspective', *Encounter*, 31 (Dec. 1968), 45.

37. This term was used by Adam von Trott zu Solz as early as 1936; letter from Adam von Trott to Shiela Grant Duff, Imshausen, 14 Sept. 1936, Klemens von Klemperer (ed.), *A Noble Combat: The Letters of Shiela Grant Duff and Adam von Trott zu Solz 1932–1939* (Oxford, 1988), 184.

38. Letter from Helmuth James von Moltke to Lionel Curtis, Stockholm, 25 Mar. 1943, in Balfour and Frisby, *Helmuth von Moltke*, 223.

39. Gerhard Gleissberg in the discussion 'Der kommende Friede und das kommende Deutschland', 10–11 May 1941, Archive of the Social Democratic Party of Germany, Bonn, AKE 21, quoted in Werner Röder, *Die deutschen sozialistischen Exilgruppen in Grossbritannien 1940–1945: Ein Beitrag zur Geschichte des Widerstandes gegen den Nationalsozialismus* (2nd edn., Bonn–Bad Godesberg, 1973), 113.

40. Letter from Helmuth von Moltke to Lionel Curtis, London, 12 July 1935; Lionel Curtis Papers, Box 28, Bodleian Library, Oxford University.

41. 'Strictly private and confidential' memorandum for the British government, end of Apr. 1942, Hans Rothfels, 'Zwei aussenpolitische Memoranden der deutschen Opposition (Frühjahr 1942)', *VfZ*, 5 (Oct. 1957), 393. The document which is composed in the 'we' form is clearly the work of various hands—Hans Schönfeld, Eugen Gerstenmaier, Trott, Hans-Bernd von Haeften, Albrecht von Kessel, and, while it cannot be said to have emanated from the Kreisau Circle, it had a distinct part in influencing its foreign policy thinking; see Ger von Roon, *Neuordnung*, 302; and Eugen Gerstenmaier, 'Der Kreisauer Kreis: Zu dem Buch Gerrit van Roons "Neuordnung im Widerstand"', *VfZ*, 15 (July 1967), 236–7.

42. It has become customary in the literature on the German Resistance to designate this cluster of groups and individuals 'conservative-national' or 'national-conservative'. (Almost all papers for the International Conference on Resistance held in Berlin in July 1984 followed the same practice; see Schmädeke and Steinbach (eds.), *Der Widerstand, passim*.) This designation is, however, altogether unsatisfactory since it does not do justice to the outlook of the younger men like Trott, Moltke, and Bonhoeffer, which was predominantly Christian, socialist, and European. There is no perfectly fitting generic term to encompass all the shadings in the non-Marxist camp. But since the attribute 'national' strikes me as particularly limiting and misleading, especially in regard to the younger men, I prefer using the term 'conservative Resistance' which allows for all shadings of conservative attitudes and positions, including the progressive ones.

43. These are Winston Churchill's words and part of a letter which he gave in August 1938 to a German emissary on a secret mission to London, Ewald von Kleist-Schmenzin, ironically upon the latter's request for some tangible evidence of the British determination to meet force by force in case of a German military move against Czechoslovakia: ' . . . Such a war, once started, would be fought out like the last to the bitter end . . .'; letter from Winston Churchill to Ewald von Kleist-Schmenzin, 19 Aug. 1938, in *Documents on British Foreign Policy 1919–1939 (DBFP)*, 3rd ser., vol. ii, ed. E. L. Woodward and Rohan Butler (London, 1949), 688.

44. Bishop Bell's information about the German Resistance came largely through his ecumenical contacts: Professor Friedrich Siegmund-Schultze, an active Christian social worker, pedagogue, and publicist, who was expelled from Germany in 1933 and kept up his ecumenical work in Switzerland. Bishop Bell and Siegmund-Schultze first met in 1925 at the Universal Christian Conference on Life and Work. Siegmund-Schultze was in close touch with Carl Goerdeler, and in May 1941—unsuccessfully—attempted to place a peace

plan of Goerdeler's into the hands of the British government (see below Ch. 4, s. 6). The Revd Dr Hans Schönfeld, Director of Research at the World Council of Churches (in Process of Formation) in Geneva, had, in this capacity, close contacts with Bishop Bell. Living throughout the war in Geneva, he continued travelling to Germany and thus was an important intermediary between Protestant Resistance circles and the outside world. In May 1942 he set out to Stockholm to meet Bishop Bell and confer about resistance matters (see below Ch. 5, s. 2). Bishop Bell first met Dietrich Bonhoeffer on the occasion of two ecumenical meetings at Geneva in August 1932, and since Bonhoeffer's tenure as German pastor in London (Oct. 1933–Apr. 1935) the two rapidly developed an intimate rapport. Bonhoeffer also appeared—independently of Schönfeld—in late May, 1942, in Sweden (Sigtuna) to inform Bishop Bell about the *Widerstand* (see below Ch. 5, s. 2). Throughout the war Bishop Bell was kept informed about the German situation by Gerhard Leibholz, Bonhoeffer's brother-in-law. He was originally a Professor of International Law at the University of Göttingen, but because of his Jewish ancestry he emigrated in September 1938 to England where he established contact with the Bishop through an introduction by Dietrich Bonhoeffer. Leibholz's insistence on distinguishing between Germans and Nazis, on the ideological rather than national nature of the war, and his opposition to the 'unconditional surrender' formula of Casablanca, coincided with the views of Bishop Bell (see esp. Eberhard Bethge and Ronald C. D. Jasper (eds.), *An der Schwelle zum gespaltenen Europa: Der Briefwechsel zwischen George Bell und Gerhard Leibholz 1939–1951*, Stuttgart, 1974, *passim*; and Sabine Leibholz-Bonhoeffer, *The Bonhoeffers: Portrait of a Family*, New York, 1971, *passim*). Also, Bishop Bell had been in contact with Helmuth von Moltke since November 1935, when the latter on a visit to Oxford sent a message to the Bishop on the state of affairs in the Confessing Church in Germany and on the plight of the Jews, asking him to hold himself ready to make some public protest (Report by Phillip Usher (chaplain of Bishop A. C. Headlam of Gloucester) 8 Nov. 1935, Bell Archive, Box 7, Lambeth Palace, London). Later Bishop Bell was instrumental in expediting the gist of Moltke's previously quoted letter addressed to Lionel Curtis from Stockholm of 25 Mar. 1943; for details see below Ch. 5, s. 2.

45. George Bell, Bishop of Chichester before the Upper House of the Convention of Canterbury, 15 Oct. 1942; quoted in Ronald C. D. Jasper, *George Bell: Bishop of Chichester* (London, 1967), 273; see also Bell's memorandum for the International Round Table Conference in Princeton, NJ, 8–11 July 1943, Bethge and Jasper (eds.), *An der Schwelle*, 294, 297.

46. Jasper, *George Bell*, 274.

47. FO 371/34415/C 8903/29/18; 371/39087/C 10028/180 G.

48. See Klaus von Dohnanyi, 'Widerstand und Menschenrechte', *Die Zeit*, 28 July 1978.

49. Willem A. Visser't Hooft, 'The View from Geneva', *Encounter*, 33 (Sept. 1969), 93.

50. George F. Kennan's thought on 'The Dissidents and Human Rights' (George F. Kennan, *The Cloud of Danger: Current Realities of American Foreign Policy*, Boston, 1977, 212–18) were no doubt trained in part on his experience as a young diplomat in Berlin when, after the departure of Alexander Kirk, the American Chargé d'Affaires from Berlin in October 1940, he kept up the connections with Helmuth von Moltke; see George F. Kennan, 'Noble Man. Helmuth von Moltke: A Leader Against Hitler', *New York Review*, 22 Mar. 1973; idem, *American Diplomacy 1900–1950* (New York, 1954), 133–4; idem, *Memoirs 1925–1950* (London, 1968), 119–22.

# I

# Resistance and Exile

## 1. The Beck–Goerdeler–von Hassell Group

The groups which formed within the military and civilian opposition against the Nazis were loose and amorphous. In reaction to regimentation, propaganda, and terror, it was natural that like-minded dissenters should have veered towards each other to consult, to strengthen each other's resolve, and to do what could be done jointly under the prevailing circumstances. As things were, even within the Resistance, the informal groupings which did take shape were looked at askance by some as being too risky and given to too elaborate theorizing.[1]

The leadership of the military and civilian Resistance fell, as if by co-option, into the hands of General Ludwig Beck and Carl Goerdeler, the head of state and chancellor-designate of the conspiracy respectively. Chief of the German Army General Staff between 1935 and 1938, Beck was not the most typical of German officers; 'not the type of the military man but rather that of a thinker', recorded Eduard Spranger.[2] Beck was a soldier steeped in the Prussian tradition of service and yet not a militarist. A student of Clausewitz, he had learnt to correlate warfare with politics and was a critic of Ludendorff's 'total war' theories. Like most of his fellow officers, he initially welcomed the advent of the Nazis and their 'national policies' aimed at overcoming Versailles and Weimar until finally he recoiled from their domestic and foreign enormities. With his resignation in August 1938, in protest against Hitler's planned Czechoslovak adventures, Beck came to rethink the limits of obedience. He, who earlier had said that 'revolution and mutiny are words not to be found in a German officer's dictionary,'[3] now became the generally acknowledged 'sovereign' of the German Resistance.[4]

Carl Goerdeler was Beck's counterpart in the civilian Resistance. Beck and Goerdeler's paths were similar in many ways, and indeed eventually they converged. Like Beck, Goerdeler was an ardent patriot, if not a nationalist, while at the same time he was committed to the higher canons of human dignity and the Christian faith. Like Beck he translated the ethos of his native Prussia into an attitude of unbending independence and open-mindedness. Also like Beck Goerdeler always remained a monarchist at heart, and it was his sense of duty rather than preference that made him enter the service of the Republic. He could never quite reconcile himself to the benefits of a freewheeling parliamentary system. But though he was active in the conservative DNVP and became a member of its governing board, he resigned from the Party over its obstructionist policies and put himself at Chancellor Brüning's disposal as Reich Commissar for Price Control. In November 1934 he followed Hitler's call to take up the same office once again. He harboured deep reservations against the Nazis, especially concerning their racial agitation, but, like many of his contemporaries, he initially hoped to be able to help the new regime to overcome its revolutionary excesses and realize its 'constructive' national and social goals.

Goerdeler was fundamentally a civil servant and not a political man. As deputy mayor of Königsberg (1920–30) and mayor of Leipzig (1930–7), he brought to his life in public service unlimited energies as well as an undaunted faith in the rationality and goodwill of mankind. This faith gave him strength, but it also left him unguarded against the realities of Nazism which he came to see as a calamity for his country and the whole world. It was during his tenure as mayor of Leipzig that Goerdeler decided to take a stand against the anti-Semitic and anti-Christian policies of Nazism. He chose to resign (in 1937) not only because the Party authorities had in his absence removed the public statue of the composer Felix Mendelssohn, a native of Leipzig, but also because, bypassing Goerdeler, they had eliminated a proposed church from the blueprint for a municipal housing project.[5]

Goerdeler's resignation propelled him into a political arena for which he was little prepared, and he had to find ways of implementing his basic rejection of National Socialism. In a setting of the ever-watchful and ruthless Nazi tyranny, however, any form of opposition was fraught with enormous difficulties. Goerdeler did not lack courage: on the contrary, he became a tireless and all too careless activist in search of a way of displacing the Nazi regime. But even as he became, in about 1940–1, the driving force of the conspiracy, and eventually its candidate for the future chancellorship, he could still toy with the proposition of openly confronting Hitler in order to persuade him to retire for the good of the country, or of merely taking him prisoner. Religious conviction made him reject the alternative of assassination. But it was Goerdeler's unshakeable belief in the self-evidence of reason which kept him from being able to fathom the full iniquity of Nazism. It has been suggested, and rightly so, that Goerdeler's tragedy was that firm faith in the workings of reason led 'this liberal conservative' down the illusionary path of irrationality.[6]

Goerdeler's ventures abroad were no less marked by the coincidence of his activism and lack of political instinct. His many forays abroad, the many memoranda which he sent out attest to his intense preoccupation with trying to secure for Germany its proper place in Europe and indeed the world. Later he reminisced that 'reared as a nationalist', and having been one until 1930, he had already established in Leipzig 'ties with the wide world' and learned on his journeys 'the vital lesson' that 'all peoples' followed ideals and that all were 'worth loving'.[7] The cementing of 'ties with the wide world' became a prime concern of his, and under the impact of Hitler's aggressive policies and ruthless conduct of war Goerdeler inched his way towards plans for a European and indeed a world federation. Coming from Germany's east, however, he could never bring himself to renounce Germany's claims for Danzig and the Polish Corridor, or to overcome a deep-seated fear of Russia. If he and his closest associates in the Resistance, such as Ulrich von Hassell and Johannes Popitz, kept insisting upon the hegemonic position of a future Germany in Europe, it was largely in order to safeguard the Continent against being overwhelmed by Soviet Russia. Once again, Goerdeler's faith in 'political reason', as has been rightly argued, made him deem unthinkable a Russian predominance over Europe.[8] Understandable as this position may have been, at least from a German perspective, and especially in view of the need for Goerdeler to win over the Generals for a coup, it failed to take into account the commitment of the Western Allies to Russia in the pursuit of the war. Thus Goerdeler gave the British, whom he so ardently wanted to reach, reason to doubt the integrity of his objectives. His difficult friend across the Channel in the British Foreign Office, the later Lord Vansittart, attested in his memoirs that Goerdeler had desired the destruction of Hitler 'with catonian simplicity' and that he was prepared to die for his *ceterum censeo*.[9] Nevertheless the question remains whether, in his quest for a hearing abroad, Goerdeler could have expected to overcome the prevailing and not altogether unfounded British suspicions that the '*Reichswehr*-Royalist-Goerdeler clique',[10] being wedded to German hegemonial ideas, differed from the Nazis in method—but not in aim—and that it therefore constituted no creditable alternative to Hitler's expansionism.

Ulrich von Hassell, a diplomat of the old school, was one of the chief foreign policy experts in the *Widerstand* and thus a leading candidate for the position of foreign minister after the hoped-for coup.[11] As ambassador to Rome (Quirinal; 1932–8) von Hassell took issue with the inclusion of Italy in the German-Japanese Anti-Comintern Pact in November of 1937, as it would inevitably lead to war. As a consequence he was retired when Joachim von Ribbentrop assumed the post of Foreign Minister in February 1938. From then on Hassell, who had been a Party member since 1933, pursued resolutely, even if too carelessly, the course of resistance. Just as Goerdeler had found financial support from the Stuttgart industrialist Robert Bosch that enabled him to cement his foreign contacts, so Hassell, with the help of Krupp's son-in-law Baron Thilo von Wilmowsky, obtained a position on the Board of the Central European Economic Conference (Mitteleuropäischer Wirtschaftstag) which served as 'camouflage' for his conspiratorial activities and especially for his journeys abroad. One of the most perceptive sources on the political scene in wartime Germany and on the thoughts and activities of the *Widerstand*, von Hassell's diaries[12] show him intrepidly at work to prevent a second world war. After its outbreak he and his friends were left in a predicament poignantly expressed in the diary:

the situation of the majority of clearheaded and reasonably well-informed people today, while Germany is in the midst of a great war, is truly tragic. They love their country. They think patriotically *as well as* socially. They cannot wish for victory, even less for a severe defeat. They fear a long war, and they see no feasible way out . . .[13]

Beck and Hassell were both members of the Mittwochs-Gesellschaft,[14] an old-established discussion group of distinguished scholars, public servants, and military men; there they met up with two fellow conspirators, the ultra-conservative Prussian finance minister Johannes Popitz and the somewhat younger economist Jens Peter Jessen, a one-time National Socialist. While the Mittwochs-Gesellschaft cannot be considered to have been wholly, or strictly speaking even a branch of, the *Widerstand*, it constituted an enclave of sorts in the landscape of totalitarianism and served the quartet as a cover for their resistance work. But even the contributions of the Resistance group within the 'Wednesday Society' were, it cannot be denied, on the whole disappointing. Only Beck's reports excel by virtue of their restraint and courage. His advocacy of a 'limitation and humanization of war' and of 'overcoming of the doctrine of total war', together with his plea that 'the leader in politics be a moral man', gave unmistakable signals to his colleagues as to where he stood.[15] Popitz's paper on the 'Reich', on the other hand, in which he stressed the importance of the *volkish* concept and concluded that a new Reich was to assert its mission in Central Europe above all by means of power,[16] as well as Hassell's on 'Mussolini' in which he characterized the Duce as combining 'energy and rationality',[17] make one wonder what kind of Germany and what kind of Europe were in the minds of these men.

Somewhat on the periphery of the Beck–Goerdeler–von Hassell group, it should be mentioned here, was Germany's financial wizard, Hjalmar Schacht. Schacht had lent his expertise to the Weimar Republic and to the Third Reich in various capacities, and his ventures into politics especially were marked by a conspicuous vanity on his part. In fact, early in the game as Hitler's Reichsbank president and economics minister, Schacht had been at odds with Goerdeler who opposed his support of Hitler's unorthodox financial policies. But thereafter, in opposition to Hitler's bellicose course, Schacht moved closer to the Resistance. In November 1937 he resigned as economics minister, and in January 1939 he was dismissed as Reichsbankpräsident, although he stayed on in the Cabinet as minister without portfolio until 1943. He was never quite trusted in the inner circles of the Resistance. 'Unfortunately he is getting a reputation', so Hassell wrote in his diary, ' . . . for talking one way and acting another.'[18] But Schacht capitalized on his foreign connections with the aim of informing the outside world about the Nazi threat and of bringing about some understanding with the Allied governments.

It should be recorded here that, while the Beck–Goerdeler–von Hassell group clearly represented the sector of the *Widerstand* which was most wedded to conservative principles and policies, it managed through Goerdeler to establish contacts with former union leaders towards the end of 1941, especially Jakob Kaiser of the Christian trade unions, Wilhelm Leuschner of the social democratic union, and Max Habermann of the white-collar workers' union. Thus in the course of time the Beck–Goerdeler–von Hassell group succeeded in broadening its popular base.[19]

## 2. The Abwehr

From their suite of offices in the massive complex of buildings of the Wehrmacht headquarters on Berlin's Tirpitzufer overlooking the chestnut trees along the Landwehrkanal, Admiral Wilhelm Canaris and his chief of staff Colonel (since December 1941 Major General) Hans Oster conducted Nazi Germany's military intelligence section, the so-called Abwehr. This organization was engaged in the line of duty in such clandestine operations as espionage and sabotage. With the appointment in January 1935 of Canaris as its chief, however, it assumed an additional function, that of the nerve centre of the *Widerstand*. Under Canaris the Abwehr became 'not only a nest of spies but also a nest of conspirators'.[20]

Ernst von Weizsäcker, the State Secretary in the German Foreign Office, wrote about Canaris as follows: 'He was one of the most interesting phenomena of the period, of a type brought to light and perfected under dictatorship, a combination of disinterested idealism and of shrewdness such as is particularly rare in Germany. In Germany one very seldom finds the cleverness of a snake and the purity of a dove combined in one personality.'[21] From beginning to end Admiral Canaris was a deeply enigmatic character. Of course it behoves an intelligence chief to envelop himself with mystery. Canaris rather enjoyed leaving his own ancestry in doubt and letting people think that he descended from the Greek freedom fighter Konstantin Kanaris, whereas in reality his family hailed from Lombardy, whence it had emigrated to Germany. Of patrician background, Canaris was not a man of particularly impressive appearance: he was of small stature and his expression was, if anything, indirect and aloof. He seemed an observer, somewhat nervous, whimsical, and, if necessary, terrifying through his probing silences, rather than a man of directness and decisive action. His political sympathies had been with the Freikorps movement of the immediate post-revolutionary era, and as a monarchist he was by no means a supporter of the Republic. While from the beginning he seemed to harbour severe doubts about the Führer and his Nazi movement, he developed close ties with Franco and in fact hung a large, inscribed portrait of the Caudillo on the wall of his office. Thus it was not a love of democracy which led him into his rejection of National Socialism but rather a basic sense of right and wrong as well as his Christian faith. It was the Nazi humiliation of General von Fritsch in February 1938[22] which finally removed all of Canaris's doubts about the depravity of the regime.

His position in the Abwehr gave Canaris the opportunity to strike against Hitler from within. He was one of those who perceived that a regime like that of the National Socialists could be, if at all, best toppled from within. Puzzling and tortured as was his political course, so was his actual role in the *Widerstand*. In fact, it can hardly be said that he was himself of the Resistance. In his conspiratorial activities he was a very cautious man, always remaining, as one of his close associates attested, 'the man behind the scenes'.[23] Though he knew of everything that went on, Canaris did not himself act. He carefully covered his own tracks. At the same time, while he plotted against the Nazis, he relentlessly pursued, as secret service chief, his intelligence operations on behalf of the German war effort, including the so-called 'England game' (*Englandspiel*) in 1942/3 which enabled him to penetrate the British intelligence operations in Holland and which led to numerous deaths and arrests on the Allied side.[24] Admiral Canaris fought with limitless imagination and cunning in a setting appropriate to his trade: a setting of multiple mirrors trained on each other. It can well be argued that the perhaps all too wily intelligence chief himself got lost in that labyrinth of mirrors even before the Nazis caught up with him in February 1944.

If Canaris remained shy of direct involvement in the conspiracy, he nevertheless acted as a shield for his younger lieutenants in the Abwehr who were of a very different temperament. Actually it was Colonel Hans Oster, Chief of the Central Department of the Abwehr[25] who was the man of action and who orchestrated the conspiracy. On basic matters there was of course agreement between him and his chief, and their relationship of trust was cemented by their common rejection of National Socialism. Oster, however, dapper, elegant, agile, was outgoing and unafraid and, if anything, singularly lacking in caution. He was the kind of officer who had a good way with people, and under the adverse circumstances in the Third Reich, prodding them into action was to him a challenge of sorts on which he thrived. The bond with fellow officers and conspirators turned out to be deceptively protective for him.

No less important than the Canaris–Oster relationship was the one between Oster and Beck.[26] Oster was the man who to begin with enlisted General Beck in the Resistance.[27] And while the latter may initially have had reasons to keep the Abwehr at arm's length,[28] there is no doubt about the fact that, beginning early in 1938, most probably under the impact of the Fritsch affair, Oster was a constant visitor in Beck's Bendlerstrasse office. There, according to the testimony of the then Deputy Army Chief of Staff, General Franz Halder, they often spent 'hours together under four eyes',[29] and in the winter of 1939/40 Oster appeared untold times at Beck's house in the Goethestrasse of Berlin-Lichterfelde,[30] presumably to urge him to take action and to establish contacts with the outside world.

For the rest, Oster, together with his friend in the Abteilung Z, the 'Special Deputy' (Sonderführer) Hans von Dohnanyi, was largely instrumental in drawing the 'right people' into the Abwehr, in placing members of the *Widerstand* in strategic positions outside Germany[31] and in giving title to the phalanx of emissaries who took the cause of the *Widerstand* abroad. Beginning in 1938 the so-called 'Oster Circle'[32] played the part of the general staff of the German Resistance and of the chief link with the outside world.

## 3. The Auswärtiges Amt

The Auswärtiges Amt, along with the army, harboured one of the old establishments which did not readily yield to the pressures of Nazification. No doubt the Führer distrusted and scorned the professionals of the Wilhelmstrasse. But even after the reshuffling of the highest echelons of the military and diplomatic command in February 1938, in the course of which Foreign Minister Freiherr Konstantin von Neurath had to yield to Hitler's protégé Joachim von Ribbentrop, the old élite still managed to maintain its position in the Office. It furnished the Third Reich with expertise and also much-needed respectability abroad. And for a long time the old foreign servants were able to deceive themselves that, for all the differences between themselves and the Nazi party-liners, they could still serve a useful function and be instrumental in 'averting the worst'.[33]

Above all it was the 'circle around Weizsäcker'[34] which was exposed to the pressures of Nazi ideology threatening the rational conduct of foreign affairs, if not the ethos of the Office and its personnel. Ernst Freiherr von Weizsäcker, elevated in April 1938 to the post of 'State Secretary' of the Auswärtiges Amt,[35] was the senior official among the old élite in the Office. As one of those who, while staying in the service, carried the burden of resisting the irresponsible policies of Hitler and his Foreign Minister Joachim von Ribbentrop, Weizsäcker has become to historians one of the most controversial figures of that period.[36] Nothing in his family background—which was Protestant, Swabian, liberal academic, and of recent nobility—nothing in his temperament—which was calm, cautious, and correct—nothing in his political outlook—which was monarchist of the enlightened Württembergensian as well as the Prusso-German variety—prepared him for the challenges which confronted him in the Third Reich.

Weizsäcker's position was in many ways analogous to that of Admiral Canaris. His naval background (1900–20) gave him a special sense of affinity and intimacy with the intelligence chief. Both Weizsäcker and Canaris chose to stay rather than to resign. As a matter of fact, it was General Beck who pleaded with his colleague in the Foreign Office to stay since in his official capacity he could do something for peace 'up to the last moment'.[37] Also like Canaris, Weizsäcker, while not in the strict sense belonging to the *Widerstand*, offered obstruction from within and resisted through 'feigned co-operation'[38] which amounted, in his own terms, to 'conspiracy with the potential enemy for the purpose of ensuring peace'.[39] Weizsäcker's genuine efforts to maintain peace, or rather to proceed by peaceful methods, have to be seen in terms of the clash between an essentially Wilhelminian statesman, still impressed by the rationality of Germany's exclusive claim to leadership in Central Europe and the irrational expansionism of Hitler and Ribbentrop. In effect the clash was one between two styles of imperialism. Weizsäcker had no qualms concerning Germany's domination of Czechoslovakia and Poland, but he was determined to attain these objectives short of plunging Europe into a major war. In this effort he kept hoping to convince even the Führer himself of the reckless adventurism of his rival Ribbentrop.[40]

Weizsäcker's resistance, however, was above all, that of a tired servant of the old school rather than of an outraged man of principle; it was resistance devoid of firm resolve and conviction. The struggle with his Foreign Minister Ribbentrop was made all the more uneven by the latter's having, in a diabolical way, the advantage of vitality and ideological commitment which the State Secretary lacked.

'Resistance in a dictatorship', said Warren Magee, co-counsel at the Nuremberg Trial for the defendant von Weizsäcker, 'is a game of assigned roles.'[41] Weizsäcker played the one assigned to him, commensurate with his personality. Cautious and timid though he was, he doggedly pursued his obstructionist course. Already before his appointment to the position of State Secretary in 1938 he had made sure of establishing intimate relations with the opposition group in the Abwehr.[42] Much like Canaris, moreover, he extended his protection over the opposition group in his office. These were mostly younger men. It might then be suggested that the problem was in part a generation one, that Weizsäcker, like the many generals, had too strong a sense of service and duty towards the state to allow himself to proceed to active resistance. His caution was tantalizing even to those who revered him and knew about his private contempt for Nazi methods and brutality and about his suffering. They did indeed revere him, and they did depend on him. And if he was thought of by his one-time private secretary Albrecht von Kessel as being of the 'silent though loyal' type, he was generally recognized among the opposition group in the *Widerstand* as the 'mentor of resistance'.[43]

Weizsäcker had a 'solid phalanx' of devoted lieutenants, and their story will unfold in the course of the following pages. They constituted a peer group of sorts, intensely loyal to their chief and held together by their common patrician and upper-class background as much as by their revulsion against what the Third Reich stood for. They have been variously referred to as constituting a *Freundeskreis* (circle of friends)[44] which also extended beyond the Wilhelmstrasse. Closest of that group to the State Secretary, according to Weizsäcker's own testimony, was Erich Kordt, a Catholic from the Rhineland. As early as 1934 he had been delegated by the then State Secretary, Bernhard von Bülow, as liaison to the upstart Ribbentrop in order to block the latter's aspiration to the post of Foreign Minister. It was largely Kordt who orchestrated the Foreign Office opposition,[45] through cementing ties with the other Resistance groups and establishing outposts abroad which would facilitate negotiations between Resistance members and foreign powers.[46] He worked with his brother Theo, his elder by ten years, who was appointed Councellor (Botschaftsrat) at the Embassy in London in March 1938 and who, one year later, when Ambassador Herbert von Dirksen was recalled to Berlin, became Chargé d'Affaires. Both brothers were indefatigably involved in Weizsäcker's efforts to urge the British government to take a strong stand against Hitler's aggressive designs.

It has by now been established beyond doubt that the objectives of the younger men in the German Foreign Office went way beyond those of their mentor Weizsäcker. In many ways resistance in the Third Reich was a generational question: in the Wilhelmstrasse as well as in the Tirpitzufer and, for that matter, also in the Bendlerstrasse. For the younger men, opposition to the Nazi pressures clearly meant more than refusal; it meant preparing the ground for resistance; and their foreign feelers in particular were initiated, unlike in the case of Weizsäcker, not merely to maintain peace, but to serve the purpose of conspiracy.[47]

One of the most important diplomatic listening posts in neutral Europe during the war, more important than the Vatican, was Switzerland.[48] This is why Theo Kordt was sent immediately after the outbreak of the war to the Legation in Berne,[49] ostensibly to safeguard the German interests in relation to Switzerland as a protective power, to take care of prisoner-of-war questions, and to deal with the International Red Cross Committee in Geneva.[50] In fact, he made it his chief task, 'upon instruction from the German opposition',[51] to re-establish the ties with the British Foreign Office and in particular to negotiate with T. Philip Conwell-Evans, the emissary of Sir Robert Vansittart, the Chief Diplomatic Adviser of the Foreign Secretary.[52]

Especially close to Erich Kordt was Hasso von Etzdorf, a dapper and fearless reserve cavalry officer (Rittmeister) who, according to Erich Kordt, was 'one of the ablest foreign servants and a convinced foe of the despotic rule'.[53] By virtue of an informal arrangement between Weizsäcker and General Franz Halder, Beck's Bavarian-born successor as Chief of Staff of the Army and, like his predecessor, deeply involved in the conspiracy, Etzdorf was appointed in October 1939 to the post of liaison officer between the Foreign Office and the Army High Command (OKH) in Zossen. This assignment turned out to be of extreme importance for the annals of the Resistance. While officially Etzdorf was delegated to inform the OKH about political matters abroad and the Auswärtiges Amt about military matters, he was confidentially commissioned by his chief to keep him informed about plans for an offensive in the West with an understanding that everything was to be done to prevent a continuation or expansion of the war. Through his counterpart in the OKH, Major Helmuth Groscurth, who served as liaison between Abwehr and the OKH, and who among the conspirators was one of the most determined ones,[54] Etzdorf was able to establish close ties with Canaris, Oster, and Dohnanyi of the Abwehr. He was in 'continuous touch' with Beck and Goerdeler, and he also maintained intimate ties with Theo Kordt in Berne and with two passionate foes of Hitler in the Foreign Office, Albrecht von Kessel and Gottfried von Nostitz, both intimate friends whom Weizsäcker had shrewdly steered to positions in the Consulate in Geneva.[55] In fact Etzdorf then contributed with considerable agility and cunning to a minimal cohesion of the otherwise rather disparate sectors of the *Widerstand*. But let it be said that he was more than a mere facilitator. As a man of character and consequence he was, together with Erich Kordt, author of the impressive 'Etzdorf–Kordt Memorandum' of October 1939 addressed to the Generals and prefaced by the heading 'The Imminent Disaster' which, in view of Hitler's design to attack in the west, called for the overthrow of his government.[56] After this brave but somewhat academic effort had run aground, Etzdorf, once again in complicity with Erich Kordt, in the following month hatched an assassination plot against the Führer which failed because the security measures following the Bürgerbräu attempt against Hitler on 8 November 1939 made the procurement of the required bomb impossible.

Among the most indefatigable activists of the *Freundeskreis* in the Foreign Office were undoubtedly Eduard Brücklmeier, Gottfried von Nostitz, Albrecht von Kessel, Hans-Bernd von Haeften, and Adam von Trott zu Solz.[57] Nostitz's early career had taken him through the usual sequence of assignments in Berlin and abroad; in fact his first foreign post was in the Belgrade Legation (1930–3) under Ulrich von Hassell, who throughout the troublesome years to come remained his 'fatherly friend'.[58] Later, in 1938–40, when back in the German capital, and serving as Foreign Office liaison officer to the OKW, Nostitz took it upon himself to act as contact between the Foreign Office conspirators and the Abwehr resistance group.[59] In May 1940 Ribbentrop seized upon an inter-office competence issue between the Foreign

Office and the OKW to press for the dismissal of Nostitz which was rescinded only upon Weizsäcker's intervention. The latter in turn urged Nostitz to stay in office, saying:

You don't wish to yield to types like this fool [Ribbentrop]? We must and we shall survive him. People like us must not abandon ship. Our people needs us today more than ever, even if often we are mere soldiers doomed at a lost post.

Eventually the State Secretary succeeded in having his protégé moved as Consul to Geneva, the seat of international organizations which, he figured, were of importance less to Nazi Germany than to 'the other, better Germany'.[60]

Albrecht von Kessel, who had developed close ties with Weizsäcker since the days when he served under him in the Berne Legation in 1935–7 and subsequently in the Office of the State Secretary in Berlin from early 1938 to early 1939,[61] also landed in the Consulate-General in Geneva,[62] thus joining his friend Nostitz in 1941. Like most of their circle of friends, these young diplomats were anything but typical bureaucrats. Highly educated, sensitive, and idealistic, they fed on a common sense of mission for which their Swiss assignment promised to offer the proper outlet. And if they did not see themselves exactly as proponents of 'democracy', their vision, as Kessel put it, was that of 'an era of European co-operation' and of 'social justice'. Their 'magic formula' was, if not 'democracy', then the *Abendland*, that is the somewhat loaded German version of the 'West' in which 'law and humanity' were to prevail.[63] As attested by William A. Visser't Hooft, the General Secretary of the World Council of Churches, their primary concern was the establishment and maintenance of connections with his organization and, against determined opposition from the Nazi Party and the Gestapo, to enable it to pursue its task of caring for prisoners of war and internees and to maintain contacts with the Churches in Germany as well as in the occupied countries. At the same time they formed a link in the so-called 'Swiss Road' which Visser't Hooft, residing in Geneva, had carefully devised in order to reach the Dutch Resistance movement.[64]

Standing before the ominous Nazi 'People's Court' on 15 August 1944, and interrogated by the 'hanging judge' Roland Freisler about his position towards Adolf Hitler, Hans-Bernd von Haeften responded without fear and hesitation: 'My conception of the Führer's role in world history is that he is a great perpetrator of evil.'[65] Hans-Bernd, the son of a learned and highly respected officer of the imperial General Staff, was a man of impressively firm character and penetrating mind. He combined a profound Christian faith with a keen interest in and understanding of politics. In the course of his short life he sought to interrelate both, which led him to explore in the realm of theology the ecumenical dimension and in that of politics the need for understanding between the nations. It may not have been incidental that

von Haeften, like a number of his friends among the younger generation of
resisters, Trott, Moltke, Berthold von Stauffenberg—the brother of Claus—
chose international law as his vocation. Patriots though they were, their
horizons extended beyond the confines of their own country.

It should be recorded here that among the formative influences upon the
young Haeften were Professor Friedrich Wilhelm Siegmund-Schultze, the
German theologian and pioneer ecumenist, who soon after the Nazi seizure
of power was arrested and forced to leave for Switzerland from where he lent
his support to the *Widerstand*; also Kurt Hahn, the great educator, who,
together with Prince Max von Baden, was the founder of the well-known
boarding school 'Salem' on the shores of Lake Constance. Hahn, who during
the First World War had worked for General von Haeften, took a keen
interest in young Hans-Bernd's future. In fact, the two became linked in a
'political friendship, indeed a veritable political passion' which was preoccupied by the search for ways of preventing the triumph of the Hitler
movement.[66] Hahn also encouraged Haeften to apply for a year off in
England[67] and to prepare himself for the foreign service which he entered in
1933.[68]

From the very beginning of the Third Reich Haeften became deeply
involved in the 'Church Dispute', identifying, in revulsion against the
National Socialist Church policy and the Nazified branch of the Evangelical
Church, the 'German Christians', with the 'Confessing Church' and becoming
particularly friendly with one of its chief spokesmen, Pastor Martin Niemöller.

After a short tour of duty in Copenhagen, Haeften's assignment to Vienna
in the autumn of 1935 as Cultural Officer made him witness independent
Austria in its struggle for survival. Far from seeing himself as a missionary
of the new Germany, he welcomed the still relatively open climate in Vienna.
Austria's survival and her contribution to an overall German (*gesamtdeut-
sche*) *Kultur*[69] might yet redeem the honour of the German people. This
assumption Haeften shared with some of the other younger members of the
German Legation,[70] including Gottfried von Nostitz whom he encountered
in Vienna and with whom he formed a close bond of friendship. In fact, it
was Nostitz who eventually brought together Haeften and the Kreisau group,
especially Moltke, Trott, and Peter Graf Yorck von Wartenburg.[71] While in
Vienna Haeften was furthermore engaged in following up his ecumenical
leanings, establishing connections with religious groups, Catholic and Protestant.[72]

Haeften's transfer to Bucharest opened up yet another chapter in his
ecumenical work. When Kessel wrote that 'our circle' was instrumental in
establishing relations with representatives of the Orthodox Churches in the
Balkan states,[73] he evidently was thinking above all of his friend Hans-Bernd
for whom this connection became a major concern even after his return to

Berlin and reassignment to the Cultural Department of the Auswärtiges Amt. A memorandum which Haeften composed for the office in November 1943 on the German policy towards Balkan Orthodoxy[74] attests to his efforts to shield the Orthodox Churches against political penetration by Nazi propaganda. By cunningly referring to the 'unfavourable impression' which the Church Dispute and the 'German Church policy' had made abroad, he sought to point out the damaging effect of the 'inner-German' influences and to resuscitate the role of the Foreign Office in conjunction with the Church Office for External Affairs (Kirchliches Aussenamt).[75] His concern until the very end, as his friend Anton Böhm wrote in an eloquent and moving sketch of Haeften's life, was to 'establish a religiously rather than politically based tie between German evangelical Christianity and the Orthodoxy of the southeast'.[76]

At no time during his foreign-service career was Haeften really in a position where he could have left a decisive mark. Yet his place in the Resistance is a central one. Among his fellow conspirators, as we have seen, there were many who at one time or another had abetted the same regime against which they eventually turned with vehemence. Haeften, on the other hand, emerges as a man of clear conviction and straight direction. From beginning to end his understanding of the Christian faith made him immune to the temptations of what he called the 'secularizing world views' of the modern age.[77] The separation of man from the divine order could not, in Haeften's view, be overcome by any false certainties but only by a rededication of man to the drama of sin and redemptive grace. And while the distant God does not enter into history, and while the Church has no business engaging in politics and being concerned with the secular order, there are points of convergence of State and Church, Haeften believed, where the citizen is brought into a position which as a Christian he cannot condone. In such a case the Church cannot—and should not—remain silent 'like a dumb dog'. A war, so Haeften argued, in which children, women, and old people are being killed by bombs and machine-guns, is no longer a war but murder, and threatens the very essence of Christianity. 'War as extermination of a people is a dreadful sin' and in such a case

it would be up to the Church (Churches) to call upon the 'Christian' soldiers and urgently to warn them against destroying the foundations of any order by ignoring the inviolable commandments of God and converting the *corpus christianum* into a *corpus diabolicum* ... When the Christian peoples are gripped, as they are today, by the madness of political demons, then the pastoral voice of the Church must sound *publicly* and bear witness *before the whole world*.[78]

These passages should be read as more than inconsequential reflections of Legationsrat von Haeften. They take us into the privacy of a mind that was struggling, in view of the abysmal horrors of the world, with the theological justification of action. From the very otherness of God he derived the need for political responsibility. 'Grace is never only a gift, but always at the same time a challenge,'[79] and ultimately the challenge meant resistance. The irenic ecumenist thus appropriated 'the severe commandments of the struggle' as he found them outlined in the Epistle of St Paul to the Ephesians: 'And take the helmet of salvation, and the sword of the Spirit, which is the word of God.'[80]

It is striking how much Haeften's thinking coincided with that of Dietrich Bonhoeffer. The two had known each other since 1921 when they were confirmed together in Berlin-Grunewald. Ever since Haeften had closely followed Bonhoeffer's doings,[81] and in turn the latter, when planning in 1935 an ecumenical office for the Confessing Church, commented on Haeften as 'much interested in this matter and ready to devote much time to it, fully in tune with us'.[82] For now it should be registered that untrained though he was in theology, in his struggle against the 'rulers of the darkness' in his own country, Haeften set an example akin to Bonhoeffer's for Christian resistance that was to have a distinct impact especially upon the ethos of the younger generation among the resisters. Haeften's part in charting the missions of the *Widerstand* abroad was also to be a crucial one.

Adam von Trott zu Solz, who became one of the leading architects of German resistance foreign policy, was one of the most colourful and complex figures of the opposition, and easily the most controversial. Like his friends in the *Widerstand* he had to make agonizing political and moral decisions and subject himself to the hardships of a split existence, which is the law of conspiracy. But with Trott, more than with the others, an 'almost too single-minded concentration' on foreign affairs, as he once put it,[83] projected the predicaments and attendant risks of resistance work into the arena of foreign affairs. On this level, love of country and rejection of its regime clashed with redoubled fury. To start with, Trott exposed himself at home to the charge of the gravest form of treason. And yet, being a patriot and not a traitor, he in turn courted misunderstanding, distrust, and rejection abroad.

It is all too tempting to assess Adam von Trott as a somewhat quixotic figure, a charming, handsome, well-bred, and well-connected aristocrat with an unusual gift for friendship, but on balance no more than 'an untrained amateur of diplomacy'.[84] Fearless and lacking in caution, however, he himself generated much of the mystery and ambiguity which were largely responsible for the 'failure' of his mission.

But the roots of the 'Trott problem' lie much deeper than that.[85] The complexity and controversiality of Trott are embedded in his background, in the nature of his assignments and the unusual conditions in which he had to perform them, and last but not least in the way in which he perceived his task.

On both his father's and his mother's sides Trott was born into a setting of public service. The Trotts were an old and distinguished Hessian noble family, and the Schweinitzes, from whom his mother was descended, were notable Prussian Junkers. But Trott's mother Eleonore was, through her mother, Anna Jay von Schweinitz, a direct descendant of John Jay, the first Chief Justice of the United States. The Hessian legacy had in the course of time merged with the Prussian tradition. But the Jay ancestry opened up the Anglo-Saxon world to Trott. His mother, keenly conscious and proud of her Puritan background,[86] once reminded him in a letter: 'Both of us have inherited, apart from our good German blood, something of the fighters against slavery in America.'[87]

Trott then belonged to two worlds, one informed by the more traditional values of country and state, and the other preoccupied with justice and humanity and reaching out to the wider world. Blending in Trott's personality were patriotism, a generous cosmopolitanism, and unyielding concern for the rights and dignity of man. At the same time his mother's outgoing religious commitment and her connection with ecumenical church leaders in Geneva steered him towards breaking out of the confines of a narrow and unduly nationalistic reading of his inherited Protestant tradition in search of, as he put it, 'international solidarity' and a 'spirit of co-operation'.[88] Transcending national loyalties, as rooted in his particular family background, Trott's position was hard to maintain in the German setting after the First World War in which international as well as ecumenical attachments were still looked on askance by many people of the upper and middle strata of society.[89] Even within the circle of his immediate family there were tensions which troubled and haunted Trott, as with his much beloved father, the one-time Prussian Minister of Education (1909–17) who could not condone his son's liberal let alone socialist orientation. Adam considered himself a socialist, and while he was not of the 'pure', scientific, 'purely rationalistic' Marxist variety, he was admittedly 'greatly impressed' by the writings of Gustav Landauer (1870–1919) whose socialism was, as Adam put it, 'personal', by which he meant humanitarian and spiritual.[90] In the Reichstag election of September 1930, in which the Nazis scored heavily, Adam voted for the Social Democratic Party which caused his distressed father to comment in a letter: 'A young man like you who cannot reconcile the canons of paternal authority, of his origins, family, and tradition to his conscience, would have acted more responsibly abstaining from voting rather than participating,' and he added that Adam should not be surprised to run into ridicule and hostility in the circles 'which we are used to consider our own'.[91]

Adam was frequently at odds also with his elder brother Werner, a strange, brooding, and strong-willed man who, deeply pessimistic over the course of Western civilization and his own fatherland, withdrew into a life of inner emigration and, in 1931, decided to join the Communist Party. Werner virtually tyrannized his younger brothers and especially Adam whom he loved, disapproving of his tendencies to follow his mother's influence, to move out into the world, and to act. To Werner the outgoing and lighthearted strain in Adam seemed wasteful and futile, and the latter's youthful spontaneity and gift for friendship downright frivolous.[92] Indeed Werner voiced fears lest, in view of the 'landslide' which had occurred in Germany in January 1933 and which he thought graver in consequence than the French Revolution, Adam would be left playing the part of a 'modern Don Quixote'.[93]

For Adam, however, action meant precisely the opportunity to break out of the excessive introspection and sequestration that prevailed in Germany after the war. Already his law studies, culminating in a thesis for the University of Göttingen on the subject of Hegel's philosophy of State and international law,[94] had pointed towards a preoccupation with international affairs. But Adam's real opening came with the years he spent at Oxford as a Rhodes Scholar (1931–3). These years were exciting and triumphant, and his trip around the world (March 1937–November 1938), which took him to the United States, Canada, China, Manchuria, and Japan, was full of discovery and adventure. To start with, he managed to obtain what he once had called *Distanz*[95] from the 'peculiar troubles and special trials'[96] that he thought were absorbing so much of the energy of German youth, as also from the troubling events in his own country. Moreover, Trott was a thoroughly political man, literally 'obsessed with politics', as a friend later recalled.[97] He agonized over the question of how he could apply himself to the service of his country, which he loved, short of surrendering his convictions. He certainly had made up his mind on this basic issue when, early in 1933, he wrote to his father that service to the rights of the individual, that is 'man', had become to him 'immeasurably more important than service to the "state"' which, he added, had come to stand for 'arbitrariness'.[98]

Adam's eventual decision to join the Auswärtiges Amt in the spring of 1940, and indeed the Nazi Party one year later, must have appeared to his brother Werner as final capitulation. But these steps made Adam's life no easier as they were designed to serve as cover for his subversive activities. Preparation for the invasion of the British Isles and sponsorship of the Indian freedom fighter Subhas Chandra Bose coincided with Trott's moving closer to the heart of the Resistance. In the Foreign Office he met up with kindred spirits who constituted the *Freundeskreis*, and through these in turn, together with his friend Hans-Bernd von Haeften, he came, in the spring of 1941, into the orbit of Moltke's Kreisau Circle. From then on Trott functioned as its chief adviser on foreign affairs. It was late in 1943 that Trott and Stauffenberg met, and soon their bond was to become an especially close one. Trott's journeys abroad, restless and acrobatic as they were in their attempt to reach the world, gained through Stauffenberg's sanction, no less than that of Moltke, a particular legitimacy of purpose, mission, and readiness for sacrifice.

A complete outsider in the Auswärtiges Amt was Albrecht Haushofer (1903–45), son of Karl Haushofer, the well-known founder of the German school of 'geopolitics' which, combining a hard-nosed correlation of geography and politics with expansionist designs, exerted a considerable influence upon Nazi ideologists. An eminently gifted, indeed brilliant, man with considerable artistic gifts, Albrecht followed in his father's footsteps and was determined to play an active part in the formulation of the foreign policies of his country. His disdain of National Socialism, its vulgarity as well as its brutality, in part precipitated by the fact that his mother was of half-Jewish ancestry, was not to stand in the way of his sense of mission, let alone his ambition. In fact, he owed his position of prominence largely to Rudolf Hess, the Führer's Deputy, who, a grateful disciple of Haushofer *père*, took it upon himself to declare Albrecht and his younger brother Heinz honorary Aryans. Albrecht then embarked upon a tortuous course between collaboration with the regime and resistance against it that left him ultimately unable to stem the tide of Nazi aggression and condemned him to the role of victim, flawed and tragic.

Haushofer's way through the labyrinth of agencies concerned with the formulation of Nazi foreign policy gave him direct access to the highest leaders of the Third Reich, especially Hess, Ribbentrop, and even Adolf Hitler. Early in 1933 he moved into *volksdeutsch* affairs, a particular concern of his father as well as of Hess. Haushofer exerted his influence throughout in the direction of moderation, trying without much success to shield the German minorities abroad against Party control and interference. While filling a teaching position in the Berlin Hochschule für Politik from 1934 and, after its dissolution in 1939, a chair in Geography and Geopolitics at the University, he obtained, through the intervention of Hess, a position in the Dienststelle Ribbentrop, a bureau under Hess's supervision designed to complement, if not compete with, the Foreign Ministry's operations. After Ribbentrop's appointment to the position of Hitler's Foreign Minister in February 1938, Haushofer was transferred, as a consultant, to the Information Section of the Auswärtiges Amt. He liked to take on secret assignments abroad, some of them commissioned by Admiral Canaris, and while he thus got the reputation of a 'grey eminence'[99] he invariably, whether it was in connection with the Czechoslovak crisis or the Japanese–Chinese war, advocated a course of rationality in the place of ideological commitment and alignment. A major task he saw himself called upon to perform was to act as intermediary between Germany and the Anglo-Saxon world and to warn his chiefs against an underestimation of the British and American resolve to take a stand against Germany's aggressive designs. His ultimate vision was the peaceful coexistence of a hegemonial Germany on the Continent with the British Empire and the United States.[100]

Haushofer's relationship with Ribbentrop was never a particularly close one. While the Foreign Minister would not forget about his aide's racial blemish and furthermore resented Hess's patronage over him, Haushofer in turn had little respect for Ribbentrop's adventurism. In March 1938 Haushofer played a decisive part in the nomination of Weizsäcker for the position of State Secretary.[101] The relations between Haushofer and Ribbentrop deteriorated seriously after the Munich Agreement of September 1938 when it became clear to Haushofer that Hitler and his Foreign Minister were not disposed to honour the agreement and that they were leading Germany into war. His work in the Foreign Office, however intensive, was thus, as he had to admit to himself, condemned to ineffectiveness.[102] Whatever tangible expectation he had left of acting as a brake and of being able cautiously to steer the foreign policy decisions of the Third Reich, he instead chose the risky path of establishing direct contacts with friends in Britain—especially the Marquis of Clydesdale.[103] Haushofer expected continued backing from Hess, but his hopes came to naught when the news broke on the evening of 12 May 1941 that two days earlier Rudolf Hess, inspired by 'supernatural forces', as he later confided to Albert Speer,[104] had set out on his quixotic solo flight across the Channel with the idea of negotiating peace with the British. The guardian angel of the Haushofers had vanished in the fogs of Scotland.

Haushofer's deep misgivings about the Nazis, however, had led him as early as 1940 into the orbit of the Resistance. Through an acquaintance, the lawyer Karl Langbehn, who, while engaged in resistance work, was on good terms with Himmler, Haushofer was brought into contact with Popitz and von Hassell, with whom he developed a close working relationship. The latter entered into his diary in mid-March 1941 that Haushofer 'now thinks as we do (after going through a few spiritual detours in the direction of Ribbentrop)'.[105] Early in the same year Haushofer also met Helmuth von Moltke and from then on repeatedly attended meetings of the Kreisau Circle; indeed on one occasion he addressed the assembled group on matters of foreign affairs.[106] At the same time he established through some of his students a link with Harro Schulze-Boysen, the leader of the Communist *Rote Kapelle* group.

A story goes that when as a young boy he was asked what his aim was in life, Albrecht Haushofer responded that he wanted to become German foreign minister. In the last months of Nazi rule, and now in Gestapo custody, returning from a hearing, Haushofer was asked by a fellow-inmate about the state of affairs. He answered that he was confronted with two menaces: 'either the firing squad or the appointment to be the last foreign minister of the Nazi Reich'.[107] With the failure of the 20 July 1944 plot, Haushofer's fate was sealed. After spending more than four months in hiding as a fugitive, he was hounded down by the Gestapo early in December. But even in captivity his double life as foreign policy expert—between resistance to and co-operation with the regime—temporarily paid dividends; he was kept alive by Himmler throughout the early months of 1945 in the expectation that he might be useful in negotiations for a separate peace with the Western Allies. But finally, in the night of 22–23 April 1945, as the Russian troops were closing in on the German capital, having been formally released from Moabit gaol together with seven of his fellow prisoners, Haushofer was herded by an SS gang to a nearby bomb site and brutally shot in the back of the neck.

Three weeks afterwards Heinz Haushofer found his brother's body at the execution site, still clutching in one hand a bundle of papers. They were sonnets, the *Moabit Sonnets*, which Albrecht had written in prison. 'Fettered hand and foot,' a friend of his later wrote, 'he at last found peace for himself and the world':

no memoranda, no geopolitics any more, but sonnet after sonnet describing his days and nights in prison, which he shared with many of his comrades of the Resistance, one after another of them to be taken away to the hangman. From there his mind soared out to the world he had known and loved: the land near and far, the men and women who meant most to him, the works of beauty he treasured above all. Sometimes he wrote in sorrow over the destruction of so much of mankind's most precious heritage, other times in anger against those who had led his people on the road to war, to the senseless suffering and death of millions upon millions in Europe, in Asia, in America. But mostly he wrote in praise and love, as he conversed with the dead and the living nearest to him.[108]

The thirty-ninth sonnet, entitled 'Guilt', ended as follows:

> I gave warning—not loud enough and clear!
> Today I know what I was guilty of . . .

## 4. The Churches

Churches are sacred institutions and on that account, it can be argued, are not the proper vehicles of political resistance. But resistance, being born of extreme situations, inevitably harbours a dimension transcending politics and involving basic human rights. In this case the Churches, precisely because they are sacred institutions, cannot escape the responsibility of taking a position. The record of the German Churches in the Nazi era is marked by this dilemma. But the by now vast literature on the subject has made it all too evident that as institutions they were neither willing nor able to overcome this dilemma. For too long they were absorbed in defending their own realms against Nazi incursions, and on balance as institutions took no part in the *Widerstand* against National Socialism.

German Protestantism had all along almost frantically subscribed to the Lutheran theory of the two realms ('Zwei-Reiche-Lehre') which separated the Kingdom of Christ from the Kingdom of the World and assigned inordinate powers to the latter. The worldly state, while not part of the divine order, was nevertheless seen as appointed by God to maintain order. The state, then, is the authoritarian state (*Obrigkeitsstaat*) and is to be obeyed. To set the record straight, it ought to be registered, however, that the German Protestants did not follow this prescription exactly during the Weimar days; the revolution of 1918 was generally perceived as an interference with a divinely established order, and as a consequence the German Protestants remained, on the whole, aloof from the Republic. All the more did they welcome the 'national revolution', as the events following the Nazi seizure of power were first labelled, and all the more did they succumb to that 'great masquerade of evil', as Dietrich Bonhoeffer called it,[109] which seemed to indicate that the interregnum of Weimar was terminated.

The German Catholics, the once much maligned 'enemies of the Reich', partly in compensation, were preoccupied during the Second Reich with proving their 'national' reliability, and, while after 1918 their Centre Party did become one of the pillars of the 'Weimar coalition', it clearly veered in the last years of the Republic towards the right. Franz von Papen, one of the last chancellors before Hitler, belonged to the increasingly influential right wing of the Centre Party and became a decisive force in engineering Hitler's seizure of power. The leader of the Centre Party, Prelate Ludwig Kaas, was no less instrumental in advocating co-operation with the Nazis and, after their seizure of power, negotiating the treacherous Enabling Act (23 March 1933) and subsequently the Concordat with the Vatican (20 July 1933). As for the German episcopate, it did not see fit, despite its obvious fundamental differences with Nazi ideology, to assume a clear-cut position against the movement. General considerations of expediency, as well as fear of a Communist dictatorship, prevailed upon it to equivocate. Early in 1930 it went as far as warning against National Socialism since it was ideologically 'not compatible' with the teachings of the Church, and even forbade its priests to co-operate with the movement. It retracted this position, however, once Hitler in his governmental declaration of 23 March 1933—in the formulation of which Prelate Kaas had a hand—assured both Christian denominations that the 'National Government' considered them 'the most important factors' for the maintenance of the people's well-being and promised to respect their rights. With the Concordat the Church finally conferred international respectability on the Nazi regime.

Meanwhile the Nazi Party vigorously set in motion the persecution of the Jews, thus making it manifest that the racial tenets of the Party programme were to be taken seriously. Both Churches, alas, kept their silence; they were not to be their Jewish brothers' keepers. But before long the Churches found out that they themselves would not be immune against attacks if they were to resist Hitler's objective to transform them into pliable instruments of state policy. The Church Dispute (*Kirchenkampf*) between the government and the Protestant Churches, then, set in with full fury in the spring of 1933, and the

Catholic Church, disarmed by the Concordat, found itself embroiled almost instantly in a struggle against systematic interference by the state and defamation from the Party. However, the opposition of the Churches was primarily institutional and reactive; they reacted to what they considered interference into their respective realms. In this respect they did no more and no less than the other traditional German establishments; like the army and the bureaucracy they offered institutional refusal. Later on Pastor Martin Niemöller, one of the most outspoken members of the Protestant opposition, had occasion to reflect on the lessons that could be learned from the Churches' response to the Nazi policy of persecution:

First the Nazis went after the Jews, but I was not a Jew, so I did not object. Then they went after the Catholics, but I was not a Catholic, so I did not object. Then they went after the trade-unionists, but I was not a trade-unionist, so I did not object. Then they came after me, and there was no one left to object.[110]

Even where the protest of the Churches assumed a dimension of principle, it remained strictly spiritual and steered away from entanglements in political resistance. It might be argued, with some justification, that at the time this was the only course open to the Churches if they were to survive as institutions. But it also must be registered that at no point did they see fit to offer general resistance against a regime that was manifestly tyrannical.

Growing out of a general perception of the fundamental evil of the movement and the regime, the call for resistance against National Socialism came from a few individual churchmen. The towering figure in this respect was the Swiss Calvinist theologian Karl Barth, the father of 'Dialectical Theology'. His basic position was his departure from the so-called 'liberal theology' of the nineteenth century which sought to correlate the modern forms of Christianity with the historical process of self-fulfilment and thus to reinterpret Lutheranism as a religious parallel to the process of human progress. But if the secularization of Christ could be made to correlate with the forces of democracy and pacifism, Barth argued, what would keep theologians from correlating it with other secular trends like nationalism—or National Socialism? Barth's dialecticism, then, insisted upon the 'otherness of God'. A basically Augustinian vision made him emphasize the contrast between creation and redemption, between the righteousness of man and God, and between justice and grace. The gap between reason and revelation was unbridgeable: God's will was not a corrected continuation of our own; it was the 'wholly other'.[111]

Thus in June 1933 Barth came out with his treatise, *Theologische Existenz Heute*,[112] in which he argued, against all temptations of secularism and worldly causes, the case for the integrity of the 'theological existence'. The basic issue, then, was not the Church Dispute, not even political dispute with the Nazis, but the affirmation by the preachers and theologians of their theological task. A few months thereafter, on the occasion of a Reformation Day lecture in Berlin, Barth followed up by issuing a resounding call for 'unrestrained and joyful resistance'.[113] As yet he was concerned primarily about not getting lost in mere tactics of Church politics. Resistance had to spring from spiritual motives, and it had to safeguard the spiritual realm of the Church.[114]

The theological firmness of Barth's summons reinforced the stand which Pastor Dietrich Bonhoeffer, the most resolute and articulate advocate of Church resistance in Germany, chose to take. He had, as a matter of fact, already defined his position on this issue before the actual Nazi seizure of power in January 1933. On the occasion of an ecumenical youth conference in July 1932 held in Czechoslovakia,[115] Bonhoeffer, already deeply troubled by the spectre of Nazi aspirations to religious as well as political control, pleaded for an ecumenism which went much further than organizational co-ordination between the various Churches. Stirring up the delegates with the statement 'there is no theology of the ecumenical movement', he argued that, unless the Church developed such an ecumenical theology, it would find itself defenceless against the threat that came from the upsurge of nationalism among German youth. In view of this threat Bonhoeffer maintained that keeping the peace could not be considered an '*absolute ideal*':

Peace commanded by God has two limits, first the truth and secondly justice. There can only be a community of peace when it does not rest on *lies* and on *injustice*. Where a community of peace endangers or chokes truth and justice, the community of peace must be broken and battle joined ... If the ordering of eternal peace is not timelessly valid ... simply because the complete oppression of truth and justice would threaten to make the hearing of the revelation of Christ impossible, then *struggle* is made comprehensible in principle as a possibility of action in the light of Christ.[116]

From the early 1930s on, then, Dietrich Bonhoeffer's life was a preparation for resistance which, immediately after 30 January 1933, took the form of his engagement in the Church Dispute for the 'Confessing Church' (*Bekennende Kirche*), in which he became the younger generation's leading spokesman against the Nazification of the Protestant Church. He took issue especially with the so-called 'German Christians', who threatened to blend the Christian message with the racist doctrines of the Nazis. But the Church Dispute was for him, after all, only what he called, a 'way station'.[117] Even the stand in Church matters taken by the Confessing Church in staving off the German Christians was not enough. The Church, Bonhoeffer judged, had remained silent (*stumm*):

She was silent when she should have cried out because the blood of the innocent was crying aloud to heaven. She has failed to speak the right word in the right way and at the right time. She has not resisted to the uttermost the apostasy of faith, and she has brought upon herself the guilt of the godlessness of the masses.[118]

It should be noted, then, that from the outset resistance for Dietrich Bonhoeffer was neither defensive nor in any way limited but principled and whole. It was to be an 'altogether different opposition' from the one of the Church which he had found wanting. To his friend Erwin Sutz he wrote that he believed 'the whole thing' would 'depend on the Sermon on the Mount' and that it was to amount, if necessary, to 'resistance to the blood'.[119] Much of Bonhoeffer's thinking and writing since the early 1930s was, in fact, dedicated to elaborate and reinforce the rationale for this position. His participation in the conspiracy against Hitler and his martyr's death on 9 April 1945 were its logical outcome.

Bonhoeffer's main premiss, like Barth's, was that of the otherness of God: 'the way of Jesus Christ, and therefore the way of all Christian thinking, leads not from the world to God but from God to the world.'[120] No man-made constructs, not even ones as benign as natural law or rationality can ultimately serve as guides for the Christian man, but *only* the gospel of Jesus Christ. And of all man-made constructs Bonhoeffer was up against the most absorbing, the most absolutist one, namely Nazi ideology. Ideology itself was the chief manifestation of man's claim to self-sufficiency and omnipotence. 'All ideological action carries its own justification within itself from the outset in its guiding principle.' But against ideological action Bonhoeffer opposed 'responsible action' which 'does not lay claim to knowledge of its own ultimate righteousness':

When the deed is performed with a responsible weighing-up of all the personal and objective circumstances and in the awareness that God has become *man* and that it is *God* who has become man, then this deed is delivered up solely to God at the moment of its performance. Ultimate ignorance of one's own good and evil, and with it a complete reliance upon grace, is an essential property of responsible historical action. The man who acts ideologically sees himself justified in his idea; the responsible man commits his action into the hands of God and lives by God's grace and favour.[121]

It was not, then, irresponsibility or a violation of his duty as a believing Christian that made Bonhoeffer take part in the conspiracy; it was, on the contrary, his awareness of himself as a Christian who had to act responsibly in the world. Indeed his action was prompted not by ideological motives, since this would have meant taking action out of God's hands, but by the awareness of the need for man to act responsibly in a world in which God has become man and in which man abandons himself to God's grace and depends on it. Certainly Bonhoeffer's entanglement in the 'worldly sector' gave him cause, as he himself admitted, 'to think',[122] and he did not dismiss lightly the reminder of his brother-in-law Hans von Dohnanyi that 'all they that take the sword shall perish with the sword' (Matthew 26: 52). In the last analysis, Bonhoeffer found his way into martyrdom as a sinner who, as such, stands before and commends himself to God. In the depth of despair he evoked the majesty of God and validated the drama of sin and forgiveness. Resistance 'to the blood' and the decision to condone tyrannicide had their place in the dispensation of the redemptive order and found their justification in the *theologia crucis*.

Both Karl Barth and Dietrich Bonhoeffer were thus instrumental in reminding the Christian community of its responsibilities that lay beyond self-interest and self-defence in the theological realm. But it was Bonhoeffer who from the start announced the 'unconditional obligation' to the victims of any ordering of society.[123] The Christian was called upon to act responsibly in a situation when any group, even if it did not belong to the Christian community, was deprived of its basic rights. This was meant not merely to remind the state of its responsibilities, not just to bandage the victims under the wheel, but 'to put the spoke into the wheel itself'. It was Bonhoeffer's deeply religious commitment that impelled him to move into the 'worldly sector'; doing so in defence of human rights left him, so he argued unequivocally, *in statu confessionis*.[124] Early in 1941 when he appeared on one of his missions for the Abwehr in Switzerland and called on Karl Barth, even the latter initially did not know what to make of his young friend who came from Nazi Germany with official sanction and swastika-stamped documents.

In the relations between the German Resistance and the outside world, Bonhoeffer assumed a distinctive and decisive function. Clearly, he did not go out, as did Ulrich von Hassell or even Adam von Trott, to negotiate conditions for peace, and if he travelled under the auspices of Admiral Canaris's organization, it was not for the purpose of transacting political business. He was a churchman who saw himself impelled to alert his Christian brethren abroad to the enormities of the Nazi menace and to remind the Protestant Churches of their obligations. Embattled as he found the German believers and the German Churches to be, Bonhoeffer turned to the wider ecumenical community with the outcry 'we need you', and, moreover, with the emphatic reminder that the affairs of the German Churches were in reality also those of the 'Church universal'.[125]

Ecumenism meant for Bonhoeffer the realization of a solidarity of the Protestant Churches, as he had stressed early in his 1932 address in Czechoslovakia, transcending mere organizational matters, but bearing witness to the *Christus praesens* and being able to account for the question 'who Christ really is, for us today'.[126]

Bonhoeffer's formula for resolving the dilemma of his Church in its encounter with National Socialism did not, however, go unchallenged. The deep and multiple divisions in the Evangelical Church over the assessment of and policies towards National Socialism flared up particularly in the realm of ecumenism. Early in 1934 the Nazi-sponsored 'Reich Bishop' Ludwig Müller set up the 'Church Office for External Affairs' (Kirchliches Aussenamt) under

Dr Theodor Heckel, who henceforth was allowed to call himself 'bishop' and who was put in charge of relations with churches abroad and especially of all ecumenical affairs. It is not surprising that his office in their effort to project the picture of a thriving German Protestantism backed by a benign state, should have distanced itself from what was considered the intransigence of such as Karl Barth and Dietrich Bonhoeffer. And while Heckel pretended to adhere rigidly to the Lutheran 'Zwei-Reiche-Lehre', he allowed his office to depend for its work abroad on substantial subsidies from the Auswärtiges Amt.

Within German Protestantism the lines were by no means clearly drawn between supporters and critics of the Nazi regime's Church policies. Heckel himself—with little success—attempted to present his course to the foreign Church leaders as reasonable and that of the hard-liners in the Confessing Church, and especially of Barth and Bonhoeffer, as exaggerated and self-defeating. The lines got more blurred, by the co-operation which Heckel obtained from two key figures in German Protestantism, Eugen Gerstenmaier and Hans Schönfeld, who, while active ecumenists, had close ties to the *Widerstand*, and thus could present themselves abroad as the authentic voice of the Church.

The active part which Gerstenmaier took in the German Resistance is a matter of record and will unfold in the later chapters of this book. While in the Auswärtiges Amt (1939–42) he worked closely with Haeften and Trott, and after being forced to leave it he found a protected assignment with the Abwehr. From 1942 he was also one of the most faithful participants in the meetings of Helmuth von Moltke's Kreisau Circle. Indeed Gerstenmaier was among the most determined and fearless conspirators in the plot against the Führer. There has been considerable controversy, however, especially over his role in the Kirchliches Aussenamt.[127]

Gerstenmaier's friend Hans Schönfeld was in a singularly sensitive post as Director of Research of the World Council of Churches, then 'in Process of Formation'.[128] A deeply religious man and a German patriot, Schönfeld was, through his station abroad, in a position to observe and collect vital information on the German Church Dispute and to warn, as he did early on, that the Church in Germany was involved, as he put it, 'in the hardest struggle since the times of the Reformation'.[129] In this grave situation he considered it his chief task to keep the lines of communication open between the World Council and all the embattled Churches, first the German one and subsequently, as the war took its course, the Churches in the occupied countries. Not only did Schönfeld have close ties with the *Widerstand*, he also often carried vital information from Geneva to the Resistance Movement in Holland.[130] At the same time he co-operated closely, on the level of Church policy, with Heckel's office and with his friend Gerstenmaier and did his best to expose the 'hypocritical arrogance'[131] of 'certain very radical circles' which, as he saw it, made all ecumenical work in his sense impossible.

The controversiality of both Gerstenmaier and Schönfeld should not be reduced to a mere matter of pastors' and theologians' infighting, as is done all too often in the literature. Their problem was a real one, namely the dilemma between, as Visser't Hooft once put it, the 'maintenance of the community' and the stress upon confession and bearing 'witness'.[132] There is no question but that their understanding of ecumenism was utterly different from that of Karl Barth and Bonhoeffer. It also appears that, while carrying out their Church diplomacy, they, and especially Gerstenmaier, all too readily lent support to Heckel's manœuvres which in effect amounted to accommodation with the Nazi authorities and certainly not to resistance in the name of the faith.

Both Gerstenmaier and Schönfeld had, no doubt, to lead a double life, and we have no reason to be scandalized by Schönfeld having been financially supported by the Auswärtiges Amt.[133] Nor should we be shocked by his cooperation with the German Consul-General in Geneva, Wolfgang Krauel,[134] and Consuls von Nostitz and von Kessel.[135] Such, we must understand, were the fruits of Weizsäcker's carefully designed *Sonderpolitik*.

The more the lines between accommodation and resistance were blurred in Germany, of course, the more difficult does the task become for the historian to assess the relative weight of the two modes of political and social behaviour. There were incidents, moreover, in the careers of Gerstenmaier and Schönfeld, such as their handling of the so-called German Christian-inspired 'Godesberg Declaration' of 4 April 1939,[136] which suggest excessive accommodation with the Nazis.

Visser't Hooft made the point that Gerstenmaier and Schönfeld, however close their working relationship, should not be wholly equated with each other.[137] This reminder is helpful. Certainly their temperaments were utterly different. Gerstenmaier was a go-getter and not above letting his boundless ambition run away with him.[138] Although his defenders have made a point of invoking his need for camouflage under Nazi rule,[139] he seems not to have been excessively burdened by the moral dilemmas which this condition created[140]—at least not in the years before he actually joined the Resistance. Schönfeld, by contrast, was a rather withdrawn and mysterious person who suffered under the burden of the conflicting pressures upon him[141] and was in the end broken by them.

A whole spectrum of attitudes and policies represented by the various shadings of German Protestants under Nazi rule thus was brought to bear on the Ecumenical Movement,[142] ranging from Karl Barth's 'crusade theology'[143] to the obfuscating manœuvres of Heckel and his friends which Karl Barth derided as 'Christianity à la mode'.[144] The leaders of the Ecumenical Movement had to sort out these disparate signals.

It should not be surprising that the latter did not themselves present a united front against the Nazi threat. The Scandinavian and the English princes of the Protestant Churches were, without exception, rooted in the tradition of liberal Christianity and in an optimistic reading of the Christian doctrine of man.[145] And quite apart from the fact that they were committed to the redress of what they considered to be the injustices of the Versailles settlement and to a reconciliation with their German brethren, they favoured a policy of appeasement even with the Nazis, whose policy of persecution they abhorred. Appeasement appeared to them an essentially Christian and moral imperative. All the leading ecumenists of the 1930s, Archbishop Erling Eidem of Uppsala, Bishop Eivind Berggrav of Oslo, Archbishop William Temple of York (and later of Canterbury), and Bishop George Bell of Chichester, saw the need for striking a 'delicate balance'[146] between maintaining unity in Christianity and standing up for the integrity of the Christian message. The World Council of Churches, despite its increasing awareness of the Nazi atrocities, was eager, moreover, to avoid giving the appearance of becoming an organ of the Western democracies.[147] As late as May 1939 Bishop Berggrav remarked: 'We must not build a Maginot line of churches.'[148]

In this setting the signals emanating from Schönfeld and Gerstenmaier seemed, to begin with at least, much more reasonable than Karl Barth's 'general-staff verdicts', as they were once called,[149] which were issued from his Basle sanctuary. In the long run, the thundering of Barth was probably less effective than Bonhoeffer's persistent and authentic witness in awakening the princes of the Churches outside Germany to the perception of the *tua res agitur*, namely that the Church Dispute was a common concern and responsibility. 'The question at stake in the German Church is no longer an internal issue,' Bonhoeffer wrote to Bishop Bell in 1934, 'but it is the question of the existence of Christianity in Europe; therefore a definite attitude of the Ecumenical Movement has nothing to do with "intervention"—but it is just a demonstration to the whole world that Church and Christianity as such are at stake.'[150]

Bonhoeffer's theology of resistance, as he had elaborated it as early as 1932, was now put to the test at an ecumenical level. Of course the Churches in Norway and Holland themselves came to feel the immediacy of the burden of Nazi oppression and thus to understand the relatedness of confession and resistance. Once the intrepid appeaser, after 1942 Bishop Berggrav was responsible for leading the Norwegian Church into resistance.[151] Visser't Hooft, hardened by the experience of the Dutch Church Dispute, made the World Council of Churches a clearing-house for Church resistance.[152] Bishop Bell, hitherto a man of conciliation, had learned in the course of the 1930s that 'the dramatic nature of the times demanded a dramatic and radical response'.[153] In war-torn England Bell became a fighter for unpopular causes, including the German Resistance. All these churchmen had learned an important lesson from a young fearless and determined German theologian,

Dietrich Bonhoeffer. They had learned above all, as Visser't Hooft reported late in 1943 to William Temple, by then Archbishop of Canterbury, that 'on the Continent had arisen what might be called a theology of Resistance'.[154] They, in turn, were now prepared to stand up for this German theologian and his friends of the *Widerstand*, granting them a recognition which abroad was otherwise stubbornly denied them.

Karl Barth proudly declared that in matters of the relationship to the European Resistance the 'trumpet' of European Protestantism had sounded a 'clearer tune' than the one of the Holy See.[155] On balance he was correct. There is therefore a paradox involved in the fact that the Church of Rome, a universal institution, should have given relatively little support to its embattled German flock. Basically, the Papacy confined itself to insistence on the implementation of the Concordat. The episcopate was further divided over the relative merits of emphasis on the prerogatives of the Church as against those of the faith. The Encyclical *Mit brennender Sorge* ('With Deep Anxiety') issued by Pius XI on 14 March 1937, that was read from the Catholic pulpits all over Germany on 21 March, contained a sharp condemnation of the National Socialist Church policies. It did not really constitute a breakthrough, however. In fact, it did not prevent the cleavages within the German episcopate from widening: especially between the accommodative Cardinal Bertram, Archbishop of Breslau, and Count Preysing, bishop of Berlin, who favoured a strong stand against the Nazis.[156] Preysing maintained close connections with individuals of the *Widerstand*, especially with Helmuth von Moltke, the head of the Kreisau Circle.[157]

But contact between the Roman Church as such and the German Resistance was sporadic. In one instance the Papacy did actually involve itself as mediator in the negotiations between the British and the *Widerstand*.[158] But the Pope remained far more wary of 'intervention' than did the Protestant ecumenical leaders. The 'missionary field'[159] about which Bonhoeffer wrote cryptically in a letter from his temporary refuge in the Benedictine monastery in Ettal, and by which he meant the relations with the enemy countries by way of Rome,[160] was not working too well. In fact, Father Max Josef Metzger, the Catholic pacifist, and founder and head of the *Una Sancta* movement, channelled his plan of 1942 for a German and European post-war order through the Protestant Archbishop Eidem of Uppsala.[161]

## 5. Conspiratorial Circles

The old establishments could, as we have seen, offer to the opposition at best some protection under their umbrella. In this setting the latter were reduced to functioning more or less by deception. But in the course of the war certain groups of like-minded people formed that allowed the individuals to converge and offered them a sense of conspiratorial community. One of the chief groups of this kind was the 'Kreisau Circle' which derived its name from the Silesian estate of its mentor, Helmuth James von Moltke. It was an informal circle of friends—the name was actually only given it later by the Gestapo—who felt that the opposition groups emanating from the old establishments, especially the Beck–Goerdeler–von Hassell group, did not plumb the depths of Germany's crisis and concentrated too much on political reform and action at the expense of spiritual renewal. The circle met sporadically, most frequently in various Berlin apartments, but also, for the more comprehensive conferences, at various landed estates such as Kreisau and the properties of the Yorck von Wartenburg and Borsig families. The very composition of the group gives one a good idea of the generously explorative spirit that animated it, for it included noblemen and commoners, Protestants and Catholics (among them three Jesuits), conservatives and socialist labour leaders. Uncommitted to party creeds, and rejecting one-sided doctrinaire positions, these men sought to learn from each other and to prepare the ground for a new synthesis that would heal all those divisions, both religious and political, that had plagued Germany in the past. Belonging for the most part to the younger generation born in the early years of our century, not old enough to have served in the Great War, but deeply affected by its aftermath, their thoughts and politics tended to be at variance with those of the Beck–Goerdeler–von Hassell group. Their thinking was marked by an exploratory, if not revolutionary, spirit, ready to part from conventional capitalist and nationalist canons.

A number of fine books have been written about both Moltke and the Kreisau Circle.[162] It remains for me here to outline the setting and the premises which instructed the formulation of Moltke and his circle's thoughts and their actions in the area of foreign affairs.

Helmuth James von Moltke was, beyond all doubt, a personage of singular presence. He was a Moltke and a proud kin of the Field Marshal of the Second Reich era. And if he was not the saintly person all too readily depicted immediately after the war, he was a man of clear direction and independence and of moral firmness and integrity. If he was a Prussian Junker, he was the most untypical of them all. To begin with, he had, like Adam von Trott, deep roots in the Anglo-Saxon world. His mother was the daughter of South Africa's Chief Justice, Sir James Rose Innes, and his ties to Britain, indeed to the whole Commonwealth, served, as his biographers put it, as a 'lifeline' to him.[163] The 'greater world'[164]—Europe, the Commonwealth of Nations—meant as much to him as did the Moltke estate whose management he took over in 1929. But what was in between, namely Germany as a political power unit, was of less and less importance to him as he watched the wave of nationalism and racism surge over his country. Moltke's vision was of a

Europe risen above power conflicts and reformed along socialist lines. And the more things in Germany took a turn for the worse, the more did he see himself as a man with a mission. It certainly was not an empty phrase when, during the war, he wrote from neutral Sweden to Lionel Curtis, his English family friend and mentor:[165]

For us Europe after the war is less a problem of frontiers and soldiers, of top-heavy organisations or grand plans, but Europe after the war is a question of how the picture of man can be re-established in the breasts of our fellow-citizens. This is a question of religion and education, of ties to work and family, of the proper relation of responsibility and rights.[166]

Moltke's mention of religion deserves some comment; it was no empty phrase. Brought up a Christian Scientist, he rebelled against this particular Church. In fact, at the time he married, his bride[167] found him to be plainly an agnostic. In the course of time, however, as the struggle with the Nazis went on, he turned increasingly to religion. In his letter to Lionel Curtis just quoted he explained that, while earlier he had maintained that belief in God was not necessary for his endeavours, now he knew that he had been 'wrong, completely wrong'. And he continued:

you know that I have fought the Nazis from the first day, but the amount of risk and readiness for sacrifice which is asked from us now, and that which may be asked from us tomorrow require more than right ethical principles, especially as we know that the success of our fight will probably mean a total collapse as a national unit. But we are ready to face this.[168]

This does not mean that in any way he minimized 'right ethical principles'. To his immediate chief in the Abwehr[169] who was arguing with him about the justification of an absolutely murderous order from the Führer, Moltke said: 'You see, Admiral, the difference between us is that I am incapable of arguing about such questions ... because for me the difference between good and evil, right and wrong exists *a priori*.'[170] However, he discovered the dimension transcending considerations of this world. 'Our lives', he wrote to his wife, 'are in God's hands.'[171] And as he took to reading the Bible with increasing pleasure, he found that, what previously he had regarded as 'all stories', at any rate in the Old Testament, had become 'real' to him.[172]

The affinity between the thinking of Moltke and Bonhoeffer is inescapable. It is not that the two were in any way personally attuned to each other. As a matter of fact, when they went on a wartime mission together to Scandinavia in 1942, they found out that they did not have much to say to each other. Moltke, the squire, was not on the same wavelength as, and indeed was a bit bored by and impatient with the man of the Book.[173] Both, however, the man of responsible action who had moved towards theology and the theologian who had chosen the way of 'responsible action' were decisive in giving the

*Widerstand* a rationale that clearly transcended pleading for class, or nation, or any other special interest. When in the well-known prison letter of January 1945 Moltke reported to his wife that he had faced his tormentor, Roland Freisler of the Nazi People's Court, not as a Protestant, not as a big landowner, not as a nobleman, not as a Prussian, not as a German . . . 'but as a Christian and nothing else',[174] he reiterated his own convictions while at the same time summarizing the spirit that had come to pervade his Kreisau Circle. Like Bonhoeffer, Moltke was an ecumenical figure in the sense of having overcome denominational and factional divisions, and in this way he lent a genuine universal sanction to his and his friends' approaches to the outside world.

It would be altogether mistaken to envisage the deliberations of Moltke's group as having been characterized by unanimity. The atmosphere at their meetings was far from cultish and solemn. We must visualize them, especially those away from the capital, as accompanied by a good deal of informality and cheer. Helmuth von Moltke's wife Freya and likewise the Countess Marion von Yorck, who was also present at these meetings, made sure that those who had travelled from far away were rewarded by good food, drink, and laughter. And there was the peacefulness of the countryside, immune from the air raids that plagued the cities. In this setting the argumentation was refreshingly lively, and the participants who, as indicated earlier, were of quite varied backgrounds and persuasions, each brought their best to bear on the discussion. Despite all the argumentation, Helmuth von Moltke was happy to record how strong was 'das Gemeinsame' which made all the differences 'bearable'.[175] And despite the informality of it all, Freya von Moltke recalls that, as she watched the group move on to its formal meetings, she had the distinct sense that somehow the future of Europe hung in the balance.[176]

Many of the figures whom we have encountered thus far in this chapter— Trott, Haeften, Kessel, Haushofer, Gerstenmaier, and also Schönfeld—found their way into the Kreisau Circle. In one capacity or another, they all contributed their share to the orchestration of Kreisau's foreign political plans and moves.[177]

Among these it was Trott in particular who made it his task to build bridges to the outside world for Moltke's group. Despite their similar backgrounds and part-Anglo-Saxon identity, as well as their common dedication to the principles of international law, Moltke and Trott were not easily attuned to each other. When they first met in February 1937 in hall at All Souls College, Oxford, A. L. Rowse, Adam's host, recorded the 'mutually appraising, slightly suspicious look' which the two gave each other 'in the increasing dangers of the later thirties'.[178] They were in any case men of quite different temperaments: Moltke serene, down-to-earth, and self-assured, and Trott impulsive, imaginative, and ever struggling for clarity. Like his eminent great-great-uncle, Moltke was given to long silences, and might initially at least have been understandably distrustful of the overflowing intellectuality of Trott. But there were more than temperamental differences standing in the way of their relationship. To start with, Moltke was never quite certain of Trott's chief in the Auswärtiges Amt, the State Secretary, von Weizsäcker,[179] whose 'feigned co-operation' was incomprehensible to him. Trott himself, concentrating on resistance foreign policy, had to adopt the same style and find continuous alibis for his missions abroad. If for the most part Moltke's role in the Abwehr could be one of admirable candour and openness, Trott, on the other hand, had to fall back on camouflage and deception. What official work he did for the AA, whether it involved preparations for the invasion of the British Isles or the sponsorship of the Indian freedom fighter Bose, all had to serve as cover for his illegal activities which took him from country to country in his restless attempts to reach the outside world.

This 'greater world' was more manifest, no doubt, to Moltke than it was to Trott, largely because of the former's readiness to dismiss that 'in between' dimension, namely Germany, as a 'national unit'. Trott would not and could not do this. Since he was more directly involved in concrete negotiations abroad, he felt duty-bound to safeguard his nation's integrity. Therefore Trott had continuously to reassess the balance between the prerogatives of the nation and of Europe. If Moltke set the tone for the ethos of the Kreisau group, it fell upon Trott to function as its 'foreign minister', and as such he was subject to the tensions between principle and practicality which are peculiar to all statesmanship.

The letters of Moltke to his wife betray no little friction between Moltke and Trott. As a matter of fact, Moltke was more attuned to Haeften and Gerstenmaier than he was to Trott. A breakthrough eventually occurred, however, in the relations between Moltke and Trott. By the late spring of 1943, when the third major Kreisau meeting took place and which was primarily devoted to Adam's area of expertise, 'foreign policy',[180] Moltke registered 'general satisfaction' about the concrete results and even a sense of 'bliss'.[181] By then he and Adam von Trott had become trusted associates, if not friends.

Among the conspiratorial circles three others must be briefly introduced here which, in one way or another, also had a bearing on the thoughts and actions of the Resistance in the area of foreign affairs. The Freiburg group goes back to the time of the infamous Crystal Night of November 1938, after which a number of professors of the Albert-Ludwig University connected with the Confessing Church decided to form the 'Freiburg Council' (Freiburger Konzil) with the objective of investigating the possibilities and duties of Christians to resist.[182] Subsequently, in October 1942, Dietrich Bonhoeffer, on behalf of the Provisional Governing Body of the Confessing Church, commissioned the group to elaborate for the occasion of an international

Church Conference, planned by the Archbishop of Canterbury and the Bishop of Chichester for the time following the cessation of hostilities, guidelines for the establishment of world peace. The reconstituted and somewhat enlarged group which from then on called itself the 'Freiburg Circle' (Freiburger Kreis) or 'Bonhoeffer Circle'[183] emerged in January 1943 with a major memorandum[184] which served as a preliminary text for the Amsterdam ecumenical conference of August 1948 during which, under the chairmanship of the Archbishop of Canterbury, the World Council of Churches, hitherto only 'in Process of Formation', was formally constituted.

Within the spectrum of the German Resistance the Freiburg group occupied a central place and possessed a considerable potential as a mediating force. Through the participation of Goerdeler a tie was established with the activist branch of the Resistance. 'He represented in our circle a natural unofficial authority,' recalled the theologian Helmut Thielicke.[185] In the Circle Bonhoeffer found a concrete outlet for his part in the Church Dispute as well as a sounding board for his work on ethics, in progress at the time, in which he elaborated the theoretical justification of resistance; he in turn was able to assure his Freiburg friends of ecumenical sanction. The message contained in the memorandum—the assumption of the integrity of the Reich in the area of foreign affairs, combined with the protection of the smaller nations, and the proposal of a federation of all European states—puts it right in the middle between the more conservative position of the group around Goerdeler and the Kreisau Circle. No substantial ties were established with the latter, however,[186] which might, as Eberhard Bethge suggests, be explained by the fact that Bonhoeffer was involved in the unfortunate disagreements on Church policies with men such as Gerstenmaier and Schönfeld.[187] In the event, there was no co-ordination between these two groups.

Some distinct ties, however, existed between the Freiburg group and the so-called Stuttgart Circle which formed around the industrialist Robert Bosch, a magnate of a rather unusual kind, 'altogether different', as Gerhard Ritter described him, from the majority of his peers in Rhineland-Westphalia.[188] A typical Swabian democrat, Bosch possessed a strong sense of political and social responsibility which led him to detest the Nazi regime. Together with his general manager, Hans Walz, and his private secretary, Willy Schloßstein, Bosch set out to attract like-minded people, to help the persecuted, to strike up relations with the Resistance, and to establish contacts with the outside world. Among his confidants was Bishop Theophil Wurm of Württemberg[189] who within the Protestant episcopate was one of the most outspoken supporters of the Confessing Church. The chief connection between the circle and the Resistance was Carl Goerdeler[190] who in 1937, after his resignation as Mayor of Leipzig, accepted Bosch's offer for a loose contractual relationship, which served as cover, and also financial backing for his opposition activities and in particular his trips abroad. Walz remembered him as 'by far the most

fiery personality of truly dynamic effectiveness'[191] among all those men who
aimed at freeing Germany and Europe from the Nazi tyranny without involving them in war. Bosch's lieutenants themselves took advantage of their
opportunities to travel abroad in order to establish ties with foreign powers.
During the Twilight War Schloßstein, upon instruction from Goerdeler, made
connection with the mysterious British Group Captain Malcolm Grahame
Christie, who, shuttling back and forth between Switzerland and the Traveller's Club in London, served as private intelligence agent for Sir Robert
Vansittart, the Chief Diplomatic Adviser to the Foreign Secretary.[192] Late in
1942 and in the following spring Walz repeatedly established contact in
Zurich with the American Consul Maurice W. Altaffer.[193]

Later in 1941 a new centre of resistance emerged, the so-called 'Goerdeler
Circle'. This actually emanated from two former labour-union leaders, Jakob
Kaiser, who in the Weimar years had headed the Christian unions in the
Rhineland and Westphalia, and Wilhelm Leuschner, one-time Social Democratic Minister of the Interior of Hesse and deputy head of the Socialist
Union (ADGB).[194] Despite their obvious misgivings about the 'reactionary'
views of Goerdeler, and repeated warnings about him from the Kreisau
people, including Moltke himself, Kaiser and Leuschner pursued, together
with some other labour-union leaders,[195] their aim of building bridges within
the Resistance.[196] In particular they sought to work towards a consolidated
union movement in Germany after Hitler. For Goerdeler, who all along had
lamented the divisions within the pre-Hitlerian German labour movement,[197]
this connection meant a welcome and important potential broadening of the
base of his schemes since it opened up prospects of a resistance backed by a
wide popular support.

In the area of foreign contacts the Goerdeler Circle also played a distinct
part. However, it must be noticed that the labour leaders took the position
that domestic affairs should have priority. Since their primary objective was
the removal of the 'system', they advocated 'greatest restraint'[198] in matters
relating to other countries. But it is by no means in contradiction to this basic
position that they were particularly keen to establish ties with Vienna. They,
like Goerdeler, were 'Greater Germans', and not even the manner in which
the *Anschluss* was accomplished by the Nazis in 1938 deterred them from
assuming that after Hitler Austria would remain united with Germany. They
found out, however, that none of their suggestions for Austria's special
position within a future Reich was able to prevent their Austrian interlocutors
from becoming increasingly confirmed in their insistence on Austrian independence.

## 6. Exiles as Auxiliaries

Exile constituted an important link between the *Widerstand* and the outer world. Exile by itself, of course, is no resistance, and while deep down in his heart almost every exile interprets his leaving as a form of resisting and as a prelude to returning home, it must be understood that the German exiles from National Socialism were a singularly varied lot. Strictly speaking, most of those who left were refugees who were forced to leave their country for religious and racial reasons. There was also, of course, the incidence of political exile which in its turn formed a by no means united front. There were the middle-class exiles of liberal-conservative persuasion, and there were the Socialists and the Communists. The connections between these groups were minimal. Also, of course, the dispersal of the German exiles into virtually all corners of the world added to their political ineffectiveness.

It would be a mistake, however, to write off altogether the exiles as a 'serious political reality' and in particular to deny their many contacts with the Resistance.[199] As a matter of fact, the connections between the exiles and the Resistance were many, intricate, and a testimony to the solicitude of the exiles, political as well as religious and racial, and also to the perceived need on the part of the resistance emissaries to stay in touch with the exiles. It simply is not right to say that 'not only the Ocean separated Count Stauffenberg from Paul Tillich ... '.[200] And when one of the most mysterious of all the exiles, the former German General Staff Captain Hans Ritter,[201] who from his Swiss outpost was deeply involved in the traffic with the resistance, dismissed the bulk of his fellow German 'emis', as he called the emigrants, as belonging to the 'dustbin',[202] he but gave understandable expression to his impatience over the inherent complexities of the operation he was involved in. There never existed a serious question of the British or the Americans favouring the formation of a German government-in-exile; likewise the odds were against the exiles themselves ever being able to return to their homeland after the war to assume political responsibilities.[203] Therefore many prominent exiles strove all the more to establish contacts with their host governments as well as to pave the way for the resistance emissaries.

In Britain the middle-class political exile[204] was left without an obvious focal point when ex-Chancellor Heinrich Brüning, in the late summer of 1939, left for good for the United States. In any case, the Foreign Office was extremely hesitant about approaching the exiles; so the main connection between them and the authorities was Sir Robert Vansittart[205] and his private intelligence service, notably Group Captain Christie. If anybody was frequently sounded out, it was Hermann Rauschning, the renegade Nazi and former President of the Danzig Senate. In an *aide-mémoire* of the early summer of 1939 the latter stated unequivocally his position that since modern

dictatorships exercise enormous powers of coercion, and leave but a very
limited field of action for resistance, 'the German opposition abroad should
to a large extent supplement the domestic opposition'.[206] Whenever in London
Rauschning had access to the Foreign Secretary, Lord Halifax, and was
consulted by the Foreign Office on questions of future policies towards
Germany.[207] Together with Otto Strasser, Hitler's one-time paladin, and Karl
Höltermann, former leader of the Republican defence corps *Reichsbanner*,
Rauschning was actually proposed by Group Captain Christie to Vansittart,
shortly after the outbreak of the war, to serve on a German Advisory
Committee.[208] Nothing came of the idea. Strasser, with whom Rauschning
did not want to make common cause,[209] was eventually, early in 1941, whisked
away by the efforts of Vansittart from his exile on the European Continent
to Canada for possible political use.

But if Rauschning and Strasser, considering their political backgrounds,
were clearly controversial figures, less compromised exiles did their share in
claiming to represent the 'other Germany'.[210] An inveterate activist on behalf
of the opposition was Dr Reinhold Schairer[211] who set himself up as 'personal
representative' of Goerdeler in Britain and conducted negotiations on his
behalf not only with the Foreign Office but also in Belgium and France,
where he had access to the highest authorities, and in the United States.[212]
But Schairer was a man without any political experience and a busybody
who exaggerated his own importance and was easily distrusted by those who
had to deal with him. There was also Sebastian Haffner,[213] a journalist
formerly connected with the Berlin *Vossische Zeitung* who in his English exile
became a leading publicist on the German question. While initially he argued
the case for a harsh future policy towards, in fact a partitioning of,
Germany,[214] he subsequently advocated a European Commonwealth under
Britain's leadership in which a post-Hitlerian Germany was to play its part.[215]
Germany was after all, he now maintained, 'merely the first Nazi-occupied
territory', and he called attention to 'those Germans who had already fought
longer against Hitler than anyone else, under much harder conditions, with
much less hope and against greater odds'.[216] Haffner then called attention
to the existence of the *Widerstand* in Germany which, he urged, needed
encouragement.

Quieter but no less insistent was the work on behalf of the German
Resistance of Ernst Jaeckh, Kurt Hahn, and Gerhard Leibholz. Jaeckh[217]
advised the Foreign Office in matters pertaining to Germany. Thus in April
1936 he transmitted a message from Schacht to the Secretary of State cau-
tioning the British government against any political or economic agreement
with Hitler's Germany until '"civilization" had been restored in Germany'.[218]
Hahn,[219] whom we have encountered earlier as a mentor of Hans-Bernd von
Haeften, never abandoned his sense of responsibility for the affairs of his old
country. Through Lionel Curtis he had access to the Foreign Secretary Lord

Halifax, on whom as late as July 1939 he urged the recognition of the legitimate needs of the German people stemming from the wrongs of the Versailles Treaty. In keeping with the thinking of the conservative German Resistance, he argued that this course, if rejected by Hitler, would have the effect of 'unmasking' him before Germany.[220] And while Hahn eventually went along with the official Allied line of 'unconditional surrender', he kept insisting throughout that the promise of a fair deal to a vanquished Germany would strengthen the hands of the Resistance.[221]

Gerhard Leibholz,[222] who was married to Dietrich Bonhoeffer's twin sister, was a Professor of International Law at the University of Göttingen. In 1938, because of his Jewish ancestry, he emigrated with his family to England and settled down in Oxford.[223] Through the mediation of Dietrich Bonhoeffer he established contact with Bishop Bell of Chichester and became during the war years the latter's chief consultant on matters pertaining to the future of Germany.[224] Leibholz's insistence on distinguishing between Germans and Nazis, and on the ideological rather than national nature of the war, led him to confirm the Bishop in his stand against the 'unconditional surrender' formula and in his interest in the *Widerstand*.

Mention should also be made here of Wilfrid Israel,[225] scion of a notable Jewish Anglo-German family and heir to the Berlin department store, N. Israel, until dispossessed by the Nazis in the mid-1930s. Israel first met Adam von Trott in 1935, and the two formed an intimate friendship. Protected by a British passport, Israel was able to stay in Germany until the eve of the war, dedicating himself to helping German Jews leave the country. In England during the war he joined the Foreign Research and Press Service of the Royal Institute of International Affairs. While he, like Hahn, eventually endorsed the 'unconditional surrender' policy, he nevertheless continually urged that Britain should 'come to the aid of the besieged opposition'[226] by promising a better future for Germany after the war. Israel's faith in his friend Trott made him overcome all the doubts which it would have been natural for a Jew to harbour concerning the integrity of the German people.[227] Approached by Bishop Bell on this matter late in 1942, he answered resolutely that for him it was a 'simple but significant fact that the German people—not only the Jews—were the first victims of Nazi oppression'.[228] It was this passage above all that Bishop Bell took over from Wilfrid Israel when, on 10 March 1943 before the House of Lords, he called attention to the existence of opposition in Germany and stated as a 'simple matter of fact' that Germany was 'the first country in Europe to be occupied by the Nazis'.[229]

In the United States of America the king pin among the middle-class exiles was of course the former Chancellor Heinrich Brüning who resided like a monk in Harvard University's Lowell House.[230] Once he had finally put the Atlantic between himself and his country in September 1939, he resigned himself to the role of witness, as in a Greek drama, to the inevitable doom ahead.[231] But cautious and circumspect as Brüning was, he acted as protector and mentor to Goerdeler, Moltke, and Trott.

Brüning had never ceased to regret that at the point of his resignation as Chancellor in May 1932 his proposal to the President to appoint Goerdeler as his successor had not been heeded. He had recommended the latter because, apart from having the confidence of Hindenburg and most of the political parties, he was 'highly thought of'[232] by the Social Democrats because of his conciliatory policies towards the labour unions. Indeed it was Brüning who in May 1933 had brought together Goerdeler and Leuschner. Later, in England as well as in the United States, the ex-Chancellor was most eager to pave the way for Goerdeler.[233] He also attempted, in the spring of 1938, to bring him together with Winston Churchill; but this encounter did not come off until the following year.[234] In February 1940 Brüning had a long session about Goerdeler with Frank Ashton-Gwatkin, head of the economic section of the British Foreign Office, during the latter's lecture tour in the United States. While Brüning was well aware of Goerdeler's all too open, 'somewhat naïve' ways, he never doubted, as he put it, 'his character'.[235]

Between Brüning and Moltke there had existed an old bond since 1927 when the young Moltke had called on the then Centrist Member of the Reichstag in Breslau to enquire into the possibilities of obtaining funding for a projected camp in Kreisau that was to bring together young workers, peasants, and students.[236] Ever since that day, Brüning later wrote to Moltke's widow, he had admired and kept an eye on Moltke.[237] The two met for the last time in Germany around the turn of the year 1933/4 and again in London late in 1937. In the autumn of 1939, when on his second American trip Adam von Trott sought a meeting with the former German Chancellor, he wrote him a formal letter on Institute of Pacific Relations stationery. In this letter Trott referred to Moltke, with whom he had spoken a fortnight before in Berlin, as having asked him to bring greetings and to discuss with him 'our common concerns'.[238] During the subsequent weeks Brüning's assistant at Harvard, Alexander Böker, whom Trott knew as a fellow Rhodes Scholar from the Oxford days,[239] was most eager to pave the way for him; Brüning, so Böker entered into his diary, already 'seemed to know of Adam and his coming as well as of his mission'.[240] Over the weekend of 11/12 November Brüning went to Washington where he stayed with the Assistant Secretary of State, George S. Messersmith, who arranged for a meeting between the German ex-Chancellor and President Roosevelt. During this meeting Brüning 'imploringly and passionately'[241] pleaded the case of his 'young friend',[242] submitting to the President all the intelligence obtained from Trott about the strength and the plans of the Resistance—but, alas, without appreciable result.[243]

From behind the scenes the ever-cautious Brüning also kept a hand in the affairs of an 'International Group in New York',[244] composed of Americans, one Englishman, and several Germans, mostly exiles, which was formed in the winter months of 1939/40 during the time of Trott's American sojourn. Trott, often referred to in the papers of the group as 'our friend from Germany' or 'friend from abroad', clearly constituted the reason for its formation, and Edward C. Carter, the Secretary General of the Institute of Pacific Relations, who to start with had been instrumental in inviting him to its November conference at Virginia Beach, was its motor. The group's primary objective was the definition of terms for a peace settlement and of a workable scheme for international co-operation in the future. Among the American contingent there was, besides Carter, Percy E. Corbett, a distinguished Professor of International Law at McGill University in Montreal, who in fact drafted its programme.[245]

The Englishman in the group was the historian John W. Wheeler-Bennett.[246] At the outbreak of the Second World War he had been assigned to the United States where he served in various official capacities. Upon instructions from the British Ambassador to Washington, Lord Lothian, late in November 1939, Wheeler-Bennett accompanied Trott to the Virginia Beach conference where the two saw a great deal of one another. Indeed soon afterwards Trott saw fit to describe his newly found friend as understanding 'one essential side of Germany probably better than anyone'[247] in Britain at that time. In a memorandum of December 1939, which Trott forwarded to England to his friend David Astor, Wheeler-Bennett had actually referred to the opposition forces inside Germany as an 'ally' of the 'Democratic Powers'.[248] In the course of the war, however, as we shall see, Wheeler-Bennett was to change his stance on the German Resistance.

The German contingent in the group included a number of distinguished exiles such as: Hans Muhle, a former official in the Prussian Ministry of Trade;[249] Kurt Riezler,[250] the one-time Chief of Cabinet in the Auswärtiges Amt under the short-lived government of Prinz Max von Baden of October/November 1918 and Director of the Bureau of the Reich President until April 1920;[251] and Hans Simons,[252] a distinguished Prussian civil servant who was retired after Chancellor von Papen's coup in Prussia of 20 July 1932.[253] Then there was Paul Scheffer, one of Germany's leading journalists, who, after the Nazi seizure of power, had succeeded the famous Theodor Wolff as editor-in-chief of the liberal-democratic *Berliner Tageblatt*. Scheffer himself was forced to resign in December 1936, however, and then moved to New York City as foreign correspondent for his old paper. After its demise early in 1939 he represented the *Deutsche Allgemeine Zeitung*. Being in possession of a valid German passport, Scheffer was not exactly an exile. A rather enigmatic and cagey person, he found himself in a basically ambiguous position. *Persona non grata* with the authorities at home, he was suspected in the United States of collusion with the Nazis. In fact, he was a German patriot who had maintained close ties with the *Widerstand*, and when Trott came to the United States in the winter of 1939, he took a particular interest in his mission.[254]

Altogether it was a motley group which formed in New York City. It would be an exaggeration to call it a 'German lobby'; its multinational composition in itself would preclude such a classification. Not even the German members were in agreement with one another. Muhle gave expression to this, for example, when he characterized Simons as 'the most modern' among them, but Riezler as being of a 'virtually fossil tradition'. He also criticized the ex-Chancellor for his ambivalence and reticence.[255] Indeed even between the two friends, Muhle and Trott, there were fundamental differences pertaining to their respective visions for a coup against the Nazi regime, inasmuch as Muhle dismissed Trott's formula of a 'revolution of the *Volksgemeinschaft*', that is one brought about by the military in conjunction with the workers, and, distrusting the former, insisted upon the central role of the latter.[256] Activated as it was by Trott's American visit, however, the group was a formation symptomatic of the period of the Twilight War when the discussion of peace aims was still an open one and when it was a foregone conclusion that the German opposition to Hitler would have a hand in the discussion.

It stands to reason that the neutral capitals would have afforded the exiles more than ample opportunity to link up with the emissaries of the Resistance. Certainly the Vatican served as a natural clearing-house. One of the leading figures in this arena was Monsignor Ludwig Kaas,[257] the former leader of the German Centre Party who, having prevailed upon his Party early in 1933 to accede to Hitler's Enabling Act[258] and having also negotiated the Reich Concordat between the Vatican and the new German regime, withdrew to Rome where he took charge of the excavation of St Peter's tomb in St Peter's Church. Being among the few to carry a key to the Pope's personal apartments, Kaas was also on 'terms of some intimacy' with Dr Josef Müller of the Abwehr[259] who in the winter of 1939/40 was to conduct the intricate negotiations in the Vatican on behalf of the *Widerstand* for an agreement with Britain. Most instrumental, however, in steering Müller in his secret Vatican mission, was Father Robert Leiber, SJ, Pope Pius XII's principal personal aide.

Since the capitulation of France in June 1940, and surrounded by Nazi-controlled territories, as the Swiss now were, exiles in Switzerland were severely curtailed in any political activities by the ever-watchful police. The exiles nevertheless found ways of getting around these difficulties. The very presence in the Swiss capital of the Allied secret services, the British Secret Intelligence Service (SIS) and, since November 1942, the American Office of Strategic Services (OSS), and furthermore the solicitous presence in Geneva of Willem A. Visser't Hooft, the General Secretary of the World Council of Churches, who was always ready to channel help and information to the

Resistance movements through Switzerland, facilitated the activities of those among the *émigrés* who saw themselves called upon to help their opposition friends in Germany.

One of the earliest German refugees of this kind was Professor Friedrich Wilhelm Siegmund-Schultze,[260] one of Germany's most active ecumenists and a confirmed pacifist who, exiled in 1933, particularly in the early phases of the war persisted in making his new home in Zurich a meeting-place between exiles and emissaries of the *Widerstand*. He maintained direct contacts in Britain with William Temple, the Archbishop of York and, from 1942, of Canterbury, and also with the Prime Minister, Neville Chamberlain, and in Germany with the group around Robert Bosch. Furthermore there was the previously mentioned ever-zealous former German Captain Hans Ritter who had taken refuge in Switzerland in order to put his services at the disposal of the intelligence operations of Sir Robert Vansittart.

The actual centre of political activity among the exiles in Switzerland, however, was the German Centrist ex-Chancellor Joseph Wirth.[261] Wirth had little in common with his peer in the United States, Heinrich Brüning, except the prestige which was attached to the high office which both had held in the Weimar days. By comparison with the painfully reticent and proud Brüning, Wirth, residing in Lucerne, made the most of his prestigious background to re-establish himself abroad and regain a position of political influence. It would not be overstating the case to say that he acted as a power-broker. Actually the exile colony in Switzerland, including such luminaries as the one-time Prussian Prime Minister, Otto Braun, and his Bavarian Social Democratic comrade, Wilhelm Hoegner, might have been conducive to the rebuilding of a nucleus of the Weimar coalition, and the plan for a post-war German government with Braun as President, Wirth as Chancellor, and Hoegner as Minister of Justice did not seem altogether unreasonable.[262] It was, however, not until April 1945 that the group, largely in response to Communist exiles' agitation in Switzerland, managed to assume a corporate identity by establishing itself as 'Das Demokratische Deutschland'. But any effective co-operation was impeded, if not by the ever-watchful eye of the Swiss police, then by the compulsive infighting on the part of Wirth.

It is wholly understandable that Wirth should have had close Vatican connections. But the ex-Chancellor got frantically enmeshed too in an absurdly intricate web of makeshift connections in Germany itself as well as with the Allies. Although immediately after his flight from Nazi Germany he wanted to 'hear nothing' of resistance,[263] before long nevertheless he got entangled in it. His main German ties were with the former Reichswehr Minister Otto Gessler who shuttled between Germany and Switzerland for the Beck–Goerdeler–von Hassell group, for Beck's successor as Chief of the Army General Staff, General Franz Halder, and the emissaries of the Stuttgart Circle. At the same time, however, Wirth kept his door open to the

Nazi authorities including Hans Heinrich Lammers, Hitler's Chief of the Reich Chancellery, reminding them of his patriotic policies while he had been Chancellor.[264] There are even indications that Wirth was in touch, indirectly at least, with Walter Schellenberg, the ever-ingenious chief (from 1941) of the Foreign Political Intelligence Service under Heinrich Himmler.[265]

Wirth's contacts with the Allies were no less bizarre. Anyone who embarks upon the path of secret-service dealings takes the risk of himself being used rather than being able to derive help from them. In any event, Wirth indiscriminately negotiated with Sir Robert Vansittart's intelligence service[266] as well as with the French secret service[267] and with the OSS in Switzerland, and, unwittingly, he even got entangled in the red espionage network in Switzerland.[268] Consumed by ambition and pride,[269] and addicted to care-lessness as well as to an excessive love of red wine, as came to be common knowledge, he was on balance of no help to his Resistance friends in Germany.

Neutral Turkey was, as has been rightly remarked, 'no place for innocents'.[270] Allied and Axis diplomatic and secret services there were com-peting with one another for intelligence; at the same time Turkey became a haven for Central European refugees. In fact, President Kemal Atatürk, taking advantage of the emigration from Nazi Germany, invited some hundred German and Austrian experts to teach in his universities, and not all of them steered clear of the political manœuvres along the Bosporus.[271]

Apart from Ernst Reuter, one of the most politically concerned exiles with a high profile,[272] Hans Wilbrandt and Alexander Rüstow most firmly lived up to the perception of the political function of the exile. The former, as an official of the Central Co-operative Funds Administration of Prussia before 1933, had been involved in the financing of the Kreisau estate and had thus become friends with Moltke. Rüstow, an economist of the 'neo-liberal' persuasion, had been head of the Economics Department of the Association of German Machine Construction Companies and, like Wilbrandt, emigrated to Turkey after the Nazi seizure of power. While maintaining ties with the German Ambassador in Ankara, Franz von Papen, Rüstow had connections with the American intelligence community there. When Moltke appeared at the Bosporus in July 1943, Wilbrandt brought Moltke and Rüstow together, and the latter in turn alerted the American secret service.[273]

## 7. The Socialists in Resistance and Exile

It stands to reason that in contacts between the resistance and the exiles the Socialists were concentrating on reaching their own comrades. But whereas the initiative in the traffic across the borders on the part of the conservative resistance came predominantly from those, such as Goerdeler, Trott, Moltke, within Germany, in the case of the Socialists it came from the exiles. The explanation for this is not hard to find. On balance, the conservatives had chosen the path of working from within the old establishments, in particular the army and the bureaucracy. This option gave them a potential hold on the levers of power, and it enabled them to survive as opposition in broad daylight, so to speak. It also enabled them in their official capacities to travel abroad relatively freely. Needless to say, it was precisely their conspiratorial entanglement with the Nazi state which involved them in serious conflicts of conscience, while on the other hand their foreign missions exposed them to distrust and rejection. For the Socialists, however, there was neither the protection nor the temptation of such camouflage. They were easily detected by the Gestapo, and only scattered groups were left trying to maintain their identity in a state of illegality.

The bulk of the Social Democratic leadership had fled in 1933 to Prague where it set up the headquarters of the Sopade;[274] in 1938 they moved to Paris and in 1940 to London. The establishment of Frontier Secretariats served the purpose of encouraging resistance, as far as possible, and also of collecting information about the political situation in Nazi Germany.[275] But the contacts between the illegal cadres at home and the exiled leadership remained minimal; the Social Democratic conspirators, in fact, avoided contact with their exiled comrades.[276]

On the other hand, the Socialist exiles in Britain who obtained active backing—until 1943—from their Labour sponsors were understandably eager to counteract the influence in Whitehall of conservatives such as Rauschning, and they even obtained—until 1941—a hearing from the British Foreign Office. Thus they had reason, in the early years of the war at least, to harbour hopes of being treated as political allies in Britain in the common struggle against Hitler.[277] In the course of the 'unwinding of appeasement', however, support for the German Socialists faded in Britain. On balance, the activities of the Sopade in London were strictly a chapter of exile politics with all its usual deceptions, frustrations, and hallucinations.

The divide between the exiled Social Democrats and the non-Socialist exiles was, as will have become already evident, not a rigid one. When the emissaries from the conservative *Widerstand* arrived abroad, they generally could count on support from the Socialists despite some fundamental policy differences involving especially the reliance of the conservatives on the military who, in the eyes of the Socialists, were the source of all evil and were bound to lead to a restoration of the old order. In New York Hans Muhle and Hans Simons, both Social Democrats, combined forces with Adam von Trott; and in Switzerland Otto Braun and Wilhelm Hoegner were initiated in Joseph Wirth's contacts in Germany. In Turkey Ernst Reuter associated with Alexander Rüstow and Hans Wilbrandt and closely followed their efforts on behalf of Helmuth von Moltke. In his Swedish exile Willy Brandt twice met

with Adam von Trott[278] in a futile effort to help him to establish a contact
with the Russian Minister. Trott's socialist leanings and his 'radical' stance,
as Brandt later recollected, as well as his mention of his association with the
Socialists of the Kreisau Circle and particularly with Julius Leber, admittedly
facilitated a meeting of minds between the two. In general, the very presence
of the Socialists in Kreisau tended to be a bridge between the Socialist and
the middle-class camps.

    An active pursuit of resistance foreign relations among the Socialists can
be registered chiefly on the part of the marginal groups and individuals of
the so-called 'New Left'.[279] Even the Socialists connected with the Kreisau
Circle, who were on the Right margin of the old Party—Julius Leber, Wilhelm
Leuschner, Theodor Haubach, and Carlo Mierendorff—were highly sceptical
about any foreign ventures. Leuschner, in fact, is quoted as having explicitly
urged the 'greatest restraint' in this matter, 'first of all since the system itself
had to be removed at all cost'.[280] The extreme Left, however, was more prone
to reach out to the world outside. Most active in this respect was the small
but tightly conspiratorial Neu Beginnen group founded in the latter years of
the Weimar Republic. Immediately after the Nazi seizure of power the group
installed a Foreign Bureau under the Austrian Karl B. Frank (alias Paul
Hagen) who moved, a step ahead of the Nazi bloodhounds, from Vienna to
Prague and thence to Paris and London. It was Frank who late in 1939
crossed the Atlantic with the primary mission of meeting Trott and of
confirming his credibility as an anti-Nazi. There were furthermore some
individuals originally connected with the radical Socialist splinter group, the
Internationaler Sozialistischer Kampfbund (ISK), notably Fritz Eberhard[281]
and Hilda Monte,[282] who persisted in co-ordinating resistance and exile, thus
overcoming the *malaise* of the Sopade circles. Hilda Monte finally paid with
her life when, in the spring of 1945, she was caught while acting as a courier
on the German–Swiss border; attempting to get away, she was shot by a
German frontier guard.[283]

# 8. The Communists in Resistance and Exile

Without doubt, the Communist Resistance was much more stubborn and
active—and costly—than was the one among the Social Democrats; at the
same time its foreign relations were much more intensive. It might be said
then that the Third International, while it was by no means prepared for the
Nazi onslaught, proved *in extremis* to be much more truly an International
than was the Second. The 'irrational fanaticism'[284] of the Communists supported their readiness for sacrifice as well as their unwavering allegiance to
the Comintern. But this latter relationship was not without its problems. The

fact was that the German Communist Party (KPD) had already in the Weimar period become directed from Moscow. This foreign dependence presented particular problems before and after the Nazi seizure of power. To begin with the KPD blindly followed the Moscow line which prevailed until 1935 and according to which the main struggle of the Communists was to be fought not against the Nazis but against the Social Democrats, who were branded as 'Social Fascists'. The proposition of a Popular Front policy and formation, which might have been an effective weapon against National Socialism, was thus eliminated. The underestimation of the Nazis also led to expectations that resistance could be pursued on a mass basis.[285] But the instant terror that followed upon the Reichstag fire on 27 February 1933 proved that the theoretical base of the Comintern strategy was altogether fallacious and that its implications were disastrous.

While by necessity the Communist leadership became divided into a *Landesleitung* in Berlin and an *Auslandsleitung* which moved from Prague to Paris, the determining factor throughout was and remained the Comintern. The discipline within the Communist movement remained intact despite some serious conflicts of interests.

The foreign relations, then, of the KPD were determined by both ideology and discipline. This caused its agents to enter into impressively daring ventures and often sent them to certain death. But at the same time the Communist stand in all its manifestations was subject to the directives of a foreign power. This fact must have dawned upon many of those who went out to fight Fascism in the Spanish Civil War. The failure of the Moscow-directed penetration into Germany of Central Committee member Wilhelm Knöchel was a clear demonstration, as has been rightly argued, that Communist resistance could not reasonably be directed from abroad in time of war.[286]

The melancholy story of the *Rote Kapelle*[287] speaks of the dangerous propinquity of resistance and treason. Men such as Schulze-Boysen and Arvid Harnack were no doubt motivated by their opposition to everything Nazism stood for. In effect, however, they became 'cogs in the machine of a foreign espionage organization'.[288]

Similarly, there was the case of the 'National Committee for a Free Germany' founded after the battle of Stalingrad at the behest of the Soviet government by a combination of German exiled Communists—Erich Weinert, Wilhelm Pieck, Walter Ulbricht—and German prisoners of war under General Walther von Seydlitz-Kurzbach, and the subsequently formed 'League of German Officers' under Seydlitz, calling for the overthrow of the Hitler regime, the ending of the war, and the retreat of the German armies to the original Reich borders of 1937. But the black-white-red frame of the National Committee's publications was designed by the Soviets merely to serve as a patriotic bait. Seydlitz found himself used by the Russians. Court-martialled *in absentia* by the Supreme Military Court of the Reich and in turn sentenced to death as a 'major war criminal' by the Soviets,[289] he, like his fellow German soldiers, was left in limbo between resistance and treason.

It would be foolish for us to pass judgement on General von Seydlitz and his like as to their motives and their failure in an unprecedented situation. It would also be wrong-headed to apply a different standard to the men of 20 July 1944 and to the rebel soldiers in Russian captivity.[290] Each man in his own way resisted. But this must be said: in the case of the captive soldiers exile vitiated the ethos of resistance. The National Committee and the League were both used for propaganda purposes and then dismissed in 1945. Colonel von Stauffenberg, speaking for the *Widerstand*, may have been right after all when he distanced himself from captive fellow officers in Russia by saying that he rejected 'proclamations from behind barbed wire'.[291]

## 9. Some Concluding Thoughts

Resistance and exile, then, as we have seen, are not exclusive of each other; indeed they are complementary. No doubt resistance which in many cases, such as in Trott's, Moltke's, and Bonhoeffer's, was a conscious alternative to exile, takes on the burden of inordinate risks. But exile is not a safe haven or a paradise either. Theodor Wolff's remark after his visit in the summer of 1935 to the Prussian ex-Prime Minister, Otto Braun, in his Ascona refuge, where he found him gardening, that 'Hannibal fled in order to act and did not plant lettuce'[292] was a harsh one. Pain and poverty were surely constant companions of Braun, as well as the frustrations over his inability to act from afar. Like resistance, exile claims for itself a legitimacy higher than the one represented by the regime it opposes; like resistance exile—in contra-distinction to much of the 'emigration' of the 1930s and 1940s[293]—is political in nature and in its ultimate aims. The political exile aims at returning and at effecting, in his own way, a change of regime at home and making common cause with the resister.

As we have seen in our story, resistance and exile constantly gravitated towards one another. There was, after all, not much more between Stauffen-berg and Tillich, so to speak, than the Ocean. For Trott the visit to the ex-Chancellor Brüning in October 1939 in Cambridge, Mass., was more than a social courtesy or a plea for help; it was meant to give sanction to Trott's mission. The Sopade always had its eyes on an internal uprising in Germany, and it explicitly distanced itself from liberation of the country by 'foreign bayonets'.[294] To Rüstow and Wilbrandt, Moltke's appearance in July and December 1943 at the Bosporus gave a ray of hope for the much longed for change at home. Of course the entanglement, if not alliance, between resist-ance and exile at best yielded little more than mutual legitimization and encouragement. Ultimately, in order to break out of its 'vast gaol', as Wilhelm Leuschner characterized the Nazi state, the German Opposition had to plunge into the open sea of foreign countries to be recognized, to explain itself, and to be listened to.

*CHAPTER 1*

1. Information from Eberhard Bethge.
2. 'Ludwig Beck in der Mittwochs-Gesellschaft', BA/K, Spranger/1, repr. as 'Generaloberst Beck in der Mittwochs-Gesellschaft', *Universitas: Zeitschrift für Wissenschaft, Kunst und Literatur*, 11 (1956), 1/2, 183–93.
3. Franz Halder in 'Protokoll aus der Verhandlung Halder [vor der] Spruchkammer X München [15.–21. September 1948]', mimeographed [Munich, 1948], 67, quoted in Peter Hoffmann, 'Ludwig Beck: Loyalty and Resistance', *Central European History*, 14 (Dec. 1981), 348; see also Erich Kosthorst, *Die deutsche Opposition gegen Hitler zwischen Polen- und Frankreichfeldzug* (2nd ed., Bonn, 1955), 52; and Ritter, *Carl Goerdeler*, 146.
4. See the testimony of Lt.-Col. Friedrich Wilhelm Heinz of the Abwehr, 11 Aug. 1952: 'For everyone it was a foregone conclusion that Colonel General Beck was the sovereign (Oberhaupt)', Kurt Sendtner, 'Die deutsche Militäropposition im ersten Kriegsjahr', in *Vollmacht des Gewissens*, ed. Europäische Publikation e.V. (Frankfurt/M., 1960), i. 437. Also: 'in dem Kreis Oster–Dohnanyi–Müller war einfach Beck der Souverän'; 'Protokoll der Besprechung mit Frau v. Dohnanyi am 1. Dezember 1952', 10; IfZ, ZS 603.
5. Dr Hans Walz, 'Meine Mitarbeit an der Aktion Goerdeler' (Nov. 1945), BA/K, Gerhard Ritter, 131.
6. Erich Kosthorst, 'Carl Friedrich Goerdeler', in Rudolf Lill and Heinrich Oberreuter (eds.), *20. Juli: Portraits des Widerstands* (Düsseldorf, 1984), 122.
7. 'Unsere Idee' (Memorandum written by Goerdeler in gaol, Nov. 1944); BA/K, Goerdeler 26.
8. Kosthorst, 'Carl Friedrich Goerdeler', 126.
9. Lord Vansittart, *The Mist Procession: The Autobiography of Lord Vansittart* (London, 1958) 513.
10. Minutes by Mr G. P. Young (Central Department), 15 Feb. 1940 to Sir R. Campbell, Paris to Sir A. Cadogan, 8 Feb. 1940, FO 371/24387/C 2339/6/18.
11. All four Cabinet lists (the ones of Jan. and Aug. 1943 and of Jan. and July 1944 name Hassell for this post; the one of August 1943 also ex-Chancellor Heinrich Brüning and the one of July 1944 also Friedrich Werner Graf von der Schulenburg, Nazi Germany's last Ambassador to Moscow); See Hoffmann, *History*, 367. In the very last days before 20 July 1944, however, Beck and Goerdeler seemed to have tipped the scales in favour of Schulenburg in desperate expectation of some settlement with the East.
12. The first edition of the diaries, hastily put together by von Hassell's widow, appeared in 1946 in Switzerland (Ulrich von Hassell, *Vom Anderen Deutschland: Aus den nachgelassenen Tagebüchern 1938–1944*, Zurich, 1946) and appeared in English translation as *The Von Hassell Diaries 1938–1944: The Story of the Forces against Hitler inside Germany as recorded by Ambassador Ulrich von Hassell, a Leader of the Movement* (New York, 1947). Meanwhile an enlarged and revised scholarly edition, arranged by the historian Friedrich Freiherr Hiller von Gaertringen has appeared in the Federal Republic of Germany: *Die Hassell-Tagebücher 1938–1944: Aufzeichnungen vom anderen Deutschland* (Berlin, 1988). In the passages of this book the quotations from the diary will be taken as a rule from the new edition; whenever possible the quotations in English will be taken from the American edition.
13. Entry of 22 Oct. 1939, ibid. 131; italics in the original.
14. See Klaus Scholder (ed.), *Die Mittwochs-Gesellschaft: Protokolle aus dem geistigen Deutschland 1932 bis 1944* (Berlin, 1982); see also Paul Fechter, *Menschen und Zeiten: Begegnungen aus fünf Jahrzehnten* (Berlin, 1949), 365–417.
15. Ludwig Beck, 'Die Lehre vom totalen Krieg (eine kritische Auseinandersetzung)' (17 June 1942) in Scholder (ed.), *Die Mittwochs-Gesellschaft*, 292–4; see also Nicholas Reynolds,

*Treason Was No Crime: Ludwig Beck, Chief of the German General Staff* (London, 1976), 232–8.

16. Johannes Popitz, 'Reich' (11 Dec. 1940), in Scholder (ed.), *Die Mittwochs-Gesellschaft*, 260–3.

17. Ulrich von Hassell, 'Mussolini' (26 Nov. 1941) in ibid. 278–80.

18. Entry of 20 Dec. 1938, *Die Hassell-Tagebücher*, 72.

19. See Ritter, *Carl Goerdeler*, 286 ff.

20. Hugh Trevor-Roper, 'Admiral Canaris: "The Hamlet of Conservative Germany"', *Listener*, 12 June 1980.

21. Ernst von Weizsäcker, *Erinnerungen* (Munich, 1950), 175.

22. The so-called Fritsch crisis brought about major changes in the military command and the Auswärtiges Amt. Colonel General Werner Freiherr von Fritsch, Supreme Commander of the Army, was dismissed on 4 Feb. 1938 on a trumped-up charge of homosexuality for his opposition to Hitler's plans for aggressive warfare, and Field Marshal Werner von Blomberg, Minister for War and Supreme Commander of the Armed Forces, was sacked under the pretext of his marriage to a one-time prostitute. Colonel General Walther von Brauchitsch was appointed to succeed Fritsch, whereas Hitler himself assumed the position of Minister for War and Supreme Commander of the Armed Forces, and Major General Wilhelm Keitel was appointed Chief of the Armed Forces High Command (OKW). At the same time Konstantin Freiherr von Neurath was replaced as Foreign Minister by Joachim von Ribbentrop.

23. 'Der Mann hinter den Kulissen'; Oberstlt. Friedrich Wilhelm Heinz, 'Von Wilhelm Canaris zur NKVD', typescript [*c.*1949], National Archive, Washington DC, microfilm No. R 60.67.

24. See Jørgen Hæstrup, *European Resistance Movements, 1939–1945: A Complete History* (Westport, Conn., 1981), 293–5.

25. Zentralabteilung, generally referred to as Abteilung Z.

26. Interview with Major General Achim Oster, 23 June 1980.

27. Reynolds, *Treason*, 181; Graf von Thun-Hohenstein, *Der Verschwörer: General Oster und die Militäropposition* (Munich, 1984), 78–9.

28. Deutsch, *The Conspiracy*, 66.

29. Letter from Colonel General Franz Halder, 6 Sept. 1952, Sendtner 'Die deutsche Militäropposition', in *Vollmacht*, i. 432.

30. Testimony of Lieutenant Colonel Friedrich Wilhelm Heinz, 11 Aug. 1952, ibid. i. 438.

31. Thus Paul Leverkühn, a Hamburg lawyer, who was the head of a distinguished law firm in Berlin, was posted by Canaris to Istanbul partly because of his American connection. Hans Bernd Gisevius, a one-time official of the Gestapo and the Ministry of the Interior who became one of the most tireless members of the *Widerstand*, was sent in the guise of 'Vice-Consul' to the Consulate-General in Zurich, his main assignment being the securing of underground channels to Switzerland. Indeed it was Gisevius who established, beginning early in 1943, a close working relationship with the newly arrived American OSS representative attached to the Berne Legation, Allen W. Dulles. In the spring of 1943 after the Gestapo had first moved against the Abwehr and Gisevius could no longer shuttle between Germany and Switzerland, a Berlin lawyer, Eduard Waetjen, was attached to the Zurich Consulate and took over his functions. In Madrid and Lisbon Otto John, legal adviser of the Lufthansa, acted as liaison with the Abwehr. After the suspension of Oster and Canaris from office (Apr. 1943, Feb. 1944) Colonel Georg Hansen, Canaris's successor, also connected with the underground, continued to guide the work of Waetjen and John.

32. See Hans Bernd Gisevius, *To the Bitter End* (Boston, 1947), 425 ff.

33. To Hitler and Ribbentrop the old élite in the Auswärtiges Amt was anathema. Hitler is known to have thought of the AA as a 'poison kitchen' (*Giftküche*), but evidently decided upon delaying a purge of the Ministry until after the war. Thus he rejected a list of about 300 foreign servants whom Ribbentrop wanted to have dismissed in 1942 or 1943. Ribbentrop of course counteracted the influence of the old guard by trying systematically to infiltrate the Foreign Office by new appointments from the Party rival organizations, namely the Foreign Division of the National Socialist Party (Auslandsorganisation der

NSDAP, abbreviated to AO) under Gauleiter Ernst W. Bohle, the Foreign Policy Office of the National Socialist Party (Aussenpolitisches Amt der NSDAP, abbreviated to APA) under the Party 'philosopher' Alfred Rosenberg, the Ribbentrop Office (Dienststelle Ribbentrop), as also from the SS and SA. While the *homines novi* were bestowed with glittering titles and high salaries, the career officials came increasingly under pressure to join the Party and its 'formations' (the SS or SA), or else they were subjected to accusations of harbouring anti-Nazi sentiments. Only a few Foreign Office servants faced the consequences of their rejection of the new regime and took the courageous step of resigning from the Office, most notably the German Ambassador to Washington, Friedrich Wilhelm von Prittwitz und Gaffron, and the Embassy Counsellor in London, Graf Albrecht von Bernstorff who eventually got involved in the conspiracy against Hitler and was subsequently shot by the Gestapo in 1945. Many of those who stayed on for whatever tortured and often honourable reasons, and even a number of those who chose to go into the Resistance, yielded to pressures to join the Party and its formations. For the latter group this meant an inevitable step designed to camouflage their conspiratorial activities; Gottfried von Nostitz, 'The Attitude of the pre-1933 Officials of the German Foreign Office during the National Socialist Aera [*sic*]', typescript, Geneva, Feb. 1946, Nostitz Papers; Hans-Adolf Jacobsen, *Nationalsozialistische Aussenpolitik 1933–1938* (Frankfurt/M., 1968); Paul Seabury, *The Wilhelmstrasse: A Study of German Diplomats under the Nazi Regime* (Berkeley, Calif., 1954).

34. See the recent monograph by Marion Thielenhaus, *Zwischen Anpassung und Widerstand: Deutsche Diplomaten 1938–1941: Die politischen Aktivitäten der Beamtengruppe um Ernst von Weizsäcker im Auswärtigen Amt* (Paderborn, 1984).

35. It should be noted here that Weizsäcker's appointment was engineered by two of his junior colleagues in the Auswärtiges Amt, especially by Albrecht Haushofer (the son of the 'geopolitician' Karl Haushofer), who at the time had the ear of Foreign Minister-designate Ribbentrop, and by Erich Kordt, the head of the Ministerial Bureau; see *Die Weizsäcker-Papiere*, 28; see also Thielenhaus, *Zwischen Anpassung und Widerstand*, 35–8; Deutsch, *The Conspiracy*, 17; Weizsäcker held the post until April 1943 when he was reassigned to the post of German Ambassador to the Vatican.

36. See esp. the fierce indictment by Sir Lewis Namier ('A German Diplomatist', *Times Literary Supplement*, 1 June 1951) of Weizsäcker as the 'German diplomatist' who 'first helped pave the way for Hitler' and later covered up for him, followed by Sir John W. Wheeler-Bennett's somewhat less intemperate charge that Weizsäcker was opposed to the Nazi policy of aggression for the same reason that many other high-ranking German officers, military and political, had been opposed to it—'because of the risks involved' (John W. Wheeler-Bennet, *The Nemesis of Power: The German Army in Politics 1918–1945*, London, 1954, 417). For an attempt at rehabilitation of the State Secretary see *Die Weizsäcker-Papiere*; however a recent monograph dealing with Weizsäcker (Rainer A. Blasius, *Für Grossdeutschland—gegen den grossen Krieg: Staatssekretär Ernst Frhr. von Weizsäcker in den Krisen um die Tschechoslowakei und Polen 1938/39*, Cologne, 1981) in turn takes a more critical view of Weizsäcker as having been opposed in the years immediately preceding the war chiefly to the adventurism of his chief but not to the 'greater German' objectives of the Nazi leadership. See also Klemens von Klemperer, 'A Kind of Resistance', *Times Literary Supplement*, 27 Feb. 1976 and Paul Kennedy, 'Approaching with Caution', *Times Literary Supplement*, 10 June 1983.

37. Von Weizsäcker, *Erinnerungen*, 173.

38. Warren E. Magee, 'Opening Statement for Defendant Von Weizsäcker', 3 June 1948, *Trials of War Criminals before the Nuernberg Military Tribunals under Control Council Law No. 10. (The Ministries Case)*, xii, Nuernberg, Oct. 1946–Apr. 1949 (Washington, DC, n.d.), 241.

39. Von Weizsäcker, *Erinnerungen*, 178.

40. See on this subject esp. Blasius, *Für Grossdeutschland*.

41. *Trials of War Criminals*, xii. 241.

42. See Deutsch, *The Conspiracy*, 61; André Brissaud, *Canaris: The Biography of Admiral Canaris, Chief of German Military Intelligence in the Second World War* (London, 1973), 24.

43. Interview with Albrecht von Kessel, 3 July 1975; the latter attribution, according to Kessel, goes back to Adam von Trott zu Solz.
44. See von Kessel, 'Verborgene Saat', 22–7; Gottfried von Nostitz, 'Abschied von den Freunden: Ein Bericht', typescript, n.d., Nostitz Papers, and Clarita von Trott zu Solz, 'Adam von Trott', 213–23.
45. In this connection the name of Eduard Brücklmeier should be mentioned, who, belonging to the *Freundeskreis* of younger Foreign Office members, worked closely with Erich Kordt under the State Secretary and who, early in October 1940, had to leave the service because of a denunciation against him. He eventually obtained a civilian post with the Armed Forces High Command (OKW) but worked intensively for the Opposition. He was finally executed after the plot against Hitler on 20 July 1944; See von Nostitz, 'Abschied' and Hans von Herwarth, *Against Two Evils* (New York, 1981), *passim*; Erich Kordt, *Nicht aus den Akten ... Die Wilhelmstrasse in Frieden und Krieg: Erlebnisse, Begegnungen und Eindrücke 1928–1945* (Stuttgart, 1950), 341–3. Mention should also be made here of Rudolf von Scheliha (1897–1942). One of the most determined opponents of National Socialism in the Auswärtiges Amt, he was apprehended by the Gestapo in October 1942 and sentenced to death by the Reich War Tribunal (Reichskriegsgericht) on 14 December for aiding and abetting the enemy, for *Landesverrat*, and for espionage. The case against him was coupled with that against the Communist 'Red Orchestra' and aggravated by the charge that he had received payment for information which he had allegedly turned over to the Russian Secret Service. Furthermore, Rudolf von Scheliha's name has not figured in the annals of the German Resistance, notably the works of Hans Rothfels, Peter Hoffmann, and Ger van Roon. Only recently has an effort been made to rehabilitate him. Ulrich Sahm's *Rudolf von Scheliha 1897–1942: Ein deutscher Diplomat gegen Hitler* (Munich, 1990), based on meticulous study of sources, constitutes an attempt to disprove the Nazi verdict on Scheliha and in turn to establish him as a daring and honourable resistance fighter. According to Sahm, one of Scheliha's main aims was to establish contacts abroad and in particular to alert the Allies to the Nazi plans for the 'final solution' to the Jewish question.
46. See Deutsch, *The Conspiracy*, 43–4.
47. See Thielenhaus, *Zwischen Anpassung und Widerstand*, 72–3.
48. Interview with Albrecht von Kessel, 3 July 1975.
49. His brother Erich, who caught Ribbentrop's ire, was banished to the Embassy in Tokyo despite Weizsäcker's efforts to place him in Lisbon.
50. 'Personalien des Dr. Theo Kordt', Kordt Papers.
51. Theo Kordt, Short Autobiography (ii), 14 ff., Kordt Papers.
52. In 1940 Theo Kordt was joined in Berne by Herbert Blankenhorn and Georg Federer who, while not actively engaged in resistance work, were firmly opposed to the Nazi regime and in constant contact with the group of young turks among the Foreign Office and Abwehr officials in Switzerland. Federer acted as liaison between the Legation and Gisevius and Waetjen. Blankenhorn especially was from 1941 in close touch with Adam von Trott and fully initiated into the designs of his missions of the *Widerstand* abroad; letter from Herbert Blankenhorn to me, Badenweiler, 10 May 1978; interview with Georg Federer, 7 Feb. 1978.
53. Erich Kordt, *Nicht aus den Akten*, 340.
54. Helmuth Groscurth, *Tagebücher eines Abwehroffiziers 1938–1940*, ed. Helmut Krausnick and Harold C. Deutsch (Stuttgart, 1970). In reaction to the inactivity of the Generals he is quoted to have exclaimed: 'If only I had my Macedonians ...'; interview with Hasso von Etzdorf, 14 Feb. 1978.
55. Much of this information is derived from a variety of sources and esp. Hasso von Etzdorf, 'Meine Tätigkeit als Vertreter des Auswärtigen Amts beim Oberkommando des Heeres (Oktober 1939–Januar 1945)', typescript, Kordt Papers.
56. See below Ch. 3, s. 3.
57. Brücklmeier, as we have seen, was soon eliminated from the roster the Auswärtiges Amt, but remained undaunted nevertheless in his substitute position in the OKW.
58. Gottfried von Nostitz, 'Mein Verhältnis zur NSDAP und Partei-Organisationen', typescript, Icking im Isartal, 10 May 1946, Nostitz Papers; see also *Die Hassell-Tagebücher*, *passim*.

59. Henry O. Malone, 'Adam von Trott zu Solz: The Road to Conspiracy Against Hitler'; diss. (University of Texas at Austin, May 1980), 561, 580; idem, *Adam von Trott zu Solz: Werdegang eines Verschwörers 1909–1938* (Berlin, 1986), 216.
60. Gottfried von Nostitz, 'Eidesstattliche Erklärung'; typescript (Stuttgart, 6 Apr. 1949), Nostitz Papers.
61. Weizsäcker later recorded: 'Albrecht von Kessel . . . since Berne had shared all my anxieties'; von Weizsäcker, *Erinnerungen*, 253.
62. He stayed there until 1943 when he rejoined Weizsäcker who had moved to the Vatican as ambassador.
63. Kessel, 'Verborgene Saat', 209–10.
64. See Willem A. Visser't Hooft, 'Eidesstattliche Erklärung', Geneva, 11 Mar. 1948; Dr Hans Schönfeld, Director of Research of the World Council of Churches, 'Bestätigung', 15 Mar. 1958; Nostitz, 'Abschied', 2; all among the Nostitz Papers; Willem A. Visser't Hooft, *Memoirs* (Philadelphia, Pa., 1973), 136–49; Jürgen Heideking, 'Die "Schweizer Strassen" des europäischen Widerstands', in Gerhard Schulz (ed.), *Geheimdienste und Widerstandsbewegungen im Zweiten Weltkrieg* (Göttingen, 1982), 143–87.
65. Film No. 3179–1, BA/K film library. For varying versions of the statement see Hoffmann, *History*, 718 n. 17.
66. Barbara von Haeften, *Aus unserem Leben 1944–1950* (privately printed, Heidelberg, 1974), 74.
67. Haeften did indeed spend the academic year 1928/9 as a student at Trinity College, Cambridge. Though the year was not a particularly happy one for him, his health was not good and he complained especially about the food, he later often commented on the importance of the sojourn in England. He had come to perceive the Lutheran tradition, in which he had been brought up, as too compliant in its relation to the magistrates, and he was impressed by the spirit of independence which informed politics in England; interview with Barbara von Haeften, 17 June 1980.
68. Letter from Barbara von Haeften to me, Tutzing, 3 Mar. 1978.
69. I deliberately chose this term. It emanates from the Austrian historian Heinrich Ritter von Srbik (1874–1951), the biographer of Metternich, whose vision of German history aimed at overcoming the traditional Austro-Prussian (*grossdeutsch-kleindeutsch*) perspectives, stressing harmony rather than struggle, and transcendence in the form of a Christian universalism. While in Vienna Haeften was an admirer of Srbik (interview with Barbara von Haeften, 27 June 1981). It might be added, however, that Srbik, while himself not a National Socialist, welcomed the *Anschluss* in 1938 and allowed himself to be honoured by the Third Reich.
70. In 1936 the Legation was elevated to the status of Embassy.
71. Interview with Barbara von Haeften, 11 Feb. 1978.
72. He maintained particular ties with a group of intellectuals connected with the Catholic youth movement Neuland which set itself the aim of rejuvenating the Church from within and redefining relations between Church and State, thus counteracting their all too close interpenetration. The men he saw most of were Anton Böhm, a publicist who as editor-in-chief of the *Rheinischer Merkur* after the war became one of the most influential Catholic journalists in the Federal Republic of Germany, and with Wilhelm Wolf, a dynamic young civil servant who, believing he could build bridges between Catholicism and German nationalism, allowed himself to be appointed Foreign Minister in the ominous Seyss-Inquart cabinet which paved the way for the *Anschluss*. Haeften's hopes that Wolf might be able to influence the course of events proved to be vain. The avalanche of the Nazi take-over left Wolf deeply disillusioned, and in the summer of 1939 he died mysteriously in an automobile accident. Among the Protestant minority Haeften was much involved with members of the 'Evangelische Michaelsbruderschaft', a fraternity founded in the 1920s by a number of theologians and laymen dedicated to the liturgical and spiritual renewal of the Church and to ecumenical concerns. He became particularly friendly with Herbert Krimm, the second pastor of the 'Dorotheerkirche' in the heart of Vienna, discussing with him theological questions and making it his task to enlighten Krimm about the seriousness of the 'Church Dispute' which went on in Germany. The connection between the two did not break up after Haeften left Vienna in 1937, and they became

involved in a lengthy correspondence of considerable theological importance; Haeften's letters to Krimm are reproduced in Barbara von Haeften, 'Aus unseren Briefen 1931–1944' (typescript, Heidelberg, 1964), 50 ff. Krimm's letters have not been preserved by Haeften who, after Vienna, lived under a continuous threat of police search or arrest. Much of the above information is derived from a letter by Barbara von Haeften to me, Tutzing, 1 Dec. 1983.

73. Kessel, 'Verborgene Saat', 212.
74. Anlage zu ZB 8/80.02/1/964/65, 'Aufzeichnung zur Frage der deutschen Politik gegenüber der Balkan-Orthodoxie', 8 Nov. 1943, Haeften Papers.
75. Actually, the Kirchliches Aussenamt was created in February 1934 by the Nazi puppet 'Reich Bishop' Ludwig Müller; its head was a senior member of the Consistory of the Evangelical Church, Dr Theodor Heckel, who was promptly made bishop. The new agency, commissioned to take charge of communications with Churches abroad thus inevitably displaced in ecumenical matters the Auswärtiges Amt whose sympathies tended to be on the side of the Confessing Church. By the time of Haeften's memorandum even the influence of the Kirchliches Aussenamt had been reduced by pressure of Himmler's Reich Security Office (Reichssicherheitshauptamt, RSHA) and the Party; see 'Aufzeichnung' and Armin Boyens, *Kirchenkampf und Ökumene 1933–1939: Darstellung und Dokumentation* (Munich, 1969), 110 and *idem, Kirchenkampf und Ökumene 1939–1945: Darstellung und Dokumentation unter besonderer Berücksichtigung der Quellen des Ökumenischen Rates der Kirchen* (Munich, 1973), 186–97.
76. Anton Böhm, 'Hans-Bernd von Haeften: Eine Skizze', typescript, n.d., Haeften Papers.
77. Letter from Hans-Bernd von Haeften to Herbert Krimm, May 1941 in Haeften, 'Aus unseren Briefen', 120.
78. Ibid. 118–20; italics in the original.
79. Letter from Hans-Bernd von Haeften to Hannes Brockhaus, Jan. 1941, Lenzerheide, ibid. 115. Brockhaus, a student of medicine serving since 1939 in Bucharest with the Abwehr, was befriended by the Haeften family.
80. Ibid.; Haeften refers to Ephesians 6: 10–17.
81. Interview with Barbara von Haeften, 11 Feb. 1978.
82. Dietrich Bonhoeffer, *GS* i. 226.
83. Clarita von Trott, 'Adam von Trott', 289.
84. Sykes, 'Heroes and Suspects: The German Resistance in Perspective', *Encounter*, 31 (Dec. 1938), 47.
85. For a systematic exposition of the 'Trott controversy' during Trott's lifetime as well as later in the literature see Malone, 'Adam von Trott', diss., 1–80.
86. In fact the Jays were originally Huguenots who left France after the revocation of the Edict of Nantes by Louis XIV in 1683 and made their way to England and the USA; see William Jay, *The Life of John Jay*, 2 vols. (New York, 1833).
87. Letter from Eleonore von Trott to Adam von Trott, 16 Aug. 1930, Trott Archive, Letters from the Parents.
88. Of particular interest in this respect is the correspondence between Trott and the Revd Tracy Strong, an American who served as Executive Secretary of the World's Alliance of Young Men's Christian Associations in Geneva. Trott's mother had arranged an invitation for Adam to Geneva, where he stayed for three weeks in the late summer of 1928 with the Strongs and met a number of other ecumenical leaders including in particular Willem A. Visser't Hooft with whom he struck up a friendship which he was able to renew later during the war on the occasion of his missions for the Opposition to Switzerland. For the correspondence with Strong see esp. the letters from Adam von Trott to Tracy Strong, Berlin, 21 Feb. 1930 and Imshausen, 9 Aug. 1932, Tracy Strong Papers, University of Washington Libraries. For Trott's 1928 sojourn in Geneva see Malone, *Adam von Trott*, 30–2; *idem*, 'Adam von Trott', diss., 124 ff.; and Christopher Sykes, *Troubled Loyalty: A Biography of Adam von Trott zu Solz* (London, 1968), 29 ff. See also Visser't Hooft, *Memoirs*, 155.
89. In fact, in 1928 the Revd Strong encouraged Trott to persuade his cousin, Viktor von Schweinitz, eldest son of his uncle Wilhelm, to apply for a scholarship to study in Geneva. But Adam had to report back that his uncle 'did not wish ... to expose his son to an

international atmosphere', adding, however, that he felt 'that in this country this sort of attitude' had ceased to be 'the ordinary one'; letter from Adam von Trott to Tracy Strong, Berlin, Wednesday [late Aug. or early Sept. 1929], Tracy Strong Papers.

90. Letter from Adam von Trott to Tracy Strong, Berlin, 21 Feb. 1930. During the short-lived Soviet Republic in Bavaria (12 Apr.–2 May 1919) Landauer served for a few days as Commissar for Propaganda ('Volksbeauftragter für Volksaufklärung') and was subsequently brutally beaten to death by the Freikorps soldiers.

91. Letter from August von Trott to Adam von Trott, 4 Oct. 1930, quoted in Clarita von Trott, 'Adam von Trott', 30.

92. Letter from Adam von Trott to Diana Hubback (now Mrs David Hopkinson), Jan. or Feb. 1937: 'He [Werner] does not understand the Anglo Saxon part, the English, and thinks my attitude to them is one of self indulgence and a dissipation of the spirit . . .', Diana Hopkinson, 'Aus Adams Briefen', typescript, 1946, 10, Julie Braun-Vogelstein Papers, Leo Baeck Institute.

93. Letter from Werner von Trott to Adam von Trott, 10 Jan. 1937, quoted in Clarita von Trott, 'Adam von Trott', 85.

94. Adam von Trott zu Solz, *Hegels Staatsphilosophie und das Internationale Recht* (Göttingen, 1932, 1967).

95. Letter from Adam von Trott to Eleonore von Trott, 2 Feb. 1929, Trott Archive, Letters to the Parents; see also 'Impressions of a German Student in England', *The World's Youth*, 5 (Nov. 1929), 135, 138; this piece was written after Trott's first sojourn in Oxford at Mansfield College during Hilary term, Jan.–Mar. 1929.

96. Ibid. 135.

97. Letter from Helmuth Conrad to Ger van Roon, Nov. 1963, Trott Archive, Chris [Bielenberg] Interviews.

98. Letter from Adam von Trott to August von Trott, 13 Feb. 1933, Trott Archive, Letters to the Parents; also Clarita von Trott, 'Adam von Trott', 46–7.

99. Hans Adolf Jacobsen, *Nationalsozialistische Aussenpolitik 1933–1938*, (Frankfurt/M., 1968), 197.

100. France did not feature in Haushofer's calculations. To him, like almost all Germans, she was perceived as the power bent upon thwarting Germany's aspirations to be a determining factor in the European balance of power.

101. See Haushofer's special report of 2 Mar. 1938 for Ribbentrop: 'Beurteilung der Diplomaten im Auswärtigen Amt', in Hans-Adolf Jacobsen, *Karl Haushofer: Leben und Werk*, ii *Ausgewählter Schriftwechsel 1917–1946* (Boppard am Rhein, 1979), 342–4, in which he characterized Weizsäcker as 'the strongest and, by virtue of his talents, character and political convictions, most commendable personality' in the Berlin Foreign Office; see Ursula Laack-Michel, *Albrecht Haushofer und der Nationalsozialismus* (Stuttgart, 1974), 171. Among the many foreign office servants subjected to scrutiny by Haushofer, Albrecht von Kessel and Hans-Bernd von Haeften emerged to be singled out for praise. For Erich Kordt's part in the appointment of Weizsäcker see *Die Weizsäcker-Papiere*, 28, 497 n. 13.

102. Jacobsen, *Haushofer*, i. 352.

103. Since 1940 the Duke of Hamilton.

104. Albert Speer, *Inside the Third Reich: Memoirs* (New York, 1970), 176.

105. Entry of 16 Mar. 1941, *Die Hassell-Tagebücher*, 232–3.

106. Rainer Hildebrandt, *Wir sind die Letzten: Aus dem Leben des Widerstandskämpfers Albrecht Haushofer und seiner Freunde* (Neuwied, 1949), 130; the meeting which Hildebrandt refers to as having taken place 'in the autumn of 1941' most likely took place on 10 Dec. of that year; see Michael Balfour and Julian Frisby, *Helmuth von Moltke: A Leader Against Hitler* (London, 1972), 146, 373 and van Roon, *Neuordnung*, 275.

107. Rainer Hildebrandt, 'Er sah die Wirklichkeit und hoffte auf die Zukunft. Zum 50. Geburtstag von Albrecht Haushofer', *Die Neue Zeitung*, 7 Jan. 1953.

108. Arvid Brodersen, 'Albrecht Haushofer 1903–1945', in Albrecht Haushofer, *Moabit Sonnets* (London, 1978), 176–7. Arvid Brodersen was himself an active member of the Norwegian Resistance.

109. Dietrich Bonhoeffer, 'After Ten Years', in *Letters and Papers from Prison*, ed. Eberhard Bethge (New York, 1972), 4.

110. *Time*, 2 Mar. 1981, 91, quoted in Ruth Zerner, 'German Protestant Responses to Nazi Persecution of the Jews', in Randolph L. Braham (ed.), *Perspectives on the Holocaust* (Boston, Mass., 1983), 66.

111. Karl Barth, *The Word of God and the Word of Man* (New York, 1957), 24.

112. Karl Barth, *Theological Existence To-day!* (*A Plea for Theological Freedom*) (London, 1933).

113. Quoted in Eberhard Busch, *Karl Barth: His Life from Letters and Autobiographical Texts* (Philadelphia, Pa., 1976), 231.

114. Only later did Karl Barth come round to justifying direct political resistance when, in September 1938, he wrote to the Czech theologian Josef Hromádka that every Czech soldier fighting Nazi aggression would do so 'also for the Church of Jesus Christ'.

115. World Alliance Youth Conference on peace in Čiernohorské Kúpele, formerly Bad Schwarzenberg, 20–30 July 1932.

116. Bonhoeffer, *GS* i. 140–1, 153–4, 159–60; *No Rusty Swords: Letters, Lectures and Notes 1928–1936 from the Collected Works* (London, 1974), 153, 155, 164–5, italics in the original; Eberhard Bethge, *Dietrich Bonhoeffer: Man of Vision, Man of Courage* (New York, 1970), 183–4; Jørgen Glenthøj (ed.), 'Dokumente zur Bonhoeffer-Forschung 1928–1945', *Die Mündige Welt*, v (Munich, 1969), 41 ff.

117. 'Durchgangsstadium'; letter from Dietrich Bonhoeffer to Erwin Sutz, London, 28 Apr. 1934, Bonhoeffer, *GS* i. 40.

118. Dietrich Bonhoeffer, *Ethics*, ed. Eberhard Bethge (New York, 1965), 113.

119. Letter from Dietrich Bonhoeffer to Erwin Sutz, London, 28 Apr. 1934, Bonhoeffer, *GS* i. 40.

120. Bonhoeffer, *Ethics*, 356.

121. Ibid. 234; italics in the original.

122. Letter from Dietrich Bonhoeffer to Eberhard Bethge, 25 June 1942 in *GS* ii. 420.

123. Bonhoeffer, 'Die Kirche vor der Judenfrage', ibid. 48.

124. Ibid. 49.

125. Letter from Dietrich Bonhoeffer to Bishop George Bell of Chichester, London, 27 Dec. 1933, Bonhoeffer, *GS* i. 182.

126. Letter from Dietrich Bonhoeffer to Eberhard Bethge, [Tegel], 30 Apr. 1944 in Bonhoeffer, *Letters and Papers*, 279.

127. It was, no doubt, a matter of poor taste that Gerstenmaier, one of the few survivors of the *Widerstand*, published in the summer of 1945 a couple of articles about the attempt of 20 July 1944 (Konsistorialrat Dr. theol. Eugen Gerstenmaier, 'Zur. Geschichte des Umsturzversuchs vom 20. Juli 1944', *Neue Züricher Zeitung*, 23 and 24 June, 1945) which solely revolved around his own person. One might say that he asked for trouble. Indeed the articles opened up a fierce polemic concerning the personality and the past Church policies of Gerstenmaier in which especially the theologians Karl Barth and Emil Brunner joined battle, the former in attack against, and the latter—Gerstenmaier's former teacher—in defence of him; Karl Barth, 'Neueste Nachrichten zur neueren deutschen Kirchengeschichte?', typescript; Emil Brunner, 'Die Wahrheit über Dr. Gerstenmaier', typescript; also Visser't Hooft's handwritten critique of Brunner's essay; all in WCC 284 (43) Germany, Archive of the World Council of Churches, Geneva (WCC ipof). See also Professor Emil Brunner, 'Zum Zeugnis für Dr. Gerstenmaier', *Neue Züricher Zeitung*, 22 July 1945; and Fabian von Schlabrendorff, 'Eugen Gerstenmaier im Dritten Reich', in 'Aus Politik und Zeitgeschichte', B41/65, *Das Parlament*, 13 Oct. 1965. See also Eugen Gerstenmaier, *Streit und Friede hat seine Zeit: Ein Lebensbericht* (Frankfurt/M., 1981).

128. From 1931 he was head of the Ecumenical Research Department in Geneva which in 1938 became the Research Department of the World Council; see Visser't Hooft, *Memoirs*, 93; Eugen Gerstenmaier, 'Zum Gedenken an Hans Schönfeld; 1900–1954', in *Reden und Aufsätze* (Stuttgart, 1962), 421–7.

129. Confidential letter from Hans Schönfeld to Henry Louis Henriod, 25 July 1933. WCC ipof, General Correspondence; see also confidential letters from Schönfeld to Bishop George Bell of Chichester, 20 and 24 Mar. 1934, ibid.

130. See copy of Willem A. Visser't Hooft, 'Eidesstattliche Erklärung', 8 Mar. 1948, Schönfeld Papers.

131. 'Pharisäische Überheblichkeit'; copy of letter from Schönfeld to Professor W. Adams Brown, New York, 30 May 1940, Schönfeld Papers.
132. Copy of letter from Visser't Hooft to Karl Barth, 19 Feb. 1943, WCC ipof, General Correspondence.
133. See the documentation in Kl. Erw. 386–3, BA/K; until July 1938 the Kirchliches Aussenamt paid a yearly sum to the World Council of Churches which in turn remunerated Schönfeld; from then on Heckel could prevail upon the AA to support him directly; the documentation for these payments accounts for the period up to and including 31 Sept. 1941. In an interview with me (28 Feb. 1978) Visser't Hooft denied having had any knowledge of these payments, asserting that, had he known, he would have asked Schönfeld for an explanation.
134. Krauel was a convinced anti-Nazi and eventually, when about to be recalled to Berlin in the spring of 1943, chose to remain in Switzerland and became an exile.
135. See Visser't Hooft, 'Eidesstattliche Erklärung', 8 Mar. 1948, as above; see also letter from Gottfried von Nostitz to Eberhard Bethge, 27 July 1961 in which he stated that, while he knew that the relationship between Bonhoeffer and Schönfeld was not the best, he had the 'closest' working relationship with the latter; Bonhoeffer Archive, Ökumene.
136. Published in the official journal of the German Evangelical Church of 4 Apr. 1939, it stressed the connection between Luther and National Socialism, the 'unbridgeable' contrast between Christian faith and Judaism and rejected unequivocally the connection between Christianity and 'supranational and international churchism'; it elicited a vigorous rejoinder from the World Council of Churches which, in turn, caused Heckel to send a telegram of protest to Geneva even before the WCC rejoinder had actually gone to press. The reason for this precipitate reaction of Heckel was that Schönfeld, in disagreement with Visser't Hooft on the matter, having 'warned' and advocated caution, broke the news on the rejoinder in an unsigned airmail special delivery letter to Gerstenmaier who then could inform the Kirchliches Aussenamt, thus enabling it to act; see WCC IX, WCC ipof, Visser't Hooft, *Memoirs*, 95–6; Bethge, *Dietrich Bonhoeffer*, 549 ff.; Armin Boyens, *Kirchenkampf und Ökumene 1933–1939*, 257 ff. and 380–1.
137. See Visser't Hooft's handwritten critique of Brunner, as above.
138. Interview with Willem A. Visser't Hooft, 28 Feb. 1978.
139. See Brunner, 'Zum Zeugnis ... '; Schlabrendorff, 'Eugen Gerstenmaier ... ', 4.
140. Visser't Hooft: 'I do not believe that the need to lie burdened Gerstenmaier as much as it should have'; Visser, handwritten critique of Brunner, as above.
141. Interview with Visser't Hooft, as above.
142. Visser't Hooft rightly reminds us that there were yet other Protestant churchmen involved in the traffic with the outside world, and he rightly mentions in particular Hans Bernd Gisevius and Paul Collmer; Visser't Hooft, handwritten critique of Brunner, as above. Gisevius, Konsistorialrat (Member of the Consistory in the Evangelical Church), a wildly ambitious man, worked in the Gestapo before being transferred to the Police Department in the Prussian Ministry of the Interior. But since, as the story goes, his aspirations could not be satisfied within the Nazi establishment, he moved, soon after the Röhm purge of June 1934, into opposition circles where he became an indefatigable, although distinctly controversial, activist. A protégé of Schacht, he was distrusted by General Beck; a confidant of Colonel Oster, he remained shunned by Admiral Canaris (see Friedrich Wilhelm Heinz, 'Erklärungen über Dr. Gisevius' and anon., 'H. B. Gisevius', BA/K, Pechel, III/9). During the war he served in the Abwehr with an assignment as Vice-Consul in the Consulate-General in Zurich where he became an important link between the German Resistance and the Americans. (See Hoffmann, *History*, 235–9; also Gisevius, *To the Bitter End*.) Paul Collmer, an official of the Evangelical Church in Württemberg, was a very different kind of a person: firm and unassuming. During 1940 he served for a short time as German adviser to the Dutch Ministry for Social Affairs, establishing connections with the incipient Dutch Resistance. A close associate of both Gerstenmaier and Schönfeld, as also of Trott and Haeften, he later became an important link between the *Widerstand* and the World Council of Churches, especially trying to impress upon Visser't Hooft the fact that Schönfeld's talk about the German Resistance amounted to more than 'clouds of thoughts'. (In my interview with Visser't Hooft of 28 Feb. 1978 he still used these words; also interview with Dr Paul Collmer, 8 Feb. 1978.)

143. This is Visser't Hoot's term; copy of letter from Visser't Hooft to Karl Barth, 19 Feb. 1943, WCC ipof, General Correspondence.

144. Karl Barth, 'Die protestantischen Kirchen in Europa: ihre Gegenwart und ihre Zukunft', typescript, p. 6, WCC ipof, General Correspondence.

145. See Peter Ludlow, 'The International Protestant Community in the Second World War', *The Journal of Ecclesiastical History*, 29 (July 1978), 311–62; Owen Chadwick, 'The English Bishops and the Nazis', Friends of Lambeth Palace Library, *Annual Report* (London, 1973).

146. M. Daphne Hampson, 'The British Response to the German Church Struggle 1933–1939', diss. (Oxford University, 1973), 29.

147. Ibid. 338.

148. Bishop Berggrav to Bishop Bell, 25 May 1939, quoted in Visser't Hooft, *Memoirs*, 106.

149. Letter from Edward Thurneysen to Karl Barth, 21 Aug. 1937, WCC ipof, General Correspondence.

150. Letter from Dietrich Bonhoeffer to Bishop Bell, London, 14 Mar. 1934, Bonhoeffer, *GS* i. 184.

151. Ludlow, 'The International Protestant Community', 324–5.

152. See Visser't Hooft, *Memoirs, passim*; see also letter from Visser't Hooft to Karl Barth, 19 Feb. 1943, WCC ipof, General Correspondence.

153. Hampson, 'The British Response', 174–5.

154. Letter from Visser't Hooft to William Temple, 15 Dec. 1943, quoted ibid. 363.

155. Barth, 'Die Protestantischen Kirchen', 10; the essay is undated but was written, to judge by internal evidence, after the spring or summer of 1941.

156. See Walter Adolph, *Kardinal Preysing und zwei Diktaturen: Sein Widerstand gegen die totalitäre Macht* (Berlin, 1971), 159 ff.

157. See ibid. 181 ff.; van Roon, *Neuordnung, passim*; Freya von Moltke, Michael Balfour, and Julian Frisby, *Helmuth James von Moltke 1907–1945: Anwalt der Zukunft* (Stuttgart, 1972), *passim*; Balfour and Frisby, *Helmuth von Moltke, passim*.

158. See below ch. 3, s. 9.

159. 'Missionsfeld'.

160. Letter from Dietrich Bonhoeffer to Eberhard Bethge, Ettal, 8 Feb. 1941 in Bonhoeffer, *GS* vi. 516.

161. See below Ch. 5, s. 2.

162. Van Roon, *Neuordnung*; Balfour and Frisby, *Helmuth von Moltke*; Freya von Moltke, Balfour, and Frisby, *Helmuth James von Moltke*; Kurt Finker, *Graf Moltke und der Kreisauer Kreis* (East Berlin, 1978); see also Eugen Gerstenmaier, 'Der Kreisauer Kreis', *VfZ* 15 (July 1967), 221–46; Golo Mann, 'Helmuth James von Moltke', *Journal of European Studies*, 4 (Dec. 1974), 368–89; see also the recent edn. of letters by Moltke to his wife Freya: Helmuth James von Moltke, *Briefe an Freya 1939–1945*, ed. Beate Ruhm von Oppen (Munich, 1988), and *Letters to Freya 1939–1945*, ed. and trans. Beate Ruhm von Oppen (New York, 1990); when quoting from these letters I have followed as a rule the translations by von Oppen. Also *Dossier; Kreisauer Kreis. Dokumente aus dem Widerstand gegen den Nationalsozialismus. Aus dem Nachlass von Lothar König S. J.*, ed. Roman Bleistein (Frankfurt/M., 1987).

163. Balfour and Frisby, *Helmuth von Moltke*, 65 ff.

164. Letter from Helmuth von Moltke to Lionel Curtis, London, 12 July 1935, Lionel Curtis Papers, Box 28, Bodleian Library, Oxford.

165. Lionel Curtis (1872–1955); fellow of All Souls College at Oxford; an untiring advocate of the Commonwealth idea; founder of the Royal Institute of International Affairs (Chatham House); author of a mammoth work with the ambitious title *Civitas Dei*, 3 vols. (London, 1934–7).

166. Balfour and Frisby, *Helmuth von Moltke*, 185.

167. Freya von Moltke. The daughter of a Cologne banker, she obtained a law degree before marrying Helmuth in October 1931. Her marriage with Helmuth was an unusually happy one. There were two sons, Helmuth Caspar and Konrad. Freya von Moltke contributed greatly to the atmosphere of cheer and harmony at the Kreisau meetings.

168. Ibid.

169. Soon after the outbreak of the war Moltke, a student of international law and connected with the Institute for Foreign Public Law and the Law of Nations of the Kaiser-Wilhelm-Institut, was posted as War Administration Counsellor (Kriegsverwaltungsrat) to the Foreign Countries Division of the Abwehr under Rear Admiral Leopold Bürkner. His main concern was to humanize the war and plead for the enforcement of the norms of the Law of Warfare which were threatened by the increasingly ideological and savage conduct of the war by the Nazis. He particularly applied himself, generally supported by Admiral Canaris, to the conditions of prisoners of war, hostages in occupied countries, and civilian internees, with the objective of alleviating their lot. He also managed to alert the Danes of impending measures against their Jews. Most of Moltke's activities in the Abwehr were performed openly and without recourse to the usual 'camouflage' which under the prevailing circumstances seemed imperative to most of his friends in the Resistance. Incidentally, he never wore a uniform, even in his official capacity; see Wilhelm Wengler, 'H. J. Graf von Moltke (1906 [*sic*]–1945)' *Die Friedens-Warte*, 48 (1948), 297–305; Christian Streit, *Keine Kameraden: Die Wehrmacht und die sowjetischen Kriegsgefangenen 1941–1945* (Stuttgart, 1978), 130–82, 231 ff.; van Roon, *Neuordnung*, 68 ff.; Ger van Roon, 'Graf Moltke als Völkerrechtler im OKW', *VfZ*, 18 (Jan. 1970), 12–61; Ger van Roon (ed.), *Helmuth James Graf von Moltke: Völkerrecht im Dienste der Menschen* (Berlin, 1986).
170. Letter from Helmuth von Moltke to Freya von Moltke, Berlin, 3 Nov. 1942, in von Moltke, *Briefe an Freya*, 429.
171. Letter from Helmuth von Moltke to Freya von Moltke, Berlin, 2 Jan. 1944, ibid. 582.
172. Letter from Helmuth von Moltke to Freya von Moltke, Berlin, 17 Mar. 1940, ibid. 126.
173. Interview with Mrs Freya von Moltke, 10 Dec. 1976.
174. Letter from Helmuth von Moltke to Freya von Moltke, 11 Jan. 1945, von Moltke, *Briefe an Freya*, 610.
175. Letter from Helmuth von Moltke to Freya von Moltke, Berlin, 18 July 1943, ibid. 508.
176. Interview with Mrs Freya von Moltke, 27 Feb. 1975.
177. There were two more men associated with the Kreisau Circle who were involved in the foreign operations of the resistance. Eduard Waetjen (1907– ), whose mother was American, was a Berlin lawyer. He had known Moltke since 1939 when the Circle was still being formed. By virtue of certain Gestapo connections he was able to forewarn his friends whenever their actions aroused suspicion on the part of the Nazi police. In January 1944, after Gisevius had come under suspicion of the Gestapo, the Abwehr arranged for Waetjen to take over the liaison between the *Widerstand* and the Americans under the guise of German Vice-Consul in Zurich. Theodor Steltzer (1885–1967) was one of the older members of the Kreisau Circle. A native of Schleswig-Holstein, he served in the army in the First World War and subsequently as administrative officer (Landrat) in Rendsburg. In the autumn of 1940 he met Helmuth von Moltke, remaining in constant touch with him until Moltke's arrest early in 1944. During the Second World War, while taking active part in the Kreisau deliberations, he was Transport Officer on the General Staff of the Commander in Chief in Norway where he established close connections with Bishop Eivind Berggrav and the Norwegian Resistance. Steltzer was a man of deep religious convictions who abhorred the hold of Nazi ideology over the German people which, he observed, was detrimental to the religious realm. Imprisoned after 20 July 1944, by good fortune he escaped the implementation of the death sentence against him and after the war became chief administrator (Oberpräsident) of Schleswig-Holstein.
178. A. L. Rowse, *All Souls and Appeasement: A Contribution to Contemporary History* (London, 1961), 95–6.
179. Interview with Mrs Freya von Moltke, 27 Feb. 1975.
180. The three major Kreisau meetings took place in 1942 and 1943: the first one 22–5 May 1942 (agenda: the possibilities of resistance; the constitution, Church-State relations, educational questions and university reform); the second 16–18 Oct. 1942 (agenda: the structure of the state and the economy); the third 12–14 June (Whitsun), 1943 (agenda: foreign policy, economic structure, the punishment of war criminals); see van Roon *Neuordnung*, 248 ff.
181. Letter from Helmuth von Moltke to Freya von Moltke, Berlin, 17 June 1943, Moltke, *Letters*, 493.

182. For the main literature on this group see Christine Blumenberg-Lampe, *Das wirtschaftspolitische Programm der 'Freiburger Kreise'. Entwurf einer freiheitlich-sozialen Nachkriegswirtschaft. Nationalökonomen gegen den Nationalsozialismus* (Berlin, 1973); *In der Stunde Null: Die Denkschrift des Freiburger 'Bonhoeffer-Kreises'* (Tübingen, 1979); Klaus Schwabe and Rolf Reichardt (eds.), *Gerhard Ritter: Ein politischer Historiker in seinen Briefen* (Boppard am Rhein, 1984).

183. The core of this group, identical with the Council, consisted of the economists Constantin von Dietze, Walter Eucken, Adolf Lampe, and the historian Gerhard Ritter; it had close ties with a number of Protestant as well as Catholic churchmen and laymen and to Carl Goerdeler.

184. 'Politische Gemeinschaftsordnung: Ein Versuch zur Selbstbesinnung des christlichen Gewissens in den politischen Noten unserer Zeit'; a loose translation of this rather Germanic title is: 'Political Commonweal: Towards a Regeneration of the Christian Conscience in the Political Time of Trouble'.

185. *In der Stunde Null*, 9.

186. Copies of the Freiburg Circle protocols were sent to Moltke's friend Count Peter Yorck von Wartenburg, and in turn Dietze took part in one meeting of Moltke's group.

187. Bethge, *Dietrich Bonhoeffer*, 682.

188. Ritter, *Carl Goerdeler*, 151.

189. It was through him that the chief bond was established between the Freiburg and Stuttgart Circles in as much as he delegated the theologian Helmut Thielicke to take part in some of the Freiburg deliberations; see ibid. 511.

190. Bosch also maintained contacts with Ulrich von Hassell whose activities he supported to the sum of between 600,000 and 800,000 Marks; 'Notizen über Unterhaltung mit Herrn Willy Schloßstein, Stuttgart, 5.1. 1953', BA/K, Ritter 131. Furthermore he financed the publication of Rudolf Pechel's periodical *Deutsche Rundschau* which was one of the few refuges of spiritual resistance in Nazi Germany.

191. Otto Kopp, 'Die Niederschrift von Hans Walz "Meine Mitwirkung an der Aktion Goerdeler"', in Otto Kopp (ed.), *Widerstand und Erneuerung: Neue Berichte und Dokumente vom inneren Kampf gegen das Hitler-Regime* (Stuttgart, 1966), 101.

192. See Christie Papers, CHRS 1/35; 180/1/35, Churchill College, Cambridge.

193. 'Precis Concerning Alleged Attempt Assassinate Hitler', 16 August 1944, NA, RG 84, 800 Germany—Subversive Movement.

194. See in particular BA/K, Ritter 131, Kaiser 73; Elfriede Nebgen, *Jakob Kaiser: Der Widerstandskämpfer* (Stuttgart, 1967), 128 ff.

195. Thus in particular Max Habermann, former Secretary of the nationalist white-collar workers' union, the Deutschnationaler Handlungsgehilfenverband.

196. They did, however, refrain from seeking any ties with people like Schacht and Popitz.

197. See Ritter, *Carl Goerdeler*, 51–2, 286 ff.

198. Nebgen, *Jakob Kaiser*, 134.

199. For the first premiss see Karl O. Paetel, 'Zum Problem einer deutschen Exilregierung', *VfZ*, 4 (July 1956), 287; for the second premiss see ibid. 300.

200. Ibid. 300. Paul Tillich (1886–1965), a German Protestant theologian, was an adherent of religious Socialism. Forced out of his position as Professor at the University of Frankfurt/M. by the Nazis, he went into exile to the USA where he had a distinguished career at Union Theological Seminary in New York, Harvard University, and the University of Chicago. During the war he engaged in exile politics and became chairman of the 'Council for a Democratic Germany'.

201. Captain Hans Ritter was a South German from Württemberg who had served during the First World War as General Staff officer. After the war he worked for the Junkers Aircraft Company as military adviser on aviation and filled the position of Assistant to the Military and Air Attachés at the German Embassy in Paris (1934–8). Subsequently he emigrated to Switzerland and entered the intelligence service of Sir Robert Vansittart. He maintained close contacts with such political exiles as Hermann Rauschning, Otto Strasser, and ex-Chancellors Josef Wirth and Heinrich Brüning as well as with the Vatican and with opposition circles in Germany—especially the Beck–Goerdeler–von Hassell group, Admiral Canaris, and the group around Robert Bosch. Ritter's lively accounts of the situation in

Germany were generally addressed to Group Captain Malcolm Grahame Christie in London, a chief aide of Sir Robert Vansittart (see below Ch. 2, s. 2). More than conventional intelligence reports, they were written in highly spiced German and reflected a spirited and politically deeply engaged personality impatient with the appeasement policy of the Chamberlain government as well as with the obsequiousness of the German Generals towards Hitler. Ritter's reports to Christie which were forwarded to Vansittart were variously signed by 'Kn.', 'Knight', 'Johnnie', and many other playful pseudonyms such as 'Alois Achselduft', 'Isaah Jammerbein', 'Immanuel Blutwurst'. Ritter's identity was confirmed to me in an interview with General Hans Speidel (14 July 1975); the latter especially stressed Ritter's close ties with Beck and Canaris. See also Rudolf Pechel, *Deutscher Widerstand* (Erlenbach-Zurich, 1947), 292.

202. Letter from 'Johnny' to 'Lieber Freund Grahame', 11 Apr. 1940, Christie Papers, CHRS 180/1/35.

203. The outstanding exceptions to this rule, of course, are Willy Brandt who returned from exile in Sweden eventually to become Mayor of West Berlin (1957–66) and Chancellor of the Federal Republic of Germany (1969–74) and Wilhelm Hoegner who returned from exile in Switzerland to become Prime Minister of Bavaria (1945–6 and 1954–7).

204. See in this connection Lothar Kettenacker, 'Der Einfluss der deutschen Emigration auf die britische Kriegszielpolitik', in Gerhard Hirschfeld (ed.), *Exil in Grossbritannien: Zur Emigration aus dem nationalsozialistischen Deutschland* (Stuttgart, 1983), 80–105.

205. 1881–1957; from 1941 Lord Vansittart, Permanent Under-Secretary of State 1930–8; thereafter in the relatively side-tracked position of Chief Diplomatic Adviser to the Foreign Secretary (1938–41); while entertaining close ties with Carl Goerdeler in the later 1930s, largely through his intelligence network, he eventually turned against him. He was the chief critic in Britain of everything German and refused to make a distinction between Germans and Nazis.

206. *Aide-mémoire* (in the French language), Paris, 8 June 1939; Christie Papers, CHRS 180/1/29.

207. See FO 800/317/H/XV/358; also Anthony Glees, *Exile Politics during the Second World War: The German Social Democrats in Britain* (Oxford, 1982), 49.

208. Memorandum from Christie to Vansittart, 'Rough Suggestions for German Advisory Committee' (28 Sept. 1939); Christie Papers, CHRS 1/31.

209. Robert H. Keyserlingk, 'Die deutsche Komponente in Churchills Strategie der nationalen Erhebungen 1940–1942: Der Fall Otto Strasser', *VfZ*, 31 (Oct. 1983), 637.

210. Mention should be made here of the formation in 1937/8 of the German Freedom Party by a number of exiles of liberal persuasion which saw itself as a link from abroad to a conspiracy in Germany. Like its counterparts in Paris and Ankara it remained without resonance.

211. 1887–1971; a German pedagogue with a Youth Movement background and with close ties to the socialist group around the *Neue Blätter für den Sozialismus*, he emigrated after the Nazis had dismissed him in 1933 and in 1937 joined the Institute of Education of London University. He also launched a bulletin, *Post aus England*, which was subsidized by the British authorities.

212. See A. P. Young, *The 'X' Documents* (London, 1974), *passim*.

213. 1907– .

214. Sebastian Haffner, *Germany, Jekyll and Hyde* (London, 1940).

215. Sebastian Haffner, *Offensive against Germany* (London, 1941); this book was written in the autumn of 1940.

216. Ibid. 107, 121.

217. 1875–1959; publicist, liberal politician, and Near East expert. From 1920 to 1933 he was President of the well-known *Hochschule für Politik* in Berlin; upon the Nazi seizure of power he emigrated to England.

218. Memorandum of Orme Sargent, 6 Apr. 1936, PREM 1/330, 1/350.

219. Kurt Matthias Robert Martin Hahn (1886–1974), one-time private secretary of Prince Max von Baden, was one of Germany's leading educators and founder of the well-known Salem boarding school whose philosophy was an unusual blend between élitism and progressivism and the balance between learning and character-building and between

idealism and pragmatism. He emigrated in 1933 to Britain and founded Gordonstoun School in Scotland after the model of Salem. In 1938 he became a British citizen.

220. FO 800/316.

221. Golo Mann, *Zwölf Versuche* (Frankfurt/M., 1973), 97. An excerpt from one of his memoranda prepared late in July 1940 for the Foreign Office, in which he pleaded for showing the Reich, in addition to defeating it, 'an honourable way out', was actually forwarded by the Assistant Under-Secretary of State R. A. Butler to Churchill; PREM/4/100/8.

222. 1901–82.

223. See Sabine Leibholz-Bonhoeffer, *The Bonhoeffers: Portrait of a Family* (New York, 1971).

224. See Bethge, Jasper (eds.), *An der Schwelle zum gespaltenen Europa*; also Gerhard Leibholz (S. H. Gerard), 'Germany between West and East', *Fortnightly*, 158 (Oct. 1942), 255–62 and Gerhart [*sic*] H. Leibholz, 'Ideology in the Post-War Policy of Russia and the Western Powers: The Study of a Contrast', *Hibbert Journal*, 42 (1944), 116–25.

225. 1899–1943; see Naomi Shepherd, *Wilfrid Israel: German Jewry's Secret Ambassador* (London, 1984).

226. Ibid. 196.

227. He is quoted as saying to the friend he and Trott had in common, David Astor, something to this effect: 'As a Jew I am sometimes tempted to hate Germany and the Germans, but then I remember Adam von Trott and that stops me'; quoted in Sykes, *Troubled Loyalty*, 277.

228. Letter from Wilfrid Israel to Bishop Bell, 28 Dec. 1942, Bell Papers, Box 28, quoted in Shepherd, *Wilfrid Israel*, 203.

229. Bishop Bell in the House of Lords, 10 Mar. 1943, Parliamentary Debates, 5th Ser. 126/26 (House of Lords, London, 1943), col. 539; see also Shepherd, *Wilfrid Israel*, 202 ff.

230. See also Thomas A. Knapp, 'Heinrich Brüning im Exil: Briefe an Wilhelm Sollmann 1940–1946', *VfZ*, 22 (Jan. 1974), 93–120.

231. See Heinrich Brüning, *Briefe und Gespräche 1934–1945*, ed. Claire Nix *et al.* (Stuttgart, 1974), 220.

232. Letter from Heinrich Brüning to Ewald Loser, Hartland, Vermont, 15 Dec. 1955, ibid. 459.

233. Goerdeler himself had, both in London and New York, 'personal representatives' who were devoted to him without reserve and acted as his intermediaries. In London it was Dr Reinhold Schairer; as a matter of fact, Brüning, who was compulsively cautious, distrusted him and told Goerdeler so; see Brüning's annotation of Mar./Apr. 1938, ibid. 187. In the USA Goerdeler's personal representative was Dr Gotthilf Bronisch, a man of Free Corps background who through his activities in the German City League (Deutscher Städtetag) had been acquainted with Goerdeler. In 1935 he settled in New York and was active during the war as Vice-President of the Loyal Americans of German Descent. Along with Bronisch, Dr Spencer Miller, Industrial Adviser to the Episcopal Church of America, acted in the USA on behalf of Goerdeler.

234. Ibid. 185–9; Ritter, *Carl Goerdeler*, 160, 164, 473.

235. Letter from Heinrich Brüning to Dannie Heineman, Lowell House, 7 Apr. 1941, Brüning, *Briefe und Gespräche*, 349.

236. Letter from Heinrich Brüning to Freya von Moltke, Andover, 10 Aug. 1946, ibid. 448; van Roon, *Neuordnung*, 31–2.

237. Letter from Brüning to Freya von Moltke, Brüning, *Briefe und Gespräche*, 448.

238. Letter from Adam von Trott to Heinrich Brüning, New York, 4 Oct. 1939; Brüning Papers.

239. Alexander Böker, who at Oxford was a member of Corpus Christi College, eventually sought refuge from Nazi Germany in the USA without, however, harbouring the intention to immigrate and become an American citizen. He considered himself a temporary political exile. After the war he returned to West Germany and joined the Foreign Office of the Federal Republic of Germany ending his career as Ambassador to the Holy See.

240. Alexander Böker, Diary entry, 20 Oct. 1939; Böker Papers.

241. Letter from Brüning to Freya von Moltke, 10 Aug. 1946, Brüning, *Briefe und Gespräche*, 450.

242. Letter from Heinrich Brüning to George S. Messersmith, Lowell House, 22 Dec. 1939, ibid. 299.

243. See, apart from the already cited letters from Brüning to Messersmith and Brüning to Freya von Moltke, Brüning's annotation of July–Sept. 1944, ibid. 417.
244. See the papers of Edward C. Carter in the Library of the University of Vermont, Burlington, Vt.; the papers of George M. Merten (formerly Hans Muhle), now in the Trott Archive, and the Brüning Papers at Harvard University, courtesy of Claire Nix.
245. 'Program for an International Group in New York', and Dr H. Muhle, 'Remarks on Mr Corbett's "Program for an International Group in New York"'; Muhle Papers.
246. 1902–75; from 1959 Sir John; he had spent a decade of his early manhood, from the mid-1920s to the mid-1930s, in Germany collecting intelligence as well as materials for his various works on 20th-cent. Germany. He also formed friendships with men such as General Hans von Seeckt and, from 1928, with Heinrich Brüning; Wheeler-Bennett was the only man in the world who could address this austere statesman as 'Harry'. His and Trott's paths would cross repeatedly in the course of the years. The two first met in September 1935 at a weekend party at Trott's friend's, Count Albrecht Bernstorff's, Schloss Stintenburg. See Sir John Wheeler-Bennett, *Knaves, Fools and Heroes in Europe Between the Wars* (London, 1974) and *Special Relationships: America in Peace and War* (London, 1975).
247. Letter from Adam von Trott to David Astor, 26 Dec. 1939; David Astor Papers.
248. 'Memorandum', 'Trott und die Aussenpolitik des Widerstandes', *VfZ*, 12 (July 1964), 316.
249. 1889–1979; he had been an old friend of Trott's since the summer of 1929 when the latter was in Berlin seeking contacts with Socialist circles (see Malone, *Adam von Trott*, 40); in 1931 he joined the Social Democratic Party. A political activist, he was dismissed by the Nazis in September 1933 and eventually, having spent six months in a Nazi prison in 1936, emigrated to the USA. There he changed his name to George M. Merten and finally went to work for the British and American Secret Services providing them with information on Nazi political and economic activities in the USA and South America; see 'Project George' in Anthony Cave Brown, *Wild Bill Donovan: The Last Hero* (New York, 1982), 206–10; the book is to be used with great caution.
250. 1882–1955.
251. In 1938 he emigrated to the USA where he first obtained a teaching position at the New School for Social Research.
252. 1893–1972.
253. He emigrated to the USA where he became Professor and subsequently Dean and President of the New School for Social Research. He knew Trott from Berlin where during the summer of 1931 Trott with the help of Hans Muhle had established contact with the group around the magazine *Neue Blätter für den Sozialismus* with which Simons was closely connected.
254. For Paul Scheffer see Margret Boveri, *Wir lügen alle: Eine Hauptstadtzeitung unter Hitler* (Olten, 1965), *passim*.
255. Letter from Hans Muhle to Adam von Trott, Bloomfield, NJ, 14 Nov. 1939, Muhle Papers.
256. Letters from Hans Muhle to Adam von Trott, Bloomfield, NJ, 14 and 23 Nov. 1939; Muhle Papers.
257. 1881–1952.
258. On 27 March 1933 the Reichstag passed (with only the votes of the Social Democrats against) the Enabling Act which gave the government dictatorial powers for four years, thus establishing the foundation for the Nazi dictatorship.
259. See Deutsch, *The Conspiracy*, 114.
260. 1885–1969.
261. 1879–1956.
262. This proposal was launched in 1942 by Heinrich Georg Ritzel, himself a former Social Democratic member of the Reichstag living in Basle since 1935; see Hagen Schulze, *Otto Braun oder Preussens demokratische Sendung: Eine Biographie* (Frankfurt/M., 1977), 806.
263. Quoted in Hugo Stehkämpfer, 'Protest, Opposition und Widerstand im Umkreis der (untergegangenen) Zentrumspartei', in Jürgen Schmädeke and Peter Steinbach (eds.), *Der Widerstand gegen den Nationalsozialismus: Die deutsche Gesellschaft und der Widerstand gegen Hitler* (Munich, 1985), 890.
264. NA Microcopy No. T-120/2541/E295391.

265. See *The Rote Kapelle: The CIA's History of Soviet Intelligence and Espionage Networks in Western Europe, 1936–1945* (Washington, DC, 1979), 207.

266. With whom his code-name generally was 'Uncle Joe' or 'Mr. Wild' and Gessler's, appropriately, 'W. Tell'; Christie Papers.

267. According to Captain Hans Ritter ('Knight') Wirth was financially wholly dependent on Dr Manfred Simon, a German émigré from Nuremberg who found refuge in France and entered the French Secret Service. He succeeded in being appointed Press Attaché to the French Embassy in Berne from where he sought to establish contact with members of the German Opposition and exiles, notably Wirth and Fritz Thyssen; Christie Papers, CHRS 180/1/35, No.29; see also *Biographisches Handbuch der deutschsprachigen Emigration nach 1933*, ed. Werner Röder and Herbert Strauss, i (Munich, 1980).

268. See *The Rote Kapelle*, 205.

269. He seems to have discouraged an overture late in 1942 on the part of a 'Wilhelmstrasse emissary' to hold himself ready to return to his native country after the war in order to participate in its political reconstruction, arguing that he would not 'go to Compiègne' to play the part of 'another Erzberger' (Matthias Erzberger, a Centrist statesman who as State Secretary without Portfolio signed, at the end of the First World War in November 1918, the armistice at Compiègne and was subsequently identified by his many nationalistic foes with the policy of fulfilment (of the terms of the Treaty of Versailles). He was finally assassinated by an extremist right-wing squad in August 1921); Telegram from Leland Harrison (American Minister to Switzerland) to Secretary of State, 14 Dec. 1942, NA, RG 59, CDF 862.00/4347.

270. Cave Brown, *Wild Bill Donovan*, 355.

271. See Jarrell C. Jackman and Carla M. Borden (eds.), *The Muses Flee Hitler: Cultural Transfer and Adaptation, 1930–1945* (Washington, DC, 1983), 24; Fritz Neumark, *Zuflucht am Bosporus: Deutsche Gelehrte, Politiker und Künstler in der Emigration 1933–1953* (Frankfurt/M., 1980).

272. 1889–1953; after the collapse of the Nazi regime, Reuter, Mayor of West Berlin, had moved in his political career from the extreme Left to Social Democracy. He was one of Weimar Germany's foremost municipal politicians. Mayor of Magdeburg in 1931, he became a member of the Reichstag in the following year until he was thrown into a concentration camp in 1933. In 1935 he found refuge in Turkey where he served first in the Ministry of Economics and subsequently as Professor of City Planning. Shortly before the war he met Carl Goerdeler, who was on one of his many trips abroad, and he did not fail to warn him that he was misguided in his reliance on the Generals to overthrow Hitler since the latter was but 'their product' (quoted in Willy Brandt and Richard Löwenthal, *Ernst Reuter. Ein Leben für die Freiheit. Eine politische Biographie*, Munich, 1973, 323). Reuter also repeatedly implored Thomas Mann in far-away California to come out as 'the voice of the spiritual, free, humane Germany' (copy of letter from Ernst Reuter to Herrn Dr Thomas Mann, Amerika, Ankara, 17 Mar. 1943, see also in Brandt and Löwenthal, *Ernst Reuter*, 314 ff.) with a persuasive political statement. Thomas Mann dismissed this proposal for its 'exile patriotism' (ibid. 317). Within Turkey Reuter was no less instrumental in attempting to politically activate fellow exiles of all persuasions.

273. Since July 1941 COI (Office of Co-ordinator of Information); since June 1942 OSS (Office of Strategic Services).

274. Sozialdemokratische Partei Deutschlands.

275. See *Deutschland-Berichte der Sozialdemokratischen Partei Deutschlands (Sopade), 1934–1940*, 7 vols. (Frankfurt/M., 1980).

276. Werner Röder, *Die deutschen sozialistischen Exilgruppen in Grossbritannien 1940–1945* (2nd edn., Bonn-Bad Godesberg, 1973), 174.

277. See the excellent treatment of the Socialist exiles in Britain in Glees, *Exile Politics*, passim; also idem, 'Das deutsche politische Exil in London 1939–1945', in Hirschfeld (ed.), *Exil in Grossbritannien*, 62–79.

278. Interview with Willy Brandt, 1 July 1980.

279. See Lewis J. Edinger, *German Exile Politics: The Social Democratic Executive Committee in the Nazi Era* (Berkeley, Calif., 1956), 71, 83 ff.

280. Odd page 'Seite 180', BA/K, Ritter 131.

281. His real name was Hellmut von Rauschenplat.

282. Her real name was Hilde Meisel.

283. The ISK also maintained a connection with the International Federation of Transport Workers under its Finnish Secretary General Edo Fimmen who in 1935 organized an international conference in Roskilde (Denmark) which was attended by 31 Germans alongside representatives from England, France, Holland, Denmark, Sweden, and Norway. The chief purpose of the conference was to impress upon the union leadership the fact that there was resistance in Germany and to reassure the Germans that they were not abandoned; see Helmut Esters and Hans Pelger, *Gewerkschafter im Widerstand* (Hanover, 1967), 43–4, Ger van Roon, *Widerstand in Dritten Reich: Ein Überblick* (Munich, 1979), 75–6. Among the unionists Fritz Tarnow who headed the German Unions Abroad (Auslandsvertretung der deutschen Gewerkschaften, ADG) kept up from Stockholm a contact with the Socialist conspirators connected with the 20 July 1944 circles; Röder, *Die deutschen sozialistischen Exilgruppen*, 75, 174.

284. Martin Broszat *et al.*, *Bayern in der NS-Zeit*, iv. 705.

285. See Hermann Weber, 'Die KPD in der Illegalität', in Löwenthal and von zur Mühlen (eds.), *Widerstand und Verweigerung in Deutschland 1933 bis 1945* (Berlin, 1982), 85. See also Allan Merson, *Communist Resistance in Nazi Germany* (London, 1985), 19, 21, 72–3, 75, 155.

286. Weber, 'Die KPD', 97.

287. The Communist intelligence organization, so designated by the Gestapo, under the leadership of Harro Schulze-Boysen and Arvid Harnack, worked in close conjunction with a widespread Soviet espionage network with the aim of opposing Fascism by conveying military information to the Russians. It was crushed by the Nazis in 1942; see Heinz Höhne, *Codeword: Director. The Story of the Red Orchestra* (London, 1970).

288. Höhne, *Codeword*, 247; for a recent attempt to vindicate Schulze-Boysen and Harnack as men of principle and patriots see Peter Steinbach, 'Ein Kämpfer, bereit, die Folgen auf sich zu nehmen', *Deutsches Allgemeines Sonntagsblatt*, 1 Sept. 1989, 18.

289. In effect his sentence was commuted to 25 years in gaol, and he was finally freed in 1955.

290. See in this connection Alexander Fischer, 'Die Bewegung "Freies Deutschland" in der Sowjetunion: Widerstand hinter Stacheldraht?', in Schmädecke and Steinbach (eds.), *Widerstand*,968.

291. SD Report of 8 August 1944 in '*Spiegelbild einer Verschwörung'. Die Opposition gegen Hitler und der Staatsstreich vom 20. Juli 1944 in der SD-Berichterstattung. Geheime Dokumente aus dem ehemaligen Reichssicherheitshauptamt*, ed. Hans-Adolf Jacobsen (Stuttgart, 1984), i. 174.

292. Hagen Schulze, 'Rückblick auf Weimar: Ein Briewechsel zwischen Otto Braun und Joseph Wirth im Exil', *VfZ*, 26 (Jan. 1978), 144–5.

293. Brüning's correspondence gives particular evidence of the divide which often separated the exile and the emigrant. His remarks on emigrants were rarely appreciative; see Brüning, *Briefe und Gespräche*, 142, 368.

294. See Glees, *Exile Politics*, 25, 39.

# 2

## Thinking for the British Empire?

### 1. Reconnaissances

There was no Resistance in Germany in the period immediately following Hitler's seizure of power. On the Right there was almost universal intoxication over the 'national resurrection', and on the Left there was dumbfoundedness in view of the instant terror of the new regime. But whereas on the Left there was near-unanimous hostility against the Nazis and among the Communists in particular the road into illegality was merely a question of time, in the conservative circles, especially those which later gravitated towards the *Widerstand*, there was confusion over the assessment of the 'national revolution' which had taken place on 30 January 1933. General Beck, for example, felt 'relief', registering that he had wished for years for 'the political revolution': 'it is the first ray of hope since 1918'.[1] Goerdeler was by no means unequivocally opposed to Hitler's assumption of power; after all, the new Chancellor promised to undo the humiliation of Versailles and to overcome the class and party struggles of the Weimar days.[2] On the other hand, in the Bonhoeffer family there was little doubt that an ominous event had happened in their country which augured war.[3] Similarly, from the very beginning Moltke was keenly aware of the fact that the coming of Hitler meant the dissolution of all constitutionality and altogether was a catastrophe.[4] Trott, at the time a student at Oxford, 'knew at once', as one of his closest friends there registered, 'that a terrible disaster had befallen his country' and that 'a bitter struggle' was ahead.[5]

But as there was no immediate organized resistance, there was nothing like a resistance foreign policy at the start. There were, however, certain early feelers afoot which should be registered here since they indicate a tendency from the beginning to break out and communicate with the world 'outside'. One of the earliest of such communications was the memorandum of September 1933 by Theodor Steltzer on conditions in Germany, addressed to the Austrian Federal Minister of Justice and later Chancellor, Kurt von Schuschnigg, upon the latter's request. Steltzer,[6] who came from an upper-class family in Holstein, having served in the First World War, occupied during the Weimar years the important administrative position of Landrat

(District Administrator) in central Schleswig-Holstein. In his preoccupation with the administration of his district, as well as with the relationship between Germans and Danes, he tended to take a critical position towards the capital. He considered himself a German patriot, though not one of the Prussian variety; hence his particular interest in Austria.[7]

In Austria the Christian Social Engelbert Dollfuss had, in May 1932, become Federal Chancellor and his Party friend Kurt von Schuschnigg Minister of Justice. In March of the following year Dollfuss established a corporative and authoritarian regime which constituted, in the view of many critics, a variety of Fascism, namely Austro-Fascism. But this particular Austrian regime, while anti-parliamentarian and certainly not democratic, also saw its mission to be the staving off of National Socialism. Its public philosophy was distinctly Christian and 'greater German' in the pre-Bismarckian, if not anti-Bismarckian, universalist tradition. From this position and under the threat of National Socialism, it launched the claim to be an outpost of and a spokesman for the 'true Germany' to which it hoped to rally in particular the German ethnic groups abroad.

Theodor Steltzer, with his appeal to Schuschnigg to take the lead,[8] chose to go outside the Reich borders in order to call attention to the danger signs at home. No doubt, Steltzer was first and foremost a romantic conservative who lamented the development of mass culture and mass politics and the prevalence of materialism and aestheticism among the German upper strata. However, this not exactly 'liberal' position led him to a strikingly astute analysis of the menace which came from the Nazis. Above all he zeroed in on the 'deification of ideology'[9] which, he warned, constituted a challenge to the realm of religion and to the limits which are set to statesmanship by the dispositions of 'a higher hand'.[10] The rejection of religion and the deification of everything ideological would lead, so Steltzer stressed, to the cult of naked power and of race.

Such considerations also led Steltzer to address himself to the Jewish problem, not exactly a priority with the Austrian addressee, to say the least. But the desertion of God on the part of the Western world could not, so he argued, be laid at the feet of the Jews. The approach to the Jewish question by the new regime violated not only 'the most elementary laws of nature' but also the *volkish* idea in the Herderian sense which preached respect for alien ethnicity as much as one's own. What was needed was the establishment in Vienna, in conjunction with leading personalities from among the Jews, of an academy for the study of nationality rights.

The reception which the memorandum found in Vienna is not known. Steltzer himself later recorded that in fact the political situation in Austria at that time had already deteriorated too much for it to have had any effect there. However, it came to the attention of the German authorities who charged him with high treason.[11] For a short time Steltzer even had to go to

gaol until the charge against him was dismissed. We shall encounter Steltzer
again later in our story. Meanwhile he was active in ecumenical work until,
in 1939, he was recalled into the army which assigned him in 1940 as Transport
Officer to Norway where, as a General Staff Officer, he belonged to the inner
circle of the Commanding Officer. Shortly before his departure for Oslo he
made the acquaintance of Helmuth von Moltke, and frequent trips to
Germany in the subsequent years allowed him to establish an intimate
relationship with Moltke and to become an integral part of the Kreisau
Circle. Steltzer's position in Norway, where he also struck up close ties with
the Norwegian Resistance movement, made him one of the lifelines of the
*Widerstand.*

In the summer of 1935 Helmuth James von Moltke in a letter to his English
friend Lionel Curtis confided his own and his German friends' sense of
isolation, assuring him that, even if for all their lives they were confined to
'a small cell', they would try to keep open the connection with the 'greater
world'.[12] Moltke was favoured by a cosmopolitan background and a wide
circle of friends and acquaintances. He was determined to make the most
of an outlook which, he knew, was 'broader and wider' than that of his
contemporaries.[13] He had kept in close touch with his South African relatives
through whom doors were opened for him to influential circles in England.
Through his family connection he first met Curtis, whose Commonwealth
idea and broader vision of a world federalism was attractive to him. Then
Moltke's decision to read for the English Bar opened up to him the need for
regular journeys to London and perhaps, if necessary, the option—of which
he later did not avail himself—of practising in England. Furthermore, while
in Berlin, he struck up a close relationship with the body of American foreign
correspondents, including Dorothy Thompson, Edgar Ansel Mowrer, and
Wallace Deuel.

Moltke's letter to Lionel Curtis of July 1935 is of considerable significance
in as much as its chief burden was an account of a conversation which the
former had had a few days earlier with Lord Lothian.[14] The latter, an
influential figure in the Royal Institute of Foreign Affairs (Chatham House),
was one of Britain's arch-appeasers.[15] The connection came obviously
through Curtis, and the talk gave Moltke precisely the opportunity he was
seeking to reach the 'greater world'. But it was unsatisfactory, not merely
because it lasted only ten minutes, but particularly because the British peer
as it turned out leaned over backwards to make apologies for the new
Germany to his German partner who knew much better.

It was Lord Lothian who confronted Moltke with a number of puzzling
propositions proceeding from the one that there was no such thing as international law but only anarchy (point 1) through the whole litany of the
appeasers: that the growth of Nazism must be attributed to England and
France's post-war policies, especially Versailles and the Ruhr (point 2); that

the Nazis were stable in power and that no revolution or change in power was feasible (point 3); that in the course of time the Nazis would be transformed into a 'respectable government' (point 4); and that a policy of concessions to the Nazis would help to transform them (point 5).

Moltke did not leave any of these propositions unanswered. A student of international law, he could not accept the actual premisses of Lothian; as one coming out of the 'small cell', he had to refute the political spin-offs. Lothian's point 3 had simply been 'pushed down' his throat by propaganda; Moltke well knew that there was no such thing as an erosion of dictatorship by its own free will; the Nazi respectability existed outwardly only. Finally, point 5 required the most elaborate response:

The more concessions you make, the less need there will be to use war as a weapon to settle international disputes; but it seems a fallacy to believe that if you yield to the threat of war, you will make the one who has threatened the war, less eager to try the same again.[16]

In his commentary to Lionel Curtis, Moltke added that it was a mistake to make the Germans count on English neutrality should a European war break out; in reality Britain was not an arbiter, but was bound to be 'a party to the struggle'.

When episodes of a given kind multiply they cease to be episodes. Certainly the bizarre ten-minute disputation between Moltke and Lothian was more than an inconsequential episode. It set the stage for a concerted effort on the part of opponents of the new German regime to enlighten the outside world, especially Britain, about its harsh realities. In this case it was the German who 'thought for the British Empire'. But there were other similar occurrences. Carl Goerdeler's restless journeys abroad, about which more will be said later on, certainly served the same purpose. Meanwhile, General Beck made a visit to Paris in June 1937. Needless to say, it was all above board. On the occasion of the funeral of King George V, General Gamelin had invited General von Blomberg to Paris who, not being able to accept, proposed that General Beck take his place. Beck reacted enthusiastically.[17] The visit, although cleared with the Auswärtiges Amt, was to be a strictly unofficial one, and Beck went on a mission of goodwill, 'as a gentleman to talk to gentlemen'.[18] While no doubt Beck's bearing in the conversations with the French was nothing short of correct, he subsequently confided to some of his German friends what really had been on his mind,[19] namely that the Radicals in the Party[20] kept pressing the Führer[21] for a *Heldentat* (heroic deed) in order to counter internal discontent—all this of course against the better judgement of the military. Some of this message evidently reached Gamelin and his colleagues;[22] it certainly penetrated, indirectly, through Christie to the British, that is to those who wanted to listen. As Christie commented: 'Only a very firm upper lip and a solid front with France and those nations who oppose war in principle can now prevent Hitler from running amok.'[23] As for Beck's official report, it also had a distinct message: it was meant to impress upon the Nazis the strength and determination of the French army and thus to deter them from adventures.[24] Hitler's predictably scornful reaction: 'Beck and Gamelin ... the two heroes of humanity met there in Paris.'[25]

It should also be mentioned here that somewhat earlier in the same year two important German documents on the deficient state of the German economy, and therefore the military unpreparedness of the country, found their way to the British Foreign Office; one was drawn up in Düsseldorf late in 1936 upon Goerdeler's initiative by the Association of Heavy Industries in the Rhineland and Westphalia (Langnamverein, so called owing to the inordinate length of its official name); the other one by Colonel, later General, Georg Thomas, head of the War Economy Staff of the Armed Forces, a sworn foe of Nazism since the Fritsch affair early in 1938. The Langnam Report evidently turned up in the British Legation in Prague whence it was forwarded to the Embassy in Berlin; its authenticity was verified for Sir Robert Vansittart by Goerdeler himself in London in July 1937. It was never presented to the Cabinet, however. Across the 'Most Secret' document printed on official light-blue paper for His Majesty's Government there appeared a curt note in Vansittart's hand: 'Suppressed by Eden'.[26] Whatever the Foreign Secretary's own views on the matter, he knew that the Prime Minister, bent on a policy of appeasement, was set on disregarding countervailing intelligence. The Cabinet thus had no opportunity to reappraise British policy towards Germany in the light of Vansittart's—and this means at this point, Goerdeler's—information and advice.

## 2. Missions to Britain (1938)

Beginning in the year 1938 the efforts of the German opposition abroad multiplied; doggedly the various individuals and groups which came together in what later came to be known as *Widerstand* kept trying to put on the brakes at home and sending emissaries abroad. On the European scene 1938 and 1939 were of course cathartic years. For too long the German dictator had had his way unchallenged by, if not with the support of, the Powers in systematically dismantling the order of Versailles. The re-establishment of German military sovereignty in March 1935 went unchallenged. It was rewarded in June of the same year by the conclusion between Britain and Germany of the Naval Pact which itself undermined the foundations of the Peace Treaties. Then of course followed the reoccupation of the demilitarized zone of the Rhineland in March 1936, again without eliciting any action on the part of the Powers. Troubled domestically, France attempted to strengthen her position *vis-à-vis* the German threat by the search for collective security and by means of bilateral treaties—with Russia and Czechoslovakia, both in mid-1935. In Britain, on the other hand, Stanley Baldwin's premiership steered the unsteady course of 'cunctation', as Sir Robert Vansittart called it,[27] vaccilating between a League policy, cautious rearmament, and bilateral negotiations with the Fascist dictatorships in the hopes of mollifying and appeasing them.

With the accession of Neville Chamberlain as Prime Minister in May 1937 the British policy became altogether identified with the appeasement course. Let it be said here that, under the impact of Hitler's unopposed annexation of Austria in March 1938, the shameful and humiliating abandonment by Britain and France of Czechoslovakia in September 1938 (the Munich Agreement), and in March 1939 the German occupation and destruction of Czechoslovakia, the term appeasement has all too readily acquired a pejorative meaning in political and historical polemics. In this sense appeasement has, quite mistakenly, been identified with the policy of yielding to the demands of the dictators, especially Adolf Hitler, without asking for reciprocal assurances. In fact, Neville Chamberlain's appeasement policy must be understood within a structural context which lent it a distinct and arguable rationale. Appeasement was not a matter of mere mismanagement and misreading, whether wanton or not, of Nazi Germany's intentions. To a large extent it was dictated by an interaction of national and international constraints such as those concerning the state of preparedness at home, economic needs, and the dependence on the Commonwealth, which prevented decisive action then and there on the part of Britain against the Fascist menace.[28] These were the circumstances which conditioned Chamberlain's pursuit of a peace policy which, measured by the limited perspective of Anglo-German relations, too readily suggested weakness and surrender. The cultivation of good relations with Nazi Germany was dependent on considerations that far transcended it.

But in 1938, certainly, the merits of the appeasement policy became a matter of intense controversy, and the debate arose between the 'appeasers' and 'anti-appeasers', as we have come to label, perhaps too sharply, the two camps. The debate raged within the Cabinet, among the various branches of the Executive, in the Houses of Parliament, as well as, of course, among the public, about the need for a reorientation of foreign policy in the light of the clear and present danger that came from Nazi Germany. In the course of this debate the positions were accentuated when the British Ambassador to Berlin, Sir Nevile Henderson, of all people, assumed the part of an extreme appeaser. Henderson's outright and admitted scepticism concerning the advisability of Britain's abiding by international obligations and the standards of morality,[29] and his open sympathies with the Nazi élite pulled the rug out from under those in Germany who were concerned about the interconnections of Hitler's sweep on the international scene and his consolidation of power at home.

At the other end of the spectrum in the Foreign Office there was Sir Robert Vansittart, who came to be known as Britain's most obsessive Germanophobe, angrily condemning any efforts to distinguish between 'good' Germans and 'bad', between Germans and Nazis.[30] Vansittart became Britain's most vociferous critic of appeasement towards Germany.

It was into this debate that the German emissaries entered. It would be foolish to assume and maintain that they were an integral part of it; they were, in fact marginal to it. But marginal as they were to the grand diplomacy, and later even more so to the conduct of the war, they can be, indeed must be, fitted into the co-ordinates of the European diplomacy of the late 1930s and early 1940s. And what is no less important, they must be fitted as well into the co-ordinates of the ideological fronts of the immediate pre-war period and of the war itself. The German emissaries came primarily from the traditional élites. Still in their positions at home, they were able to secure alibis to get out of the country without prejudice. Their accreditation was of course rather questionable. They came out of the blue, so to speak, recommended to one or the other British dignitary, and occasionally penetrating even to the centres of power. They were listened to with a mixture of sympathy, distrust, horror, and altogether puzzlement. But in the precarious situation in which Britain found itself in those years, these members of the German opposition, whether regarded as patriots or traitors, were at least welcomed as good sources of information. Ultimately, they had a distinct impact upon the orientation, that is the reorientation, of British foreign policy. As we shall see, it was more in spite of them than because of them that Whitehall initially saw itself confirmed in its appeasement course.

It is important to realize, however, that at this time most of these conservative German critics of the Nazi regime had barely begun to disengage themselves from it. Certainly the Fritsch crisis of February 1938 had given them a jolt. But whatever their disagreements were with the Nazis, whether these concerned the general lawlessness, the policy towards the Churches and the Jews, or foreign policy, they did not as yet add up to a resolve to make a clean break. Almost everyone still harboured illusions that the excesses of the past half-decade were passing phenomena and that the traditional élites were strong enough to assert themselves and to 'tame' the wilder Nazis. This assumption was often combined with the expectation that the 'reasonable' elements in the Party, of whom Hermann Göring of all people came to be regarded as the protector, would be able to assert themselves ultimately in Party and government counsels.[31] In short, as yet the opposition did not add up to all-out resistance.

In the controversy over appeasement in London, the officials at 10 Downing Street and Whitehall were themselves mesmerized by the distinction between what they called the 'moderates' and the 'extremists' among the Nazis, and were in a quandary as to what weight to assign to the former. The contours of these groups were by no means clear, except that British officialdom accepted the view of Sir Eric Phipps, Henderson's predecessor as British Ambassador to Berlin, that Schacht was 'more or less' the leader of the 'moderate party' supported by Neurath, the Army, and the Civil Service. Phipps also called attention to what he termed 'very helpful points of contact with General Göring, who is an old army officer with few Nazi proclivities in his saner moments'.[32] Ribbentrop, Goebbels, and Himmler and his SS were considered among the chief extremists. It was thought in Britain, so Rauschning suggested with tongue in cheek, that Göring was the only Nazi with *Kinderstube* (manners) and who did 'not pick his teeth during diplomatic talks like Herr Hitler'.[33] Göring might at least be suitable for a 'transitional' government.[34] But the lines were not clearly drawn in the British perception of the two groups; in fact they were so blurred as to make the distinction almost absurd. As for Hitler, he was generally perceived as remote and likely to be swayed by one or the other party.

The speculation, if not confusion, over the German 'moderates' and 'extremists' was the fuel, so to speak, in the many encounters between the British and the German opposition. Before long the question posed itself as to how acceptable the 'moderates' would be, and indeed whether they would be preferable as spokesmen for Germany to Hitler himself, if not the 'extremists'. No doubt, the efforts of the conservative emissaries were designed to counteract the policies of Hitler and the Party and indeed to compromise and shake them. Their efforts were clearly coupled with, if not subordinated to, a strategy of opposition and eventually to resistance and conspiracy. In this matter the primacy of domestic concerns (*Primat der Innenpolitik*) was in operation, and *Aussenpolitik* in the form of feelers abroad was made to bolster the domestic effort and to serve as its instrument.

In any case, it must be stated emphatically that a proposal for appeasement, in the sense of yielding to Hitler's demands, did not come from the side of the Opposition.[35] As stated from the very start by Goerdeler, the German message was consistently for France and Britain to stand firm, and it was thus understood in the Foreign Office.[36] As we shall see, the most decisive anti-appeasers, will be found in the ranks of the German Opposition, and their advice to the Foreign Office was not altogether unrealistic. Thus there is no reason not to fit the foreign feelers, however cautiously, into the co-ordinates of the European diplomacy of the late 1930s and early 1940s.

In this connection a second look at Vansittart is in order who was one of the principal contacts before the outbreak of the war with Carl Goerdeler, the Opposition's chief traveller abroad. The former's attitude towards appeasement in general and towards Germany in particular was a rather complex one. In relation to Fascist Italy at least Vansittart had been one of the foremost advocates of appeasement. His close involvement in the abortive Hoare–Laval Pact of December 1935, by the terms of which Mussolini would have been appeased in Abyssinia, was the cause of his waning influence in Whitehall. It was also Vansittart's impetuous and compulsive style, as much as his insistence upon conducting a personal policy, which led in December 1937 to his dismissal by the Foreign Secretary from the position as Permanent Under-Secretary in the Foreign Office and to his transfer, in fact demotion, to the high-sounding but rather anonymous position of Chief Diplomatic Adviser to the Foreign Secretary,[37] in which he doggedly urged a draconian policy against the German menace.

But even on this score Vansittart's position was not altogether unequivocal. He had been among the many Britons who were deeply impressed by the injustices of Versailles and had 'always wished', as he wrote to Sir Eric Phipps, his brother-in-law, 'to see minimized the imprudences then committed'.[38] In fact, in order to counter all the 'violent prejudices' attributed to him and to 'dispel the absurd but widely held idea in Germany' that he was 'possessed by a blind and unreasoning hatred' of Germany, Vansittart made a point of visiting Phipps in Berlin on the occasion of the Olympic Games in the summer of 1936 and of scheduling meetings with 'all the principal members of the German Government from the Chancellor downwards'.[39]

According to the testimony of Phipps, these meetings turned out to be 'long and most friendly'.[40] Vansittart, so it seems, made quite an impression in official Berlin; at least we have a report that he was thought of as a 'he-man' who had spoken for Great Britain 'openly and courageously' in contrast to the many 'yes-men' who previously had flooded into Germany from England.[41] As for Vansittart, he left satisfied, and 'with better hopes', than he had arrived with.[42] He was keenly aware, however, of the fact 'that undue optimism would be out of place'.[43]

Vansittart's ambivalence towards Germany found expression in, and was nourished by, a network of agents which he established on his own and which reached deep into Germany. Generally known in Whitehall as 'Van's private detective agency',[44] its function was in effect a much broader one than this designation suggests; it was in effect an instrument of its chief's private diplomacy. Not without justification, however, another designation was current at the time in official circles. In the light of the Germanophobe label usually attached to Vansittart, it was a paradoxical one: the men in Vansittart's service were dubbed his 'Germanophiles'.[45]

Vansittart's two chief aides in this enterprise were Group Captain Malcolm Grahame Christie and T. Philip Conwell-Evans. Both were men of extraordinary enterprise and ingenuity. They were also men with views of their own, especially on Anglo-German relations, and not mere tools. Much of Christie's life (1881–1971) revolved around Germany. After obtaining an engineering degree in Aachen, he worked in the Ruhr until the outbreak of the First World War when he joined the Royal Flying Corps. After the war he served in the RAF, first as Air Attaché in Washington (1922–6) and subsequently in the same capacity in Berlin (1927–30). In Washington Christie met Vansittart, who at the time was head of the American Department at the Embassy; in Berlin he struck up a friendship with Göring which carried over into the Nazi period.[46] When upon his retirement in 1930 he left Germany, he wrote to an acquaintance that he would remain 'a good "Ambassador without Portfolio"' for Germany, though adding mysteriously that he realized it would be difficult to convince the latter of this.[47] The same year he went into the service of 'Van' with the special assignment of investigating the political situation in Germany and Central Europe. A man of independent means, Christie steered his own course, enjoying continued close ties with the Nazi potentates, ties which, of course, he knew enabled him 'to get entrée to the Nazi camp and keep watch'.[48]

By Vansittart's own description 'one of the most ardent germanophiles', if not '*the* most ardent germanophile' in Britain,[49] was Oxford-educated Conwell-Evans (b. 1891). After lecturing at the University of Königsberg on diplomatic history from 1932 to 1934, he returned to England to become one of the central figures in appeasement circles. He acted as Joint Honorary Secretary of the Anglo-German Fellowship, accompanied Lord Lothian in 1935 and Lloyd George in the following year on their Hitler pilgrimages, and developed a close friendship with Ribbentrop. Tom Jones, the Deputy Secretary to the Cabinet, who met him in 1936, commented upon Conwell-Evans's 'passionate hostility' to the British Foreign Office 'because of its attitude to Berlin'.[50] It was only later, in the summer of 1938, that he saw the light and changed his attitude towards Germany, making it his business to warn the Foreign Office about Nazi Germany's intentions.

It was through Christie and Conwell-Evans, then, that Vansittart was able to establish ties with the German power élites and was encouraged in his illusion of being in the position of an arbiter on German affairs, on Anglo-German relations, and indeed on the question of war or peace. The irony was, of course, that the agents of this compulsive Germanophobe were actually outspoken Germanophiles. They had certainly been sobered by National Socialism, and their continued preoccupation with, indeed passion for, Germany led them to strike up connections with opposition circles and to plead their case with 'Van'.

But which were these opposition circles? They were those conservative groups in Germany which, especially since the Fritsch crisis of February 1938, had begun to disengage themselves from the broad consensus of the early years concerning the Nazi regime. Through Goerdeler 'Van's' agents reached the economic and the military sectors; and for the latter, of course, the mysterious Hans Ritter with his many aliases was especially helpful. Through the Kordt brothers was established the connection with the Auswär-

tiges Amt. Then there were the particularly close ties with the House of
Bosch. Wirth, Rauschning, and Otto Strasser were always ready sources of
information, though clearly much of the intelligence from the exiles had to
be discounted. Then there was a most unusual source, Prince Max Egon
zu Hohenlohe-Langenburg[51], descendant of one of Germany's illustrious
princely houses and a naturalized citizen of Liechtenstein, who owned large
estates in the Sudetenland as well as in Spain and Mexico. While maintaining
close connections with Göring, the heads of the Gestapo, and the Nazi
Minister of the Interior, Frick, Hohenlohe presented himself as wholly out
of sympathy with the Nazi Party and especially the policies of Hitler's Foreign
Minister, Ribbentrop. Early in September 1938, shortly before Munich, he
sought, not without self-interest, a role in pleading the Sudeten German case
with the investigative Runciman mission from Britain in August 1938. Being
'furiously fond of England and the English people',[52] he offered his services
in the following year, before and after the outbreak of the war, to mediate
between the British and the Germans.[53]

In any event, 'Van's' agents made themselves eloquent advocates of the
'moderates', whoever they were, and so their chief, Vansittart, in his struggle
against the appeasement policy and especially against the Ambassador in
Berlin, became, initially at least, a passionate apologist of these 'moderates'.
'I disagree with Sir N. Henderson profoundly,' he minuted in August 1938,
'and so do all moderate Germans ... If Sir N. Henderson had his way there
would be an end to all moderate Germans and to any hope whatever of a
moderate Germany in the future.'[54] And in February 1939 he noted defiantly:
'The truth blows Sir Nevile Henderson's fallacious cobweb into the limbo
where it belongs ... People like Professor Conwell-Evans, Colonel Christie
and myself ... really know what was going on in Germany.'[55] The two
Germanophiles had, temporarily at least, made Vansittart depart from his
unbending anti-Germanism.

The flow of German emissaries abroad was initiated by the man who
turned out to be one of the most untiring travellers of the Opposition, Carl
Goerdeler. After his resignation as Mayor of Leipzig, he was given a haven
by Robert Bosch in the form of a loose contractual arrangement which
enabled him to enter actively into opposition activities and especially served
as a cover for an elaborate schedule of foreign journeys.[56] Whether or not
Goerdeler's tour was approved by Admiral Canaris, as is claimed by one of
his biographers,[57] he travelled, as the Germans say, 'auf eigene Faust',[58] that
is, without any particular legitimation. This should not in any way detract
from Goerdeler's diplomatic mission, as he conceived of it; much to the
contrary.[59] His kind of foreign policy was by definition foreign policy without
the usual formal mandate. He went out on his own and had to rely on private
contacts, which he had in abundance. But the British Foreign Office was
puzzled to begin with about his accreditation: 'He seemed to me an honest

fellow,' commented Frank Ashton-Gwatkin, when Goerdeler first appeared in London in June 1937, 'but I could not make out in whose interests he was travelling or with what precise purpose.'[60] Sir Orme Sargent, the Assistant Under-Secretary of State for Foreign Affairs, guessed that Goerdeler had come over 'as the unofficial emissary and representative of the Reichwehr'.[61] One thing was quite evident at the Foreign Office, namely that while Goerdeler did not appear there on an official mission, he was not a purely private person either. In fact, wherever he went, he was received as a person of consequence and given much attention.

Starting in June 1937, Goerdeler's grand tour took him to Belgium and Britain, and after a brief return to Berlin, to Holland and France and thence in August to Canada and the United States and back to France. A second trip in March and April 1938 led again to France and Britain, and a third one, beginning in August 1938, to Switzerland and via Italy to Yugoslavia, Romania, and Bulgaria. A fourth trip, in March and April 1939, took him to France and Algeria, and finally a fifth one, in the spring and summer of 1939, to Britain, Libya, Egypt, Palestine, Syria, Turkey, and Switzerland. About all these journeys Goerdeler wrote elaborate reports[62] which were addressed to Krupp, Bosch, Göring, Schacht, Generals Fritsch, Beck, Halder, Thomas, and, initially, also to Captain Wiedemann.[63]

Strikingly urbane and sane documents, Goerdeler's reports are master-pieces of political and economic observation as well as analyses of the state of affairs in the countries visited. At the same time they conveyed a distinct political message: that the countries visited, especially the great Powers, were strong economically and politically and not to be under-estimated and, while geared for peace, determined to stand up for their legitimate interests. In his attempt by such indirect means to influence the course of German policies, Goerdeler also stressed such features on the German scene as the persecution of the Jews and especially of the Churches, which were instrumental in turning public opinion abroad against his country.

This is as far as Goerdeler could go in sticking out his neck; and as we know, his message, while serving to encourage and convince 'the converted' at home, as Peter Hoffmann put it,[64] had no impact upon German government policies. Goerdeler did, however, have more intimate discussions in the capitals of Europe and in America of which understandably he made no mention in his reports.[65]

Of considerable significance was Goerdeler's sojourn in England in June/July 1937. Until the very end, he never ceased in his attempt to reach the powers-that-be in Britain on the assumption that they really were his friends and allies. On this particular visit he had his first major encounter with Sir Robert Vansittart,[66] the man who was to become his friend and foe, certainly his sparring partner, in the months to come.[67]

Fundamentally, the two men hit it off well. Vansittart, in fact, liked and respected the German, and the latter was sufficiently sanguine about having found the right contact on whom to unburden his concerns. Their relations, however, were rocky, certainly on Vansittart's part: first admiration and then the parting of the ways and rejection. Later, after the war, Vansittart nevertheless spoke of his one-time friend with at least residual respect, if not affection: Goerdeler was 'the only genuine German conspirator' whom he 'admired' for his convictions and his readiness to die for them, that is, to die 'bravely, horribly'.[68]

The meeting in 1937 between these two men was a distinctly amiable one; indeed Vansittart, after two interviews with his German visitor, one in the Foreign Office and the other at his house, noted that 'Herr Goerdeler' was 'an impressive person, wise and weighty, a man of great intelligence and courage, and a sincere patriot'. Vansittart seemed to appreciate Goerdeler's precarious position, 'offering his advice and criticism at home' and 'making any but blindly favourable comment abroad' and thus, in Goerdeler's own words, 'putting his neck in a halter'.[69] And even though it must have been evident to Sir Robert that, notwithstanding all Goerdeler's candour about conditions at home and insistence on 'firmness', he still harboured some illusions about Marshal Göring[70] and also, rather vaguely, took a revisionist position on the questions of Austria, the Sudetenland, and the Polish Corridor.[71] Vansittart was nevertheless persuaded to take on, for the moment at least, the patronage of the German 'moderates' against the 'extremists' of the Party. Concessions, if any, should be made to them and not to Hitler. Goerdeler did not get anywhere, however, with his all-too-optimistic faith in Göring, nor was Vansittart listened to in Whitehall.

Goerdeler's visit to America, which lasted from August to December 1937, was marked by a rigorous schedule of political visits and public lectures. In Washington he did not fail to pay his respects to the German Embassy and also had meetings with American men of affairs.[72] Ever ready to pave the way for the 'moderates', ex-Chancellor Brüning recommended him to his friend, the English historian, John W. Wheeler-Bennett, who resided in Virginia. As mentioned earlier, the latter had a particular interest in matters German; he had already met Goerdeler during his German years. Now, having suffered a heart attack in the course of his travels, Goerdeler spent a number of weeks as the guest of Wheeler-Bennett in Virginia.

Not much transpired from all these encounters, but enough to inform us that Goerdeler did not conceal his distaste for the regime at home. Of course he met with a good deal of suspicion. Might he not after all be an instrument of the Nazis? But George S. Messersmith, recently appointed to his State Department post and who kept his ears to the ground, attested that during his conversations with Goerdeler the latter indicated 'in strict confidence' that he was out of sympathy with his government, which he saw 'bringing ruin to Germany and others'. The general impression in Washington was that Goerdeler was there on behalf of Schacht 'and probably conservative elements in Germany' to endeavour to find out 'to what degree changes would have to be made in German internal and external policy, and probably in government, in order to put Germany in a position to deal with other countries on a normal basis'.[73] From Wheeler-Bennett we know that his German visitor made him familiar with 'the general ideas at that time current among the conspirators for an alternative government in Germany', and also projected the restoration of a monarchy on a constitutional basis.[74]

From Goerdeler's American trip one of his important early memoranda is extant. He was in the habit of writing memoranda, rather elaborate ones, in which he explained, to himself as much as to the addressees and to posterity, his convictions and political and economic schemes; many such memoranda were to follow in subsequent years and even into the days of his captivity after the failure of the plot in July 1944. Theoretical as they are, they form an important source for an understanding of Goerdeler's personality and views. This particular one, dated 1 December 1937, has come to be known as Goerdeler's 'Political Testament'; he turned it over to his confidant in New York, Gotthilf Bronisch, for safe keeping and eventual publication upon his instructions or in case 'something should happen to him'.[75]

The primary purpose of the 'Political Testament' was to counteract the general underestimation of National Socialism which Goerdeler had encountered in his previous journeys abroad. It was intended to open the eyes of the world to the dangers of Nazism. Goerdeler's indictment of the 'condition of lawlessness, of moral disintegration, of economic unreality and financial irresponsibility' in the Third Reich[76] was as unequivocal as his condemnation of those who had helped the Nazis into the saddle.[77] However, the root of the evil, Goerdeler insisted, was the hardships of the Versailles Treaty and the ensuing economic crises. What then followed was a rather moving tribute to the policies of Stresemann and especially of Brüning, that is an identification with their policy aimed at the revision of the Treaty system. On this basis, and on this basis alone, Goerdeler envisaged 'a pacified Europe' on its way to an 'ever-expanding economic unity'.[78] But the question still altogether unresolved in his mind at the time of the writing of this document was, who was to be the beneficiary of the new revisionism: a modified and chastened Nazi government or one that would have to take its place? Goerdeler had not yet wholly made the break with the regime; in any case, he spelled out what he thought were the legitimate claims of his country.

The next trip to a centre of power took Goerdeler in the spring of 1938 to Paris[79] where he met, through the mediation of Reinhold Schairer, Pierre Bertaux, Professor of German Studies and at that time Chef de Cabinet in the Education Nationale section of the French Ministry of Culture. Bertaux in turn helped him to obtain an interview early in April with the Secretary General of the French Foreign Ministry, Alexis Léger.[80] In the meeting with

Léger, which lasted two hours and in which Bertaux also participated, Goerdeler once again urged an unyielding stand against Hitler. The Frenchman, however, knowing that Goerdeler reported back to Göring and Wiedemann, remained extremely cautious and non-committal. Not only was Goerdeler an enigma for him, but the hard fact was that France was not prepared to accept the consequences of Goerdeler's advice, which would have meant war. The country was deep in a political crisis, and a few days after the interview the last Popular Front government of Léon Blum fell.

The openness which initially existed between the British Foreign Office— especially through Vansittart—and Goerdeler, soon gave way to contretemps and suspicion in the Foreign Office. Goerdeler's return trip to Britain in March 1938 did not come off at all well. The Fritsch crisis in Germany early in February 1938 opened British eyes to the fact that, if anything, the position of the 'moderates' had been dealt a serious blow and that Goerdeler and his friends were not the best of bets. Goerdeler's persistent optimism was registered in the Foreign Office as ill-founded. Now that he had virtually made the break with the Nazi regime, he talked compulsively abroad about army and industrialists' revolts and *putsches* which never came off.[81] No wonder, then, that the word spread in Whitehall that 'Dr. Goerdeler and Dr. Schairer are allowing their wishes to be fathers of their thoughts'.[82]

No less aggravating was the fact that during this visit Goerdeler spoke candidly, in his talks with Vansittart, about his claims to the Sudeten area. Not satisfied with autonomy, as suggested by Vansittart, he pleaded for its incorporation into the Reich since the area had a common frontier with it.[83]

Goerdeler was not much of a diplomat. His way was always, almost naïvely, forthright. He thought that the propositions which he considered right and reasonable were best brought out into the open and would thus ultimately prevail. That his friend 'Bobby', as he frequently referred to Vansittart, would take exception to these claims for his country, even assuming that they were not to benefit the Nazi regime but its successor, Goerdeler simply could not fathom.[84] In any event, Vansittart did take exception. He had come to perceive that his German friend differed from the Nazis only in method. It was from this time on that Sir Robert began to have doubts as to whether Goerdeler could still be counted as being one of the 'moderates'.

Nevertheless the traffic between German opposition members and the British if anything intensified. Many communications reached Sir Robert Vansittart, and he did not miss the opportunity to point out that the Embassy in Berlin had been of no help in this matter. Vansittart reported to the Foreign Office the intelligence obtained by himself or his agents from such sources as 'a prominent German officer', 'a very well informed Sudeten Deutsch source', 'a highly-placed German official',* 'a leading industrialist in Germany', 'a serving German diplomat',* 'a German friend whom he has long known',* 'an old and intimate friend in close touch with the Wilhelmstrasse', 'a trusted old friend, a reliable source', and a 'distinguished German economist' whom Vansittart's agent thought to be 'himself the virtual leader of the whole [opposition] movement'.[85] The general strategy, if one can call it such, of the Germans was to impress upon the British the futility of making concessions to Hitler and the need to pursue a hard course which, in turn, they could build on in order to destabilize Hitler's position at home and thus create the necessary preconditions for a coup.

Captain (retired) Victor von Koerber, by occupation chief correspondent in Berlin for the *Neues Wiener Journal* and contributor to a number of German newspapers, such as the Berlin *Vossische Zeitung*, clearly acted on his own when, early in August, he called repeatedly upon the British Military Attaché in Berlin, Colonel F. N. Mason-MacFarlane[86] to inform him about both Hitler's war plans against Czechoslovakia and a fast-growing opposition inside Germany.[87] Koerber got a sympathetic hearing from Mason-Mac-Farlane and no more. Understandably he did not cut much ice with Whitehall with his avowed preference for a Hohenzollern restoration and his advocacy of a revolution under tradition black-white-red auspices.[88] Koerber's approach in itself would have been a negligible episode had it not been for the fact that it brought out once again a fundamental divergence between the German and British positions. For the latter a revival of the Kaiser's Germany was understandably no proper alternative even to Nazism. Besides, Henderson took the opportunity to warn emphatically against any 'outside interference' into German affairs which would only defeat its own purpose.[89]

A considerably more orchestrated venture was the mission to London of 18–23 August by Ewald von Kleist-Schmenzin,[90] a Pomeranian Junker, deeply religious, conservative to the bone, and fiercely opposed to the Nazis. Though he had participated in the 1920 Kapp *putsch* in his district capital and had been a member of the DNVP, he opposed the Party leadership's policy of co-operation with the Nazis. In fact, in 1932 he published a pamphlet on National Socialism as a 'menace'[91] which from a staunchly conservative, if not reactionary, vantage-point predicted that the consequence of a National Socialist government would inevitably be chaos.[92]

Shortly after Hitler's annexation of Austria in March 1938, Kleist had approached, in the exclusive Casino Club located on Berlin's Bendlerstrasse, a British acquaintance Ian Colvin, the *News Chronicle* correspondent for Central Europe, who had close ties with the Foreign Office in London. Without much ado Kleist outlined to him Hitler's aggressive plans and impressed upon him the need for the British government to throw a 'sheet anchor' to the German Generals by issuing 'a firmly spoken word'. This conversation was eventually related to Sir George Ogilvie-Forbes, Counsellor and Chargé d'Affaires at the British Embassy, who took careful notes and, so Colvin assures us, forwarded the information to London.[93]

The August trip to England was a sequel to this earlier episode. In all probability the idea for it emanated from Kleist himself; Oster—and most likely Canaris too—took him up on it, thinking that the time had come for the *Widerstand* to present its case to the British. Colvin paved the way for it,[94] General Beck gave it his blessing,[95] and even Sir Nevile Henderson saw fit to announce in London the imminent arrival of a Herr von Kleist as emissary of 'the moderates in the German General Staff'.[96]

Kleist called on three people, Lord Lloyd,[97] Sir Robert Vansittart, and Mr Winston Churchill.[98] His encounters with the latter two were the really important ones for Kleist. Both were 'anti-appeasers', and while Vansittart stubbornly sought to ignore his demotion in the Foreign Office, Churchill was a back-bencher in the House of Parliament.

Though Kleist saw neither the Prime Minister nor the Foreign Secretary, the two were kept informed by Vansittart and Churchill on their discussions with the German emissary. We are in a position therefore to compare in particular the reactions of the 'anti-appeasers' with those of Neville Chamberlain; and they were noticeably different. It was not flattery on the part of the visitor when initially he said to Vansittart that he, Vansittart, was one of the few people in England with whom he wished to speak and would be able to speak freely. They shared the position that only a policy of firmness on the part of Britain and France, and not of concession towards Hitler's aggressive plans, was in order. This was the message which had reached Vansittart persistently from the other German 'moderates' including Goerdeler, and he thought it 'essentially reasonable'.[99]

The encounter with Churchill was marked by a basic mutual respect between two formidable conservative gentlemen of the old school and yielded the well-known letter, requested by Kleist, from Churchill and cleared by the latter with Lord Halifax. For the benefit of the conspirators in Germany, Churchill expressed in this letter his appreciation of Kleist's being 'ready to run risks to preserve the peace of Europe and to achieve a lasting friendship between the British, French and German peoples for their mutual advantage'. The letter also gave Kleist the requested assurance that Nazi aggression would mean war.[100]

Thus far and no further would and could Vansittart and Churchill go, however. There were substantial differences between them and Kleist which, in the long run, were decisive. In the course of the meeting with Churchill it was Kleist who brought up the issue of the Polish Corridor because, as Churchill understood him to argue, it 'was the matter that affected them [his friends] most'.[101] Not even Churchill's rejoinder that after all it had been 'officially dropped' by Germany,[102] and that 'this was certainly not the moment to discuss it', would persuade Kleist. But neither Churchill nor Vansittart[103] were prepared to go along with this position. Here, then, was yet another instance of German revisionism to which Vansittart had earlier taken exception when Goerdeler insisted on the German claim to the Sudetenland. Whatever the merits of Kleist and his friends' objection to the Corridor, it became evident that, in this instance at least, the territorial aspirations of the *Widerstand* exceeded those of even the Nazis.

Altogether different, however, were Henderson and Chamberlain's reactions to Kleist. The Ambassador, who in his reports to London had consistently played down the information obtained from the 'moderates', in this case had especially advised London against receiving the German visitor in official quarters.[104] The Prime Minister was dismissive. Van's report to him on Kleist merely elicited the curt analogy that the latter reminded him 'of the Jacobites at the Court of France in King William's time', and he was thus disposed to 'discount a good deal' of what Kleist had said.[105] Neville Chamberlain, no doubt, was a painfully cautious and correct man to whom the close-to-treasonous approaches of Kleist were incomprehensible. In the capacity of Prime Minister, moreover, he could hardly plunge into a commitment with a group that seemed not much more than a phantom to the Foreign Office and the support of which could have meant an incalculable risk. 'We have had similar visits from other emissaries of the Reichsheer, such as Dr Goerdeler,' minuted Sir Ivo Mallet of the Foreign Office on the occasion of the Kleist mission,

but those for whom the emissaries claim to speak have never given us any reason to suppose that they would be able or willing to take action such as would lead to the overthrow of the regime. The events of June 1934 and February 1938 do not lead one to attach much hope to energetic action by the army against the regime.[106]

The action that His Majesty's Government saw fit to take was little. The day after Kleist's departure on 23 August it was decided to recall Sir Nevile Henderson from Berlin for consultation, and the Chancellor of the Exchequer, Sir John Simon, was authorized to give a public address—the Lanark speech of 27 August—in which essentially he reiterated the Prime Minister's statement in the House of Commons of 24 March[107] in which he had hedged on the question of British readiness to back up France in case of German aggression against Czechoslovakia. The speech certainly did not meet Kleist's desideratum put before Vansittart for a firm statement. As for the deliberations with Henderson in London, the Ambassador managed to have his way and was sent back with instructions which eventually paved the way to Berchtesgaden, Bad Godesberg, and Munich which turned out to be Neville Chamberlain's stations of the cross. Allowing for an understanding of the very precarious situation in which the Prime Minister found himself, one wonders whether some more imaginative way, even if surreptitious, could not have been found to engage and to keep open channels to the *Widerstand*.

Upon sending Kleist off on his mission, General Beck had said that, through yielding to Hitler, the British government would lose 'its two main allies', the German General Staff and the German people.[108] No doubt, Beck's assessment of the two had been all too sanguine, indeed singularly illusory. An imagined and at best partial convergence of interests between two parties does not have the makings of an alliance. No wonder, then, that Kleist returned empty-handed to Berlin on 24 August. He had found 'no one in London ... prepared to wage a preventive war'.[109] Also, travelling upon his return 'from one general to another', urging them to act on the strength of the Churchill letter, drew no appreciable results.[110] Furthermore, he learned that during the very day of his departure to England General Beck himself had resigned.

Nevertheless the Opposition persevered in its efforts to reach Britain under the aegis of Beck's successor as his plans for action at home matured. General Franz Halder was no less hostile to the Nazis than his predecessor, but more ready to plunge into action. The approaching crisis over Czechoslovakia and Hitler's war preparations propelled him, an officer through and through, to countenance a coup after all. With the help of the ever-ready Oster, Halder was initiated into the ways of conspiracy. Immediately after he had assumed office as Chief of Staff on 1 September 1938, Oster approached him with the proposal to dispatch someone to London with instructions to inform the British of the plans of the Opposition and to urge upon them a firm stand against Hitler's further foreign political aspirations. Actually, the general plan for this particular mission began with Beck. But now the initiative was with the new Chief of Staff who, together with Oster, settled on a Lieutenant Colonel (ret.) Hans Böhm-Tettelbach. The latter was an industrialist and *Stahlhelm* leader who was well acquainted with Beck, Halder, and Oster[111] and at the same time was thought to have good connections in England.

On 2 September Böhm-Tettelbach[112] was on his way to London. There, unlike Kleist, about whose previous mission he had not been informed,[113] he did not penetrate to any personages of political consequence. His chief contact was Julian Ito Piggott, with whom he had made friends in the early 1920s when Piggott was British Commissioner at Cologne of the Inter-Allied Rhineland High Commission. He met his one-time friend, now a prosperous businessman, accompanied by 'a major of the Secret Service of the English General Staff'[114] in a 'club near St James's Theatre'. Apparently the two Britons emerged 'deeply moved' from this experience of a German seeking help from abroad against his own head of state, and the major left with a touching 'God bless you'.[115] Böhm-Tettelbach's message supposedly was conveyed later to Sir Robert Vansittart.[116]

But this was all. Upon his return there was nothing left for Böhm-Tettelbach but to report back to Oster in Wuppertal, as we are told, 'during the dark of night'[117] about the failure of his mission. Oster in turn reported to Halder. Undeniably the visit had been insufficiently prepared and ill-co-ordinated with the Kleist mission. Nevertheless it deserves attention as yet another effort on the part of the German Resistance to communicate with a foreign power in the hope of eliciting international support for a domestic coup.

## 3. Von Weizsäcker and his Lieutenants in a Search for Alternative Policies

Another set of overtures towards Britain emanated from the Auswärtiges Amt. But in this venture also it was Oster who was the catalyst. He had a good rapport with the State Secretary, von Weizsäcker, but especially with the latter's Chief of the Ministerial Bureau, Erich Kordt. It was the Fritsch crisis which had led Kordt to move closer into the orbit of Oster in whom he saw 'the most active among the opposition'.[118] To start with, Oster sent Kordt late in August on a mission to the Commander-in-Chief of the Army, Colonel General Walther von Brauchitsch to intervene with him and put before him the information on the diplomatic isolation of Germany and the likelihood of British and French intervention in the event of a German move against Czechoslovakia.[119] This mission, which had the blessing of Kordt's chief, received a polite hearing from Brauchitsch but nothing more.

The State Secretary also availed himself of the help of Carl Jakob Burck-hardt, the League of Nations High Commissioner for Danzig, who on 1 September happened to be in Berlin *en route* to Geneva. Weizsäcker spoke, so Burckhardt recollected, 'with the frankness of a man in despair',[120] asking him to make a stop in the Swiss capital and to transmit to the British Legation his urgent request for London to deter Hitler from his aggressive plans by means of 'unmistakable language'. In fact, he proposed the sending of an 'uninhibited, undiplomatic Englishman, such as some General with his riding crop', to Hitler and thus to impress him with the delivery of a special message from the Prime Minister.[121] At the same time the State Secretary initiated Burckhardt into his plans to engage the Kordt brothers in a scheme to approach the British government directly and thus to engage, as he put it in retrospect, in 'conspiracy with the potential enemy for the purpose of ensuring peace'.[122]

Once again, it was Oster who arranged the next *démarche* in Britain which was to be undertaken by the Kordt brothers. Time was of the essence, particularly in view of the Nuremberg Party Congress scheduled to begin on 5 September. The British government was to be urged to use firm language against Hitler in order to call his bluff. The British as well as the French should be informed about the unpreparedness of the German army for war as well as about the general unwillingness on the part of German public opinion to support a war. It was time to call a halt to Hitler's series of political triumphs abroad, and a yielding on his part to foreign pressure in this case would affect his prestige and strengthen the position of the opposition. In the event, however, that Hitler should ignore the warnings, the Opposition would stand ready to act. Oster's briefing to Erich Kordt went as follows:

In case the British government would provide us by means of an energetic declaration with arguments which would make sense to the man in the street, then you could reveal to the British government that the military fronde headed by Beck would know how to prevent an outbreak of war. In that case there would be no more Hitler ...[123]

Erich Kordt, who thought it appropriate to stay close to the centre of action, devised a plan to dispatch a cousin of his, Susanne Simonis,[124] as courier to his brother Theo, the Chargé d'Affaires in London. On the night of 3/4 September he then composed, after consultation with Weizsäcker, an exposition of the crisis which, so he argued, by comparison with the one in 1914, called for an unequivocal stand on the part of Britain that, in turn, would allow the opposition to deploy its 'forces'.[125] Susanne Simonis then committed the message to memory and, arriving in London on 5 September, delivered it to her cousin Theo who subsequently set things in motion. On the following day Theo Kordt got in touch with Sir Horace Wilson, Chief Industrial Adviser to His Majesty's Government and one of the Prime Minister's main counsellors on foreign affairs,[126] who, after a two-hour conversation arranged for the now well-known meeting on 7 September between Kordt and Lord Halifax at 10 Downing Street. To avoid publicity, the German was asked, in the best E. Phillips Oppenheim style, to approach through the garden entrance.[127]

The message which the German Chargé conveyed to the British Foreign Secretary, however, exceeded the instructions of Weizsäcker. Indeed, after consultation with General Beck,[128] the latter had given his blessings to the venture of the Kordts. But Weizsäcker's concern was plainly the maintenance of peace, and consequently he was opposed to a public warning which would have unduly encouraged the Czechs[129] and involved too much risk of war. Theo Kordt in contrast, identifying himself explicitly not as the German Chargé d'Affaires but as 'speaker for political and military circles in Berlin' which 'by all means' wanted to prevent a war[130] asked for a 'public declaration' to the German people by means of radio to enable 'the leaders of the army' to 'move against Hitler's policies by force of arms'.[131]

Weizsäcker no doubt pursued what Hans Rothfels called a *Sonderpolitik*[132] designed to protect the integrity of the Foreign Service and especially to counteract the aggressive plans of the Foreign Minister, von Ribbentrop, and thus to prevent the 'great war'. Weizsäcker followed this path with cunning and determination and to the point of committing 'treason for the sake of maintaining the peace'.[133] But Weizsäcker's divergence from the official policies went no further than this. He engaged in 'social refusal' rather than resistance. Also his determination to preserve the peace did not really present an alternative to the political objectives of the Führer and his Foreign Minister. To their plotting war, Weizsäcker opposed merely his cherished but not much less questionable formula for the 'chemical dissolution' of the Czechoslovak state.[134] Weizsäcker was, in fact, a German counterpart of Sir Nevile Henderson. As such he was one of the architects of the appeasement policy which, even though in opposition to the Foreign Minister, aimed to benefit the expansionist aims of a more respectable Reich. The *Primat der Aussenpolitik*, to which he subscribed, in his case meant the pursuit of a rational foreign policy devised to establish a German hegemony in East Central Europe as against an irrational and somnambulist one.

The divergence between Weizsäcker's conception for the Kordt mission and its actual execution by the Kordts is undeniable. It cannot be ascertained with certainty what exactly caused the brothers to exceed their authority, that is whether they misunderstood their instructions or whether they on their own reinterpreted them by urging a 'public declaration'.[135] It must be remembered, however, that the man who had initiated the mission was not Weizsäcker but Oster, who was by then fully committed to the removal of Hitler. And Oster was in close touch with the younger Kordt. The two were of a different generation from the State Secretary and thus were no doubt more activist in temperament. Furthermore it is understandable that the elder Kordt, further away from the Wilhelmstrasse, would have felt less inhibited and disposed to caution than did Weizsäcker. It can be assumed that the priority not only of Oster but also the Kordts and their young friends in the Auswärtiges Amt, was not 'social refusal' but resistance, and for them the maintenance of peace was not an end in itself. Rather it was to serve the preparation of a coup. They proceeded beyond the conduct of mere *Sonderpolitik* to a conduct of foreign affairs which distinctly had the marks of a resistance foreign policy. In this context Kordt's quotation from Hamlet's monologue, when assuring Lord Halifax that the political and military circles for which he spoke would 'take arms against a sea of troubles and by opposing end them', assumed the character of a moving plea to be recognized and understood by the Foreign Secretary.[136] And it might have been expected that the voice of the German Chargé d'Affaires would carry more weight than did that of Kleist or the other earlier unofficial emissaries.

There were a number of parallel moves that emanated from the environment of Weizsäcker. In 1938 Erich Kordt himself repeatedly sought out the French journalist Pierre Maillaud, Deputy Chief of the Havas Agency in London, in an attempt to influence, indirectly at least, French policies.[137] Kordt also initiated a clandestine *démarche* on the part of a young Second Secretary at the Moscow Embassy and private secretary to the Ambassador Count Friedrich Werner von der Schulenburg, Hans von Herwarth,[138] to leak information to the diplomatic community there. In Berlin in August 1938,

Herwarth was briefed by Eduard Brücklmeier, upon Erich Kordt's instructions, about the frictions between the Führer and his Foreign Minister on the one hand and the professionals in the Wilhelmstrasse on the other. Also he was informed of the readiness of Generals Beck and Erwin von Witzleben, at the time Commander of the Berlin Military District (*Wehrkreis* III), to strike against the regime. Herwarth then proceeded to talk with the Third Secretary of the British Embassy in Moscow, Fitzroy Maclean[139] as well as with some members of the French Embassy.[140] He impressed upon them, in line with the other emissaries of the opposition, the need to stand firm and to talk to Hitler 'with utter brutality' if necessary.[141] To Viscount Chilston, Herwarth also divulged the possibility of an impending coup; in any case, he assumed that his instructions came ultimately from Weizsäcker.[142]

Similarly under instruction from Weizsäcker were the approaches by his confidant Albrecht von Kessel, at the tail end of the Nazi Party Congress, to the Second Secretary of the British Embassy, Mr G. W. Harrison. In a dining-car especially reserved for diplomats, and at a safe distance from a table occupied by a party of SS men, Kessel engaged Harrison over several whiskies in a long talk, impressing upon him the need for Britain to cease to appease Hitler even while recognizing Germany's legitimate 'historically and ethnographically founded aspirations'.[143] With this stance Kessel faithfully reflected his chief's awkward position. Harrison seemed 'deeply moved' and subsequently, so Kessel ascertained, conferred with the Ambassador until deep into the night. We can assume that it was to this encounter that Sir Nevile Henderson referred when he reported to London that some of the Germans had been talking 'a lot of treason'.[144]

Meanwhile, one of the junior officers at the German Embassy in London, Edward C. W. von Selzam, took steps of his own. Well connected in England, he took advantage of his relationship with Group Captain Christie, whom he considered one of his 'oldest and most reliable British friends',[145] to reinforce the message of the Kordts. Also, married to an American, Selzam sought to gain access to the American Embassy. Through Herschel V. Johnson, Counsellor at the Embassy,[146] he obtained access to the Ambassador Joseph P. Kennedy whom he urged, in an interview that took place on 13 or 14 September,[147] to induce President Roosevelt to threaten Germany with war in case of an attack on Czechoslovakia. Theo Kordt, while correctly being of the opinion that the American Neutrality Act militated against such a move, did encourage Selzam's venture since 'no leaf was to remain unturned to realize the objectives of Herr von Weizsäcker'.[148] In any case, Selzam approached the wrong man,[149] and his venture was fruitless.

The cold fact is that none of the many efforts on the part of the German emissaries bore any fruit. The crucial two-month period of August and September 1938, which might have yielded an understanding between the British and the German Opposition in view of the danger that loomed from

Hitler and Ribbentrop's policies instead led along the road to the Munich Agreement of 29 September when the Western Powers capitulated to Hitler's demand for the Sudetenland. Lord Halifax, in fact, soon after Munich said to Theo Kordt: 'We were not able to be as frank with you as you were with us. At the time that you gave us your message we were already considering sending Chamberlain to Germany.'[150] A special effort on the part of Vansittart to double-check with Goerdeler, and to ascertain his views on the German situation by commissioning the British industrialist Mr A. P. Young to engage him in a number of secret meetings beginning early in August, did not help to change the course of events.[151] On the contrary, 'X's', that is Goerdeler's, call for a *firm* and *open* pronouncement by Great Britain and France regarding Czechoslovakia, coupled with his spelling out of what he called 'the life problems' of Germany, including the colonial question and 'Central Europe' was destined only to confuse the authorities in Britain.[152].

## 4. The Generals' Plot and the Munich Agreement between the Powers

Meanwhile the preparations for the coup did proceed. It was, as we have seen, to be the acid test of all the foreign ventures of the Resistance. The cold fact is that the coup did not materialize, and our chief problem now is to attempt to answer the question: why was this the case? Clearly, the conspirators did not lack determination. Indeed, Halder's assumption of the position as Chief of Staff of the Army signalled an intensification of the conspiratorial activities and a systematic assembling of a network to implement them. In its centre were men such as Oster, Gisevius, Schacht, and among the high military the Generals von Witzleben and Walter Graf von Brockdorff-Ahlefeld, commander of the 23rd Division stationed in Potsdam. Its immediate objective was the occupation of the chief nerve centres of the capital, such as the Chancellery and the key Ministries, the communication installations, and above all the headquarters of the SS and Gestapo. As for the fate of Hitler, the plotters were not in full agreement, though a group of younger activists under Major Friedrich Wilhelm Heinz, a Freikorps veteran and former Stahlhelm leader now working for the Abwehr, formed a 'conspiracy within a conspiracy'[153] involved in hatching plans for the assassination of the Führer.

Every conceivable preparation, then, for swift and effective action was made. Everyone's part in the venture was well understood and assigned. There was also a general understanding among the conspirators on the objectives other than the immediate one of toppling the regime: a military dictatorship, serving as a temporary device, was to prepare the ground for a constitutional monarchy and to yield at the earliest opportunity to the convocation of a national assembly and the formation of a parliamentary government.[154]

It can be argued also that the coup was planned in the context of a public mood that was possibly favourable to it. None of the pressures of terror and propaganda could immunize the population from the naked reality that a war was imminent, and by all accounts its mood was apprehensive. When Hitler staged the 'grand parade' of troops through the capital on 27 September, we are told that in the workers' quarters they were greeted with 'clenched fists',[155] and as they defiled before their Führer looking down on them from the famous balcony of the Wilhelmstrasse Chancellery, there was icy silence. The sight of the troops called out to impress the masses as well as the staff of the British Embassy located only a few buildings away did not impress the spectators. Rather, they seemed frightened—much to the disgust of Hitler who, we are told, poured out his anger on Goebbels, saying: 'I can't lead a war with such a people.'[156] For the moment at least he got the message right. For Goebbels it underscored the need for more 'intensive enlightenment', while the conspirators understandably derived encouragement from it for their venture.

Despite the fact that the chief prerequisites for a successful coup were met in these tense weeks of September 1938, and thus it has been argued with reason that the so-called 'Halder–Witzleben–Oster action plan' was 'the most promising attempt to overthrow Hitler',[157] it did not even come to the take-off point. It may be argued, as indeed it has in the literature, that General Halder lacked the necessary resolve for action.[158] There may be some grounds for this charge. Whatever the flaws may have been in his gifts of leadership, however, they were not the decisive factor in explaining the failure of the venture. To begin with, Halder himself later explained his caution with his fear of unleashing a civil war, in itself an undeniably responsible consideration.

The chief explanation for the fiasco of the plot, however, can and must be found in its basic strategy, namely in the designed interdependence between the domestic effort of the *Widerstand* and its foreign policy. On general grounds the latter was, as we have seen, considered by the conspirators an indispensable instrument for the former. The calculations behind the foreign ventures were of course varied. They ranged from a fundamental sense of solidarity transcending border lines among free men in view of the obvious threat of National Socialism to less elevated and more tangible considerations of a distinctly political nature. Above all it seemed imperative to the conspirators, considering the strong popular backing of the Nazi regime, to play on the general war weariness in Germany by exposing Hitler's bellicose designs and making him back down by pressure from the Powers. At the same time, lest they be saddled with a renewed stab-in-the-back legend, the plotters had to seek assurances from abroad which would identify them as defenders of the national interest. They were particularly conscious of the fact that, in order to activate the Generals, they were obligated to exact some basic guarantees for them lest the Allies exploit the German crisis and impose drastic terms on Germany.[159] Such considerations, however, instead of furthering the cause of the conspiracy, in effect made it all the more difficult and on balance contributed to its failure.

The gospel of firmness which the Germans proclaimed virtually unanimously abroad did not serve to bring them closer to their British interlocutors. Shortly before Munich, and at the height of the crisis over Czechoslovakia, Goerdeler, witnessing with deep misgivings the drift of events in the direction of concessions to the dictator, exclaimed in dismay that it was not after all his task 'to think for [sic] British Empire'.[160] He felt himself rebuffed and losing out in his efforts to construct a 'well-balanced Europe' which, he was convinced, could have been achieved only in conjunction with the British. The hard fact was that neither Goerdeler nor his friends were on the same wavelength as the British. The utter candour of the Germans was disarming not to the other side but to themselves. As they put on the table the German claims to the Sudeten area and the Corridor, with Goerdeler also raising the colonial question, they caused suspicion, if not consternation, in Whitehall. In all fairness, the 'moderates' raising the issue of the Sudetenland might well be seen in the context, if not of the canons of self-determination, of the fact that the British government itself had since the spring of 1938 written it off.[161] And what was wrong with questioning the sanity of the Corridor 'solution'? Sir Robert Vansittart, however, the great 'friend' in the Foreign Office of the 'moderates', was extremely sensitive to any revisionist claims that came from Germany. The revision of the Treaty of Versailles, of course, was at the basis of all foreign-politicy thinking of the conservative *Widerstand*, and it was clearly wedded to notions of a hegemonial position of the Reich in Central Europe.[162] It was over this issue that 'Van's' alliance with the 'moderates' and, alas, his fragile friendship with Goerdeler crumbled.

As for the Prime Minister and his immediate advisers on the Czechoslovak question,[163] they were determined above all to maintain the peace which, they came to conclude, was on balance threatened more by the pressures from the 'moderates' than by the German dictator. What the German emissaries had to offer appeared to Whitehall, as Hermann Graml has put it aptly, as 'another partner and yet not another policy'.[164] In some ways indeed their claims seemed to go further even than Hitler's. And while in the Foreign Office the distinction between the essentially rational approach of the *Widerstand* and the somnambulism of Hitler was properly registered, the former, distinctly reminiscent of the dreaded German imperial past, loomed as a tangible menace,[165] while the latter emerged as a lesser evil. Hitler talked, after all, the language of self-determination which had not yet lost its magic in Britain,[166] and, given the right treatment, he might yet turn out to be a 'good boy'.[167] Furthermore he was a reliable bulwark against Communism, whereas the *Widerstand* with its heralded but unpredictable coup might only precipitate internal disorder, if not civil war, in Germany, thus all the more conjuring up the danger of Communism.[168] Altogether the Nazis appeared to Whitehall a preferable risk to the one of a traditionalist rule by the Generals.

Just as the strategy for the plot was flawed so were the tactics designed for the actual realization. It necessarily was to coincide with the last phase of the crisis over Czechoslovakia. It was upon General Halder's insistence that the so-called 'setback theory'[169] was adopted according to which the uprising could be realized only as a result of a drastic blow that was to come from outside. No event on the domestic scene, he figured, could have a comparable effect. This theory amounted to pure brinksmanship, in as much as it presumed the risk of a German mobilization which was to be met by a declaration of war on the part of the Western Powers that would call Hitler's bluff. The coup, then, was to take place in the brief breathing spell between Hitler's issuing the marching orders to his troops and the first exchange of shots. But could the war machine, once set in motion, be stopped at will? Would Hitler retreat from his bluff and would Britain and France in turn, assuming the coup succeeded, revoke their declaration of war for the benefit of a new German government?

The calculation of the 'action plan' was downright 'frivolous'[170] and irresponsible, and no British government in its senses would have acceded to it. Indeed it was in reaction to the momentous risks which a 'firm policy' towards the Nazis and reliance on the *Widerstand* would have involved that the famous British 'Plan Z' was implemented which provided for a visit of the Prime Minister to Hitler.[171]

Chamberlain's itinerary led, as is well known, from Berchtesgaden (16 September) to Bad Godesberg (22–4 September) to Munich (29 September). From the start, when the plan was hatched, 'Van', who was called in for consultation, uttered the right word: 'Canossa'.[172] Among the Resistance people, so it seemed, the first trip of the Prime Minister was still interpreted as being 'merely a tactical gesture', with the British 'temporizing in order to "pass the ball"' to the Generals and 'to show Hitler as glaringly in the wrong'.[173] But the events following disabused them of such illusions. In particular the special mission of Chamberlain's confidant, Sir Horace Wilson, Chief Industrial Adviser to His Majesty's Government, to Hitler on 26–7 September smacked of surrender.[174] Munich, then, was an anticlimax. The 'peace in our time' which Chamberlain erroneously thought he had brought about left the *Widerstand* out in the cold. Peace was indeed kept for the moment, and war was adjourned. But the *coup d'état* did not take place.

The settlement of Munich did not correspond to the optimal designs of Hitler who had hoped to settle the affairs of Central Europe without the interference of Britain and France.[175] But out of the deal he emerged as a 'champion of peace against his own will'.[176] Certainly, for the moment at least, his Foreign Minister who, backed by the SS, had been prepared to go to war,[177] found himself deflated. 'In the internal German scramble for power', Albrecht von Kessel commented, 'Munich was a victory for the Auswärtiges Amt under Herr von Weizsäcker over the Party with its war-mongers'.[178] As for Weizsäcker, he had fought for the preservation of peace and he had reason therefore, in retrospect, to recall Munich as 'the last happy day' of his life.[179] His younger lieutenants, however, had reason to assess Munich differently. Being wedded to what their chief called 'Solution I', meaning a coup,[180] they had a sense of being left high and dry by the settlement. Erich Kordt gave expression to this feeling when, immediately after the Munich accord, talking over the telephone with his brother in London, he somewhat impulsively appraised Munich as 'the second best solution'.[181]

The reactions among the conspirators ranged from despondency to despair. As for General Halder, he was found by Captain Gerhard Engel, Hitler's military Adjutant, 'collapsed over his desk'[182] after the meeting at Munich became known to him. Goerdeler, who, incidentally, was initiated in this particular phase of the conspiracy only afterwards,[183] reacted with 'deep disappointment, if not almost despair'.[184] In a letter to an 'American politician' he maintained that, if England and France had only taken the risk of a war, Hitler would have backed down. If they had heeded all the warnings, a 'purified' Germany, that had rid itself of its dictator, would with a government of 'decent men' have been prepared to solve 'promptly', together with the Western Powers, the Spanish problem, the removal of Mussolini, and to bring, in conjunction with the United States, peace in the Far East.[185]

'Chamberlain saved Hitler', so Gisevius summarized the Munich events.[186] This statement has been frequently echoed in the literature on the German Resistance.[187] The corollary to this assumption is of course that the Generals' plot would have succeeded had the Prime Minister not left the conspirators in the lurch. However, the evidence does not support such a conclusion. The hazards of Resistance foreign policy simply were overwhelming as were, in the game without rules, the dangers of being detected at home and misunderstood abroad. And how could one reasonably have expected the British and French to have risked a war for the benefit of a foreign opposition of whose objectives they were by no means certain and whose strength and efficacy was indeterminate?[188] The fact is that neither Britain nor France was in a position to risk a war at the time of Munich. The policy of appeasement, as pursued by Chamberlain, was predicated upon the failures of earlier governments and, far from being a mere matter of weakness and irresponsibility, it was a considered policy for safeguarding the interests of the British Empire.

At the same time an all-too-ready indictment of the part played by the

German Resistance in the prologue to Munich is not justified. No doubt its councils were divided, but so were those in the British Foreign Office.[189] How can one expect a group of people, under the unprecedented conditions of Nazi oppression, to take upon itself the establishment of clandestine ties with the potential foreign foe, to speak with one voice, and to have a co-ordinated policy?[190] Even granted the fact that the opposition emissaries to Britain were of a predominantly conservative cast and that their foreign political objectives raised some eyebrows in Whitehall, might not their basic goodwill and extraordinary bravery have been recognized and encouraged and indeed translated into political action?

But the hard fact is that most choices that statesmen must face are not between the safe course and the dangerous one but between different kinds and degrees of danger. The encounters between the German emissaries and the British were a singularly hard test of statesmanship for both sides. By virtue of their unorthodoxy they forced the two parties into illusionary positions that made failure of the venture all the more certain. The German illusion was the assumption of a common cause with Britain; but the British needed peace rather than an alliance with an uncertain group of German dissenters. The very need of the conspirators for outside help was their undoing, and the particular formula of 'no peace, no war' added up to brinksmanship and virtually forced Chamberlain into rebuffing them. The British illusion finally lay in the failure, as Keith Middlemas wrote, 'honestly to face the stark question of the inevitability of war, and in their persistent belief that co-existence with [Nazi] Germany was still within the limit of practical politics'.[191] In any case, a major effort on the part of the German Resistance to make an end of the Nazi scourge in its early phases by means of Anglo-German co-operation and short of resorting to war came to naught.

## 5. After Munich: The US State Department and the 'Moderates'

At the time of Munich, when the European Continent was on the brink of war, and when German war planes roared over Berlin in ominous formations, the north-east coast of the United States was preoccupied with digging itself out of the devastating September hurricane. This difference is symptomatic of the distance, political as well as geographic, between the two continents. America was still a far-away continent as far as European affairs were concerned and protected against them, moreover, by the wall of the Congressional Neutrality Act.

But if America was still a sleeping giant, it was soon to be awakened to its wider responsibilities by the challenge of Nazidom.[192] Isolation clearly was no longer tenable. And as America entered the arena of European affairs in the late 1930s, so the issue of appeasement or containment of Nazi Germany began to be acute there also. Like the British Foreign Office, the State Department had its appeasers,[193] and anti-appeasers,[194] and the distinction between 'moderates' and 'extremists' in Germany reverberated in Washington as in London.[195]

In the United States the argument over appeasement and anti-appeasement had, to begin with, distinctly economic overtones. Actually both groups, appeasers and anti-appeasers, were agreed upon the vital importance of ensuring a liberal trade policy. Both groups likewise were distrustful of Chamberlain's economic policies which, they suspected, might lead to an Anglo-German agreement and a division of spheres between a British imperial economic bloc and a German-dominated *Mitteleuropa*. And while the anti-appeasers sought to counter a German autarchic dominion by working towards an economic collapse of the Reich, the appeasers sought to appeal to the German 'moderates' in the expectation that they would favour a German alignment within an open capitalist world economic order.[196]

It would be an exaggeration to maintain that the German 'moderates' played anything close to a central part in American appeasement before 1938.[197] However, among the 'moderates' Hjalmar Schacht enjoyed a considerable reputation in the State Department. To be sure, until his resignation in November 1937 from the Ministry of Economics over disagreements with Göring and over the war-bound course of the Führer, Schacht was still very much one of the pillars of the Nazi establishment. But he appeared to the Americans as a reasonable contact with whom to negotiate an overall economic settlement which would include especially the grant to Germany of the much coveted sources of raw materials and thus obviate the need for a bellicose policy by the Third Reich. The scepticism of the anti-appeasers in Washington prevailed before long, however, and certainly when later in 1937 it became evident that Schacht had been outmanœuvred by Göring. Whereas in 1938 the British Foreign Office still kept toying with a Göring alternative, the State Department never succumbed to that illusion. Certainly its Ambassador in Berlin, William E. Dodd, was infinitely sharper and firmer than his British counterpart, Sir Nevile Henderson.

Meanwhile, Carl Goerdeler's gospel of firmness against Hitler made its way to the United States. During his visit late in 1937 he had already taken pains to convey the message that Hitler meant war. Later on, after Munich, in the spring of 1939, as we shall see, Goerdeler was in a position to have a more tangible impact, however momentary, upon the formation of American policies. This occurred when an idea of his for an international peace conference reached the White House and was reformulated there in the form of the presidential peace initiative of 14 April that was aimed at weakening Hitler's domestic position.

## 6. After Munich: Continued Contacts with Britain (1939)

Britain remained the main stage for the renewed efforts abroad of the German dissidents. Munich at first had given rise, in Britain as well as in the United States, to euphoric expectations that the foundation had been laid for an overall peaceful world settlement. But the effect of Munich upon the men of the *Widerstand* was, on balance, paralysing. While it can of course be argued that the Agreements meant 'victory for the Auswärtiges Amt' which could now point to the fact that war had been averted, to the conspiratorial group consisting largely of younger men, Munich was a blow. Their preferred solution—the removal of Hitler—had given way to the 'second best' one, and those who had hoped to expose the madness of Hitler's policies found the rug pulled from under their feet. The Führer's peaceful sweep across the scene of European diplomacy, for this is how it appeared to the German public at least, was fully under way. And under those circumstances who would want to oppose him?

Symptomatic of this mood was the statement, as handed down to us, of General Halder, the chief of the aborted September coup: 'What are we supposed to do now? He [Hitler] succeeds in everything!'[198] From this time on Halder himself shed much of his zeal for resistance and conspiracy, all the more so as some of his closest erstwhile fellow conspirators had been removed from the centre of action.[199]

Halder's often-quoted statement that the opposition had been 'decimated'[200] by Munich can be explained by his own perspective; but it was not completely accurate. Certainly Goerdeler, who at first could not help but be affected by the general climate of disappointment, quickly bounced back into activity as did the younger members of the original conspiracy. This was especially true in the case of Hans Oster and his Abwehr friends and also the conspiratorial group in the Auswärtiges Amt.

When A. P. Young met Goerdeler again two weeks after Munich, he found him 'distraught'; Goerdeler confided to his British friend that he had not slept for two weeks ever since the signing of the agreement.[201] But he was not a man to be easily discouraged. On the contrary, Munich, that 'sheer capitulation of France and England to puffed-up charlatans',[202] as he called it, was to be a new challenge for him. In no time Goerdeler resolutely went to work to design a containment policy against the Third Reich in which the German Resistance was to take its proper place. Through the mediation of 'the firm of Reinhold [Schairer] and Edgar [Bronisch]', as he once put it,[203] and by means of his contacts with Christie and Young he bombarded the British Foreign Office with wide-ranging schemes that both stunned and antagonized them.

Goerdeler was an expert of sorts in writing memoranda. To begin with he had the kind of mind that preferred to put down his thoughts systematically in writing, and furthermore his precarious and isolated position in Germany made it imperative for him to explain himself to himself as well as to those to whom he addressed his pieces. But to those on the receiving end they could easily appear extravagant.[204]

'One of the obvious difficulties with which the friends of X have for long been confronted', so recorded A. P. Young after the mid-October meeting of 1938 with Goerdeler, 'is their inability to get others in high places to appreciate the full importance of his views.' Young lamented that it had not been possible for the 'great moral strength radiating from his powerful personality' to influence those in high places.[205] Indeed the high moral purpose speaking from Goerdeler's memoranda and from his insistence upon a 'well-balanced Europe'[206] is inescapable. The reader of his many memoranda cannot escape a consistent concern on his part for a supranational order, whether in the form of a 'Europe-League' based on the 'voluntary and organic' co-operation of all civilized peoples, and specifically the European ones,[207] or of a proposal for a small world conference spearheaded by Great Britain with the purpose of 'ushering in a new era based on the eternal moral code'.[208]

To the professionals in the Foreign Office, however, such horizons were too distant and unreal. If the style of the Foreign Office minutes means anything, it betrays a coolness, if not an antagonism, towards Goerdeler's rather apocalyptic messages. The survival of the British Empire was not to depend upon advice from Germany, albeit opposition Germany. In any case, notwithstanding Goerdeler's arguments to the contrary, the form of government in Germany was an 'internal question', so Sir Alexander Cadogan argued, in which Britain had no right to intervene.[209]

Goerdeler's major proposal called 'Heads of Agreement between Britain and Germany' of 4 December 1938[210] turned out to be the decisive document determining his connections with Whitehall. Entered into the Foreign Office files as 'Secret', it was one of the most comprehensive statements by Goerdeler to reach Britain. Once again, it had a distinct global dimension, now in the form of a projected new League of Nations under the leadership of England, France, and Germany.[211] Prominent were Points 1 to 3, however, that addressed themselves to the questions of the Polish Corridor,[212] to Germany's recovery of colonial territory,[213] and to a no-interest gold-loan to the amount of 4–6 billion Reichsmark (£400–£500 million).

Point 4, to the effect that 'further rearmament shall be stopped at once' came at the time, after Munich, when Britain had to give priority to rearmament plans. Point 5, in which Goerdeler offered an assurance that Germany aimed at no hegemony in south-eastern Europe, was followed by a reminder that Germany, having to pay 'the greatest attention to developments on her eastern frontier', was interested in restoring, in conjunction with the Great Powers, including the United States of America, a 'reasonable order' in

Russia.[214] Points 7 and 8 dealt with the questions of a peaceful settlement in Spain[215] and of a re-establishment 'fully and promptly' of 'the rights and position of the white races in East Asia'.[216]

The very discrepancies between the copy that found its way into the Foreign Office files and the draft that reached Christie, yield an insight into Goerdeler's thinking and working habits. Wide-ranging as both documents were, neither one was in any way meant to be definite. They amounted to feelers from across the Channel on the part of a deeply troubled German patriot in search of a common language among those who were aware of the menace to Europe of totalitarian regimes from both the Right and the Left.

The reactions from Whitehall were, alas, predominantly negative. Only Ashton-Gwatkin noted that there was in Goerdeler's programme nothing that appeared to him inadmissible, indeed that there was much that would bring Britain 'immense advantage'. The Corridor question was put at the head of the others, he explained, in order to 'win the Generals'. In sum, Ashton-Gwatkin pleaded for 'careful consideration' and a 'favourable reply' to Dr Goerdeler.[217] It was William Strang, the head of the Central Department of the Foreign Office, who led the chorus of critics. To begin with, he remarked on the 'family likeness' of the plan to others by the 'so-called "moderates" in Germany', and clearly the prominence of Point 1 that proposed 'to sell the Polish corridor behind Poland's back' prejudiced him against the plan. In sum, he wrote: 'I am sure that we ought to have nothing to do with this,'[218] and Sir Alexander Cadogan concurred largely on the grounds that the 'standstill in armament' signal emanating from the power which had established the lead in the race was suspect to him.[219]

Most fierce was Vansittart's reaction. It was not an accident that Goerdeler, calling for action, in an earlier frantic message to Schairer shortly after the anti-Jewish pogrom of 9 November, should have added towards the end: 'do inform Bobby';[220] neither was the endearing reference to Vansittart a mere matter of coding. But the relationship between the star-crossed friends was not to last much longer. Vansittart took the occasion of the December memorandum of his friend from among the 'moderates' to lash out fiercely against him. Goerdeler's demand for the Polish Corridor reminded him unpleasantly of the Kleist visit. In any event, Vansittart had for some time suspected Goerdeler was 'merely a stalking-horse for German *military* expansion', and now he came down hard on him: 'Do not trust Dr Goerdeler except as an occasional informant. He is quite untrustworthy;' and he added: 'I do not count Dr Goerdeler as a German moderate.'[221]

The matter was not yet quite closed, however, even with this barrage. Dr Schairer and Mr A. P. Young considered pressing the case of their client by calling on Ashton-Gwatkin in the morning of 10 December, with Schairer revealing the prospect of yet another Generals' coup in Germany which, he argued, depended largely upon a favourable British reply to Goerdeler's programme. Vansittart's hysteria, alas, was readily matched by Schairer's enthusiastic inventiveness; neither, of course, benefited Goerdeler's cause. But for the moment at least it got another hearing; indeed this time the case went for consideration all the way up to the Prime Minister and Secretary of State.[222] The minutes, hastily and thoughtlessly as they may have been dashed down, betray a whole range of viewpoints on how to cope with the Goerdeler case. The Permanent Under-Secretary, himself to begin with extremely critical of the venture,[223] came to understand that the German '*may* want something merely to show his fellow conspirators that we shan't fall upon a divided Germany'.[224] Here, for once, a senior British Foreign Servant reacted positively towards a concern which was—and was to remain throughout the war years—crucial for the *Widerstand*. Cadogan even drafted a corresponding 'very non-committal' message that might be sent to Goerdeler via A. P. Young:[225] 'I don't believe much in this,' he added in the privacy of his diary, 'But if there is anything in it, it's the biggest thing in centuries.'[226]

Sir Alexander Cadogan's flash of euphoria, however, had to yield to the hard routine of statecraft. On 11 December Cadogan, upon instruction from Lord Halifax, saw the Prime Minister who 'would have nothing to do with it' and thought that any message, to be of any use to Dr Goerdeler and to make the difference between success and failure, would by necessity expose Britain to dangers from which it 'might not recover'.[227] Things remained there. As though adding insult to injury, Sir Orme Sargent entered into the Foreign Office files: 'A straightforward and efficient military dictatorship might even be more dangerous than the present Nazi regime, struggling as it is with all sorts of financial and economic disabilities.'[228]

By the end of 1938 Goerdeler's stock in the Foreign Office had definitely declined. While the appeasers were unwilling to take the chance of complicity with an opposition group abroad, and thus continued to pursue the course of doing business with the official Germany, the anti-appeasers, notably Vansittart, came to the conclusion that Goerdeler stood for traditional German hegemonial aspirations which were not compatible with Britain's political interests.[229]

The so-called '"X" Documents' also found their way to Washington; A. P. Young passed them on to the Assistant Secretary of State, George S. Messersmith, who from his years in the early 1930s as Consul-General in Berlin, was acquainted with Goerdeler. In February 1939 the USA made direct contact with Goerdeler who outlined to 'a representative' from across the Atlantic the domestic situation in Germany, namely the economic crisis, the increasing control of the 'extremists', the increasing preparedness of the Opposition, the need for the democracies to take a firm stand against Hitler, and the danger of war.[230] But it was Goerdeler's last encounter with A. P. Young, immediately following upon the Nazi occupation of Czechoslovakia, which had a distinct, if passing, impact upon the American President's policies. Goerdeler came forth with a 'Plan of Action' that pleaded against a recognition by the three great democracies of the annexation of Czechoslovakia and for the recall of their ambassadors as well as of a British trade mission from Berlin. He then proposed a general conference that would both define guarantees for peace and make a 'clear differentiation between the Rulers of Germany and the German people'.[231] His expectation was that Hitler would reject the guarantees but thereby so antagonize the German people as to encourage the opposition elements in Germany. Via A. P. Young who was attending an industrial conference in Washington, DC, the document found its way to Messersmith as well as to the Secretary of State, Hull,[232] and, in fact, it inspired Roosevelt to proceed with his peace initiative of 14 April.[233]

It is a tribute to Goerdeler's indomitable spirit that he kept composing these memoranda. But the hard fact of the annexation of Czechoslovakia on 15/16 March and the subsequent offer of 31 March by the Prime Minister in the House of Commons, in the name of the Western Powers, of a guarantee of the Polish state[234] made the task of the German Resistance to get a hearing abroad all the more difficult. And while therefore these memoranda appear understandably frenzied, if not delirious, in tone, and reflect a desperate and isolated man confined to engaging in dialogue with himself, they attest to his never having given up in his attempt to reach the outside world. Quite bizarre, in fact, was Goerdeler's appeal for a general peace based upon Christian premisses which, under the leadership of the Pope was to overcome the threat of totalitarian Nazism as well as its Italian counterpart. 'All Peoples want and need Peace',[235] the document begins, and while the word *Papst* (Pope) is consistently misspelled,[236] it must be seen as a pioneering ecumenical piece by a deeply religious author:

It must be proclaimed that the world can obtain a true, just and happy and lasting peace once it frees itself from the people who in opposition to God's law and Christ's word aim at using the world for the benefit of vain power lust and who would ultimately destroy it. Such a proclamation should be presented to the world especially by the Churches under the leadership of the Pope.

Furthermore Goerdeler asked for economic sanctions against the dictators in the form of a rerouting of the raw materials hitherto destined for them, after the establishment of a real peace, to the needy and peaceful peoples for peaceful purposes:

Only the sword which protects the peaceful plough is sanctioned by God, and not the one which is forged in order to destroy His work and to turn free men into slaves

There is no way of knowing whether this moving appeal ever reached its destination.[237] More memoranda were to follow, however, all persistently addressed to the British and the French.[238] There lies an irony in the fact that at the very point when the doors in Britain had closed to Goerdeler, he emerged with an unequivocally and unmistakably European programme.[239]

Goerdeler had previously been to France to present his case to the Prime Minister, Edouard Daladier, and the Secretary General of the Quai d'Orsay, Alexis Léger, from whom he obtained, if we are to believe Ashton-Gwatkin, 'considerable encouragement'.[240] In London he paid a call on Winston Churchill, and once again he saw Sir Robert Vansittart. He also had three long conversations with Frank Ashton-Gwatkin. But this was to be his swan-song in London. He never returned.

Having rebuffed Goerdeler, the British Foreign Office was by no means ready to dissociate itself from the 'moderates'. 'We must not discourage the moderates' was a motif running through the Foreign Office minutes in the spring of 1939,[241] and in his hot-headed way Vansittart even ventured to add an annotatation that 'it will be quite disastrous' if Britain lost the moderates.[242] But, with Goerdeler dismissed, who was left with whom to negotiate? Schacht, still the prototype of that increasingly fuzzy category of the German 'moderates', had, of course, fallen from grace with the Nazis since his dismissal as Reichsbank President in January 1939. Thus he was all the more willing to activate his foreign contacts. Earlier, in fact, shortly after the German seizure of Prague, he had met with Gisevius, Goerdeler, and the latter's 'intermediary' Dr Schairer[243] in Ouchy near Lausanne and had prepared a brief on the German situation that was to be transmitted by the 'intermediary' to the British and French.[244] Somewhat later, upon the prodding of his friends, Schacht approached his British colleague, the Governor of the Bank of England, Montagu Norman, in order to reveal the truth about the Third Reich and thus to warn against any further appeasement. But the British Prime Minister, if we are to believe Gisevius, sent a message to the effect that, since he considered Schacht devoid of political influence at home, he felt obliged to deal directly with Hitler.[245]

Rudolf Pechel, a distinguished German publicist and editor of the Bosch-financed cultural periodical *Deutsche Rundschau*,[246] one of the prime examples of literary 'inner emigration' under Hitler, also repeatedly went abroad. After a visit to Paris in 1938, he went to London four times in 1939.[247] Through the Passport Control Officer, Major Francis Edward Foley, he obtained a visa valid for the duration of one year for himself and his wife. Later he claimed that he had been 'called' to England not on his own initiative. Be this as it may, once in London he landed in the Christie–Vansittart circuit and otherwise conferred, coached by ex-Chancellor Brüning, with a whole range of personalities: anti-appeasers such as Vansittart; appeasers such as James Louis Garvin, the editor of the *Observer*; Conservatives and Labour people; German exiles such as Hermann Rauschning and—on his May visit—members of the German Embassy, notably Theo Kordt and Ambassador Herbert von Dirksen.[248] But there the matter rested.

In June the members of the German Opposition once again went into top gear in search of a dialogue with London. Unlike the late summer of the previous year there was no coup in the offing to be secured. But the immediacy of a crisis over Poland, and furthermore the spectre of a German–Russian *rapprochement* that threatened to overtake the efforts towards a British–French–Russian agreement, made the danger of a confrontation between Germany and the Western Powers all the more acute. Weizsäcker, though not directly involved in the Russo-German secret negotiations, thought that the maintenance of a 'tenuous balance'[249] was recommendable which, with Moscow settling neither with the Western Powers nor with Hitler, would secure the peace at least over the summer. Furthermore, through his friend Carl Burckhardt, the Swiss League of Nations High Commissioner in Danzig, he channelled the message to the British that they were to observe an attitude of '*un silence menaçant*' in order to disabuse Ribbentrop of his conviction that the British would not march.[250]

Once again, as in the preceding year, the Kordt brothers went beyond their chief's position. Theo, who had been ordered to Berlin on 5 June, got in touch with his friend Pierre Maillaud of the Havas Agency on his return to London. According to the report which reached Whitehall through Mr William Ridsdale of the Foreign Office News Department, Kordt, without any reference to a 'tenuous balance', argued the case of an Anglo-Russian agreement as an instrument to maintain peace. Furthermore he urged a public statement to enlighten the German public about the dangerous German foreign-policy course. Kordt also gave information about important troop movements that were to take place in Germany[251] which, according to his own testimony, he had obtained from Canaris and Oster before his departure.[252] Symptomatic of Sir Robert Vansittart's continued solicitude for the 'moderates' is his reaction to a proposal by Sir Orme Sargent to inform Sir Nevile Henderson that the Foreign Office was receiving information 'from Germans in official positions'; especially in view of what Vansittart called Henderson's 'notorious indiscretion', he opposed the proposal as a 'betrayal of confidence' that would make the Germans 'dry up at once'.[253]

Erich Kordt in turn arrived in London on 15 June, supposedly on a holiday trip to Scotland. He lost no time in proceeding, with his brother Theo, to the Kensington home of Philip Conwell-Evans where he met up with the inevitable Sir Robert Vansittart. Speaking explicitly for the 'German Opposition',[254] Kordt, one of Vansittart's 'diminishing band of German moderates',[255] took the occasion to break the news of the Führer's intention to enter into a friendship treaty with the Soviet Union. While the Prime Minister's exposé of 7 June in the House of Commons on negotiations between the Western Allies and the Soviet Union may have been ill-advised, as it strengthened the German fear of encirclement, there was no choice left now but for Great Britain to continue on this path and beat Hitler to the punch. A

German–Russian alliance would mean certain war. Vansittart then assured the Kordts that Britain would assuredly bring the negotiations with Soviet Russia to a conclusion.[256] The following day Erich Kordt repeated his message during a luncheon meeting with Pierre Maillaud who forwarded the information to Whitehall. The files of the Foreign Office unmistakably document the fact that a German patriot in high official position took the risk of coming over to convey a message which, in effect, amounted to treason against his own country. And from the Prime Minister downwards, as the minutes attest, everyone was in the know.[257]

In the late spring of 1939 the mission to Britain of a young lawyer, Fabian von Schlabrendorff, arranged by Admiral Canaris, went almost unnoticed by official London. He saw Lord Lloyd and Winston Churchill, both Conservative back-benchers, and his warnings concerning an imminent Nazi–Soviet pact and a German attack on Poland were duly registered and no more. In one way, though, this particular visit is of some significance. In his talk with Churchill at the latter's country estate at Chartwell, Schlabrendorff made a point of making reference to the German Opposition. Although, upon Churchill's insistent prodding, he had to concede that there was little likelihood of a successful coup in Germany, at least he had informed the man who eventually was to be Britain's wartime Prime Minister of the existence of resistance in Germany, and who, for the moment at least, took it in.[258]

Another visitor caused a much greater stir. This was Lt. Col. Count Gerhard von Schwerin, a German General Staff officer, who in the Army High Command Intelligence Department on Foreign Armies was head of the section 'Foreign Armies West', responsible for the British and American armies. He was not exactly an unknown quantity in London. Repeated reports had reached the War Office about confidential conversations which, earlier in the year, Schwerin, then a Major, had held with the British Assistant Military Attaché in Berlin, Major Kenneth W. D. Strong. In these conversations Schwerin had expressed unmistakably the view that the Munich Agreement meant little more than 'scraps of paper' to those in power in Germany who were aiming at further Eastern domination and in the end would not refrain from turning against Great Britain. He also correctly predicted that, while at the time of Munich the German army was not behind the Führer, in the next crisis it would support him as it had no choice in the matter. Schwerin therefore urged upon Britain a firm and determined stand and specifically advocated the adoption of conscription in Britain as a deterrent to the 'small clique of primitive beings' who ruled his country.[259]

The Foreign Office minutes on Schwerin were predominantly dismissive. 'As usual the German army trusts us to save them from the Nazi regime,' minuted Frank K. Roberts, whereas Sir Orme Sargent wondered whether this 'gross treasonable disloyalty by a Senior Army officer', however 'significant', might not be a 'Machievellian [*sic*] lie'.[260] But it must be recorded that the reports on Schwerin's warnings reached the highest authorities.[261] Indeed his intercession was not altogether without effect. His and the other moderates' views on the need for conscription in Britain were carefully registered in Whitehall, and when the Prime Minister announced the Military Training Act to the House of Commons on 26 April 1939, he did so to no little degree in order to comply with the urgings of the 'moderates' that something be done to prove to the Nazi authorities that Britain was in earnest.[262]

In the late spring of 1939 Lt. Col. von Schwerin, travelling in mufti, arrived in London on what he later characterized as an 'altogether normal vacation trip'.[263] Every member of the Foreign Armies Department was encouraged to spend his vacation in a country of his professional concern,[264] and Schwerin's immediate superior officer, General Kurt von Tippelskirch, or for that matter anyone in the General Staff, knew of the trip. But at the same time it was cleared with, if not commissioned and sanctioned by, General Beck as well as Admiral Canaris and Colonel Oster of the Abwehr. They alone knew of the traveller's ulterior objective to obtain proof of the fact that Britain stood with her 'back to the wall' and was bound to get involved in a war in the case of a German attack on Poland.[265]

Since Schwerin had some difficulty in establishing contact with official London circles, David Astor, well-connected but, by his own rather self-deprecating admission, 'an entirely unqualified twenty-seven-year-old',[266] after consulting with his friend Adam von Trott,[267] decided to help and act as the German's mentor. The array of people Schwerin met proved impressive as it included leading people from the intelligence community, the Foreign Office, the business world, and Members of Parliament. Lord Lothian entered the act by regaling the visitor with a somewhat pathetic caricature of his earlier conversation with Helmuth James von Moltke of July 1935. Wondering aloud whether he, Lothian, should stress 'the great ethical principles for which the Anglo-Saxon race stood' or dwell on Britain's military strength, he was told by the visitor that 'British ideals and ethics were of no interest whatsoever to anyone of any importance in Germany'.[268] As for the rest, the sessions yielded a good deal of common ground. In particular Admiral J. H. Godfrey, Director of Naval Intelligence, who met repeatedly with Schwerin, paid much attention to what he had to say. Godfrey found him 'a very acceptable type of German' with 'charming manners', 'unobstrusive and receptive', and 'a good mixer'.[269] The dialogue between the British and the German was, as was somewhat impatiently noticed by the British, all too repetitive on the part of the German, urging his hosts to resort to a show of strength as the only thing likely to impress the German General Staff and government. And while Gladwyn Jebb, Cadogan's Private Secretary, after a luncheon arranged by Admiral Godfrey on 3 July, remarked that the British members of the party were clearly 'preaching to the converted',[270] Schwerin's visit nevertheless was not without consequence. On 14 July Frank K. Roberts of the Foreign Office Central Department minuted the following:

Count von Schwerin said much the same thing to everyone and we are fully alive to the various points he made. It is to be hoped that the mobilisation of the fleet announced yesterday and the RAF flights to France will have helped to convince Germany that we mean business.[271]

These measures, high on the list of Schwerin's desiderata, must have been to no little extent direct results of his pleadings.

Admiral Godfrey records that later in the year, after war had been declared, an anonymous message 'of unmistakeable origin' reached him via Switzerland to the effect that 'the message had been delivered but not believed';[272] Schwerin later denied, however, having been responsible for it.[273] He did in the end write a report about his journey for his superiors which went up as far as the Chief of the High Command of the Armed Forces, Colonel General Wilhelm Keitel. But though Tippelskirch found it 'extraordinarily interesting', the General Staff ruled that Schwerin, having 'by far exceeded his authority',[274] was to be dismissed from its ranks.[275] He was subsequently reassigned to a command post in the tank corps.

In the Foreign Office files there is a copy of a letter written to Group Captain Christie, and deposited by Sir Robert Vansittart, from an anonymous German, a 'very old' friend of both, according to 'Van's' own testimony, who referred to the German 'moderates' as 'your great ally in Germany'.[276] But alliances are usually contracted between sovereign units, and clearly the German Resistance was anything but sovereign. Had they represented a sovereign unit warning against a common menace from a third party outside, it is not a mute question whether the 'moderates' would have qualified as allies of the British. One of the chief considerations on the part of the Prime Minister—and even more of Sir Nevile Henderson—in rejecting the offer of the German emissaries was, as a matter of fact, the fear that it might compromise British relations with the Nazi state which was a sovereign state with which Britain was maintaining regular diplomatic relations. Neville Chamberlain was therefore loath to hurt the susceptibilities of the Nazi leadership.[277]

Moreover, an alliance requires, at least temporarily, a common cause or compatibility. The question is whether such common interest existed between the 'moderates' and the British, or, at least, whether the clear and present danger that threatened from the Third Reich should not have made the offer that came from the German dissidents, whatever their differences with Britain's interests, acceptable, if not welcome. The common interests between the British and the German Opposition were certainly negative: their distaste for National Socialism. It might even be argued that the Chamberlain government was not averse to a division of spheres that would have allowed a German predominance in Central Europe alongside a salvaged British Empire.[278] In that light, Goerdeler and Kleist-Schmenzin's territorial preferences were not all that objectionable. But the Foreign Office as a whole was still effectively shaped by the tradition of Sir Eyre Crowe and his 1907 Memorandum to Sir Edward Grey on Britain's relations with France and Germany in which he had argued that German designs upon Europe could be countered only by a forceful defence by Britain of her foreign interests. In this light the German 'moderates' territorial proposals seemed to Whitehall no less a threat than Hitler's aggressive course. This consideration also left the German emissaries out in the cold. As immediate witnesses of the enormity of the Nazi menace they did not carry sufficient weight. They were politely received, and they served as useful informants. They scored, as in the case of Schwerin, very minor breakthroughs. At best they were left in a state of ambiguity—both courted and ignored. They certainly were not accepted as allies.


## 7. Adam von Trott Goes It Alone

Among all the missions emanating from the German dissidents in the spring of 1939, Adam von Trott's visit to England early in June 1939 was probably the most mysterious one. It is still shrouded in mystery today and a subject of intense controversy among historians;[279] at the same time it was the one occasion when a person connected with the German Resistance came into close contact with the levers of power in Britain.

The road into resistance is an unpaved one; it generally leads through all sorts of stages marked by hope—even hope against hope—and doubt, and by acceptance—indeed the desire to accept—and revulsion, by loyalty, and by treason. In most instances resistance is not even a matter of a clear decision. Resistance, the momentous step, is mainly a matter of gradual and intensified awareness translated into political action which, in turn, is propelled by chance as much as by conviction. In any case it becomes operative at the point when the burden becomes so unsupportable as to sweep away all considerations of conforming and coasting along and to call for the leap into extreme counter-action.

In the case of Adam von Trott the preconditions for resistance were clearly present. While he came from a deeply conservative family, and while he himself was a passionate patriot, his Anglo-Saxon ties as well as the ecumenical orientation inherited from his mother, his strong sense of justice and fairness, and last but not least his socialist leanings predisposed him to a hostile stand against the Nazi regime. Accordingly, he was from the very beginning unequivocally opposed to the Third Reich, and since neither conformity nor emigration were the right prescriptions for him, he was destined sooner or later to veer in the direction of resistance.

Trott's trip around the world to the United States and the Far East (March 1937–November 1938), of which mention has been made earlier, afforded him the opportunity to escape the pressures of Nazi society. The New World with all its vitality and turbulence served him as a priceless political apprenticeship, and his conversations with leading public figures, as well as his keen observations of daily life around him, opened his eyes to politics as challenge and action.[280] The sojourn in China allowed him to study the broader dimensions of a world heading for war[281] and, moreover, to explore the Confucian sources of political wisdom. Steeping himself in a very distant and alien world, he sought to find the composure and strength to face up to a future in Germany which, he knew, would be a grim one. Indeed he returned from his Far Eastern trip resolved to take an active part in the opposition to Hitler.[282]

Trott's extensive correspondence across the seas with his family and friends, especially with his old Oxford friends Shiela Grant Duff and Diana Hubback,[283] was in itself the record of a young German setting out to construct, as he put it, 'a new common Europe'[284] despite all the clouds on the horizon. He liked to think of a 'great European alliance'[285] centred on the British–German relationship. But the correspondence, in particular the one with Shiela Grant Duff, already unfolded all the ambiguities and tensions of that relationship. For Miss Grant Duff, foreign correspondent who had witnessed with dismay the expansion of Nazi Germany's influence over the European Continent and the weaknesses of the British appeasement policy, her German friend's careful balance between an uncompromising hostility against National Socialism and a pronounced German patriotism was increasingly incomprehensible. It is therefore not surprising that, when, shortly after his return to Germany from the Far East, Trott wrote a—carefully coded—letter to her to convey what he knew about the abortive Generals' Plot of September 1938, she should not have understood.[286] But what matters here is that Trott was initiated into the affairs of the Resistance.[287]

Soon after his return Trott set out purposefully to put into effect the role for which he had prepared himself for so long, as self-styled ambassador from Germany, his native country, to Britain, which virtually had become his country by adoption. He took the first steps at a time when there were storm signals everywhere. After the anti-Jewish pogrom that had taken place in the Reich on 9/10 November 1938, followed by Hitler's seizure of Czechoslovakia of mid-March 1939, Trott was likely to find that much of the goodwill he had hitherto encountered in England had vanished. During a brief visit to Oxford in February he noted a certain coolness towards him particularly on the part of his contemporaries, and three months later he lamented that a number of his English friends seemed to 'identify the evils of Europe with Germany as such'.[288]

As a matter of fact, of all the unofficial missions of the spring of 1939 across the Channel from Germany, Trott's can least be read as having taken place upon the instruction of any of the centres of the *Widerstand*. While it cannot be maintained that he went out as an *Einzelgänger*, that is as an altogether solitary witness, the initiative for this particular venture came from him and him alone. In the course of time he had become almost obsessed by the fear of a general European war as a calamitous fratricide reminiscent of that of the Greek cities.[289] Furthermore, his immediate objective, in keeping with this general premiss, was to stave off the threat of war by a combination of pressure from without, particularly Britain, and gestures of goodwill towards Germany which, if not accepted by the Führer, as Trott expected would be the case, would convince the army and the people at large of Hitler's irresponsibility and thus benefit the Opposition. Trott's reasoning came down to the message that peace had to be maintained at all cost and that only under those circumstances would a plot against the Nazi regime have a chance to succeed.[290]

Trott was determined to put this scheme before his English friends. Its elaborate and baroque features give it away as a rather personal one, out of tune with those of Goerdeler, his friends in the Auswärtiges Amt,[291] and Schlabrendorff and Schwerin. Even though it is very likely that Trott got clearance for his trip from State Secretary von Weizsäcker, he did not go out with his backing. Somehow Trott managed to obtain through two distant cousins an introduction to Walther Hewel. The latter, an old Nazi from the days of the Hitler Putsch of November 1923, was the Chief of the Personal Staff of Ribbentrop and Liaison Officer between the Foreign Office and the Führer. But while Hewel was an unquestioning admirer of Hitler, he kept his own council, especially on the question of war and peace; and being determined to prevent an Anglo-German confrontation, he was interested in supporting Trott's journey to gather information about British foreign-policy objectives. Hewel thus declared his willingness to give Trott an informal association with the Auswärtiges Amt and to finance his venture.[292] All this, however, should not detract from Trott's daring, since Hewel, for all his anglophile leanings, was a devoted Nazi who remained faithful to his Führer to the end and who, had he got wind of Trott's real political intent, would have denounced him.

In England it was Trott's old friend from Balliol College, David Astor, who welcomed him and paved his way to the people of influence he sought. Astor asked his parents, Lord and Lady Astor, to arrange a party for the weekend of 3/4 June at Cliveden, their grand country seat, with among the fellow guests Lord Halifax, the Foreign Secretary, Lord Lothian, recently appointed to be Ambassador to the United States, and Sir Thomas Inskip, the Secretary of State for the Dominions. At the grand dinner on Saturday Lady Astor placed the young German visitor next to Lothian and opposite Halifax to allow him to unfold his ideas to them.

After dinner, for three solid hours at least, Adam von Trott had the ear of the British statesmen. What was said in the course of this conversation is not easy to reconstruct, especially since the main document on this episode is Trott's official report to the Auswärtiges Amt, written with the help of his friend Peter Bielenberg,[293] rendering account to Hewel—and indirectly to Hitler—of the fact-finding mission to England.[294] Here is a classic case of camouflage as a way of getting around political repression. The style of the document certainly was couched in Nazi jargon; Peter Bielenberg in fact recalled that he and Trott had 'a good many laughs at writing a lot of Goebbels language'.[295] But the latter should not deceive the historian. The very fact that Trott identified himself in the report with the German 'deep-seated bitterness and hostility', as he put it, towards Britain's '"guarantee" for Poland' and 'relentless policy of rearmament',[296] allowed him in turn to outline and underscore the British concerns about German policies, especially the occupation of Prague; the '"destruction" of the Czech nation' he identified as 'the decisive turning point'[297] in the British attitudes towards Germany.

Upon close inspection, the document is a shrewd piece of dialecticism designed to convince the opponent, namely the Nazis, of the British readiness to fight. At the same time, in the staging of the argument, Lord Lothian assumed a special role in as much as he became the mouthpiece for Trott's plans.[298] In particular he was made in the report to launch, in strictest secrecy, a proposal by which the rump of Czechoslovakia, namely Bohemia and Moravia, was to have its independence restored on condition of 'an effective limitation' of armaments and 'economic cooperation with Germany'[299] in return for a solution of the Danzig and Corridor issues.

We can now safely move from the report to the event itself. A wholly disinterested account of the Cliveden conversations from another source should indeed give us more reliable and direct guidance on Trott's part in them. William Douglas-Home, another guest at the dinner party, who overheard the discussion about international politics, recollected that

Von Trott, as passionate an anti-Nazi as he was a patriot, spoke with a perfect mastery of English, of the aspirations of the German nation as a whole. While allowing for the mistrust engendered in the British mind by the activities of the Nazi leaders—a mistrust which he fully shared—he seemed to be trying to impress upon the Minister [Lord Halifax] the necessity for an immediate adjustment to the *status quo*. He argued that some gesture of goodwill, not verbal, but actual, should be made towards Germany, not only to satisfy her just desire for a revision of the Versailles Treaty, but also—and this might be decisive—to remove some of the planks from Hitler's political platform and thus pave the way to power for those who had the interests of the world, as well as Germany, at heart. This young man, who a few years later was to die a martyr's death in opposition to the Nazi regime, spoke with a deep sincerity and a sense of urgency. Listening to him, I understood how it was that so many Germans, loathing and despising Hitler as they did, yet felt that in his insistence on the rights of Germany, he was voicing the wishes of the people ... Be this as it may, it was the future, rather than the past, with which von Trott concerned himself that night. He saw the disaster ahead, and he felt that, with mutual co-operation and sacrifice, the danger might yet be averted, and the problem solved by peaceful means ...[300]

There is no reason for us not to go along with this sober assessment of Trott's predicament and position.

As for the question of Danzig and the Corridor, Trott's scheme must be seen in the broadest of contexts. Even though his journey had not been commissioned by the State Secretary, there can be no doubt but that this particular scheme was somehow co-ordinated with him.[301] The settlement of the Danzig and Corridor questions had been foremost on the agenda of the German revisionist policy since the days of Gustav Stresemann. So it remained among the professionals in the Auswärtiges Amt under Weizsäcker as well as, as we have seen, among the emissaries of the conservative Resistance. Weizsäcker, as a matter of fact, explicitly recorded that back in December 1938 he had sought to divert Ribbentrop from the Czech problem and in turn to direct him towards the 'North-East problem', namely the Polish one. In the spring of 1939 he argued, moreover, that the occupation of Prague had been a mistake since, before Prague, Poland had been 'abandoned by the whole world' and no one would have raised a finger then for Poland.[302] The convergence between Weizsäcker's and Trott's patterns of thought is too close to be ignored; the Trott initiative may be understood finally to have been a 'trial balloon' by Weizsäcker.[303]

Lord Astor was sufficiently taken by Trott's presence to arrange a meeting for him with the Prime Minister in 10 Downing Street. It took place on 7 June and lasted half an hour, allowing Trott to sharpen the argument which he had presented at Cliveden. The Prime Minister, so we are told, emerged favourably impressed by the German visitor, seeing in him a welcome mediator between Britain and Germany.[304]

The day after his return from England Adam von Trott sent an exultant letter to his mother:

In order for you to rejoice with me and to pray for a beneficial progress of my work, I should like to inform you briefly that the turn in Anglo-German relations which is just now under way goes back directly to my intervention. Eight [in fact seven] days ago I had in Clivedon [*sic*] a four-hour-long talk with Lord Halifax, and on Wednesday one lasting half an hour with Mr Chamberlain. Meanwhile I have not been idle. Tonight I worked until 3 o'clock and in a few hours I shall see Herr von Ribbentrop and possibly also Hitler.[305]

Thus it seems that momentarily, at least, the red carpet treatment in England had gone to the head of the not yet 30-year-old Trott. There was in fact no question of his being received by Hitler and Ribbentrop; they did not care to see him. With Göring, on whom Trott pinned most of his hopes,[306] he had an appointment for Sunday, 11 July at the latter's country seat in the Schorfheide. This visit was, however, foiled by Ribbentrop who insisted upon his prerogative to conduct foreign affairs.[307]

On the British scene the one follow-up of the Cliveden talks was Lord Halifax's often-quoted so-called Chatham House speech of 29 June before the Royal Institute of International Affairs.[308] Impressed by Trott's arguments during the evening of 3 June, Halifax had asked Thomas Jones, the Deputy Secretary of the Cabinet, to take notes on what was said. The Foreign Secretary underscored the British commitment to Poland—as well as to Turkey, Greece, and Romania—and the British resolve, following 'the inevitable line of its own history'[309] to stand up against the wish of any single power to dominate Europe at the expense of the liberties of other nations: 'Great Britain is not prepared to yield either to calumnies or force.'[310] But Halifax continued to assure his audience that 'if the doctrine of force were once abandoned . . . all outstanding questions would become easier to solve'[311] and that in an atmosphere of peace his country 'could examine the colonial problem, the questions of raw materials, trade barriers, the issue of *Lebensraum*, the limitations of armaments, and any other issue that affects the lives of all European citizens'.[312]

The Chatham House message, then, served as a secret language between the British government and the Opposition in Germany. In part inspired by Trott, it was also recognized by the Opposition as an encouraging signal. It was most likely this speech by Lord Halifax that Trott and his friend Peter Bielenberg read about as they picked up a newspaper at the Berlin Wittenbergplatz. To their satisfaction, they recognized the arguments Trott had made the Secretary of State.[313] Count Schwerin also showed himself 'very much impressed' by the speech.[314]

Adam von Trott, alas, left behind him a trail of doubt and suspicion. A follow-up trip to London and Oxford in mid-June did not dispel this. On the contrary, Trott left his old friends at Balliol and All Souls Colleges wondering whether he had gone over to the Nazis after all and was playing a double game.[315] Was it that on his first June visit he had appeared in a semi-official capacity which made him suspected of acting as an 'agent of Ribbentrop'?[316] Was it that he was so closely associated with the so-called 'Cliveden Set'[317] and its appeasement course? Was it that his preoccupation with Hegel was a source of irritation to his Anglo-Saxon friends, who held this responsible for the ambiguity which they detected in him?[318]

All these factors undoubtedly had their share in making Trott appear in a questionable light. But it is undeniable that his basic situation, as well as the strategy of his argumentation, were at the root of his ambiguity. By the time he went out on his mission to England Trott had cast his lot with resistance to the Nazi regime; but he was not wholly resolved how best to translate this course into the area of foreign affairs, his chosen field of expertise. The Cliveden talks were in effect a rehearsal for his tasks ahead, and they betrayed all the risks and flaws that are inherent in the kind of unorthodox diplomacy he had outlined for himself.

To anyone who took pains to listen to Trott it must have been clear that he was not Ribbentrop's man, but his semi-official attachment to the Auswärtiges Amt was bound to raise suspicion abroad. Trott's effectiveness, however, like that of his fellow conspirators, was predicated upon working from within the official Establishment which would serve as camouflage. In order to resist he had to collaborate. But the chances were that his friends abroad would not exhibit the necessary understanding for his predicament, all the more so at a time when feeling against Germany ran increasingly high.

Nor did this passionate anti-Nazi, who at the same time was a passionate patriot who identified himself with German revisionist policy, come across well in an England that after the March days of 1939 was determined to dig in its heels against further claims from Germany. Trott, in turn, had a way of digging in his heels also whenever he felt the honour of his country slighted. He felt that he had to make a point of legitimizing his dissent against National Socialism by a profiled defence of what he considered the rightful interests of his country. He firmly rejected the 'whole *jargon* of mutual national blame'[319] as belonging to the past. Thus his angry outbursts in his correspondence with Shiela Grant Duff or his angry reaction to Commander King-Hall's *News-Letter*[320] which early in the summer of 1939, circulating by mail in German translation, staged a major attack against the Nazi regime and, so Trott thought, the Germans.[321] He could not tolerate, so he wrote to his friend David Astor, the tone of moral superiority and 'condescension' on the part of the British.[322]

Now for the question of Trott as appeaser or anti-appeaser. At first glance it looks as though his position fitted in with Neville Chamberlain's policies. Indeed, shortly after Munich, he had written to Lord Lothian about 'Mr. Chamberlain's courageous lead'[323] and in turn he had declined an offer to meet Winston Churchill whom he saw as a 'warmonger'.[324] Trott's persistent advocacy in England of Göring as a reasonable partner for negotiations[325] also coincided with the negotiations in London between Göring's Four Year Plan Commissioner Helmut Wohlthat, and the Chief Industrial Adviser to the British government, Sir Horace Wilson, which marked the last chapter in economic appeasement.[326]

Trott's peace policy, however, was not equal to appeasement. The objective of his manœuvres was distinctly not to settle with Hitler but to stave off war and thus to obtain conditions for change in Germany. But what change? No doubt Trott was still toying with thoughts of an erosion of National Socialism: 'The real way to end Nazism ... is first to remove its sting and secondly to out-mode it in Germany.'[327] To a few of his Oxford friends, such as David Astor and C. M. Bowra, he actually revealed his connection with the Resistance and his ultimate aim, the coup.[328] But what is the connection between the erosion of National Socialism and resistance to it? Trott himself was still groping for a clear strategy. To most of his English interlocutors—with the notable exception of David Astor and a few others—he was incomprehensible. Sir Orme Sargent of the Foreign Office minuted Trott's scheme as being 'rather woolly'.[329] C. M. Bowra actually showed him the door when Trott could not satisfy him on the question of territorial claims of the German Generals; Trott, he decided, was playing a 'double game'.[330]

The Trott mission to England in June 1939 was ill-starred; it was a mistake. He had misjudged the mood in Britain. What was a rehearsal for the young man who thought he could virtually change the course of Anglo-German relations single-handedly met after all with a rebuff and left a trail of suspicion which followed his reputation in subsequent years. Not even he who seemed uniquely predestined to cope with the complexities of the Anglo-German relationship fared any better than Goerdeler, the brothers Kordt, and Count Schwerin.

## 8. The Spectre of the Nazi–Soviet Pact and the Road to War

The Nazi–Soviet Pact, signed by Ribbentrop and Molotov in Moscow on 23 August 1939, constituted an important point of orientation for the men of the *Widerstand*. The mutual soundings between Germany and Russia went back as far as the early months of 1939, and the displacement on 3 May of Litvinov by Molotov as Foreign Commissar was a straw in the wind, auguring a reorientation of Russia's foreign policy. Trade negotiations eventually led to political ones, and attempts at a 'gradual normalization'[331] led to a political-military conspiracy. Furthermore, the ongoing negotiations between Great Britain, France, and the Soviet Union were a decisive element in propelling Hitler to take the big step and, overcoming ideological differences with Bolshevik Russia, to enter into an agreement with her that would relieve his eastern flank and allow him to settle accounts with Poland.

Actually, one of the chief negotiators of the Pact was Friedrich Werner von der Schulenburg, and his part was decidedly no mere matter of routine. He was a German diplomat of the old school who had a basic respect for the Russians whom he considered the best actors, chess players, and mathematicians and therefore unbeatable in politics.[332] Committed to the Rapallo policy of the Weimar era, Schulenburg had, since his assignment in 1934 as

German Ambassador to Moscow, established a good rapport with the Soviet authorities which he put to use in the course of the negotiations. But his concept of the Pact differed fundamentally from that of Hitler. The Ambassador, who envisaged an agreement with the Soviet Union as a long-range proposition and an end in itself, had to recognize that for Hitler and Ribbentrop it was merely a tactical move aimed at immobilizing Stalin in the face of the German designs upon Poland.[333] Schulenburg came to perceive the Pact, concluded in Moscow on 23 August 1939, as the inevitable prelude to a world conflagration which would lead to the *finis Germaniae*. It was his tragedy, as has been remarked, that he fully understood that he had helped to bring this about.[334]

More independent and enterprising than Schulenburg in the period preceding the Nazi–Soviet Pact was his young attaché Hans von Herwarth. As in August of 1938, but this time on his own initiative, Herwarth went into action to cross his government's policies. Despite his basic understanding with his Ambassador, he did not reveal to him that, beginning in May 1939, he established contacts with friends in the Italian, British, French, and American Embassies with the objective of precipitating an intervention by Mussolini along the model of August 1938. This, he hoped, would galvanize the British and French to come to an accommodation with Russia to prevent the conclusion of the imminent Pact between Hitler and Stalin that, he knew, would lead to war.[335] However, Herwarth's personal *démarches* were no more effective than the efforts of Weizsäcker to stave off a settlement with the Russians and of the Kordt brothers to torpedo it.[336]

However daring, these attempts to thwart the Nazi–Soviet negotiations were but uncoordinated rearguard actions on the part of a small group of dissenters. They were, as we have seen in the case of Weizsäcker and the Kordts, not even attuned to each other. Even Trott, who unambiguously counted himself by that time as belonging to what he called, the 'new opposition',[337] assessed the German–Russian understanding as an 'astonishing and welcome' political achievement.[338] No doubt, German conservative circles, whether in opposition or not, were residually wedded, as Trott himself pointed out,[339] to the Bismarckian tradition of securing the Reich's flank in the east. But the Nazi–Soviet Pact constituted an altogether new chapter in German relations with Russia. Those among the German dissenters who grasped this fact, understood the full impact of the threatening Soviet penetration into eastern Europe. Apart from such political misgivings about the alliance with Russia, however, they also had serious reservations that were of a more fundamental nature. These stemmed from their distrust of the plebeian features of Nazism. Both National Socialism and Bolshevism were akin by virtue of their constituting different forms of mass democracy. Thus the Pact between the two regimes all the more conjured up the prospect of a bolshevization of Germany. Von Hassell thought that the advance of Bolshevism along the whole front of the German borders, together with the necessary socialist consequences of the war economy, would also have 'political results of the most dangerous nature inside Germany'.[340] He added that Goerdeler was of the same opinion.[341] An Abwehr document of the period immediately following the conclusion of the Nazi–Soviet Pact warned against Germany's proceeding from the first, the Nazi revolution, to the second, the Bolshevik one, and against her thus becoming an 'adjunct of the Russian world revolution'.[342]

There were nevertheless, so Hassell and Goerdeler figured, some possible advantages to be derived after all from the unwanted Russo-German accord. It might open the eyes of the Germans, especially the 'better elements' within the Party; moreover the spectre of Germany's bolshevization might induce the Western Powers to build bridges to a 'healthy, vigorous Germany'.[343] But nothing of the sort materialized. Quite the contrary, there was no way for the Opposition to halt the war machine, and there was no question but that the outbreak of war, in fact, would make the position of the domestic opposition increasingly difficult.[344] It was fallacious, moreover, to think that fear of Russia would swing Britain into the arms of Germany, no matter how regenerated a Germany it was.[345] And in the long run, it should be added, a deep irony hung over the efforts of the spokesmen of the *Widerstand* who urged upon the Western Powers the importance of bringing their negotiations with Russia to a positive conclusion. It was precisely the eventual cementing of the Grand Alliance after the German attack on Russia in June 1941 which virtually condemned to failure all approaches of the German Resistance abroad.

On the very eve of the war, on a mission in Stockholm evidently for the Robert Bosch firm, Dr Goerdeler[346] took the opportunity to send last-minute messages to the British. Meeting with the British Military Attaché, Colonel Reginald Sutton-Pratt, on 30 August, Goerdeler outlined his analysis of the crisis over Poland while also proffering his advice.[347] His message combined the usual urgent plea for firmness with a proposal for a conference with a demilitarized Germany, that would offer Germany herself 'a fair and just solution' and to Czechoslovakia the restoration of her independence on the basis of the principle of self-determination, that is, along the lines of the Munich Agreement. For the rest, the message contained a not uncharacteristic for Dr Goerdeler dose of wishful thinking—that the army, as well as the German people, was unwilling to fight a 'major war', other than one against Poland over Danzig, and that before long Germany would 'crack' and would rise and overthrow the Party.

Late at night on the same day Goerdeler also sent a direct telegram to the Foreign Office:

Chief manager's attitude weakening. Remain completely firm. No compromise. Take initiative only for general settlement under strong conditions.

It was seen by the Prime Minister and the Secretary of State, as well as by Sir Alexander Cadogan.[348]

Clearly the momentum on the question of war or peace came from Berlin. All the attempts on the part of Weizsäcker and Hassell,[349] as well as Göring and his Swedish intermediary, the industrialist Birger Dahlerus,[350] were shattered by the Führer and his Foreign Minister's determination to foil any compromise. The 'Sixteen Point Programme',[351] hastily elaborated late in August in the Auswärtiges Amt upon Hitler's orders and proposing a solution of the Danzig-Corridor and the German–Polish minority problems was, as quickly as it had been composed, overtaken by Ribbentrop's precipitous actions towards the British and Polish ambassadors to Berlin. Hitler and Ribbentrop clearly had decided on war.

While there is no particular need to document Hitler and Ribbentrop's determination here, and while clearly all the efforts of the German Opposition to break it were ineffective, one episode should be included here to register the length to which it was willing to go to counteract the policies of its government. On 22 August Hitler had called together the leaders of the Armed Forces on the Obersalzberg, treating them to an intemperate harangue in which he, the self-styled latter-day Genghis Khan, outlined his plans to crush Poland and to redistribute the world together with his soon-to-be soulmate, Stalin.[352] Among the several transcriptions of Hitler's speech one found its way into the hands of Louis P. Lochner, Bureau Chief of the Associated Press in Berlin.

The question is, of course, from whom he got it and what he did with it. The person—referred to as 'my informant' in Lochner's book,[353]—was Hermann Maass, a Social Democrat who in the Weimar years had been engaged in the co-ordination of German youth organizations and who was well known to Lochner as an ardent anti-Hitlerite active in the underground against the Nazis.[354] Maass came a week before the assault on Poland—it must then have been on 24 August—'at the suggestion of Col. Gen. Beck' to turn over to the American the three-page typed manuscript of the Hitler diatribe. The text, Maass said, had been taken 'surreptitiously' by 'one of the high officers present'. The officer in question who was responsible for the particular version of the Hitler speech which reached Lochner was, as has been meanwhile established, none other than Admiral Canaris. Seated in a corner, Canaris at first merely took notes for transmission to Beck, but then, realizing that Hitler was saying outrageous things of enormous potential consequence, he shifted over to verbatim stenographic reporting of the latter part of the proceedings.[355]

Lochner thereupon, on 25 August, offered the document to the American Chargé d'Affaires, Alexander Kirk, asking him to take it into safe custody and of course to forward its contents to Washington, only to be told that it was 'dynamite' especially in view of the fact that at this date Hitler was still in the process of negotiating with the British Ambassador, and that he should take it away 'at once'.[356] Kirk, in fact, kept reporting to the Secretary of State on Sir Nevile Henderson's continued efforts at pacification[357], but concerning the meeting at the Obersalzberg he remained silent. In contrast, his British colleague, Sir George Ogilvie-Forbes, to whom Lochner proceeded to show the document, was on the job and reported the Führer's speech of 22 August in detail to London.[358] One way or the other, it would not have made much difference; the switches had been set by Hitler for war, and the British knew it all too well. But in the turmoil of the preparations for war another fact also got drowned out which was contained in the intelligence from Mr Lochner, namely that there were highly placed Germans who were willing to go to the limit of treason to oppose the manifest danger emanating from their own country.[359]

In London on the night of 31 August Theo Kordt found himself closeted with Vansittart and Conwell-Evans in the latter's flat at 31 Cornwall Gardens. But in view of the precipitate events in Berlin they found that there was not much official business left to be discussed. Once again the German Chargé d'Affaires became a partisan of the German Underground, taking up his interlocutors on their proposition to keep up the contact with the German Opposition for the purpose of bringing an end to the 'European civil war' because, so Kordt later quoted Vansittart, 'it would mean the death of thousands instead of millions'.[360] In view of Kordt's expectation of being transferred, upon the outbreak of war, to a post in a neutral capital, the group made arrangements for future secret meetings upon Kordt's initiative. He was to send, of course without signature, a postcard either to Vansittart, Conwell-Evans, or Vansittart's secretary, carrying a coded message in the form of a verse by Horace. Two weeks from the stamped date of the card Vansittart would send Conwell-Evans to the locality printed on the postmark. The Horatian verse, carefully chosen, was appropriate to that night's dramatic circumstances:

Si fractus illabatur orbis impavidum ferient ruinae.
[Yea, if the globe should fall, he [the just man] will stand serene amidst the crash.][361]

On 1 September, the day when Hitler's troops marched into Poland, Group Captain Christie sat down to write on Traveller's Club stationery a farewell letter to Theo Kordt:

Dear Friend,
I hope you do not mind my addressing you thus, for friend you have been and are to your great people, to us Britons, and to all who are struggling to restore the conception of honour and integrity amongst nations. I am writing you these few lines to wish you a deeply felt *'Auf Wiedersehen'*. If you must leave us soon, ours is the loss: if a miracle should keep you here, ours is to rejoice.

Thank you a thousand times for all your noble work: Come what may, we shall regard you always as a great gentleman and a great Christian.

Believe me

Yours ever

M. Grahame Christie.[362]

A shorter, somewhat more sober but no less friendly note, written on Foreign Office stationery by R. A. Butler, the Under-Secretary of State for Foreign Affairs, reached Theo Kordt on the eve of his departure from London.[363] He returned to Berlin in the forenoon of 6 September and was promptly moved by Weizsäcker to Berne with the official assignment of dealing with the Swiss authorities in their capacity of having assumed the role of safeguarding German interests in the enemy countries. It was also Weizsäcker's calculation that this new post would afford Theo Kordt a maximum opportunity to resume from Berne the conversations with the British.

Once again, as at the time of Munich, the attempts on the part of members of the Resistance to synchronize their efforts with the *grosse Politik* came to naught. This time, however, the army was no longer a factor that could be counted on for support, and thus the power base of the emissaries abroad was reduced to the Weizsäcker circle and, very much behind the scenes, the Canaris outfit. Once again, also, their messages were ill-co-ordinated. Nevertheless it can reasonably be argued that, if the British had lent more credence to the German warnings about the imminence of the Nazi–Soviet Pact,[364] they would have taken more pains to arrive at some settlement with the Russians. It was, to say the least, within the realm of possibility that the disaster thus could have been avoided. In that case it stands to reason that the men of the *Widerstand* would have left a major mark on events. But the Nazi–Soviet Pact was in fact the prelude to war, and the German Resistance, for the moment, receded into a state of disarray.

*CHAPTER 2*

1. Quoted in Nicholas E. Reynolds, *Treason Was No Crime: Ludwig Beck, Chief of the German General Staff* (London, 1976), 44.
2. See Ritter, *Carl Goerdeler*, 61–2.
3. See Eberhard Bethge, *Dietrich Bonhoeffer: Man of Vision, Man of Courage* (New York, 1970), 91 ff.
4. See Freya von Moltke, Michael Balfour, and Julian Frisby, *Helmuth James von Moltke 1907–1945. Anwalt der Zukunft* (Stuttgart, 1972), 57.
5. Charles E. Collins, 'Notes on Adam von Trott', 19 Nov. 1946, Astor Papers; also Christopher Sykes, *Troubled Loyalty: A Biography of Adam von Trott zu Solz* (London, 1968), 79.; Henry O. Malone, *Adam von Trott zu Solz. Werdegang eines Verschwörers 1909–1938* (Berlin, 1986), 86–7.
6. 1885–1967.
7. See van Roon, *Neuordnung*, 132 ff., esp. p. 133.
8. 'Auszug aus der Denkschrift "Grundsätzliche Gedanken über die deutsche Führung"'; Theodor Steltzer Papers; see also the reprint of the memorandum in Theodor Steltzer, *Sechzig Jahre Zeitgenosse* (Munich, 1966), 270–84.

9. Ibid. 275–6; the German word here is *Weltanschauung*, and it is clearly used in the strict sense of an all-encompassing scheme of ideas and concepts about human nature furnishing the base of a political programme.

10. It might be noted here that a few years later Dietrich Bonhoeffer developed similar thoughts in his *Ethics* in which he drew the sharp contrast between 'ideological action' and 'responsible action'; see above p. 41.

11. Steltzer, *Sechzig Jahre*, 114 ff.

12. Letter from Helmuth von Moltke to Lionel Curtis, London, 12 July 1935; Lionel Curtis Papers, Box 28.

13. Letter from Moltke to Curtis, 19 Nov. 1937; Curtis Papers, Box 28.

14. Philip H. Kerr (1882–1940), since 1930 Marquis of Lothian; Secretary to the Rhodes Trust 1925–39; Ambassador to the United States 1939–40.

15. He had just recently, in February, been on a 'pilgrimage' to Hitler and emerged satisfied that the 'Führer' was 'sincerely anxious for peace'; T. P. Conwell-Evans (who accompanied Lord Lothian on the trip), *None So Blind: A Study of the Crisis Years, 1930–1939*, priv. printed (London, 1947), 37.

16. Letter from Moltke to Curtis, 12 July 1935, Curtis Papers, Box 28.

17. See for the following Reynolds, *Treason*, 111 ff.

18. Conwell-Evans, *None So Blind*, 91.

19. There are two versions extant, only slightly differing in the wording, of Beck's 'unofficial' account which must have reached the British Foreign Office via the 'Knight'–Christie channel: (1) Christie, Very Secret 'Gist of conversation between General Beck, Chief of the German Army General Staff and one or two *intimate* friends (officers) on his visit to Paris. June/1937'; Christie Papers, CHRS 180/1/21; one of these friends was evidently 'Knight' who at the time still was Assistant to the Military and Air Attachés in Paris; (2) Conwell-Evans, *None So Blind*, 91–2.

20. He mentioned Goebbels, Himmler, Heydrich, Ley, Rosenberg, 'and sometimes Göring'.

21. Beck characterized the Führer as 'pathologisch und völlig unberechenbar' (pathological and altogether unpredictable).

22. See Reynolds, *Treason*, 111.

23. Conwell-Evans, *None So Blind*, 92.

24. Ludwig Beck, 'Beck's Visit to Paris, 16–20 June 1937 (a translation from the German of Beck's official report)'; NA, Modern Military Section, MS B-819, quoted in Reynolds, *Treason*, 114, 297, nn. 78, 85.

25. Reynolds, *Treason*, 115.

26. FO 371/20733/C 5933/165/18; Vansittart Papers, VNST 1/20, Churchill College (the same file also contains an 'Extract from Report of Oberst Thomas'); Christie Papers, CHRS 180/1/16, Churchill College; Ian Colvin, *Vansittart in Office* (London, 1965) 151 ff.

27. See Keith Middlemas, *Diplomacy of Illusion: The British Government and Germany, 1937–1939* (London, 1972), 41–3.

28. See in this connection especially the works by Maurice Cowling, *The Impact of Hitler: British Politics and British Policies 1933–1940* (Cambridge, 1975); Gustav Schmidt, *England in der Krise: Grundlagen und Grundzüge der britischen Appeasement-Politik (1930–1937)* (Wiesbaden, 1981); Wolfgang J. Mommsen and Lothar Kettenacker (eds.), *The Fascist Challenge and the Policy of Appeasement* (London, 1983).

29. Sir Nevile Henderson to Secretary of State about the *Anschluss* and the Czechoslovak question, 16 Mar. 1938, FO 800/313/H/XV/14.

30. Lord Vansittart, *Lessons of My Life* (London, 1943); *The Mist Procession* (London, 1958); Aaron Goldman, 'Germans and Nazis: The Controversy over "Vansittartism" in Britain during the Second World War', *Journal of Contemporary History*, 14 (Jan. 1979), 155–91.

31. For the Göring problem see especially Stefan Martens, *Hermann Göring. 'Erster Paladin des Führers' und 'Zweiter Mann im Reich'* (Paderborn, 1985).

32. Sir Eric Phipps, Report, Berlin, 4 Nov. 1936, Phipps Papers, Churchill College, File 4.

33. Memorandum from Sir Campbell Stuart on Conversation with Dr Rauschning on 14 Nov. 1939, FO 371/23013/C 19119/53/18.

34. Minute by Lord Halifax on Conversation with Dr Rauschning, 15 Dec. 1939, FO 800/317/H/15/358.

35. I write this especially in response to the article by Hedva Ben-Israel, 'Im Widerstreit der Ziele: Die britische Reaktion auf den deutschen Widerstand', in Jürgen Schmädeke and Peter Steinbach (eds.), *Der Widerstand gegen den Nationalsozialismus* (Munich, 1985), esp. pp. 734–5; see also in relation to Adam von Trott, Sykes, *Troubled Loyalty* and Shiela Grant Duff, *The Parting of Ways: A Personal Account of the Thirties* (London, 1982).

36. Account of conversation by A. E. Barker (*The Times*, 4 July 1937) with Carl Goerdeler and minutes by Sir Alexander Cadogan (then Deputy Under-Secretary of State for Foreign Affairs), 7 July 1937, FO 371/20733/C 4882/165/18; see also A. P. Young, *The 'X' Documents* (London, 1974), 115; Sidney Aster, *1939: The Making of the Second World War* (London, 1973), 39.

37. See Middlemas, *Diplomacy*, 77–8.

38. Letter from Vansittart to Sir Eric Phipps, 5 Mar. 1935; Phipps Papers, File 8.

39. Telegram from Sir Eric Phipps to Eden, Berlin, 13 Aug. 1936, Phipps Papers, File 4.

40. Ibid.

41. Christie: 'Germany. Rough Notes 30/12/36' after his talks with State Secretaries General Erhard Milch and Paul Körner of the Air Ministry; Christie Papers, CHRS 180/1/17.

42. Account by Sir R. Vansittart of a visit to Germany in August 1936, 10 Sept. 1936 in *DBFP* 2/xvii. 772.

43. Telegram from Phipps to Eden, 13 Aug. 1936, Phipps Papers, File 4.

44. Middlemas, *Diplomacy*, 91. Its reports frequently found their way into the files of the FO; however it had no formal connection with the Secret Service.

45. 'Possible German Intentions', Cabinet Paper FP36(74) in FO 371/22961/C 939/15/18; see also Sir Thomas Inskip, about Vansittart's 'two "Germanophiles"'; diary entry, 23 Jan. 1939; Inskip Papers, Churchill College, Cambridge.

46. Göring coveted, as he put it, 'man to man' talks with Christie about Anglo-German relations; letter from Göring to Christie, Rominten, 9 Jan. 1937; Christie Papers, CHRS 1/6, No. 8.

47. Letter from Christie to 'Herr Geheimrat', 24 Mar. 1930, Christie Papers, CHRS 1/2, No. 15.

48. Undated draft in Christie's handwriting; Christie Papers, CHRS 1/3, Nos. 8–10.

49. Vansittart to Secretary of State, 30 Aug. 1938, Vansittart Papers, VNST 2/42, Churchill College.

50. Entry of 4 Sept. 1936, Thomas Jones, *A Diary with Letters, 1931–1950* (London, 1954), 242.

51. For a biographical sketch of Hohenlohe see Bernd Martin, *Friedensinitiativen und Machtpolitik im Zweiten Weltkrieg 1939–1942* (Düsseldorf, 1974), 85.

52. Minute by Frank Ashton-Gwatkin, 3 Dec. 1938; FO 371/21658/C 13956/42/18.

53. See Christie Papers, CHRS 180/1/26; 180/1/28.

54. Minutes by Vansittart, 10 Aug. 1938 to a letter from Henderson to the Secretary of State, 3 Aug 1938: '... I cannot bear the thought of losing a single British life to either Sudeten or Czechs.' FO 800/314/H/XV/58.

55. Cover note by Vansittart to 'A Report by Professor Conwell-Evans', 21 Feb. 1939; FO 23006/C 2762/53/18.

56. See Ritter, *Carl Goerdeler*, 151 ff. Goerdeler's passport had been confiscated by the Gauleiter of Saxony Martin Mutschmann; however, he succeeded in having it returned by the intervention of Hermann Göring who, while not knowing the extent of Goerdeler's disaffection, was interested in obtaining information about attitudes abroad towards the Nazi regime. All this does not mean that Goerdeler travelled as 'Göring's emissary'; Michael Krüger-Charlé, 'Carl Goerdeler and Great Britain 1937–1939: A Revision of Versailles without a Great War', 7; paper delivered at the Anglo-German Conference on the German Resistance and Great Britain in Leeds, England, 6–9 May 1986. It was to start with the idea of Captain Fritz Wiedemann, Hitler's unruly adjutant, that Göring be engaged in countermanding Mutschmann's order; both Wiedemann and Goerdeler hoped that this might be a way of winning over Göring for the cause of peace. Goerdeler in particular saw in Göring's interference in this matter a 'ray of hope'; his calculation was a political one, and it involved the risk of playing a double game; information from Frau

Marianne Meyer-Krahmer, née Goerdeler, 21 May 1986. Anyway, having to report to Göring was a price worth paying for Goerdeler to be able to go abroad; to his wife he reported that to get his passport returned he had ventured into the 'lion's den'; see Marianne Meyer-Krahmer, *Carl Goerdeler und sein Weg in den Widerstand* (Freiburg i. Br., 1989), 97–9. The funding for Goerdeler's foreign journeys was provided by Krupp.

57. Colvin, *Vansittart in Office*, 150.
58. See Ritter, *Carl Goerdeler*, 154; Klaus-Jürgen Müller, 'Zur Struktur und Eigenart der nationalkonservativen Opposition bis 1938', in Schmädeke and Steinbach (eds.), *Der Widerstand*, 337.
59. See Ritter, *Carl Goerdeler*, 157.
60. Letter from Frank Ashton-Gwatkin (Foreign Office) to S. D. Waley (Treasury), 25 June 1937, FO 371/20733/C 4714/165/18.
61. Minute by Sir Orme Sargent, 6 July 1937, ibid.
62. 'Reisebericht Belgien, 12. Juni 1937'; 'England, 15. Juli 1937'; 'Frankreich, 3. August 1937'; 'Kanada, 28. Sept. 1937'; 'USA, 2. Januar 1938'; 'England und Frankreich, 30. April 1938'; 'Jugoslawien, November 1938'; 'Rumänien, November/Dezember 1938'; 'Bulgarien, Dezember 1938'; 'Schweiz, 13. Dezember 1938'; 'Italien, 19. Dezember 1938'; 'Schluss-betrachtung zu den Reisen Schweiz-Italien-Jugoslawien-Bulgarien-Rumänien, Dezember 1938'; BA/K, Goerdeler 14.
63. Captain Fritz Wiedemann owed his position as Hitler's adjutant to the fact that during the war he had been Hitler's company commander. He was frequently entrusted with unofficial diplomatic missions abroad, but since he belonged to the 'peace party' in the Reich Chancellery (Erich Kordt, *Nicht aus den Akten* (Stuttgart, 1950), 234) and let on in Berlin to his views, in agreement with General Beck, that Britain in case of war would not remain neutral, he fell into disgrace and was moved, in fact banished, in 1939 to San Francisco where he functioned as Consul-General; see also Ritter, *Carl Goerdeler*, 474–5 and Hassell, *Die Hassell-Tagebücher*, 81.
64. Hoffmann, *History*, 55.
65. In fact, between September 1938 and March 1939 he made a number of secret trips to Switzerland to confer with an emissary of Sir Robert Vansittart of which we have obtained information only much later through British sources; Young, *The 'X' Documents*.
66. He also had meetings with the Governor of the Bank of England Montagu Norman (by introduction of Schacht), the Secretary of State Anthony Eden, Frank Ashton-Gwatkin of the Foreign Office, and the Lord Privy Seal Viscount Halifax.
67. A. P. Young records the fact that at the occasion of a dinner at the National Liberal Club in June 1937 Sir Wyndham Deedes, Director of the National Council for Social Service, introduced Goerdeler to Vansittart; A. P. Young, *The 'X' Documents*, 24–5. But according to Vansittart's memoirs he began meeting Goerdeler as early as 1935; see also Colvin, *Vansittart in Office*, 150; Norman Rose, *Vansittart: Study of a Diplomat* (London, 1978), 136.
68. Lord Vansittart, *The Mist Procession*, 315–16.
69. Most Secret Report Sir Robert Vansittart to the FO, 6 July 1937, FO 371/20733/C 5933/165/18.
70. In fact at the end of his first ten days in London he briefly interrupted his stay and flew over for a few hours to Berlin to report about the state of his negotiations with the British to Göring whom he thought to be a counterbalance against the 'extremists' led by Himmler and Heydrich; account of conversation by A. E. B. Barker, FO 20733/C 4882/165/16.
71. Letter from F. Ashton-Gwatkin to S. D. Waley, 25 June 1937, FO 371/20733/C 4717/165/18.
72. Goerdeler had talks with the Secretary of State, Cordell Hull, the Secretary for Agriculture, Henry A. Wallace, the Under Secretary of State, Sumner Welles, the Assistant Secretary of State, George S. Messersmith, the former President, Herbert Hoover, the later Secretary for War, Henry L. Stimson, the Secretary of the Treasury, Henry Morgenthau Jr., the industrialist Owen D. Young; see Ritter, *Carl Goerdeler*, 160–1. He was to meet Messersmith and Welles again later.
73. Messersmith wrote this in a letter to Hamilton Fish Armstrong in preparation for Goerdeler's appearance before the Council on Foreign Relations in New York City (Letter

from George S. Messersmith to Hamilton Fish Armstrong, Esquire, 12 Nov. 1937; from the Archive of the Council on Foreign Relations, New York City). Goerdeler did address the Council in a closed session on 6 December.

74. John W. Wheeler-Bennett, *The Nemesis of Power: The German Army in Politics 1918–1945* (London, 1954), 386; *idem, Special Relationships: America in Peace and War* (London, 1975), 55.

75. Ritter, *Carl Goerdeler*, 161. The document was eventually published by Bronisch, after the death sentence had been imposed upon Goerdeler by the People's Court in September 1944 but before the actual execution on 2 February 1945, in four instalments of the *New Yorker Staats-Zeitung* of 22, 29 Oct. and 5, 12 Nov. 1944 and reprinted subsequently in *Goerdelers Politisches Testament: Dokumente des anderen Deutschlands* ed. Friedrich Krause (New York, 1945), 19–46. See also 'The Testament of Goerdeler', 30 Nov. 1944, Number N-115, OSS, Foreign Nationalities Branch.

76. *Goerdelers Politisches Testament*, 42.

77. Ibid. 22–3; he explicitly also distanced himself from Schacht who 'had supported and condoned the political solution of 30 January 1933'; ibid. 23.

78. Ibid. 46.

79. For this episode I rely largely on Hoffmann, *History*, 56; his account has been verified by an oral presentation of M. Pierre Bertaux at the International Conference on the German Resistance in Berlin, 2–6 July 1984.

80. The poet Saint-John Perse; Goerdeler also had talks with Edouard Daladier, Minister of National Defence, who on 10 April was to become Prime Minister, and Paul Reynaud who was about to become Minister of Justice; but no details are known about them.

81. See 'Germany: Internal Situation', based on conversation between Ashton-Gwatkin and Dr Schairer, 7 Feb. 1938; FO 371/21660/C 876/62/18; 'Germany: Internal Affairs', FO 21662/C 579/62/18, Minute by F. K. Roberts (Central Department), 4 Apr. 1938 according to which Goerdeler said that, had the Austrian Chancellor Kurt von Schuschnigg been able to postpone for a fortnight the plebiscite preceding the *Anschluss* in March, 'an internal revolt would have been staged by the Army and Hitler and the present Nazi Government would have been swept away'.

82. Minute by F. K. Roberts, 2 July 1938 to 'Germany: Internal Situation (Dr Schairer)'; FO 371/21663/C 6577/62/18.

83. Ritter, *Carl Goerdeler*, 164; Colvin, *Vansittart in Office*, 205–6; see also Carl Goerdeler: 'I have stressed everywhere that as a German I considered certain changes of the political scene (the Sudeten question, the Polish Corridor) necessary, but that I detest Hitler's methods and that the German people would turn away from him once it learned the truth;' 'Vorwort zur Wirtschaftsfibel', typescript, p. 6; BA/K, Kaiser, 135.

84. Gerhard Ritter's verdict that, making this claim, Goerdeler came 'dangerously close to that policy of "appeasement at all price" which eventually Chamberlain conducted after Munich' (Ritter, *Carl Goerdeler*, 165) is too harsh and not justified. 'Appeasement' in this case was not for its own sake, and certainly not to benefit the Third Reich. Goerdeler's aim was throughout, as Ulrich von Hassell at a later date recorded, to negotiate abroad conditions of peace 'which Hitler could not swallow' and thus to effect his overthrow; entry of 19 Oct. 1939, *Die Hassell-Tagebücher*, 133.

85. The sources who approached Vansittart directly are marked by an asterisk; 'Czecho-slovakia: Communications to Sir R. Vansittart', 9 Aug. 1938; FO 371/ 21736/C 9591/1941/18.

86. Rudi Strauch, *Sir Nevile Henderson. Britischer Botschafter in Berlin von 1937 bis 1939. Ein Beitrag zur diplomatischen Vorgeschichte des zweiten Weltkrieges* (Bonn, 1959), 134–8; for the Embassy reports about Koerber see *DBFP* 3/ii. 65–7.

87. He derived his intelligence from, among others, General Thomas; Strauch, *Sir Nevile Henderson*, 136.

88. Furthermore, by mistake, Mason-MacFarlane reported to London that Koerber had played a part in the Hitler Putsch of 1923, whereas he had merely witnessed it as a journalist and not as a participant; ibid. 135.

89. *DBFP* 3/ii. 108, n. 2.

90. See *DBFP* 3/ii. 683–9. Also Bodo Scheurig, *Ewald von Kleist-Schmenzin. Ein Konservativer*

*gegen Hitler* (Oldenburg, 1968); Colvin, *Vansittart in Office*, 222 ff.; Helmut Krausnick, 'Vorgeschichte und Beginn des militärischen Widerstandes gegen Hitler', in *Vollmacht des Gewissens*, ed. Europäische Publikation e.V. (Frankfurt/M., 1960, 1965), i. 330 ff.; Ian Colvin, *Master Spy* (New York, 1951), 57 ff.; Fabian von Schlabrendorff, *The Secret War against Hitler* (London, 1966), *passim*; Middlemas, *Diplomacy*, 275–8; Hoffmann, *History*, 60–2; Wheeler-Bennett, *The Nemesis of Power*, 410–13.

91. Ewald von Kleist-Schmenzin, *Der Nationalsozialismus: eine Gefahr* (Berlin, 1932), reproduced in Scheurig, *Ewald von Kleist-Schmenzin*, 255–64.

92. Ibid. 263.

93. The one source on this episode is Colvin; Colvin, *Vansittart in Office*, 210–11.

94. See the letter from Colvin to Lord Lloyd, 3 Aug. 1938 in Colvin, *Vansittart in Office*, 221.

95. 'Bring me certain proof that England will fight if Czechoslovakia is attacked and I will make an end of this regime'; Colvin, *Vansittart in Office*, 223.

96. *DBFP* 3/ii. 683.

97. Lord Lloyd of Dolobran (1879–1941), President of the Navy League (1930) and Chairman of the British Council (1936); Lloyd, to whom Kleist carried a letter from Colvin, was in sympathy with him but felt that, not being a political person, he, Lloyd, could be only of limited help and sent the visitor on to the more influential Vansittart.

98. For whom Kleist also brought a letter from Colvin.

99. From report by Vansittart to Halifax, 18 Aug. 1938 in Colvin, *Vansittart in Office*, 226; see also *DBFP* 3/ii. 685.

100. *DBFP* 3/ii. 688–9. The letter was sent by diplomatic pouch, for the sake of security, to the Embassy in Berlin and then turned over to Kleist. In the literature there is a divergence concerning the question as to who picked up the letter at the Embassy; both Colvin (Colvin, *Vansittart in Office*, 229) and Fabian von Schlabrendorff (von Schlabrendorff, *The Secret War*, 95) claim to have done so. Kleist, in turn, passed on copies made by Schlabrendorff to General Beck and Admiral Canaris. The letter was also, in the form of excerpts, worked into an Auswärtiges Amt memorandum on the possible reactions of the powers to a conflict over Czechoslovakia; also, allegedly, the gist of it was used by Canaris in a report to the Führer; Bernd-Jürgen Wendt, *München 1938: England zwischen Hitler und Preussen* (Frankfurt/M., 1965), 40; cf. also Wheeler-Bennett, *The Nemesis of Power*, 413. The original of the letter was deposited by Kleist in Schmenzin where, following his arrest after the unsuccessful plot of 20 July 1944, it was found by the Gestapo and used against him in the proceedings of the Nazi People's Court leading to his execution on 9 April 1945.

101. *DBFP* 3/ii. 688.

102. In view of the German–Polish Non-Aggression Pact of January 1934.

103. Vansittart years afterwards to Colvin:' Of all the Germans I saw, Kleist had the stuff in him for a revolution against Hitler. But he wanted the Polish Corridor . . .'; Colvin, *Master Spy*, 70–1.

104. *DBFP* 3/ii. 683.

105. *DBFP* 3/ii. 686–7.

106. Minute by Sir I. Mallet, 22 Aug. 1938, FO 371/21732/C 8520/1941/18.

107. *Parliamentary Debates*, House of Commons, 5th ser., vol. 333, 6th vol. of Session 1937–8 (London, 1938), cols. 1405–6.

108. Colvin, *Master Spy*, 67.

109. See Colvin, *Vansittart in Office*, 234.

110. Colvin, *Master Spy*, 75.

111. He knew Beck from way back when he served together with Beck, still a young lieutenant, in the Field Artillery Regiment No. 15 in Straßburg. His acquaintance with Halder and Oster went back to the year 1933 when in his capacity as Stahlhelm Gauführer he visited Münster where he reported to Halder, then Chief of Staff of Military District (*Wehrkreis*) VI in Münster and to his lieutenant Oster about the Stahlhelm opinions on National Socialism; letter Hans Böhm-Tettelbach to Colonel (ret.) Johannes Rohowsky, 14 Mar. 1954; BA/MA, Rohowsky N124/3. He evidently had preliminary meetings on 15 Aug. 1938 with Halder and Oster in the course of which the plan for the mission was hatched; letter from Rohowsky to Gerhard Ritter, 18 Mar. 1954, BA/MA, Rohowsky N124/9.

112. See esp. Krausnick, 'Vorgeschichte,' in *Vollmacht*, i. 339–40; Hoffmann, *History*, 63; Wheeler-Bennett, *The Nemesis of Power*, 413–14 (Wheeler-Bennett mistakenly assumed that Böhm-Tettelbach met Vansittart and the head of the Press Department of the Foreign Office); Colvin, *Master Spy*, 88 is altogether mistaken on the Böhm-Tettelbach mission which he dates June 1939.

113. Letter from Böhm-Tettelbach to Dr Helmut Krausnick, 1 July 1955; IfZ, ZS 633.

114. 'Ein Mann hat gesprochen. Oberstleutnant a.D. Böhm-Tettelbach über seine Rolle im September 1938', *Rheinische Post*, 19 July 1948; IfZ, ZS 635 I.

115. Ibid.

116. In this case, might the unidentified 'major' have been Group Captain Christie? After the war Vansittart responded to an enquiry by Böhm-Tettelbach that he did not remember the episode. As we shall see subsequently, he reacted in a similarly evasive fashion to requests to testify on behalf of the Kordt brothers. Neither the Vansittart Papers nor the Christie Papers contain any references to Böhm-Tettelbach.

117. Hans Böhm-Tettelbach, 'Eidesstattliche Erklärung', 19 Jan. 1948, quoting Achim Oster's recollection of his father's account; BA/MA, Rohowsky, N124/7.

118. Kordt, *Nicht aus den Akten*, 240; also Reichsgraf Romedio von Thun-Hohenstein, 'Hans Oster. Versuch einer Lebensbeschreibung', diss. (Christian-Albrechts University, Kiel, 1980), 84–5.

119. Kordt, *Nicht aus den Akten*, 241–4.

120. Carl J. Burckhardt, *Meine Danziger Mission 1937–1939* (Munich, 1960), 182.

121. Burckhardt indeed made his way instantly to Berne where, arriving on 2 Sept., he called on the British Minister Sir George Warner, telephoning from the Legation to Lord Halifax's Parliamentary Secretary; a few days later he elaborated his concerns orally to Sir Ralph Claremont Skrine Stevenson, a British foreign servant who in turn reported back in a long letter dated 8 Sept. to William Strang, the Head of the FO Central Department. In a letter dated 8 May 1962 to the historian Leonidas E. Hill, Lord Strang confirmed the fact that he was well aware at the time that Burckhardt's anonymous informant was Weizsäcker; *Die Weizsäcker Papiere*, 506 n. 127. The General with the riding crop considered for the mission was Sir William Edmund Ironside, ADC-General to King George VI, a particularly tall and corpulent person. See Burckhardt, *Meine Danziger Mission*, 181–7; *DBFP* 3/ii 689–92.

122. Ernst von Weizsäcker, *Erinnerungen* (Munich, 1950), 178; the same passage in Burckhardt, *Meine Danziger Mission*, 181–2 is obviously derived from Weizsäcker.

123. Kordt, *Nicht aus den Akten*, 248.

124. Susanne Simonis while in Berlin worked for the *Deutsche Allgemeine Zeitung*. She lived with Erich Kordt and, not asking any questions about his work, considered herself as a sort of 'lightning rod' for him. After the war she herself joined the diplomatic service, her last assignment being the one of Consul-General in Vancouver; interview with Mrs Susanne Simonis, 10 July 1975.

125. 'Machtmittel'; ibid. 250–1.

126. Theo Kordt had met Sir Horace previously at the end of August in the house of Conwell-Evans, on which occasion he had already revealed to him Hitler's and his friends' war plans and urged him to impress upon the Prime Minister the need for a 'consistent policy' on the part of the British government; ibid. 279.

127. Ibid; see also Theo Kordt, 'Wir wollten den Frieden retten', *Stuttgarter Rundschau*, 8 (1948), 10–13.

128. Interview of Harold C. Deutsch and Harold C. Vedeler with Dr Erich Kordt, 15–16 Dec. 1945, Washington, DC, State Department Special Interrogation Mission, NA 679, Roll 2.

129. Weizsäcker annotation 10 or 11 Sept. 1938 in *Die Weizsäcker-Papiere*, 142; see also Weizsäcker, *Erinnerungen*, 178. For a summation of the problem see Rainer A. Blasius, *Für Grossdeutschland—gegen den grossen Krieg* (Cologne, 1981) 141–4; Marion Thielenhaus, *Zwischen Anpassung und Widerstand: Deutsche Diplomaten 1938–1941* (Poderborn, 1984), 60 ff.

130. Kordt, *Nicht aus den Akten*, 279; also Theo Kordt, 'Diplomatische Autobiographie', mimeograph, Bad Godesberg, 23 July 1949, 39; Kordt Papers.

131. Kordt, *Nicht aus den Akten*, 281; see also diary entry by Sir Alexander Cadogan, Wed., 7

Sept. 1938: 'Herr X [Theodor Kordt] ... wants us to broadcast to the German nation ...';
Sir Alexander Cadogan, *The Diaries of Sir Alexander Cadogan, OM 1938–1945*, ed. David
Dilks (New York, 1972), 95.

132. Hans Rothfels, 'Adam von Trott und das State Department', *VfZ*, 7(1959), 319.

133. See Marion Grafin Dönhoff, 'Hochverrat um des Friedens willen', *Die Zeit*, 22 Nov.
1974.

134. *Die Weizsäcker-Papiere*, 128–9, 131, 133, 144, 167, 502 n. 67; see also Blasius, *Für Grossdeutschland*, 29 ff.

135. For a discussion of this problem see Wendt, *München*, 70; Blasius, *Für Grossdeutschland*,
61, 141 ff.; Thielenhaus, *Zwischen Anpassung und Widerstand*, 73–4; Hoffmann, *History*,
551 n. 76.

136. Kordt, *Nicht aus den Akten*, 280; Colvin, *Vansittart in Office*, 236.

137. Kordt justified the failure of the anti-Nazi conspirators to make their disclosures to official
French circles by their 'notorious indiscretion'; Interview by Deutsch and Vedeler with
Erich Kordt.

138. Hans von Herwarth, *Against Two Evils* (New York, 1981), 123 ff.

139. See Fitzroy Maclean, *Eastern Approaches* (London, 1949), 178; see also Letter from
Ambassador Viscount Chilston to Mr Laurence Collier, Northern Department of the
Foreign Office, *DBFP* 3/ii. 140 ff.

140. He first approached Baron Gontran de Juniac, the Second Secretary, and subsequently
Baron Maurice Dayet, the First Secretary.

141. Von Herwarth, *Against Two Evils*, 130. Herwarth was assured by the two French diplomats
that the information was forwarded under Dayet's signature to Alexis Léger, the Permanent
Under-Secretary at the Quai d'Orsay. Also, partly to cover himself, partly to scare the Berlin
warmongers, he prepared a number of memoranda, to be forwarded by his Ambassador
to Berlin, calling attention to the distinct possibility of French and British support of
Czechoslovakia in the event of a German provocation; ibid. 132–4; see *DBFP* 3/ii. 656–7,
666–7.

142. Letter from Hans von Herwarth to me, 13 Oct. 1982; also interview with Hans von
Herwarth, 9 May 1986.

143. Von Kessel, 'Verborgene Saat', 86–7.

144. *DBFP* 3/ii. 654; see also Leonidas Hill, 'Three Crises, 1938–1939', *Journal of Contemporary
History*, 3 (Jan. 1968), 116.

145. Edward von Selzam, 'Eidesstattliche Erklärung', NA, US Mil. Trib. IV (IVA) Nürnberg,
Case 11, *US v. Ernst von Weizsäcker*, Defense Exhibits Weizsäcker. Exhib. No 7, Doc. 159.

146. He was First Secretary and Counsellor at the American Embassy in London from 1934 to
1941 and then became Minister to Stockholm whence he reported to the State Department
on the Swedish visit of Adam von Trott in June/July 1944.

147. Selzam, 'Eidesstattliche Erklärung'. Theo Kordt may not be correct in dating this meeting
23 Sept.; Kordt, 'Diplomatische Autobiographie', 56.

148. Selzam, 'Eidesstattliche Erklärung'.

149. By supporting Chamberlain's appeasement policy, Kennedy was altogether at odds with
the President who at that time was working his way out of the American appeasement; see
Callum A. MacDonald, *The United States, Britain and Appeasement 1936–1939* (New
York, 1981), 92 ff.

150. Evidence given by Theo Kordt in the Wilhelmstrasse Trial, 14 July 1948, *Wilhelmstrassenprozess*, Protokoll vom 14. Juli 1948, minute 12029; see also Rothfels, *The German
Opposition*, 68; Wheeler-Bennett, *The Nemesis of Power*, 418, n. 3; Hoffmann, *History*, 67,
551 n. 77.

151. Arthur Primrose Young, 1885–1977. A Scot by birth, he was a distinguished electrical
engineer and Manager of the Rugby Works, British Thomson Houston Co. Ltd. As a
friend of Robert Bosch, he was a sensible choice for the encounters with Goerdeler to
whom he took quickly and whom he came to appreciate as 'a fine Christian man'. But
Young had no previous experience in the art of diplomacy and, trusting and kindly as he
was, never felt at home in that 'world of international intrigue, unsavoury politics, secrecy,
fear ...', as he himself put it (*Across the Years: The Living Testament of an Engineer with
a Mission* (London, 1971), 17), into which he was catapulted. The mounting suspicions in

the Foreign Office against Goerdeler and his friends were beyond his understanding. This assessment of Mr Young is, in part, based on a lengthy meeting which I had with him on 23 Mar. 1974 in Leamington Spa; see also A. P. Young, *The 'X' Documents*.

152. These proposals were made in the course of the first secret meeting of 6–7 Aug. in Rauschen Düne, a small Baltic resort near Königsberg where Mr Young sought out Goerdeler who was on holiday with his family. In the course of a second meeting between the two preceding Munich which took place on 11 Sept. in Zurich, Goerdeler essentially elaborated on the position which he had stated earlier; ibid. 50 ff. and 75 ff.

153. Oberstlt. Friedrich Wilhelm Heinz, 'Von Wilhelm Canaris zur NKVD', typescript [*c.* 1949], National Archive, Washington, DC, microfilm No. R60. 67, p. 99; see Hoffmann, *History*, 92.

154. Hoffmann, *History*, 87, 91; Ritter, *Carl Goerdeler*, 189–90; on the question of the candidate for the throne, however, there was some disagreement in as much as the younger officers in the conspiracy were set upon the eldest son of the former Crown Prince, Prince Wilhelm of Prussia, instead of the second son, Prince Louis Ferdinand, Goerdeler's candidate, who seemed to Heinz and his friends too close to the tradition of the Second Reich from which they sought to escape.

155. Hans Bernd Gisevius, *To the Bitter End* (Boston, 1947), 324.

156. Ibid.; Kordt, *Nicht aus den Akten*, 265 ff.; Ruth Andreas-Friedrich, *Berlin Underground 1939–1945* (London, 1948), 12; William L. Shirer, *Berlin Diary: The Journal of a Foreign Correspondent 1934–1941* (New York, 1941), 142–3; Sir Nevile Henderson, *Failure of a Mission* (New York, 1940), 165–6; Weizsäcker, *Erinnerungen*, 188.

157. Hoffmann, *History*, 96; see also Ritter, *Carl Goerdeler*, 196.

158. See Hoffmann, *History*, 81–2, 555 n. 5.

159. See e.g. the Minute of M. J. C. Creswell (3rd Secretary of the British Embassy in Berlin) of 28 Sept. 1938 on the position of an Austrian *émigré* friend of his, Erwin Schüller, who had taken an interest in the German Resistance and was initiated into its affairs; 'Support of anti-Nazi influences in German Army circles', FO 371/21664/C 11614/62/18.

160. Letter from Goerdeler to A. P. Young, Sept. 21, 1938 in Young, *The 'X' Documents*, 101.

161. See Wendt, *München*, 26, 130 n. 18.

162. See esp. Graml, 'Die aussenpolitischen Vorstellungen', in Walter Schmitthenner and Hans Buchheim (eds.), *Der deutsche Widerstand gegen Hitler*, (Cologne, 1966), 19 ff.; Wendt, *München, passim*.

163. During the crisis over Czechoslovakia the Prime Minister 'ruled' with an improvised inner group, the Committee on the Czechoslovak Question consisting of himself, Lord Halifax, Sir John Simon, and Sir Samuel Hoare advised by Sir Alexander Cadogan, Sir Horace Wilson and, occasionally, Sir Robert Vansittart, since from this group he could promise himself a 'safer consensus' than from the established Foreign Affairs Committee; Ian Colvin, *The Chamberlain Cabinet* (London, 1971), 146 ff.; Middlemas, *Diplomacy*, 300.

164. Graml, 'Die aussenpolitischen Vorstellungen', in Schmitthenner and Buchheim (eds.), *Der deutsche Widerstand*, 25.

165. See esp. Wendt, *München*, 17 ff.

166. See Sir Alexander Cadogan's diary entry for 16 Sept. 1938: 'Quite clear that nothing but "self-determination" will work. How are we to get it—or give it? I know Halifax will, by hook or crook. So will P[rime]. M[inister]. [Sir]J[ohn]. S[imon]. trying to evolve a semblance of quid pro quo. I think we'd better not try. Make the gesture to Hitler—we've never made one before [sic!]—and trust to the result'; *The Diaries of Sir Alexander Cadogan*, 99. Even the French Prime Minister Edouard Daladier in the sessions of 18 Sept. at 10 Downing Street with the representatives of the British Cabinet including the Prime Minister and Foreign Secretary spoke of independence and not territorial integrity of Czechoslovakia; his chief concern was some sort of guarantee that Hitler should not go beyond the claim to the Sudetenland; ibid. 100–1; *DBFP* 3/ii, esp. 387 ff.; see also Colvin, *The Chamberlain Cabinet*, 157–8.

167. *DBFP* 3/i. 604; 3/ii. 257; in both cases this was Sir Nevile Henderson's expressed expectation.

168. See Wendt, *München*, 104 ff.

169. Gisevius, *To the Bitter End*, 292 ff., 299.

170. Helmut Krausnick, 'Vorgeschichte und Beginn des militärischen Widerstandes gegen Hitler', in *Vollmacht*, i. 350.
171. *The Diaries of Sir Alexander Cadogan*, 96 ff. For the genesis of the plan see Wendt, *München*, 80; see also Colvin, *The Chamberlain Cabinet*, 151 ff.
172. *The Diaries of Sir Alexander Cadogan*, 95.
173. Gisevius, *To the Bitter End*, 321.
174. See *DBFP* 3/ii. 554 ff., 564 ff. *Documents on German Foreign Policy 1918–1945 (DGFP)*, Series D, ii. 963 ff.; Telford Taylor, *Munich: The Price of Peace* (New York, 1979), 870 ff.; Ritter, *Carl Goerdeler*, 193–4.
175. For Hitler's 'without England' concept see Josef Henke, *England in Hitlers politischem Kalkül 1935–1939* (Boppard am Rhein, 1977), 304; see also Blasius, *Für Grossdeutschland*, 69; Thielenhaus, *Zwischen Anpassung und Widerstand*, 83.
176. Kordt, *Nicht aus den Akten*, 272.
177. See entry of 9 Oct. 1938, *Die Weizsäcker-Papiere*, 145; for Ribbentrop's 'against England' course see Wolfgang Michalka, *Ribbentrop und die deutsche Weltpolitik 1933–1940* (Munich, 1980), 240.
178. Von Kessel 'Verborgene Saat', 94.
179. Weizsäcker, *Erinnerungen*, 193.
180. The distinction between 'Solution I' (the coup) and 'Solution II' (the Munich Agreement) goes back to Weizsäcker (ibid.). It is generally understood in the recent literature on Weizsäcker that he, claiming to have pursued both solutions simultaneously, did not literally mean this but referred by 'Solution I' to the activities of the Kordt brothers; Blasius, *Für Grossdeutschland*, 143 n. 11; Thielenhaus, *Zwischen Anpassung und Widerstand*, 81 n. 134.
181. Kordt, *Nicht aus den Akten*, 272; Weizsäcker, *Erinnerungen*, 193; see also Selzam, 'Eidesstattliche Erklärung', 6.
182. The story was told soon after the event by Engel and recorded by Nicolaus von Below, Hitler's Luftwaffe Adjutant, in his memoirs (Nicolaus von Below, *Als Hitlers Adjutant 1937–1945*, Mainz, 1980, 130). Only later, when Below had heard about Halder's part in the projection of the coup, did he understand.
183. Gisevius, *To the Bitter End*, 327.
184. Ritter, *Carl Goerdeler*, 198.
185. Carl Goerdeler, 'Brief an einen amerikanischen Politiker', 11 Oct. 1938 in *Goerdelers Politisches Testament: Dokumente des anderen Deutschland*, ed. Friedrich Krause (New York, 1945), 57–64. Concerning Neville Chamberlain, he and his 'clique of noblemen' were themselves Fascists of sorts who hoped to salvage the 'capitalistic profit system' with the help of National Socialism. It might be noted here that, ironically, similar charges have been levelled later in the revisionist historiography on the *Widerstand* against the traditional German élites, of which Goerdeler was a prime representative, which all too long co-operated with the Nazis; see Klaus-Jürgen Müller, 'Nationalkonservative Eliten zwischen Kooperation und Widerstand', in Schmädeke and Steinbach (eds.), *Der Widerstand*, 26, 29.
186. Gisevius, *To the Bitter End*, 326.
187. See esp. Hans Rothfels, 'The German Resistance, in its International Aspects', in 'Record of General Meeting held at Chatham House' (London, 14 Mar. 1958), 488, commenting about the 'bitter irony of history' that the Western Allies virtually co-operated not with the German Resistance but with Hitler. See also Gerhard Ritter, 'The Foreign Relations of the Anti-Hitler Plot in Germany', ibid. (London, 31 Oct. 1949), 5; Helmut Krausnick and Hermann Graml, 'Der deutsche Widerstand und die Alliierten', *Das Parlament* (19 July 1961), 12; Kordt, *Nicht aus den Akten*, 283.
188. It must be registered here that the French Prime Minister Edouard Daladier claimed not even to have known until during the Nuremberg Trials that a conspiracy had been afoot in Germany. In answer to the proposition that 'Chamberlain and Daladier strangled the conspiracy of the German generals' he protested: 'Neither Chamberlain nor Halifax, who knew of it from its beginnings from the emissaries to London, informed me of it'; from a number of drafts in Daladier's handwriting dealing with the Generals' Plot; Fondation Nationale des Sciences Politiques. Service des Archives d'Histoire Contemporaine.

Archives Edouard Daladier, 2 DA, Dr 2, sdrc, f—La conspiration des généraux; courtesy Professor Philip C. F. Bankwitz. But General Gamelin, the Chief of Staff of the French Army, at the occasion of an interview which he and Daladier had with Chamberlain on 26 September raised the issue of the state of preparedness of the German Resistance; the British Prime Minister is quoted to have responded: 'who guarantees us that Germany would not afterwards turn Bolshevik?'; Wendt, *München*, 104, 144 n. 1.

189. Even within the fold of Vansittart there was little co-ordination. A. P. Young was altogether unaware of the activities of Christie and Conwell-Evans; interview with A. P. Young, 13 Mar. 1974.

190. See the argument of Klaus-Jürgen Müller in a paper: 'On the Genesis and Nature of the National-Conservative Opposition to Hitler before the Second World War' (pp. 11, 14), delivered at the Anglo-German Conference on the German Resistance and Great Britain in Leeds, England, 6–9 May 1986, concerning the 'lack of uniformity' among the German contacts which left the British with a picture of their desiderata which was 'far from uniform'. But the fact alone that someone like Captain Wiedemann, in an at least semi-official capacity, was also involved in the British–German dialogue, should not have prevented the British FO from sorting out the various Germans who came over. For a similar charge of ambivalence among the British caused by the Germans see Hedva Ben-Israel, 'Im Widerstreit der Ziele: Die britische Reaktion auf den deutschen Widerstand', in Schmädeke and Steinbach (eds.), *Der Widerstand*, 732–49.

191. Middlemas, *Diplomacy*, 307.

192. See William L. Langer and S. Everett Gleason, *The Challenge to Isolation 1937–1940* (New York, 1952) and *The Undeclared War 1940–1941* (New York, 1953).

193. Thus in particular Sumner Welles, the Under-Secretary of State, and Adolf A. Berle, Assistant Secretary of State.

194. Thus Cordell Hull, the Secretary of State, George S. Messersmith, Assistant Secretary of State, William E. Dodd, the Ambassador to Berlin.

195. See Arnold A. Offner, *American Appeasement: United States Foreign Policy and Germany, 1933–1938* (Cambridge, Mass., 1969); MacDonald, *The United States, Britain and Appeasement*.

196. See Callum A. MacDonald, 'The United States, Appeasement and the Open Door', in Mommsen and Kettenacker (eds.), *The Fascist Challenge*, 400–27; also Bernd-Jürgen Wendt, *Appeasement 1938. Wirtschaftliche Rezession und Mitteleuropa* (Frankfurt/M., 1966).

197. MacDonald, *The United States, Britain and Appeasement*, ix.

198. Walter Görlitz, *Der deutsche Generalstab: Geschichte und Gestalt 1657–1945* (Frankfurt/M., 1950), 481; Gert Buchheit, *Soldatentum und Rebellion: Die Tragödie der deutschen Wehrmacht* (Rastatt/Baden, 1961), 192.

199. Thus especially General von Witzleben who, promoted to the rank of Colonel General, was transferred to a command post with headquarters in Kassel.

200. Quoted in Krausnick, 'Vorgeschichte' in *Vollmacht*, i. 370; Krausnick and Graml, 'Der deutsche Widerstand', 12.

201. Young, *The 'X' Documents*, 125.

202. 'Das Weltfriedensprogramm' in *Goerdelers Politisches Testament*, 59.

203. Copy of letter from Carl Goerdeler to Reinhold Schairer (from Switzerland), 19 Oct. 1938, BA/K, Goerdeler 9.

204. See the minute by Sir Orme Sargent of 12 Feb. 1939 to one of Goerdeler's many memoranda: 'It is a pity that D.G. [*sic*] tries to curdle our blood by overstating his case; Secret Report: 'Germany: Internal Affairs; Foreign Policy'; FO 371/22963/C 1290/15/18.

205. Young, *The 'X' Documents*, 123.

206. Ibid. 120.

207. Carl Goerdeler Memorandum 'Deutsches Ziel ...', 8 Oct. 1938; Christie Papers, CHRS 180/1/26.

208. Young, *The 'X' Documents*, 120–1.

209. Minute Sir Alexander Cadogan, 10 Dec. 1938, FO 371/21665/C15438/62/18.

210. FO 21659/C 15084/42/18.

211. Point 9 of the Heads of Agreement.

212. 'England recognises that the Polish Corridor is a source of continuing disturbance to the justified national feelings and interests of the German people. She therefore agrees that the Corridor be liquidated and guarantees every suitable support to Germany for this end . . .'; only as an afterthought, in point 8, did Goerdeler state that 'Poland's access to the sea can be assured in another way'and mention France along with England as an interested party. As a matter of fact, in his letter to Schairer of 19 Oct., in which he enclosed a text of the document, he stated flatly that 'France anyhow is to be written off'; copy of letter from Carl Goerdeler to Reinhold Schairer, 19 Oct. 1938, BA/K, Goerdeler 9.

213. 'Germany receives a colonial territory as far as possible interconnected and as far as possible capable of development which Germany will administer according to the recognised principles of International Law. England will undertake that all interested parties contribute to establish this situation without delay . . .'; in his draft for Group Captain Christie, Goerdeler specified that the 'interconnected' colonies were to be in western Africa, which would mean most likely the territory between the former German colonies of the Cameroons and German South West Africa, and affect the holdings of France, Belgium, and Portugal; Carl Goerdeler Memorandum, 8 Oct. 1938; Christie Papers, CHRS 180/1/26.

214. In the draft for Christie this particular item is stated as follows: 'Germany and England jointly aim at . . . the restoration of a reasonable order in Russia and . . . at a removal of the pestilence of Bolshevism by means of a constructive effort short of a war of intervention . . .'; ibid.

215. The draft for Christie spells out, in this connection, an 'alliance against Italy'.

216. The draft for Christie specifies an 'alliance against Japan'.

217. Minute by, F. A. Gwatkin, 6 Dec. 1938, FO 371/21659/C 15084/42/18.

218. Minute by W. Strang, 7 Dec. 1938; ibid.

219. Minute by Sir Alexander Cadogan, 10 Dec. 1938; ibid.

220. Copy of letter from Carl Goerdeler to Reinhold Schairer (in capital letters, coded telegram style), 17 Nov. 1938; BA/K, Goerdeler 9; see also FO 371/21665/C 14809/62/18.

221. Minute by Sir Robert Vansittart, 7 Dec. 1938; FO 371/21659/C 15084/42/18.

222. FO 371/21665/C 15438/62/18; FO 371/22961/C 864/15/18.

223. Goerdeler's message looked to him, so he entered in his diary, 'too much like "Mein Kampf"'; entry of 10 Dec. 1938; *The Diaries of Sir Alexander Cadogan*, 128.

224. Ibid. Also: 'We shall never attempt to take advantage of any troubles arising in Germany. We should be ready to cooperate with, and if desired, assist any German Govt. of whom we could be assured that they desired to live in peace with their neighbours and work for better conditions in Europe'; Minute by Sir Alexander Cadogan, 10 Dec. 1938; FO 371/21665/C 15438/62/18.

225. Ibid.

226. Entry of 10 Dec. 1938, *The Diaries of Sir Alexander Cadogan*, 128.

227. Minute by Sir Alexander Cadogan, 23 Dec. 1938, FO 371/21665/C 15438/62/18.

228. Minute by Sir Orme Sargent, 12 Dec. 1938, FO 371/22961/C 864/15/18.

229. See in this connection Oswald Hauser, 'England und der deutsche Widerstand 1938 im Spiegel britischer Akten', in Heinz Dollinger, Horst Gründer, and Alwin Hauschmidt (eds.) *Weltpolitik, Europagedanke, Regionalismus* (Münster, 1982), 525–7.

230. 'Record of a Conversation which a Representative had with Mr. X. on February 21st, 1939'; Messersmith Papers, 1170.

231. 'Memorandum Recording a Conversation with X. on Thursday March 16th, 1939', Messersmith Papers 1172; see also A. P. Young, *The 'X' Documents*, 173 ff.

232. Letter from Messersmith to Hull, 25 Mar. 1939, Messersmith Papers, 1178; Hull had already received a copy of the document from another source; MacDonald, *The United States, Britain and Appeasement*, 151, 200, n. 61.

233. 'Roosevelt calls for Peace in Europe', *New York Times*, 15 Apr. 1939; 'Roosevelt asks Dictators for 10 Years Peace', ibid., 16 April 1939. The official German response was that the American President had delivered his proposal to the 'wrong address'.

234. This decision was prompted not a little by a mission of Ian Colvin who, upon the urging of Beck and Oster, travelled to London on 29 March in order to brief Cadogan, Halifax, and the Prime Minister on the threat of a German aggression against Poland; Wheeler-Bennett, *The Nemesis of Power*, 437; Gerhard Ritter, quite unnecessarily, makes a point

of minimizing the part played by the German Opposition in the British decision; it stands to reason that, momentous as it was, it was taken on the grounds of more evidence than the one offered by a journalist, however well connected; see Ritter, *Carl Goerdeler*, 223.

235. 'Alle Völker wollen und brauchen Frieden', 23 Mar., 1939; BA/K, Goerdeler 16.
236. 'Pabst' instead of 'Papst'.
237. See also Ritter, *Carl Goerdeler*, 215. Goerdeler—'a very high standing German'—did see at about that time Professor Adolf Keller, a prominent Swiss ecumenical figure, about the same matter, hoping that he would go 'at once' to Rome and transmit the statement to the Pope; but Keller commented that, though he could have access to the Vatican, he found it 'too dangerous and a little bit too naïve to hope that the Pope could start such an action'; 'very confidential' letter from Prof. D. Adolf Keller to the Revd Dr H. S. Leiper (Associate Secretary, Federal Council of Churches, New York), Geneva, 24 Mar. 1939, Messersmith Papers, 1177. On 6 April Leiper forwarded the document to the American Assistant Secretary of State Francis B. Sayre; letter from Henry Smith Leiper to Francis B. Sayre, New York, 6 Apr. 1939, NA, RG 59, CDF 862.00/3842.
238. 'Die nächsten praktischen Schritte'; the dating is uncertain; Michael Krüger-Charlé settles for Jan.–March 1939, Ritter for the spring or summer 1939; most likely late spring, possibly May, is the correct date since at the end of the month during his last visit to England (25–30 May) Goerdeler submitted to his friend in the FO Ashton-Gwatkin a 'Plan for a Peace Partnership in Europe' which contains a number of key passages from the German version; BA/K, Goerdeler 16; Ritter, *Carl Goerdeler* 215, 484 n. 22; FO 371/22973/C 8002/15/18; 371/32008/C 7729, 7769/53/18. Memorandum without heading or date, starting with 'England, Frankreich und Deutschland ...', most likely of the summer of 1939; BA/K, Goerdeler 16; Ritter, *Carl Goerdeler*, 216–18, 484 n. 25. 'Zur Lage Ende Juli 1939', possibly written in Turkey; BA/K, Goerdeler 16; Ritter, *Carl Goerdeler*, 229, 487 n. 54.
239. To judge from the detailed German version of his mid-1939 position, he reiterated his earlier proposal for a union of England, France, and Germany as the 'core of a new European federation' while in his specifics modifying at least the phrasing concerning the thorny issues of the Polish Corridor and Czechoslovakia. The status of the Corridor was to be changed within the framework of a German–Polish compromise ('Dieser Status wird daher so geändert werden, dass die deutschen und polnischen Interessen ausgeglichen werden ...'), and Czechoslovakia with the frontiers of the Munich Settlement was to become a neutral state after the Swiss model and guaranteed by the Powers. Except for an insertion calling for protection by the three Powers of the South Tyroleans against 'tyrannical arbitrariness', the other stipulations are substantially identical with Goerdeler's earlier 'Heads of Agreement'; Goerdeler, 'England, Frankreich und Deutschland ...'.
240. Minute by Ashton-Gwatkin, 30 May 1939, FO 371/22973/C 8004/15/18; according to a memorandum in the Messersmith Collection Goerdeler spent late in April or early in May 'a busy week' in Paris during which he conferred with the French Prime Minister; Messersmith Papers 1188.
241. See the minute by Ivone Kirkpatrick (Central Department; until 1938 First Secretary of the British Embassy in Berlin), 3 Apr. 1939; FO 371/22968/C 4495/15/18.
242. Minute by Sir Robert Vansittart, 27 Mar. 1939, ibid.
243. Gisevius, *To the bitter End* 345; *Trial of the Major War Criminals before the International Military Tribunal, Nuremberg 14 November 1945–1 October 1946* (Nuremberg, 1947), xii. 221–2.
244. See also 'Unterhaltung mit H.B. Gisevius, 16.1.54'; BA/K, Ritter 131.
245. Gisevius, *To the Bitter End*, 348 ff.
246. See Karl-Wolfgang Mirbt, 'Methoden Publizistischen Widerstandes im Dritten Reich nachgewiesen an der "Deutschen Rundschau" Rudolf Pechels', diss. (Free University, Berlin, 1958).
247. (1) 26 Feb.–14 March; (2) 20–5 April; (3) 13–22 May; (4) August; typescript 'Eine der letzten Arbeiten Rudolf Pechels ...' (1961) BA/K, Pechel, II, 120; Heinrich Brüning, *Briefe und Gespräche 1934–1945*, ed. Claire Nix *et al.* (Stuttgart 1974) 245–6, 281.
248. 'Eine der letzten Arbeiten Rudolf Pechels ...'.
249. 'Schwebelage', von Weizsäcker, *Erinnerungen*, 232–3; in the American translation the term is translated as 'a period of uncertainty', *Memoirs*, 188; see in particular Blasius, *Für*

*Grossdeutschland* 92 ff.; Thielenhaus, *Zwischen Anpassung und Widerstand*, 116 ff.

250. 'Ein drohendes Schweigen'; Burckhardt, *Meine Danziger Mission*, 286; Weizsäcker expressed this idea to Burckhardt in an interview in Berlin of 1 June, and Burckhardt in turn conveyed it to Roger M. Makins of the FO Central Department at a meeting in Basle of 11 June; Memorandum by Mr Makins, 12 June 1939, *DBFP* 3/vi. 41 ff. See also Aster, *1939*, 234; Blasius, *Für Grossdeutschland*, 103; Thielenhaus, *Zwischen Anpassung und Widerstand*, 117.

251. FO 371/22973/C 8408/15/18. See Blasius, *Für Grossdeutschland*, 147–8; Thielenhaus, *Zwischen Anpassung und Widerstand*, 120.

252. Erich Kordt, *Nicht aus den Akten*, 310; see Thielenhaus, *Zwischen Anpassung und Widerstand*, 120.

253. Minutes by Sir Robert Vansittart, 20 and 21 June, FO 371/22973/C 8408/15/18.

254. Kordt, *Nicht aus den Akten*, 314; Theo Kordt, Short Autobiography (i), 12, Kordt Papers.

255. Minute by Vansittart, 16 June 1939, FO 371/23009/C 8923/53/18, quoted in Aster, *1939*, 274.

256. For the meeting between the Kordts and Vansittart see Kordt, *Nicht aus den Akten*, 313 ff.; Theo Kordt, Short Autobiography (i), 12–13; Aster, *1939*, 274–5; Colvin, *Vansittart in Office*, 325; Rose, *Vansittart*, 236–7; Thielenhaus, *Zwischen Anpassung und Widerstand*, 122.

257. Secret Memorandum by W. Ridsdale, 16 June 1939, FO 371/22973/C 8924/15/18.

258. Von Schlabrendorff, *The Secret War*, 95–8; Schlabrendorff in Lothar Kettenacker (ed.), *Das 'Andere Deutschland' in Zweiten Weltrieg* (Stuttgart, 1977) 94–5.

259. On the conversation between Count Schwerin and Major Strong of 25 Jan. 1939 see FO 371/22963/C 1291/15/18; on the one of 28 Mar. 1939 see FO 371/22968/C 4819/15/18.

260. FO 371/22963/C 1291/15/18.

261. The report on the January conversation went up to the Foreign Secretary for deliberation at the Cabinet meeting of 1 Feb. and the one on the March conversation was initialled by Lord Halifax on 18 April and by Neville Chamberlain on 23 April.

262. 2nd Meeting, Committee on Foreign Policy, 14 Nov. 1938, PRO, FP(36), CAB 27/624; FO 800/294/C 2/39/13; 22968/C 4495/15/18; 22968/C 4819/15/18. See *Parliamentary Debates*, 5th ser., vol. 346, House of Commons, 6th vol. of Session 1938–9, 26 Apr. 1939 (London, 1939), cols. 1150–3; H. M. D. Parker, *Manpower: A Study of War-Time Policy and Administration* (London, 1957), 55. During the week preceding 26 April Christie had an interview with Rauschning in the course of which the latter also proposed, along with various other tactical measures to impress Nazi Germany, the introduction of national conscription; 'Allgemeine Lage' (handwritten note by Christie), 24/4/39, Christie Papers, CHRS 180/1/29; see also Secret Report Christie to Vansittart, 26 Apr. 1939, Christie Papers, CHRS 180/1/29. In his announcement to his Cabinet of 22 April the Prime Minister referred to the great pressure from France and also the USA on his country to introduce some scheme of compulsory military training; MacDonald, *The United States, Britain and Appeasement*, 152.

263. Letter from Count Gerhard von Schwerin to me, Rottach-Egern, 3 Aug. 1974; also interview with Count Gerhard von Schwerin, 29 May 1974.

264. Schwerin had spent the year 1930/1 in the USA on a study trip and had never yet been in England.

265. According to Schwerin there existed a *Führerbefehl* according to which the General Staff was prohibited from disseminating any reports contravening the official Ribbentrop line to the effect that Britain would not get involved in a European conflict; in other words he well knew that he was risking expulsion from the General Staff; letter from Gerhard Graf von Schwerin to Gero von S. Gaevernitz, Rottach am Tegernsee, 30 Oct. 1948, BA/MA,N 524 (Gero von S. Gaevernitz), Bd. 19.

266. David Astor, 'Adam von Trott: A Personal View', in Hedley Bull (ed.), *The Challenge of the Third Reich* (Oxford, 1986), 25.

267. Trott, quite correctly characterizing the German staff officer as 'not a Nazi, although not necessarily an anti-Nazi', urged David Astor to meet him; ibid.

268. Secret 'Interview with Officer of the German General Staff' by Brigadier F. E. Hotblack, WO, 22 June 1939; FO 371/22974/C 9819/15/18.

269. 'The Naval Memoirs of Admiral J. H. Godfrey', v (1939–1942), 17–18; Churchill College.
270. Minute by Mr Jebb, early July 1939, FO 371/22974/C 9818/15/18.
271. Minute by Frank K. Roberts, 14 July, FO 371/22974/C 1819/15/18. *The Times* of 7 July reported on the plan for long-distance training flights of RAF bombers over France; they in fact started on 11 July; 'Spreading the Wings: New Plan for R.A.F. Training', 'Showing the Wings: 100 R.A.F. Bombers over France', *The Times*, 7, 12 July 1939, both p. 14. On 14 July it brought the news that on the previous day the Prime Minister in the House of Commons had announced the mobilization of the Reserve Fleet; 'A Fleet in Being', *The Times*, 14 July 1939, 14.
272. Godfrey, 'The Naval Memoirs', v, 18.
273. Letter from Count von Schwerin to me, 3 Aug. 1974.
274. Actually Winston Churchill had expressed an interest to see Schwerin, but the latter declined since he thought that this would go beyond his authority and be too sensational.
275. Interview with Count von Schwerin, 29 May 1974.
276. Sir Robert Vansittart to the Secretary of State, 27 Mar. 1939; 'My dear Friend', 22 Mar. 1939; FO 371/22968/C 4495/15/18.
277. This term was, as is well known, actually used by Geoffrey Dawson, the editor of *The Times* when he censured the dispatches of Norman Ebbutt, his paper's Berlin chief correspondent who was critical of the Nazis; letter from Geoffrey Dawson to H. G. Daniels (Geneva), 23 May 1937; *The Times* Archive, Geoffrey Dawson Papers.
278. See letter from Halifax to Phipps, 1 Nov. 1938: 'Henceforward we must count with German predominance in Central Europe. Incidentally I have always felt that once Germany recovered her normal strength, this predominance was inevitable for obvious geographical and economic reasons'; Phipps Papers 1/21, No.57; Churchill College; see also Wendt, *Apppeasement 1938*.
279. See Malone, 'Adam von Trott', diss., 29, 70 nn. 109–13.
280. It might be recorded here that in the course of his American trip Trott befriended among others Roger Baldwin, co-founder of the American Civil Liberties Union, Edward C. Carter, Secretary-General of the Institute of Pacific Relations, Colonel William J. Donovan, the later head of the United States Secret Service (OSS) and Felix Morley, the editor of the *Washington Post*.
281. See Trott's paper 'Ostasiatische Möglichkeiten' (July 1938; the English version: 'Far Eastern Possibilities', Sept. 1938) in which he proposed a peace plan for the Far East in which British and German interests, threatened by Japanese expansion and Russian inroads into China, could be safeguarded by Anglo-German co-operation involving the recognition of the Chiang Kai-shek government as well as by support of legitimate Japanese economic and political interests; the English version is reproduced in Malone, 'Adam von Trott', diss., 586–602; see also 522–8; *idem, Adam von Trott*, 202 ff. A work of a novice in international relations and especially in the field of Far Eastern affairs, it betrays nevertheless an impressive coherence of view and a broad political vision; particularly astute was the recognition of the central part which the Far East played in British policy planning. One motive certainly emerges in the paper, central to all Trott's thinking on foreign policy, namely the firm resolve to build a world order on the basis of Anglo-German understanding.
282. See David Astor's reference to a letter by Trott to him—which has unfortunately not survived—from China in which he revealed this resolve; David Astor, 'Why the Revolt against Hitler Was Ignored', *Encounter*, 32 (June 1969), 7.
283. See Klemens von Klemperer (ed.), *A Noble Combat: The Letters of Shiela Grant Duff and Adam von Trott zu Solz 1932–1939* (Oxford, 1988); the correspondence with Diana Hubback (1932–42) has been deposited in the Library of Balliol College, Oxford. Trott's letters to Diana Hubback have been incorporated into Diana Hopkinson, 'Aus Adams Briefen', typescript, 1946, Julie Braun-Vogelstein Collection, Leo Baeck Institute, New York; see also Shiela Grant Duff, *Fünf Jahre bis zum Krieg (1934–1939): Eine Engländerin im Widerstand gegen Hitler* (Munich, 1978), *The Parting of Ways: A Personal Account of the Thirties* (London, 1982); Diana Hopkinson, *The Incense-Tree: An Autobiography* (London, 1968).
284. Letter from Adam von Trott to Shiela Grant Duff, Peking, undated but most likely 8 Aug. 1938, von Klemperer (ed.), *A Noble Combat*, 323.

285. Letter from Adam von Trott to Shiela Grant Duff, Berlin, 5 Feb. 1937, ibid. 209.
286. The pertinent passages of the letter read as follows: 'The attempt to couple the venture with a general overhaul and readjustment of the inner gears of the machine was frustrated by your clever Neville [Trott, then, identified with the "Chamberlain saved Hitler" explanation for the failure of the plot] and the only alternative is another "venture" or an overhauling in the garage in which many chaps only disguised as mechanics would have to be squeezed out of the door ... At present the door is shut, the engine stinks and puffs the evillest poisons, suffocating all the more sensitive lungs while everybody gets more and more uneasy. Although some will still not believe that the gas is poisonous, all seem to agree that something must happen soon ...'; letter from Adam von Trott to Shiela Grant Duff, 30 Dec. 1938, ibid. 347.
287. He most likely was informed by his friend Count Albrecht von Bernstorff; furthermore he was in close contact with Schacht; see Malone, *Adam von Trott*, 297 n. 3. and letter from Adam von Trott to Shiela Grant Duff, 30 Dec. 1938.
288. Clarita von Trott, 'Adam von Trott', 160; Diana Hopkinson, 'Aus Adams Briefen', 134.
289. See letter from Adam von Trott to Lord Lothian, Peking, 4 Dec. 1937; Rhodes Trust; see also letters from Adam von Trott to Eleonore von Trott, Peking, 15 June 1938, Berlin, 13 Mar. 1939, Trott Archive, Briefe von Adam an seine Eltern. Interview with the Hon. David Astor, 2 Apr. 1974.
290. Letter from David Astor to Heinrich von Trott, 29 June 1956; Trott Archive, Über Adam; Henry O. Malone, 'Between England and Germany: Adam von Trott's Contacts to the British', 20; paper delivered at the Anglo-German Conference on the German Resistance and GB in Leeds, England, 6–9 May 1986.
291. See Albrecht von Kessel's reading of Trott's position after his return from China: 'Apart from a basic rejection of National Socialism, his political views were not altogether in agreement with ours; he thought that the Anglo-German gulf could be bridged once again by negotiations without the overthrow of our regime—perhaps his assessment of England was more correct than ours was at that time; however he certainly was mistaken in connection with the possibility of swaying the Nazis with rational arguments'; von Kessel, 'Verborgene Saat', 139.
292. See Clarita von Trott, 'Adam von Trott', 162–3; Sykes, *Troubled Loyalty*, 232 ff.; Peter Bielenberg, 'Critique of Sykes', Trott Archive.
293. Peter Bielenberg, a native of Hamburg, and his English-born wife Christabel were intimate friends of Trott's. They had planned to emigrate to Ireland, but Trott persuaded them to stay, arguing that opponents of the regime should remain in Germany in order to work there for their cause. Peter Bielenberg subsequently obtained a position in the Reich Ministry of Economics; see Christabel Bielenberg, *The Past is Myself* (London, 1970).
294. *DGFP* D/vi. 674–85.
295. Bielenberg, 'Critique of Sykes', 6, Trott Archive.
296. *DGFP* D/vi. 674–6.
297. Ibid. 677.
298. See Bielenberg, 'Critique of Sykes', 6, Trott Archive.
299. *DGFP* D/vi. 679.
300. William Douglas-Home, *Half-Term Report: An Autobiography* (London, 1954), 113.
301. Sykes's conjecture that the 'new appeasement plan' was 'presumably drawn up by Weizsäcker' (Sykes, *Troubled Loyalty*, 237) has been recently challenged by Marion Thielenhaus who considered Weizsäcker's authorship 'almost impossible'; Thielenhaus, *Zwischen Anpassung und Widerstand*, 127. Blasius, by not dealing at all with the Trott visit to England, implicitly denies the connection with the Auswärtiges Amt.
302. 'Mitte Oktober 1939 [Ein Rückblick über 1938 und 1939]', in *Die Weizsäcker-Papiere*, 173, 175.
303. Thielenhaus goes as far as to concede this possibility; Thielenhaus, *Zwischen Anpassung und Widerstand*, 127. Here the reader might also be reminded of the fact that even from the Czech perspective Trott's proposal could not have been as shocking as it was made out to be by the Czechoslovak political emigration (see esp. the fiercely negative reaction of the Czechoslovak publicist Hubert Ripka who was a close friend of Shiela Grant Duff; Sykes, *Troubled Loyalty*, 252–3). Since the mid-1930s the Prague Foreign Office had consistently

striven to disconnect the Czechoslovak question from the Polish one to the point of even casting doubts concerning the viability of the Polish Corridor, and when late in 1936 Albrecht Haushofer, with Ribbentrop's authorization, initiated negotiations in Prague towards a German–Czech non-aggression pact, Eduard Beneš proposed the inclusion into the system of Yugoslavia and Romania but not Poland; see F. Gregory Campbell, *Confrontation in Central Europe: Weimar Germany and Czechoslovakia* (Chicago, 1975), 145; Piotr S. Wandycz, *France and Her Eastern Allies 1919–1925: French–Czechoslovak–Polish Relations from the Paris Peace Conference to Locarno* (Minneapolis, 1962), 337; Gerhard L. Weinberg, 'Secret Hitler–Beneš Negotiations in 1936–37', *Journal of Central European Affairs*, 19 (Jan. 1960), 366–74; Piotr S. Wandycz, 'The Foreign Policy of Eduard Beneš, 1918–1938', in Victor S. Mamatey and Radomír Luža, *A History of the Czechoslovak Republic 1918–1948* (Princeton, NJ, 1973), 232. It should furthermore be pointed out here that John Foster Dulles in a Confidential Memorandum of 1942 on a visit to England (28 June–25 July 1942) upon the invitation of the Archbishop of Canterbury reported that Beneš favoured a cutting-down of Poland's pre-war frontiers so as not to incur German and Russian hostility; also a restoration of Poland's 1939 frontiers could turn out to be too much of a liability for Czechoslovakia; it certainly would 'over-balance' Czechoslovakia in a Polish–Czechoslovak federation; 'Confidential Memorandum Prepared by John Foster Dulles and Walter W. van Kirk on their Recent Visit to England', WCC ipof, XIII (Section I of the Memorandum on foreign policy was prepared by Dulles).

304. See Sykes, *Troubled Loyalty*, 251. Winston Churchill was apprised of Trott's proposal through Hubert Ripka who was outraged by Trott's 'obscure political goals' (ibid. 253). Churchill, less agitated than Ripka, thought that they would come to naught anyway (ibid. 254.)

305. Letter from Adam von Trott to Eleonore von Trott, Berlin W.15, Sonnabend, [10] Juni 39, Trott Archive, Briefe an die Mutter.

306. Still at that time Trott entertained expectations, widespread also among conservative Resistance people as well as in British official circles, that Göring would emerge as a force of moderation within the Nazi establishment; see Stefan Martens, 'Hermann Göring: Der "Zweite Mann" im Dritten Reich?', in *Francia: Forschungen zur Westeuropäischen Geschichte* (Sigmaringen, 1985), 488.

307. See Clarita von Trott, 'Adam von Trott', 170–1.

308. *Documents on International Affairs 1939–1946*, ed. Arnold J. Toynbee (London, 1951), i (Mar.–Sept. 1939), 297–304.

309. Ibid. 297–8.

310. Ibid. 298.

311. Ibid. 301.

312. Ibid. 303.

313. Clarita von Trott, 'Adam von Trott', 166–7.

314. From the notes made by a British businessman after an interview with Schwerin and forwarded to Lord Halifax on 7 July 1939 by Viscount Trenchard; FO 800/316.

315. Interviews with Sir Isaiah Berlin (29 Apr. 1974), Sir Stuart Hampshire (10 Apr. 1974), Christopher Hill (8 Nov. 1977), Sir Con O'Neill (12 Apr. 1974). See also C. M. Bowra, *Memories 1898–1939* (Cambridge, Mass., 1966), 305–6; A. L. Rowse, *All Souls and Appeasement: A Contribution to Contemporary History* (London, 1961), 91 ff.

316. See interview with Sir Con O'Neill.

317. The term 'Cliveden Set' was coined by the British radical publicist Claud Cockburn who in his journal *Week* (17 Nov. 1937) thus labelled the circle around the Astor family, including men such as Lords Halifax and Lothian, Geoffrey Dawson (editor of *The Times*) and J. L. Garvin (editor of the *Observer*); see Claud Cockburn, *A Discord of Trumpets* (New York, 1956), 258 ff.; Martin Gilbert and Richard Gott, *The Appeasers* (London, 1963), *passim*

318. See esp. Rowse, *All Souls*, 94; also interviews with Sir Isaiah Berlin, Sir Stuart Hampshire.

319. Letter from Adam von Trott to Shiela Grant Duff, Shanghai, 6 Oct. 1938; von Klemperer (ed.), *A Noble Combat*, 330.

320. (William Richard) Stephen King-Hall, from 1966 Baron, edited since 1936 the *King-*

Hall *News-Letter Service* (later *National News-Letter*), a weekly of liberal internationalist outlook.

321. Actually Trott had not read the *News-Letter* itself but the elaborate and indignant rejoinder by Nazi Propaganda Minister Dr Goebbels in the *Völkischer Beobachter* of 14 July.
322. Copy of letter from Adam von Trott to David Astor, 15 July 1939, BA/K, Rothfels 28, Bd.7a; see also Sykes, *Troubled Loyalty*, 272–3.
323. Letter from Adam von Trott to Lord Lothian, Shanghai, 11 Oct. 1938; Rhodes Trust.
324. Letter from Adam von Trott to Shiela Grant Duff, Canton, China, 31 Aug. 1937; von Klemperer (ed.), *A Noble Combat*, 270.
325. See esp. David Astor's report to Lord Halifax of 9 July 1939 on a talk he had in Berlin with Trott and some of his friends; FO 800/316.
326. See Aster, *1939*, 243 ff.
327. FO 800/316.
328. David Astor, 'The Man who plotted against Hitler', *New York Review* (28 Apr. 1983), 19.
329. FO 800/316.
330. Bowra, *Memories*, 306.
331. Strictly Secret Memorandum by Ernst von Weizsäcker, 30 May 1939 in Raymond James Sontag and James Stuart Beddie, *Nazi–Soviet Relations 1939–1941* (New York, 1948), 14.
332. He made a statement to this effect to Axel von dem Bussche at the occasion of a meeting of the two men in 1941 or 1942; information from Freiherr Axel von dem Bussche-Streithorst, 24 June 1981.
333. Von Herwarth, *Against two Evils*, 152.
334. Ibid. 166. Later, when finally it became quite clear to Schulenburg that the German attack upon Russia had been decided upon by the Führer, he embarked upon a policy of what has been called 'diplomatic resistance'; G. Grafenco, *Préliminaires de la Guerre à l'Est: De l'accord de Moscou (21 août 1939) aux hostilités en Russie (22 juin 1941)* (Fribourg, 1944), 39, quoted in Ingeborg Fleischhauer, *Der Widerstand gegen den Russlandfeldzug: Beiträge zum Widerstand 1933–1945* (Berlin, 1987), 15. Much in the manner in which State Secretary von Weizsäcker had warned the British before the outbreak of the war in 1939, he, together with his commercial attaché Gustav Hilger, now conducted a policy of advising the Russians of the impending danger and urging them to take measures that would stem the tide. But not even at this eleventh hour were the two Germans, 'knowingly and deliberately incurring the greatest danger for the purpose of making a last effort to save the peace', listened to by their Russian counterparts; Gustav Hilger and Alfred G. Meyer, *The Incompatible Allies: A Memoir-History of German–Soviet Relations 1918–1941* (New York, 1953), 330–1; also Fleischhauer, *Der Widerstand*, 20. After the German invasion of Russia in June 1941 Schulenburg moved into the orbit of the conspiracy against Hitler, and he made himself fully available to it in mid-1943. Because of his connection with the plot of 20 July 1944 he was ousted from the Nazi Party, which he had joined in 1934, and executed.
335. See von Herwarth, *Against two Evils*, 140 ff. Herwarth's American partner was Charles Eustis Bohlen (later, from 1953–7, US Ambassador to Moscow); for the latter's encounters with 'Johnny' see Charles E. Bohlen, *Witness to History 1929–1969* (New York, 1973), 69 ff.
336. Admiral Canaris also went independently into action. He informed the Italian Military Attaché in Berlin of Hitler's plans for an attack on Poland in the hopes of an interference on the part of Mussolini; Herwarth, *Against Two Evils*, 159.
337. Memorandum by Adam von Trott, 'Inner Political Situation in Germany Today', 2, written for David Astor, 24 Aug. 1939, Astor Papers. This memorandum was sent to David Astor through a friend in the British Embassy; see also Sykes, *Troubled Loyalty*, 284.
338. Letter from Adam von Trott to Clarita von Trott, 24 Aug. 1939; Trott Archive.
339. Memorandum by Trott, 'Inner Political Situation', 1.
340. Entry of 11 Oct. 1939, *Die Hassell-Tagebücher*, 126.
341. On 6 May the British Foreign Office had received a message from 'an emissary of Dr. Goerdeler' about 'a new and unexpected offer from the Soviet Union which might entirely change the situation'; *DBFP* 3/v. 433.
342. Captain Franz Liedig, 'Die Bedeutung des russisch-finnischen Zusammenstosses für die gegenwärtige Lage Deutschlands' (Dec. 1939), in Helmuth Groscurth, *Tagebücher eines*

*Abwehroffiziers 1938–1940*, ed. Helmut Krausnick and Harold C. Deutsch (Stuttgart, 1970), 513; see also the memorandum of another Abwehr officer, Dr Franz Etscheit, 'Die innere und äussere Lage' (1 Jan. 1940), ibid. 514–18.

343. *Die Hassell-Tagebücher*, 126; see also Etscheit memorandum in Groscurth, *Tagebücher*, 517.

344. All the more puzzling is the note therefore struck by Alfred Duff Cooper, Britain's First Lord of the Admiralty until his resignation in 1938, in protest over the Munich Agreement, who, arriving in New York on 22 Oct. for a lecture tour in the USA, commented on the embitterment on the part of German 'conservative elements' over the alliance with Soviet Russia and predicted with considerable assurance the coming of a 'conservative revolution' in Germany; *New York Times*, 23 Oct. 1939.

345. See also Graml, 'Die aussenpolitischen Vorstellungen', in Schmitthenner and Buchheim (eds.), *Der deutsche Widerstand*, 34 ff.

346. Ritter, *Carl Goerdeler*, 231, 489 n. 57.

347. Sutton-Pratt, in turn, forwarded the gist of the interview by means of a King's messenger to Ashton-Gwatkin; FO 371/22981/C 12789/15/18 (by mistake the file is headed 'Dr. Schairer'; but it was clearly Dr Goerdeler who talked to the Military Attaché; see the annotation on fo. 236 in Ashton-Gwatkin's handwriting: 'Just received from Col. Sutton-Pratt, Military Attaché in Stockholm who saw Dr. Goerdeler there yesterday').

348. Ibid.

349. See *Die Hassell-Tagebücher*, 116 ff.; *Die Weizsäcker-Papiere*, 162–3; Aster, *1939*, 339 ff.; Thielenhaus, *Zwischen Anpassung und Widerstand*, 142 ff.

350. See Johan Birger Essen Dahlerus, *The Last Attempt* (London, 1948); Walther Hofer, *Die Entfesselung des zweiten Weltkrieges* (Frankfurt/M, 1964), 336 ff.; Martens, *Hermann Göring*, 174 ff.

351. *DGFP* D/vii. 447 ff.; *DBFP* 3/vii. 459 ff.; see also Hofer, *Entfesselung*, 345, 368 ff.

352. See esp. *Nazi Conspiracy and Aggression*, U S Government Printing Office (Washington, DC, 1946), vii. 752–4; *Trial of the Major War Criminals before the International Military Tribunal, Nuremberg 14 November 1945–1 October 1946* (Nuremberg, 1947, 1949), xxvi. 338–44, 523–4; ibid. (1949), xli. 16–25; also Louis P. Lochner, *What About Germany?* (New York, 1942), 1–6; for a critical analysis of the various transcriptions of the Führer's speech which actually was delivered in two instalments, one in the morning and the other in the afternoon, see Winfried Baumgart, 'Zur Ansprache Hitlers vor den Führern der Wehrmacht am 22. August 1939: Eine quellenkritische Untersuchung', *VfZ*, 16 (Apr. 1968), 120–49.

353. Lochner, *What About Germany?*, 1 ff.

354. Letter from Louis P. Lochner to Lt.-Col. John Learmont, MBE, Lebanon, Pa., 16 July 1949, Louis P. Lochner Papers, Correspondence, British Embassy. Maass, who worked particularly closely with the Socialist Resistance leader Wilhelm Leuschner, was executed after the failed plot of 20 July 1944.

355. Ibid.; Baumgart, 'Zur Ansprache Hitlers', 139–40. Actually Maass, who discovered that the name of the 'reporting officer' appeared in one place of the manuscript, quickly cut it out lest he put Lochner into an embarrassing position in case of a possible Gestapo inquisition. The question whether in the chain of transmission of the document there was another link—possibly Oster—cannot be ascertained.

356. Letter from Louis P. Lochner to Lt.-Col. John Learmont, MBE, Lebanon, Pa., 24 July 1949, Louis P. Lochner Papers, Correspondence, British Embassy; Testimony of Mr Lochner taken at Berlin, Germany on 25 July 1945 by Colonel John H. Amen IGD, NA RG 238, Lochner, *What About Germany?*, 4–5.

357. *Foreign Relations of the United States: Diplomatic Papers* (*FRUS*) (1939), i. 379, 384–5.

358. Letter from Sir George Ogilvie-Forbes to Mr Kirkpatrick, Berlin, 25 Aug. 1939, *DBFP*, 3/vii. 257–60, 316–17.

359. All too cryptically Lochner even revealed that his 'informant' not only gave him 'the zero hour' for the outbreak of the Second World War, but also the exact day and minute for the attack on Crete and subsequently the invasion of Russia; Lochner, *What About Germany?*, 1.

360. Theo Kordt, 'Offener Brief an den Sehr Ehrenwerten Robert Gilbert Baron Vansittart', mimeograph, n.d., Kordt Papers.

361. Theo Kordt, Short Autobiography (i), 15 (ii), 14, Kordt Papers; *Nicht aus den Akten*, 338. The verse is from the Odes of Horace, bk. III, Ode 3, 'The Apotheosis of Romulus'. Although the only evidence for this episode comes from Theo Kordt himself, there is no reason to doubt its veracity. Vansittart's later categorical affidavit to the effect that the Kordt brothers 'served Hitler and Ribbentrop until the Nazi tyranny was clearly beaten' and took no part whatsoever in resisting the Nazi regime is in obvious conflict with the historical record and must be explained in terms of the part which he took on compulsively during the war as Britain's chief German-hater; Affidavit by Lord Vansittart, 12 Aug. 1948 for the Nuremberg Trial, Kordt Papers. See also Erich Kosthorst, *Die deutsche Opposition gegen Hitler zwischen Polen- und Frankreichfeldzug* (2nd. edn., Bonn, 1955), 73; Aaron Goldman, 'Germans and Nazis: The Controversy Over "Vansittartism" in Britain during the Second World War', *Journal of Contemporary History*, 14 (Jan. 1979), 155–91. By contrast to Vansittart, Lord Halifax attested in Nuremberg to the effect that Theo Kordt, in giving information to Vansittart had taken 'very great risk' and in so doing 'gave very practical evidence of his active opposition to the criminal policy of Hitler'; Lord Halifax, Affidavit, 9 Aug. 1947, Kordt Papers; see also Kosthorst, *Die deutsche Opposition*, 73–4.
362. Kordt Papers.
363. 'Personal' letter from R. A. Butler to Theo Kordt, London, 4 Sept. 1939, ibid.
364. For the confusions of British intelligence over the German–Russian negotiations see Aster, *1939*, 317 ff. and David Dilks, 'Appeasement and "Intelligence"', in David Dilks, *Retreat from Power: Studies in Britain's Foreign Policy of the Twentieth Century* (London, 1981), i. 162–4. For the problems involved in the Anglo-French negotiations with the Russians see the late Lord Strang, 'The Moscow Negotiations, 1939', in ibid. 170–86.

# 3

## 'Make a Revolution in Germany for the German People'?

### 1. Fighting the Germans or the Nazis?

The outbreak of the war did not discourage the *Widerstand*; nor did it close the books on its traffic with the British. On the contrary, as the Twilight War with all its uncertainties unfolded, it raised expectations on the part of both the British and the Resistance that some mutual understanding and arrangement was after all within the realms of possibility. In fact, the Twilight War constituted a high point for resistance foreign policy; it precipitated on both sides a flurry of feelers and activities, official and unofficial.

The British Prime Minister, however cautiously, set the tone for his government's policy to reach out to the 'other Germany' by stressing in his address to the House of Commons of 1 September the distinction between the German people with whom, he elaborated, the British had 'no quarrel',[1] and the Nazi government. He was echoed by the speakers for the Labour Party and the Liberals[2] as well as by the Foreign Secretary in the House of Lords.[3] Indeed, on the day following the British Declaration of War against Germany, the Prime Minister in his broadcast appealed directly to the German people:

In this war we are not fighting against you, the German people, for whom we have no bitter feelings, but against a tyrannous and forsworn regime which has betrayed not only its own people but the whole of Western civilisation and all that you and we hold dear.[4]

It was partly in implementation of this policy that the government refrained from an official statement of war or peace aims. While it insisted that more than a removal of Hitler and his entourage was called for to prevent the re-emergence of German militarist and expansionist ideas, it discouraged any suggestion that it intended the dismemberment of Germany and the disruption of its unity.[5] Undoubtedly this position was meant, in part at least, to serve as a signal to the German Opposition.[6] Both Neville Chamberlain and Lord Halifax kept setting their sights on an internal disruption within Germany.[7] 'Every means', Sir Alexander Cadogan urged the Foreign Secretary, had to be tried for 'helping G[ermany] to beat herself'.[8] As late as

February 1940 Halifax confided to his chief how he hankered after a German revolution.[9]

## 2. The Conspiracy Reactivated

As for the German opposition, it regrouped in the autumn of 1939. Catapulted into action by the Führer's manifest determination to proceed with an attack in the west, General Halder once again took the initiative by directing Colonel Oster to revive and bring up to date the plans for the coup of the late summer of 1938.[10] For once the military and civilian sectors of the Opposition were ready to co-ordinate their efforts, despite the fact that army headquarters had recently been moved from Berlin to Zossen, eighteen miles to the south of the capital, thus adding to complications of communication. But the zest and determination of a number of younger men made up for this. Besides Oster, Major (since 1 October Lieutenant Colonel) Helmuth Groscurth, a sworn foe of Nazism and a man with unusual verve, was this time the moving spirit. A General Staff officer, he was delegated by Admiral Canaris to be the liaison between the Abwehr and the Supreme Command of the Army (OKH). In Hasso von Etzdorf he found a counterpart who was appointed by Weizsäcker, by agreement with Halder, to the position of liaison between the Auswärtiges Amt and the OKH. Groscurth and Etzdorf developed an easy working relationship, and they in turn established ties with General Beck and Goerdeler as well as with the Foreign Office opposition group.[11] The contact between Weizsäcker and Canaris was kept up by Freiherr Bernd-Otto von der Heyden-Rynsch, head of the specially created Referat Pol IM in the Auswärtiges Amt and his trusted lieutenant Gottfried von Nostitz.[12] Also a particularly active member of this network was Hans von Dohnanyi, Bonhoeffer's brother-in-law, who, after a tour of duty with the Supreme Court in Leipzig, had been conscripted in August 1939 to serve under Oster in the Abwehr with the particular assignment of enlisting a wider circle of personalities including the Generals for the Resistance. Impatient with the Generals' continuous hesitations, Dohnanyi sought to goad them into action by pointing out to them that by their prescription 'they would have to wait for Hitler as Supreme Commander himself to give the command for his removal'.[13]

The critical element in the setting-up of the reconstructed conspiracy was indeed the Army High Command, and while it was certainly informed about the preparations for a coup, the question was to what extent it was ready to lend its hand and to get actively involved. In the upper echelons of the OKH the opposition to Hitler's war plans was virtually unanimous. But there were the tortuous questions involving the soldier's oath which they had sworn to the Führer and concern lest the Allies might take advantage of an internal upheaval in Germany to stage an offensive of their own. While still in office during the Fritsch–Blomberg crisis, Beck himself, pushed into action by his then Quartermaster-General Halder, had responded that revolution and mutiny were words not to be found in a German officer's dictionary. But now that Beck was out of office and Halder had succeeded him as Chief of Staff, it was Beck who did the pushing and Halder who was cautious. The latter now carried the burden of having to prepare an army for war. Could he and should he at the same time lend his hand to the opposition venture that would, of necessity, jeopardize the same war effort? The question which the OKH group had to face up to was how far it could block Hitler's policy by means of professional persuasion, or whether it had to yield to the group of conspiratorial activists and join in the preparation of a coup.

An 'intensive discussion' took place between von Brauchitsch and Halder on 14 October over these very issues in the course of which they weighed the three specific options open to them: 'attack [against the enemy, as desired by Hitler], wait [for an attack by the enemy], fundamental changes [undoubtedly a coup]'.[14] The latter course, envisaging a coup, was brought into the discussion by Halder who felt committed to explore its possibilities, even though such a step constituted for him a last resort. Brauchitsch, however, did not go along with him. The need, then, for the 'active general' which Popitz voiced about that time to von Hassell[15] had clearly not been resolved. And the more the Führer harassed his generals, as he did Brauchitsch on 5 November, with tirades against the defeatist 'spirit of Zossen',[16] the more he left them intimidated and dispirited.

## 3. 'The Imminent Disaster'

With the objective of convincing the senior generals of the calamitous consequences of the Führer's designs, Etzdorf, together with Erich Kordt, composed a memorandum entitled 'The Imminent Disaster'.[17] Sounding a call for the overthrow of Hitler and his regime, the authors set out to remove all possible objections to such a course on the part of the Generals, including the crucial issue of the oath. The 'relative unpopularity' of the venture among the population, and indeed in the army, was to be met by a necessary measure of 'civil courage' that in the long run was to be rewarded. Such a bold move, they argued, was to pave the way for a 'peace with honour' which, backed up by an 'intact army', would guarantee to the Reich its ethnographic borders roughly conforming to the Munich Agreement. It would include an overland passage to East Prussia as well as the incorporation of the Upper Silesian industrial district.

It can be safely assumed that the memorandum, carefully designed in content and form to satisfy those to whom it was addressed, namely the Commander-in-Chief of the Army, the Chief of Staff and other high-ranking officers,[18] expressed the consensus among the conservative Resistance circles concerning a settlement that would ensure, as the phrasing went, Germany's 'decisive influence' in what was left of Czechoslovakia and Poland. Once again it was not the foreign-policy objectives of Hitler that were called into question, but his resort to aggression. All too caustically did Sir Lewis Namier, one of the harshest critics of the Kordt brothers' resistance stance, comment that these 'good Germans' thus revealed themselves as 'Hitler's profiteers'.[19] We must be aware of the fact that at this time the peace aims of the British government were still not really at variance with those of the *Widerstand*. To be sure, the discussions on that crucial matter were just beginning at 10 Downing Street as well as between the British and French governments.[20] Pushed by the Quai d'Orsay, the British acknowledged that the combined effort should aim at the prevention of 'the re-emergence of German militarist and expansionist ideas', but they nevertheless persisted in drawing a distinction between the German government and the German people. Late in December 1939, as a matter of fact, His Majesty's Government, in the hopes that 'a German Government can be found which is willing and able voluntarily to accept their [the British and French] terms', justified its having been 'careful not to define in precise terms' what it implied by the restoration of independence to Poland and Czecho-Slovakia (*sic*), and to limit itself to referring 'in general terms' to the recovery by the Polish, Czech, and Slovak peoples of their liberties.[21] There was, then, a convergence of ideas between the British and the German Resistance on more than the mere removal of Hitler and Nazism.

## 4. The Vansittart–Theo Kordt Lifeline

Actual contacts between the British Foreign Office and the German opposition were swiftly re-established after the outbreak of the war. The Vansittart–Kordt lifeline once again was activated, now in a climate of both unreality and urgency. The war was on, but the German attack in the west was still to come. Early in October Theo Kordt made contact with his friends in Berlin, in particular Weizsäcker and Oster, for new instructions. Late that same month, 'Philipos', as Conwell-Evans identified himself in a note from London to his German friend,[22] made his first visit to Berne. This was to be followed by at least three others[23] until the last one, scheduled for 12 April, was overtaken by the *fait accompli* of the German invasion of Norway and Denmark three days earlier.

The chief point on the agenda for the talks was indeed what Erich Kordt called a *Stillhaltezusage*[24] namely British assurance of military restraint in case of a German coup. The statement to this effect that Theo Kordt obtained in the course of the October sessions has been subjected to elaborate analysis in the historical literature.[25] Jotted down by Conwell-Evans, the supposed coveted assurance from the Prime Minister was in fact a hasty and not altogether accurate transcription of the latter's address to the House of Commons of 12 October. In this address he had declared that it was no part of the British policy to exclude from her 'rightful place in Europe a Germany which will live in amity and confidence with other nations' and that it was not with vindictive purpose that Britain embarked on war but simply in defence of freedom, desiring 'nothing from the German people which should offend their self-respect'.[26] Together with Conwell-Evans's oral assurances this statement was taken by the German as a 'solemn obligation strictly to be observed towards any trustworthy government which would replace the Nazi regime'.[27] Kordt in turn initiated his British friend into plans for a German coup against Hitler scheduled presumably for November.[28]

Namier's dismissal of the episode in Berne as a 'comedy'[29] is excessively harsh. No doubt Theo Kordt exaggerated the firmness of the British commitment and likewise the authenticity of its source.[30] One certainly must wonder why it should not have occurred to Kordt, a seasoned diplomat, that the 'assurance' obtained was no more than a passage from a warmed-up public address by the Prime Minister. The encounters in Berne, however, must be seen against the background of a policy on the part of the British government which was still stalling on a commitment to an all-out war and which was still supported in this course by British public opinion.[31] It cannot be ascertained that Chamberlain and Halifax, as Theo Kordt asserted, went as far as 'condoning' the Conwell-Evans mission.[32] If Lieutenant Colonel Groscurth identified Halifax as having sent messages to Kordt,[33] this was most likely a conjecture on his part. But it fitted in to their design, and it clearly took place upon instruction from Vansittart. It should be noted that in this instance the British, by means of the Vansittart secret service, pursued alternative channels to reach the other side and that for the first time it was a British emissary who approached a German of the Resistance in order to explore a common path. It was an untrodden one in a hazardous landscape, of course, and the chances that it would lead anywhere were minimal.

## 5. The 'Reichenau Incident'

Distinctly bizarre by comparison, and altogether without tangible consequence, was the so-called 'Reichenau Incident',[34] which is nevertheless worth recounting because of the broader context within which it took place. Colonel General Walter von Reichenau, who was known for his unquestioning loyalty to the Führer, was among those general officers who took the lead late in October and early in November in trying to dissuade him from his determination to stage the attack in the west set for 12 November. The attack, as is well known, was postponed time and again until it was finally launched on 10 May. To be sure, Reichenau resorted to the most unorthodox methods in order to press his point about seeking to establish contact with the British for the purpose of encouraging them and the Dutch to take visible countermeasures that would discourage the German army command from going ahead with its plans.

About that time Reichenau seems to have approached Carl Goerdeler in order to consult with him about the implementation of his scheme. A meeting took place between the two in the home of Fritz Elsas, one of the mayors of Berlin until 1933, and a close associate of Goerdeler.[35] It was Elsas who found the way to expedite Reichenau's message abroad by sending an emissary to an acquaintance in Denmark by the name of Hans Robinsohn.

Before his emigration to Denmark in November 1938, Hans Robinsohn, a German-Jewish businessman, was a leading spirit of one of the few bona fide liberal German Resistance circles which, centred in Hamburg, set out as early as 1924 under the name of 'Klub vom 3.Oktober' to stem the trend of the Republic towards the Right.[36] This group, which comprised some sixty members, persisted in its activities after the Nazi seizure of power in 1933, concentrating, as did the Kreisau Circle in later years, on long-range planning for a post-Hitlerian Germany rather than on immediate subversive action. It built bridges to other centres of resistance such as the Beck–Goerdeler–von Hassell group, the Abwehr and the military Opposition, Protestant as well as Catholic circles, and former union leaders. After leaving Germany, Robinsohn also sought to establish ties with England.

Negotiations which Robinsohn, together with three other members of his German circle, conducted with agents of the Secret Service in London late in May 1939, brought no results. However, in keeping with the chief objectives of the group, he composed a lengthy memorandum during the months preceding the outbreak of the war, 'The German Opposition: Activities and Aims',[37] designed to present the case of the German Resistance to the world. In the task of removing the Hitler dictatorship, the 'German Opposition' had to face up to forming a civilian organization, if necessary without the support of the army, with the aim of establishing law, freedom, and order in Germany and of bringing peace and 'common progress' to Europe.[38] It should be noted that this is one of the few documents emanating from the German Resistance to call for Franco-German political as well as economic co-operation as a prime condition for European stabilization.[39] For the moment, however, the 'European mission' of the Opposition was to consist of alerting world opinion to the Nazi menace.[40] Robinsohn's memorandum, alas, never reached its intended destination, but it deserves nevertheless to be remembered as a striking document of constructive planning and political sanity.

When the message from Reichenau came, Robinsohn was ready to go into action. As for General von Reichenau himself, like most of the military *fronde*, he folded up in the face of the Führer's insistent tirades against the defeatist 'Spirit of Zossen' and came to 'wobble ... tempted by the prospect of easy success against France and England' and to see the need after all, as he took pains to explain to Goerdeler, of 'going through with it'.[41] But Reichenau's message reached its destination.[42] It was on the very day of the 'Venlo Incident', which will be discussed in the following paragraphs, that Robinsohn was informed by a British agent in Copenhagen that his information had been forwarded to London.[43] For his part Robinsohn could at least derive satisfaction from the fact that he had lived up to the resolve spelled out in his memorandum to fit the émigré group into the frame of the Opposition at home, thus making it serve as an 'auxiliary force in the struggle for the liberation of Germany from the Hitler dictatorship'.[44]

## 6. The Venlo Incident

The operations of the German Resistance, it should be interjected here, were seriously hampered by two incidents which took place in close succession in the early November days of 1939. One was the unsuccessful assassination attempt on Hitler's life by Johann Georg Elser in the Munich Bürgerbräukeller on 8 November. Though Elser, a carpenter with Communist affiliations, was a solitary resister, the Nazis insisted upon attributing the deed to the British Secret Service and to Otto Strasser. In any case, the event put the Nazis on guard against any possible recurrences, and indeed it was instrumental in preventing the performance of Kordt's part of the 'deal' with Conwell-Evans, namely the coup against the Führer.

In the setting of stepped-up preparations for the German attack against Belgium, Holland, and Luxembourg, scheduled for 12 November, the urgency of a coup became once again apparent to the conspirators. As a matter of fact it was Erich Kordt who, having easy access to Hitler's quarters in the Chancellery, was chosen by Oster to trigger it off, and who, after careful self-examination declared himself ready to perform the task by throwing a bomb at the Führer.[45] After the Bürgerbräu attempt, however, the regulations for the issue of explosives had been tightened up, and not even Oster was in a position to procure what he needed for Kordt.[46] Since Kordt's proposal to attempt assassination by means of a pistol was vetoed by Oster for its 'madness', he was left with pangs of conscience and the cold comfort that the attack in the west had for the moment been postponed to 19 November.

The other incident took place in Venlo, the Dutch border-town on the German frontier on the day following the Munich bombing. The 'Venlo Incident' saw two British Secret Service officers, Major Richard H. Stevens and Captain Sigismund Payne Best stationed in The Hague, in expectation of meeting with representatives of the dissenting German Generals, overwhelmed and spirited across the border into Germany. The SS Security Service (SD), under the direction of Major Walter Schellenberg, the head of its counter-intelligence section, had penetrated the British Secret Intelligence Service (SIS), and thus administered a major blow to it. Hitler himself had ordered the kidnapping[47] since, shaken by the Bürgerbräu attempt at his life, he was convinced of its connection with the British Secret Service. He took a special interest in the interrogations of Stevens and Payne, and they were subsequently kept in German custody until liberated at the end of the war.

There was more to the 'Venlo Incident', however, than a duel between two intelligence services.[48] It has to be understood in the context of intensive efforts, Scandinavian, Dutch, and Belgian as well as Italian, towards a compromise peace,[49] and Whitehall's determination to follow these up. Furthermore there was the hope for a deal with 'even the nebulous German generals'.[50]

Venlo was indeed a chapter of Twilight War diplomacy. Even on the German side, unbeknown to the British, Himmler was involved in exploring peace terms that would avert the threatening all-out war in the west from which, he thought, only Bolshevik Russia would emerge as a beneficiary.[51] But in Venlo the major initiative came from the British; its chief significance lies in its having been, alongside the Conwell-Evans approaches to Theo Kordt, yet another British attempt actively to seek out German dissidents rather than passively awaiting their initiative.[52] The operation was authorized and closely supervised by the Foreign Office.[53] The latter certainly followed up on the spade work done by SIS, and while initially Sir Alexander Cadogan was distrustful of 'C's',[54] that is Admiral Sir Hugh Sinclair's, 'German General friends', suspecting them to be Hitler's agents,[55] he quickly got drawn into the Prime Minister and the Foreign Secretary's determined pursuit of the venture,[56] registering that 'there's *something* going on in Germany'.[57] Before long the War Cabinet became involved, however reluctantly, and even Winston Churchill got 'nobbled' by Halifax.[58] On 7 November the latter, in strict secrecy, initiated the French Ambassador Monsieur Corbin into the negotiations with 'the German military elements'.[59] Above and beyond all doubts concerning the identity of the Germans, Halifax seemed to have managed to convey to the Frenchman 'that something was in the wind'.[60] Unbelievable as this may now read, on 16 November, that is one week after the kidnapping at Venlo, a note composed by Cadogan and approved by the

Secretary of State on 'what might be said to M. Daladier about the "Generals"' ended as follows:

It seems that German representatives crossed the Dutch frontier on November 10th [sic] and met our agent at the frontier. Unfortunately the party appears to have been killed or kidnapped by Germans who came over from the German side of the frontier, but it has been impossible to obtain precise details. It is not certain that the last message summarised above [the need to change the German regime] reached the German side.

The same elements in Germany have however in the last few days contrived to get into touch with us through another channel and the message has now been repeated to them.[61]

Nevertheless, still on 18 November, the Prime Minister took the trouble to sketch out an outline of a reply to go to the Germans.[62] On 22 November, however, a radio message from Berlin made it clear to the British that the Gestapo had taken over the communications with the 'Generals'.

In Venlo the SD staged, without doubt, a major coup. Although for the moment Schellenberg's swift action frustrated Himmler's efforts to send out feelers of his own for a separate peace, it reached one of its major objectives, to find more evidence for subversive activities of 'German reactionary circles'[63] about which they had general though little concrete knowledge.[64] Among these circles Venlo understandably caused concern, and it is not surprising that Admiral Canaris, apprehensive about what had come to light about his own Abwehr men, was kept in the dark by his SD rival Reinhard Heydrich.[65] Still, as of 15 November, Groscurth entered into his diary that Heydrich had not turned over to Canaris the thrice-promised report about Venlo.[66]

## 7. More Negotiations: Group Captain Christie's 'Southern Connection'

After Venlo the cloud of unreality which had hung over all the negotiations between London and the German dissidents thickened. On one hand the commitment of Whitehall to the exploration of openings to the German Resistance was too firm to deter it from this course; neither the Munich Bürgerbräu attempt nor Venlo made an end to further negotiations. These, in fact, intensified. However, there was no question but that in Venlo the SD had administered a major blow to the British Secret Service, and henceforth fears of 'another Venlo'[67] did affect the already precarious exchanges. There was also the question of the multiplicity of German approaches, and the fact that some of the contacts, like the one of Göring's Swedish peace emissary Birger Dahlerus, were of at least a semi-official nature. Even Christie, who rather enjoyed the game of the foxes, had occasion to complain that 'the wires were getting badly crossed' and that the opposition 'seemed to be working in water-tight compartments'; could not 'one clear reliable channel' be established?[68] Finally Vansittart was prompted to confide to the Secretary of State that no one really believed that there was 'even the faintest possibility of these manœuvres leading to any result'. Before long all the experiments, 'whether the will-o'-the-wisp dances in the name of phantom generals or of a fat field-marshal with neutral go-betweens', had to yield to the realization that the war had to be won, and that it could 'only be won by fighting'.[69]

The confusion of signals was not diminished by messages which reached London from none other than General Erwin von Witzleben. In contrast to von Reichenau, Witzleben who, until his forced retirement from active service early in 1942 occupied commanding positions in the army, had been deeply involved since 1938 in the various phases of the conspiracy against Hitler. The intelligence which reached the British[70] concerned the opposition of the German Generals to Hitler's invasion plans and more far-reaching peace proposals,[71] a scheme for the re-establishment of a constitutional monarchy in Germany under Prince Wilhelm of Prussia, the eldest son of the ex-Crown Prince, along with a purge of the Nazi Party of its radical elements, and finally a vision of an alliance, allegedly sanctioned by Göring and Mussolini, to include London, Paris, Rome, and Berlin 'in a common front against Moscow'. To that mirage even a general disarmament scheme, launched by Prince Max von Hohenlohe in an eight-hour session with Christie in mid-November[72] seemed preferable. The intelligence coming from the German Generals, Christie commented,

does reveal what difficulties lie ahead for the best-minded Moderates who want to utilise Goering and the Generals as a transitory means of crashing the Nazi Party. They may find Siegfried an equally awkward problem after persuading him to rid them of Fafner the dragon.[73]

Meanwhile, negotiations proceeded in all directions. The Kordt–Conwell-Evans exchanges continued apace, and Christie set out early in February for a fortnight's scouting expedition to Switzerland in the course of which, occasionally joined by his fellow 'Germanophile', he met up with the all too beguiling and wily Prince Max von Hohenlohe, former Reichskanzler Joseph Wirth, ex-Nazis Fritz Thyssen and Hermann Rauschning, and his 'old friend Kn. [Hans Ritter]'. Christie hoped to disentangle the wires coming from Germany.[74]

The negotiations with Joseph Wirth clearly transcended the fact-finding dimension. They were prompted by an overture on his part to Neville Chamberlain that called for further exploration. On the day before Christmas 1939 Wirth, 'formerly and for many years Chancellor and Minister of the Reich' had addressed a letter to the Prime Minister on behalf of the 'middle class [bürgerlich] opposition' in Germany. In this he urged the Prime Minister to take the opportunity of his forthcoming 'great speech' scheduled for 9 January to state unequivocally 'that England has not been drawn into war in order to break the German people to pieces with the axe of war as though it were a block of wood, but in order to free the people who are the victims of aggression'.[75] While upon advice from the Foreign Office the Prime Minister had not honoured the letter with a direct reply, he had made a point of incorporating Wirth's suggestions into the foreign-policy parts of the speech in question:

We on our side have no ... vindictive desires. (Cheers) To put it about that the Allies desire the annihilation of the German people is a fantastic and malicious invention which can only be put forward for home consumption.

Chamberlain continued to stress, moreover, 'the desire of the Allies for an essentially human, just, Christian settlement'.[76] In fact, then, the Mansion House speech of 9 January was designed to serve in its own way as a reply to Wirth's initiative,[77] and it was expected to be understood as such by the Opposition.

But things did not end there. Indeed in the following weeks a lively exchange developed in Switzerland between Wirth and Vansittart's men, the story of which can only now be properly told.[78] It is as easy to exaggerate its importance in the light of the concrete proposals which actually emanated from the British side, as it is to play it down in the light of the altogether negative outcome. But whatever justified misgivings there were in the Foreign Office about Wirth's reliability and his addiction to drink, he was, as ex-Chancellor, a man of no little consequence. Also he had, as Christie was soon to ascertain, important contacts with German opposition circles. Wirth's chief liaison to them was the former Republican Reichswehr Minister, Otto Gessler,[79] who, in the service of the Abwehr, was able to commute between Germany and Switzerland and thus to act as intermediary between Wirth, General Halder, and the Generals. Wirth furthermore had connections with other Opposition groups including the circle around Robert Bosch whose general manager, Hans Walz, frequently visited Switzerland. Most important of course were Wirth's ties with the Vatican.

Altogether four meetings took place between Christie and Wirth in Switzerland—at whose initiative cannot be clearly resolved.[80] In any event, when Christie first called on the German in Lausanne-Ouchy on 11 February, he stressed that he did so 'purely unofficially'. In particular because Wirth, somewhat to the puzzlement of Christie, was accompanied by a Frenchman by the name of Dr Simon,[81] it was generally agreed to consider the whole conversation 'a mere private talk'. As a matter of fact, this particular encounter served largely explorative purposes, as did the second one of 13 February.[82] Surprisingly, unlike in almost all the previous talks between the British and German emissaries, the question of frontiers was not raised—apart from a

German commitment to 'a new Polish State and a new Czechoslovak State'—but rather the nature of a future Germany. Wirth, however, presuming to speak for 'Halder & Co.', proposed a federalization of the Reich, a reduction of Prussia to its component states, and even the removal of the capital from Berlin. In turn he asked for a verbal message from the Prime Minister that Germany would not be divided up into small states.

Meanwhile 'Kn.' was in a position to convey to Christie a message from Goerdeler repeating his request for assurances on the part of the British government to a post-Hitlerian government and he even, in the name of the military, raising the possibility of a federal Germany. Thereupon Christie entered in his Memorandum: 'I am never too happy when Goerdeler buts in.' The Wirth–Gessler–Halder channel represented for once, by contrast to all the previous ones, a Southern German one, and this may well have been the chief reason why Christie decided to 'refer the matter back to W'.[83]

It was only at this point that the Wirth negotiations turned into what can be termed an affair of state. In the course of the third meeting of 14 February, which took place in Lucerne, Christie prevailed upon Wirth to address a letter, based upon the latest instructions from Berlin, to the Prime Minister via Lord Halifax, to be posted 'probably' in a week's time at the British Legation in Berne. For the moment Christie returned to London to await the course of events.

On 12 March Christie finally reappeared in the company of Conwell-Evans in Lausanne-Ouchy for the last meeting with Wirth, in the course of which they were also joined by 'Kn.'[84] The former German Chancellor had to apologize for not having sent the promised letter to London after all, explaining that he had had to await the arrival of ex-War Minister Gessler, 'the friend of the General Staff', whom he expected on the following day. He also took the opportunity to announce one correction of his position in the previous conversations pertaining to the question of the capital which now, he stated, 'might even remain in Berlin provided Prussia were sufficiently reduced territorially'.[85] Christie in turn presented Wirth with 'the document' which, he told Wirth, had been given to him by Vansittart but had received 'higher' approval.[86]

The Vansittart–Christie–Conwell-Evans network seemed after all to prove its worth.[87] The 'document' included an assurance 'that the British government will not by attacking in the west use to Germany's military disadvantage any passing crisis which may be connected with action taken by the German Opposition' (pt. 1); the readiness on the part of the British government to 'work with a new German government which has its confidence', with the aim of securing a lasting peace and to give Germany the necessary financial aid (pt. 2); the need to co-ordinate 'further assurances' (concerning frontiers?) with the French government (pts. 3, 4). Furthermore, if the German Opposition should wish their action made easier through a 'diversion' by the

Western Powers, the British government would be ready 'within the bounds of possibility' to meet that wish.[88]

The major terms which German emissaries had for months attempted to exact from the British were now granted, and for once Wirth was now presented with a concrete and authoritative British proposal to the conspirators that promised to bring to a positive conclusion that uncertain and tortured relationship between the German Opposition and the British Foreign Office. Meanwhile Gessler had indeed arrived, as heralded, in Switzerland, there to be briefed by Wirth on 'the Premier's generous offer'[89] and to take it back to 'the Generals'.

The two friends discussed the tasks ahead in the light of the message from England.[90] While both were in agreement that the ' "inner evolution" aiming at the removal of the tyrants' would require 'much patience', Wirth saw himself committed to press for the end of April as a deadline for action. He thereupon proceeded to reveal the terms agreed upon in Lausanne 'point by point', underlining, as he later stressed, 'several points' and indicating 'the historical significance of the grave words [Stimme] coming from England'. He concluded with the following admonition:

If in a comparatively short time (naturally not a question of days for an event of world importance) England fails to be convinced that the Generals are taking the initiative to carry out the evolution, the 'fair chance' just offered by England, for which we should thank our destiny, will be shamefully and lightheartedly thrown away. The military must not burden itself with a new historical guilt.

Gessler, we are told, was 'greatly moved' by this communication, and Wirth parted from him convinced 'that he will do his best'. It is all the more puzzling that nothing came of this venture, and that the Wirth connection, like the Kordt connection, broke at the very moment when the omens seemed most auspicious. I shall attempt to address myself to this question in connection with the other ventures yet to be discussed, which were afoot about that time and which involved Ulrich von Hassell and the Abwehr emissary to the Vatican, Josef Müller. But for now some preliminary comments and questions are in order. To start with, it is more than puzzling that Gessler, upon subsequent enquiry from Gerhard Ritter, should have protested ignorance of his part in the Lausanne transactions.[91] Be this as it may, does not Wirth and Gessler's vocabulary alone, that is the reference to an 'inner evolution', suggest a certain half-heartedness and ambivalence towards the regime they were set upon overturning? Furthermore, there is reason to wonder how closely the southern connection, for which Christie for the moment opted, was plugged into the heart of the conspiracy? Gessler had no contact with Goerdeler,[92] and, as far as we know, Wirth did not either; and the relations between Generals Beck and Halder were anything but close.[93] Might it then be inferred that Wirth, in his dealings with the

British, exaggerated his and his friends' place in the conspiracy just as Christie tended to exaggerate his own role on the British side? It may well be that, opting for the southern connection over the *Preussengeist*, Christie renounced access to the innermost centre of the conspiracy. In any case, he had learnt from both Gessler and 'Kn.' that the 'Generals' were marking time, and he therefore had to admit to himself that 'it is difficult to be in any way sanguine as to the effect of the "message" which he [Gessler] has promised to convey to them [the Generals], or of the long conversations which Dr. W. and I had at Lucerne and Lausanne'.[94]

Shortly after his negotiations with the British, Wirth embarked upon what was to be a parallel journey to Paris. Having previously cleared his visit with the French Embassy in Berne, as well as with the Quai d'Orsay, he conferred with a number of French officials including M. Ernest Pezet, Vice-President of the Commission on Foreign Affairs of the Chamber of Deputies, to whom we owe a detailed account of his session with the German ex-Chancellor of 19 April.[95] As in his talks with the Britons, Wirth came in order to exchange information as well as assurances for a future settlement between the Allies and a post-Hitlerian Germany. Not surprisingly the discussion yielded nothing substantially conclusive.[96] What is of particular interest, however, is the mandate with which Wirth claimed to have come. Apart from his emphasis on his close ties with the Vatican, he mentioned the self-exiled German industrialist Fritz Thyssen, 'General' Gessler and the latter's 'protector', Halder. Neither Thyssen nor Gessler can by any stretch of the imagination be counted as having been part of the German Opposition, and Halder was certainly not in the centre of it. Even assuming that Wirth would not have wanted to divulge the names of its moving spirits, he offered not the slightest hint of their existence.[97] Furthermore, the proposition of the Wittelsbach restoration in no way reflected the thinking of the mainstream of the *Widerstand*. All this but reveals the marginality of the Wirth missions to the affairs of the German Resistance. The evidence derived from his session with Pezet merely reinforces the assumption that in his talks with the British, ex-Chancellor Wirth misrepresented his place in the conspiracy and that, in short, the British government wasted its assurances on him.

Finally, one fact should be especially registered here, namely that Wirth's mission to France constituted one of the few instances, along with earlier feelers in Paris on the part of Goerdeler—in August 1937, and March and April 1939—of someone approaching the French in matters pertaining to the German Resistance.

## 8. Ulrich von Hassell on the Wrong Trail in Switzerland

If the story of the negotiations which proceeded concurrently in Switzerland between Ulrich von Hassell and an Englishman, J. Lonsdale Bryans, bears telling, it is more to record the determination on the part of the German Opposition to put their case before the British than the British eagerness to reciprocate.[98] It stands to reason that von Hassell, the former Ambassador to the Quirinal and one of the foremost experts in the Resistance on foreign affairs, should have welcomed an opportunity to impress his position on Germany's place in the European order after Hitler, and moreover to play his part in ascertaining, if not influencing, Allied attitudes towards a coup in Germany.

Just about that time, early in 1940, Ulrich von Hassell, in consultation with Beck, Goerdeler, and Popitz, had drafted an elaborate statement on measures to be taken in the event of a change of regime in Germany.[99] The major parts of the document were concerned with the displacement of the 'unbearable Party rule' by a temporary regency that was to pave the way for a vindication of 'law and justice' as well as 'decency, morality, and true freedom'. But there were also some references to the realm of foreign affairs, Hassell's particular domain, which added up to a sweeping indictment of the adventurous character of Nazi foreign policy since 1938 and its misleading version of *Realpolitik* which was in disregard of 'all principles and agreements'. Hassell was an old-school practitioner of *Realpolitik* in the Bismarckian tradition, and especially in view of the Führer's somnambulism, it was incumbent upon him to recapture the ethos of *Realpolitik*, calling on the other side to join Germany in securing a peace that would respect the territorial integrity of the German Reich and people.[100] Like the many memoranda which Goerdeler addressed to the British, this one was an honest and candid restatement of the Prussian ethos. For better or worse it breathed *Preussengeist*. Its propositions were rational and unsentimental if not chilling. Our question now is how these premises served Hassell in his ventures into the untested terrain of resistance foreign policy.

The right opportunity, so it seemed, presented itself when von Hassell's son-in-law-to-be, a young Italian by the name of Detalmo Pirzio Biroli, who had been initiated into von Hassell's concerns, struck up an acquaintance late in 1939 with an Englishman, J. Lonsdale Bryans. The latter identified himself as a roving diplomat, well connected in Britain and with a special entrée to Lord Halifax,[101] and he declared himself more than willing to play the part of establishing the desired connection between the German Opposition and the British Foreign Office.

Lonsdale Bryans had certain features in common with Christie and Conwell-Evans. All three were Germanophile adventurers who through good fortune landed on the right side in Britain's struggle with Nazism. But somehow Vansittart's rigour drew his men into performing essential functions in wartime Britain, albeit at one remove from the mainstream of things. Undoubtedly they had fun doing what they did; but they did it responsibly. Lonsdale Bryans, though, never came down to earth; whatever cause he adopted, such as the double danger of Nazism and Bolshevism, became an obsession with him. Certainly the professionals in foreign affairs, like Sir Alexander Cadogan, saw him as a lightweight and a busybody and thus eyed him with deep suspicion.

Lonsdale Bryans, however, possessed the talent of establishing a certain rapport with Halifax and of drawing him out. Thus what started out as an 'altogether private' venture, assumed the nature of a 'government-sponsored' mission before it folded up in disgrace and the 'official ostracism' of Lonsdale Bryans.[102] He first formally called on Halifax on 8 January 1940 with a Hassell-inspired message from Pirzio Biroli which was to open a dialogue with the British. Halifax allowed himself to say, however cautiously, that, speaking only for himself, he 'personally' would be against the Allies taking advantage of a revolution in Germany to attack the Siegfried Line 'if the revolution looked like being a genuine affair and producing a different regime in Germany, in which it might be possible to place some confidence in honest dealing'.[103] He also bestowed upon Lonsdale Bryans the benefit of 'full diplomatic facilities'[104] and furthermore facilitated his return flight to Rome[105] to make from there the necessary preparations for a meeting with von Hassell. Of course Halifax made it plain to Lonsdale Bryans that his, Halifax's, name 'must be kept completely out of any public notice' and that, if it should ever come to public notice, he would 'deny having said anything' except that he had listened and expressed the view that the Allies could not be satisfied with any patched-up peace.[106] Furthermore, the Ambassador to Rome was to be informed that Lonsdale Bryans had 'not, of course, been sent on any kind of mission by him'.[107]

In the course of the meetings which took place between 'Charles'[108] and 'Mr X'[109] on 22 and 23 February in Arosa—Hassell could not very well visit Rome without having to call on Mussolini—they agreed that Hassell should send a statement to Lord Halifax on the conditions for peace that would be acceptable to the Generals. This in turn would constitute the basis for a British assurance not to exploit in any way a change of regime in Germany and to be ready to enter into peace negotiations with a new German government.

The statement,[110] accompanied by a signed cover note, started with the resolve to make an end to 'this mad war' which threatened the complete destruction of and, in particular, the bolshevization of Europe. Europe indeed was not a mere 'chessboard of political or military action'; it had 'la valeur d'une patrie' which was to be assured permanent pacification and protection against a revival of warlike tendencies. Among the specific territorial conditions which would ensure the recovery of Europe, Hassell listed the confirmation of the union of Austria with the Reich; the continued union of the Sudetenland with the Reich was to be consistent with the re-establishment of an independent 'Czech' Republic, just as a settlement of the German-Polish border, 'more or less' identical with the German frontier of 1914, was to go with the re-establishment of an independent Poland; Germany's frontiers in the west were to remain intact.[111] This settlement was to be informed by some general guide-lines such as the principle of nationality—'with certain modifications deriving from history'—a general reduction of armaments, economic co-operation, and above all Christian ethics, justice, and law as fundamental elements of public life, social welfare, effective control of executive power of the state by the people, 'adapted to the special character of every nation', and, finally, liberty of thought, conscience, and intellectual activity.

In his oral comments to Lonsdale Bryans, von Hassell emphasized that such a settlement could only be effective before major military operations had taken place. While assuring Lonsdale Bryans that a statement from Halifax would get to the right people, he declined to give any of their names and cautioned emphatically against non-German sources demanding a change of regime in Germany: 'this must be an exclusively German affair.'

While von Hassell's claim upon Austria and the Sudetenland was not likely to cause great shock in 10 Downing Street, the proposition for the re-establishment of a 'Czech' Republic, implying an endorsement of the dismemberment of Czechoslovakia, was not likely to be welcomed in London. As for the stipulation about Poland, von Hassell's demand for the frontiers of 1914 clearly amounted to a rather generous 'modification', to say the least, of the principle of nationality. In this respect he went beyond the terms of the Etzdorf-Kordt memorandum of October 1939. Also, the Allies had after all gone to war over Poland and could hardly be expected to make concessions in that area. But if Europe had for von Hassell and his friends 'la valeur d'une patrie', the Reich was one of its chief columns and it was to function moreover as the hegemonial power in Central and East Central Europe.[112]

London's reaction to the strange mix of Lonsdale Bryans's amateurism and von Hassell's *Realpolitik* was understandably negative. Cadogan, to whom Lonsdale Bryans turned over von Hassell's statement, while officially thanking him for his services, must have been hard put to disguise his irritation and boredom. In his diary for Wednesday, 28 February he made the following entry: 'Lonsdale Bryans, with his ridiculous stale story of a German opposition ready to overthrow Hitler, if we guarantee we will not "take advantage". Let him talk, and then broke it to him that this was about the 100th time I had heard this story … I couldn't get him out of my room …'[113] In mid-March Halifax, Vansittart, and Cadogan finally 'settled to put

[the] kybosh on him',[114] and that is what Cadogan had to do on the following day.

Cadogan, however, enabled Lonsdale Bryans to return once again to Switzerland in order to wind up matters there;[115] in other words, he closed the books on this particular action. Lonsdale Bryans called on von Hassell in mid-April, again in Arosa, without the hoped-for official British assurance. But in the post-mortem between 'Charles' and 'Mr X' there seemed to be one ray of hope: Lonsdale Bryans was 'given permission'[116] in London[117] to explain to von Hassell that the official British assurance could not be offered because it had already been given 'through another channel just a week before'.[118] Von Hassell, while not completely sure what this was all about, assumed that it concerned 'a serious action' known to him, which might well have been the Wirth–Gessler action;[119] in this case he could only heartily welcome Lonsdale Bryans's information as 'a kind of confirmation'.[120] But for Hassell's expressed hope that London still wished 'to arrive at a decent peace with a *national*, but not emigrant, Germany, which would employ other political methods than those used by the present regime'[121] there was little justification.

Thus ended von Hassell's escapade into active resistance foreign policy. Not only did it lack co-ordination with the other ventures of the same kind, but Hassell, the seasoned exponent of *Realpolitik*, had allowed himself to be coupled with a British partner of most questionable credentials who enjoyed virtually no backing at home. In any case, a mere change of 'political methods' would not have satisfied Whitehall. The German invasion of Denmark and Norway, moreover, had taken place on 9 April, leaving the British in no mood to compromise or to negotiate.

## 9. Agreement within Reach: The Vatican Exchanges

The most high-powered contacts between the German Opposition and the British, proceeding more or less simultaneously with the negotiations discussed earlier in this chapter, were the 'Vatican Exchanges'. This time the initiative came from the German military Opposition. In its determination to prevent the offensive in the west by means of a coup and to obtain the necessary assurances from the other side that would prevent it from taking advantage militarily of the temporary turmoil in the Reich, the Opposition chose to approach the Vatican to play the part of intermediary with the British. It was the indefatigable Oster who, acting upon Beck's instructions, enlisted the Munich lawyer Dr Josef Müller for this task. At about the same time Oster also enlisted Dietrich Bonhoeffer into the service of the Abwehr, his objective in both cases being to activate the relations with both Churches, thus drawing them into the orbit of political resistance.[122]

Captain Best, who towards the end of the war found himself sharing Nazi captivity with Müller, with perhaps some exaggeration, called him 'next to Cardinal Faulhaber, probably the most influential representative of Roman Catholicism in Germany'.[123] This heavy-footed person with sparkling sky-blue eyes, who had popularly become known as the 'Ochsensepp',[124] was undoubtedly an important personage in Bavaria, and he knew it. He was a close associate of Heinrich Held, the last Bavarian Prime Minister of the Weimar era, and indeed enjoyed close ties with Cardinal Faulhaber. Oster's choice fell on Müller, however, because of his special relations with the Supreme Pontiff and with the Vatican. Müller had known Eugenio Pacelli, later Pius XII, since the latter's years as Papal Nuncio in Munich between 1917 and 1920. He had also performed a number of special missions when Pacelli became Cardinal Secretary of State in the 1930s.[125] Furthermore he was on intimate terms with two key figures at the Vatican, Monsignor Ludwig Kaas, the former Chairman of the German Centre Party, who, in his Roman exile was assigned the care of St Peter's Cathedral and who, of course, was well informed about German affairs. Also he knew Father Robert Leiber, SJ of the Università Gregoriana in Rome who, in the personal service of the Pope, had his full confidence and ready access to him. Müller's connections with the Pope and the Vatican appeared all the more important to the German conspirators in view of the fact that the truth about the conditions in Germany could not be expected to penetrate to Rome through the channel of Nuncio Cesare Orsenigo in Berlin who was known for his latent sympathies with the Nazi regime.

Müller's initiation into the plot took place at Abwehr headquarters at the Tirpitzufer where he was received by Oster and Dohnanyi. Canaris, with whom he had the original appointment, was not present; but Oster left no doubt in Müller's mind that he acted upon General Beck's orders. Beck, who was well acquainted with Pacelli since the latter's tenure as Nuncio in Berlin in the 1920s, was convinced that, the Pope, if anybody, who had such close ties to Germany, would be the best agent to impress upon the Western Powers the existence of the German Opposition and its objectives. Moreover, as Oster put it succinctly to Müller: 'His wish is our command.'[126] Müller was subsequently assigned as first lieutenant to the Munich branch of the Abwehr with the supposed assignment of monitoring the political developments in Italy.

Müller instantly accepted the challenge and late in September 1939 embarked upon his first trip to the Eternal City taking up quarters at the Hotel Flora. This confirmed Catholic now proceeded at the instigation 'exclusively of Protestants',[127] to sound out the Pope as to his willingness to play a part as intermediary in an unprecedented venture that was altogether risky for the Church. The Pontiff's readiness to go along with this can be reckoned, as the historian Harold C. Deutsch rightly stressed, 'among the most astounding events in the modern history of the papacy'.[128]

Because of their unusual sensitivity these 'Vatican Exchanges' were fraught with as many difficulties for the actors then as they are now for the historians. To begin with, utmost secrecy had to be maintained in order to protect all three parties involved. If only for this reason no 'negotiations', in the strict sense of the term, took place between the Pope and Müller and between the Pope and the British once the latter had consented to enter into the exchanges. During the war, as a matter of fact, Müller never saw Pius XII in person. Instead, an intricate but tenuous chain of communications was established that extended all the way from Berlin via the Vatican to London. After generally obtaining his instructions in Berlin from Oster and Dohnanyi, Müller would travel to Rome[129] where he would see primarily Prelate Kaas and Pater Leiber. Early on in the 'negotiations' Kaas imparted to Müller the Holy Father's wish that Leiber was to serve as the main liaison between the two, namely that, as the Pope expressed himself, 'Pater Leiber should be our common mouth'.[130] Thus Müller would meet with this modest, self-effacing, and utterly discreet Jesuit in the protective grounds of the Gregoriana where they were immune from the ever-watchful eyes of the Nazi Secret Service. From Leiber in turn the agenda would be turned over to the Pope who would convey them to the British Minister to the Holy See, Francis d'Arcy Osborne, for forwarding to the Foreign Office in London. All agenda were transacted mostly in the form of oral questions and answers which were eventually to form the basis for negotiations.

For the historian the sensitivity of these 'Vatican Exchanges' has produced a formidable problem of evaluation and interpretation.[131] To begin with, most of the communications between the Pope and Leiber and in their turn between Leiber and Müller were oral. Occasionally they exchanged written notes, but these were usually destroyed as a matter of precaution.[132] After the event, that is after Müller's return late in February or early in March from one of his trips to Rome which, he thought, had marked a decisive breakthrough in the understanding with the British, Dohnanyi set about composing, on the basis of information and various annotations obtained from Müller, an elaborate summary report which he hurriedly dictated to his wife Christine. Designed to serve as an account of Müller's missions, and at the same time to stir the Generals into action, it has gone down in the annals of the German Resistance as the 'X-Report' since it consistently substituted for Müller's name the code 'Mr X'. Disregarding the repeated urgings of Pater Leiber and Müller to destroy the Report after use, Dohnanyi, conscious of its historical importance, deposited it in the safe in Zossen. This safe, however, was raided by the Gestapo on 22 September 1944, and thus the 'X-Report' fell into the hands of the Nazis. Subsequently it was lost, presumably burned in 1945 along with other Gestapo files. For Müller, the discovery by the Gestapo of the 'X-Report' along with the two documents mentioned earlier, meant elaborate interrogations in a concentration camp. For the historian the loss of this crucial document has meant a great deal of uncertainty as to what exactly its contents were and what exactly was transacted in Rome. Also, all of Müller's papers relating to the Vatican Exchanges, including his reports to the Abwehr in Berlin, were destroyed by his secretary in the days after his arrest on 5 April 1943.[133] As for the British document-ation, it was for a long time thought to have been destroyed, so an unproved story went, at the Pope's request in June 1940 when a German invasion of the British Isles seemed imminent. As a matter of fact, the relevant Foreign Office Papers have surfaced, and they therefore afford us the most reliable guidance for the reconstruction of the Rome negotiations.[134]

There is no question about the readiness with which the British entered into the Vatican Exchanges and the importance which they, that is the Prime Minister and the Foreign Secretary more than the civil servants in the Foreign Office, attributed to the role of the Pope as mediator. The Germans made no attempt to approach the French. The general understanding, however, was that the British would keep the French government informed.[135] This was done rather sparingly. In Rome both French embassies were kept in the dark, although Osborne was a close friend of the French Ambassador to the Holy See, F. Charles-Roux.[136] It was Halifax's resolve to take no steps in the matter 'except in conjunction with France',[137] but this in fact meant talking on behalf of the French and keeping them minimally informed rather than letting them enter into the exchanges.[138]

First and foremost, the Rome talks were *Friedensgespräche*, that is to say they were designed to bring about peace before the fury of war could be unleashed by a major German attack in the west. But no less central to the talks was the installation in Germany of what was understood to be a *verhandlungsfähige Regierung*, namely 'a government with which it is possible to negotiate',[139] by means of a coup against the Nazi regime. These constituted the *conditio sine qua non*, as Dohnanyi's widow later summarized,[140] stipulated by the Pope for his entering into the act of mediation.

As for the more specific terms which were transacted between the Germans, the Pope, and the British, one thing can be said with certainty: no definite agreement was reached on anything, and it is not really possible to talk about the exchanges having come to any 'result'. They were preliminary and no more than tentative. After all, negotiations about concrete issues were only to be taken up later with a new German government. This does not mean, however, that there was not a general understanding or even a 'gentleman's agreement'[141] which emerged in the course of the intricate mutual soundings. Thus, with all the caution necessary in view of the delicate documentation, it can be assumed that there was agreement that the territorial integrity of the German Reich as of 1937 was to be respected.[142] In retrospect certainly

Müller made a point of emphasizing that there was agreement between General Beck and himself to the effect that Germany was to abandon the *Faustpfandtheorie* favoured by a large segment in the military opposition, according to which it would have held on as a matter of security to the territories annexed since 1938. [143] This was to yield to a policy of restraint and magnanimity and eventually to a 'European solution' within which adjustments of frontiers could be effected by means of plebiscites.[144] In keeping with the latter provision, the understanding included the continued existence of the 'Reich *plus* Austria' with the condition that the Austrians should decide for themselves freely whether or not they were to maintain the union with Germany.[145] The principle of self-determination at this point did play a modest role in the Vatican talks. As for the question of Czechoslovakia, the assumption was that the Munich Agreement would after all be respected. This was in effect Müller's position; and, if his later recollection served him right, also that of the Pope.[146] The British themselves made allowance for the 1937 frontiers to be stretched to exclude only 'non-German Czechoslovakia',[147] and as in the past the Foreign Office was still ready, as Sir Orme Sargent noted, to 'slur over the fate of the Sudetenland'.[148] About the 'restoration of Poland', so it seems, nothing specific was mentioned on either side.[149]

Among the other eight or nine points which, Müller thought he remembered, featured in the agenda for the peace talks [150] there were also personnel questions. We are assured by Müller that Göring's name was never specifically mentioned; a political future for him was never introduced more than 'inferentially' in the Vatican transactions.[151] Schacht, however, was mentioned as a candidate for the position of Minister of Economics and Finance, and Ulrich von Hassell for the position of Foreign Minister. In the case of Hassell, though, the British seemed to have balked, since in Whitehall he was—wrongly—identified as a protagonist of the Berlin–Rome Axis. The inclusion of Brüning in a new German government also came under consideration. All in all, however, these personnel questions played no more than a secondary part in the transactions. Müller in particular was sceptical at making up a cabinet roster at this point: the person who was needed at this time was the assassin.[152].

On one count Müller evidently did not get full satisfaction in the course of his Rome talks, namely the question of an assurance that the Western Powers on their part would not stage an offensive during disorders in Germany precipitated by a coup. For the German Resistance this had all along, as we have seen, been a crucial item in its dealings with the British; and Müller accordingly seems also to have raised the issue. Indeed, Pater Leiber at one point was said to have assured him that England, in case of an overthrow of Hitler, was prepared to stand *Gewehr bei Fuss*.[153] But beyond this there is no evidence to support the assertion that the British government gave the German military Opposition 'well-founded' encouragement along those lines.[154] There is no indication in the Foreign Office Papers of any concrete assurance given to the emissary of the Generals. It may well be that the French were balking at this proposition, and if this was the case, it might be conjectured that they were more ready to go ahead with it a couple of weeks later when the British were involved with that 'other channel', that is ex-Chancellor Wirth, who was a known quantity in Paris.

All in all, the Roman exchanges yielded an impressive readiness on all sides to come to terms—and this despite the series of events such as the Bürgerbräu attempt on Hitler's life and especially the Venlo affair which might easily have torpedoed the transactions.[155] They were, indeed, interrupted for four to five weeks; and it was eventually the Pope who, vouching for the integrity of the German emissary, managed to re-establish communications between the two parties.[156]

A most vexing and virtually unsolvable problem, however, is the discrepancy between the terms of the Vatican 'gentleman's agreement' as extracted from Müller and Hassell's recollections and from the British documents, and those that are related to us by the recipient of the X-Report, General Halder and by General Thomas who, as we shall see, was delegated by the Opposition to deliver the report to the Chief of Staff. One must wonder what happened to the ill-fated document, undated and unsigned as it was, on the way to its destination? To begin with, it was a tortuous way. Von Hassell was at first designated by the military Opposition to present it to General Halder. At the request of Oster and von Dohnanyi, Gottfried von Nostitz of the opposition group in the Auswärtiges Amt appeared about noon on 16 March at Hassell's. He asked the latter to call on General Beck in the afternoon, which, of course, he did. Before long the two were joined by Oster and Dohnanyi, and it was on this occasion that Hassell was commissioned to be the messenger.[157]

Meanwhile Halder was put under pressure by Goerdeler who, at the behest of General Beck, virtually besieged him, calling on him three times in the period from 17 March and 1 April,[158] urging him to proceed with a coup against the regime. Halder finally wrote Goerdeler a letter in which he firmly outline his own course: 'The German army will do its duty for the Fatherland even against the Hitler government if and when the situation calls for it.'[159] But Halder insisted that only after a serious set-back of the Hitler regime would the situation be ripe for a coup.[160]

For the moment Halder decided to shake off not only Goerdeler but all civilians, and he cancelled an appointment that had been scheduled with Hassell. Instead, General Thomas, having easy access to headquarters in Zossen, was commissioned by the Opposition to forward the X-Report to Halder; and he did so on 4 April.[161] Along with the X-Report he also delivered some related papers, among them a memorandum by von Dohnanyi in which he, together with a small group that included his brother-in-law Dietrich Bonhoeffer, had summarized arguments for decisive action.[162] Thomas himself, however, was not initiated in the intricacies surrounding the undated and unsigned key document. Not being able to explain matters, he encountered understandable distrust concerning the whole affair on the part of the Chief of Staff.

By the time that the X-Report was transmitted by General Thomas to General Halder, its terms (if we are to follow the recollections of Halder) were at considerable variance from the ones that had been (as far as we can ascertain) agreed upon by Müller in Rome. According to Halder, the report, while stipulating the 'removal of Hitler' and 'if possible of the whole NS-regime',[163] called for the restitution to Germany in the west of Alsace-Lorraine and in the east of the borders of 1914.[164]

The discrepancy, then, between the 'gentleman's agreement' as it seems originally to have been spelled out in the X-Report, and the documentation of German hegemonic claims, which Halder—and Thomas—remembered to have been handed over, is inescapable. It is certain that the British would never have gone along with the version of the report as recollected by Halder and Thomas. The *'furor Germanicus* of Hitlerism' which Osborne cited to Lord Halifax[165] would thus have been validated in a slightly changed disguise. Nor would the Pope have been party to such a deal.[166] It is equally doubtful that Müller, from all we know about him, would have identified himself with such outrageous propositions. On the other hand, even accepting the fact that General Halder was disposed to play down the seriousness of the troubling X-Report,[167] it can hardly be assumed that he—and for that matter General Thomas—invented its hegemonic bias.

Since the hard and fast documentary evidence for a resolution of our problem is clearly missing, we shall have to resort to some conjectures which might help narrow the gap between the two versions of the X-Report and which might possibly also account for the existence of both versions of the report. To begin with, there were certain grey areas which may have had the effect of blurring issues. One involved the question of the political dispensation to follow the coup in Germany; what exactly was meant by the stipulation *verhandlungsfähige Regierung*? Did it imply the removal of the Nazi regime, or, as a transitional step, would the replacement of Hitler and his worst lieutenants be acceptable? This latter consideration once again raised the question of Göring. Actually, Halder and Thomas's recollections of the X-Report in this respect were not wholly out of line with Müller's recollections on the matter. Müller's assurance that Göring's name was never specifically mentioned in the Rome talks, and that his political future was never introduced more than inferentially, has to be read in conjunction with Leiber's—and therefore the Pope's—understanding of the meaning of a government capable of negotiating, namely 'any government without

Hitler'.[168] Indeed, in his communication to the Foreign Office in the early stages of the Vatican Exchanges, Osborne reported that, according to Mgr. Kaas, Göring was said to share the 'apprehensions of conservative military circles' concerning the rapid growth of Communism in Germany and to 'accept the idea of secret negotiation for a "fair and honourable peace" over the head of Hitler and Ribbentrop'.[169] Although Göring had by that time lost much of his credit in opposition circles, and especially at the Tirpitzufer, the problem 'with or without Göring', as von Hassell stated it succinctly,[170] at that time still featured among the calculations of the German Opposition as much as it did among the speculations of the British Foreign Office.[171] The proposition of Goebbels as an alternative to Hitler is downright absurd; he was never remotely considered in this connection.

The other grey area was the one for the settlement in Eastern Europe. On territorial questions in general there were undoubtedly two positions even among the conspiratorial Generals: Beck, if we accept Müller's account, seems to have been prepared for Germany to divest itself voluntarily of the occupied territories for the benefit of the 'European solution'; on the other side there were those, undoubtedly in the majority, who were determined to hold on to the German conquests as a matter of security.[172] On the specific question of the 'restoration of Poland', Halder's reading of the X-Report— namely the reduction of Poland to the frontiers of 1914—and Thomas's reading—namely the solution of all Eastern questions 'in favour of Germany'—seems, offhand, to deviate from Müller's reading of the understanding reached through Papal mediation. But it was not wholly out of step with it. According to Müller's own testimony, he and Leiber had agreed on the formula of a 'free hand for negotiations in the east'[173] which, they assumed, was accepted in London. But precisely this formula, indistinct as it was, might well have lent itself to readings favouring more far-reaching German claims in the east.[174] Far removed as these readings undoubtedly were from the original intent of the Vatican Exchanges, they may well have been encouraged by the vagueness of its formulation.[175]

We cannot, however, dismiss the possibility that the document, once it reached General Halder, had gone through a series of revisions. Pointing to the fluidity of the Rome exchanges, Josef Müller actually reminded us that he saw himself in a bargaining situation and that, 'corresponding to the strength of Germany's position', he attempted as time went along to exact more favourable terms for a new German regime.[176] Thus it can be argued that he himself started the stiffening of the terms on the German side. Accordingly, the possibility cannot be dismissed that the X-Report was doctored at the Tirpitzufer, possibly by Oster and Dohnanyi themselves, in the weeks between its original composition and its delivery in order to be more persuasive in Zossen.[177] In any case, the document which Halder thought he saw, or indeed did see, was at considerable variance from the original intent of the X-Report. It is reasonable to conclude, therefore, as Müller does, that everything that exceeded the 'well-considered concessions' of the British was bound to elicit Halder's distrust and so to diminish the effect-iveness of the 'original X-Report'.[178] Assuming the document had been doc-tored to suit the Generals, the effort in this instance boomeranged; it was Halder who saw through the futility of it all.

The reception of the X-Report in Zossen was chilly. Halder promptly put it before his Commander-in-Chief later in the same day that he received it, asking him to study it in order to talk it over the following morning. He found Brauchitsch in a grim mood, however. Brauchitsch swept the 'scrap ['Fetzen'] without date and without signature',[179] as he put it, across his desk and tore charged into Halder:

You should not have put this before me. This amounts to plain betrayal of the country [*Landesverrat*]. For us this is out of the question. We are at war; to establish ties with a foreign power in peacetime may be within the realm of the permissible. During times of war this is impossible for a soldier. Besides, in this case it is not a matter of a war between governments but of a dispute between ideologies [*Welt-anschauungen*]. The removal of Hitler would therefore be of no avail.[180]

Brauchitsch subsequently asked Halder to identify the author of the report and to have him arrested. Halder however, maintaining that 'in view of the catastrophic situation' one might differ on this matter, refused to divulge any name and snapped back at his chief: 'if someone is to be arrested, then please arrest me!'[181] This Brauchitsch did not do. Somehow this encounter had cleared the air between the two men. Neither one, after all, had an interest in bringing the existence of the conspiracy to the attention of the authorities, and both were now resolved to go ahead with their business as warlords.

The Vatican Exchanges had thus brought about an unprecedented degree of understanding between the British authorities and the German conspirators. While the feelers between Theo Kordt and Conwell-Evans broke down pri-marily over the question of the German evacuation of Poland,[182] while the road via Wirth had turned out to be a dead end, and while von Hassell in his encounters with Lonsdale Bryans had clearly stumbled upon a partner who, barely tolerated by the British Foreign Office, was without any weight, the mission of Josef Müller came very close indeed to yielding results which satisfied the basic needs of the German Opposition as well as those of the British, still bent upon striking a peaceful settlement with the 'other Germany'. But it was precisely those other 'similar approaches' which had taken place that had 'vitiated', as the Pope expressed it in an audience with the British Minister, the prospects of favourable developments through the Vatican.[183] The very fact that different opposition groups had entered the fray accounted for the lack of co-ordination as well as of agreement. Fur-thermore, this particular operation, largely because of its elaborate and intricate nature, was bedevilled by all sorts of complications on the German side. Less eager for action than the Zossen–Tirpitzufer activists, the Generals of the OKH evidently demanded a greater price for their participation in the conspiracy; this was the most likely explanation for the X-Report in the version which Halder and Thomas remembered. But the British were of course not apprised of the doctoring of the report, if indeed it happened, or at any rate of the perversion on the German side of the gentleman's agreement.

The postscript to the Vatican talks is important. Once again, late in April, Josef Müller set out for Rome. On 9 April the German war machine had started rolling against Denmark and Norway, and it was clearly only a matter of weeks before the much heralded attack in the west would materialize. Upon instructions from General Beck, Müller conveyed to the Pope through Pater Leiber the 'regret' of his friends in Berlin that the 'negotiations' could not be continued with any prospect of success. Thanking the Pope for what he and the Church had done for the cause of peace, Müller had to concede that the Generals unfortunately were unable to decide upon action against the Nazi regime. He also added that the imminent attack on the Low Countries would involve the violation of their neutrality: 'In the name of the decent Germany we repudiate this breach of neutrality, and we are convinced that the greater part of the German people, if it could decide freely, would condemn this violation of international law.'[184] While admitting failure, Beck at least sought with this message to explain matters to the Pope and moreover to protest the good faith and integrity of the Resistance and thus leave the door open for a resumption of exchanges in the future.[185] As for the impending German military offensive, it was common knowledge in all European capitals. Beck and Müller's imparting this information to the Vatican, however, is a measure of the lengths to which the German Opposition was willing to go: it did not shrink from committing acts that bordered on treason against a regime which did not represent the true interests of their country. The 'Oster Case', which will be discussed shortly, did before long bring this problem fully into focus.[186]

## 10. The von Trott Mission to the United States

Meanwhile, in the latter part of September 1939, Adam von Trott had set out on another of his one-man diplomatic missions, this time to the United States. Once before, in the first half of 1937, he had visited America before embarking on his extended study trip to the Far East. While fully aware of growing pains and tensions marking life in the United States, Trott had emerged from his four months' sweep across the North American continent impressed by its wealth and vitality and 'wide spaces', and speculated that Washington might become a 'focus' [of power?] one day.[187] By the time he returned to the United States in 1939 he was ready to attest to America's 'tremendous authority in helping to decide the character of a future European and world peace'.[188] The outward occasion for this journey across the Atlantic was an invitation to a conference on 'Problems of the Pacific' scheduled for the late autumn of 1939 at Virginia Beach, Virginia organized by the New York-based Institute of Pacific Relations (IPR). The Secretary General of the Institute, Edward C. Carter, had befriended Trott during the latter's earlier American journey and had become impressed by his grasp of Far Eastern affairs.[189] A German participant, so Carter figured, might present to the Conference a new point of view. The outbreak of the war did not daunt this energetic entrepreneur; so he sent a carefully worded cable of invitation to Trott that would pass the scrutiny of even the German authorities.[190]

In contrast to his mission to England of the previous year, Trott's wartime mission to the United States thus could take place with the official backing of the Auswärtiges Amt.[191] What Theo Kordt was meant to do on behalf of Weizsäcker from his new post in Switzerland, Trott was encouraged to do in the New World, namely to explore the possibilities for a peaceful settlement of the Twilight War that would, so Weizsäcker and his lieutenants figured, be a prerequisite for the removal of Hitler and his regime.[192]

In the winter of 1939/40, however, the United States turned out to be no less hazardous ground for Trott than England had been in the months before the outbreak of the war. Though Washington was caught in the quandary of resisting being drawn into the war while at the same time not wanting to be left out of it,[193] a visitor from Germany advocating peace was not exactly welcomed; whatever his ultimate objective, he was suspect. To be sure, during his previous trip to the United States Trott had established important contacts which now could be activated, and furthermore one of his chief British mentors, Lord Lothian, now Britain's Ambassador to the United States, was presumably accessible to him. But would Trott's youthful persuasiveness and aristocratic charm be enough to serve him this time as he was catapulted into a diplomatic mission of almost unprecedented sensitivity? His semi-official status only added to the air of mistrust surrounding him, especially as he chose, even if only 'as a hedge', to maintain a connection with the German Embassy in Washington.[194] On the other hand, his actual assignment as emissary for the Opposition made him all the more vulnerable to the long reach of the Gestapo. He was keenly aware of that fact, and, as he confided to George S. Messersmith of the State Department, he was 'putting his neck into a noose'.[195] Once again Trott was caught in the predicament of having to walk the tightrope between ostensible collaboration and actual resistance. Once again also he found himself up against the challenge of representing abroad a position that, while firmly anti-Nazi, had nevertheless to be reconciled with fundamental German national interests.

As far as we know, Trott left Germany without any specific instructions from either Weizsäcker or his aides as to what and with whom he was to negotiate. Engaged in an explorative mission, he was left to his own devices. Trott threw himself into his task with astonishing self-assurance, resourcefulness, and fearlessness. He was perfectly willing to take risks: 'one should continously impose upon oneself and others tasks to which to begin with one is *not* equal.'[196] Being now too secretive, now too careless and even indiscreet, he doubtless made many mistakes. But he was on an uncharted course, embarking on a chapter of resistance foreign policy with all its anomalies and hazards; he was bound to run into serious obstacles just as he had in the course of his mission to England in the spring of 1939.

For better or worse, the Trott mission was a prime case of co-operation between exile and resistance. The kingpin in this relationship was ex-Chancellor Heinrich Brüning, despite the fact that he tended to keep as much distance from official Washington as he did from the emigration group. Distrustful and resentful of the former and condescending towards the latter, Brüning was also deeply apprehensive about retributive measures on the part of the vigilant Gestapo against any of his German visitors. When it came to matters of German resistance, however, he was ready to overcome his reserve and stand by the resisters. Always ready to support Goerdeler, he was now all too willing to give fatherly advice and guidance to young Trott. There were also the other German members of the 'International Group in New York', among them especially Paul Scheffer, along with Hans Muhle, Kurt Riezler, and Hans Simons, all of whom took a keen interest in Trott's mission. Quite apart from Trott's American cousins—the Schieffelins and Bosanquets—and friends—such as Roger Baldwin and Felix Morley—there were his various friends among the emigrants—namely Julie Braun-Vogelstein,[197] Hasso von Seebach,[198] and Ingrid Warburg,[199] who stood by him, giving him a sense of the familiar in the rough and unfamiliar climate of American urban life.

Clearly, the Conference in Virginia was only a pretext for Trott's political agenda in the United States. The centre of his activities was in the New York-based International Group which included a number of distinguished German professorial and political refugees. Elaborate discussions among them yielded a Memorandum which was to serve as a vehicle with which to approach the American authorities about the objectives and projected needs of post-Hitlerian Germany.

For a long time there has been uncertainty concerning the authorship of the Memorandum.[200] There is no doubt, however, that it was the result of elaborate discussions with Trott among the group of Germans, most of whom were exiles, including Brüning,[201] Scheffer, Riezler, Simons, and Muhle. While

Scheffer was the most likely author of the original draft, Trott was clearly the activating and driving force. Scheffer described him as 'a magnet'.[202] As Scheffer later explained things to the historian Hans Rothfels, the Memorandum goes back to an article which he originally had written for the *Atlantic Monthly*, but whose editor Edward Weeks subsequently got cold feet. When Trott appeared on the scene, Scheffer, once he had sized up his young friend, pulled out the draft again and found him 'in all his vehemence ... wholly captivated by the text',[203] except that he voiced reservations on 'one point'. In any case, the two agreed that for the purpose of obtaining signatures for the document and presenting it in Washington, Trott should pose as its author. As correspondent for a German newspaper, Scheffer was well aware that he was under suspicion as a 'Nazi journalist'. He caricatured himself thus[204] among the exiles and, of course, in official American quarters.[205]

The basic tenets of the Memorandum[206] argued for a 'constructive and fair peace, as a pledged aim of Allied war efforts'. Only a timely clarification of definite war aims along these lines could strengthen the hand of the Opposition in Germany and thus contribute to the downfall of the Nazi regime and at the same time set in motion a machinery for European co-operation. Invoking the tradition of Woodrow Wilson, the framers of the document appealed to the United States to take the lead and redeem the European Continent: 'not being involved in the immediate implications of warfare, America may find herself in a better position than any of the belligerents in the task of defining the fundamentals of a lasting peace.'

The survival of Scheffer's original version of the Memorandum, which he entitled 'A Practical Vision of the Future Peace as an Integral Part of the Present Conduct of War',[207] affords us an insight into the intent behind the document as well as into the difference (or differences) between Scheffer's and Trott's attempts to influence official Washington. The one reservation which Trott voiced at the time related to Scheffer's predicating his arguments for a future peace upon a German defeat. Scheffer, as a matter of fact, thought it opportune for the German group to come out with a clear statement to the effect that a German defeat was preferable to an entrenchment of the Nazi regime, and thus to overcome possible American suspicions about the venture. But he finally deferred to Trott, not without speculating about his lack of political instinct and wisdom.[208] Trott's patriotic idealism, then, carried the day against Scheffer's clever tactical considerations. In any case it is more than doubtful whether either approach would have made any difference in influencing the White House.

There are other notable discrepancies between the two versions of the Memorandum. In the final one a paragraph has been inserted conjuring up the spectre of the German people seeking a union with Soviet Russia if the Western Powers insisted on yet another crushing peace settlement reminiscent of the humiliations of Versailles. This passage was most likely of Trott's making;[209] he was to use this argument time and again in his subsequent communications directed at the Allies. But was it to be at all persuasive?

There was also one passage, in the early version, on a territorial settlement. In the name of an implementation of the Wilsonian message with a 'maximum of precision'[210] it proposed an Allied commitment to Germany and her neighbours' ethnographic integrity involving a recognition of the frontiers of Germany as of December 1938 that would include Danzig, certain parts of the Corridor and Upper Silesia, Sudeten Germany and Austria, 'if her people vote for inclusion in the Reich',[211] as also some form of German participation in the colonial field. In this instance, we must comment, Scheffer's own political instincts abandoned him. At any rate, the final Memorandum called modestly for an assurance of the territorial status of 1933.[212]

The Scheffer–Trott Memorandum, as we should call the document, made the rounds in the capital. To start with, Brüning did his best to pave the way for Trott. He was in close touch with Messersmith whose guest he was in Washington over the weekend of 11/12 November,[213] and he made a point of vouching for Trott as an 'honest man' who 'really represented responsible, potentially powerful, conservative forces in Germany'.[214] The German ex-Chancellor even got as far as President Roosevelt in order to further the cause of his 'young friend'.[215]

It is certain that the Memorandum made its way to the top echelons of the State Department. William T. Stone, the Washington representative of the Foreign Policy Association and an admirer of Adam von Trott, took the document to the Under Secretary of State, Sumner Welles, and to Messersmith. The latter in turn turned over a copy to the Secretary of State, Cordell Hull.[216]

The reception of the Scheffer–Trott Memorandum in the State Department was, according to all evidence, favourable, despite lingering suspicions on the part of Messersmith. The latter, as a matter of fact, had further copies made for distribution to influential persons, encouraging the German visitor to call on the recipients in person.[217] In subsequent weeks, Trott was, on 20 November and 8 December, also given an opportunity to call on Messersmith. In the course of the first visit Trott actually surprised Messersmith with the statement that, 'while the memorandum represented his views on the whole', he had reservations about the appropriateness of the statement of Allied peace terms or conditions at that time. 'This was not an idea', Messersmith noted, 'that he was pressing himself, for the most dangerous thing, he said, which could happen, was a premature settlement which would leave the present Government or something similar to it in power in Germany.' Trott was all the more concerned about this because, he thought, there was still a very powerful group in England which could not be trusted and which might be prepared to make peace 'on terms which would be disastrous all round'.[218]

Trott therefore had partially at least to disown the Memorandum, and he thus displayed, Scheffer's criticism of his style notwithstanding, a good deal of political instinct after all.[219] It is not devoid of irony, then, that at just about that moment Trott's mission should have run into serious trouble.

It is generally maintained that it was Trott's visit to the Justice of the Supreme Court, Felix Frankfurter, that was responsible for his misfortune in the United States. Without doubt, the meeting between the two ended on an unfortunate note. Their earlier encounter on the occasion of Trott's first American visit in 1937 had gone very well, but now something went wrong. It may have been an inconsiderate remark by Trott which angered the judge.[220] The causes for the failure of this meeting, however, went deeper. The wall of distrust against the German peace emissary thickened and indeed linked up with, and reached back to, Trott's ill-fated mission to England in the spring of 1939—indeed to his relations with everything English which had been increasingly put to the test by the animosities and suspicions engendered by the oncoming war. As a matter of fact, the rebuff which Trott had suffered from C. M. Bowra in June 1939 now carried over to the American scene in as much as Bowra, upon hearing that Trott was going to the United States, wrote to influential friends there, including Felix Frankfurter, warning them against him.[221] To his loyal friend in England, David Astor, Trott wrote a long letter from New York defending himself against the 'ill-deserved reputation of an appeaser' who was 'out for another Munich', and he identified 'certain "clever" quarters in Oxford' hanging on to 'Felix and his friends here'.[222] But the wall of distrust against Adam von Trott was thickening mercilessly. When Frankfurter forwarded his suspicions to Messersmith[223] and, so it seems, also to the President,[224] the game was up for Trott in America.

The IPR Conference, then, turned out in fact to be but an epilogue to Trott's mission. The 'German member', as he was tactfully referred to in the proceedings, elaborated elegantly on the thesis that only a peaceful solution in the Far East could guarantee a free China, free also from the domination by the Western democracies.[225]

An epilogue also, and a rather curious one at that, was the close relationship—not to call it friendship—which developed between Trott and John W. Wheeler-Bennett during the days at Virginia Beach. Lord Lothian, with whom Trott had a secret reunion about the middle of October in the Washington Mayflower Hotel, had delegated Wheeler-Bennett, an expert on German affairs, to attend the meetings for the express purpose of monitoring Trott, and there was hardly a meal that the two did not take in common, as well as repeated horseback rides which they took together on the bridle path of the Cavalier Hotel.[226]

The following passages are from the letter dated 26 December 1939 from Trott to his friend in England David Astor:

I have derived considerable comfort and encouragement from one of your god-father's[227] immediate co-operators in the capital, whom you must see at some length when he comes to England this spring. His name is Wheeler-Bennett and he understands, as you will soon discover, one essential side of Germany probably better than anyone in your country at the moment ... he should be very carefully listened to. He has the implicit trust of a number of important people in Germany; though he is obviously as British as he could be. ... He is a close friend of Anderson's[228] ... He will come to you with a special message from me, and if he has not done so otherwise, you should insist on his seeing your uncle Edward[229] ... I have asked WB to send you personally a memorandum (enclosed in this letter) that he has written; we have discussed it here at length and in detail and I would consider it *very important* that it should be taken seriously before it is too late. Perhaps your knowledge of the situation tells you that it is too late already or impossible because of the Latin friends.[230]

This meeting of minds that developed between the German and the Englishman on neutral ground must have been a great boost to Trott's otherwise dampened spirits. Wheeler-Bennett gave Trott new hope after all. When late in 1939 Trott, attempting to 'recover lost ground',[231] prepared a memorandum for Lord Halifax pleading for an understanding 'over the warring frontiers' in the crusade against Nazi oppression that should aim at a peace based on justice and equality, he was undoubtedly advised by Wheeler-Bennett.[232]

The Memorandum by Wheeler-Bennett to which Trott referred in his letter to David Astor constitutes one of the rare records emanating from the British side appealing to the solidarity of interests between the Democratic Powers and their 'ally' within Germany, namely those 'high patriots' engaged in the 'War for the Liberation of the German People'.[233] While hitherto the Prime Minister, and the Foreign Secretary, had only in all-too-general terms attempted to reassure the German people that Great Britain was not fighting against the German people but against 'a tyrannous and forsworn regime', it now behoved the Allies, so Wheeler-Bennett argued, to make an unmistakable public commitment to a 'just and generous treatment' of a 'New Reich' that had thrown off the Nazi yoke.

It seems that Wheeler-Bennett at that time was even considering going to England himself in order to explain the views and aims of the German Opposition to the British government.[234] In any case, trying to secure his flank, he sent with the Memorandum a lengthy covering letter[235] to Sir Robert Vansittart, appealing, as it were, to his earlier role as protector of the German Opposition. But as he pulled out all the stops, indeed too many stops, in his argument on behalf of the Opposition in Germany—including the ills of Versailles, the spectre of the Germans turning eastwards, the eventuality of Britain having to bring pressure to bear on a recalcitrant France—Wheeler-Bennett got nowhere. Vansittart's minutes merely played down the role of the 'so-called German moderates'.[236] After paying due respect to the historian's 'admirable books', Sir Alexander Cadogan vaguely suggested underground channels to explore the possibility of a new regime in Germany, also, however, adding the old refrain: 'But I hope it won't lead us to another Venlo!'[237] And there the matter rested. Wheeler-Bennett himself soon afterwards was to change his tune on the German Resistance. The helping hand that came from him was after all but a mirage for Trott.

The hard fact was that the mission to America, like the one to England of June 1939, was a failure; in fact the two were but different chapters of the same story. The obstacles in the way of Trott's kind of diplomacy turned out to be insuperable, mistakes or no mistakes. A cloud almost of delirium hung over Trott's last weeks in New York. He was, and felt like, a hounded animal. And whether the agents following him were from the FBI or the Gestapo— and those whose records we have were from the former—he sensed that he was in deep trouble if not in mortal danger. His friends in England as well as America implored him not to return home. David Astor even devised the ruse of working on Trott to join a—fictitious—circle of distinguished British public figures to search for an equitable peace settlement. He also got together with one of the leaders of the radical left-wing German Resistance group Neu Beginnen, Karl B. Frank,[238] in an effort to persuade Trott that his usefulness would be much greater outside Germany as a planner for the future than inside Germany as a revolutionary.[239] In December, then, Frank, with at least the sanction of the British authorities, crossed the Atlantic with the express purpose of assuring himself of Trott's political reliability.[240] It is intriguing to speculate on what would have happened if he had struck up any ties with the young German who was clearly one of the most active foreign-policy agents of the conservative resistance; perhaps some sort of co-ordination of foreign feelers and a salutary paring down of objectives might have been effected. But nothing much came out of the encounter between the two. The substantial differences between them turned out to be insuperable, and even if Frank emerged with a positive verdict on Trott and, as Richard Löwenthal claims, 'reported' back accordingly, nothing at this juncture could have vindicated Trott's reputation in Britain.

In any case, Trott was determined to return to his country. 'It is humiliating to be an emigrant—and this I think I least want to be,' he had written in the early days of Nazi rule to his friend Shiela Grant Duff.[241] He never wavered in his conviction that, for better or worse, his place was at home.[242] Besides, he felt committed to those who had enabled him to go on his mission and whose positions, if not lives, would have been endangered by his failure to return. Although he had benefited while in America from the interplay between exile and resistance, he became at the same time aware of the gulf that separated these two conditions. It did not escape the FBI that Trott was in possession of a letter of introduction dated 3 December from his 'colleague' Edward C. Carter to the Russian Ambassador Constantine Oumansky and that three days later the 'subject' was sighted, coming from the Mayflower Hotel, approaching the Russian Embassy in Washington. 'He approached the door and stood in the portico without having knocked or having been approached by a doorman and left immediately and went to the Lee House Hotel located at 15th and L Streets . . .'[243] He got his application in for the Russian visa anyway and finally departed on 12 January aboard the SS *President Cleveland* for Honolulu and Japan to continue his long voyage home via China and Russia. From Hawaii he posted a letter to an English friend, writing that this time he left America 'with a certain sigh of relief', and adding: 'They don't really partake in anyone's troubles.' Approaching the Pacific hemisphere, he had begun to feel a liberation from the 'hopeless superstructures of prejudice and morose hatreds' of the West:

Don't think of me as depressed or desperate whatever happens; I have the least right to grumble on my own account, and as to my surroundings I feel these wider worlds have equipped me with far greater resources of joy, independence and power of resistance than I could have possibly hoped for.[244]

Back in the United States, after the departure of the enigmatic visitor, the President sent the following Memorandum to Felix Frankfurter:

For Heaven's sake! Surely you did not let your Trott friend get trotted out of the country without having him searched by Edgar Hoover. Think of the battleship plans and other secrets he may be carrying back. This is the height of indiscretion and carelessness on your part! FDR.[245]

As in the case of the mission to England in early June 1939, Trott sent a report to Berlin. This one was written in the form of a letter from Tokyo to Walter Hewel who had made the trip possible to begin with.[246] Having read in the Japanese press about the forthcoming European visit of Sumner Welles, Trott took this occasion to brief Hewel on the American Under Secretary of State and subsequently to outline alternatives for the foreign policy of the United States, as he saw them. This document, like the earlier one of the spring of 1939, presents a problem of interpretation for the historian. Once again it was couched in the jargon of Nazi chauvinism, referring to the 'odious and warmongering'[247] wing of the American government, to which President Roosevelt supposedly gave the nod, to the 'alarming stirring up'[248] of the population against Germany, and signing off with the obligatory 'Heil Hitler'. But however apprehensive Trott may have been about the impending Welles mission, he did not use this language in his private conversations, as recorded by the FBI, or correspondence.[249] The jargon was, we can assume, put on for Nazi consumption. The analysis given in this report of the inter-relatedness of Roosevelt's domestic and foreign policies was skilful, as was the account of the President's vacillation between the roles of peacemaker and, *in extremis*, the one man to stand up against the 'imminent disaster'. It was left to Trott also with his Far Eastern interests to spell out the dangers perceived in America of a German–Russian–Japanese combination and a spreading of Russian influence in the Far East.

It is a fair assumption that, while Trott's 1939 report was designed to impress the authorities at home with the British preparedness to fight, he now sought to convince them of Roosevelt's determination, after the Presidential election, to swing his nation towards war. In this respect, also, the Trott mission to England and the one to America were but different chapters of the same story. But it was the country of his great ancestor which was to become the greatest impediment to his and his friends' efforts to get a hearing abroad.


## 11. The Sumner Welles Mission to Europe (February–March 1940)

Adam von Trott, still on his long voyage home, hearing that the American President had decided to dispatch his intimate foreign policy adviser, Under Secretary of State Sumner Welles, on a mission to the major capitals of Europe with the objective of 'advising the President and the Secretary of State as to present conditions in Europe',[250] was not the only one who was puzzled and apprehensive lest behind this cautious statement there were some 'disquieting' ulterior purposes at play.[251] Nourished by the ambiguities of past policies towards the European crisis, both isolationists and interventionists voiced objections, each in their own way. Among the various capitals, London and Paris in particular were distrustful of such 'sensational intervention', as the British Prime Minister called it.[252] In view of the mounting rumours about a major German offensive in the west, was it not reasonable to assume that some plans were afoot in Washington for yet another Munich, this time under American aegis? As for the men of the German Resistance, their concerns were spelled out by Goerdeler: the Welles visit might give the Generals the impression 'that the other side was ready *after all* to negotiate with Hitler and therefore one dared not deprive him of his chance'.[253]

All misgivings about Sumner Welles's forthcoming visit notwithstanding, von Hassell entered the arena and invited the American Chargé, Alexander Kirk, over to his house in order 'to put him on the right track', urging him to have Welles meet other than strictly official personages.[254] As a matter of fact, the only 'unofficial' person to meet the American visitor was, upon the latter's express desire, Hjalmar Schacht.[255]

Of course Welles did have a session with Weizsäcker in the Auswärtiges Amt, the greater part of which took place in the afternoon of 1 March in the centre of the office, at the latter's direction, to evade detection by Gestapo microphones in the walls. But the ever-cautious and correct State Secretary could not let himself go beyond insinuations of deep policy differences between himself and his Foreign Minster, with whom Welles had had a thoroughly unsatisfactory meeting earlier in the day. When, after one hour, the American took his leave he saw that tears had come into the German's eyes.[256]

During his own meeting with Welles, which took place on 3 March in the private house of Kirk, Schacht did not beat about the bush.[257] Some initial remarks concerning his personal predicament of living under dictatorship[258] led to revelations 'in a whisper' on the 'movement' that was under way, headed by leading generals, to supplant the Hitler regime. Reiterating the basic refrain of all his friends of the Opposition on their missions abroad, Schacht stressed that for the successful execution of their plans the Generals depended on 'positive guarantees to Germany' that she would be permitted to regain her 'rightful place in the world' and not be treated as she had been in 1918. He furthermore assured the American that, since military action on either side would impede the plans of the conspirators, they would do their utmost to prevent, or at least delay, the threatening German offensive.

Sumner Welles might have derived the same message from the Scheffer–Trott Memorandum, but somehow he did not put two and two together. However open-ended the objectives of his mission were, he certainly had not been sent over by the President to get involved in what the historians William L. Langer and S. Everett Gleason harshly termed 'an intrigue'.[259] But they were right in pointing out that Schacht, however respected he was all over the world as a financial and economic expert, had an equally widespread reputation for 'being slippery'. In fact, Trott's ill-fortunes during his American mission might well have been, in part at least, caused by the fact that it was known in Washington that Schacht was one of his sponsors. In any case the contacts between the German resisters and Americans remained purely private ones: Trott cherished his friends such as Roger Baldwin and Felix Morley; but that was that. In Berlin the Chargé d'Affaires, Alexander Kirk, kept up regular secret meetings with Helmuth von Moltke, and before leaving the German capital in October 1940 he turned over this contact to the First Secretary of the Embassy, George F. Kennan, for whom the encounters with 'this lonely, struggling man, one of the few genuine Protestant-Christian martyrs of our time', as he later recalled, became a decisive human and political inspiration.[260] Kennan never reported to Washington, however, what he knew about Moltke. Official Washington was in no way prepared to deal with something as intangible as a German Resistance.

In Paris (Welles's next stop after Berlin) Premier Daladier in the course of their two-hour talk on 7 March conceded, so the American reported back home, that, while France and England would insist on a peace which provided for the 'restoration of an independent Poland' and for the 'independence of the Czech people', in his own judgement 'there was every reason why the really German peoples of Central Europe should live under German rule, provided they so desired'. Danzig, Daladier added, was 'clearly a German city' and the Germans of the Sudetenland or of Western Poland 'should be afforded the opportunity of uniting with the Reich if they so desired'.[261] In London, where Welles was exposed to a wide variety of people and opinions, the Prime Minister in the course of the session with him on 13 March called for the evacuation of German-occupied Poland, and of Bohemia and Moravia as 'indispensable' for any negotiations with the Hitler regime. Britain would not, he added, be intransigent with regard to the ultimate frontiers of Poland, nor with regard to the frontiers of a new Czech state. Slovakia was now divorced from 'Czechia', and he saw no reason to change that situation. Danzig and the really German minorities of the old Poland might well be included in the new German Reich. As for Austria, a free and impartial plebiscite should satisfy the canons of self-determination.[262]

These positions taken by Daladier and Chamberlain were, on their face value at least, exceedingly moderate. They were, of course, coupled with proposed stipulations on disarmament which was to begin with Germany, in which case Chamberlain even raised the issue of a formal Anglo-French undertaking to the United States not to attack Germany. Also, he firmly stated that it would be impossible to deal with the existing regime in Germany and that he aimed at 'the restoration of liberty to the German people'.[263] The irony here is that the conditions on territorial settlement, the Allies holding out a prospect of not attacking Germany and of course the refusal to deal with the Nazi regime, did by and large agree with the terms that also emanated from the German conspirators. Even if the territorial aspirations of some of them, like Theo Kordt, von Hassell, and those who, for whatever reasons, 'doctored' the X-Report, went further than those the French and British Prime Ministers outlined to the American Under Secretary, it stands to reason that they would probably have been all too ready to negotiate and compromise, especially since their main concerns were the overthrow of the Hitler regime coupled with the Allied guarantee not to take advantage militarily of a German coup. But this convergence went unnoticed. The German Opposition was not a factor in the discussions which Welles conducted during his European trip. Still wavering between the alternatives of a 'deal with the existing German regime',[264] that is appeasement, and, in extremis, 'not [to] remain indifferent', as Welles expressed himself to von Weizsäcker,[265] the United States diplomacy was totally indifferent to the predicament as well as the political potential of the Opposition in Germany.

## 12. Treason as Patriotic Imperative: Ewald von Kleist-Schmenzin and Hans Oster

All resistance borders on treason. By itself treason is not an honourable deed as it connotes betrayal of trust and, in the public domain, an offence against the interests of one's own country. The context of resistance, however, tends to lend dignity to and thus to redeem treason. Political resistance in itself is an extreme act in an extreme situation in which the citizens are denied recourse to legal procedure or to open political opposition. In such a setting treason becomes an extreme manifestation of resistance.

Although all resistance, therefore, borders on treason, and although treason tends to be redeemed by resistance, their interrelationship nevertheless in all circumstances is marked by tension and ambiguity. This was particularly the case in the German setting during the Nazi regime. To begin with, the German legal distinction between *Hochverrat* and *Landesverrat*, while lending a certain grudging respectability to the former, settles the latter with a singular stigma: it jeopardizes the very integrity of the state. Annelies von Ribbentrop, the Nazi Foreign Minister's widow, was therefore ready to hit hard when, in defence of her husband's policies leading up to the outbreak of the war, she lashed out against 'the permanent *Landesverrat* of the German Resistance Movement against Hitler' that, she argued, could be traced 'step by step' from the year 1938.[266] This argument was a way for her to tarnish, if not to destroy, the reputation of the Resistance. Moreover, in the German case especially the tensions between resistance and treason were accentuated by the fact that during the war resistance was bound to come into conflict with what appeared, conventionally at least, to be the national interest. It had to oppose the war and the triumphs of the German armies as well as, as a last consequence, victory itself. It was, to be sure, not an easy matter for a patriot like Ewald von Kleist-Schmenzin to arrive at the position that, as he put it to Ian Colvin, 'the shortest way to defeat' would be 'the most merciful'.[267] And whether or not Dietrich Bonhoeffer actually said that he prayed for the defeat of his country,[268] he would not have done so light-heartedly. In any case he and his co-conspirators were caught up in a painful conflict between their love of country and their distaste for the Nazi regime, which each individually had to resolve within his own conscience.

There is no doubt that virtually each and every one of the conspirators who in matters of resistance turned to foreign lands for help, was hovering on the threshold of the graver charge of treason. But the 'co-ordination with foreign powers'[269] was, as Hans von Dohnanyi explained, an imperative for a coup lest it lead to civil or foreign war. He thus furnished an extreme moral and political, if not juridical,[270] legitimation of resistance foreign policy. When General Beck played out the text of the Hitler diatribe on the Obersalzberg of 22 August 1939 on the coming war with Poland to Louis P. Lochner for forwarding to the American State Department and, again, when he sent out Josef Müller late in April 1940 to Rome with the message revealing the scheduled attack in the west and the imminent violation of the neutrality of the Low Countries, he was not far from committing *Landesverrat*. But his motive for this most unusual action for a German officer was to prevent a far greater evil. It can be said of Admiral Canaris that he was playing the 'game of the foxes' all along, when, after the invasion of Poland, he whisked Halina Szymańska, wife of the former Polish Military Attaché to Berlin, to Berne with the idea that she should establish contact there with the British Secret Service and convey messages to it, first from Canaris himself and subsequently from his agent in Zurich, Vice-Consul Hans Bernd Gisevius.[271] Canaris and Goerdeler were also the 'friendly contacts' with the Swedish Military Attaché in Berlin, keeping him abreast of German intentions about Sweden throughout the war.[272]

Surveying his chosen course later, however, Goerdeler protested that 'it is not a matter of *Landesverrat*; the country was not to be betrayed but saved. ... It is a matter only of *Hochverrat*.'[273] Theo Kordt's response to the charge of treason was that under a totalitarian regime the dissenter has the choice between inactivity and 'active', that is, 'illegitimate' resistance. Hitler and Ribbentrop were the ones who had committed 'treason against the highest interests of the German people', and Kordt and his friends had established contact with the British government 'not to serve the interests of British policies but to save Germany and the West from a catastrophe'.[274] Virtually all the men engaged in the foreign operations of the *Widerstand* explained themselves in much the same way as Goerdeler and Kordt.

If now we move into a discussion of the 'treason' cases of Ewald von Kleist-Schmenzin and Colonel Oster, it should be understood that they were by no means isolated or exceptional phenomena; they constituted simply the most highly profiled incidences of the frantic efforts of the Resistance to avert the imminent German attack in the west and its consequences for Europe at large and, of course, Germany. Kleist went abroad once again, with Beck and Canaris's backing, late in August 1939, this time to Sweden. In Berlin he had established close ties with the Counsellor at the Swedish Legation, Kurt Herbert Damgren, and now he made the rounds in official quarters in Stockholm, as he had done the year before in London, to warn against the Nazi menace and to call attention to the existence of resistance in Germany.[275] But in January 1940, driven by a sense of urgency, and being unable to leave Germany, Kleist resumed his contacts with the Swedish Legation. Alarmed by what he had learned about the Führer's diatribe before the Wehrmacht commanders of 23 November, overwhelming them with his determination for an attack in the west, Kleist went to inform the Legation about the details of the planned offensive as well as, with some exaggeration, about the misgivings on the part of 'the majority' of the army commanders about its feasibility. While a failure of the German offensive would open the doors to action against the Nazi regime on the part of the top military leaders, they were, Kleist reported, understandably concerned about the Allied response to this situation. He took this occasion to plead for 'neutral mediation' from the Allies and to enquire whether the readiness for such mediation would stand a better chance with a new German regime than with the present one. In any case, Kleist concluded that 'resistance is a patriotic duty'.[276]

Oster who, as we have seen, had been the driving force in all resistance activities since the autumn of 1938 and always conscious of the need to secure foreign understanding, if not support, for the Resistance, undertook one of the most daring feats himself in the months before the German offensive in the west in a frantic effort to deroute it in co-ordination with Germany's neighbours in the west and thus to save the honour of his country. He was consumed by hatred of the Führer, whom he referred to customarily among his close associates in the Abwehr as 'the pig' or simply as 'Emil', especially since the outrageous dismissal in February 1938 of General von Fritsch who earlier had been his Commanding Officer in the Second Artillery Regiment in Schwerin and for whom he harboured feelings of admiration and unquestioning loyalty.[277] Behind a rather unconventional, breezy, and often improvident exterior there was an officer rooted in a firm religious upbringing who cared deeply and became increasingly apprehensive of the Nazi policy against the Churches and the Jews. After the victorious campaign in the east, he became agitated by the atrocities committed by the SS against the Poles and followed with great misgivings the systematic expansion of the role in the Third Reich of Hitler's élite guard.

Early in October 1939 Colonel Oster promised his friend, the Dutch Military Attaché, Major Gijsbertus Jacobus Sas, concerned about the fate of his country in the case of a German attack in the west, that he would look into the matter and 'inform' him once he had learnt about the operational plans against Holland.[278] In so doing, Oster had in fact taken a step that completely violated the traditional code of honour of the German officer and even set him apart from the daring ventures of his various friends in the Resistance. In short, he had set out to commit what, conventionally, seemed to be a clear case of *Landesverrat*.

The close relationship between Oster and Sas goes back to the time of the Olympic Games in Berlin in 1936[279] when Sas first functioned as a Military Attaché. He was recalled to The Hague in 1937 to take up an important post on the Dutch General Staff but was reassigned to Berlin in April 1939 after the German annexation of the rump of Czechoslovakia, since, as he was told by the Commander-in-Chief, his 'connections' made him the only person eligible for this position. Sas's renewed presence in Berlin henceforth enabled Oster to inform him step by step about the German preparations for the offensive in the west. Not only were the Dutch authorities to be, and, in fact were, alerted; the understanding between the two men was that Sas was to transmit the pertinent information to his Belgian friend and colleague, the Military Attaché, Georges Goethals.[280] In fact, the latter was also kept abreast of the German threat to his country by General Alexander von Falkenhausen who, after the German invasion of Belgium, accepted in May 1940 the post of Military Governor of Belgium and Northern France.[281]

First, however, it was the turn of Denmark and Norway to be invaded, and Oster asked Sas, on 3 April, to forward this intelligence not only to the Danes and Norwegians, but 'above all' to the British Intelligence.[282] To make doubly sure that the Allies were alerted, at about the same time Oster went to the length of commissioning Josef Müller to put the Vatican into the picture by telephone.[283]

Of the German preparations for 'Case Yellow', which was the German codeword for the attack in the west, Oster kept Sas informed step by step, and up to the last possible moment the German stayed in touch with his Dutch friend. On the evening of 9 May the two were still together. They went into town for dinner—Sas later referred to it as 'more or less a funeral meal'[284]—and then Oster once more stopped at the Armed Forces head-quarters in the Bendlerstrasse to check on the latest developments while Sas waited outside in the car. After twenty minutes Oster returned saying: 'My dear friend, now it is really all over. ... The pig has gone off to the Western front, now it is definitely over. I hope that we shall meet again after this war ...'.[285] The Dutchman then spent a hectic night engaged in alerting his Belgian colleague and telephoning last-minute coded warnings to The Hague. Early the following morning the German tanks started rolling across those Dutch bridges that had not been blown up.

These three, Kleist, Oster, and Sas, were men who knew their minds and who were resolutely following their consciences against all odds. Sas himself did not have an easy time of it. The Dutch *Enquête*, which was carried out after the war concerning his activities as Military Attaché in Berlin, revealed the wall of disbelief and distrust which he encountered in the Army High Command in his own country.[286] To his Commander-in-Chief, General Reynders, he was a nuisance with his periodical warnings of the German prep-arations; and as the dates for the attack were continuously postponed by the Germans, Sas lost much of his credibility and he came to be dismissed as an alarmist. It must be remembered, however, that Sas was in the end vindicated by the turn of events. He was proved to have done his duty, and the Chairman of the *Enquête*-Commission had reason to state that the case had been 'fully cleared up'.[287]

Our particular concern here, however, should be the evaluation of the deeds of Kleist and Oster—as well as, of course, their friends—over whom, for their persistence in alerting the outside world, the cloud of suspicion continues to hang. It must be reiterated that, in contrast to someone like Sas who clearly acted to save his country, Kleist and Oster opened themselves up to the charge of having risked the defeat of their own country. In Oster's case, the more extreme of the two, even those who were to benefit from his revelations suspected him. The Dutch Commander-in-Chief, Reynders's successor General Winkelmann, thought him to be a 'miserable fellow', while a high official in the Belgian Foreign Office suspected him of being an *agent provocateur*.[288] Even Gerhard Ritter, one of the most engaged historians of the conservative *Widerstand*, felt compelled to ask whether Oster did not 'knowingly' hurt the army when he exposed it to great danger and whether his 'duty to his people and his own comrades' should not have taken precedence over 'any duty to the foreigner?'[289] The basic fact, of course, is that they were confronted by the extreme situation of a criminal regime at home and were therefore entitled, if not obliged, to resort to extreme steps in the name of a higher canon that transcended immediate national interests. It was a matter of an 'order of values', as Hans Rothfels expressed it so well,[290] which prompted both Oster and Kleist to resort to their deeds, deeds which no doubt were born of despair. Their 'intent', certainly, was anything but to harm their country; on the contrary, it was to save their country from tyranny and degradation. 'One might say that I am a traitor' [*Landesverräter*], Oster said to Sas, 'but in reality I am not; I consider myself a better German than all those who run after Hitler. It is my plan and my duty to free Germany, and at the same time the world, of this plague.'[291] Neither Kleist nor Oster can be considered guilty of having committed *Landesverrat* in any way. They may have been engaged in 'high treason' (*Hochverrat*) by endangering the safety of their government; but high treason, it has been said, enjoys the air of being a 'gentleman's delict'.[292]

On the part of both Kleist and Oster, there were also quite realistic considerations at work. While both departed from the assumption that a prevention of the attack in the west would facilitate the preparations for the coup—Oster especially was eager to let the Vatican talks take their course. Late in 1939 when Oster became convinced that the Army High Command and the Commanders of the Army Groups were committed to the offensive rather than the coup, he fell back upon the so-called 'set-back theory', originally identified with General Halder, which meant that it would take a failure of the offensive to stir the Generals into action. The idea was that a swift set-back might bring about a swift coup and prevent not only an expansion of the war and the loss of millions of lives[293] but also the destruction of the Reich.

Gerhard Ritter's verdict on 'Oster's treason' is harsh: he called it 'superfluous'.[294] Ritter might, by inference, have said the same about the steps undertaken by Kleist. There is, certainly, no way of arguing that the two affected the course of events in any tangible way. Kleist's *démarches* with the

Swedish foreign-office civil servants seem to have gone *ad acta*, and no further. Ritter is correct that Oster's persistent transmission of intelligence benefited 'neither Danes nor Norwegians, Dutch nor Belgians'. The Danes were in no position even to hope to offer serious resistance; the Norwegians, left in the dark by their own Attaché, were caught unawares when the invasion actually took place; the Dutch had to pay the price for their disbelief in the reliability of the Oster–Sas channel; and the Belgians mobilized their troops all too late.[295] As for the British, they were not kept informed, Oster's expectations notwithstanding, either by The Hague or by Oslo. They were taken by surprise when the Germans invaded Denmark and landed in Norway; it is very likely that Oster's intelligence, had it reached them, might have made a difference. As for the information on the attack in the west, it did penetrate to London, possibly by way of Theo Kordt.[296] The American Embassy in Berlin reported, on the eve of the invasion, that the Netherlands government had been advised 'from confidential sources in Berlin' on the exact date and hour of the imminent advance of the German troops into Holland.[297]

But once all this is said, it must be added that success should not be the only measuring rod for judging what Kleist and Oster, as of course also their co-conspirators, did. To be sure, they were political men and wanted results. But the odds against them were enormous, and they were fully aware of this fact. Kleist said to his Swedish friend Damgren: 'I am now all alone.'[298] Something of the same sort, the reader will remember, was said by Adam von Trott to his friend Julie Braun-Vogelstein while in New York. Kleist and Oster's message (concerning the attack in the north) did not arrive either, at least in the places which really mattered; and if it did, as in the case of the attack in the west, the message got lost in the confusion of distrust and the whirl of often-conflicting intelligence that reached London, Paris, The Hague, and Brussels.[299] Kleist and Oster were indeed all alone. It was left to them to make a statement, and this in itself is of importance. The statement which they made was that the 'other Germany' was in solidarity with the countries threatened by the Antichrist and ready to make sacrifices for them.

In connection with the Oster case there is finally one more dimension, a very down-to-earth one, to be considered, which has been pointed out by Klaus-Jürgen Müller.[300] It will be remembered that late in April 1940 Beck sent Josef Müller once again to the Vatican 'in the way of a gesture of loyalty' towards the Pope to convey the message that no coup could be expected in Germany before the offensive in the west, and that the latter was scheduled to violate the neutrality of the Low Countries.[301] Oster's persistent revelations to the countries threatened by Hitler have to be seen in this context. Like General Beck he was determined to save the honour of the *Widerstand* and to salvage its credibility for future exchanges.

Finally, it should be remembered here that it was at about this time that

Oster and Dietrich Bonhoeffer first met. Bonhoeffer knew from Dohnanyi about Oster's activities, and he condoned them. According to Bonhoeffer, treason, normally regarded as a blemish, in an extraordinary situation such as the one that existed in Nazi Germany, became 'true patriotism', whereas what was normally patriotism had become treason.[302] Thus the deeds of Oster and of his fellow conspirators received understanding and indeed sanction from the man who became the chief theologian of the *Widerstand*. They had acted as responsible Christians.

## CHAPTER 3

1. *Parliamentary Debates*, 5th ser., vol. 351, House of Commons, 11th vol. Sessions 1938–9 (London, 1939), col. 131.
2. See Ibid., cols. 135, 137.
3. *Parliamentary Debates*, 5th ser., vol. 114, House of Lords, 4th vol. of Session 1938–9 (London, 1939), col. 917.
4. *Keesing's Contemporary Archives*, iii (1937–40), col. 3718.
5. On this score, during the first months of the war, a distinct rift became evident between the British and the French positions, but Frank K. Roberts of the FO Central Department shrewdly minuted that, while the divergence between British and French views was 'a fundamental issue ...', there will be more sympathy here with the French view after the war has gone on for some time'; minutes by F. K. Roberts, 26 Sept. 1939, FO 371/22948/C 14579/62; see also FO 371/22946–22948 *passim*.
6. The proposal by Group Captain Christie that a German Advisory Committee be formed under the roof of the Ministry of Information, to be directed by Conwell-Evans and to include Rauschning, Otto Strasser, and the leader of the former Republican defence corps Reichsbanner, Karl Höltermann, even though backed by Vansittart, did not get anywhere; Memorandum by Christie to Vansittart, 'Rough Suggestions for German Advisory Committee', 28th Sept. 1939, Christie Papers, CHRS 1/31; see also unsigned and undated typescript 'If the victory ...', most likely from the autumn of 1939 and authored by Christie, proposing the participation of 'moderate German elements' in the formulation of a peace programme to be adopted by the Allied Powers with the ultimate objective of 'gaining the support of Germans in Germany'; ibid. From the FO Papers it also becomes quite clear that the proposition of Strasser's entry into the United Kingdom was vetoed from on high; letter from Sir Campbell Stuart to Sir Alexander Cadogan, 17 Nov. 1939 with minute by F. K. Roberts: 'This had been suggested by Sir R. Vansittart', FO 371/23013/C 19119/53/18.
7. Peter W. Ludlow, 'The Unwinding of Appeasement,' in Lothar Kettenacker (ed.), *Das 'Andere Deutschland' in Zweiten Weltkrieg*, (Stuttgart, 1977) 20 ff.
8. Entry of 1 Nov. 1939, *The Diaries of Sir Alexander Cadogan O.M. 1938–1945*, ed. David Dilks (New York, 1956), 228.
9. Letter from Neville Chamberlain to Ida Chamberlain, 10 Sept., 5 Nov. 1939, Chamberlain Papers, Birmingham, NC 18/1/116, 1129; letter from Lord Halifax to Neville Chamberlain, 13 Feb. 1940, ibid., NC 7/11/33/74; see also Ludlow, 'The Unwinding of Appeasement', 21–2; Lothar Kettenacker, 'Die britische Haltung zum deutschen Widerstand während des Zweiten Weltkriegs', in Kettenacker (ed.), *Das 'Andere Deutschland'*, 52 ff.
10. Hans Bernd Gisevius, *To the Bitter End* (Boston, Mass., 1947), 385; Graf von Thun-Hohenstein, *Der Verschwörer*. *General Oster und die Militäropposition* (Berlin, 1982), 164; *Aufstand des Gewissens: Der militärische Widerstand gegen Hitler und das NS-Regime 1933–1945* (Herford, 1984), 373; Hoffmann, *History*, 129–30; see Helmuth Groscurth, *Tagebücher eines Abwehroffiziers 1938–1940*, ed. Helmut Krausnick and Harold C. Deutsch (Stuttgart, 1970), 222–3.
11. Hasso von Etzdorf, 'Meine Tätigkeit als Vertreter des Auswärtigen Amts beim Oberkommando des Heeres (Oktober 1939–Januar 1945)', typescript, 1946, Kordt Papers; Groscurth, *Tagebücher*, 46–7.

12. That is, until in mid-1940 when first von Nostitz and then von Heyden-Rynsch were reassigned to other duties by the suspicious Foreign Minister.

13. Typescript of 20 pp. by Christine von Dohnanyi on her husband's resistance activities; no title, no date; Dohnanyi Papers.

14. Franz Halder, *Kriegstagebuch*; *tägliche Aufzeichnungen des Chefs des Generalstabes des Heeres, 1939–1942*, i: *Vom Polenfeldzug bis zum Ende der Westoffensive (14.8.1939–30.6.1940)*, ed. Hans-Adolf Jacobsen (Stuttgart, 1962); entry of 14 Oct. 1939, 105. Kosthorst's reading of the Halder diary passage (*Die deutsche Opposition gegen Hilter* (2nd edn. Bonn, 1955) 38) giving two alternatives 'wait for attack' and 'fundamental changes' is in error; see also Klaus-Jürgen Müller, *Das Heer und Hitler: Armee und nationalsozialistisches Regime 1933–1940* (Stuttgart, 1969), 479–80.

15. Entry of 19 Oct. 1939, *Die Hassell-Tagebücher*, 133.

16. Kosthorst, *Die deutsche Opposition*, 95–6; Müller, *Heer und Hitler*, 521. He repeated this tirade on 23 Nov. in a command performance with Brauchitsch and Halder; Hoffmann, *History*, 137, 143.

17. As for the date of the memorandum, the evidence from Groscurth's diary makes it quite clear that it, 'the memorandum' (most likely the Etzdorf–Kordt memorandum; diary entry of 19 Oct. 1939, Groscurth, *Tagebücher*, 219) was completed by 19 Oct.; it can be assumed that, composed, as it was, 'in a hurry' (Erich Kordt, *Nicht aus den Akten ... Die Wilhelmstrasse in Frieden und Krieg. Erlebnisse, Begegnungen und Eindrücke 1928–1945* (Stuttgart, 1950), 358), it was written in the course of 2 days (see also Deutsch, *The Conspiracy*, 205 and Marion Thielenhaus, *Zwischen Anpassung und Widerstand* (Paderborn, 1984), 158). The major parts of the memorandum were retrieved by Groscurth when on 5 Nov., after von Brauchitsch's and Halder's audience with Hitler, the bulk of the compromising materials was burned in Zossen upon Halder's orders (Deutsch, *The Conspiracy*, 205). The full text, as far as it has been salvaged, is from the BA/MA N 104/2 and reproduced in Groscurth, *Tagebücher*, 498–503; the text reproduced in Kordt, *Nicht aus den Akten*, 359–66 is incomplete. For a summary of the memorandum by Etzdorf see Etzdorf, 'Meine Tätigkeit'.

18. See Kordt, *Nicht aus den Akten*, 358; Thielenhaus, *Zwischen Anpassung und Widerstand*, 158–9.

19. Sir Lewis Namier, 'Erich and Theo Kordt', in *In the Nazi Era* (London, 1952), 101.

20. See FO 371/22947; 22948.

21. Response of the British government to a French *aide-mémoire* of 23 Oct. 1939, 20 Dec. 1939; WP(G) (39) 150; see also Kettenacker, *Das 'Andere Deutschland'*, 159 ff. and Eleanor M. Gates, *End of the Affair: The Collapse of the Anglo-French Alliance, 1939–40* (Berkeley, 1981), 24–5.

22. Letter from Conwell-Evans to Theo Kordt, London, 20 Oct. 1939, Kordt Papers.

23. The evidence for these meetings is taken from Kordt, *Nicht aus den Akten*, 367 ff. and the two 'Short Autobiographies' by Theo Kordt (i: 21pp.; ii: 22pp.), Kordt Papers. The first set of meetings took place on 25, 27, and 29 Oct. (i. 15; ii. 15); the second encounter early in Dec. 1939 (i. 17; ii. 17; Kordt, *Nicht aus den Akten*, 379, however, dates it 18 Dec.); the third one possibly on 27 Jan. 1940 (ibid.; although in i.18, ii. 17 Theo Kordt voices uncertainty as to whether it has taken place at all), followed by a number of meetings between 13 and 17 Feb. (Kordt, *Nicht aus den Akten*, 379; also Kosthorst, *Die deutsche Opposition*, 87) and in Mar. 1940 (i. 18; ii. 17).

24. Kordt, *Nicht aus den Akten*, 367.

25. For the statement itself see ibid. 367–8 and the facsimile in the appendix to the volume; see also i. 16; ii. 15–16; for analyses see Kosthorst, *Die deutsche Opposition*, 78 ff.; Deutsch, *The Conspiracy*, 160–1; Namier, *In the Nazi Era*, 102–3.

26. *Parliamentary Debates*, 5th ser., vol. 352, House of Commons, 12th vol. of Session 1938–9 (London, 1939), cols. 565–6.

27. Kordt, *Nicht aus den Akten*, 368. In fact there is no way of interpreting it to have amounted to a formal commitment to military restraint on the part of the British government; see also Kosthorst, *Die deutsche Opposition*, 81; Müller, *Heer und Hitler*, 505–6.

28. On this Kordt is most likely to have derived his intelligence from Oster; however, it has been pointed out that while Kordt's revelation to his British friend was made in good faith,

it was over-optimistic and therefore misleading; see Kosthorst, *Die deutsche Opposition*, 80; Müller, *Heer und Hitler*, 506. It is to be noted also that the information on the negotiations between Theo Kordt and Conwell-Evans was presented by Erich Kordt and Oster to Beck, who was distinctly buoyed by it; but it apparently was not brought to the attention of General Halder; Kordt, *Nicht aus den Akten*, 368–9; Kosthorst, *Die deutsche Opposition*, 81–2; Müller, *Heer und Hitler*, 506–7.

29. Namier, *In the Nazi Era*, 103.

30. See also Kosthorst, *Die deutsche Opposition*, 81.

31. See Michael Balfour, *Propaganda in War 1939–1945: Organisations, Policies and Publics in Britain and Germany* (London, 1979), 152 ff.

32. Theo Kordt, Short Autobiographies, (i), (ii). 15.

33. Groscurth entry in his service diary, 15 Nov. 1939, *Tagebücher*, 311.

34. Wolfgang Benz, 'Eine liberale Widerstandsgruppe und ihre Ziele: Hans Robinsohns Denkschrift aus dem Jahre 1939', *VfZ*, 29 (July 1981), 443; the whole story of the incident has for the first time been told in Deutsch, *The Conspiracy*, 74 ff.

35. According to Deutsch (ibid. 74) the meeting occurred on 6 Nov.; another meeting between Reichenau and Goerdeler seems to have taken place on 10 Dec.; 'Nachrichten aus Deutschland und Italien bis zum 10.1.1940', 11. Jan. 1940; Secret Letter from Christie to Vansittart, 16 Jan. 1940, Christie Papers, CHRS 180/1/33.

36. Benz, 'Eine liberale Widerstandsgruppe', 437–71.

37. 'Die deutsche Opposition: Tätigkeit und Ziele', ibid. 447 ff.; the approximate date of its composition was after March and before Sept. 1939.

38. Ibid. 466.

39. Ibid. 464.

40. Ibid. 471.

41. Diary entries 30 Dec. 1939, 28 Jan. 1940, *Die Hassell-Tagebücher*, 155, 161.

42. Via Dr Walter Jacobsen, a former member of the Hamburg circle who had emigrated to Sweden and who in turn had contact with Peter Tennant, Press Attaché at the British Legation.

43. According to Deutsch (*The Conspiracy*, 76–7) London had the message confirmed by another source by way of Switzerland. The Foreign Office certainly was informed, through whatever source, about the meeting that had taken place in Nov. between Reichenau and Goerdeler; Secret Letter from Ashton-Gwatkin to Gladwyn Jebb, 31 Dec. 1939, FO 371/24386/C 297/6/18.

44. Benz, 'Ein liberale Widerstandsgruppe', 467. Once more, in Jan. of the following year, Dr Jacobsen approached Peter Tennant, the British Press Attaché in Stockholm, this time with a peace proposal contingent on the assurance that his group was now ready to take over complete control of Germany in 24 hours, with the collaboration of the army. The plan was for the army to occupy all key points and to arrest all the Nazi chiefs and to cope with the SS, which was expected to be the only serious opposition. A transitional military dictatorship was to yield to responsible popular government with a constitution protected by the armed forces. Meanwhile the Allies were not to exploit the temporary weakness of Germany during such a coup to their military advantage. The proposal then provided for a restoration of Poland as a 'small and independent state', of Czechoslovakia with frontiers subject to international determination, and for Austria to remain in the Reich; it furthermore held out for nothing less than a 'crusade' against Russia with the objective of overthrowing the Stalin regime; Secret Report Victor A. L. Mallet (British Minister to Sweden) 21 Jan. 1940 including detailed minute by Tennant, FO 371/24405/C 2577/89/18, and Peter Tennant, 'German Resistance as seen from the British Legation in Stockholm', paper delivered at the Anglo-German Conference on the German Resistance and Britain in Leeds, England, 6–9 May 1986. G. P. Young of the FO Central Department minuted 'nothing of importance', and Tennant later recorded in a deadpan manner that nothing came of this approach which 'joined the files of intelligence which piled high as the war progressed'. Later, during the critical days around 20 July 1944 one of the founding members of the Hamburg group, the lawyer Ernst Strassmann, was on a secret mission in Stockholm where he established contact with the British; Official Dispatches USTRAVICH—OSS, 22 July, 12 Aug. 1944, NA, RG 226, Entry 99, Box 14.

45. Kordt, *Nicht aus den Akten*, 369 ff.
46. Ibid. 374; Major Erwin Lahousen, head of Section II (Sabotage and Infiltration) of the Abwehr, 'Eidesstattliche Erklärung', Seefeld/Tirol, 1. July 1947, Kordt Papers; Hoffmann, *History*, 256–7; see also Anton Hoch, 'Das Attentat auf Hitler im Münchner Bürgerbräukeller 1939', *VfZ*, 17 (Oct. 1969), 383–413.
47. Walter Schellenberg, *The Schellenberg Memoirs* (London, 1956), 94; Groscurth, *Tagebücher*, 228–9.
48. In its origins, the affair throws some interesting light on the not necessarily salutary role played by exiles in their dealings with Nazi Germany. To begin with it was a questionable *emigré*, in fact an SD double agent, by the name of Franz Fischer who offered his services as intermediary to Captain Best. But his reliability was vouched for insistently by Dr Carl Spiecker, a left-wing Centrist journalist, politician, and civil servant of the Weimar era, who emigrated in 1933 to France, then after the German invasion to Britain and finally in 1941 to Canada; ex-Chancellor Dr Heinrich Brüning, who was not a friend of Spiecker, made the charge that throughout his exile he was in the pay of the French and British intelligence services, and Brüning correctly maintained that, having 'inspired' the Venlo adventure, Spiecker had played the Gestapo game; letter from Heinrich Brüning to Dr (Hermann Josef) Schmitt, Lowell House (Cambridge, Mass.), n.d. (most likely 1948 or 1949), BA/K, Pechel II, 89; see also Christopher Andrew, *Secret Service: The Making of the British Intelligence Community* (London, 1985), 434–5.
49. See Bernd Martin, *Friedensinitiativen und Machtpolitik im Zweiten Weltkrieg 1939–1942* (Düsseldorf, 1974), esp. pp. 132 ff.; Thielenhaus, *Zwischen Anpassung und Widerstand*, 185 ff.
50. This epithet apparently goes back to Lord Halifax, FO 371/22985; for the story of that file see below. See also Ivone Kirkpatrick's (First Secretary, FO) minute dated 12 Dec. 1939: 'that nebulous entity "the generals"' in FO 371/22987/C 19636/15/18.
51. See Callum A. MacDonald, 'The Venlo Affair', *European Studies Review* 8 (Oct. 1978), 443–4.
52. By no means therefore the only attempt, as maintained by MacDonald; ibid. 460.
53. Ibid. 445; Captain S. Payne Best, *The Venlo Incident* (London, 1950), 7; Francis Harry Hinsley *et al.*, *British Intelligence in the Second World War: Its Influence on Strategy and Operations* (London, 1979), i. 57.
54. Such was the designation of the head of the Secret Service (SIS) since the days of its first chief Captain Mansfield Cumming.
55. Entry of 23 Oct. 1939, *The Diaries of Sir Alexander Cadogan*, 226.
56. Lord Halifax, so it seems, was swayed to take this course by yet another memorandum from Carl Goerdeler, sent early in Oct. from Brussels to a FO official. Contained in FO 371/22985, it has been closed until the year 2015, not because of its admittedly 'innocuous' contents, but because of a series of internal minutes from Sinclair; interview with F. H. Hinsley, 15 Dec., 1975; see also Andrew, *Secret Service*, 436–7.
57. Entry of 31 Oct. 1939, *The Diaries of Sir Alexander Cadogan*, 228; italics in the original.
58. Entries of 1 and 6 Nov., ibid. 228–9; see also Andrew, *Secret Service*, 436–7.
59. Secret 'Extract from Conversation between Lord Halifax and Monsieur Corbin: 7th November, 1939', Neville Chamberlain Papers, NC 8/29/4.
60. Ibid.
61. Sir Alexander Cadogan to the Prime Minister, 'Most Secret Note of what might be said to the "Generals"', 16 Nov., 1939; NC/8/29/2, 3. The 'other channel' alluded to was most likely 'K', frequently referred to in Cadogan's diaries of those particular days, and 'K' most likely stood for Theo Kordt; David Dilks's conjectures on the identity of 'K' in *The Diaries of Sir Alexander Cadogan*, 227 (Canaris, spelled 'Kanaris', or an informer of Ivone Kirkpatrick back in mid-Dec. 1938) are not convincing.
62. Entry of 18 Nov. 1939, ibid. 232.
63. Official Diary entry of 15 Nov. 1939, Groscurth, *Tagebücher*, 309.
64. See Deutsch, *Conspiracy*, 247–8.
65. See ibid. 248–9.
66. Groscurth, *Tagebücher*, 309.

67. See e.g. Cadogan's minute of 24 Jan. 1940 to a Memorandum by John W. Wheeler-Bennett of 27 Dec. 1939 to Vansittart on 'future attitude of Allies towards Germany': 'But I hope it wouldn't lead us to another Venlo!'; FO 371/24363/C 1545/267/62; see also CAB 65/11, WM(40) 16th concl., Minute 8, Conf. Annex.
68. Secret Memorandum Christie to Vansittart 19 Feb. 1940; FO 371/24389/C 3439/6/18.
69. Vansittart to Secretary of State, 11 Mar. 1940, ibid.
70. Registered in a document dated 30 Nov. 1939 ('Nachrichten aus Deutschland bis zum 28.11.39', 30 Nov. 39, Christie Papers, CHRS 1/33 and Most Secret Report Christie–Vansittart, 13 Dec. 1939, Christie Papers, CHRS 1/30), it was 'vetted and guaranteed by Kn.'. He (Hans Ritter) named as his sources Generals von Witzleben and Richard Ruoff, both 'active Corps-Commanders' and Count von Soden, a friend of ex-Crown Prince Rupprecht of Bavaria. There is, however, no indication as to the exact date when the information was proffered. (Ruoff was Commanding General of Fifth Corps and Commander of Military District V, Stuttgart. As for Witzleben, he was Commanding General of Third Corps and Commander of Military District III, Berlin, until mid-1939; by the time of the Polish campaign he had become Commanding General of 1st Army.) There is no indication either in the document in question as to how exactly the information reached Ritter, whether directly or indirectly.
71. '(a) The whole present-day territory held by the Reich, including Austria, but excluding the Protectorate of Bohemia-Moravia and a rump-state Poland. (b) The existing authoritarian form of State, which will guarantee a wide measure of freedom of action to the German combatant forces, and ensure them a position of priority in the Annual Budget. (c) Germany's sovereign rights over its own measures for defence to be unimpaired by any considerations of foreign policy ("die aussenpolitisch unbeschränkte Wehrhoheit Deutschlands").'
72. Christie notes, 'I met my friend on Wednesday, November 15th', 17 Nov. 1939, Christie Papers, CHRS 180/1/33.
73. Letter from Christie to Vansittart, 13/12/39, Christie Papers, CHRS 1/30.
74. For his elaborate Secret Memorandum see FO 371/24389/C 3439/6/18.
75. Translation of letter from Joseph Wirth to Neville Chamberlain, Lucerne, 24 Dec. 1939, FO 371/24386/C 297/6/18.
76. The Times, 10 Jan. 1940.
77. Letter from J. R. Colville to I. A. Kirkpatrick Esq., CMG, 12 Jan. 1940; Minute by Frank K. Roberts, 18 Jan. 1940; FO 371/24386/C 297/6/18.
78. We owe the rudimentary information on this exchange to Gerhard Ritter (Carl Goerdeler, 252–3, 495, n. 253) on the basis of an interview which he had with Wirth and of a written deposit from an unnamed person who, however, can be identified as having been Hans Ritter. There is, alas, no record of either in the BA/K Ritter Papers. Meanwhile, however, the availability of the FO and Christie Papers allows a much closer insight into the sequence of events and therefore also into the nature of the exchange. Peter Hoffmann's version (History, 154) is altogether derivative from Gerhard Ritter.
79. In most of the Christie Papers Wirth is referred to in proper secret service style as 'Dr. Wilde' or 'Onkel Joe', and Gessler as 'Wilhelm Tell'.
80. Wirth's supposed intimation to the French Embassy in Berne that the initiative had come from the British side has been contradicted by Sir Alexander Cadogan (signed statement 19 Mar. 1940, FO 371/24389/C 4379/6/18) as well as by Christie himself (Secret Memorandum of 19 Feb. 1940, FO 371/24389/C 3439/6/18).
81. He was identified in one of the rare Secret Service documents which found its way into the now open Foreign Office files—wrongly—as a financial pundit formerly with the Bank of International Settlement, living in Ascona, and a friend of M. Léger; Most Secret 'Reference the memorandum dated the 19th February ...', FO 371/24389/C 3439/6/18. As a matter of fact he was Dr Manfred Simon; see above Ch. 1 n. 267.
82. This second meeting took place most probably in Lucerne after Wirth had received the visit of 'an important emissary from the Opposition and from the General Staff in Germany', also identified as a 'big industrialist': Hans Walz from the Bosch works? In any case, this emissary promised 'in a day or two's time' detailed written instructions from Berlin; Secret Memorandum, 19 Feb. 1940, FO 371/24389/C 3439/6/18.

83. Sir Robert Vansittart expressed his particular approval of Christie's contact with the 'South German group'; Minute by Sir Robert Vansittart, 20 Jan. 1940, FO 371/22986/ C19495/15/18. The preference of the 'good' Southern Germans over the 'wicked' Prussians was widespread in Britain and also shared by Winston Churchill.

84. Christie, 'My meeting with Dr Wirth ...', 16 Mar. 1940, Christie Papers, CHRS 180/1/35.

85. Ibid.

86. Ibid.; once again, in a letter to Vansittart, Christie referred, somewhat mysteriously, to 'the "documents"', Secret Letter from Christie to Vansittart, 18 Mar. 1940, CHRS 180/1/35. The 'document' is undoubtedly identical with the 5-point proposition reproduced by Gerhard Ritter (*Carl Goerdeler*, 253). It was, however, not sprung on Wirth, as suggested by Ritter, in mid-Feb. by 'two Foreign Office representatives'. On the contrary, it constituted, as we have seen, the climactic feature of the Christie-Wirth negotiations, begun as 'purely unofficial' and 'private' soundings in mid-Feb., and ending with the official proposal of 12 March. Gerhard Ritter finds support for his dating by reference to his having obtained (from Wirth or 'Kn.'?) one of a number of copies, which Christie and Conwell-Evans gave to Wirth or his friend, of the supposedly forthcoming Birmingham address of the Prime Minister that was to stress that the British did not desire the destruction of any people. In fact, by the time of the encounter between Christie, Conwell-Evans, Wirth, and 'Kn.' the Birmingham address was in the past. Christie's Memorandum of 16 Mar. 1940 quite unmistakably sets the record straight: 'We [he and "Kn."] parted cordially after I had given him two printed copies of the Prime Minister's speech of February 24th and of Lord Halifax's recent address at Oxford'; 'My meeting with Dr Wirth ...'. The only work in which at least the approximate date, 'the middle of March', of the meeting between Christie, Conwell-Evans, and Wirth is given is Thielenhaus, *Zwischen Anpassung und Widerstand*, 182.

87. The text as given by Ritter (*Carl Goerdeler*, 253) is the only one extant; he most probably obtained it in the form of a German translation from Hans Ritter with whom he was in correspondence about the matter or from Wirth himself whom he interviewed (ibid. 495, n. 47). Actually, Christie recorded that after his and Conwell-Evans's session with Wirth he allowed the latter's 'friend and confidant Kn.', who had been waiting in an adjoining room, to make a few pencilled notes on the contents of the document, after which Conwell-Evans went into the next room to burn the whole paper ('My meeting with Dr. Wirth ...'). But it has not surfaced among the BA/A Ritter Papers (although Ritter claimed that it was 'still in existence'). As for the Wirth Papers, they have not yet been released. Notwithstanding the cloak and dagger ways of Conwell-Evans, it is odd that the original of the document should not be among the files of the FO since there is no doubt that the authorization came from on high. See also the rather carefully phrased but firm statement by Cadogan concerning the degree to which the French Ambassador had been initiated into the matter: 'Monsieur Corbin did not ask whether we had made any response to the request from Dr. Wirth for assurances and I did not tell him that we had made any'; Cadogan, Signed Statement 19 Mar. 1940, FO 371/24389/C 4379/6/18.

88. In the course of the ensuing conversation some stipulations were added, namely that, as far as the British government was concerned, all these assurances were to be considered binding until the end of April; that a new German government, to be trustworthy, would have to abandon all expansionist policies and the *Preussengeist* (Prussian spirit) and to undertake corresponding organizational measures, especially as regards the armed forces; and that it was to exclude any member of Hitler's government, including Göring.

89. Secret Letter from Christie to Vansittart, 18 Mar. 1940.

90. 'Translation of Memorandum by ex-Reich Chancellor Wirth, describing his talk with ex-Reich War Minister Gessler on 13 March 1940', Lucerne, 14 Mar., 1940, Christie Papers, CHRS 180/1/35.

91. Ritter, *Carl Goerdeler*, 495–6, n. 49; apart from the multiple documentation of Gessler's involvement, notice also the entry of 22 Mar. 1940 in the von Hassell diary: 'I saw Gessler yesterday. He has been to Switzerland on what appeared to be a similar mission' (see below for von Hassell's negotiations in Switzerland); *Die Hassell-Tagebücher*, 182.

92. 'Gessler has not had any negotiations with Goerdeler, but he has heard nothing to his

disadvantage. He will make closer enquiries about him'; 'Translation of Memorandum by ex-Reich Chancellor Wirth ...'.

93. Beck's persistent efforts to prod Halder into action led to a meeting between the two generals on 16 Jan. 1940 which from beginning to end was marked by acrimony; 'Aufzeichnungen zum Gespräch zwischen Herrn Generaloberst a.D. Halder und Dr. Uhlig am 2.6.53 in Königstein', IfZ, ZS 240; see also Müller, *Heer und Hitler*, 556–7; Nicholas Reynolds, *Treason Was No Crime: Ludwig Beck, Chief of the German General Staff* (London, 1976) 197–8.

94. Secret Letter from Christie to Vansittart, 18 Mar., 1940.

95. Ernest Pezet, 'Contre Hitler et la guerre: Une mission secrète du chancelier Wirth à Paris (Avril 1940)', *Revue Politique et Parlementaire*, 224 (Apr. 1958), 289–305; see also D. C. Watt, 'One Man's Opposition: Dr. Wirth's Anglo-French Contacts, 1939/40', *Wiener Library Bulletin*, 16/1 (1962), 14.

96. Although the panacea of a European and German federalism, launched by the German, seemed to have established a rapport of sorts between the two men, Wirth's proposition of a restoration of the Wittelsbachs in Bavaria only elicited a plea of 'ignorance' of the problem and 'indifference', and while on the one hand Wirth had come to reassure himself that the French were not out to strike Germany from the map of Europe, he in turn assured Pezet of the German readiness to have the Austrians decide their own future by means of a plebiscite and to guarantee full sovereignty to Poland and Czechoslovakia. For the settlement of the Czechoslovak question he proposed a meeting with Eduard Beneš, the exiled President of Czechoslovakia.

97. See also for this argument Watt, 'One Man's Opposition'.

98. See esp. J[ames] Lonsdale Bryans, *Blind Victory* (*Secret Communications Halifax–Hassell*) (London, 1951); *idem*, 'Zur britischen amtlichen Haltung gegenüber der deutschen Widerstandsbewegung', *VfZ* 1 (Oct. 1953), 347–51; *Die Hassell-Tagebücher*, 168–73, 188–91.

99. '"Programm" für erste Massnahmen bei einem Umsturz', ibid. 451–4; the authorship of the 'Programme' is not altogether certain. While there is no reference in the Diaries to the document, there is sufficient evidence from a number of Diary entries to the effect that Hassell had discussed at that time with Beck, Goerdeler, and Popitz measures to be taken in case of a change of regime in Germany; ibid. 449.

100. The 'Programme' specifically referred to the 'old Reich frontier', i.e clearly the one of 1914 with Poland.

101. Returning in late August 1939 from a journey to the Far East, he had indeed made his way straight to the FO where he happened to run into Halifax and Cadogan among others, engaging them in a conversation which, so we are told, left the Foreign Secretary 'rather impressed'; Lonsdale Bryans, *Blind Victory*, 17.

102. Lonsdale Bryans, 'Zur britischen amtlichen Haltung ...', 350; Report by J. Lonsdale Bryans to Lord Tyrrell, 12 July 1943, FO 371/34449/C 7963/155/18.

103. Lord Halifax minutes after the Lonsdale Bryans visit on 8 Jan. 1940; FO 800/326/H/XLIII/4.

104. Lonsdale Bryans, 'Zur britischen amtlichen Haltung ...', 348.

105. FO 800/326/H/XLIII/4.

106. Lord Halifax minutes, 8 Jan. 1940, ibid.

107. Copy of letter from R. C. Skrine Stevenson to Sir Percy Loraine, 9 Jan. 1940, FO 800/326/H/XLIII/6.

108. The code-name given to von Hassell in Lonsdale Bryans's dealings with the FO.

109. The code-name for Lonsdale Bryans in von Hassell's Diaries.

110. *Die Hassell-Tagebücher*, 172.

111. That is, as stipulated in the Treaty of Versailles.

112. See in this connection especially Walter Schmitthenner and Hans Buchheim (eds.), *Der deutsche Widerstand gegen Hitler* (Cologne, 1966), 30 ff.

113. *The Diaries of Sir Alexander Cadogan*, 256–7.

114. Entry of 13 Mar. ibid. 263.

115. R. C. Skrine Stevenson arranged with the Air Ministry to have Lonsdale Bryans flown from London to Paris, after which he was to proceed by train to Switzerland; he also got

a stipend to the amount of £50; Stevenson: 'After this I think we should do nothing more for Mr. Bryans'; FO 800/326/H LXIII/14.

116. Report of Bryans to Lord Tyrrell, FO 371/34449.

117. Von Hassell understood Lonsdale Bryans to have said that he had given Hassell's notes to Halifax who, allegedly without mentioning his name, had shown them to Chamberlain; entry of 15 Apr., *Die Hassell-Tagebücher*, 189.

118. Ibid.

119. Gerhard Ritter's hypothesis (*Carl Goerdeler*, 257) that it was the British message to Wirth that was meant has been questioned by various people; see esp. Hoffmann, *History*, 583 n. 27. While Wheeler-Bennett's assumption (*The Nemesis of Power*, 490) that the reference was to the Vatican talks (see below) finds tentative support from Deutsch (*The Conspiracy*, 170), it is dismissed by Kurt Sendtner ('Die Militäropposition', in *Vollmacht des Gewissens*, ed. Europäische Publikation e.V. (Frankfurt M., 1960), 472–3 n. 88); the Vatican negotiations had been wound up certainly by the end of Feb. The explanation that the 'other channel' meant the negotiations with Wirth, however, finds further support, if not confirmation, by Lonsdale Bryans's reference in his Report to Lord Tyrrell to his having been given permission to ask von Hassell 'whether he had heard anything of the démarches that had been made by the professional Foreign Office agents who ... had lately been entrusted with a written message ...'. As for the dating problem, the last meeting between Cadogan and Lonsdale Bryans took place on 14 March, and it is most likely that this was the occasion when the latter was informed that a written assurance had been given via another channel 'a week before'. The assurance to Wirth, as we have seen, was given by Christie and Conwell-Evans—the 'professional Foreign Office agents'?—on 12 March, and it is reasonable to assume that it was decided upon and formulated just about a week before 14 March.

120. *Die Hassell-Tagebücher*, 189.

121. Italics in the original; ibid. 189.

122. Summary by Christine von Dohnanyi, IfZ, ZS 603.

123. Best, *The Venlo Incident*, 181.

124. When attending the *Gymnasium* in Bamberg, having to earn some of his own upkeep, he was sighted by his fellow students driving an oxen-drawn dung cart; thus the nickname 'Joe the Ox'; Josef Müller, *Bis zur letzten Konsequenz: Ein Leben für Frieden und Freiheit* (Munich, 1975), 20.

125. See Deutsch, *The Conspiracy*, 112–13.

126. Müller, *Bis zur letzten Konsequenz*, 80. The Pope, so it seems, reserved to himself the conduct of affairs pertaining to Germany; Deutsch, *The Conspiracy*, 108, 115–16; see also Sendtner, 'Die deutsche Militäropposition', 444 ff.; Thun-Hohenstein, *Der Verschwörer*, 149.

127. Later, in May 1945, Pius XII, on the occasion of a private audience granted to Müller, reminded him that his co-operation with Oster, the son of a Protestant pastor, marked the beginning of the ecumenism; upon Müller's remark that he was under attack in Bavaria for his ecumenical course, the Pope smiled, got up, and tended his right hand to the German; interview with Dr Josef Müller, 17 Feb. 1978; see also Müller, *Bis zur letzten Konsequenz*, 291 ff.

128. Deutsch, *The Conspiracy*, 121.

129. The exact dates and the number of Müller's missions to Rome cannot be reconstructed; between late Sept. and late Dec. 1939 he made the trip at least five times; early in 1940 he was 'constantly *en route*' and in one week alone he flew three times to Rome and twice to Berlin, once landing in Munich (Müller, *Bis zur letzten Konsequenz*, 107); the final visits to Rome then took place towards the end of April and early in May 1940.

130. Ibid. 85; the Secretary of State, Cardinal Luigi Maglione, and his entire office were not kept informed about the Pope's part as a mediator, in part because it was known that a secret agent of the Axis Powers had worked his way into the Secretariat of State; Owen Chadwick, *Britain and the Vatican during the Second World War* (Cambridge, 1986), 88.

131. See also Sendtner, 'Die deutsche Militäropposition', 442–3, 455.

132. Two written communications, however, were not destroyed: a calling card including a message from Leiber and a letter from Leiber to Müller. They were put to use in Berlin by

Oster to impress upon Halder the authenticity of the reports about the Rome exchanges. But these documents were discovered in the autumn of 1944 by the Gestapo at OKH headquarters in Zossen; ibid. 453–4.

133. The only extant contemporary German documents on the Vatican Exchanges are Josef Müller's 'Besprechungen in Rom beim Vatikan, 6.–9. [in fact 12.] 11. [1939]', IfZ, ZS 659, I and BA/K EAP 21 X 15/2; excerpts reproduced in Groscurth, *Tagebücher*, 506–9 (the names mentioned in the report are coded, thus 'Gregor' for Pater Leiber, 'Onkel Ludwig' for Mgr. Kaas, 'Diplomat' for Minister Osborne); see also von Hassell's diary entry of 19 Mar. 1940, *Die Hassell-Tagebücher*, 179–80. Important of course is Müller's autobiography *Bis zur letzten Konsequenz*. Subsequently subsidiary German sources on the Vatican Exchanges have been created by means of later depositions and interrogations among which the following are of special importance: 'Protokoll der Besprechung mit Frau v. Dohnanyi am 1. Dezember 1952', IfZ, ZS 603; 'Die römischen Friedensgespräche: Befragung des Staatsministers a.D.Dr. Josef Müller am 2. September 1954', IfZ, ZS 659, II; 'Aussagen Staatsminister a.D.Dr. Josef Müller, München, den 4. Juni 1952', IfZ, ZS 659, II; 'Aussagen des Staatsministers a.D.Dr. Josef Müller, München, den 11. Juni 1952, Fortsetzung 20. Juni 1952', IfZ, ZS 659, II; 'Befragung des Staatsministers a.D.Dr. Josef Müller am 2. September 1954', IfZ, ZS 659, II. For the main secondary literature see Deutsch, *The Conspiracy, passim*; Hoffmann, *History*, 158 ff.; Kosthorst, *Die deutsche Opposition*, 127–38; Klaus-Jürgen Müller, *Heer und Hitler*, 558–69; Ritter, *Carl Goerdeler*, 257 ff.

134. See esp. Peter Ludlow, 'Papst Pius XII., die britische Regierung und die deutsche Opposition im Winter 1939/40', *VfZ*, 22 (Juli 1974), 299–341.

135. See in this connection 'Die römischen Friedensgespräche'.

136. Chadwick, *Britain and the Vatican*, 88.

137. Letter from Lord Halifax to Osborne, 17 Feb. 1940, FO 800/318.

138. See on this point Deutsch, *The Conspiracy*, 138–9 and Ludlow, 'Papst Pius XII.', 332–3.

139. Letter from Osborne to Lord Halifax, 12 Jan. 1940, FO 800/318; 'Die römischen Friedensgespräche', 11, IfZ, ZS 659, II.

140. Minutes by Christine von Dohnanyi, II, p. 3, IfZ, ZS 603; see also Hans von Dohnanyi Papers.

141. This term has been used in this connection by Klaus-Jürgen Müller, *Heer und Hitler*, 559 and has also been taken over by Josef Müller as most accurately reflecting the spirit in which the exchanges were carried out (*Bis zur letzten Konsequenz*, 126).

142. Such stipulation, if strictly adhered to, would have served as an assurance to Germany's eastern neighbours as well as a protection for Germany itself against possible French claims to the Rhine frontier; see Müller, *Bis zur letzten Konsequenz*, 126; Sendtner, 'Die deutsche Militäropposition', 462; Ludlow, 'Papst Pius XII.', 334.

143. For an example of the invocation of the *Faustpfandtheorie* see the Memorandum by General Wilhelm Ritter von Leeb warning against an attack against France and England by violating the neutrality of Holland, Belgium, and Luxembourg, which he sent to von Brauchitsch on 11 Oct. 1939; 'Denkschrift über die Aussichten und Wirkungen eines Angriffs auf Frankreich und England unter Verletzung der Neutralität Hollands, Belgiens und Luxemburgs', in Kosthorst, *Die deutsche Opposition*, 155–64.

144. 'Aussagen des Staatsministers', 11 June 1952, IfZ, ZS 659, II; see Müller, *Bis zur letzten Konsequenz*, 126.

145. Lord Halifax was particularly attracted by the proposition of a 'decentralized and federal' Germany which, so Osborne reported to London, the German military circles were ready to envisage; within its confines Austria conceivably could take its place; Osborne to Halifax, Rome, 7 Feb. 1940, Halifax to Osborne, 17 Feb. 1940, FO 800/318; Sargent to Halifax, 15 Feb., FO C 2522/89/18, in Ludlow, 'Papst Pius XII.', 336; see also *Die Hassell-Tagebücher*, 179. Müller in turn considered a plebiscite over the future of Austria a concession on his part to the British; he cleared this matter with Beck, but they agreed that preferably the referendum was not to take place immediately after the conclusion of a peace 'because of the bad performance of the Nazis in Austria'; after a span of approximately five years, they figured, a plebiscite would result in Germany's favour; 'Aussagen Staats-

minister', 4 June 1952, 17, IfZ, ZS 659, II; see also Müller, *Bis zur letzten Konsequenz*, 126, Sendtner, 'Die deutsche Militäropposition', 462.

146. Müller, *Bis zur letzten Konsequenz*, 126; 'Aussagen des Staatsministers ... Fortsetzung', 20 June 1952, 5, IfZ, ZS 659, II.
147. Osborne to Halifax, Rome, 7 Feb. 1940, FO 800/318.
148. Sargent to Halifax, 15 Feb. 1940, FO C 2522/89/18 in Ludlow, 'Papst Pius XII.', 336.
149. Osborne to Halifax, 12 Jan. 1940 and 7 Feb. 1940, FO 800/318.
150. 'Aussagen Staatsminister', 4 June 1952, 18, IfZ, ZS 659, II.
151. Deutsch, *The Conspiracy*, 294–5.
152. 'Aussagen Staatsminister', 4 June 1952, 16–17, IfZ, ZS 659, II; also Deutsch, *The Conspiracy*, 295–6, Müller, *Bis zur letzten Konsequenz*, 102; Sendtner, 'Die deutsche Militäropposition', 470. Müller was particularly critical of Goerdeler for whom the making up of such lists was a favourite pastime. He was generally considered by his fellow conspirators to be too careless, and this was a reason why he was not drawn into this phase of the operation.
153. 'Die römischen Friedensgespräche', 4. But this very metaphor, it should be noted, is inherently ambiguous, as it suggests 'holding fire' as well as 'standing ready for action' or 'waiting for the word to go'.
154. Sendtner, 'Die deutsche Militäropposition', 471.
155. As a matter of fact, the effect of Venlo on the exchanges was 'disastrous' (Müller, *Bis zur letzten Konsequenz*, 92); thus even on 12 January 1940 Osborne reminded the Secretary of State that the 'whole thing' was 'reminiscent of the Venloo [*sic*] affair'; Osborne to Halifax, 12 Jan. 1940, FO 800/313.
156. See Deutsch, *The Conspiracy*, 136–7; Sendtner, 'Die deutsche Militäropposition', 458.
157. Entry of 19 Mar. 1940, *Die Hassell-Tagebücher*, 179; see also entry Monday, 18 Mar. 1940: 'With Dohnanyi at Oster's home; we again discussed the matter of informing Halder of the Pope's action'; ibid. 181.
158. See Kosthorst, *Die deutsche Opposition*, 138 ff.; Deutsch, *Conspiracy*, 306 n. 160.
159. Fabian von Schlabrendorff, *The Secret War against Hitler* (London, 1966), 108; Ritter, *Carl Goerdeler*, 260, 498 n. 62; the letter fell into the hands of the Gestapo which in 1944 confronted Halder with it; it has since been lost. On 3 April Goerdeler showed von Hassell, who had just arrived in the capital from his home in Bavaria, a letter from Halder in which he refused for the time being to take action: 'England and France', so von Hassell paraphrased in his Diary the argument in the letter, 'had declared war on us, and one had to see it through. A peace of compromise was senseless. Only in the greatest emergency [come, now!] could one take the action desired by Goerdeler'; entry of 6 Apr. 1940, *Die Hassell-Tagebücher*, 184. It is not clear whether the letter alluded to here is the same as the one mentioned and quoted above.
160. For the 'set-back theory' see Deutsch, *The Conspiracy*, 304 and Thun-Hohenstein, *Der Verschwörer*, 182, 188.
161. Halder diary entry 4 Apr. 1940: 'General Thomas: Insight into intelligence materials'; Halder, *Kriegstagebuch*, i. 245.
162. Eberhard Bethge, *Dietrich Bonhoeffer: Man of Vision, Man of Courage* (New York, 1970), 578; Deutsch, *The Conspiracy*, 308 ff.; Sendtner, 'Die deutsche Militäropposition', 477–8.
163. 'Aufzeichnungen zum Gespräch zwischen Herrn Generaloberst a.D. Halder und Dr. Uhlig am 2.6.53 in Königstein', 3, IfZ, ZS 240; see also Kosthorst, *Die deutsche Opposition*, 135; Sendtner, 'Die deutsche Militäropposition', 466.
164. It should be pointed out that Halder was twice confronted with the report: first in April 1940 and again during the Gestapo hearings after 20 July 1944. Also, his reading of the X-Report has been partly corroborated by General Thomas, who in the course of the Gestapo hearings after the coup in the summer of 1944, was shown a 'minute' discovered in the Dohnanyi Zossen files, presumably identical with the X-Report. This version of the X-Report allowed for the 'removal of Hitler and Ribbentrop' and a 'formation of a new Government (person of Göring acceptable)' as well as the solution of all Eastern questions 'in favour of Germany'; General Georg Thomas, 'Gedanken und Ereignisse', *Schweizer Monatshefte*, 25/9 (Dec. 1945), 546; see Sendtner, 'Die deutsche Militäropposition', 465–6.

165. Osborne to Halifax, Rome, 23 Feb. 1940, FO 371/24405/C 3044/89/18.
166. A report in the Prague Communist newspaper *Prace* of 14 Jan. 1946 which came out with the revelation that in the course of Vatican talks the Pope had consented to a solution of all Eastern European problems in favour of Germany and had even given his assent for Goebbels to succeed Hitler as Germany's Führer was met by a categorical denial in the *Osservatore Romano* of 11/12 Feb.; Müller, *Bis zur letzten Konsequenz*, 141–2. Pater Leiber denied categorically that the Pope would have been party to a dissolution or partition of Poland; such a proposition he called 'freely invented'; Robert Leiber, 'Pius XII.', *Stimmen der Zeit*, 163 (1958/9), 98.
167. See Deutsch, *The Conspiracy*, 301; Hoffmann, *History*, 163, 586 n. 67.
168. Deutsch, *The Conspiracy*, 294.
169. Secret Telegram from Osborne to Foreign Office, London, 1 Dec. 1939, FO 371/23100/C 19745/13005/18.
170. Entry 30 Dec. 1939, *Die Hassell-Tagebücher*, 153.
171. For this topic see esp. Deutsch, *The Conspiracy*, 291 ff.
172. See above the so-called *Faustpfandtheorie*.
173. Müller, *Bis zur letzten Konsequenz*, 131.
174. It should be noted here that even Christine von Dohnanyi recollected that the original version of the X-Report called for Germany's 'free hand in the east' ('freie Hand im Osten'); Minutes by Christine von Dohnanyi, ii. 3, IfZ, ZS 603.
175. A control function of sorts on this item is exercised by the testimony of SS Standartenführer (Colonel) Walter Huppenkothen who as a member of the 'Special Commission 20 July 1944' and prosecutor of Dohnanyi, Oster, and Canaris had made a careful study of the report. According to his recollection, landing somewhere in the middle of the argument, the 'German-speaking areas' were to remain in the Reich, which would probably have involved the German retention of Danzig and some adjustments in the Corridor region; Deutsch, *The Conspiracy*, 298–9.
176. 'Die römischen Friedensgespräche', 8.
177. This is the position of General Halder ('Aufzeichnungen zum Gespräch', IfZ, ZS 240. 3) and also of Pater Leiber (Robert Leiber, 'Pius XII.' 98); see Deutsch, *The Conspiracy*, 299–300; Kosthorst, *Die deutsche Opposition*, 134–5; Müller, *Bis zur letzten Konsequenz*, 132; Klaus-Jürgen Müller, *Heer und Hitler*, 562–4; Sendtner, 'Die deutsche Militäropposition', 455, 460 ff. For the problem of the hiatus between the composition and the delivery of the X-Report see Deutsch, *The Conspiracy*, 303–4 and Sendtner, 'Die deutsche Militäropposition', 483 ff.
178. Müller, *Bis zur letzten Konsequenz*, 132–3.
179. Deutsch, *The Conspiracy*, 312.
180. Sendtner, 'Die deutsche Militäropposition', 479. According to Kosthorst, who had his information directly from General Halder, Brauchitsch used the words 'qualified betrayal of the country' (*qualifizieter Landesverrat*); the version 'qualified high treason' (*qualifizierter Hochverrat*), found in 'Aufzeichnungen zum Gespräch', IfZ, ZS 240. 3 is obviously in error.
181. See for this episode also ibid.
182. Sir Robert Vansittart instructed Conwell-Evans to hold out for the immediate evacuation of Poland after the expected coup in Germany; Kordt's rejoinder that in view of the threat of a Soviet occupation of Western Poland this was not feasible, but that General Beck anticipated the withdrawal of German troops 'as soon as possible' (Kordt, *Nicht aus den Akten*, 383) did not satisfy the British and led to the closing of this particular channel.
183. Osborne to Lord Halifax. Rome, 3 Apr. 1940, FO 800/318.
184. Müller, *Bis zur letzten Konsequenz*, 139–40; see also 'Aussagen Staatsminister', 4 June 1952, 21–3, IfZ, ZS 659, II; Deutsch, *The Conspiracy*, 336–7.
185. Beck as well as Oster and Dohnanyi were particularly concerned lest the break-up of the exchanges might evoke memories of Venlo in Britain; 'Aussagen Staatsminister', 4 June 1952, 22, IFZ, ZS 659, II; see also Müller, *Heer und Hitler*, 571.
186. Müller, in retrospect, emphasized that, in contrast to Oster, he did not reveal the time of the impending attack, 'also', as he put it, because he did not know it; 'Aussagen Staatsminister', 4 June 1952, 23, IfZ, ZS 659, II.

187. See an extremely perceptive 19-page travel report 'Amerikanische Eindrücke' which he wrote in California in July 1937; Trott Archive, Berichte; also letter from Adam von Trott to Shiela Grant Duff as from California [about 10] May 1937 in Klemens von Klemperer (ed.), *A Noble Combat: The Letters of Shiela Grant Duff and Adam von Trott zu Solz 1932–1939* (Oxford, 1988), 230.

188. Scheffer–Trott Memorandum, FO 371/34449/C 5218/155/18, reproduced in Hans Rothfels, 'Adam von Trott und das State Department', *VfZ*, 7 (July 1959), 328.

189. He had been one of the recipients of Trott's treatise 'Far Eastern Possibilities' (Sept. 1938) written during his Asian trip for Rhodes House; for the Carter–von Trott relationship see letter from Edward C. Carter to Allen W. Dulles, 11 Oct. 1946, Allen W. Dulles Papers, Box 203, Princeton University.

190. The text of the cable was as follows: 'INSTITUTE EXPLORING POSSIBILITY EXPANDING FAR EASTERN INQUIRY TO RELATE UNOFFICIAL SCHOLARSHIP TO GENERAL POST-WAR SETTLEMENT. IN VIEW OF YOUR KNOWLEDGE PRESENT INQUIRY REGARD IT UTMOST IMPORTANCE YOUR COMING THIS COUNTRY EARLIEST POSSIBLE MOMENT FOR CONSULTATION. HOPE THIS CAN BE REGARDED AS YOUR FIRST NATIONAL SERVICE CABLE EDWARD CARTER'; Clarita von Trott, 'Adam von Trott', 175. A slightly different version was copied, obviously hastily, by an FBI agent from Trott's papers in New York; Teletype, 31 Oct. 1939, FBI Trott file, vol. ii. The last sentence, so Carter explained later, was particularly designed to spare Trott embarrassment with the Nazi authorities and thus to enable him to obtain the necessary travel permit; letter from Carter to Dulles, 11 Oct. 1946.

191. Once again the permission to travel depended on Walter Hewel, but he was persuaded by Weizsäcker and Kessel to let Trott go. While Kessel, in his memoirs, flatly stated that 'Trott was sent by the Foreign Office to America, where he was invited to a Conference by the Institute of Pacific Relations' (von Kessel, 'Verborgene Saat', 175), Erich Kordt elaborated more precisely on the real state of affairs: 'In those days one of ours, the young Adam Trott zu Solz went to the United States. He was scheduled to take part in a conference of the Institute of Pacific Relations and to get in touch with Brüning as well as with the British Ambassador to Washington, Lord Lothian, on behalf of the German Opposition. I enabled him to depart by way of Italy ...'; Kordt, *Nicht aus den Akten*, 341. In fact for the purpose of this mission Trott was given a temporary assignment in the Information Section of the Auswärtiges Amt. It should be added that Hjalmar Schacht has repeatedly been mentioned as having been behind the Trott mission; 'Bericht George M. Merten 1963 über Trott', Trott Archive, Chris Interviews; the FBI reports also repeatedly referred to 'Dr Schott (probably Hjalmar Schact [sic])', thus in Office Memorandum, 23 Jan. 1956, FBI Trott file, vol. ix; see also letter from J. Edgar Hoover to Adolf A. Berle, 17 Nov. 1939, FBI Trott file, vol. iii.

192. See Weizsäcker's own account of his policies during the winter of 1939/40: ' ... my only idea was peace. Hitler, I thought, could be shaken off before, during, or after the conclusion of peace, just as the circumstances permitted'; Ernst von Weizsäcker, *Erinnerungen* (Munich, 1950), 272.

193. *The Economist*, 17 Feb. 1940, referred to in William L. Langer and S. Everett Gleason, *The Challenge to Isolation 1937–1940* (New York, 1952), 343.

194. FBI report 24 Nov. 1939, FBI Trott file, vol. iii; on 20 November in the morning Trott called on the German Chargé d'Affaires, Hans Thomsen, and on the same day dined with the Press Attaché Heribert von Strempel; cf. also Christopher Sykes, *Troubled Loyalty: A Biography of Adam von Trott zu Solz* (London 1968), 295. Hans Rothfels made a point of registering that in the official American—State Department as well as FBI—files the Trott case was kept under the heading 'Espionage', thus implying a complete misreading of his position and objectives. As a matter of fact, although there was much puzzlement in Washington about the nature of Trott's mission, the proposition that he was spying for Nazi Germany was readily dismissed. Assistant Secretary of State George S. Messersmith, while harbouring doubts as to how a man permitted to leave Germany in those days could be a free agent, identified Trott nevertheless as 'a young man who arouses confidence', considered to be 'in touch with conservative elements in Germany who view with concern the course of the German Government in various spheres of activity' and who are 'very much interested in the establishment of a stable peace' (letter from Messersmith to Alex-

ander C. Kirk, 8 Dec. 1939, NA, RG 59, CDF 862.20211, Trott, Adam von/8). J. Edgar
Hoover, the FBI Director, who ranked the case ('DR. ADAM VON TROTT, with aliases, Adam
Von Trott zu Solz, Adam Von Tropp zu Solz, Adam Von Trott Zu Sole—ESPIONAGE', as
it was carried in the FBI files), 'of great importance' and who in the period between 12
October 1939 and 18 January 1940 kept him under 'physical surveillance', assigning no
fewer than 46 agents to him, informed the President and other branches of the Executive
that Trott was 'reported to be soliciting the assistance of a number of prominent individuals
in the United States in support of a movement involving the overthrow of the present
regime in Germany (John Edgar Hoover to Special Agent in Charge, Los Angeles, Calif.,
24 Oct. 1938, FBI Trott file, vol. i; see also letter from J. Edgar Hoover to General Watson,
18 Dec. 1939 incl. 35-page memorandum concerning the activities of Trott, FBI Trott file,
vol. v; E. A. Tamm, Memorandum for the Director, 23 Feb. 1940, FBI Trott file, vol. viii;
letters from J. Edgar Hoover to General Edwin M. Watson, 18 Dec. 1939, 16 Jan. 1940,
J. Edgar Hoover to Henry Morgenthau, Jr., 27 Feb. 1940, FDR Library, Hyde Park, NY,
Official File, Cont. 10b, Morgenthau, Cont. 243. If anything, Hoover harboured suspicions
concerning Trott's left-wing leanings and acquaintances. It has also been suggested that
the 'espionage' label had been attached to the Trott case to protect him against Nazi
detection; letter from Heinrich Kronstein (Georgetown University Law Centre) to Hans
Rothfels, 18 Jan. 1962, BA/K, Rothfels 28–2; as a source for this proposition Kronstein
mentioned Hugh Cox who was Assistant to the Attorney General between 1939 and 1943
and became Assistant Attorney General in 1943.

195. G. S. Messersmith to the Secretary—The Under Secretary, 20 Nov. 1939, NA, RG 59,
CDF 862.20211, Trott, Adam von/3; reproduced in Hans Rothfels, 'Adam von Trott und
das State Department', 331.

196. Italics in the original; letter from Adam von Trott to Hasso von Seebach, Kyoto, 12 Feb.
1940, Julie Braun-Vogelstein Papers, Leo Baeck Institute; italics in the original.

197. Widow of the German socialist Heinrich Braun; a wealthy Jewish lady of strong personality
and broad interests. She was a prolific author, especially in the field of art history and
biography. Trott met her at her home outside Berlin in the winter of 1934–5. A relationship
of mutual confidence developed between them, and while Trott initially featured as her
protector against Nazi harassments, in subsequent years she became a mother figure and
patron to him. She emigrated to the USA where in the spring of 1937 and again in the
winter of 1939–40 Trott saw a great deal of her. After Pearl Harbor she was for a time
imprisoned and under constant FBI surveillance because of suspicions emanating from
misconstrued FBI monitorings of her telephone conversations with Trott.

198. One of Trott's socialist friends and a protégé of Julie Braun-Vogelstein; the two had
emigrated together to the USA where he worked with the 'American Friends of German
Freedom', an organization closely linked with the left-wing Neu Beginnen Resistance
group; Seebach's particular assignment was to maintain relations with conservative circles
in order to utilize their sources of information; Minutes of the Research and Information
Service of the American Friends of German Freedom, 27 Dec. 1940, Julie Braun-Vogelstein
Papers IV. After the war Seebach returned to Germany.

199. Of the Hamburg bankers' family. Trott became friends with her in 1935 while in Hamburg.
She emigrated in 1936 to the USA; see her recently published autobiography: Ingrid
Warburg-Spinelli, *Die Dringlichkeit des Mitleids und die Einsamkeit, nein zu sagen. Lebens-
erinnerungen 1910–1989* (Hamburg, 1990).

200. Both Gerhard Ritter (*Carl Goerdeler*, 495 n. 43) and John W. Wheeler-Bennett, who was
a member of the Conference in Virginia and at the time close to Trott as well as to his
group, later in his *The Nemesis of Power: The German Army in Politics 1918–1945* (London,
1954), 487–8 attributed it to Kurt Riezler and Hans Simons. Hans Rothfels in the first
edn. of his work (*The German Opposition to Hitler: An Appraisal*, Hinsdale Ill., 1948, 136–
7) attributed it to Trott, whereas later (*Die deutsche Opposition gegen Hitler: Eine Würdigung*,
Frankfurt/M., 1958, 203 n. 18) he elaborated further that Paul Scheffer, Riezler, and
Simons also contributed to the document. Meanwhile Hans Simons has emphatically
denied having had any part in the formulation of the Memorandum (Letter from Hans
Simons to Dr Clarita von Trott zu Solz, New York, 18 July 1957, Trott Archive, Berichte)
and moreover Paul Scheffer has emerged with an elaborate and, on the whole, convincing,

exposé on the metamorphosis and authorship (Letter from Paul Scheffer to Hans Rothfels, Woodstock, Vt., 6 Oct. 1958; BA/K, Rothfels 28, Bd. 7b) which Rothfels has finally also taken over in his article 'Adam von Trott und das State Department'.

201. Brüning's part in the discussions has been stressed by his then Assistant at Harvard, Alexander Böker; letter from Alexander Böker to Dr Clarita von Trott zu Solz, 28 Apr. 1958, Trott Archive, Berichte; see also letter from Trott to Brüning, 1 Nov. 1939, FBI Trott file, vol. viii.

202. Letter from Scheffer to Rothfels.

203. Ibid.

204. Ibid.

205. As for Trott, while quietly going along with this proposition, at the proper time he revealed the fact that he was author of the manuscript 'only in parts'; letter from Adam von Trott to David Astor, 26 Dec. 1939, David Astor Papers.

206. 'Memorandum' in Rothfels, 'Adam von Trott und das State Department', 322–9; see also FO 371/34449/C 5218/155/18.

207. Trott deposited the typescript with his friend Julie Braun-Vogelstein; it is prefaced by an annotation in Trott's handwriting: 'Erste Fassung eines später stark veränderten Memo-randums von P. Scheffer', Trott Archive, Julie Braun-Vogelstein.

208. Letter from Scheffer to Rothfels.

209. The paragraph in question starts as follows: 'If, on the other hand, the German people—groping for some bearable alternative to Hitler—are met with continued vagueness and intransigence from the Western powers, their desperate hopes are bound to turn eastwards once more. The ensuing resurgence of popular unrest forms as yet a remoter possibility than might be taken as the obvious immediate implication of the Nazi–Soviet threat . . .'; Rothfels 'Adam von Trott und das State Department', 325. The FBI report of 2 Dec. 1939 reproduced a conversation which took place on 4 Nov. between Trott and Miss Anne Boardman of the Institute of Pacific Relations which proceeded as follows: 'Then apparently MISS BOARDMAN dictated corrections for the memo as follows: "If on the other hand the German masses, groping for some venerable alternative from Hitler, are met with continuing vagueness from the western powers, their desperate hopes are bound to turn eastward once more and inevitably press in the direction of the East." Von Trott then suggested these two sentences: "This institutes a much remoter possibility as is implied in the general propaganda regarding the Soviet Pact. This ensuing resurgence of Communistic thinking is as yet a much remoter possibility than is implied in the German–Soviet Pact." A lengthy discussion then followed as to how this sentence was to be constructed . . .'; FBI report on Adam von Trott of 2 Dec. 1939, 22, FBI Trott file, vol. iv. Even the prism of FBI surveillance, always somewhat mysterious, points to Trott's part in the formulation of the paragraph.

210. 'A Practical Vision', 11.

211. Ibid. 12.

212. Rothfels, 'Adam von Trott und das State Department', 327. The early version also calls for an American guarantee of the projected stipulations or, as an alternative, at least a moral commitment to them on the part of the Holy See or the 'Oecumenical Council of the Christian Churches'; but this whole complex was dropped in the final version; it is to be noted though that this is the first instance—the first draft goes back to July 1939—in which a role for the Vatican and also the Council of Churches as mediators on behalf of the German Resistance was considered.

213. Brüning, Briefe und Gespräche, 297.

214. G. S. Messersmith to the Secretary—The Under Secretary, Nov. 20, 1939, Rothfels, 'Adam von Trott und das State Department', 329.

215. See letter from Heinrich Brüning to George S. Messersmith, 30 Nov. 1939 in Brüning, Briefe und Gespräche, 296; annotation by Brüning, July–Sept. 1944, ibid. 417. Also, according to the diaries of Felix Morley, the editor of the Washington Post and an unwavering admirer of Trott, Brüning visited the White House—the date given is Dec. 1939—and registered that, initially at least, Roosevelt showed 'interest in the appeal for support of the German Underground'; Alexander B. Maley, 'The Epic of the German Underground', Human Events, 3 (27 Feb. 1946); Morley was co-editor of this journal, and

while much of the material for this specific article was collated by Maley who had been a naval intelligence officer during the war, it was actually written by Alexander Böker, Brüning's Assistant at Harvard who actively engaged himself on behalf of Trott during his visit to the USA; Letter from Alexander Böker to Dr Clarita von Trott zu Solz, Bonn, 28 Apr. 1958, Trott Archive, Berichte.

216. There is a dating problem here. In a note dated 14 Nov. Messersmith himself related to Welles that he had obtained the copy of the Memorandum 'yesterday'. While an FBI teletype of 13 Nov. confirmed this date, according to another FBI document, a taped telephone conversation of the afternoon of 10 Nov. between Stone and Trott, Stone reported to Trott in great detail his sessions of the same day in the State Department with Welles and Messersmith; FBI teletype, 13 Nov. 1939, FBI Trott File, vol. ii; FBI Report on Adam von Trott, 2 Dec. 1939, entry for 10 Nov., 29–31, FBI Trott File, vol. iv. Since, however, according to the telephone conversation Messersmith identified Trott before Stone had mentioned the source of the Memorandum which he had delivered, it can be assumed that he did this on the strength of his previous briefing from Brüning over the weekend of 11/12 Nov.

217. Copy of letter from Paul Scheffer to Margret Boveri, n.d., Trott Archive, Berichte; see also Sykes, *Troubled Loyalty*, 302–3.

218. G. S. Messersmith to the Secretary—the Under Secretary, 20 Nov. 1939.

219. See also Margret Boveri's interpretation of this episode along the same lines in Margret Boveri, 'Critique of Sykes', 18–19, Trott Archive.

220. Frankfurter evidently did not agree with the assumption that held the ills of the Versailles Treaty responsible for the rise of Hitler; but Trott made some remark to the effect that the American Jews should refrain from taking a prominent part in the question of a peace settlement with Germany; see Sykes, *Troubled Loyalty*, 303–4.

221. C. M. Bowra, *Memories 1898–1939* (London, 1966), 306.

222. Letter from Adam von Trott to David Astor, 26 Dec. 1939; David Astor Papers.

223. G. S. Messersmith to the Secretary—the Under Secretary, 20 Nov. 1939.

224. This according to the diary of Felix Morley as related by Alexander Böker; letter from Alexander Böker to Dr Clarita von Trott.

225. Kate Mitchell and W. L. Holland (eds.), *Problems of the Pacific, 1939* (New York, 1940), 93–4.

226. Report on Adam von Trott, 2 Dec. 1939, FBI Trott file, vol. iv.

227. Lord Lothian.

228. Heinrich Brüning.

229. Lord Halifax.

230. The 'latin friends': the French; letter from Adam von Trott to David Astor, 26 Dec. 1939, David Astor Papers; italics in the original.

231. Sykes, *Troubled Loyalty*, 314.

232. See Deutsch, *The Conspiracy*, 156; the Memorandum was turned over by Trott in New York to his cousin by marriage Charles Bosanquet to be taken to Britain, and it was delivered by him to the FO. I have not been able to find the document in the Public Record Office; for the text of the Memorandum see Hans Rothfels, 'Trott und die Aussenpolitik des Widerstandes', *VfZ*, 12 (July 1964), 313–15; see also 305.

233. FO 371/24363/C 1545/267/62, dated 28 Dec. 1939; Rothfels, 'Trott und die Aussenpolitik', 316–18; see also 307.

234. Alexander Böker diary, entry of 26 Dec. 1939; Alexander Böker Papers.

235. Dated 27 Dec. 1939.

236. Minute by Sir Robert Vansittart, 23 Jan. 1940.

237. Minute by Sir Alexander Cadogan, 24 Jan. 1940.

238. He directed the Auslandsbüro of his group from London.

239. Letters from David Astor to Adam von Trott, London, 27 Oct., 10 Nov. 1939, Trott Archive.

240. Werner Röder's assertion, based primarily on Richard Löwenthal's testimony, to the effect that Frank was sent over by the Foreign Office is not verified by documentary evidence and seems exaggerated; in fact it has been explicitly denied by David Astor.; Werner Röder, *Die deutschen sozialistischen Exilgruppen in Grossbritannien 1940–1945*, 2nd edn. (Bonn-

Bad Godesberg, 1973), 39, 174; Richard Löwenthal, *Die Widerstandsgruppe 'Neu Beginnen'* (Berlin, 1982), 13–14; interview with the Hon. David Astor, 22 May 1982.

241. Letter from Adam von Trott to Shiela Grant Duff, Glasgow, 22 July 1933, von Klemperer (ed.), *A Noble Combat*, 18.

242. In the summer of 1939 Dietrich Bonhoeffer found himself in a similar predicament. In the course of his visit to New York his friends there urged him to stay on and to take up the post as a pastor of the Protestant exiles. He decided, however, to return to his homeland, for he was convinced that he had to share the trials ahead with his own people.

243. FBI Report on Trott, 11 Dec. 1939, pp. 14, 23, FBI Trott File, vol. iv.

244. Letter from Adam von Trott to Diana Hopkinson, mid-Jan. 1940, Hopkinson, 'Aus Adams Briefen', 147–50.

245. Memorandum of President Roosevelt to Felix Frankfurter, 17 Jan. 1940, Morgenthau Papers 238, FDR Library, Hyde Park.

246. Draft of letter from Adam von Trott to Walter Hewel, 11 Feb. 1940, Trott Archive, Briefe an Andere.

247. 'gehässigen und kriegstreiberischen'.

248. 'erschreckende Verhetzung'.

249. See letter from Adam von Trott to Hasso von Seebach, Kyoto, 12 Feb. 1940, Julie Braun-Vogelstein Papers.

250. *New York Times*, 10 Feb. 1940.

251. Letter from Adam von Trott to Hasso von Seebach, Kyoto, 12 Feb. 1940, Julie Braun-Vogelstein Papers.

252. Quoted in Langer and Gleason, *The Challenge to Isolation*, 362.

253. Entry of 14–17 Feb. 1940, *Die Hassell-Tagebücher* 165.

254. Ibid. 167; von Hassell suggested, besides Schacht, Erwin Planck, and Popitz; the former had been State Secretary in the Reich Chancellery under von Papen and von Schleicher, left the government service after the Nazi seizure of power, and became active in resistance activities for which he was executed after the unsuccessful coup of 20 July 1944.

255. He had been, it will be remembered, dismissed from the Reichsbank Presidency in January 1939, but remained Minister without Portfolio until January 1943.

256. For the 'Report by the Under Secretary of State (Welles) on His Special Mission to Europe' see *FRUS*, 1940, i. 21–117; for his stop in Berlin, 33–58; for his meeting with Weizsäcker, 42–3; see also Sumner Welles, *The Time for Decision* (New York, 1944), 73–147, 90–120, 99–100 respectively. Welles's book, Weizsäcker pointed out in his *Erinnerungen*, 277, appeared during wartime, and might have greatly damaged Weizsäcker; it was only due to good fortune that it or at least the potentially incriminating passages did not come to the attention of Ribbentrop.

257. *FRUS*, 1940, i, 56–8; cf. also Hjalmar Schacht, *My First Seventy-Six Years* (London, 1955), 408–10.

258. 'I cannot write a letter, I cannot have a conversation, I cannot telephone, I cannot move, without its being known.'

259. Langer and Gleason, *The Challenge to Isolation*, 367.

260. Michael Balfour and Julian Frisby, *Helmuth von Moltke: A Leader Against Hitler* (London, 1972), 141, 168–9; George F. Kennan, *Memoirs 1925–1950* (Boston, Mass., 1967), 122.

261. *FRUS*, 1940, i. 63.

262. Ibid. 88–9.

263. Sir Ernest Llewellyn Woodward, *British Foreign Policy in the Second World War* (London, 1970), i. 169–70.

264. Ibid. 169.

265. Von Weizsäcker, *Erinnerungen*, 276.

266. Annelies von Ribbentrop, *Die Kriegsschuld des Widerstandes: Aus britischen Geheimdokumenten 1938/39*, ed. Rudolf von Ribbentrop (2nd edn., Leoni am Starnbergersee, 1975), 135. But such crude indictment is altogether out of place if only in the light of a succinct definition of *Landesverrat* by the Supreme Court of the Reich in 1931 which identified intent as the decisive criterion for *Landesverrat*, namely the 'determination and the will to administer harm to the German war potential' which in turn have to be evaluated in the context of the 'general motivation'; as a consequence the Court ruled that, assuming

214

the latter was informed by the objective to prevent yet greater damage to the war potential of the Reich than would be caused by the treasonous act, the charge of *Landesverrat* would not apply. This Supreme Court decision, issued on 20 Oct. 1931, settled once and for all a legal battle over the charge levelled by a right-wing journalist against the former German President Friedrich Ebert to the effect that, by supporting a munition workers' strike during the war in January 1918, he had committed the crime of *Landesverrat*; see Hans Jürgen von Kleist-Retzow and Fabian von Schlabrendorff, 'Landesverrat'? in *Deutsche Rundschau*, 84 (Oct. 1958), 927–32; Fabian von Schlabrendorff, 'Sub specie aeternitatis', Bruno Heck (ed.), *Widerstand, Staat und Kirche: Eugen Gerstenmaier zum 70. Geburtstag* (Frankfurt/M., 1976), 19–39; Peter Hoffmann, *Widerstand gegen Hitler: Problem des Umsturzes* (Munich, 1979), 64.

267. Ian Colvin, *Master Spy* (New York, 1951), 125.

268. This statement, attributed to Bonhoeffer by Willem A. Visser't Hooft (*Memoirs*, London 1973, 153), has meanwhile been questioned by Bonhoeffer's friend and biographer Eberhard Bethge (Amtsgericht Heilbronn, Strafsache gegen Manfred Röder, 'Verunglimpfung eines Verstorbenen', 27 July 1976).

269. 'Sicherung des Auslandes'; 'Protokoll der Besprechung mit Frau v. Dohnanyi am 1. Dezember 1952'; IfZ, ZS 603.

270. However, his bold follow-up argument that of necessity *Hochverrat* had to be combined with *Landesverrat* was as much out of step with the 1931 Supreme Court decision as was the one of Annelies von Ribbentrop. The German Resistance strictly speaking did not meet the criteria for *Landesverrat*.

271. Józef Garliński, *The Swiss Corridor: Espionage Networks in Switzerland during World War II* (London, 1981), 84–97; see also Nigel West, *MI6: British Secret Intelligence Service Operations 1909–45* (New York, 1983), xiv; Colvin, *Master Spy*, 100–5.

272. Most Secret Report by Victor A. L. Mallet. 1 Sept. 1944, FO 371/43503/N 56131/767/42.

273. Carl Goerdeler, 'Mein letzter Wille', 4 Nov. 1944; BA/K, Kaiser 135.

274. Theo Kordt, 'Wir wollten den Frieden retten', *Stuttgarter Rundschau*, 8 (1948), 13.

275. Bodo Scheurig, *Ewald von Kleist-Schmenzin. Ein Konservativer gegen Hitler* (Oldenburg, 1968), 169–70.

276. The particulars of Kleist's argumentation have been recorded in a letter of 5 Jan. 1940 by the Swedish Minister to Berlin Arvid Gustav Richert to the Chief of the Political Department in the Swedish Foreign Office, reproduced in 'Widerstand ist vaterländische Pflicht' Aus den Akten des schwedischen Ministerium des Äusseren, *Politische Studien*, 10 (July 1959), 435–9.

277. Thun-Hohenstein, *Der Verschwörer*; Hermann Graml, 'Der Fall Oster', *VfZ*, 14 (Jan. 1966), 26–39; also Interview with General Achim Oster 23 June 1980.

278. Enquêtecommissie. Regeringsbeleid 1940–1945. Verslag houdende de Uitkomst van het Onderzoek, Deel 1 c: Algemene Inleiding/Militair Beleid 1939–1940. Verhoren, Derde Druk (Staatsdrukkereij-en Uitgeverijbedrijf/'s Gravenhage, 1949), IfZ, ZS 1626. p. 8.

279. The two men had actually first met in 1932.

280. The main source for the Sas reports to his General Staff and Government is IfZ, ZS 1626; for the Sas transmissions to the Belgians see Vicomte Jacques Davignon, *Berlin 1936–1940: Souvenirs d'une Mission* (Paris, 1951; Jean Vanwelkenhuyzen, 'Les Avertissements qui venaient de Berlin', unpubl. MS, Brussels, 1979, cited in Thun-Hohenstein, *Der Verschwörer*, 287 n. 37.

281. Hsi-Huey Liang, *The Sino-German Connection: Alexander von Falkenhausen between China and Germany 1900–1941* (Amsterdam, 1978), 155. Falkenhausen, a chivalrous officer of the old school, was a determined foe of National Socialism. To Trott, with whom he shared an interest in China, he wrote cryptically early in April 1940: 'Many developments are contrary to my wishes, and I have my own thoughts about them; but all this is said better orally. In any case, I believe we have done everything possible. This at any rate is a consolation, however slight.' (Letter from Alexander von Falkenhausen to Adam von Trott, Dresden, 5 Apr. 1940, Trott Archive, quoted ibid. 155.) Beck and Canaris advanced his name to Brauchitsch for the post of Military Governor of the occupied Netherlands where he could be useful to the Resistance; however, this position was awarded to the Austrian Nazi Arthur Seyss-Inquart. As for Falkenhausen's governance of Belgium and

Northern France, it is fair to say that, while involved in the execution of hostages and deportation of Jews, he minimized the reprisals and brutality decreed from Berlin and sought to bring the area under his command through the war 'with the least possible damage' (ibid. 156). Though he was too conservative himself to take part in conspiracy, he maintained ties with many of its leaders. In the planning among the Resistance leaders for a future German government his name was repeatedly proposed for key positions including the chancellorship. After 20 July 1944 he spent nine months in Gestapo captivity; in 1951 he was convicted by a Belgian military tribunal, sentenced to 12 years' imprisonment but released after three weeks; Falkenhausen Papers, esp. Eu 2/6, 4/2, 5/3, NP 47/2, 50/22, 50/26, 51/1.

282. Deutsch, *The Conspiracy*, 320; the Norwegian Counsellor of Legation, Ulrich Stang, whom Sas sought out the following day at the bar of the Hotel Adlon, was incredulous; only later Sas learned from Oster that Stang was an adherent of the Norwegian Nazi leader Quisling. The Danish Military Attaché, Kjølsen, on whom Sas called in the afternoon, did forward the information immediately by courier to Copenhagen. As for the message to London, it was not forwarded by the Dutch; ibid. 320–2; Thun-Hohenstein, *Der Verschwörer*, 188. According to a reliable but unconfirmed account, Goerdeler on his part sent warnings about the impending German landing in Norway directly to London; 'Aufzeichnung Dr. Schloßstein', Stuttgart, 15 Sept. 1945, BA/K, Ritter 131. It should be mentioned in this connection that as early as shortly before Christmas 1939 Hasso von Etzdorf had taken the occasion of a luncheon at Berlin's Horcher Restaurant with Prince Otto von Bismarck, eldest grandson of the Chancellor, and the Swedish banker Jacob Wallenberg to warn the latter of Hitler's plans to invade Denmark and Norway. Wallenberg of course related this piece of intelligence to his Foreign Minister, Christian E. Günther, through whom, in turn, it was forwarded to the Norwegian Minister in Stockholm: The information, however, made as little impression on government circles in Norway as it did on those in Sweden; letter from Jacob Wallenberg to Professor Arvid Brodersen, postmarked 22 Feb. 1980, courtesy Professor Brodersen; letters from Mr Hasso von Etzdorf to me, 4 July 1978, 9 Jan., 11 Sept. 1981.

283. But the message evidently did not reach Paris; the incompleteness of British documentation does not allow any clues as to whether or not the Pope informed Osborne; Deutsch, *The Conspiracy*, 319, 334–5.

284. IfZ, ZS 1626. p 20.

285. Ibid. According to Harold C. Deutsch, information about the forthcoming attack, derived from General von Reichenau's headquarters in Düsseldorf, also was forwarded, on 8 May, by a Socialist refugee from Germany, Alfred Mozer, to the leader of the Dutch Social Democrats who, upon reaching the War Ministry, was told that the same information had been obtained from the Military Attaché in Berlin but that it was not believed; Deutsch, *The Conspiracy*, 328.

286. IfZ, ZS 1626.

287. Ibid. 23; by the time the *Enquête* was conducted—in March 1948—Sas was a Major General and Military Attaché to the USA.

288. Davignon, *Berlin*, 196; see also Jean Vanwelkenhuyzen, 'Die Niederlande und der "Alarm" im Januar 1940', *Vfz*, 8 (Jan. 1960), 32.

289. Ritter, *Carl Goerdeler*, 264. I might add here that in my interview with General Hans Speidel, Rommel's last Chief of Staff who had close connections with the Resistance, when asked to discuss the Oster case, preferred not to do so; interview with General Hans Speidel, 14 July 1975.

290. Hans Rothfels, *Die deutsche Opposition* (1958), 90.

291. IfZ, ZS 1626. p. 9.

292. 'Kavaliersdelikt'; Kleist-Retzow, Schlabrendorff, 'Landesverrat?', 927.

293. According to Lieutenant Colonel Friedrich Wilhelm Heinz, a close associate of Oster in the conspiracy, the scenario was that the offensive, stopped short by the coup, would cost in the environs of 40,000 dead; Sendtner, 'Die deutsche Militäropposition', 512–13. For Oster and the 'set-back theory' see Graml, 'Der Fall Oster', 38–9; Thun-Hohenstein, *Der Verschwörer*, 182–3.

294. Ritter, *Carl Goerdeler*, 265.

295. For the Belgians see Hoffmann, *History*, 171. It should be mentioned here that earlier, on 10 Jan., a Luftwaffe machine had to make an emergency landing near Malines in Belgium. The two majors who had been aboard and who carried plans for the German attack in the west, managed to destroy some of the documents, but not enough to conceal from the Belgian authorities the German intentions to invade Holland and Belgium. Of course the German plans were subsequently changed and the attack was postponed anyway, partly as a result of the swift Belgian mobilization, giving the Low Countries a respite until May; Vanwelkenhuyzen, 'Die Niederlande', *passim*.

296. A Memorandum by G. P. Young of 30 Apr. 1940, identifying among various possible German moves the attack through Holland and Belgium as the 'most probable' one, mentions as a source of information a person alternately referred to as German Counsellor at Berne and Chargé d'Affaires [earlier in London] as giving the intelligence to the British Minister David Kelly; FO 371/24381/C 6543/5/18.

297. Donald R. Heath to Secretary of State, Washington, Rush, 10 May 1940; the message was received by the Division of European Affairs of the Department of State early in the morning, but there is no indication that the Secretary of State saw it; NA, RG 59, CDF 740.0011 EW 1939/2778; see also Alexander Kirk to Department of State, Rush, 7 May 1940, NA, RG 59, CDF 740.0011 EW 1939/2707; even at this late date he suggested possible action by the American President towards peace.

298. Scheurig, *Ewald von Kleist-Schmenzin*, 176.

299. See Woodward, *British Foreign Policy*, i. 174–6.

300. Klaus-Jürgen Müller, *Heer und Hitler*, 571–2.

301. Klaus-Jürgen Müller's assumption (ibid. 571) that this gesture was addressed as well to the British partners of the Vatican Exchanges seems far-fetched. Another question is whether the Vatican forwarded the information to Osborne; but we do not know.

302. Bethge, *Bonhoeffer*, 579–80.

# 4

# Widerstand *and the Forging of the Grand Alliance*

## 1. Winston Churchill and 'Absolute Silence'

The German offensive in the West brought to a close a phase of intense activity in the foreign efforts of the German Resistance. The initiative to the many feelers had come, as we have seen, not only from the German side. Both the British and the Germans hoped to avert the worst, and behind all the exchanges there loomed the hope somehow to co-ordinate the prevention of a shooting war with a change of regime in the Reich. Vansittart, the old 'friend' of the 'moderates' in Germany, had gone on record early on in a grandiloquent memorandum entitled 'The Nature of the Beast' to remind the Foreign Office that the British were fighting 'the *character* of the German people' and to urge upon it an unbending policy towards everything German.[1] But Chamberlain and Halifax had never quite abandoned the prospect of a deal with the German 'Generals', and the Foreign Office through the early months of 1940 still kept calculating on the political potential of the anti-Nazi exiles.[2] As late as the early part of July 1940 Hugh Dalton, Britain's Labour Minister of Economic Warfare in the new Churchill government, and about to be commissioned to head the Special Operations Executive (SOE) that was to 'set Europe ablaze' in support of anti-Nazi underground movements everywhere, included the 'anti-Nazi elements in Germany and Austria', along with all the others, as being 'on our side'.[3]

The stock of the German Resistance, however, was clearly plummeting abroad. To begin with, it had spoken with many, in fact too many voices. And should not the German Generals be held to account for the fact that the breathing spell of the Twilight War had not yielded any results? Instead of staging the coup, they launched attacks first in the north[4] and then in the west. The Vansittart proposition, moreover, that the emissaries of the *Widerstand*, however firmly opposed to Hitler, had not shed their aspirations to German expansion in the west as well as east could not be altogether dismissed in London. The supreme effort on the part of the conspirators in channelling vital military intelligence abroad was not registered with any particular appreciation, it was merely registered for what it was worth there, namely information. It remained for Beck, Kleist-Schmenzin, and Oster to reconcile their grand gesture with their consciences. As for the American diplomats, they were in no position to appreciate one way or another the few signals they received, via Trott, Schacht, and Lochner; George Kennan, as we shall see, had good reason to remain silent about his contacts with Moltke. As yet the United States were too remote from and undecided about the European scene.

It has been rightly argued that during the period following the German victory over France, British diplomacy enjoyed maximum latitude in coping with feelers from the other side since it was no longer encumbered by restraints from the French and not yet by restraints imposed by an alliance with Russia or, for that matter, America.[5] But the appointment on 10 May of Winston Churchill to the post of Prime Minister of Britain made an end to all his predecessor's irresolutions, including the one relating to the dealings with feelers from the German Underground. The Battle of Britain, unleashed by the German Luftwaffe early in July, only strengthened the determination of the new government, as well as the population at large, and had the effect of playing down the 'search for the "Good German" '.[6] Although in the summer of 1940 Lord Halifax still presented to the War Cabinet the proposition that, with the French out of the picture, Britain could safely return to the policy line that Germany, once rid of Hitlerism, could 'take her place in a new and better Europe',[7] and although Churchill himself never subscribed to the Vansittart argumentation which, 'darkened by hatred or obscured by sentiment', he thought 'silly',[8] one by one all distinctions between Germans and Nazis faded.

A direct sequel to the mood of resolution in Britain was a directive issued by Winston Churchill on 20 January 1941. The immediate occasion was a peace feeler coming from a Swedish Baron by the name of Knud Bonde. A contact of Göring's, he had approached Lord Halifax in December 1939 in the name of the former with a peace feeler. The Secretary of State responded evasively, but not without affirming his government's willingness to negotiate with a German government which they could trust and which was prepared to right the wrongs Germany had done.[9] After Baron Bonde appeared in January of 1941 at the British Legation in Berne with a similar message, Churchill sent to his new Secretary of State, Anthony Eden,[10] the following communication:

I presume you are keeping your eyes upon all this. Your predecessor was entirely misled in December 1939. Our attitude towards all such enquiries should be absolute silence ... WSC 20.1.41.[11]

Similar instructions were sent to posts where peace feelers had been received in the past.

Baron Bonde's was a peace feeler, certainly. Not all the approaches that came from the German Opposition were primarily peace feelers; some were, others were not. Paramount in its considerations was the aim of toppling the Nazi regime. Now, however, peace feelers and Resistance overtures alike were indiscriminately thrown together, and the Churchillian command of 'absolute silence' applied to both. What irony that Weizsäcker's original prescription of the *silence menaçant* to be maintained by the British towards the Nazis was now turned against the German Resistance feelers. Churchill was understandably resolved to see the war through to the end by military means and by forging a Grand Coalition against 'That Man', as he frequently called Hitler. Meanwhile, negotiations of any sort, even with Resistance emissaries, seemed to him distractions from that objective. Churchill in effect thus anticipated President Roosevelt's 'unconditional surrender' formula, which became a major stumbling block to the continuing efforts of the German conspirators to reach the outside world.

## 2. Nazi Triumphs and the *Widerstand*

The German offensive in May 1940 and the swift German victory in the west altogether transformed the relations between the German Opposition and the British. Of course the French were now out of the picture. As the mood in Britain shifted in the direction of survival and ultimate victory rather than negotiated peace, so for the German resisters the German military triumph created an entirely new situation calling for a rethinking of their position and their plans. To begin with, Ulrich von Hassell was right when he noted that 'nothing is more successful than success'.[12] Once again Hitler's 'invincibility' had been demonstrated, and the sceptics among the military who had warned against the campaign had in turn been proved wrong. Weizsäcker's annotation at the time of the German advance is significant in this respect: 'Even those generals who before 10 May 1940 had misgivings about an offensive against the West are now convinced of its appropriateness, talk disparagingly of the enemy, and do not like to be reminded of their previous judgements.'[13] Even Weizsäcker himself, however troubled about the prospect of a New Order under Nazi auspices, consoled himself with the thought 'that very often in history great transformations have been wrought by criminals'.[14] Moreover, those at the core of the conspiracy were keenly aware of the fact that the task of staging a coup on top of victory was virtually impossible. While von Hassell vowed not to throw in the sponge and 'to fight on [against Hitler] under changed conditions',[15] and while Goerdeler, however 'shaken', was equally resolved not to give up the battle, the immediate reaction among the conspirators was one of utter dejection and despair.[16] In his down-to-earth style Helmuth von Moltke registered at about this time that from day to day he felt more and more nauseated.[17] But in view of 'the triumph of evil', he knew a primary condition for overcoming it was to reassure oneself continuously of what is good and what is evil.[18]

With action on the part of the Resistance at a virtual standstill, the traffic with the outside world of course also shrank to a trickle. A carry-over, so to speak, of the days before the offensive was a letter which Adam von Trott received shortly after the fall of France from his old friend, the British Ambassador in Washington, Lord Lothian, urging him to engage himself in the cause of an Anglo-German reconciliation.[19] Trott, however, was not certain what exactly Lothian had in mind, that is, whether he included the possibility of a deal with the Nazi regime. At this point, of course, any form of 'reconciliation' was out of the question, and Trott was obviously in too junior a position to be burdened with such a mammoth task. In any event, particularly because of the ambiguity of the message from Lothian, Trott made no attempt to follow it up; indeed he did not mention the existence of the letter to anyone.[20]

Trott's friend Helmuth von Moltke, for the moment at least, also wound up his personal contacts with friends in Britain, and in December 1940, when one of his American journalist friends from Berlin, Wallace Deuel of the *Chicago Daily News*, had to leave Germany, he sent an oral message through him to Lord Lothian, of whom he really did not think too much, and to the South African Ambassador in Washington.[21] Moltke's message was that his views were still the same as they had been before the war, and that they were shared by others. He was pessimistic about the opportunities open to him and to those who shared his views for active resistance, particularly since little reliance could be placed upon the Generals; and that in the long run Hitler would compromise all Germans, so that there would be nobody with whom the Allies could or would make peace. The message was delivered.[22] For the moment at least, it served as an epilogue of sorts.

On the whole the momentous events of May 1940 constituted a divide also in the foreign affairs of the *Widerstand*. Not only did 'relations' with officials or agents abroad come to a virtual standstill, but also, with the swift triumph of the German armies and victory over France, the residual national pride surfaced even among the ranks of the conspirators. Their thinking about Germany's hegemonic place on the European Continent hardened. The new formula was defined, as it were, by Kurt Hahn who, since 1938 a British subject, circulated a number of memoranda in Whitehall; 'our aims', he argued, 'are certainly incompatible with the prestige of Hitler, but not with the honour of Germany.'[23] But the question is what exactly the honour of Germany would imply?

## 3. Ex-Chancellor Joseph Wirth's Folly

Ex-Chancellor Wirth in fact caricatured the honour of Germany, when in September in the name of Gessler, acknowledging that the Battle of Britain was not going well and envisaging the need for an accommodation between Germany and Great Britain, he proposed to the British Military Attaché in Berne a peace settlement that would include German retention of the Channel ports from Dunkirk to Boulogne for a period of years and 'a free hand in the east'.[24] At any rate, the War Office had by then come to the conclusion that Wirth had become a 'back number' in Germany and that he was 'addicted to drink'.

## 4. Albrecht Haushofer's Peace Plans

All the foreign feelers which were initiated in the months following the German offensive in the west by members of the German Resistance ran aground. The evidence we have from that period of foreign-policy activity and planning in Resistance circles is one primarily of memoranda from authors who were reduced to soliloquizing. But the effort, so it seemed, was still worth making; even the faintest prospect of negotiating peace had to be followed up. There was, moreover, a continuing need for the conspirators to clarify their own position, if only towards each other.

Albrecht Haushofer's entry into the arena of foreign feelers may well have been helped by his having one foot in the Nazi establishment; his increasingly critical stance, though, towards Hitler's policies led him early in the summer of 1940 to establish relations with opposition elements. He shared with the protector of his family, the Führer's Deputy, Rudolf Hess, if not with the Führer himself, a basic sense of the need for co-operation between the Germanic peoples, and in particular between the Germans and the Anglo-Saxons,[25] as a prerequisite for the survival of the white 'race'. Thus the war appeared to him even more suicidal.

With the Reich at war with Britain, Haushofer took it upon himself to make a last-ditch effort at reconciliation. One might say that he took on the chase of the horse that had escaped from the stable. But what constituted on one level a way of making up for the adventurous policies of the Foreign Minister and indeed of salvaging the Third Reich, turned more and more into a scouting venture on behalf of his friends in the Resistance.

It all started with a walk which Rudolf Hess and Karl Haushofer took on the last day of August 1940 in a spa of Upper Austria where Hess was on holiday. In the course of this walk Hess expressed the need to find ways of coming to an accommodation with the British and thus preventing the threatened invasion of the British Isles. Haushofer *père* allowed little time to elapse before, on 3 September, he wrote a letter to his son calling upon him, also in the name of 'Tomo'—the code name for Rudolf Hess in the correspondence between the Haushofers[26]—to step on to 'the larger stage' once again and find a way of 'stopping something which would have such infinitely momentous consequences'.[27] The next step was for Albrecht Haushofer himself to call on the Führer's Deputy on 8 September, with the letter from his father in his hand. According to the Top Secret summary written by Haushofer of the two-hour-long conversation,[28] Haushofer told him candidly that 'not only Jews and Freemasons but practically all Englishmen who mattered, regarded a treaty signed by the Führer as a worthless scrap of paper'. He went on to itemize a series of treaties signed and broken by Hitler and went as far as saying that the Führer was regarded, even in the Anglo-Saxon world, as 'Satan's representative on earth' who had to be fought. Haushofer went on to argue that not merely the English assessment of Hitler and of 'Herr von R.', who, as they saw things, had 'informed the Führer wrongly about England', but indeed 'a fundamental [difference in] outlook' was responsible for the fact that the English were bound to reject any German peace feeler. Nevertheless Haushofer ventured into the ways that might be explored to reach the ears of the British: the Minister to Budapest Sir Owen O'Malley; or the Ambassador to Madrid Sir Samuel Hoare; or preferably Lord Lothian, the darling of all German Anglophiles. 'As the final possibility' he mentioned 'the young Duke of Hamilton' who, he claimed, had 'access at all times to all important persons in London, even to Churchill and the King'. But at the very end of the conversation Haushofer managed to insert a remark on the eventuality that he himself 'might possibly have to make a trip alone'.

In a follow-up letter of 19 September[29] Haushofer once again focused on the Anglo-German problem which, as he put it, was to be traced to 'a most profound crisis in mutual confidence'. Once again also he went over the various possible ways of establishing contacts in neutral capitals with Britons such as the Duke of Hamilton, Lothian, and Hoare.[30] But this time he so elaborately spelled out the obstacles in the way of these approaches that the assumption is justified that he did so in the hope that Hess would come round to commissioning him, Haushofer, to undertake the mission.[31] As in the earlier talk with Hess, in this letter the partisan of the Opposition was lurking behind the loyal adviser to the Führer's Deputy. If enabled to undertake the trip himself, Haushofer could have put before his British friends the case of the Opposition, and the peace feeler could have been made to serve the cause of the overthrow of 'Satan's representative on earth'.

The next step for Haushofer was to draft, in the summer of 1940, a Peace Plan, which was addressed to the British.[32] It was clearly written without Hess's *imprimatur*; it was for once an unmistakable document of resistance and most probably written in concurrence with the group around von Hassell and Popitz with which Haushofer had become associated since the spring of 1940. Despite his deep pessimism about the future of the European Continent and especially about the future of Anglo-German relations, he rallied to produce one of the most comprehensive and far-reaching proposals on foreign policy that ever came from the orbit of the *Widerstand*.

In its first part[33] it proposed that 'for an understanding with Britain' the evacuation of all western and northern territories under German occupation was to be accepted 'as a basis'.[34] As for the German borders with France, the future of Alsace-Lorraine was to be subject to Franco-German discussion, but in case these provinces were to remain within the confines of the Reich, the frontiers were to be moved still further west than before 1914. Germany was to be guaranteed her 'special interests' in south-eastern Europe without, however, in any way endangering the sovereignty of the countries concerned. And her eastern frontier, regarded by the Germans as a special problem, was to be settled in conjunction with the states in question and without the participation of other nations.[35]

The second part of the proposal,[36] lofty in design, projected the creation of a European Economic Council[37] to work towards the abolition of customs frontiers, a redrafting of frontiers along the lines of 'effective ethnological, geographical and cultural facts', the creation of a European police force and of a joint air command, a subordination of all navies—including the German one—under British command, and a joint European colonial association linked with the British Empire.

If this document was clearly out of tune with Hitler's vision of a Nazi New Order, can it be termed a peace plan of the German Resistance?[38] Albrecht Haushofer was, as we have seen, an outsider in any case even among his friends in the Resistance; and though this particular Plan may have been composed in conjunction with the group around von Hassell and Popitz, and even discussed with Helmuth von Moltke,[39] it bore more than anything the marks of his father's influence. In all its extravagance it was a variant of sorts of geopolitical thinking in extended continental blocs; Germany was to be the master of Central and East Central Europe.[40] But in its departure from the scheme of the old Haushofer it conjured up a grandiose division of spheres between German continental and British maritime interests. Albrecht Haushofer's genuflections towards the British, other than making embarrassing reading, were certainly miscalculated. Who in his senses, after March and September of 1939, could have expected Britain to be prepared to sell Czechoslovakia and Poland down the river?

In any case, hoping against hope, Haushofer sought to place this document into the hands of the British. His former disciple, Heinrich Georg Stahmer, serving in the Madrid Embassy, was to turn it over to the British Ambassador there. Yet as far as we know, Sir Samual Hoare, the Ambassador, and his staff would have 'nothing to do with any peace negotiations'.[41] To judge from the contents of Haushofer's message, however, it may have been just as well that it did not arrive.

In the spring of the following year Haushofer was to make further attempts to reach the British. Early in March, at a meeting with Popitz and von Hassell in the former's house, the three discussed ways as to how Haushofer, who was still used by Hess for occasional missions, could manage to capitalize on his Swiss connections in order to obtain assurances from the Allies about peace negotiations following a change of regime in Germany.[42] Haushofer indeed obtained from Hess the green light for a trip to Switzerland there to confer with Professor Carl J. Burckhardt, the former League of Nations' High Commissioner for Danzig and later President of the International Red Cross. On the grounds of his contacts with British diplomats, Burckhardt still thought himself justified in holding out to his friends among the German Resistance hopes for some reasonable settlement with a new German regime.[43] Travelling with two faces, ostensibly for Hess but actually for the Resistance, Haushofer expected Burckhardt to put to work his contacts with leading Allied statesmen. He returned from Geneva with empty hands, however.

At about the same time Haushofer tried once more, again through Stahmer, to reach Sir Samuel Hoare who seemed more amenable to German overtures than official London.[44] But this was the time of Hess's flight to Scotland. Actually, on the night of 10/11 May, Stahmer dispatched a telegram to another former student of Haushofer, now working in the Information Department of the Foreign Ministry,[45] to the effect that the lecture of 'the Professor' before the Academy of Sciences in Madrid was to take place on 12 May. It has been conjectured that the intent of this message was to whisk Haushofer away from Germany and out of the reach of the Gestapo; but it is not possible that Stahmer at that time could have known about the Hess escapade. The assumption is all the more possible that the 'lecture' in fact stood for a contact with the British Embassy; and if Hoare did not make himself available for an interview with the German visitor, perhaps one of his subordinates did.[46] In any case, Albert Haushofer was taken into custody on 12 May and flown to the Obersalzberg where he composed a tortured *apologia* for his recent ventures.[47] Thereafter he was moved to the ominous Berlin Gestapo prison in the Prinz Albrechtstrasse to be grilled by the Gestapo, notably SS Gruppenführer Heinrich Müller and Reinhard Heydrich himself. Although there was obviously enough incriminating information on Haushofer concerning his foreign contacts and his impact on Rudolf Hess, he was set free after two months in prison. He might, so both Hitler and Himmler figured, become useful at a later date.[48] The time to do away with him had not yet come.

## 5. The Rigi-Kaltbad Memorandum

Less grandiose than the Haushofer compositions in design, but not much less restrained in its foreign-policy aims, was the memorandum commissioned by Weizsäcker and composed in February 1941 for General Beck by the brothers Kordt together with their cousin Susanne Simonis at Rigi-Kaltbad in Switzerland.[49] It advocated 'urgent measures' at home that would free the Reich from its irresponsible regime by turning it over to a temporary dictatorship of the army as 'the only organization that has been relatively immune to the general maladministration of things'. Ultimately it envisaged a 'state based on freedom and social justice' that would rely neither on dictators nor political parties but on a strong Executive co-opting a Senate with consultative functions and on a parliament with distinctly limited powers in questions of finance. In the foreign realm the Memorandum projected an 'honourable' peace leaving Germany 'intact' with 'its' ethnographic borders. In the event, however, that 'foreign want of understanding' should deny Germany such a peace, 'all resources of the nation' were to be deployed to the utmost. Also, in a rather fuzzy way, the Memorandum called for 'co-operation in the European frame as well as with the ethnically related peoples outside Europe'.

After the war Theo Kordt pleaded that the ideas and the language of the Memorandum should be understood in terms of the conditions prevailing at the time of its composition.[50] They certainly serve as a key to the passages on domestic as well as foreign affairs. The rejection of the Nazi dictatorship was as firm as was the refusal to return to the Weimar 'rule of the parties';[51] and the army, while assigned temporary dictatorial functions, was recognized as the 'taskmaster' of the people. The emphasis in the Rigi-Kaltbad Memorandum on the 'honourable' peace clearly meant a peace from the position of strength and, combined with the insistence on ethnographic borders, reflected the intent of the authors for a Germany without Hitler to benefit from the gains, west and east, brought about by Hitler's foreign-policy adventures as well as by military force.[52] The Kordts were brave men who had not shied away from going to the limit of committing treason in order to prevent the outbreak of the war and at the same time to make an end to the reign of terror at home. But equally they were political men and patriots. Now that the German Reich had clearly established itself as the major power on the Continent, should they or General Beck have surrendered all the gains? As they seem to have viewed the problem, it was at that juncture not one of right or wrong, not one of political ethics, but one of practicality and of political realism. For them an 'honourable' settlement was distinctly compatible with, indeed dependent on, a righting of the wrongs of Versailles, even though the righting had been accomplished by the despised tyrant himself.

## 6. The Indomitable Carl Goerdeler

If anyone disproved the compelling universal validity of the Shakespearian maxim that 'conscience does make cowards of us all', it was Carl Goerdeler. He was a man of thought, moral scruples, and deep religious convictions; at the same time he was a man of action, 'sanguine', as von Hassell repeatedly characterized him, to the point of 'imprudence'.[53] The victories of the German armies in the west certainly brought into focus for Goerdeler the dilemma of being a patriot and at the same time having to come to terms with the 'moral condition' precipitated by the unleashing of the war.[54] While acknowledging the 'outstanding planning' behind the German attack and the brilliant accomplishments of the Wehrmacht, he insisted that 'great power' gained in victory called for 'all the greater responsibility'. Goerdeler remained unimpressed by a war which had been unleashed by a 'system' of living by 'financial madness, economic coercion, political terror, lawlessness, and immorality . . .'. His conscience, then, impelled him to press relentlessly for action against the regime that had brought victory to his country. It was during these very months following victory in the west that Goerdeler, hitherto a loner of sorts in the Resistance, moved into its centre[55] and became, among the civilians in the Resistance, 'the indefatigable motor',[56] as SD-chief Ernst Kaltenbrunner later described him, of all efforts leading up to 20 July 1944.

In the period starting in the summer of 1940 Goerdeler took to writing a whole set of memoranda on the future of Germany and Europe.[57] These may betray a certain theoretical bent and even an obvious inclination to sermonize on his part;[58] primarily, however, they forced him to come to terms with his unwavering condemnation of Nazi aggression. It is interesting that in support of his position he should have cited as a precedent for resistance against Hitler the Freiherr vom Stein's advice of 12 October 1808 to his king to resist Napoleon.[59] Thus he sought to legitimize resistance as a patriotic deed and to reconcile, especially in view of the German victory over France, the moral position of resistance against Hitler with a claim for an 'enlightened organization of free peoples under German leadership'.

It should be noticed, however, that, whatever dissonance there may have been in Goerdeler's reasoning between his firm rejection of the Nazi policies and his call for German leadership on the European Continent, it was resolved by his insistence on the safeguarding of the honour and political freedom of the European peoples, albeit under German tutelage. As he elaborated it in his memoranda,[60] his programme marked a firm rejection both of a narrow German nationalism and a levelling and oppressive hegemonic design in favour of a European federalism under the leadership of a new, enlightened Germany. Gerhard Ritter was not far off the mark in suggesting that Goerdeler's vision may well have been inspired by the example of the British

Commonwealth.[61] In any case, the memoranda of the early 1940s show that his thinking had by that time evolved distinctly in the direction of a commitment to a European solution. Among the Allies, however, even this position was bound to be regarded as suspect and was, in short, unacceptable; what amounted in Goerdeler's mind to a clear alternative to the Nazi schemes and policies was bound to appear across the trenches to amount to little more than a variation on them.

The acid test for Goerdeler's ruminations about the European order of the future came in mid-1941 when he managed to persuade an old acquaintance, the ecumenical publicist, Friedrich Wilhelm Siegmund-Schultze, then living in Swiss exile, to intervene with the British authorities on behalf of the *Widerstand*.[62] Siegmund-Schultze had good connections with political and religious circles in England. He even claimed that in the early stages of the war the British government had twice offered to fly him over from Switzerland to discuss possibilities of concluding peace, but that, having unsuccessfully insisted on backing by the Wehrmacht, he felt obliged to refuse.[63] Siegmund-Schultze's chief connections in the Church of England were Archbishop William Temple of York and Bishop George Bell of Chichester. Around Easter 1941, after lengthy negotiations between Goerdeler and Siegmund-Schultze, in which officials of the Robert Bosch firm (including Hans Walz and Willy Schloßstein), repeatedly acted as intermediaries,[64] a document was agreed upon by the two men for approval by the Wehrmacht leadership and subsequent transmission to London.

On the Friday before Pentecost, that is on 30 May, Schloßstein then appeared at Siegmund-Schultze's in Zurich with the document that bore, so Siegmund-Schultze assures us, von Brauchitsch's much coveted initial and was therefore ready to be turned over to the British.[65] Although Siegmund-Schultze thought, in view of Churchill's widely known hard stand on peace feelers, that this was the 'least opportune' moment for such an overture, he consented to get it under way anyway. As expected, he found that the officials in the British Legation whom he approached would not accept the document from him, not even in the form of a letter to the Archbishop of York. Siegmund-Schultze had reason to believe, however, that the gist at least of his oral communications to them was forwarded by telephone to Whitehall. Furthermore, after an interval of approximately six weeks, he was informed that the British Consul-General in Zurich had been instructed to accept the documents.[66]

Goerdeler's Peace Plan, which thus found its way to London, projected the same design as his earlier memoranda, combining an acknowledgement of Germany's predominance on the Continent with a vision of an enlightened international order.[67] Also it was quite in harmony with the Statement of von Hassell to Lord Halifax of February 1940. While holding out the prospect of a change of government in Germany involving a repudiation of National

Socialism, it called for peace negotiations 'in accordance with earlier assurances from the British government'. Specifically, it called for the confirmation of the *Anschluss*, the German acquisition of the Sudetenland and Memel, and the restoration of the 1914 German frontiers with Belgium, France, and Poland. It also stipulated the restoration of complete sovereignty to neutral countries occupied by the belligerents during the war, 'the establishment of European frontiers on the basis of national right of self-determination', and a reordering of international affairs along the lines of co-operation, adjudication, and mutual consultation. It furthermore proposed the return of the German colonies or equally valuable colonial territory within the framework of an international mandatery system.

The reception of the plan is interesting inasmuch as its contents elicited a minimum of comment. A sense of *déjà vu* made Frank K. Roberts of the British FO Central Department assume that the people behind the document were 'our old friends the "reasonable" Generals, Dr. Goerdeler and possibly Dr. Schacht'; and while it was generally assessed as marking 'an advance on anything previously suggested', its proposals concerning frontiers and also on the colonial question were dismissed as 'quite unacceptable'.[68] But muted as the reaction was, it yields sufficient evidence to belie the conjecture, as stated by Gerhard Ritter, that in the light of the prevailing conditions it was not considered 'over-presumptuous' across the Channel.[69] It can safely be assumed that it was thought futile to enter into argument over any proposals that came from the other side.

In any event, the elaborate file on the Goerdeler peace approach is predominantly concerned with the procedural issue of the advisability of accepting the document. The intervention of the Archbishop of York did not exactly help the Foreign Office to make a clear decision on the matter. He protested his full confidence in his German ecumenical contact, although adding that he had reason not to have equal confidence, in his judgement, in the reliability of the people with whom he was dealing.[70] He even drafted an answer to Siegmund-Schultze which he hoped could be forwarded through the Legation in Berne, expressing his 'warm' approval for some of the propositions and at the same time suggesting that others required 'further explanation'.[71] With all due respect to the Archbishop, however, his draft ran into solid opposition from the Foreign Office and most firmly from the Secretary of State. The latter had actually made one attempt to break through the Churchillian 'absolute silence' barrier earlier in September when, in a memorandum to the Prime Minister, he listed various recent feelers from Germany, including the one by 'a Dr. Schultze of Zurich to the Archbishop of York', asking for authorization to accept some of them through a neutral intermediary, in so far as they threw 'interesting light on internal difficulties and tendencies in Germany'.[72] But the Foreign Secretary was in turn firmly reminded by the Prime Minister of his directive of January:

I am sure we should not depart from our policy of absolute silence. Nothing would be more disturbing to our friends in the United States or more dangerous with our new ally, Russia, than the suggestion that we were entertaining such ideas. I am absolutely opposed to the slightest contact . . .[73]

So the Foreign Secretary was brought into line again. He finally shelved the case of Siegmund-Schultze, minuting that 'under no circumstances' could they have anything to do 'with this or any other peace negotiation'.[74] Thus no answer whatsoever was sent from the Archbishop to Zurich;[75] the Minister in Berne was merely authorized by the Foreign Secretary to convey to 'Schultze' an 'intimation' that Temple had received the initial letter.[76] 'Schultze' had been right from the beginning concerning his misgivings about entering into the venture at all. But he consoled himself with the thought that in subsequent public addresses Eden actually used one sentence of his letter to the Archbishop of York.[77]

## 7. The Atlantic Charter and Abortive American Contacts

As early as the winter of 1939/40 Trott had experienced the reticence, if not hostility, prevailing in Washington towards Germany; even the opposition's messenger was hounded by suspicion.

Back in Berlin, meanwhile, Helmuth von Moltke saw a great deal of the colony of American foreign correspondents, among them Dorothy Thompson, Edgar Ansel Mowrer, and Wallace Deuel. He managed moreover to establish a channel to the American Chargé d'Affaires, Alexander Kirk. The two men hit it off well enough to make a practice of visiting each other periodically. Kirk called on the Moltkes in their apartment in town in the Derfflingerstrasse as frequently as the Moltkes went out to the American's elegant mansion in the Grunewald district. Even if Kirk was clearly not authorized to enter into any dealings with German opposition circles, and even if Moltke could scarcely speak for anyone except himself and the group of friends he was about to assemble in the 'Kreisau Circle', the two men struck up a relationship of mutual confidence and understanding. To Moltke in particular it afforded the opportunity to establish the much coveted 'connection with the greater world'. But he was at the same time a realist and intent upon using the American to convey to Washington, short of betraying any military information, the message that, despite the initial German military triumphs, the war would end badly for his country. He hoped also to discourage any form of appeasement of Nazi Germany.[78]

When Kirk had to leave Germany in October 1940,[79] he turned over this 'most delicate and valuable of his clandestine "contacts" among the German oppositionists'[80] to his young colleague in the Embassy, George F. Kennan.[81]

In the course of their subsequent meetings, held secretly and alone, Kennan came to develop great admiration for Moltke, 'this lonely, struggling man', as he later reminisced, 'a pillar of moral conscience and an unfailing source of political and intellectual inspiration'.[82] When Kennan himself was finally getting ready to return to the United States, he 'accepted', so Moltke wrote to his wife, a 'proposal' from him, promising 'to devote himself to this task'.[83] What exactly Moltke had meant by the 'proposal', we do not know; most probably he had hoped that Kennan would use his influence to persuade the American and British governments to establish some sort of workable contact with the Resistance in Germany.[84] Kennan, however, when he finally reached the United States, decided against following up Moltke's 'proposal' after all. Having learnt that the British also had been apprised of Moltke and his friends' plans, Kennan figured that any additional revelations concerning them would in some way get back to the Gestapo and endanger their security.[85]

Meantime President Roosevelt had been steering the United States steadily closer to taking a position on the war. The Lend–Lease Act, passed by Congress on 11 March 1941, empowered the President to provide goods and services to those nations whose defence he deemed vital to that of the United States. In the first half of August, the American President met with the British Prime Minister, the 'Former Naval Person', as he was called in code, off the shores of Newfoundland aboard the American cruiser *Augusta* and the British battleship *Prince of Wales*. On the 14th the two statesmen issued a Joint Declaration, the so-called 'Atlantic Charter', in which they made known 'certain common principles' in the national policies of their respective countries on which they based 'their hopes for a better future for the world'. In their eight-point message they announced that they were seeking no aggrandisement, territorial or other, and no territorial changes that did not accord with the freely expressed wishes of the peoples concerned, and that they respected the right of all peoples to choose the form of government under which they would live (pts. 1–3). 'After the final destruction of Nazi tyranny', they pledged to establish a peace which would afford all nations the means of dwelling in safety within their own boundaries and all men in all lands freedom from fear and want (pt. 6); to further the enjoyment by all states, 'victor or vanquished', access 'on equal terms' to the trade and raw materials of the world; to bring about the fullest collaboration between all nations in the economic field; to ensure free navigation (pts. 4, 5, 7) and to establish a 'permanent system of general security' (pt. 8).[86]

Our question here, of course, is how the proclamation of this Atlantic Charter was received among the German dissidents. Hugh Dalton, the British Minister of Economic Warfare, brought out the position of the Charter's signatories most vividly when he wrote that their aim was to make Germany 'fat but impotent'.[87] The Prime Minister himself had carefully spelled it out in his world broadcast of 24 August in which he distinguished between the applicability of the provisions for armament and the economy. Concerning armament the characteristically Churchillian formula was 'disarming the guilty nations while remaining suitably protected ourselves'. Concerning the economy the Prime Minister emphatically reiterated the proposal in point 4 of the Charter to the effect that economic prosperity was to be shared by victor and vanquished alike; it was not in the interest of the world and of Britain and the United States in particular that any large nation should be 'unprosperous or shut out from the means of making a decent living for itself and its people by its industry and enterprise'.[88]

It should be no surprise, then, that the reception of the Atlantic Charter in German Resistance circles was, on balance, positive. Ulrich von Hassell thought the Joint Declaration of Churchill and Roosevelt to be, compared with President Wilson's fourteen points, 'in substance ... generally milder and, above all, more elastic'.[89] He was, however, concerned about the reading of the clauses on disarmament (pt. 8) which would be interpreted by the Generals as making no distinction between Germany and Hitler and would also make Germany defenceless; but, he added, that while this was a very plausible interpretation, it was by no means the only one possible.[90] Helmuth von Moltke's reaction to Churchill's radio address of 24 August was close to rhapsodic:

Churchill has made a really great speech. Another one of the speeches that will enter world history as classics. It is less actual content than form and sovereign grasp that raise it to its heights. One feels, reading it, that the man is speaking past us, down on the low ground of history, to the great statesmen of the classical past.[91]

More guarded, but by no means negative, were the reactions of his Kreisau friends, Adam von Trott and Theodor Steltzer.[92] As late as December 1942 Goerdeler composed a response to the Atlantic Charter[93] in which he virtually paraphrased its ideals and terms, emerging on his part with a bona fide proposal for a sovereign state system within a European federation, no longer under German leadership, that was as a final goal to have its own joint defence force.[94]

Hoping against hope, then, the men of the German Resistance sought to give the most favourable reading possible to Allied pronouncements on war and peace aims lest the door be slammed in their face and all their efforts to reach the outside world came to naught. With considerable apprehension von Hassell noted that 'the process of identifying Germany with Hitler was making progress daily throughout the world'.[95] Under those circumstances it was not incidental that feelers to the United States were explored with particular eagerness. Since Churchill's directive on 'absolute silence', Britain's traffic with the German dissenters had virtually come to a standstill, and then the Agreement for Joint Action concluded between Great Britain and the

Soviet Union on 12 July 1941 committed both governments to 'neither
negotiate nor conclude an armistice or treaty of peace except by mutual
agreement'.[96]

Von Hassell's connection with Washington was a rather tenuous one. Since
early in 1941, however, Frederico Stallforth, an American businessman with
a somewhat chequered background,[97] had been eager to meet him. Stallforth
himself, evidently 'fired by the thought that the fight against Bolshevism
would give the isolationists in America an extraordinary boost',[98] was determined to build bridges between Berlin and Washington; and in the course of
a number of visits to Germany he had struck up all kinds of connections.
From the time when he had been involved in the mid-1930s in some economic
arbitration between American and German interests Stallforth had a certain
entrée with Göring,[99] and he also cultivated contacts with von Ribbentrop.
On the other hand, so von Hassell found out, he left von Weizsäcker and
Schacht doubtful about him.[100] Stallforth gave von Hassell to understand,
however, that the American President's objective was the downfall of Hitler
followed by a conclusion of peace, and also that the American reaction to a
restoration of monarchy in Germany under Prince Louis Ferdinand of
Prussia would be distinctly positive.[101]

In the course of his various visits to Germany Stallforth also navigated in
the highest military circles, encountering men such as Luftwaffe General
Ernst Udet and Marshals von Brauchitsch and Keitel. However it was the
younger field officers, 'not the top officers, but the second men' whom he was
able to sound out on the eventuality of a displacement of the Nazi regime.[102]
But it was with von Hassell that he came to explore this possibility most
concretely. In October 1941 Stallforth conveyed to him, somewhat mysteriously, the message that the 'proposition' had been well received in Washington and the suggestion for him to make his way to Lisbon to meet there
with an 'authorized person'.[103] There is no way of ascertaining for certain
what was meant by the 'proposition'. It can be safely assumed that the
question of a Hohenzollern restoration, at this juncture at least, would not
have been considered a matter ripe for negotiation by either party. But there
is evidence to the effect that von Hassell, in the name of Generals Beck and
von Hammerstein,[104] managed to send a peace proposal through Stallforth
to the White House. The terms called for (1) resignation, voluntary or
enforced, of Hitler and all his government; (2) withdrawal of German forces
to the borders of the Weimar Republic, except the Saar, Danzig, and Austria;
(3) settlement of the Polish Corridor issue along the lines suggested by
Marshal Pilsudski (exchange of the Corridor for the four eastern districts of
East Prussia); (4) no reparations asked for by either side.[105]

At face value these terms surely must have sounded 'most moderate'.[106]
But the same man from whom these supposedly 'moderate' proposals came
had about this same time published an article on the restructuring of south-

eastern Europe, calling for a replacement of the principles of '"balance" or general "equality of rights"' by the one of 'order', and for 'unequivocal leadership—namely German leadership', albeit in the setting of 'free co-operation'—in that area.[107] We can assume this fact went unnoticed in Washington. The von Hassell connection was not sufficiently central to its policy moves. In any case, Stallforth was unable to see the President before 7 December, when the Japanese assault on Pearl Harbor dashed all his hopes.

An even more concerted effort to reach the President of the United States was made in the autumn of 1941 through Louis P. Lochner, head of the Berlin Associated Press Bureau. The latter had a special place, as he saw it,[108] among the American colony in Berlin, for the friendly feelings which he harboured towards Germany.[109] He made it his particular task to work in the midst of 'this horrible war' for a *rapprochement* between Germany and America. He had also been befriended by Prince Louis Ferdinand of whose eldest son, Friedrich, he was a godfather. The Prince, in turn, as we have seen, enjoyed a long-standing friendship with the Roosevelt family.

It was therefore not far-fetched for the people of the Resistance to devise a plan to establish a direct link between Prince Louis Ferdinand and President Roosevelt through Louis Lochner.[110] The idea was hatched in various consultations between Otto John,[111] also an intimate friend of the Prince, and Popitz, Beck, Oster, Dohnanyi, and Canaris. The group decided to convey to the President a message, accompanied by a covering note from the Prince, to the effect that: (1) it was endeavouring to overthrow the regime with the help of disaffected generals, to end the war as rapidly as possible and to re-establish as rapidly the rule of law; (2) it requested the enemy powers, in the event of a rising, not to exploit internal unrest for strategic purposes; (3) the rights of the oppressed peoples and persecuted persons would be restored; (4) it expected that the Western Powers would conclude peace with the German people only after it was purged of Nazism; and (5) it requested support from the President in the interest of rapid termination of hostilities.[112]

John and his friends subsequently arranged for a clandestine gathering to meet Lochner, on a night in November, at the house of Josef Wirmer. The latter was a lawyer and former Centrist politician who had been associated since 1936 with an opposition group of former union leaders and later in 1941 with the group around Carl Goerdeler.[113] At this gathering Lochner met a cross-section of Resistance leaders, some twelve to fifteen people, among whom were some—most likely John, Klaus Bonhoeffer, and Justus Delbrück[114]—who represented Canaris and Beck.[115] Lochner's resolve to take the message from the group to the President, including a 'secret code' designed to help the anti-Hitler forces in Germany, was frustrated by the German Declaration of War against the USA following the Japanese attack on Pearl Harbor and the subsequent internment of all American journalists stationed in Germany. As soon as he reached the United States in June 1942, however,

Lochner made arrangements to see Roosevelt. He got as far as the President's Administrative Assistant,[116] but in a circuitous way he was finally informed by the Washington AP Bureau that his insistence was viewed by official sources as 'most embarrassing'.[117] Mrs Roosevelt, whom he eventually did get to see, was no less discouraging. In official Washington at this juncture, all doors were quite clearly closed to any dealings with Germans, even those opposed to the Nazi regime.

In the spring of 1942, Dorothy Thompson went on the air in New York with the first of a series of weekly addresses sponsored by Columbia Broadcasting System and transmitted over its short-wave facilities to Europe. The title of the series, which extended into September, was 'Listen, Hans'.[118] Hans, was an 'old friend' and a man whose mind was, so she insisted, 'thoroughly familiar' to her. It has always been assumed that 'Hans' was in fact none other than Helmuth James von Moltke whom she had befriended in the course of her earlier assignments in the late 1920s in Vienna and Berlin.[119] Hans, Miss Thompson reminisced affectionately, was a German patriot, but 'not a Nazi'.[120] She even acknowledged that she knew, as she put it, of 'others in your ... group' who had attempted to reach people in England.[121] Nevertheless, for the rest, she taunted him by the collective 'you', i.e. 'your whole propaganda', 'your military gains', and in the broadcast of 14 August she bombarded him with a shower of invectives:

Today young Germans under your command stumble and fall dead on the soil of a country that they love—Russia. *You* drive them farther and farther into limbo. Under *your* orders, populations are slaughtered from Oslo to Rostov. Under *your* orders, innocent hostages are shot. Under *your* orders, trainloads of helpless Jews are transported to the Polish swamps, there to perish. Under *your* orders, young men whose only crime is love and loyalty to their own motherlands are ruthlessly executed.[122]

It is obvious how far the emotions of the war had torn Dorothy Thompson from an understanding of her friend. It was just as well that he did not hear the broadcasts. Moltke sent messages to her twice more during the war, once through a Swedish woman and once through a friend in Switzerland, indicating that he had not changed his social or political views;[123] but there the matter rested.


## 8. Otto Strasser and the Mirage of the New World

A mere episode, but nevertheless worth relating here, was Otto Strasser's Canadian venture.[124] Among the political exiles from Hitler's Germany he was one of the most persistent ones, never resigning his political role, arguing the case of German resistance wherever possible and indeed lobbying for the establishment of a German government-in-exile. Escaping the reach of the

Nazis, this inveterate activist moved from Vienna (May 1933) to Prague (July 1933) and on to Zurich (October 1938), to Paris (November 1939) and, on the eve of the German occupation of Paris in June 1940 to Portugal (May 1940). Considering his own Nazi background as well as the eagerness of the Nazis to lay their hands on him, Strasser was a comfortable guest nowhere but instead a controversial figure. He did, however, have some supporters in Britain, such as Douglas Reed, the former Central European correspondent for *The Times*,[125] and Commander Stephen King-Hall, who in the summer of 1939 had caused a minor diplomatic stir by sending a German edition of his weekly 'News-Letter' directly to German citizens to inform them about British opinion on Hitler's Germany.[126] Indeed it was Sir Robert Vansittart of all people who approached the Canadian High Commissioner, Vincent Massey, to grant Strasser admission to Canada pending his obtaining a permit to enter the United States. The idea was that Strasser could be instrumental from there in rallying the German exiles in the struggle against Hitler and also in counteracting the American hesitations to get involved in the struggle. Within twenty-four hours the Canadian visa was granted, and thus Strasser's odyssey could continue. It took him first to Bermuda from where he applied for the American visa. Despite backing from prominent people such as Heinrich Brüning and the American Ambassador to France, William C. Bullitt, he was refused. Nevertheless Strasser moved on to Canada, arriving by ship in April 1941 at St John's, New Brunswick. From there he proceeded by train to Toronto and thence to Montreal.

In Canada Strasser set out to propose himself as the leader of the self-styled 'Free Germany Movement' in which he claimed to be able to mobilize politically all the German exiles as well as the growing number of German prisoners of war. Eventually, Strasser claimed, this might form the pool for the formation of a 'Free German Legion' to take part in the actual fighting against Hitler.[127] Strasser furthermore developed an intense campaign designed chiefly to educate the public concerning the distinction between Germans and Nazis. He achieved ample news media coverage in the United States as well as in Canada. While initially his claims to represent a world-wide German underground were readily swallowed, and while he enjoyed some influential backers in Ottawa,[128] the truth soon became evident that, in fact, he drew for his activities largely on exiled members of his old 'Black Front' organization in North and South America.[129]

This 'welcome ally' in the war against Hitler, as the *Toronto Star* had initially praised Otto Strasser,[130] was before long unmasked as an unregenerate foe of Western-style democracy. As a consequence he fell from grace, and before long the Canadian authorities, late in 1942, dropped him. The 'prisoner of Ottawa' continued living in Canada[131] under surveillance and severe restrictions.

In September 1942 the Foreign Secretary, Anthony Eden, saw fit to instruct his Ambassador in Washington that the official version of Strasser's rescue by Canada was to be that it was purely a humane gesture.[132] Vansittart himself, who from the beginning has assumed a major behind-the-scenes responsibility for the Strasser escapade, now hastily resumed his official role of the passionate Germanophobe.[133] In his volume of memoirs, published soon after, he guardedly alluded to the Strasser episode:

I see from time to time some large headline in a newspaper, particularly in the American Press, to the effect that some fugitive German is the leader of a vast underground movement in Germany. Such tales are, of course, untrue, and it is fortunate indeed for us that they are not true. Militarism with a Socialist label on it is the worst form of political hooch. You go blind if you swallow it; indeed you have to be blind to swallow it at all.[134]

We are left to wonder whether Lord Vansittart was, temporarily at least, blinded when he persuaded the Canadians to grant admission to Otto Strasser?

The New World venture of Strasser turned out to be no more than a mirage. In Vansittart's case, it turned out to have been but an index of his confusions, for it certainly represented the last act of his private foreign policy going back to the days of his always ambiguous relationship with Carl Goerdeler and Theo Kordt. Before long all had become victims of Vansittart's pathological venom. As far as government policy towards Germany goes, it would be altogether mistaken to argue that the dropping and disavowal of Strasser in 1942 signified a departure from a supposed initial strategy of Churchill, during the years 1940–2, to support the 'national elements' in Germany with the aim of precipitating a domestic uprising against Hitler.[135] Such had been the policy of Chamberlain and Halifax. While Churchill had a certain respect for the chivalry of someone like Ewald von Kleist-Schmenzin, and in turn had little patience with Vansittart's anti-German philippics and had thought them 'silly',[136] ever since the time in May 1940 when he took over the helm, he made his position crystal clear that his priority was the pursuit of the war and victory on the battlefield. Any attempt at negotiation, even with a German opposition group, only detracted from this goal. The great divide in the attitude towards the German Resistance was thus between the policies of the Chamberlain and Churchill governments. Chamberlain was still hoping for that internal stirring in Germany to allow for a negotiated peace with the 'other Germany'; Churchill's preference from the very start was 'absolute silence'. The Strasser episode was but a final confirmation of the fact that Churchill was on course.

## 9. The Icy Waters of 'Unconditional Surrender'

From Churchill's directive of 'absolute silence' to the proclamation at the Casablanca Conference in January 1943 between President Roosevelt and Prime Minister Churchill of 'unconditional surrender' there was but one step. For all practical purposes the British had shut the door to all Germans after the failure of the Vatican talks. America, seemingly uncertain and hesitant about getting involved in the war and all the more a puzzle to the German resisters, became therefore, for a short time at least, a substitute target. Then came Pearl Harbor on 7 December 1941 which brought an abrupt end to American vacillation.[137] To those in the German Resistance who were preoccupied with taking their case abroad it gave an unmistakable sign. If the Atlantic Charter had still allowed for a reading that might have given them some room for action, the event of Pearl Harbor itself slammed shut all doors. At Casablanca they were finally locked.

The literature on the German Resistance has dealt extensively with the supposedly disastrous effects upon it of the Allied 'unconditional surrender' policy.[138] But while the causal connection between the two is inescapable, it should be remembered that the formula to start with was not designed with the Resistance in mind; the latter was clearly too tangential for Allied strategic planning. The fact was that the fortunes of war had changed dramatically since the end of 1942. On the African front the British Eighth Army under General Montgomery had succeeded in halting the advance of General Rommel's Afrika Korps and reconquered Tobruk on 13 November. On the Eastern Front the Russians were tightening their grip around the German Sixth Army at Stalingrad. President Roosevelt and Prime Minister Churchill—the self-styled 'Former Naval Person'—then were all the more resolved to concentrate on cementing the Grand Alliance with Russia and pursuing the war militarily to its finish. At the same time they were committed to rejecting any prospect of negotiating or bargaining over peace terms with the enemy.[139] All this does not mean that this policy did not have an impact upon the Resistance in Germany. It was more in the nature of a fall-out, however, which can be properly assessed only by means of a thorough understanding of the origins of and the degree of commitment in the Allied camp to the prescription of 'unconditional surrender'.

To begin with, the Casablanca Conference was attended by Roosevelt and Churchill, but not by Stalin. Late in 1942 the British Prime Minister had, in his and the President's name, sent a telegram to 'Uncle Joe', urging him to attend a Three-Power Conference in January 'somewhere in North Africa' for the purpose of deciding 'at the earliest moment the best way of attacking Germany with all possible force in 1943'. Stalin answered that, while welcoming the idea of such a meeting, he was to his 'great regret', especially in

view of the impending decisive action at Stalingrad, not in a position to leave
the Soviet Union 'even for a day'.[140] In a subsequent message to the American
President, Stalin followed up with a pointed reminder to the Western leaders
that he expected them to fulfil their promises to open up a second front in
Europe preferably in the spring of 1943.[141] Stalin, in short, was, as has been
remarked, 'more interested in action than discussion'.[142]

'Unconditional surrender' was, no doubt, Roosevelt's idea. It has even
been argued that the phrase was an impromptu creation of the President's at
the now famous luncheon of 23 January attended by, apart from himself,
Harry Hopkins, Churchill, and the President's youngest son Elliott. The
latter was a frequent companion of his father at international conferences
and thus a chronicler of this particular event.[143] At noon of the following
day, at a Press Conference, the President, to everyone's surprise, emerged
with the announcement of the new policy which was to have such a decisive
impact upon Allied strategy. The declaration was made, as has been maintained by Professor Michael Howard, one of its most vociferous critics,
'without any of the forethought and careful consideration which should have
gone to the framing of so major an act of Allied policy'.[144] No reference to
it was made even in the official communiqué at the close of the Conference.

The formulation of 'unconditional surrender', however, was not quite as
precipitous as has been often assumed. To begin with, the issue had been
discussed in a State Department Subcommittee on Security Problems of the
Advisory Committee on Post-War Foreign Policy which, in the course of its
proceedings, 'rapidly reached the consensus that nothing short of unconditional surrender' by the principal enemies of the Allies could be accepted.[145]
The Subcommittee's chairman, Norman H. Davis, also President of the
prestigious Council on Foreign Relations, reported to the President late in
1942. The recommendation came, to be sure, from the Subcommittee and
not from the Department of State. Furthermore, one week before the con-
vening of the Casablanca Conference, the President, at a meeting of 7 January,
brought the new formula before the Joint Chiefs of Staff,[146] and later in
Casablanca General Marshall once again raised the issue before the same
body. As far as we are informed, however, there was no discussion, and the
Chiefs did not express any views on the matter, thus leaving the decision to
the Commander-in-Chief.[147] As far as the British side is concerned, the Prime
Minister did dispatch on 20 January a telegram to the Deputy Prime Minister
and the War Cabinet asking for their reaction to his and 'Admiral "Q"'s
(the President's) inclusion in the final press conference of the demand for
'unconditional surrender' of Germany and Japan.[148]

It is all the more striking therefore, in the wake of the announcement of
'unconditional surrender', that the American President should have found so
much incomprehension at home as well as in Britain. His own Secretary of
State took occasion in his Memoirs to register that he was 'as much surprised

as Mr. Churchill' when at the press conference the principle was announced, and that he and many of his associates had been opposed to it.[149] No less dumbfounded were the officers of the American propaganda community under the umbrella of the Office of War Information as well as their British counterparts of the Political Warfare Executive.[150]

The most puzzling British reaction was that of Winston Churchill. Although he had sounded out the War Cabinet on 20 January on the matter, and although at the luncheon immortalized by Elliott Roosevelt he is recorded to have, as he listened to the President's proposition, 'thought, frowned, thought, finally grinned' and then announced: 'Perfect! And I can just see how Goebbels and the rest of 'em 'll squeal!',[151] Churchill must nevertheless have been surprised at the announcement to the Press. In the final communiqué of 26 January, as a matter of fact, no reference was made to 'unconditional surrender', and when challenged at a later date in Parliament by Ernest Bevin, Churchill explained himself in the following way:

The statement was made by President Roosevelt without consultation with me. I was there on the spot, and I had very rapidly to consider whether the state of our position in the world was such as would justify me in not giving support to it. I did give support to it, but that was not the idea which I had formed in my own mind. In the same way, when it came to the Cabinet at home, I have not the slightest doubt that if the British Cabinet had considered the phrase, it is likely that they would have advised against it, but working with a great alliance and with great, loyal and powerful friends from across the ocean, we had to accommodate ourselves.[152]

The Deputy Prime Minister, Clement Attlee, who witnessed the proclamation of 'unconditional surrender' from the London perspective, echoed Churchill:

Roosevelt more or less blurted it out and after he'd said it we had to agree. It may have been referred to in some document earlier on, but if so I don't recollect it. It was certainly never discussed. I don't think it was very wise, but I don't think it necessarily did much harm.[153]

The Allied leaders, then, had their signals crossed on 'unconditional surrender'. No more than very rudimentary staff work had gone into a decision which was momentous in its effects. But quite apart from the question whether or not it was, or turned out to be, a wise decision—and opinions on this varied greatly—it was anything but a frivolous act and distinctly more than a 'careless Yankee phrase', as Harold Nicolson once called it.[154] It was indeed an 'American decision'.[155] General Marshall was reported to have said to Field Marshal Sir John Dill that the British were 'up against an obstinate Dutchman' who had brought the phrase out and did not like to go back on it.[156] President Roosevelt knew his own mind and he was determined not to repeat the 'mistakes' of Woodrow Wilson whose armistice terms after the First World War had given the Germans, once confronted with the harshness of the Versailles Treaty, cause to charge the Allied and Associated Powers with betrayal. He was therefore resolved to avoid a premature commitment to peace terms. Churchill himself, one year later, underscored this position, arguing that a frank statement of what was going to happen to Germany would not necessarily have a reassuring effect upon the German people and that 'they might prefer the vaguer terrors of "unconditional surrender"'.[157] Roosevelt was also preoccupied with allaying the Russians' displeasure over the Western Allies' failure as yet to implement the Second Front on the European Continent, for which the Allies had held out a prospect in mid-1942.[158] Above all the American President had intuitively seized on a formula which was to commit American public opinion, as well as the Allies, to a war to the finish. 'Unconditional Surrender' thus became a 'clarion call'[159] for victory at home and abroad. More than an official phrase, it came to represent, as even Harold Nicolson, one of its persistent critics conceded, 'the united will of the American and British nations'.[160]

If the Prime Minister had misgivings about it, he was wise enough to put them aside and to yield to the President. The hard fact was that America was emerging as the chief architect of the Grand Strategy, and the balance within the Western Alliance was shifting in favour of the United States on whose mobilization the continued war effort and ultimate victory depended. Great Britain had no choice but to fall into line with the directives from across the Atlantic.

Throughout the war 'Unconditional Surrender' thus remained the unquestioned guide-line of Allied policy towards Germany. While both Roosevelt and Churchill repeatedly explained that it did not spell the enslavement of the German people, and that it committed the victors to the canons of humaneness and Christian ethics,[161] they never modified it despite mounting pressure from the foreign service departments, the intelligence and war propaganda communities, and the military leadership both in the United States and in Britain. These were concerned lest a rigid insistence on the formula would have the effect of discouraging any schemes among the Germans themselves to rid themselves of Hitler and of thus virtually forcing them to rally behind him. Above all, it would prolong the war. When, indeed, on the occasion of the so-called 'Trident' Conference at Washington in May 1943, when President Roosevelt thought of issuing a statement to the effect that 'unconditional surrender' meant that the Allies would never negotiate an armistice with the Nazi government, the German High Command, or any other organization or group or individual in Germany, it was Churchill who dissuaded him from doing so.[162] Churchill himself also warned his Foreign Secretary—*pro domo*, to be sure—that there was no need for Britain to discourage the process of disintegration of the Nazi machine by continually uttering the slogan 'Unconditional Surrender': 'We certainly do not want, if we can help it, to get them all fused together in a solid desperate block for

1. Overseas patrons of the Widerstand: (*left*) Willem A. Visser't Hooft, General Secretary of the World Council of Churches in Process of Formation. (*right*) George Kennedy Allen Bell, Bishop of Chichester.

2.  The horizon of European diplomacy: (*top*) Theo Kordt, German Chargé in London and Prime Minister Neville Chamberlain in London, 1938. (*bottom*) Sir Robert Vansittart, Chief Diplomatic Adviser to the Foreign Secretary.

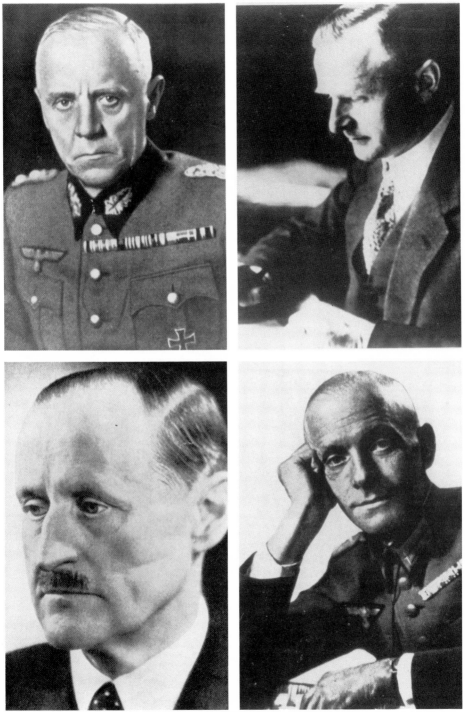

3. The Men of the Widerstand (I): (*top left*) Colonel General Ludwig Beck. (*top right*) Carl Goerdeler. (*bottom left*) Ulrich von Hassell. (*bottom right*) Major General Hans Oster.

4. The men of the Widerstand (II): (*top left*) Helmuth James von Moltke. (*top right*) Adam von Trott zu Solz. (*bottom left*) Dietrich Bonhoeffer. (*bottom right*) Albrecht Haushofer.

5. The Men of the Widerstand (III): (*top left*) Josef Müller. (*top right*) Otto John. (*bottom left*) Claus Schenk Graf von Stauffenberg. (*bottom right*) Julius Leber.

6. Intelligence chiefs: (*top left*) 'C', Major
General Sir Stewart Menzies, Chief of the British
Secret Intelligence Service (MI6). (*top right*)
Major General William J. Donovan, Director of
the OSS. (*bottom left*) Admiral Wilhelm Canaris,
Chief of the Abwehr. (*bottom right*) Allen W.
Dulles, Chief of the OSS in Berne, and his
assistant Gero von Schulze Gaevernitz.

7. From the Nazi People's Court: (*left*) Roland Freisler, President of the People's Court. (*right*) Carl Goerdeler facing the People's Court.

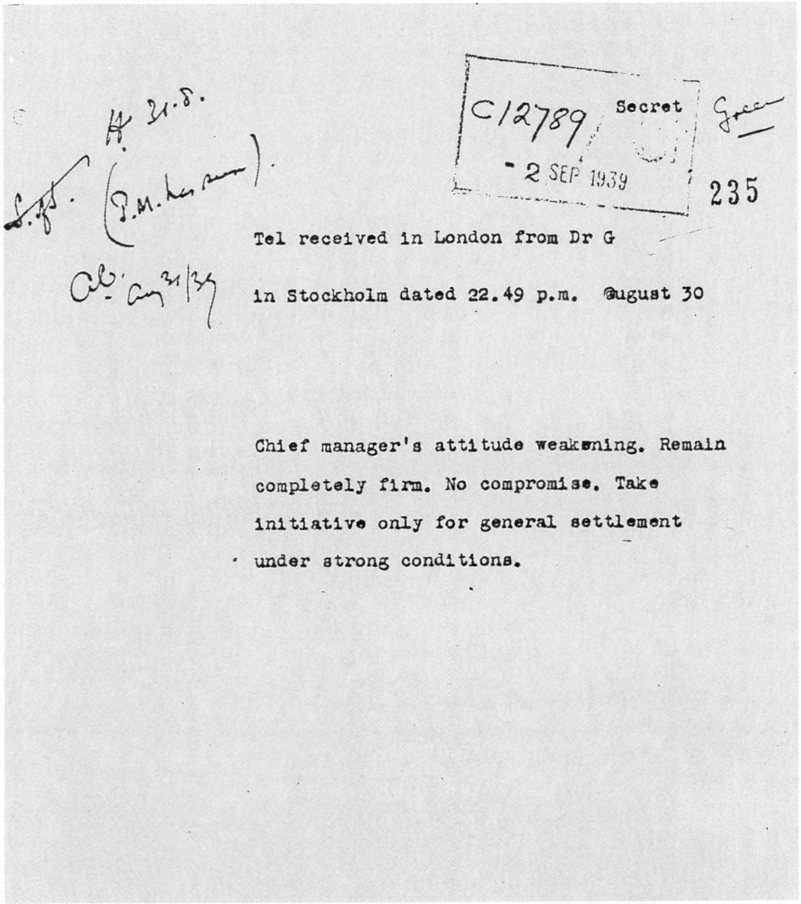
C12789 Secret

- 2 SEP 1939

235

Tel received in London from Dr G

in Stockholm dated 22.49 p.m. @ugust 30

Chief manager's attitude weakening. Remain completely firm. No compromise. Take initiative only for general settlement under strong conditions.

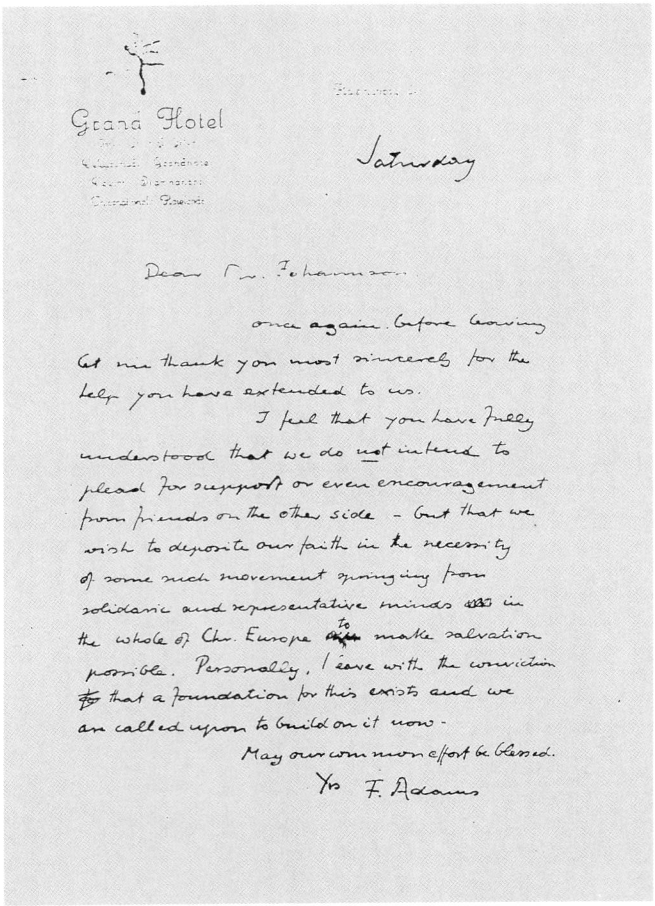
Grand Hotel

Saturday

Dear Dr. Johansson

once again before leaving let me thank you most sincerely for the help you have extended to us.

I feel that you have fully understood that we do not intend to plead for support or even encouragement from friends on the other side – but that we wish to deposite our faith in the necessity of some such movement springing from solidaric and representative minds in the whole of Chr. Europe to make salvation possible. Personally, I leave with the conviction that a foundation for this exists and we are called upon to build on it now.

May our common effort be blessed.

Yrs F. Adams

8. Documents: (*left*) Telegram from Carl Goerdeler to the British Foreign Office, 30 August 1939. (*right*) Farewell letter from Adam von Trott (pseudonym F. Adams) to Dr. Harry Johansson of the Nordic Ecumenical Institute in Sigtuna, Sweden, 26 September 1942.

whom there is no hope', and he continued speculating that the weakening of their resistance would mean 'the saving of hundreds of thousands of British and American lives'.[163] The Foreign Office thereupon made haste to draft a circular telegram to the British representations in Lisbon, Madrid, Tangier, Angora (Ankara), Berne, and Stockholm—with an explanation to Washington and Moscow—to the effect that, while the basic policy had not changed, a certain 'elasticity' in its execution was now also to be adopted in regard 'to German and other feelers'.[164] But there the matter rested.

The argument that the German Resistance was discouraged by the issue of 'unconditional surrender' is both correct and incorrect. Quite correctly the declaration was read in resistance circles as a refusal by the Allies to deal with Nazi and anti-Nazi groups and individuals alike in Germany, with the effect of severely hampering the efforts on their part to involve the Generals. Albrecht von Kessel delivered the most unequivocal condemnation of the Casablanca formula: the Allies thereby bailed out Hitler from his disaster in Stalingrad: the demand 'jeopardized, if not destroyed, the work of six years' of active opposition.[165] Goerdeler, Hassell, Trott, and initially also Moltke, likewise registered concern and voiced to their contacts abroad their deep misgivings about the Allied policy. Admiral Canaris, we are told, while not surprised when it was announced, thought it to be a 'calamitous mistake' since it was prone to prolong the war; 'our generals', he allegedly said, 'will not swallow that'.[166] On the other hand, however, the Generals had vacillated all too long before Casablanca, and it thus cannot be argued that the Conference was a decisive factor in their continued loyalty to the Führer. For too long the British in their dealings with the emissaries of the Resistance had been advised of the need to assuage the Generals, and the Generals as resisters proved to be a myth. For all practical purposes the High Command had, in the winter of 1939/40, abdicated its part in the Resistance.

Nevertheless, the Casablanca proclamation did not stop the foreign activities of the Resistance. The latter still kept manœuvring in the 'icy waters of unconditional surrender', as one of its chief critics in Britain, Lord Hankey, put it.[167] There were some warmer currents still flowing underneath that surface. F.D.R.'s fiat on 'unconditional surrender' could not altogether cancel widespread misgivings concerning the wisdom of the policy, and these, in turn, were likely to work in favour of opening up, after all, some channels to the German Resistance.

The doubts among the Allied military establishment concerning 'unconditional surrender' were by no means exclusively of a strategic nature. Those of General Eisenhower and of his Chief of Staff, General Walter Bedell Smith, were;[168] but the British Chiefs of Staff in their plea for a clarification of the term were guided by the consideration that it would 'at least strengthen the hands of the many who do not feel themselves irreparably committed to Party policy' and 'encourage a withdrawal of support from the regime'.[169]

There were, moreover, the Intelligence heads in both Britain and the United States, namely Sir Stewart Menzies, the chief of the 'Secret Intelligence Service' (MI6) and General William Donovan, the Director of the Office of Strategic Services (OSS), who, while distinctly not in policy-making positions, nevertheless persisted in keeping some contacts—however tenuous—with their German counterpart Admiral Canaris. The latter, they figured, and not without good reason, might be instrumental in overthrowing Hitler and thus in bringing the war to an early end. Thus both Menzies and Donovan saw the 'unconditional surrender' formula as seriously impeding their work. No more than the British and American Foreign Services, however, were they in a position to assert themselves effectively against the firm directives from on high.

Otherwise the German conspirators had reason to count on support from two opposing European quarters in their attempt to have the 'unconditional surrender' clause modified: the Papacy and Moscow. In fact, shortly after Casablanca General Beck commissioned Josef Müller to travel to Rome in order once again to engage the Pope in a mediation effort with the British.[170] They realized that the situation had radically changed since the Vatican Exchanges of the days of the Twilight War, but they felt justified in pursuing this venture in view of an impending action on the part of the conspirators against Hitler[171] who, they kept insisting, needed assurances from abroad for an equitable peace settlement. While this time around the Pope, as could have been expected, did not succeed in eliciting any response from the other side, he at least could lend encouragement to the German plotters by indicating, as usual through Pater Robert Leiber, his own misgivings about 'unconditional surrender' and also by holding out the prospect to the group that after a successful coup he would be prepared to acknowledge his benevolence towards the new regime. Indeed, in the summer of 1943 and on the occasion of his Christmas message of the same year, Pius XII went public with his misgivings concerning 'unconditional surrender'.[172]

Furthermore, a sleeping partner, so to speak, of the German conspirators turned out to be Marshal Stalin himself. Though 'unconditional surrender' had to begin with been formulated by F.D.R. and condoned by Churchill, largely in order to assuage their Russian ally, Stalin was by no means enthralled by it. He had all along made a point of maintaining a distinction between the Germans and the Hitlerites. On 23 February 1942, the Day of the Red Army, he had in an Order of the Day once and for all rejected the proposition that the Soviet army was aiming at an annihilation of the German people: 'It would be ludicrous to identify Hitler's clique with the German people, with the German State. The experience of history indicates that Hitlers come and go, but the German people and the German State remain.'[173] Stalin followed this up on 6 November 1942, shortly before his troops encircled Stalingrad, by saying that it was not the Russian aim to destroy all organized military force in Germany. This would be not merely impossible but also inexpedient from the Soviet point of view: 'but Hitler's army can and must be destroyed'.[174] Indeed, Bishop George Bell of Chichester in the House of Lords took the occasion of these two Russian pronouncements to put, on 10 March 1943, a question to the government: was it willing to make the same distinction as had Premier Stalin between the Hitlerite State and the German people?[175] Predictably, Lord Vansittart took issue with the Bishop, arguing that of the small, indeed very small, contingent of 'good Germans' one had 'heard so much and seen so little'.[176] Eventually, however, the Lord Chancellor, Viscount Simon, responded for the government that it agreed with Premier Stalin that, while the Hitlerite State was to be destroyed, 'the whole German people' was not thereby doomed to destruction. Of course, he hastened to add, the demand for 'unconditional surrender' would stand.[177]

Stalin publicly endorsed 'unconditional surrender' once, on May Day 1943: 'only the utter routing of the Hitlerite armies and the unconditional surrender of Hitlerite Germany' can bring peace to Europe.[178] Yet, at the Allied Tehran Conference of November/December 1943, he is reported by Anthony Eden to have said to the President that it was 'bad tactics *vis-à-vis* Germany' and that it would be better for the Allies to work out terms of surrender and let them be made known to the German people.[179] The signals that went out from Moscow, then, were ambiguous, and we have no reason to assume that this was for lack of direction. Clearly Stalin had distanced himself from the Western Allies with his repeated distinctions between Hitler and the German people and state. Now, after Stalingrad and Casablanca, Soviet wartime diplomacy entered into a most intriguing phase[180] in which feelers went out in the direction of both official and opposition Germany. The following section of this volume will deal with them. For now it suffices to register that they gave to the conspirators a renewed, however deceptive, glimmer of hope. If the Western Powers had locked the doors on them, Russia might possibly open them. Thus a fall-out, so to speak, from Casablanca, an 'Eastern solution', or at least a playing out of the East against the West, became an option in the charting of Resistance diplomacy. It soon, however, turned out to be an illusion.

If the ultimate message of Casablanca was wholly discouraging to the German resisters, nevertheless it did not stop their attempts to reach the outside world; in a way it acted as a special challenge to them. About that time the younger generation of officers and civilians—men such as Oster, Colonel Henning von Tresckow, Trott, Moltke, Bonhoeffer, and eventually Stauffenberg—moved into centre stage of the *Widerstand*. They were determined to go ahead with their plans come what may, and ready, in the foreign realm, to circumvent the seemingly tight interdict of Casablanca. The mounting news of Nazi atrocities that had come from the Eastern Front had lent their plans a special sense of urgency. Not that they were simply daredevils; some were, and others were not. But the more the success of their cause seemed doubtful, the more did an essentially ethical impulse impel them to go ahead in trying to clear their country's name and, in their relations with the outside world, to get the very basic message across that there was indeed a resistance in Germany.

## 10. Despite Casablanca: Feelers from Russia. The Mission of Peter Kleist and the 'Free Germany' Movement

There was a certain paradox inherent in the fact that after the Russian victory at Stalingrad Soviet diplomacy should have extended feelers in the direction of the other side and opened up visions of a separate deal not only with the official German regime but also with the Resistance. Through the President's Special Representative in Berne, Allen W. Dulles, the Americans themselves in the late winter and early spring of 1943 actually got involved in separate negotiations with Prince Max von Hohenlohe, one of the most slippery figures on the international scene who, while an emissary of the SS, also pretended to represent the interests of the *Widerstand*. It may well be that the Russians got wind of these talks and therefore felt all the more justified in exploring a course independent of the Western Allies.

Of course there were deeper reasons which impelled the Russians to court the Germans. While it would be too strong to talk in terms of a crisis of the Alliance, the latter showed distinct cracks at this time. Cracks do exist within the web of any alliance; but in this case they were sufficiently marked to propel the Russians into action. To begin with, Stalin, as we have seen, had not been a party to the Casablanca decisions, and not until after the landings in Normandy in June 1944 did he unequivocally commit the Soviet Union to the 'unconditional surrender' formula.[181] Furthermore the Russian leadership had distinct aspirations concerning guarantees for future Russian control of the territories acquired as a result of the Nazi–Soviet Pact of 1939, but had found itself consistently rebuffed on this score by the Western Allies. Then there was, of course, the issue, of paramount importance for the Russians, of the opening up of a second front. Stalin had become impatient at what he interpreted to be procrastination on the part of the Western Allies to launch it. Stalin, then, clearly had enough cause to go on a fishing expedition in German waters and thus to explore ways of exerting pressure on the Western Powers.

Our particular task here, however, is to determine, as far as possible, what Stalin's venture meant in terms of Russia's policy towards Germany. Had it really been initiated with the objective of reversing the course of Russian foreign policy and to conclude a separate peace, and especially what part did it assign to the forces of resistance in Germany and how, in fact, did it affect them?

The Russian readiness to enter into negotiations with the Third Reich goes back to the autumn of 1942. It was partly through the mediation of the Japanese, who were still maintaining diplomatic relations with the Russians, that the Germans learned that a change of course of the Soviet policy was not outside the realms of possibility.[182] In any case, early in December, Dr Peter Kleist, one of Ribbentrop's chief advisers in the Foreign Office on East European affairs and who had recently been transferred to Alfred Rosenberg's Ostministerium, arrived in Stockholm in order to probe into the possibilities of a 'radical reversal' of German policies and subsequently its possible effects on the Western Powers.[183] But while Kleist's efforts in this direction did not lead anywhere, he found to his great surprise that Stockholm offered better chances for an opening in the other direction, namely Russia. Kleist was not merely an emissary of Ribbentrop but also of Admiral Canaris who schemed to bring pressure to bear upon Hitler through the Auswärtiges Amt to launch a peace overture in the east.[184] His chief contact in this wild goose chase was a thoroughly questionable character, Edgar Klaus, [185] a native of Riga who, while of Jewish origin, was also in the employ of the Abwehr and at the same time under suspicion of being an agent for the Russians.[186] In any case Klaus was reputed to have a close connection with the Russian Minister to Stockholm, Madame Alexandra M. Kollontay, as well as with her Legation Counsellor Vladimir S. Semyonov.[187]

The talks between Kleist and Klaus belong to that realm of secret diplomacy so entangled with secret service manœuvres as to deserve a place in one of E. Phillips Oppenheim's thrillers.[188] While undoubtedly on an official mission, Kleist was really on an assignment from Canaris, and, like all secret agents, he let himself be guided in his encounter with Klaus by his own sense of exploration and adventure. Klaus in turn, while in the employ of Canaris, presented to Kleist a Russian peace plan, proposing to Germany a settlement on the 1939 frontiers. It came, if not from Mme Kollontay, then from the Attaché at her Legation, Andrej M. Alexandrow[189] who, on behalf of the Soviet Secret Service, was to explore avenues towards peace in Stockholm. Apart from all this criss-crossing of mandates and responsibilities there was also a tie-up with the *Widerstand* in this Stockholm operation. To start with Admiral Canaris had a hand in it, as we have seen, and the least that can be said about his involvement was that he conducted a special policy of his own. But both his men, Kleist and Klaus, were aware of the plans of the Resistance,[190] Kleist moreover, once he learned that the proposition of a separate peace with Russia, broached by Ribbentrop to Hitler, had been angrily rejected by the latter,[191] then consulted on the matter with Adam von Trott and the former Ambassador to Moscow, Count Friedrich Werner von der Schulenburg. Both favoured a keeping up of the contacts with Russia.

Trott, who had so far tried in vain, as he admitted, to find an avenue in Sweden to the enemy camp, said: 'We must ... follow up every, however uncertain, possibility that offers itself.'[192] Disappointed over the rebuffs of the German Resistance overtures to the West, he came round in the course of the war to seeing the need for carefully balancing Germany's interests between West and East. Schulenburg, an old hand in dealing with the Russians, thought it within the realm of possibilities that Stalin was ready to come to terms with the Germans in order either to put pressure on his allies or to turn towards the domestic consolidation of his country.[193] In any case, both Trott and Schulenburg distinctly favoured following up this lead as long as it held out the prospect of stopping the Red Army before the gates of Europe.[194]

Kleist's two subsequent encounters with Klaus in Stockholm in June and September 1943,[195] more than the first one, amounted to semi-official soundings furthered by Ribbentrop on the one hand and Mme Kollontay and Semyonov on the other.[196] They belong to the chapter of Russo-German Separate Peace Feelers.[197] It was their failure, however, which impelled the Soviets to embark upon yet another venture, the creation of the 'National Committee for a Free Germany'[198] and the 'League of German Officers'[199] which once again brought the Russian feelers into the orbit of the German Resistance.

The Soviet sponsorship of the 'Free Germany' movement was clearly intended to serve as yet another weapon of Stalin to put pressure on the Western Allies. While the overall objective of the Russian initiative was, as repeatedly stated, to force the removal of Hitler, to testify to the desire for peace of the German people and to bring the war to a quick end, the barb against the Allies was inescapable. It was of course recognized as such in Washington and London.[200]

The new venture, however, must be understood as nothing less than a new chapter in the Soviet policy towards Germany. Under the sign of the imperial German black–white–red colours the Russians now brought together Communist exiles and anti-Fascist writers as well as German officers and soldiers, most of them survivors of the German Sixth Army routed at Stalingrad, under the leadership of General Walther von Seydlitz-Kurzbach, scion of one of Germany's most illustrious military families. For the moment at least these disparate elements joined forces in a commitment to, so read the 'Manifesto to the German Army and German People' of 19 July, 'a strong democratic order which will have nothing in common with the impotence of the Weimar regime'.[201] The Manifesto addressed itself to 'all sections of the German people', and it singled out the army to play 'an important part' in the fight for liberation. In turn the army officers who identified with the 'Free Germany' movement felt all the more encouraged to evoke the patriotic lore of the Tauroggen Convention of 1812,[202] and also the Russo–German Rapallo

Treaty of 1922,[203] thus conjuring up the mirage of a renewed Russo–German alliance, independent from the Western Powers, against the German dictator.

The Manifesto naturally also had to come to terms with the question of resistance. As a matter of fact, it stated unequivocally that it was up to the German people to stage resistance, and that only thus could 'the existence, the liberty, and honour of the German nation' be saved. Indeed the literature of 'Free Germany' was not wanting in appeals to the Germans, and specifically to the Generals, to overthrow Hitler. Undoubtedly the sponsors of the newly launched movement intended it to play the part of a resistance and to connect with the Resistance in Germany and encourage it to strike. It is also beyond doubt that many of the prisoner-of-war officers and soldiers had come around to seeing themselves as part of a bona fide resistance movement in which they, and not the Communist exiles like Wilhelm Pieck and Erich Weinert, were to carry the torch.[204] Since the founding of the League which was especially to accentuate the imperial German black–white–red character of the enterprise, the officers had reason to believe that they had prevailed over the Soviets as well as the Communist exiles in their advocacy of, not subversion, but an orderly retreat of the German troops to the frontiers of the Reich. Thus they hoped to maintain the Wehrmacht intact for the purpose of linking up with the German Resistance.[205] From captivity in far-away Russia, then, even co-operation with the former enemy could appear to these German officers as a patriotic deed.

As for the Western Allies, they were wholly surprised by the formation of the 'Free Germany' Committee.[206] Moscow had deliberately kept Washington and London in the dark. The British Ambassador to Moscow, Sir A. Clark Kerr, expressed 'complete surprise', whereas the American Ambassador, Admiral William H. Standley, admitted he was 'baffled',[207] and Molotov made haste to explain that the NKFD was purely a propaganda device. The reactions in the British Foreign Office ranged from conveniently accepting this version to admitting embarrassment and acknowledging that this 'tiresome development' was 'in complete opposition' to the unconditional-surrender policy and that a 'really solid discussion with Stalin' on points of disagreement was in order.[208]

The bishop of Chichester, ever-critical of the British failure to distinguish between 'good' and 'bad' Germans, now grabbed the bull by the horns, so to speak, and addressed, 'with some trepidation',[209] an elaborate Memorandum to the Foreign Secretary, pointing out 'the complete gulf' between what he thought the Russian position to be and the Anglo-American policy of 'unconditional surrender'. Lest Russia and Communism emerge supreme in Germany and over all Eastern Europe, the Bishop urged the Allies to come out into the open at once with a proposal for a 'new order for Europe which is neither the New Order of the Nazis nor the Communist system, but a liberal and democratic system'.[210] The Memorandum was predictably received in the Foreign Office with *déjà vu* boredom if not annoyance. 'Our good German Bishop', as William Strang dubbed him, was thought to be alarmist. Bishop Bell may have been naïve in taking the Manifesto from Moscow at its face value. He was, however, one of the few people in Britain who, having in the spring of the previous year conferred in Sweden with the two German pastors, Dietrich Bonhoeffer[211] and Hans Schönfeld, and also being in contact with Helmuth von Moltke, was informed about the German Resistance and was deeply impressed by the moral commitment of these young men. He was also one of the few men in Britain who had the guts to speak up on their behalf and to try to impress the public with the need to recognize and support them.

Actually, however, the connections between the captive generals in Russia and the Resistance circles in Germany were virtually nil.[212] There was much that might have brought together the two groups. Both were committed to putting an end to the Nazi tyranny and to a reconstruction of the Reich that was to improve over the Weimar legacy, and the black–white–red trimmings of the 'Free Germany' movement should have appealed strongly to the conservative conspirators inside Germany. The captured generals and officers did address letters to people in Germany whom they believed to be involved in conspiracy; but these were not sent on by their captors.[213] Of course the men of the *Widerstand* were aware of 'Free Germany' and especially of General von Seydlitz's BDO. But, on balance, they remained sceptical towards them. The opening to the east, however tempting in the light of the Tauroggen tradition and in particular in the light of the futile efforts on the part of the Resistance to obtain any satisfaction from the Western Powers, was nevertheless viewed, especially by General Beck, as fraught with danger. Goerdeler seems to have been more receptive to Seydlitz's course,[214] whereas Ulrich von Hassell, while assessing the 'Free Germany' Committee 'important as a symptom' and in a Bismarckian mood ruminating about the inevitability of some sort of German 'game' (*Mühlespiel*) between East and West, clearly stated his preference for the West.[215] However, Count von der Schulenburg who, if anyone among the conspirators, was an 'Easterner' and who had enormous respect for the Russians and was thought to have a special relationship transcending ideology with Stalin, tended to see the twin committees in Russia more favourably. If we are to believe an unconfirmed report from East Germany, he even favoured establishing a connection with the leading personalities of the NKFD and especially with General von Seydlitz in order to reach some sort of preliminary accord.[216] Later on, during his last trip to Sweden in June/July 1944, Trott managed to obtain a copy of the original Manifesto of the 'Free Germany' Committee, but he came to the conclusion that it added up to little more than propaganda. On balance, the German conspirators came to concur with the verdict attributed to Stauffenberg who rejected 'proclamations behind barbed wire'.[217]

Stauffenberg's verdict turned out to be the correct one. Stalin had played a duplicitous game. By the end of the year it became clear that the Soviets' fishing in the national-patriotic waters, in any event, had not worked. The German troops did not take the bait; they did not, as anticipated in Moscow, respond to the 'Free Germany' propaganda and did not on their own withdraw to the old borders. They kept fighting to the finish while retreating westward, thus in fact defying the Soviet propaganda that had called upon them to turn against the Nazi regime along with the survivors of the Sixth Army.

It was the Tehran Conference of 28 November–1 December which was decisive in making an end to the Soviet fishing expedition in German waters. The three warlords, Roosevelt, Churchill, Stalin, now met for the first time with the objective of removing past disagreements, tensions, and suspicions. The Western leaders, notably the American President, appeared singularly eager to appease their Russian counterpart who had for too long, and so far, in vain, clamoured for the opening of a second front. Now, within the framework of an overall settlement on war strategy Stalin succeeded in obtaining satisfaction on his major desiderata: the Western Allies now committed themselves to launch 'Overlord', the Western invasion, in May 1944 while Stalin in turn would begin a major offensive in the east. Also, the Western leaders gave way to Stalin's demand for a westward push of Poland's frontiers. This latter stipulation remained secret for the moment,[218] but nothing could hide the fact that it clearly meant a selling down the river of the very country for whose defence Britain and France had gone to war to begin with. However, with Stalin having accomplished his chief objectives at the conference table and with the Grand Alliance having been mended, the NKFD and the BDO had lost most of their usefulness; they had after all served only propaganda purposes, and none too successfully. In any case, they had served Stalin as the 'trojan horse', as Edgar Klaus put it, enabling him to storm the American fortress.[219]

All this does not mean that we can dismiss the part played by the 'Free Germany' movement in the landscape of resistance.[220] For someone like General von Seydlitz, if he was to act effectively from captivity against the Hitler regime, there was no choice but to take an active part in the Russian-sponsored movement. His was a decision reached after agonizing self-examination, and for it he incurred much hostility among those of his fellow officers who chose otherwise. In the train repatriating him in October 1955 he was avoided by a number of generals who saw in him a 'miserable traitor'.[221] Seydlitz had moved, no doubt, close to the threshold of treason, but, like Hans Oster and Ewald von Kleist-Schmenzin, his 'treason' was designed to save his country. In a setting of total or near-total domination all resistance of necessity borders, as we have seen, on treason; in that case Seydlitz's decision and experience should be examined in the context of resistance. His was obviously an extreme case of a German general officer placing himself in a position of serving the 'enemy' in order to accomplish his patriotic objectives. Also, if exiles are identified as having served from abroad as auxiliaries of the Resistance, Seydlitz and his men also should be recognized as having been part of the German Resistance. Undoubtedly they perceived themselves as resisters who, thoroughly abused by their Führer, were hoping to spare the rest of the German soldiers on the Eastern front and the German people at large the fate of the Sixth Army.[222]

We simply have to be prepared, as Alexander Fischer put it, to 'broaden the spectrum'[223] of the military arm of the German Resistance. In this case, of course, a reversal of roles had taken place since for once the initiative went out from the captive officers and soldiers abroad attempting to sway the commanders in the field and at home. But, as so often before, the Wehrmacht generals did not choose to act. This time round they may have had better reasons for not doing so for, alas, the sponsors of their comrades in captivity, the Soviets, were plainly not in earnest.

*CHAPTER 4*

1. 'The Nature of the Beast', 14 Mar. 1940, FO 371/24389/C 4229/6/18; the memorandum was actually occasioned by Vansittart's concerns about the mission of Sumner Welles who, by favouring disarmament of the belligerents as a precondition for the return of confidence, so Vansittart argued, was putting the cart before the horse. As a matter of fact, Goerdeler's 'representative' in the USA, Gotthilf Bronisch, reportedly interpreted the Welles stop-over in Berlin as ostensibly only intending to take stock of the overall situation but in reality having been designed to get in touch with the anti-Hitler forces in Germany; Frank Ashton-Gwatkin to Sir Alexander Cadogan, 25 Mar. 1940; FO 371/24407/C 5287/89/18; minuted by G. P. Young from the FO Central Department, not without reason: 'This is typical for the Goerdeler–Schairer clique that they regard any international development as centring around themselves.'
2. Anthony Glees, *Exile Politics during the Second World War: The German Social Democrats in Britain* (Oxford, 1982), 51.
3. Letters from Hugh Dalton to Lord Halifax and Clement Attlee 2 July 1940, Dalton Papers, quoted in David Stafford, 'The Detonator Concept: British Strategy, SOE and European Resistance After the Fall of France', *Journal of Contemporary History*, 10 (Apr.1975), 200.
4. The disillusioned Captain Hans Ritter wrote to Group Captain Christie on 15 Apr. 1940: 'The "Generals" have confirmed my previous assessment of these gentlemen. While they have used the good Herr Tell [Gessler] and Uncle J. [Wirth] to throw sand into your eyes, they cheerfully prepared the invasion of Norway and Denmark ... I am deeply ashamed of ever having worn the same uniform which these gangsters now soil. Pfui Teufel!'; Letter from Johnny to Lieber Freund Grahame, 15 Apr. 1940, Christie Papers, CHRS 180/1/35.
5. Lothar Kettenacker, 'Die britische Haltung', in Lothar Kettenacker (ed.), *Das 'Andere Deutschland' im Zweiten Weltkrieg* (Stuttgart, 1977), 59.
6. Michael Balfour, *Propaganda in War 1939–1945* (London, 1979), 167–70.
7. WM 213 (40) 26 July 1940, CAB 65/18.
8. W.S.C. to Vansittart, 7 Jan. 1941; PREM 4/23/2.
9. Secret 'Summary of Principal Peace Feelers September 1939–March 1941', FO 371/26542/C 4216/610/G.
10. Since 23 Dec. 1940.
11. FO 371/26542/C 610/324/P.
12. Entry, of 29 May 1940, *Die Hassell-Tagebücher*, 195.

13. Note of 23 May 1940, *Die Weizsäcker-Papiere*, 204.
14. Ibid. 195–6.
15. Of course the possibility of future American involvement did not escape the experienced diplomat, though he wondered whether the USA might not look upon the effort of the Western Powers as a lost cause and a bad investment.
16. See entry of 29 May 1940, *Die Hassell-Tagebücher*, 196–7.
17. 'Mir wird alle Tage übler'; Helmuth von Moltke to Freya von Moltke, 24 May 1940; von Moltke, *Briefe an Freya*, 136.
18. Helmuth von Moltke to Freya von Moltke, Berlin, 1 June 1940, ibid. 142–3.
19. This information comes from Marie ('Missie') Vassiltchikov, a Russian exiled princess who during the war found employment in the Auswärtiges Amt where she worked closely with the conspirators against Hitler and befriended Trott. He confided to her the story of the message from Lord Lothian two days after the coup against Hitler of 20 July 1944 and shortly before his arrest by the Gestapo; Marie Vassiltchikov, *The Berlin Diaries 1940–1945 of Marie 'Missie' Vassiltchikov* (London, 1987), 200–1.
20. Later, when revealing the receipt of the letter to the Russian princess, he also revealed to her that afterwards he had often wondered whether he had not been wrong; ibid. 201.
21. Ralph William Close.
22. Deuel saw Lord Lothian—who died soon afterwards on 12 Dec.—at the British Consulate-General in Chicago and the South African at the Embassy in Washington. Later in the war Deuel received two messages from Moltke mailed from Italy and Turkey, neither signed by his real name, both without return address; letter from Wallace R. Deuel to Ger van Roon, Washington, 2 June 1963, IfZ/Ger van Roon, ZS A-18; van Roon, *Neuordnung*, 301–2.
23. Kurt Hahn, 'Balance Sheet', 19 July 1940, PREM 4/100/8.
24. However, he indicated that he and his friends might be prepared to bargain; Secret 'Summary of Principal Peace Feelers September 1939–March 1941'; FO 371/26542/C 4216/610/G; also FO 371/24408/C 9635/89/18.
25. For Hitler's changing ideas about and policies towards England see Andreas Hillgruber, 'England in Hitlers aussenpolitischer Konzeption', *Historische Zeitschrift*, 218 (Feb. 1974), 65–84.
26. From Tomodachi, the Japanese word for friend.
27. Letter from Dr Karl Haushofer to Dr Albrecht Haushofer, Munich, 3 Sept. 1940, *Akten zur deutschen auswärtigen Politik 1918–1945*, Serie D (1937–1949), vol. xi (Bonn, 1964), 13–15.
28. 'Gibt es noch Möglichkeiten eines deutsch-englischen Friedens?' BA/K, Nachlass Haushofer, HC 833; also Walter Stubbe, 'In Memoriam Albrecht Haushofer', *VfZ*, 8 (July 1960), 245–8; 'Are There Still Possibilities of a German–English Peace?', Berlin, 15 Sept. 1940; *DGFP*, D/xi. 78–81.
29. Top Secret letter A.H. to Herr Hess, BA/K, Nachlass Haushofer, HC 833; *DGFP* D/xi. 129–31; Stubbe, 'In memoriam', 248–9.
30. Haushofer did actually send a letter to the Duke of Hamilton. It was dated 23 Sept. and dispatched through the brother of Rudolf Hess, Alfred; see the ref. to the letter by the Duke in Report on Interview with Herr Hess by Wing Commander the Duke of Hamilton on Sunday, 11 May 1941 in *Trial of the Major War Criminals before the International Military Tribunal, Nuremberg 14 November 1945–1 October 1946*, vol. xxxviii (Nuremberg, 1949), 175; for a draft of the letter see *DGFP*, D/xi. 131–2.
31. Stubbe, 'In memoriam', 250.
32. 'Peace Plan drawn up by Albrecht Haushofer in the summer of 1940 for the German Resistance to Hitler', in James Douglas-Hamilton, *Motive for a Mission: The Story Behind Hess's Flight to Britain* (London, 1971), 251–4. The document was turned over after the war to the Duke of Hamilton by Haushofer's former student Heinrich Georg Stahmer, then Legation Secretary at the German Embassy in Madrid and later German Ambassador in Tokyo.
33. 'Proposal for a provisional solution of problems'.
34. This stipulation was to apply to Norway, Denmark, Belgium, and Holland.
35. Other stipulations in the document addressed themselves to the Italian demands for a

revision of her borders with France, to her eastern borders and demands for the eastern coast of the Adriatic, to her borders in the north and also her demands for Tunisia (in all these cases Haushofer recommended against the recognition of Italy's claims since he did not consider her capable of playing the part of a great power); furthermore the document called for the safeguarding of Britain's access to India and the recognition of her special interests in the Eastern Mediterranean and the Near East.

36. 'Constructive Peace Plan for Europe'.
37. It might be noted also that in this connection the suggestion was made for small states to be conceded a double voting right lest they fear being smothered by the big powers.
38. Ibid. 115.
39. This latter assumption has been stated with emphasis by Dr Rainer Hildebrandt, a close associate of Haushofer. Haushofer was an admirer of Moltke and it is more than likely that in his positive assessment of the British Empire he let himself be guided by Moltke; letter from Dr Rainer Hildebrandt to Ger van Roon, Berlin, 10 Jan. 1963, IfZ/Ger van Roon, ZS/A-18.
40. In this respect the concession of sovereignty to Norway, Denmark, Belgium, and Holland is deceptive. While the stipulations concerning France were left indeterminate, no words were lost over the re-establishment of sovereign states along Germany's eastern borders. Haushofer thus went beyond the terms of von Hassell's Statement for Lord Halifax of Feb. 1940 which called for the re-establishment of an independent Poland (with its western frontier as of 1914) and of a Czech Republic.
41. Rt. Hon. Sir Samuel Hoare (Lord Templewood), *Ambassador on Special Mission* (London, 1946), 105; the passage in the Memoir, while entered in a chapter on the year 1941, mentions 'repeated efforts' by one of Ribbentrop's staff in the German Embassy and most probably refers to Stahmer's various efforts, including the ones of the previous year.
42. Entry of 16 Mar. 1941, *Die Hassell-Tagebücher*, 232–3.
43. Entries of 3 Feb., 18 May 1941, ibid. 228, 252. As a matter of fact von Weizsäcker also played his part in the venture by arranging for Haushofer a 'silent' departure lest the Auswärtiges Amt, and esp. Ribbentrop, got wind of it; Rainer Hildebrandt, 'Eidesstattliche Erklärung', 5 Apr. 1948, NA, US Mil. Trib. IV (IV A) Nürnberg, Case 11, US vs. Ernst von Weizsäcker, Box 134, Defense Exhibit No. 249, Doc. 229.
44. See Bernd Martin, *Friedensinitiativen und Machtpolitik im Zweiten Weltkrieg 1939–1942* (Düsseldorf, 1974), 434–5.
45. Walter Stubbe.
46. For this episode see Ursula Laack-Michel, *Albrecht Haushofer und der Nationalsozialismus* (Stuttgart, 1974), 233–4; Stubbe, 'In memoriam', 251; Martin, *Friedensinitiativen*, 435.
47. 'Englische Beziehungen und die Möglichkeit ihres Einsatzes', in Stubbe, 'In memoriam', 252–5.
48. Later, in Nov. 1941, Albrecht Haushofer drafted yet another Peace Plan. While he had been dismissed from the Auswärtiges Amt by Ribbentrop on 28 May, he submitted the memorandum to Weizsäcker, expecting it to be forwarded directly to Hitler. It amounted to a more elaborate version of the earlier plan of the summer of 1940 and reflected his own personal precarious position between life and death, as well as lingering hopes to be able to win over Hitler to a last-minute gesture towards Britain and peace. Extravagant as this plan was—dividing the world into vast spheres of interest, the British–American power alliance, the Japanese orbit, the Great Russian hold over at least Russia's Asian possessions, and the German-controlled area of 'large parts' of continental Europe—it constituted an attempt to reconcile a strongly hegemonic version of resistance aspirations with reformed Nazi policies. Haushofer's conflict between loyalty to his country and his deep revulsion against the Nazi ethos and policies seemed for once resolved in a somewhat delirious fusion. It must be remembered, of course, that in Nov. 1941 the German war effort was at its height; this fact might have encouraged Haushofer in his imperialistic schemings. It seems that Hitler actually read the peace memorandum; but he was clearly in no mood to concede a decisive role in world politics to the British–American alliance and to abandon his determination to crush Russia. For the moment, however, he made sure he was kept informed by one of Haushofer's assistants, 'Frau U.', about his thoughts on relations with Great Britain; he had, he signified to her, 'a special interest' in Haushofer; for the Peace

Plan of Nov. 1941 see BA/K HC 833; reprinted in Laack-Michel, *Albrecht Haushofer*, 382–95; English version in Douglas-Hamilton, *Motive for a Mission*, 255–69; for general commentaries see ibid. 211–18; Martin, *Friedensinitiativen*, 487–90; for Hitler's interest in Haushofer see Hildebrandt, *Wir sind die Letzten*, 131–2; Martin, *Friedensinitiativen*, 487–8, n. 222.

49. 'Memorandum für Beck, Februar 1941', Kordt Papers; by the time of the composition of the Memorandum Erich Kordt had already been informed by the Foreign Minister about his reassignment, against his own and Weizsäcker's will, to Tokyo, which amounted to a form of banishment from Berlin. The Memorandum was handed over to Beck on the occasion of a farewell dinner for Kordt at the home of Admiral Canaris late in March at which, besides the brothers Kordt and Beck, Oster was present; Kordt, *Nicht aus den Akten*, 410–14; Thielenhaus, *Zwischen Anpassung und Widerstand*, 215–16.

50. Theo Kordt, Short Autobiography (ii), 21, Kordt Papers.

51. As a matter of fact, the stipulation that only such majorities were to be in a position to check or replace the Executive which themselves were able to form an Executive anticipated the 'constructive vote of no-confidence' of the Basic Law of the Federal Republic.

52. See also Marion Thielenhaus, *Zwischen Anpassung und Widerstand: Deutsche Diplomaten 1938–1941* (Paderborn, 1984), 216.

53. 'sanguinisch'; entries of 17/18 Aug. 1939, 19 Jan., 20 Sept. 1941, *Die Hassell-Tagebücher*, 109, 223, 273.

54. See untitled typescript, 1 July 1940, BA/K Pechel I/64; taken over into the memorandum 'Das Ziel' ('The Aim', end of 1941), 8 ff. under the heading 'Moralischer Zustand' ('Moral Conditions'); see also BA/K Goerdeler 18; cf. also Ritter, *Carl Goerdeler*, 267–8, 499, n. 267.

55. See Erich Kosthorst, 'Carl Friedrich Goerdeler', in Rudolf Lill and Heinrich Oberreuter (eds.), *20. Juli. Portraits des Widerstands* (Düsseldorf, 1984), 119.

56. '*Spiegelbild einer Verschwörung*'. *Die Opposition gegen Hitler und der Staatsstreich vom 20. Juli 1944 in der SD-Berichterstattung. Geheime Dokumente aus dem ehemaligen Reichssicherheitshauptamt*, ed. Hans-Adolf Jacobsen (Stuttgart, 1984), i. 178.

57. See Ritter, *Carl Goerdeler*, 266 ff.

58. Ritter reminds us that this was the most likely reason why Ulrich von Hassell in his diaries used for him the—not exactly complimentary—code-name 'Pfaff' (a somewhat derogatory German word for 'priest'); ibid. 500 n. 10.

59. Goerdeler, 'Moralischer Zustand'.

60. See esp. the already cited 'Moralischer Zustand'; furthermore 'Grundsätze für die Friedenswirtschaft' ('Principles of a Peace-Time Economy', Oct. 1940), BA/K, Pechel I/64 and Goerdeler 18, and 'Gesamtlage' ('The Overall Situation', Nov. 1940), BA/K, Goerdeler 18; cf. also Ritter, *Carl Goerdeler*, 270 ff., 499 n. 5; Walter Lipgens (ed.), *Europa-Föderationspläne der Widerstandsbewegungen 1940–1945* (Munich, 1968), 109–11. All these served as partial drafts for Goerdeler's major programmatic memorandum 'Das Ziel' ('The Aim'), composed in consultation with Beck, Popitz, and others late in 1941; for the text see Wilhelm Ritter von Schramm (ed.), *Beck und Goerdeler: Gemeinschaftsdokumente für den Frieden 1941–1944* (Munich, 1965), 81–166; see also Hans Mommsen, 'Gesellschaftsbild und Verfassungspläne des deutschen Widerstandes', in Walter Schmitthenner and Hans Buchheim (eds.), *Der deutsche Widerstand gegen Hitler* (Cologne, 1966), 133, 269–70 n. 109.

61. Ritter, *Carl Goerdeler*, 270.

62. The two men had met already before the Nazi seizure of power in the Berlin home of Wilhelm and Hanna Solf. Wilhelm Solf, a distinguished German public servant, served in 1918 as the last Imperial and the first Republican Foreign Secretary and from 1920–8 as Ambassador to Tokyo; he died in 1936. Hanna Solf became the centre of a salon in which opponents of the Nazi regime, most of them members of the Auswärtiges Amt, came together. Largely because of Wilhelm Solf's international reputation the Circle maintained connections abroad. Late in 1943 the Gestapo succeeded in infiltrating the so-called 'Salon Fronde', and subsequently most of its members were taken into custody and eventually executed. Helmuth James von Moltke was one of those imprisoned as a result of the Gestapo investigations of the Circle.

63. 'Unterredung mit Prof. Siegmund-Schultze an der Sozialakademie Dortmund am 29.7.1953', BA/K, Ritter 131.
64. See letter from Siegmund-Schultze to Gerhard Ritter, Stockholm, 28 Mar. 1954, BA/K, Ritter 131; also Ritter, *Carl Goerdeler*, 316 ff.
65. Siegmund-Schultze's later testimony ('Unterredung' and letter to Gerhard Ritter of 28 Mar. 1954) is the only evidence extant for von Brauchitsch's initial. The Commander-in-Chief's curt rejection of the 'X-Report' when it had been presented to him a year before by his Chief of Staff certainly indicated a disassociation on his part from the affairs of the Resistance. It is possible, however, that von Brauchitsch was reconsidering his attitude towards the Resistance in the spring of 1941 when he took exception to the so-called *Kommissarbefehl* of Hitler according to which, in the forthcoming Russian campaign, all Soviet commissars were to be liquidated; see von Schlabrendorff, *The Secret War against Hitler* (London, 1966), 124; also Ritter, *Carl Goerdeler*, 513–14 nn. 6 and 7. Also according to von Hassell, in March 1941 Goerdeler thought that a new approach to von Brauchitsch was in order; entry of 19 Jan. 1941, *Die Hassell-Tagebücher*, 223. See also John S. Conway, 'Between Pacifism and Patriotism—A Protestant Dilemma: The Case of Friedrich Siegmund-Schultze', in Frank Nicosia and Lawrence D. Stokes (eds.), *Germans against Nazism, Nonconformity, Opposition and Resistance in the Third Reich: Essays in Honour of Peter Hoffmann* (New York, 1990), 99, 112 n. 29.
66. Siegmund–Schultze actually had also called on him shortly after his unsuccessful visit to the Legation and found him 'personally interested' in the matter; indeed the Consul-General did accept the documents from the German, including the letter to Archibishop Temple, locking them in his desk pending instructions for them to be forwarded to London.
67. FO 371/26543/C 9472/610/G, and Ritter, *Carl Goerdeler*, 569.
68. Minutes of F. K. Roberts 24 Aug. 1941 to Mr [David]Kelly, Berne—Sir Alexander Cadogan, 'Peace Moves', 5 Aug. 1941, FO 371/26543/C 9472/324/18. On the translated document itself that circulated in the FO there is hardly any critical comment; a mere dead-pan elucidation by the hand of William Strang, the former head of the Central Department and now Assistant Under-Secretary of State, appears next to the item referring to the German 1914 frontiers: 'i.e. No Alsace-Lorraine for France. No Corridor or Posnania for Poland'.
69. Ritter, *Carl Goerdeler*, 317.
70. Letter from William Ebor (Archbishop of York) to Sir Alexander Cadogan, 25 Sept. 1941, FO 371/26543/C 10855/610/G.
71. Draft of letter from William Ebor to Siegmund-Schultze, 26 Sept. 1941, ibid.
72. 'Peace Overtures', Anthony Eden to Prime Minister, 10 Sept. 1941, ibid.; Eden listed (*a*) a July message of Goerdeler to the British SIS agent in Switzerland, (*b*) the Siegmund-Schultze approach, (*c*) an Aug. proposal via Stockholm from the 'Free Reconstruction Movement' (the Kreisau Circle?), and (*d*) a Sept. message through a Swedish industrialist from Dr Kurt Schmitt—short-term Minister of Economics in the early phases of the Nazi regime—on behalf of Göring. From among these he singled out two as worthy of being pursued. Unfortunately an obvious typing error in the memorandum to the Prime Minister—'cases (*c*) and (*c*)'—does not allow us to identify which cases he had in mind.
73. Most Secret W.S.C. to Foreign Secretary, 10 Sept. 1941, ibid.
74. Minute initialled 'AE', 4 Oct. 1941; ibid.
75. Letter from Siegmund-Schultze to Gerhard Ritter, Stockholm, 28 Mar. 1954.
76. Letter from Sir Alexander Cadogan to Archbishop Temple of York, 8 Oct. 1941; FO 371/26543/C 10855/610/G.
77. A passage in the Foreign Secretary's speech of 8 May 1942 in Edinburgh was meant to strike a note of encouragement of dissident elements in Germany: ' ... if any section of the German people really wants to see a return to a German state which is based on respect for law and for the rights of the individual, they must understand that no one will believe them until they have taken active steps to rid themselves of their present regime'; *The Times*, 9 May 1942; Summary of Principal Peace Feelers, Apr. 1941 to June 1942, PREM 4/100/8.
78. For the Kirk–Moltke relationship see von Moltke, *Briefe an Freya*, 38–9, 206–7; George

F. Kennan, *Memoirs 1925–1950* (Boston, 1967), 112–15, 119–20; van Roon, *Neuordnung*, 305–6; also interview with Freya von Moltke, 9 Dec. 1976.

79. Kirk and Moltke were, as matters turned out, never to meet again; see below Ch. 6, s. 2.

80. Kennan, *Memoirs*, 119.

81. For the Kennan–Moltke relationship see von Moltke, *Briefe an Freya*, 287–8; Kennan, *Memoirs*, 119–22; van Roon, *Neuordnung*, 306–7.

82. Kennan, *Memoirs*, 122.

83. Letter from Helmuth James von Moltke to Freya von Moltke, Berlin, 13 Sept. 1941 in von Moltke, *Briefe an Freya*, 287. After Pearl Harbor and the subsequent German declaration of war against the USA Kennan was interned in Germany for months before being able to return home in May 1942.

84. This is according to Kennan's later reconstruction of a situation, the particulars of which he had forgotten; letter from George Kennan to Ger van Roon, Belgrade 14 Mar. 1962, IfZ, ZS A-18, vol. 4; see also van Roon, *Neuordnung*, 307.

85. See von Moltke, *Briefe an Freya*, 288 n. 1; van Roon, *Neuordnung*, 307.

86. See *Dokumente zur Deutschlandpolitik* I. Reihe, Band 1: *3. September 1939 bis 31. Dezember 1941: Britische Deutschlandpolitik*, ed. Rainer A. Blasius (Frankfurt/M., 1984), 438 ff.; Ernest L. Woodward, *British Foreign Policy in the Second World War*, ii (London, 1971), ii. 198 ff.

87. Diary entry of 26 Aug. 1941, printed in *Dokumente zur Deutschlandpolitik*, I, 1, 450.

88. A World Broadcast, 24 Aug. 1941, in Charles Eade (ed.), *The War Speeches by the Rt. Hon. Winston S. Churchill* (Boston, 1953), ii. 62. The statement attributed to Winston Churchill by Hans Rothfels that 'the Atlantic Charter was not intended to include obligations of any kind towards enemy countries' (*The German Opposition to Hitler*, London, 1970, 141–2), also cited by Hoffmann (*History*, 211) was not made at the time. At a much later date, i.e. after the adoption of the 'unconditional surrender' formula in Casablanca in January 1943, the Prime Minister stressed before the House of Commons that there was 'no question of the Atlantic Charter applying to Germany'; it 'in no way' bound Great Britain about the future of Germany as it was no 'bargain or contract' with the enemy; but he added that, while 'unconditional surrender' gave the enemy no rights, it relieved Britain of no duties; Speeches to the House of Commons, 22 Feb. and 24 May 1944 in *The War Speeches*, iii. 91, 151–2; cf. also CAB 65, WM (44), 34. President Roosevelt similarly differentiated repeatedly between the validity of the principles inherent in the Atlantic Charter and their realization. In short, the Atlantic Charter was never repealed; it was, as Günter Moltmann put it, even though theoretically valid, not, for the time being, applicable to Germany; Günter Moltmann, *Amerikas Deutschlandpolitik im Zweiten Weltkrieg: Kriegs- und Friedensziele 1941–1945* (Heidelberg, 1958), 38–9.

89. Entry of 18 Aug. 1941, *Die Hassell-Tagebücher*, 266. Von Hassell's comparison alone of the 8 points with Wilson's 14 points ran diametrically counter to the British as well as the American view. Churchill spelled out in his broadcast the intent of the signatories to reverse the developments towards the end of the First World War when Germany was not effectively disarmed but brought close to economic ruin; see also *FRUS*, 1941, i. 365–6, 369.

90. Entry of 18 Aug. 1941, *Die Hassell-Tagebücher*, 266; it might be of interest to note here that Friedrich Stampfer, a leader of the Socialist exile in the USA, upon a visit to England in the autumn of 1941, expressed a similar view; Glees, *Exile Politics*, 118.

91. Letter from Helmuth James von Moltke to Freya von Moltke, 25 Aug. 1941, von Moltke, *Briefe an Freya*, 277.

92. In a memorandum written in Sweden in Nov. Steltzer acknowledged that the Atlantic Charter 'explicitly assures each people to decide on its own form of government' ('Momente zu einer Denkschrift', Nov. 1942, courtesy Ger van Roon). Trott was if anything more apprehensive; in his extensive interview of Sept. 1942 with the editor-in-chief of the *Svenska Dagbladet*, Ivar Anderson, he insistently voiced his misgivings about the Atlantic Charter's 'heavy sentence upon a defeated Germany' (Ivar Anderson, *Från det Nära Förflutna: Människor och Händelser 1940–1955*, Stockholm, 1969, 91). See also Ger van Roon, 'Der Kreisauer Kreis und das Ausland', 'Aus Politik und Zeitgeschichte', B 50/86, *Das*

*Parlament*, 13 Dec. 1986; see also Margret Boveri, 'Adam von Trott zu Solz', 7, Trott Archive, Berichte.

93. 'Erklärung zur Atlantic-Charta', 13 Dec. 1942; '*Spiegelbild*', i. 235–9; *20. Juli 1944*, ed. Bundeszentrale für Heimatdienst (Bonn, 1961), 55–60; excerpts in Lipgens (ed.), *Europa-Föderationspläne*, 143–6.

94. The territorial proposals exhibit an appreciable evolution in Goerdeler's thinking since his Peace Plan of the previous year. While in the east, Germany was still to obtain the frontiers as of 1914, Poland–Lithuania was to be established as a federal union with internal autonomy and common access to the sea; the border between France and Germany was to be determined by the criterion of language, with most of Alsace reverting to Germany and most of Lorraine to France; Poland and Czechoslovakia were to emerge as independent states, choosing their own economic relations with other states; the Germans were to commit themselves to the reconstruction of Poland and to do their part in redressing the human injustices done to her; Italy was to cede the ethnically German South Tyrol to Germany—a stipulation which indicates that Goerdeler continued to take the absorption of Austria into Germany for granted.

95. Entry of 30 Aug. 1941, *Die Hassell-Tagebücher*, 267.

96. *Dokumente zur Deutschlandpolitik*, 410–11. In the subsequent year, on 26 May 1942, this stipulation was confirmed in the formal Anglo-Russian Treaty of Alliance.

97. During the First World War, in connection with a Federal Court investigation of a German agent, he was briefly gaoled for refusal to answer questions on grounds of possible self-incrimination; in the 1920s he served on the Dawes Commission; during the early years of the Second World War, he went on several special missions to Europe, including Germany, for the State Department and, as we shall see, he maintained ties with the Office of the Co-ordinator of Information, the predecessor of the OSS.

98. Entry of 13 July 1941, *Die Hassell-Tagebücher*, 260.

99. 'Memorandum of Conversation Mr. Frederick (or Frederico) Stallforth with the Chief of the European Desk of the Department of State', 19 Aug. 1940; NA, RG 59, CDF 740.0011 EW 1939/6061. Indeed in the summer of 1940 he took it upon himself to forward to Washington a peace proposal from Göring, supposedly approved by Hitler (maintenance of the British Empire, except for certain colonies to go to Germany; political independence for France, Belgium, and Holland, except for Alsace-Lorraine and Luxembourg to go to Germany; Germany to have a free hand in the east, including Poland and Czechoslovakia) which of course was turned down; Colonel William J. Donovan to President Franklin Delano Roosevelt, 1 Oct. 1941; W. D. Whitney to Donovan, 1 Oct. 1941; FDR Library, PSF Safe File 4, repr. in Hoffmann, *History*, 742–4.

100. Entry of 20 Sept. 1941, *Die Hassell-Tagebücher*, 272. During the same period Lonsdale Bryans, of old repute, made efforts to reactivate his Hassell connection; he twice called on Sir Nevile Henderson, but of course got nowhere. By then he had acquired the reputation in the Foreign Office of an 'objectionable individual' (see a minute by Ivo Mallet, Assistant Private Secretary to the Secretary of State, 31 Jan. 1941, FO 371/26542/C 1072/324/18); ever since his earlier efforts on behalf of von Hassell he had been kept 'at a very long arm's length', as Cadogan put it. However, a lonely minute, initialled 'C.B.' suggested that 'on the face of it' the Foreign Office seems to have adopted 'a cowardly role'; Sir Nevile Henderson to Sir A. Cadogan, 20 (or 28?) Aug. 1941; Sir A. Cadogan to Sir Nevile Henderson, 2 Sept. 1941, FO 371/26546 B/C 9935/324/18.

101. Entry of 20 Sept. 1941, *Die Hassell-Tagebücher*, 272–3. Prince Louis Ferdinand, second son of the German Crown Prince—his elder brother Wilhelm fell in battle in May 1940 in the invasion of France—had consistently kept a distance from National Socialism. Having spent many of his bachelor years in America, among other things working in the Ford factory at Dearborn, Mich., he struck up a close friendship with the family of Franklin Delano Roosevelt; in resistance circles he appeared therefore particularly well qualified to assume the crown in Germany after a coup against Hitler.

102. He finally showed them 'the eight points', obviously meaning the Atlantic Charter, the text of which he had obtained from the Embassy in Berlin, and met with general approval except on 'the last point on disarmament'; Whitney to Donovan, 1 Oct. 1941.

103. Entry of 4 Oct. 1941, *Die Hassell-Tagebücher*, 276.

104. Colonel General (1934) Kurt von Hammerstein-Equord was Chief of the Army Command 1930–4 and resigned from this position in January 1934 because of his opposition to the Nazis. In 1939 he was reactivated. He was in close contact with the conservative Resistance and worked out a plan to take Hitler prisoner during a troop inspection; but he was dismissed before being able to realize this scheme. He died on 25 April 1943.

105. The source for this is the article signed by an American naval intelligence officer, Alexander B. Maley, in fact written by Alexander Böker, 'The Epic of the German Underground', *Human Events*, 3, 27 Feb. 1946, 6; see also Hoffmann, *History*, 213, 595–6 n. 9.

106. Ibid. 213.

107. Ulrich von Hassell, 'Die Neuordnung im Südostraum', *Berliner Monatshefte*, 1941, 611; this article was based on a lecture which he had given in June at Breslau University before an assemblage of some 200 foreigners, students, and others; see entry of 16 June 1941, *Die Hassell-Tagebücher*, 257–8.

108. 'Sonderstellung'.

109. He himself referred to his 'Deutschfreundlichkeit'; letter from Louis P. Lochner to Prince Louis Ferdinand and Princess Kira, Berlin-Charlottenburg, 2 June 1941, Lochner Papers.

110. The main source for this venture is Otto John, *Twice through the Lines: The Autobiography of Otto John* (New York, 1972), 69–74; also Louis P. Lochner, *Always the Unexpected: A Book of Reminiscences* (New York, 1956), 295; in greater detail see *idem*, *Stets das Unerwartete: Erinnerungen aus Deutschland 1921–1953* (Darmstadt, 1955), 355–7; for Prince Louis Ferdinand's relations to the *Widerstand* see his memoirs, *The Rebel Prince* (Chicago, 1952), 306–24.

111. Dr Otto John, who from 1937 worked for the German Lufthansa, was introduced to Resistance circles by his chief, Klaus Bonhoeffer, elder brother of Dietrich Bonhoeffer. His position of Legal Adviser for the airline, which he had held since 1939, served him as cover for work in conjunction with the Abwehr for the overthrow of the Hitler regime. Throughout the war he was incessantly engaged in attempts to reach American and British authorities by way of his connections in Madrid; for a profile of Otto John see Hoffmann, *History*, 246–8; see also below Ch. 6, s. 4.

112. John, *Twice through the Lines*, 72.

113. For a profile of Josef Wirmer see Rudolf Lill, 'Josef Wirmer' in Lill and Oberreuter (eds.), *20. Juli*, 335–47.

114. Klaus Bonhoeffer's brother-in-law.

115. See John, *Twice through the Lines*, 72–3; Rothfels, *The German Opposition*, 133; they did invite Prince Louis Ferdinand to join them, but he wisely declined, saying: 'Better not, because you might want to talk about me there.'

116. Letter from Louis P. Lochner to Lauchlin Currie (The White House), Chicago, 19 June 1942, FDR Library, Hyde Park, OF 198a.

117. Lochner, *Always the Unexpected*, 295.

118. Dorothy Thompson, *Listen, Hans* (Boston, 1942).

119. In a letter to Mother Mary Gallin of 23 Dec. 1953 Dorothy Thompson confirmed that with 'Hans' she had indeed meant Moltke; IfZ/Ger van Roon, ZS A-18.

120. Thompson, *Listen, Hans*, vii–viii.

121. Ibid. 261; it is not possible to identify the persons in question. But Dorothy Thompson had also met Adam von Trott in November 1939 (Letters from Alexander Böker to Adam von Trott, Cambridge, Mass., 14 Nov. 1939, Adam von Trott to Alexander Böker, New York, 16 Nov. 1939, Alexander Böker Papers; letter from Alexander Böker to Adam von Trott, 24 Nov. 1939, forwarded by J. Edgar Hoover to Brigadier General Edwin M. Mason, Secretary to the President, FDR Library, OF 10 b.).

122. Thompson, *Listen, Hans*, 174, 245, 271–2; italics in the original.

123. IfZ, Ger van Roon, ZS A-18.

124. The following passages on Strasser rely heavily for factual information, though not for interpretation, on Robert H. Keyserlingk, 'Die deutsche Komponente in Churchills Strategie der nationalen Erhebungen 1940–1942. Der Fall Otto Strasser', *VfZ*, 31 (Oct. 1983), 614–45.

125. See Douglas Reed, *The Prisoner of Ottawa: Otto Strasser* (London, 1953). Reed was a fierce anti-Communist and an anti-Semite in addition.

126. It is interesting that at the time Adam von Trott, after reading a rejoinder to King-Hall in the *Völkischer Beobachter* of 14 July, wrote a letter to his English friend David Astor, complaining about Britain interfering in German affairs and assuming the function of a judge in international morality; quoted in Christopher Sykes, *Troubled Loyalty: A Biography of Adam von Trott zu Solz* (London, 1968), 272–4; here was an instance where even a position, like the one of Commander King-Hall, with which substantially he most probably was in agreement, offended him for the way in which it was broached to the German public.

127. On 18 June 1941 Commander King-Hall, who was an MP, asked the Foreign Secretary in the House of Commons whether he would give favourable consideration to the creation of the status of 'Free German', and was given the answer that he, Eden, did not regard such a proposition as 'either practicable or advantageous'; *Parliamentary Debates*, 5th Ser., vol. 372, House of Commons, 6th vol. of Sessions 1940–1 (London, 1941), cols. 619–20; see also FO 371/26559/C 2951/2951/18. In the USA Democratic Congressman from Ohio William Richard Thom advocated granting Otto Strasser recognition as leader of a Free German Movement with wide scope; but his scheme remained unanswered by the government; see Reed, *The Prisoner*, 211.

128. His most influential supporter in the Canadian government was Norman Robertson, since 1941 Under-Secretary of State for External Affairs.

129. See Kurt P. Tauber, *Beyond Eagle and Swastica: German Nationalism Since 1945* (Middletown, Conn., 1967), i. 109–10, ii. 1030, n. 114; also *Biographisches Handbuch der deutschsprachigen Emigration nach 1933*, ed. Werner Röder and Herbert A. Strauss (Munich, 1980), i. 742.

130. 'Would organize German Prisoners against Hitler', *Toronto Star*, 22 Mar. 1941, quoted in Keyserlingk, 'Die deutsche Komponente', 631.

131. Otto Strasser finally was able to return to West Germany in March 1955.

132. Secret Telegram from Anthony Eden to Viscount Halifax, London, 16 Sept. 1942, referred to ibid. 635.

133. In Nov. and Dec. 1940 Vansittart had given a series of seven talks on the BBC overseas service, soon thereafter published under the title *Black Record: Germans Past and Present* (London, 1941), which constituted the fiercest attack yet in Britain against the German national character and the persistent tradition of German aggressiveness. His eccentric position on Germany was shared by neither Churchill nor Eden and nor for that matter, in general, in the upper echelons of official London (see Norman Rose, *Vansittart: Study of a Diplomat* (London, 1978), 247, 254–5) and led, among other things, to his resignation in June 1941 as Chief Diplomatic Adviser and, having been created a Peer in 1941, to the transference of his agitation to the House of Lords.

134. Vansittart, *Lessons of My Life* (London, 1943), 70–1.

135. This is the position of Robert H. Keyserlingk; the very title of the article reflects this thesis; see esp. pp. 615, 620, 622, 634, 635, 636, 640.

136. 'If your policy means anything, it is the extermination of 40 or 50 million people. This is silly'; Winston Churchill to Sir Robert Vansittart, unsigned, undated; about Jan. 1941; PREM 4/23/2.

137. See William L. Langer and S. Everett Gleason, *The Undeclared War 1940–1941* (New York, 1953).

138. See esp. Ritter, *Carl Goerdeler*, 323–7; Rothfels, *The German Opposition*, 142–51; Anne Armstrong, *Unconditional Surrender: The Impact of the Casablanca Policy upon World War II* (New Brunswick, NJ, 1961), ch. 4.

139. Already on 1 Jan. 1942, on the occasion of the so-called 'Arcadia' Conference between Roosevelt and Churchill in Washington, DC, the Allies had committed themselves not to make a separate armistice or peace with the enemy.

140. Telegrams Churchill to Stalin, 3 Dec. 1942 and Stalin to Churchill 6 Dec. 1942 in Winston S. Churchill, *The Second World War*, iv: *The Hinge of Fate* (Boston, 1950), 665–6.

141. Telegram Stalin to Roosevelt, about mid-Dec. 1943, ibid. 667.

142. Chester Wilmot, *The Struggle for Europe* (New York, 1952), 117.

143. Elliott Roosevelt, *As He Saw It* (New York, 1946), 117–9; for the genesis of the 'unconditional surrender' formula see Günter Moltmann, 'Die Genesis der Unconditional-Sur-

render-Forderung', in Andreas Hillgruber, *Probleme des Zweiten Weltkrieges* (Cologne, 1967), 171–98.

144. Michael E. Howard, *Grand Strategy*, iv: *August 1942–September 1943* (London, 1972), 284–5, quoted in A. E. Campbell, 'Franklin Roosevelt and Unconditional Surrender', in Richard Langhorne (ed.), *Diplomacy and Intelligence during the Second World War* (Cambridge, 1985), 219; see also the critique of the surprise element in the presidential declaration by another distinguished military historian, Hanson Baldwin, 'Churchill Was Right', *Atlantic*, 194 (July 1954), 27.

145. *Postwar Foreign Policy Preparation 1939–1945*, Department of State (General Foreign Policy Series 15) (Washington, 1949), 127.

146. General Eisenhower in his memoirs merely mentioned that it was mentioned in the Minutes JCS meeting, 7 Jan. 1943. OPD Exec. 10, Item 45, Department of the Army; Dwight D. Eisenhower, *Crusade in Europe* (New York, 1949), 489 n. 7.

147. See General Albert C. Wedemeyer, *Wedemeyer Reports!* (New York, 1958), 186–7; see also the official volume of the *United States Army in World War II* series by Maurice Matloff and Edwin M. Snell, *Strategic Planning for Coalition Warfare 1941–1942* (Washington, DC, 1953), 380: 'No study of the meaning of this formula for conduct of the war was made at the time by the Army staff, or by the Joint Staff, either before or after the President's announcement.' The British–American Combined Chiefs of Staff, as an American member Admiral William D. Leahy recorded, had not discussed the policy at all; William D. Leahy, *I Was There* (New York, 1950), 145.

148. Churchill, *The Hinge of Fate*, 684; see CAB 65/37 (WM 43) Confid. Annex. As a matter of fact, in its answer the War Cabinet took up the issue of Italy, urging the Prime Minister to include that country under the provision of 'unconditional surrender'.

149. Cordell Hull, *The Memoirs of Cordell Hull* (New York, 1948), ii. 1570.

150. Alfred Vagts, 'Unconditional Surrender: vor und nach 1943', *VfZ*, 7 (July 1959), 299.

151. Elliott Roosevelt, *As He Saw It*, 117.

152. *Parliamentary Debates*, 5th ser., vol. 467, House of Commons, 11th vol. of Sessions 1948–9 (London, 1949), col. 1594.

153. Francis Williams, *A Prime Minister Remembers: The War and Post-War Memoirs of the Rt. Hon. Earl Attlee, Based on his Private Papers and on a Series of Recorded Conversations* (London, 1961), 52–3.

154. Harold Nicolson, *Spectator*, 23 Mar. 1945, quoted in Vagts, 'Unconditional Surrender', 297.

155. See John L. Chase, 'Unconditional Surrender Reconsidered', *Political Science Quarterly*, 70 (1955), 258.

156. Entry of 16 Apr. 1944, *The Diaries of Sir Alexander Cadogan*, 620.

157. 'Note by the Prime Minister', 10 Jan. 1944, PREM 3/197/2, quoted in Martin Gilbert, *Winston Churchill*, vii, *Road to Victory 1941–1945* (London, 1986), 643.

158. Churchill, *The Hinge of Fate*, 341–2.

159. Wilmot, *The Struggle*, 123.

160. Harold Nicolson, 28 Oct. 1943, FO 371/34452/C 13245/155/18.

161. F.D.R. on 12 Feb. before the White House Press Correspondents Association; Churchill on 22 Feb. before the House of Commons; see Herbert Feis, *Churchill, Roosevelt, Stalin: The War They Waged and the Peace They Sought* (Princeton, NJ, 1957), 113; Churchill, *The Hinge of Fate*, 690–1; Moltmann, 'Die Genesis', 177; Chase, 'Unconditional Surrender', 265.

162. Robert E. Sherwood, *Roosevelt and Hopkins: An Intimate History* (New York, 1948), 791.

163. WSC to Foreign Secretary, 14 Aug. 1943, FO 371/34450/C 9706/155/G; this minute was written by the Prime Minister in reaction to a report from Ankara to the effect that the German Ambassador Franz von Papen expected to be recalled to Berlin to replace von Ribbentrop and then to initiate an approach to the Allies.

164. Minute of Frank K. Roberts, 27 Aug. 1943 and Secret draft telegrams initialled 'FKR', 31 Aug. 12 Sept.; ibid.

165. Von Kessel, 'Verborgene Saat', 229–30. Also in retrospect Edward von Selzam, Legation Counsellor in Berne from July 1940 to the end of 1942 and a close associate of Theo Kordt, maintained that 'the declaration of 'unconditional surrender' had the worst possible effect'

on the conspirators' efforts to gather followers within their groups; Edward C. W. von Selzam, 'The Surrender Terms', Letter to the Editor, *New York Times*, 31 July 1949.

166. For Goerdeler's remarks on the matter to the Swedish banker Jacob Wallenberg in Feb. 1943, see Allen Welsh Dulles, *Germany's Underground* (New York, 1947), 144, and Ritter, *Carl Goerdeler*, 328. In his diaries Hassell voiced concern lest Casablanca meant that the 'other side' was now holding out for complete destruction of Germany; actually the original text is ambiguous: 'Die Bösartigkeit der Lage kommt dabei darin zum Ausdruck, dass die gleichzeitigen Nachrichten von der "anderen Seite" immer stärkere Zweifel ergeben, ob diese nicht nun auf der Zerschmetterung ganz Deutschlands bestehen wolle' (entry of 22 Jan. 1943, *Die Hassel-Tagebücher*, 345); the passage, most probably written hurriedly, lends itself to two opposite readings: 'doubts whether' or 'concerns lest', but the context calls for the latter interpretation. For Trott's protestations in Sweden in Oct. 1943 against 'unconditional surrender' see Henrik Lindgren, 'Adam von Trotts Reisen nach Schweden 1942–1944: Ein Beitrag zur Frage der Auslandsverbindungen des deutschen Widerstandes', *VfZ*, 18 (July, 1970), 277 and van Roon, *Neuordnung*, 316; for Trott's Memorandum written in Stockholm in June 1944 for the British secret-service agent David McEwan see Lindgren, 'Adam von Trotts Reisen', 281, 289–91. For Moltke's misgivings concerning 'unconditional surrender' as stated to Bishop Eivind Berggrav in Oslo in March 1943 see Ger van Roon, 'Der Kreisauer Kreis und das Ausland', 43; for Moltke in Turkey where in July 1943 he was persuaded by his friend Alexander Rüstow to drop his objection to the formula see van Roon, *Neuordnung*, 319–20 and Michael Balfour and Julian Frisby, *Helmuth von Moltke: A Leader Against Hitler* (London, 1972) 270. The Canaris statement on 'unconditional surrender' is reported by Ian Colvin, *Master Spy* (New York, 1951), 192–3, to have been made in the course of a conversation which he had held with his Abwehr aide, Col. Erwin von Lahousen. The one person among the conspirators who from the very start faced up squarely to the necessity of accepting the Allied demand was Otto John; John, *Twice through the Lines*, 100, 136.

167. Lord Hankey, 'Unconditional Surrender', typescript, 20 Apr. 1943, Hankey Papers, Churchill College.

168. Under Secretary of State (Stettinius) to the Secretary of State, London, 13 Apr. 1944 in *FRUS* 1944, i. 507–9.

169. Secret JIC (43) 527 (Final), PREM 3/193/5; F.D.R. reacted altogether negatively to such a proposition; he preferred to leave things as they were for the time being; he thought that not enough was known about opinions within Germany itself 'to go on any fishing expedition'; Roosevelt–Churchill, 6 Jan. 1944 in *Roosevelt and Churchill: Their Secret Wartime Correspondence*, ed. Francis L. Loewenheim *et al.* (London, 1975), 411–12.

170. 'Notizen über eine Aussprache mit Dr. Josef Müller am 4.1.1953', BA/K, Ritter 131; Josef Müller, *Bis zur letzten Konsequenz. Ein Leben für Frieden und Freiheit* (Munich, 1975), 158–62; Hermann Graml, 'Die deutsche Militäropposition vom Sommer 1940 bis zum Frühjahr 1943', in *Vollmacht des Gewissens*, ed. Europäische Publikation e.V. (Frankfurt/M., 1965), ii. 469–74.

171. A group of staff officers of Army Group Centre headquarters near Smolensk, led by its Operations Officer Colonel Henning von Tresckow, was planning an attempt on the Führer on the occasion of his inspection trip to the Russian front. Tresckow's adjutant, 1st Lieutenant (Res.) Fabian von Schlabrendorff, volunteered to smuggle a time bomb aboard Hitler's plane on his return flight, which, however, failed to go off; Fabian von Schlabrendorff, *The Secret War*, 229–39.

172. Josef Becker, 'Der Vatikan und der II. Weltkrieg', in Dieter Albrecht (ed.), *Katholische Kirche im Dritten Reich* (Mainz, 1976), 182–3; see also Walter Lipgens (ed.), *Documents on the History of European Integration*, ii: *Plans for European Union in Great Britain and in Exile 1939–1945* (Berlin, 1986), 702.

173. 'Order of the Day of the People's Commissar for Defence, No. 55', 23 Feb. 1942 in Andrew Rothstein (ed.), *Soviet Foreign Policy During the Patriotic War: Documents and Materials* (London, 1944), i. 37.

174. 'Twenty Fifth Anniversary of the Great October Socialist Revolution', ibid. 49; see also Vojtech Mastny, 'Stalin and the Prospects of a Separate Peace in World War II', *American Historical Review*, 77 (Dec. 1972), 1372.

175. *Parliamentary Debates*, 5th ser., vol. 126, House of Lords, 2nd vol. of Sessions 1942–3 (London, 1943), col. 536. Originally he had meant to ask the question on 29 Nov., occasioned by some British propaganda leaflets and a BBC broadcast which made the same kind of distinctions which Stalin had made; however, Lord Cranborne, on behalf of the Foreign Secretary, dissuaded the Bishop from doing so, since a parliamentary debate about the contents of the leaflets and the broadcast would not be in the public interest. Bishop Bell then consented to ask the question at a later date on the general government policy towards Germany and the Nazi State, and it was then scheduled for the first suitable opportunity on 10 March; Ronald C. D. Jasper, *George Bell: Bishop of Chichester* (London, 1967), 273–4; letter from Bishop Bell to Gerhard Leibholz, Chichester, 17 Dec. 1942, Eberhard Bethge and Ronald C. D. Jasper (eds.), *An der Schwelle zum gespalteten Europa: Der Briefwechsel zwischen George Bell und Gerhard Leibholz 1939–1951* (Stuttgart, 1974), 78–9.
176. *Parliamentary Debates*, vol. 126, Lords, col. 550.
177. Ibid., col. 575; for the whole episode see also Hermann Fromm, *Deutschland in der öffentlichen Kriegszieldiskussion Grossbritanniens 1939–1945* (Frankfurt/M., 1982), 172–3.
178. 'Order of the Day of the Supreme Commander-in-Chief, No. 195', 1 May 1943 in Rothstein (ed.), *Soviet Foreign Policy*, i. 58.
179. Foreign Secretary to the Foreign Office, 30 Nov. 1943, PREM/197/2; 'Unconditional Surrender: Memorandum by the Secretary of State for Foreign Affairs', 19 Feb. 1944, W.P. (44) 125; see also Gilbert, *Winston Churchill*, vii, 581. It is of interest to note that President Roosevelt had no recollection of 'U.J.'s' remark, while Churchill registered that he 'certainly' heard it, and 'with great interest' (Churchill–Roosevelt, 2 Jan. 1944, *Roosevelt and Churchill*, 410–11); indeed he thought that Stalin's was 'a better suggestion' (Most Secret Cypher Telegram Foreign Secretary-FO, 1 Dec. 1943, FO 371/34453/C 14544/155/18. As for Anthony Eden, he minuted about 'this disappointing development': 'To the best of my recollection, Marshal Stalin raised this at dinner with the President and I heard it then. I cannot have invented it.' ('Peace Moves: Proposed Allied Declaration', 24 Dec. 1943; Eden minute 26 Dec.; FO 371/34453/C 15131/155/18).
180. Mastny, 'Stalin', 1372–3.
181. Ibid. 1384.
182. Alexander Fischer, *Sowjetische Deutschlandpolitik im Zweiten Weltkrieg 1941–1945* (Stuttgart, 1975), 38–9.
183. Peter Kleist, *Zwischen Hitler und Stalin 1939–1945: Aufzeichnungen* (Bonn, 1950), 235; in an updated edn. *Die europäische Tragödie* (Göttingen, 1961), 207.
184. Ingeborg Fleischhauer, *Die Chance des Sonderfriedens. Deutschsowjetische Geheimgespräche 1941–1945* (Berlin, 1986), 108 ff.
185. Such was his signature; in the official German files he appears as Claus, Clauß, and Clauss; ibid. 30.
186. Ibid. 41.
187. Madame Kollontay, the *grande dame* of Russian diplomacy, was the daughter of a Tsarist general; an 'Old Bolshevik' and a *confidante* of Lenin, she had fallen from grace under Stalin and was therefore sent off to Sweden. Partly because of her intransigent and independent position *vis-à-vis* Stalin, she became a legend abroad and kept attracting all sorts of diplomatic dreamers and freelancers who expected her to influence Soviet policies from her neutral post. She was, however, in ill health and had to spend much of her tenure in a sanatorium and leave the conduct of affairs to Semyonov; see Fleischhauer, *Die Chance*, 58 ff. and Fischer, *Sowjetische*, 181, n. 24; see also Isabel de Palenzia, *Alexandra Kollontay: Ambassadress for Russia* (New York, London, 1947), and Beatrice Farnsworth, *Aleksandra Kollontai: Socialism, Feminism, and the Bolshevik Revolution* (Stanford, Calif. 1980). As a matter of fact, Semyonov turned out to be by far the more important figure in the Soviet Embassy.
188. For the most recent, all too sensationalized, account of the Klaus episode see Alexander Slavinas (a former Soviet Secret Service man), '"Treff" und "Joker". Widerstand in letzter Minute: Agenten im Schatten der Diktaturen', *Die Zeit*, 9 Juni 1989.
189. Fleischhauer, *Die Chance*, 65–5.
190. As for Kleist, he recorded that he was 'cognizant' of the initiatives taken by 'the Opposition'

via Switzerland, Portugal, and Sweden; Kleist, *Zwischen Hitler und Stalin*, 232. Klaus was briefed in April 1941 by an Abwehr officer, Captain Hans-Ludwig von Lossow, about the state of the *Widerstand* and its plans; Fleischhauer, *Die Chance*, 43. Klaus also was, so it seems, in direct touch with 'influential members of the Resistance circles'; ibid. 45.

191. Joachim von Ribbentrop, *Zwischen London und Moskau: Erinnerungen und letzte Aufzeichnungen*, ed. Annelies von Ribbentrop (Leoni am Starnbergersee, 1953), 262–4.

192. Kleist, *Zwischen Hitler und Stalin*, 242–3; see also Fischer, *Sowjetische*, 41; Fleischhauer, *Die Chance*, 111.

193. Ibid. 112.

194. Kleist, *Zwischen Hitler und Stalin*, 243.

195. See Fleischhauer, *Die Chance*, 161 ff., 190 ff.; H. W. Koch, 'The Spectre of a Separate Peace in the East: Russo-German "Peace Feelers", 1942–44', *Journal of Contemporary History*, 10 (July 1975), 531–49.

196. It should be noted that by the time of the Sept. encounter the Russians had upped their stakes, stating as their objective the restoration of the Russo-German frontiers as of 1914, a free hand in the Straights question and in the whole of Asia, and the establishment of extensive economic relations between Germany and the USSR; Fleischhauer, *Die Chance*, 191; Koch, 'The Spectre', 536.

197. In the summer of 1943 Himmler also sent his lawyer Carl Langbehn, whom he knew to be affiliated with the Opposition, to Stockholm to explore possibilities of a separate peace with a Germany led by himself and the military; Heinz, 'Von Wilhelm Canaris zur NKVD'.

198. *Nationalkomitee 'Freies Deutschland'*, NKFD (12, 13 July 1943).

199. *Bund Deutscher Offiziere*, BDO (11, 12 Sept. 1943).

200. For a succinct and meticulous assessment of the part assigned to the 'Free Germany' Movement in the Soviet designs as well as of its place in relation to the German Resistance see Alexander Fischer, 'Die Bewegung "Freies Deutschland" in der Sowjetunion: Widerstand hinter Stacheldraht?', in Schmädeke and Steinbach (eds.), *Der Widerstand*, 954–73; see also Kai P. Schoenhals, *The Free Germany Movement: A Case of Patriotism or Treason?* (New York, 1989).

201. 'Manifest des Nationalkomitees "Freies Deutschland" an die Wehrmacht und an das deutsche Volk', *Freies Deutschland*. Organ des Nationalkomitees 'Freies Deutschland', No. 1, 19 July 1943, microfilm, Yale University Library; the text trans. in John W. Wheeler-Bennett, *The Nemesis of Power: The German Army in Politics 1918–1945* (London, 1954), 716–18.

202. At Tauroggen General Ludwig Yorck von Wartenburg, with the assistance of one of Seydlitz's ancestors, without authorization of his king, disengaged his army corps from its service to Napoleon to enter into a neutrality pledge to Russia, thus initiating the secession of Prussia from Napoleon.

203. See Bodo Scheurig, *Free Germany: The National Committee and the League of German Officers* (Middletown, Conn., 1969), 149, 164.

204. See Fischer, 'Die Bewegung' in Schmädeke and Steinbach (eds.), *Der Widerstand*, 963–4, 967.

205. Scheurig, *Free Germany*, 99, 103.

206. FO 371/34414/C 8626/29/18.

207. Glees, *Exile Politics*, 190–1.

208. FO 371/34414/C 8626/29/18. Later, in December, the British Embassy in Washington also forwarded to the Central Department an analysis of the 'Free Germany' movement written in Sept. by the German exiled political scientist Arnold Wolfers at Yale University who argued that at the root of the problem was the Russian advocacy of peace negotiations, non-occupation, and equality, whereas the Western Powers called for unconditional surrender, occupation, and unilateral disarmament. Nevertheless he still envisaged the possibility of the gap being narrowed down with 'much good will on both sides' and by means of 'hard bargaining'; 'Dr. Arno Wolfers' analysis of the "Free Germany Committee" Manifesto', 1 Sept. 1943, FO 372/34416/C 14723/29/18.

209. Letter from Bishop Bell to Gerhard Leibholz, Chichester, 3 Aug. 1943, Bethge and Jasper (eds.), *An der Schwelle*, 119.

210. Memorandum on the 'National Committee of Free Germany', 30 July 1943, FO 371/34415/C 8903/29/18.

211. Since 5 Apr. 1943 Bonhoeffer had already been gaoled by the Nazis.

212. See in particular Ritter, *Carl Gordeler*, 381, 535, n. 89; Scheurig, *Free Germany*, 159–82.

213. Ibid. 159.

214. Ibid. 170.

215. Entry of 15 Aug. 1943, *Die Hassell-Tagebücher*, 382.

216. This report goes back to Colonel Job von Witzleben, living after the war in the German Democratic Republic, who claims to have been informed about Schulenburg's views and intentions by his older and much revered relation, Field Marshal Erwin von Witzleben, when he visited him in the autumn of 1943; Job von Witzleben, 'Am Rande der Verschwörung gegen Hitler. Erinnerungen eines Zeitgenossen', MS, pp. 6–8, quoted in Kurt Finker, *Stauffenberg und der 20. Juli 1944* (East Berlin, 1978), 246–8. It is very likely that Colonel Albrecht Ritter Mertz von Quirnheim, a close associate of Stauffenberg's who was a brother-in-law of Major General Otto Korfes, a leading member of the BDO, was favourably disposed to the National Committee and did not dismiss the possibility of establishing a connection with it; SD Report 29 Nov. 1944, '*Spiegelbild*' i. 507; see also Sigrid Wegner-Korfes, 'Der 20. Juli 1944 und das Nationalkomitee "Freies Deutschland"', *Zeitschrift für Geschichtswissenschaft*, 24 (1976), 541–3; Finker, *Stauffenberg*, 254–5; Ritter, *Carl Goerdeler*, 535 n. 89. In general, the Marxist-Leninist literature tends to make a case for the connection between the group around Stauffenberg, assigned to the 'progressive' sector of the *Widerstand*, and the twin committees founded in Russia, which, however, is never sufficiently backed up by documentary evidence (see Finker, *Stauffenberg*, 439–40 n. 166; Daniil Melnikow, *20.. Juli 1944: Legende und Wirklichkeit* (Berlin, 1968), 157). The Kaltenbrunner Report's more cautious approach to the problem probably comes closer to the truth; while admitting that 'immediate connections' did not exist, they emphasize the basic 'political-ideological' affinity between the military men fighting with the Wehrmacht and those in captivity; SD Reports of 10 Aug. and 29 Nov. 1944, '*Spiegelbild*', i. 190–1, 507–8.

217. SD Report of 8 Aug. 1944, '*Spiegelbild*', i. 174; see also Joachim Kramarz, *Stauffenberg* (New York, 1967), 164; Ritter, *Carl Goerdeler*, 535 n. 89.

218. Largely upon the insistence of F.D.R. who was concerned about its possible effect upon the Polish vote in the impending Presidential election in his country.

219. Kleist, *Zwischen Hitler und Stalin*, 280.

220. See in this connection the fierce discussion which erupted in the Federal Republic of Germany on the occasion of the opening on 19 July 1989 of the Museum in Berlin 'Resistance against National Socialism' which also makes a place for the NKFD and the BDO; the opponents of their inclusion in the permanent exhibit, among them five members of the Stauffenberg family, argued that the members of the NKFD and BDO could not qualify for consideration as part of the *Widerstand* since they were essentially tools of Communism and also since they did not incur the risk of fighting the Nazi regime from within Germany. The assumption on the part of these critics was that the captives who had joined the NKFD and BDO had been engaged not in resistance but in unadulterated treason; Letter from Nina Schenk to Gräfin von Stauffenberg, Berthold Heimeran, Franz Ludwig Graf Schenk von Stauffenberg and Konstanze von Schulthess Rechberg-Regierender Bürgermeister Walter Momper, 15 July 1989; see also Enno Loewenstein, 'Helden und Handlanger', *Die Welt*, 20 July 1989, 2; the different positions were argued out by Georg Meyer, Peter Hermes, and Professor Peter Steinbach (the latter being the '*wissenschaftlicher Leiter*' of the Museum) in *Rheinischer Merkur/Christ und Welt*, 28 July 1989, 3–4.

221. Bodo Scheurig, *Walther von Seydlitz-Kurzbach—General im Schatten Stalingrads* (Berlin, 1983), 26.

222. See Letter to the Editor by Professor Dr Alexander Fischer, 'Das "Nationalkomitee Freies Deutschland"', *Frankfurter Allgemeine Zeitung*, 28 July 1989, 8.

223. Fischer, 'Die Bewegung', 969.

# 5

## Ecumenical Dialogue or
## 'The War Behind the War'

### 1. In Switzerland

'Absolute silence' and 'unconditional surrender' did not put an end to the attempts of the German plotters to break out of their isolation. If anything, these dictates, followed by the surrender of the German Sixth Army at Stalingrad early in February 1943, acted as a challenge making for redoubled efforts on the part of the Germans to get their message out.

This redoubling of efforts was not only a matter of redirecting the traffic to the east and opening up visions of what Ulrich von Hassell called a capricious *Mühlespiel* between east and west, but rather of following up another kind of avenue. The closing of the 'official' channels of diplomacy served as a reminder to the conspirators of the spiritual sources of their resistance. Their very stand against the Nazi ideology committed them to persevere, if only to get the basic message to the world outside, that there was a resistance in Germany. Quite apart from the consideration of facilitating a coup through foreign assurances which hitherto had predominantly informed the feelers abroad, their primary concern came to be to bear witness themselves to the 'other Germany' and thus to clear the name of their country which had become so deeply tainted with guilt.

It hardly needs stressing that even the earlier statements of, and missions abroad on behalf of, the *Widerstand* did not lack that essentially apolitical note of bearing witness to the world outside. Thus from the very start Theodor Steltzer's memorandum of September 1933 written for Schuschnigg amounted to an appeal to the conscience of the German nation, no more and no less. As early as 1935, when Helmuth von Moltke wrote to his English friend Lionel Curtis about his determination to maintain the 'connection' with the 'greater world', he understood this to be a gesture, no less and no more. For him and his friends this might mean living out their lives in 'a small cell'. Basically, then, Moltke's maintenance of connection with people outside his country was meant to be a gesture. But likewise the memoranda of Carl Goerdeler rarely lacked this same spiritual dimension and the commitment to the 'eternal moral code'[1] which made some of his admirers abroad, such as Frank Ashton-Gwatkin of the British Foreign Office and Mr A. P.

Young, overlook the otherwise questionable nature of his concrete political propositions. It is, then, not surprising that Goerdeler's rather high-toned memorandum of March 1939, 'All Peoples want and need Peace',[2] should have found its way to the offices of the World Council of Churches in Geneva, clearly not an agency concerned with matters of diplomacy; there it was assessed as a 'very important document'.[3]

Not only the closing of the 'official' channels to the overtures of the German Resistance, however, was responsible for inducing it to fall back on its spiritual resources, but also the fact that since early 1943 the initiative within the *Widerstand* was taken over increasingly by members of the younger generation. In the area of its foreign affairs the driving forces became men like Bonhoeffer, Trott, and Moltke who on balance were preoccupied in their missions with bearing witness at least as much as with obtaining tangible results. They steered the foreign operations of the Resistance towards neutral Switzerland and Sweden, both of which in the course of the war had become sites of intensified ecumenical activity. Under their influence, then, the foreign relations of the Resistance turned into an ecumenical dialogue with the leadership of the World Council of Churches (WCC) in Geneva[4] and of the Nordic Ecumenical Institute in Sigtuna near Stockholm[5] and last but not least, via Sweden, with the ever-concerned Bishop George Bell of Chichester. The result of all this was that matters of political planning were increasingly displaced by fundamental questions of an ethical if not religious nature.

The Ecumenical Movement, like the League of Nations, came into being after the First World War as part of a general effort to heal the wounds of the Great War. But in the very year when its organizational structure was consolidated in the form of the World Council of Churches, albeit still 'in Process of Formation', in Geneva, the League closed its doors. Quite clearly, the World Council did not constitute yet another international organization. Its chief objectives were to bring about unity among the divided Christian communities and denominations and to bring Christian ethics to bear on international relations.[6] Indeed it understood itself to be not the Churches' League of Nations, but a society with primarily sacred functions. In particular in view of the progressive secularization of the world and the emergence of new secular creeds in the form of totalitarian ideologies of the Left as well as the Right, the World Council of Churches aspired towards an 'essential togetherness of all Christians' under the sign of *Christus Victor*.[7]

We must be aware, however, of the fact that from the very start, when Hitler seized power in Germany in January 1933, the leadership of the Ecumenical Movement was by no means of one mind concerning the attitude to take towards the Nazi regime and its potential threat to the Churches. Parallel to the debate about political appeasement of the Third Reich that preoccupied most European capitals, and in particular that of Britain, there also ensued a debate among the princes of the European Protestant Churches on the advisability of maintaining lines open to official Germany in the hope of exerting influence upon it and thus diverting it from its course of religious persecution. They were clearly caught in a dilemma between the impulse to air their apprehensions and the need of keeping channels open into Germany. Keeping silent would have meant compromising their consciences. But speaking out would not only have jeopardized relations with the German authorities but also endangered those on whose behalf intercession was contemplated. In effect, then, the bulk of the ecumenical leadership—in Britain Archbishops Cosmo Lang of Canterbury and William Temple of York and Bishop George Bell of Chichester, in Sweden Archbishop Erling Eidem of Uppsala, in Norway Bishop Eivind Berggrav of Oslo—supported appeasement of Nazi Germany, and Visser't Hooft, the Secretary General of the World Council of Churches, himself also favoured a policy of caution.

Of course the ecumenists were particularly apprehensive about the Church Dispute in Germany. But on this score too a 'wait and see' attitude was indicated. It was dictated by the fact that the German Protestant Churches were fragmented and that even the leadership of the Confessing Church kept protesting its loyalty to the Nazi revolution. Although determined to fend off the incursions of the 'German Christians' upon the integrity of Protestant theology and establishment, it refrained from taking issue with the Nazi regime on general humane and political grounds. Moreover the faction within German Protestantism that most resolutely called for resistance against National Socialism was theologically out of step with the 'liberal theology' that prevailed in the international Protestant community, especially among the British and Scandinavian bishops. These could muster little understanding for Karl Barth's and Dietrich Bonhoeffer's rigorous dialecticism which in the name of 'confession' abjured any compromise even with natural-law theology that called for involvement of the Church in state and society. Barth and Bonhoeffer took a stand against National Socialism on the grounds of revelational and confessional integrity and not on political or social grounds, and by these terms they called upon the Ecumenical Movement to break its 'silence'. Ecumenism too, Bonhoeffer urged in April 1934, had to decide: 'Confession ... is the issue today in Germany, and confession must be the issue today just the same for ecumenism.'[8]

If in the course of the war the leadership of the World Council of Churches did respond to Barth's and Bonhoeffer's persistent proddings, it was largely due to the personality and efforts of its Secretary General, Visser't Hooft. The latter, it should be remembered, was a disciple of Barth and in continuous communication with him, and he, no less than Barth, was highly critical of the 'liberal theology' in the Anglo-Saxon countries.[9] In this connection it might well be recalled that Visser't Hooft's ascendancy in Geneva coincided with the emergence in the Ecumenical Movement of a number of Calvinist churchmen[10] who, like Visser't Hooft, were disposed to listen to Barth's battle cries and press for a more distinct position of the World Council on events in Nazi Germany as well as on issues of war and peace. They certainly formed the appropriate background for the activities of Visser't Hooft. A statesman as much as a cleric, and a vigorous and enterprising man of the world, he made his initially rather ill-defined and provisional organization into an umbrella for all the world's major Christian denominations—except for the Roman Catholic one—and a formidable voice of conscience in a war-torn world.

The outbreak of the war finally jolted Visser't Hooft into sorting out the many and often contradictory pressures that had come upon him from within his far-flung organization and moulding them into what amounted to an ecumenical consensus. He designed a course that was to lift the World Council out of its impasse and that was to ensure the maintenance of the integrity of the Church as an ecumenical Church. Among the main alternatives before the ecumenical leadership about what course to take was withdrawal in the face of the European cataclysm to an otherworldly position with the objective of salvaging the identity of the Christian Churches. This choice, Visser't Hooft came to understand, would have reduced them to irrelevance. Certainly appeasement of Nazi Germany had by September 1939 ceased to be an option; the prospect of reforming the Nazis gave pride of place to everyone's civic and patriotic commitment to war. On the other hand, no degree of sympathy with and confidence in the Allied cause could have prompted the ecumenical leadership to identify with it and its war and peace aims. The Churches could not afford to become a branch of the Allied war effort without losing their sacred identity.

In April 1940 Visser't Hooft launched the formula which, identifying the special mission of the Churches in time of war, set the World Council on course: the Churches were engaged in a 'war behind the war'.[11] As a matter of fact, it had begun long before September 1939. What he meant to express was that at the root of the evil was the apostasy of the world from the message of Christ which had been merely intensified by the 'anti-Christian ideologies' in the form of Communism and National Socialism. In other words, the war which the Christian Churches were engaged in was, strictly speaking, not the war of the Western democracies against the Nazi threat and certainly not the war among nations in the name of 'national interests'. It was, rather, the war of the Churches against the 'great Counter-Churches'.[12]

There was no question, to be sure, as to where the loyalties of the leaders of the Ecumenical Movement lay in that war which began in September 1939. However, the 'war behind the war' which in fact was a 'world civil war' gave them, whether from their neutral posts or from seats in belligerent or occupied countries, a somewhat extraterritorial status which made them examine in their own way the official friend–foe alignment. Nor were the causes of the war to be laid at the feet of the Germans alone; nor was the war seen as one against the German people as a whole. War and peace aims were not, moreover, to be defined simply in terms of total defeat of the Germans. The formulae of 'absolute silence' and 'unconditional surrender' had no currency among Church circles which tended to insist upon the distinction between Nazis and Germans and to acknowledge the fact that even in Nazi Germany— as also in Soviet Russia—there were thousands who, as Visser't Hooft put it, were eager 'to stem the tide towards spiritual and moral nihilism',[13] just as there were anti-Christian forces at work in countries that still called themselves Christian. The 'world civil war', then, cut, as it did also for the German Social Democrats,[14] across frontiers. This Christian perspective was bound to open up and to keep open channels to Germany, and it allowed, in particular after Casablanca, a natural convergence between the men of the *Widerstand* and the Protestant leadership abroad. The newly arisen 'theology of resistance', as Visser't Hooft once characterized it,[15] awakened the ecumenical leadership to the dimension of the 'war behind the war' in which a continued dialogue across the battle lines became an essential feature.

The groundwork for contacts between the World Council in Geneva and the Resistance in Germany was laid by State Secretary von Weizsäcker who, by means of a systematic personnel policy, succeeded in placing some of his younger protégés in various positions in Switzerland.[16] Their presence in Switzerland was to benefit the liaison between the Auswärtiges Amt, as well as the Confessing Church, with that vital neutral post and to counteract the activities of the Nazi secret services in that area. In January 1940 Weizsäcker actually worked out, together with Consul-General Krauel, a secret ordinance that gave the Consulate-General in Geneva sweeping powers to facilitate travel to Germany without Nazi Party interference by representatives of the World Council; to forward confidential ecumenical reports to Germany, and later also to the occupied countries and thus to encourage communications among the members of the International Protestant Community; and also to further ecumenical work on behalf of prisoners of war. Among the many beneficiaries of this unusual ordinance were, on their respective trips between Germany and Switzerland, Hans Schönfeld and Adam von Trott.[17]

Visser't Hooft's contacts with the German Resistance go back to the time of the 'Battle of Britain' in September 1940 when Adam von Trott paid a call on him in Geneva.[18] In the course of this call Trott outlined to him the plight of the opposition forces in Germany in the face of a solidified Nazi regime, also asking him to forward a summary of his observations to friends in England, among whom of course he named David Astor.[19]

The tone of Trott's message was altogether sombre. But while he had to admit that the Opposition, consisting of the Socialists, the Catholics, the Protestants, and the Conservatives, was 'weak and disorganized',[20] he also emphasized that resistance to Hitler by force was 'absolutely necessary'[21] since it was the only hope of changing the regime. Proceeding to the question of peace aims, Trott reiterated the refrain of all the Resistance emissaries not to 'do Germany down'[22] lest the whole nation rally behind Hitler; he therefore proposed to secure Germany's ethnographic frontiers.

In the message that was to be conveyed to his English friends Trott also raised the topic of a German invasion of England. After all, during the summer months following the fall of France, Great Britain was left confronting the Nazi war machine alone. Operation 'Sea-Lion', the code-name for the invasion of the British Isles, had become a real possibility. As a matter of fact, Trott himself, since June a member of the Information Section of the Auswärtiges Amt, had in late August been delegated to the Division preoccupied with preparations for the landing in England. Trott's advice to his friends in England reflected none of the fighting ethos that came from Winston Churchill across the Channel:

In the event of Britain's being defeated efforts should be made to secure that some of the best elements in the country co-operate with the new regime. A policy of non-cooperation would be disastrous. In the two countries there are many people with fundamental social ideals in common, who must try to co-operate.[23]

We have been told by a colleague of Trott's in the German Foreign Office that, while engaged in work on the German invasion, he was aware of the existence of a Nazi blacklist containing the names of those who, following the occupation, were to be apprehended, and that his concern was to prevent this plan from being implemented. Trott and a friend of his, having succeeded in obtaining permission from the authorities to be flown to London immediately after the end of hostilities, hoped thus to be able to act upon a white list of sorts of their own that contained the names of personages who were to be saved.[24] There can be no question of Trott's resolve to oppose and outwit the Nazi regime. A question can, however, be asked concerning Trott's judgement in giving the kind of advice he did to his English friends. Somehow, despite the hard political realities of a new war between his native and his adopted countries, and despite the clear and present danger of an invasion of one by the other, he kept harbouring thoughts of that 'great European alliance' as well as of the erosion of Nazism. His vision of co-operation among the 'best elements' in both countries still seemed realizable to him provided the worst, namely the Churchillian 'fight for every inch of the ground in every village and in every street'[25] was avoided. David Astor read the message from his German friend as meaning just that: a call neither for armed resistance nor for collaboration but rather the conjuring up of Trott's dream of that 'international network' which had been shattered by the reality of the war.[26]

As for Visser't Hooft, he did not take exception to Trott's reasoning. On the contrary, the conversation helped him to clarify his own thoughts on resistance. Like Trott he envisaged the distinct possibility of a British defeat in the battle against Germany, and like Trott he came around to endorsing the need for resistance: 'the struggle will have to go on on the interior battle-front'.[27] And Trott's advice to the people of Britain to 'co-operate with the new regime' which, coming from a German, might have seemed perplexing, if not suspect, came across, coming from the Dutchman, as an unmistakable blueprint for 'co-operation and close contact ... between those Germans who are struggling against nihilism and for a European order and those in the occupied and annexed territories who have the same aims and purposes'.[28]

Visser't Hooft detected in Trott a kindred spirit since he too saw the struggle in the last analysis to be a spiritual one:

Adam felt strongly that all those who held the same fundamental Christian convictions about the social and international order were on the same side in this war, even if their governments were on opposite sides. I shared this conviction and this gave our friendship a strong basis.[29]

Visser't Hooft, we might conclude, thus knew Trott better than Trott knew himself. Trott's argument was tortured because the situation in which he found himself was torturous. But Visser't Hooft was in a less ambiguous position, and he may also have been more clear-headed than his impulsive, visionary young German friend. In any event, the conversation clarified his thoughts about that 'war behind the war' which was to bring together in a common struggle the opposition groups everywhere, including those in Germany.

Trott furnished a much more substantial contribution to defining the 'war behind the war' when in June of the following year, in the course of a visit to the World Council, he composed, upon Visser't Hooft's instigation and evidently in the name of an ecumenical study group, a programmatic letter to his friends in America.[30] At this point, that is on the eve of the German invasion of Russia, Trott still saw the need of challenging the 'presupposition of a "democratic" victory' and of insisting that any discussion of post-war problems had likewise to figure on the opposite assumption.[31] For the rest Trott outlined a generous, and in some ways Keynesian, vision of a European federation that was to include Russia;[32] and he insisted that any post-war planning had to face up to what he called the 'European revolution'[33] which precluded a falling back on the model of a liberal economy but called for planning in a modern industrial society:

A more detailed exposition of post-war European possibilities must ... include some review of the completely new fabric of governmental functions and institutions, of corresponding changes in the relationship of state and citizen and of the new and in many respects socialist significance of the masses in public life. All these and other permanent factors are bound to make certain changes in the constitutional structure of post-war national and international society inevitable. ... The degree to which authorities will be able to deal with immediate emergencies of civilian life with justice and efficiency will be of decisive importance. The whole machinery of public control will have to be turned over ... to the stupendous and urgent tasks of recreating a consumption economy, of rebuilding transport on land and sea and of alleviating the worst of the housing, clothing and food problem.

In sum, 'the new emphasis on social and economic planning will encourage the growth of federal thinking in Europe'.[34]

Along with Trott, Dietrich Bonhoeffer was Visser't Hooft's main contact with the German Resistance. Knowing these two men, 'both deeply involved', the Dutch theologian later attested, made him believe in the seriousness of their cause.[35] Bonhoeffer, who in the autumn of 1940 had been conscripted, with the help of Oster and Dohnanyi, to work for the Abwehr, took off on his first foreign assignment to Switzerland on 24 February 1941 where he stayed one month. He went with the purpose of re-establishing ecumenical links as well as to explore for the Resistance in Germany what peace terms might be expected.[36] Among others, Bonhoeffer called upon Karl Barth, who initially was puzzled how in the middle of the war a pastor of the Confessing Church could have come over with official papers, and Siegmund-Schultze; but his main destination was the World Council of Churches in Geneva where he renewed his ties with its General Secretary. Visser't Hooft had no trouble renewing a relation of mutual trust with the German pastor 'with his round, almost boyish, face, his cheerful expression'.[37]

The upshot of Bonhoeffer's sojourn in Geneva from 8–15 March was an elaborate document of 12 March entitled 'Some Considerations concerning the Post-War Settlement'.[38] It pleaded for the Churches to take the initiative, in view of the political and cultural void created by the war, in countries such as Germany, France, and Italy, in the exploration of peace plans. These, indicating a radical departure from the outworn forms of national sovereignty and unrestricted capitalism and even from the forms of democracy which had been found wanting in the era between the wars, aimed at an 'evangelization' of the masses.

High-minded, if not high-flown in its tone, Bonhoeffer's memorandum was designed to carve out what Visser't Hooft called, 'the minimum conditions' on which peace would be possible and which in particular would benefit the Resistance in Germany.[39] Archbishop Temple brought it somewhat down to earth when, in his reaction to the document, he listed the disappearance of the Nazi regime, the evacuation of all occupied countries including Czechoslovakia and Poland, and the cessation of 'that type of tyranny which is represented by the Gestapo', as constituting 'minimum conditions'.[40] Visser't Hooft considered this reaction of the Archbishop as 'relatively encouraging'.[41] He had reason to believe that in his contact with Bonhoeffer he had at least established a convergence between the prerogatives of the Ecumenical Movement and the group behind Bonhoeffer. But if by mid-1940 he for his part had clearly succeeded in rallying the World Council behind him, he never seems to have asked himself this question: how much of the German Resistance was committed to the lofty tenets with which he identified his young German friends? John Foster Dulles, it might be added, upon receipt of Visser't Hooft's document, responded politely but not without ambivalence, that he found it of 'special interest' and that it seemed to reflect thinking which 'while idealistic is also realistic'.[42]

In any event, Visser't Hooft persisted in cementing his bonds with the German dissidents. In the late summer of 1941 Dietrich Bonhoeffer once again travelled to Switzerland.[43] Meanwhile, since his first visit, the German armies had been unleashed upon Russia. But Bonhoeffer appeared before his Dutch friend to assure him, much to his surprise, that precisely these developments indicated the beginning of the end in Germany and that they had therefore, if anything, strengthened the domestic Opposition.[44] The two men therefore felt all the more encouraged to draft a statement on a post-war order for the benefit of their friends in Britain and the United States. To get matters started, Visser't Hooft gave Bonhoeffer a copy of a book, *The Church and the New Order*, by William Paton which had been recently published in England and which addressed itself to the questions of their common concern.[45] The book was a product of the deliberations of the so-called Peace Aims Group which Visser't Hooft had set in motion in Great Britain early in the war and which met periodically throughout the war with the objective of preparing the position of the Churches in defining peace aims.[46] If Wheeler-Bennett is to be believed, Paton's book had 'a wide illicit circulation' in Germany, especially among the army, and was distributed in Norway by the German troops.[47]

The basic approach of Paton appealed to Visser't Hooft and Bonhoeffer: Hitler had defined the terms of his 'New Order'. But the Allied side owed it to itself to come forward with peace aims of its own, and Paton's concern was to spell out above all what should be the Christian contribution to their formulation. Apart from the general tenor of the book, calling for an equitable treatment of a defeated Germany that had rid herself of her present rulers,[48] it contained some particular passages which spoke directly to the concerns of Bonhoeffer.

It may be urged as conceivable that the totalitarian systems might collapse from internal causes, but there seems little hope that the anti-totalitarian forces which exist can become effective except after a major reverse.

and

Yet I suppose that few who have known the Confessional [*sic*] Church leaders would doubt that there are no Germans with whom fellowship in the post-war talks will be so quickly resumed.[49]

Paton's work served Bonhoeffer as a challenge to commit to paper a statement of his own that would, alongside Paton's exposition, outline the same issues as seen by a German clergyman. His Dutch friend then composed a final version designed to express the two men's combined views.[50]

The Bonhoeffer draft, of which only fragments have been preserved,[51] revealed all the tensions between the theologian and the conspirator that had built up in him since he joined the Abwehr. Although he could not help but register initially the absence in Paton's rather pragmatic argument of an other-worldly, eschatological orientation that would have relied wholly upon God's guidance,[52] he moved right into the 'worldly sector' by way of a justification of the military coup as, under the circumstances in Germany, the only possible way of removing the Nazi regime. The same man who, according to Visser't Hooft's recollection, upon arriving in Geneva had confessed to his friends that he prayed for the defeat of his country,[53] now proceeded to argue the case of a new order for his own country which, in lieu of the 'omnipotence of the state', was to fall back on 'genuine loyalties' such as family, friendship, *Heimat, Volk*, authority, humanity, science, and work.[54] What mattered was that in Germany a public order was to be realized which considered itself responsible to the commandments of God. But then Bonhoeffer rightly wondered whether England and America would be ready to negotiate with a new government that 'to begin with' did not seem democratic 'in the Anglo-Saxon meaning of the word'.[55]

Bonhoeffer's draft, as much as has been preserved, reveals the theologian and the conspirator as well as the ecumenist and the patriot at war. It was a tortured document which attests little to the clarity and serenity which usually mark Bonhoeffer's thought and writing. It was a fuzzy piece and, in particular in its attempt to differentiate between the Western and the German understanding of freedom, it fell back on some of the worst features of German political romanticism which extolled the separateness of the German tradition in thought and politics in comparison with that of the Western world.[56] Once again, however, as in the case of the 'Memorandum' on his conversation with Trott of September 1940, the ingenious Visser't Hooft jumped into the breach and edited Bonhoeffer's 'Gedanken'. Perhaps, as in the case of Trott, we may say that Visser't Hooft knew his German friend better than the latter knew himself? In any event, he edited Bonhoeffer's draft so as to make it emerge as a document composed by 'two Continental Christians from two nations which are on opposite sides in this war'[57] and which would speak to friends in Britain and the United States.

The final draft, mutually agreed upon, while giving due recognition to Bonhoeffer's apocalyptic theology, claimed for the Church a place in defining the post-war order. The absence of any explicit mention of the Atlantic Charter recently signed in Newfoundland by the Western Allies is striking. While the two churchmen left no doubt that they were committed to a British victory in the war, and while they went on paper calling for evacuation of *all* occupied territories, the ousting of all Nazi leaders and the willingness to disarm,[58] they set forth their own agenda for a settlement of the war issues. It was the Church's responsibility, so the draft read, to

remind the nations of the abiding commandments and realities which must be taken seriously if the new order is to be a true order, and if we are to avoid another judgement of God such as this present war.[59]

This guide-line, then, called for caution against a mere restoration of the pre-war political and economic system. 'Drastic changes' in these two domains were called for: in the political domain the effective limitation of national sovereignty, and in the economic domain the limitation of economic individualism and planning for economic security of the masses.[60] In this document, as in Trott's letter to his friends in America of some three months earlier, Visser't Hooft's 'war behind the war' assumed distinct features; and even though it may be considered wholly out of tune with the official mood of the time, it manifestly anticipated the thinking which surfaced in the programmes of the various European Resistance movements somewhat later in the war.[61] Concerning the treatment of a defeated Germany, the two churchmen agreed on emphasizing the importance of a 'positive policy'.[62] Disarmanent of Germany, though imperative, should be seen in the context of a 'much wider programme' which would ensure 'a certain amount of political and economic security for a disarmed Germany' and 'the acceptance by all nations of a certain supra-national control of their armaments'.[63] Occupation, however necessary, was to be considered no panacea for the solution of the German problem. The political objective then, wholly disregarded in the formulations of the Atlantic Charter, was to enable Germany to 'find its way back to a system of government which is acceptable to the Germans' and thus 'to be an orderly member of the family of nations'.[64]

In the the final section Visser't Hooft took up an issue which Bonhoeffer had already raised in his draft, namely the threat of the Soviet Union to a European peace.[65] Short of taking issue with the Anglo-Russian agreement concluded in July 1941, Visser't Hooft allowed himself to be carried away by the anti-Communist argument. Not only did he voice concern lest Eastern Europe revert to Russian control after the war, but on these grounds he also saw fit to justify 'authoritarian, though non-Fascist' regimes in that area after the war and the strengthening of the non-Nazi elements in Germany able to form a new government there.[66]

Visser't Hooft sent the document on to London with hopes that it would circulate among interested people there and also be forwarded to the United States.[67] But the reactions were altogether muted. In New York Henry P. Van Dusen of Union Theological Seminary assessed it as one of the most valuable documents on issues of the peace that had reached him, and he handed it on to John Foster Dulles,[68] but that was that. In Britain only the inveterate supporter of the German Opposition Bishop Bell of Chichester, seconded by his German exile-friend Gerhard Leibholz, endorsed it whole-heartedly.[69] As for Paton, he reported that he had distributed it among 'very important people'.[70] However with Paton and his friends and the 'very important people' doubts prevailed as to whether there really existed in Germany an opposition group strong enough to be effective; besides, Paton himself voiced his doubts about the 'real danger of bolshevization of Europe'.[71] The 'Continental reaction' of the two clergymen to Paton's challenging book, then, wholly out of tune with the official war policy of Britain, did not get any further. And when, in the spring of 1942, on the occasion of a journey to England Visser't Hooft took it before the assembled Peace Aims Group, it caused no stir; another half-year had gone by without any evidence of the much-heralded uprising in Germany.[72]

At no point did Dietrich Bonhoeffer abandon his essentially theological responsibilities. Even when on a political mission, he was guided throughout by the need to reconcile it with the imperatives of the Ten Commandments. The Abwehr scout faithfully kept within the bounds of the Ministry of Christ, even at the risk that the particular rationalization of his political role would not convince even the London ecumenical circles.

Altogether different in motivation and style was Trott's appearance in Geneva. He was an essentially political man, and in the course of time he had trained himself 'in an almost too one-sided concentration' to serve his country's interests abroad. Because there were no precedents for the kind of foreign policy, resistance foreign policy, that he conducted, he had to throw himself into it, like an acrobat, taking chances, defying hazards—and all the while under him was the abyss.

In order to follow the strategy of Trott's moves we shall have to retrace our steps, however briefly, to a quixotic episode in his dual life of working at the same time both in an official capacity and for the Resistance. This episode involved him in the cause of India's independence and had a distinct impact upon the effectiveness, or rather lack of effectiveness, of his attempt to reach London by way of the World Council in Geneva. When it became known in Berlin that Netaji Subhas Chandra Bose, leader of the radical wing of the All-India Congress, had early in 1941 escaped from India, the Auswärtiges Amt entered the act of exploring ways of utilizing him in the struggle against Britain.[73] Before long Trott found himself assigned to a newly established Section for Indian Affairs (Sonderreferat Indien). Its chief function was to assist Bose, who arrived in Berlin early in April, and above all to assemble, from among the Indian prisoners of war taken in the North African theatre of war, an Indian Legion that was eventually to be deployed in the battle for a free India.

Strangely, the Sonderreferat turned out to be a refuge for anti-Nazis.[74] For

Trott in particular the Sonderreferat served as an alibi to cover the pursuit of his clandestine activities abroad. At the same time he no doubt threw himself into his official work. While he did not particularly care for the person of 'His Excellency', as Bose had to be addressed by instructions from on high, here was for once someone who, like Trott himself, had ventured into that hitherto unknown realm of resistance foreign policy. Also Trott was in tune with Bose's socialist and anti-imperial policies.[75]

His work for the mysterious Indian freedom fighter from the distant East, and in particular the organization of the Indian Legion,[76] became a special challenge, indeed a sport of sorts for Trott, as it did for his colleagues.[77]

Trott's involvement in Indian affairs had a distinct, though melancholy, relevance for the conduct of his resistance ventures. On 11 March 1942 the British Prime Minister announced to the House of Commons the impending departure for Delhi of the Lord Privy Seal and Leader of the House, Sir Stafford Cripps, an old friend of Trott's,[78] in order to persuade the Congress to accept a settlement of the Indian problem involving self-government short of full independence. But the venture ended in failure. The Cripps mission was bound to put Trott in a quandary. He had taken the position all along that 'no compromise' between India and England was possible, and for propaganda purposes he advocated the emphasis on the liberation of suppressed peoples, the highlighting of the social motive, and the exposure of the 'empty phrases of democracy and humanity'.[79] The Cripps mission to India was to be met with disruptive reports.[80]

It is not hard to detect the camouflage aspect in these official dispatches. Be this as it may, it can and must be argued that Trott's calculations were bound to backfire. By his inflammatory anti-British stance he probably thought of protecting his conspiratorial activities.[81] But while this course may have protected him from detection from the Nazis, it had the effect of ruining his standing with the British on whose support his intricate scheme depended. It was entirely Trott's own business, to be sure, that he little reciprocated the friendship and loyalty of Cripps, and according to the later testimony of his widow, he suffered greatly from the awareness that he may have had a part in the failure of the Cripps mission.[82] Indeed he was at the time cautioned by his friend Helmuth von Moltke to keep his hands off the Bose business and that 'nothing good' could come of it.[83] What he gained in his credibility with the Nazis, he was bound to lose in credibility with the British who probably were informed about Trott's involvement in the Bose affair.[84] It is of course doubtful whether, had he managed to stay out of it, his stock in London would have risen and whether this would have made any appreciable difference in favour of his overtures. In any case, he could not break out of the complexities inherent in his resistance foreign policy, and the Bose folly no doubt had the effect of augmenting British suspicions against Trott and his German co-conspirators.[85]

But in the spring of 1942 Trott went into top gear in Switzerland. By way of his ecumenical connections[86] he managed to establish a connection with Miss Elizabeth Wiskemann, an Oxford-trained historian and journalist who was on the staff of the British Legation in Berne with the assignment of assembling all possible non-military information about all the enemy nations and enemy-controlled nations of Europe.[87] Whatever their mutual attraction was, for Trott this connection opened up another possible channel to London; she, in turn, might obtain some valuable information on German affairs from him.[88] Miss Wiskemann, however, had put herself at risk even by meeting with Trott, since of course she, like all British diplomats, was subject to the command of 'absolute silence'. There was nothing she could do for her fellow Oxonian. Later she recorded that anyway she seldom got from him 'anything but his own political theories'.[89]

It is of interest to note that since Trott was not excessively careful in the neutral capital crawling with secret agents from everywhere, it was, back in London, Sir Stafford Cripps who, getting wind of the connection between the two, tried to come to the rescue of his German friend by sending out a request that Miss Wiskemann 'cool off' from further communication with Trott since he was thought 'by certain people' to be too valuable. This move in turn prompted one of the members of the Foreign Office Central Department, G. W. Harrison, to minute that this was not in the British interest 'since his [Trott's] value to us as a "martyr" is likely to exceed his value to us in post-war Germany'.[90]

On the occasion of his journey to England in the spring of 1942, Visser't Hooft undertook a major effort to act as intermediary for his friends of the German Resistance by taking along a memorandum, handed to him by Adam von Trott during his April visit to Geneva, which was to be turned over to the Lord Privy Seal, Sir Stafford Cripps. The memorandum,[91] written in the first-person plural, was, actually, a product of co-operation among young members of the Resistance, most of whom were associated with the Kreisau Circle.[92] The authors of the document proceeded from the conviction that the German penetration into Russia was bound to be checked before long and that the time had come, 'at the heights of German power', to approach the British government in order to obtain from it assurances that would encourage the German Generals to stage a coup.[93]

But the document distinctly bears Trott's imprint; especially when, conceding uncertainty about the outcome of the war, it refers to the 'so-called "victor"' in the struggle which he had always feared would be fratricidal. Europe, if not the whole world, was threatened by (1) 'Intensified mass destruction of life and economic substance', (2) 'Increasingly totalitarian control of national life everywhere' and (3) the 'trend toward anarchical dissolution'. In view of this situation, the memorandum appealed to a sense of solidarity among responsible groups in the West with those forces in

Germany which had consistently fought against nihilism and its National Socialist manifestations. Inspired by a 'militant Christianism', these groups were striving for political and constitutional reconstruction in terms of a 'practical application of the Christian European tradition to modern human needs'. Concretely, their message was federalism on a German as well as European scale and the realization of 'socialist principles' in all sectors of political and economic life.

The pronounced religious note may have entered into the memorandum by way of Gerstenmaier or Haeften, which does not mean that it had not in the course of the war entered into Trott's thinking. Furthermore the statement that the group did not intend to justify its own position but was ready to accept its 'due share of responsibility and of guilt' spoke, as we shall see, the same language as Dietrich Bonhoeffer when in May of the same year he met in Sweden with Bishop Bell of Chichester.

However, all these high-spirited premises were doubtless of less interest to the hard-headed professionals in Whitehall than were the provisions that bordered on foreign-policy questions. It certainly did not help the reception of the memorandum that, with its identification of the Soviet Union as an unmitigated threat, it circulated in London at just about the time that the Treaty between Britain and the Soviet Union was signed, and that, while proposing to reconstitute 'a free Polish and a free Czech state', it insisted upon ethnographic frontiers. But Britain had not entered the war in 1939 in order to accept yet another partition of Poland.[94]

Immediately upon his arrival in London, which he reached via southern France, Spain, and Portugal early in May, Visser't Hooft handed the Memorandum over to Sir Stafford Cripps who, upon hearing that it came from Trott, showed 'genuine interest' and promised to put it before the Prime Minister.[95] We are told by Visser't Hooft that, according to Cripps, Churchill did study the document carefully, entering underneath the words: 'very encouraging'.[96] But this cryptic entry in no way was to indicate that he was impressed by what he read.[97] The territorial proposals of Trott and his friends were clearly unacceptable to Whitehall; but above all there was the hard rule of 'absolute silence' which Churchill would have been the last one to break. It is most likely he was encouraged by the fact that there was dissension among the leadership of the Reich, a portent of its demise. But for Trott there was, so Sir Stafford had to report back to Visser't Hooft, 'no answer'.[98]

If there was an answer for Trott, it was contained in a much-noticed speech which the Foreign Secretary gave four days after Visser't Hooft's arrival in England. It cannot be ascertained whether he had been apprised of the Trott Memorandum, but he addressed himself to the question of resistance in Germany, and this is what he said:

If any section of the German people really wants to see a return to a state which is based on respect for law and for the rights of the individual, they must understand that no one will believe them until they have taken active steps to rid themselves of their present regime.[99]

By making Allied encouragement of the German conspirators contingent upon decisive action on their part at home, Anthony Eden thus reversed the priorities to which Trott and his friends thought they had to cling. In other words, Eden's answer to Trott, if it was to be an answer, was no answer at all.

Subsequently the Trott Memorandum made its way through the regular mill of the Foreign Office where it was subjected to the scrutiny of the professionals.[100] Whereas Visser't Hooft himself, of course, easily passed review with the authorities as being, as Anthony Eden put it, 'a man above reproach or suspicion',[101] the name of Trott once again conjured up and indeed hardened old suspicions. An elaborate confidential statement on Trott, entitled 'Freiherr Adam von Trott', for the Foreign Office, composed by his one-time Oxford friend Richard H. S. Crossman,[102] characterized him as being 'as high-minded as he is woolly' and the document that his Dutch friend brought over as a 'perfect specimen' of Trott's thought, 'ingenious in its politics and unaware of its intellectual and political dishonesty'. This assessment, if nothing else,[103] certainly allowed the Foreign Secretary to dismiss the case without much ado: Trott was, he wrote confidentially to 'My dear Stafford', 'a curious mixture of high-minded idealism and political dishonesty';[104] and he summarized Trott's position with supreme curtness, if not insensitivity, 'not untypical of a number of young Germans in the German Ministry of Foreign Affairs who, profoundly anti-Nazi in upbringing and outlook, have never quite been able to bring themselves to pay the price of their convictions and resign from the service of the Nazi regime'.[105] As for Sir Stafford, he was not satisfied with this dismissal of his German friend and instantly sent a rejoinder to 'My dear Anthony' charging him with 'a complete failure to understand' either Trott or what he stood for, explaining that Trott 'felt strongly that it was his duty as a German, in spite of the imminent personal risks, to go back to Germany'. 'It is not a question', so Cripps lectured his fellow member in the War Cabinet, 'of his bringing himself to pay the price of his convictions by resigning from the service of the Nazi regime, like that of many émigrés which would have been a very simple solution. He paid the far higher price in risk in refusing to join the Nazi regime, but going back to Germany to fight for the things which he believed to be right.'[106] Thus indeed did Cripps keep faith with his German friend.

Even among the members of the Peace Aims Group, which was predisposed to listen to dissident voices from Germany, doubts were voiced in particular concerning the passages in the Memorandum concerning Soviet Russia: 'it was "useless" and "indecent" to talk about linking up with any German government to defend the West against Russia; the British public would not accept an anti-Russian policy.'[107] However, so the Peace Aims Group was told, Visser't Hooft remained unruffled by these criticisms: these men of the Resistance felt so keenly the iniquity of the regime, he insisted, 'that they ought to go on even if they got no encouragement from the Allies. This was a vital point morally.'[108]

Otherwise, one of the few men whom Visser't Hooft canvassed about the matter while in England and who showed a more positive interest in the message that had come from the German conspirators, was Bishop Bell of Chichester.[109] He was about to undertake a mission to Sweden where he would, quite unexpectedly, meet two German churchmen, Hans Schönfeld and Dietrich Bonhoeffer, who were to present him with messages very much like the one that had come from Trott.

To Trott, who visited Visser't Hooft in Geneva soon afterwards, in June, the news of the negative reaction to his message to Britain came as a blow.[110] The vision of the solidarity of the best elements across the front lines which were to join in constructing a radically new Europe beyond nationalism and capitalism had to yield to the hard realities of power politics and war policies. There was no doubt now left in his mind as to where the British stood in relation to a German coup. The conspirators were expected to act on their own and could meanwhile count on no sympathy or help from abroad.[111] For Trott the whole venture meant the failure of yet another mission. The tangible effect of his disappointment now was to nourish doubts in him about the usefulness of further approaches to the Western Powers and in turn to encourage him to explore avenues towards Russia.[112]

Upon a later visit by Trott to Geneva early in January 1943, Visser't Hooft found that the rebuffs his German friend had experienced from the Western Allies had indeed left a deep mark on his thinking. In a lengthy conversation[113] Trott related to Visser't Hooft that the Opposition was 'deeply disappointed, even shocked' by the lack of encouragemant from the other side. There was, he volunteered, no further use in talking as long as the British and American propaganda ignored the fact that 'they', the Germans themselves, were also an 'oppressed people'.

Disillusionment with the West, then, drove Trott to fall back on the consideration of some sort of 'game' (*Mühlespiel*) between East and West. Von Hassell, when somewhat later he coined this concept[114] thought that Trott was in full agreement with him. But Trott's world was less Bismarckian, and, moreover, he always remained emotionally and even politically committed to the Anglo-Saxon world.[115] Now, however, he felt all the more disappointed at being misunderstood by it. His projection of a German eastern orientation came out of the depth of an eastern mystique common to many young Germans of his generation. As a matter of fact, upon his first meeting with Visser't Hooft in 1928 Trott had, as mentioned earlier, confided in him that, having had an overdose of religious nourishment in his family, he had found religious inspiration in the novels of Dostoevsky.[116] In Trott's mind Dostoevsky now blended with long-standing socialist inclinations which, two years earlier, in his letter to Professor Percy E. Corbett,[117] had emboldened him to speak of the 'European revolution'. As if in answer to Dostoevsky who in his time had appealed to the Germans to turn east against the decadent west, Trott now exclaimed: 'Europe is becoming increasingly anti-Western' and predicted the 'fraternity of the *oppressed common* people' of Europe which would form the basis of a new Europe. Undoubtedly thinking of his friends in England, he even conceded that in London also a part of the future Europe was in preparation, and that it was a question, finally, of finding a synthesis between the two Europes: the 'democratic pre-mass Europe' and the 'democratic post-mass Europe'.[118]

Such were the thoughts of a confused, desperate, and in some ways brilliant and visionary mind. The saintly, very sane Visser't Hooft was sufficiently exercised over the burden of Trott's argument to communicate it to Allen Welsh Dulles, the American Secret Service (OSS) chief, who in November 1942 had set up shop in Berne with the special assignment, among others, to develop and maintain contacts with Germany's anti-Nazi and underground movements. On behalf of the Opposition in Germany, the Secretary General pleaded for a less 'high-handed' propaganda and policy towards the Germans:

the question to be faced in political warfare seems to be: Are the United Nations willing to say to the opposition: 'If you succeed in overthrowing Hitler and if you then prove by your acts (punishment of Nazi leaders and Nazi criminals, liberation of occupied territory, restoration of stolen goods, installation of a regime which respects the rights of men, participation in economic and social reconstruction) that you have wholly broken with National Socialism and militarism, we would be ready to discuss peace terms with you?' As long as that is not clearly and definitely said, the process of development of an anti-Western, anti-liberal complex is likely to go on. And, as long as that is not said, large groups in Germany, who are psychologically prepared to join the opposition, will remain hesitant and wonder whether, after all, Hitler is not a lesser evil than total military defeat.[119]

## 2. In Sweden

In the course of the war Scandinavia moved ever more centre stage of the ecumenical activity. This development was due to the active interest which the northern Churches took in the German Church Dispute, and especially due to the personality of Bishop Berggrav whose dynamic leadership had given shape since the late 1930s not only to the Scandinavian, but equally to the international, Protestant community.[120] Also the German victory over France in the spring of 1940 had affected the ready accessibility of Switzerland. Particularly after 11 November 1942, when the German troops moved into unoccupied France, Switzerland found herself altogether isolated and cut off from contacts with the Allied countries.[121] Thus increasingly did Scandinavia, and in particular the Nordic Ecumenical Institute in Sigtuna, emerge as the outpost for ecumenical exchanges as well as for the dialogue with the German dissidents.

On 13 May 1942 Bishop George Bell of Chichester was the single passenger in an aeroplane with a Norwegian pilot and two crewmen, making his way to Stockholm. Early in the year, under government auspices, air communications had been restored on a limited scale between Great Britain and Sweden, and the Ministry of Information was anxious to resume cultural contacts between the two countries.[122] For a fortnight the Bishop toured his host country as a messenger of Christian fellowship, bringing greetings from all the Churches of Britain, including the Roman Catholic and the Greek Orthodox Churches, delivering sermons to curious crowds and addressing many meetings both public and private.[123]

The public drama was followed by a distinctly more secretive one, however, when later in the month, much to Bishop Bell's surprise, he found himself face to face with two German pastors, Hans Schönfeld and Dietrich Bonhoeffer, who, having learnt of his presence in neutral Sweden, and independently of each other, had made their way north in order to put before him the case of the German Resistance.[124]

All along, war or no war, Bishop Bell had kept an intense interest in German affairs and in particular, of course, in the tribulations of the Confessing Church. He had been acquainted with Hans Schönfeld for many years, ever since their common ecumenical concerns had first brought them together. But their relations had never been close. From his post in Geneva, ever since the early days of the Nazi regime, Schönfeld had been singularly preoccupied with keeping the channels open between the German Protestant Churches and the outside world. He had chosen to do this by way of maintaining connections with Bishop Heckel's Church Office for External Affairs which, for good reason, was suspected abroad of being a front for Nazi policies. Bishop Bell was now to discover that Schönfeld actually came on behalf of the *Widerstand*.

Bishop Bell's relations with Bonhoeffer, however, were of a very different kind. The two had first met late in 1933, when Bonhoeffer came to London to serve there as vicar of the German Church in the south London suburb of Forest Hill; he had been in London barely three weeks when he was invited to visit the Bishop in the Palace of Chichester. To the prince of the Anglican Church the young German pastor may initially have seemed all too impetuous with his rigid theology and uncompromising emphasis on the integrity of confession over the advisability of converting and thus accommodating the Nazis. Bell soon, however, had occasion to appreciate Bonhoeffer's integrity and depth of Christian commitment, and to understand that his sombre assessment of German affairs, far from being alarmist, was accurate. Bonhoeffer thus became one of Bishop Bell's chief advisers and informers on the state of the Church Dispute in Germany, and if the Bishop in turn became one of the few men in wartime England who called attention to the German Resistance, it was mainly because of his awareness of Bonhoeffer's resolute stand against Nazism: 'He was one of the first as well as one the bravest witnesses against idolatry', the Bishop later recollected about his young friend. 'He understood what to choose, when he chose resistance . . . I learned the true character of the conflict, in an intimate friendship . . . He was crystal clear in his convictions; and young as he was, and humble-minded as he was, he saw the truth, and spoke it with a complete absence of fear.'[125]

In his biography of Bonhoeffer, Eberhard Bethge wrote about the 'riddle of the two messengers',[126] and a riddle it certainly was for Bishop Bell, as to why two emissaries of the Resistance should have travelled to see him in Sweden on a similar errand, but independently of each other and with, to the best of his knowledge, neither knowing about the other's coming. We are left, then, with a number of questions. Assuming that, in fact, Bishop Bell's perception was correct, why the lack of co-ordination, and on whose behalf, then, did each pastor come? But nor can we exclude the possibility that the Bishop's perception may not have been altogether correct and that some connection between the travellers may have existed after all.

It was Schönfeld who was the first to arrive in Stockholm. He had learnt back in early May that Bishop Bell was to visit Sweden,[127] and scheduled a week's stop-over in Berlin before his own projected arrival in Stockholm. Precisely what Schönfeld did in Berlin we do not know, but the likelihood is that he was in touch with members of the *Freundeskreis* in the Auswärtiges Amt[128] and that through them he kept abreast of the sentiments in Kreisau.[129]

There is convincing evidence to the effect that Hans-Bernd von Haeften was the one to brief Schönfeld before his departure for Sweden, on what the Kreisau Circle expected from the much-coveted contacts with England.[130] But there is every reason to assume that, at least when he left Berlin on 25 May, Schönfeld was uninformed about similar plans for Bonhoeffer.[131]

The bishop of Chichester had two sessions with Schönfeld on 26 and 29 May in the course of which he was given by the German pastor a comprehensive brief concerning the general composition and the chief objectives of the German Resistance which subsequently, upon the Bishop's request, he put on paper on 31 May in an elaborate document known as 'Statement by a German Pastor at Stockholm'.[132] It must be noticed that the explicit preamble of Schönfeld's performance was an appeal, not to national interest, but to 'human rights'. There was, he said, in an unmistakable allusion to the Kreisau Circle, 'a block of Christians belonging to both confessions who were strongly speaking of three human rights—the right of freedom, the right to the rule of law, and the right to live a Christian life'.[133] Clearly Schönfeld spoke not just for himself, nor was his written 'Statement' a mere improvisation on his part. His reference to a European Federation built on the 'fundamental principles of Christian Faith and life', together with the reconstruction of the economic order 'according to truly socialistic lines', was distinctly in line with his Kreisau friends and the *Freundeskreis*[134] and in particular with the Trott Memorandum of the end of April. Also, the omission of the ethnographic principle concerning definition of the borders of the 'Free Czech' and 'Free Polish' nations may well have reflected the thinking at Kreisau. The proposal for a 'real solution of the colonial problem along the lines of a true mandate system', however, is closer to the concerns of Goerdeler than to those of Kreisau.[135] The conciliatory note which Schönfeld struck on the question of the 'Russian Problem'[136] may well be attributable to the influence of Ambassador von der Schulenburg.[137] An altogether surprising revelation on the part of Schönfeld, finally, was that the SS under Himmler was ready to stage a coup of its own which, however, would serve as an opening for the Opposition to stage a follow-up coup of its own against Himmler and the SS. This particular, and to say the least, hazardous calculation might well have been inspired by the circle around Johannes Popitz to which Carl Langbehn, a Berlin lawyer and former Nazi turned anti-Nazi, who exploited his intimate personal connection with Himmler to kindle his ambitions to displace his Führer, belonged.[138] If all the above assumptions are correct, it becomes evident that Schönfeld's presentations to Bishop Bell, both oral and written, constituted a composite of the positions taken by the various groups in the Resistance. It is quite likely, as has also been suggested by Hans Rothfels,[139] that it was an effort to summarize the consensus among them.

In the spring months Bonhoeffer went into top gear travelling abroad on conspiratorial business. In Norway the dispute between the Church and the newly appointed Nazi-puppet Prime Minister, Vidkun Quisling, had come to a head when on Easter Day an overwhelming number of the pastors resigned from their offices, and Bishop Berggrav, who had become the prime mover of the Church resistance,[140] was taken to prison by the authorities. Since the summer of 1940 Theodor Steltzer was stationed as Transport Officer in Oslo; there he belonged to the intimate circle of General Nikolaus von Falkenhorst, the German Armed Forces Commander. A patriot, Steltzer was also, as we have seen, a determined foe of National Socialism and, while officially a member of the occupation, he made it his task to become, in fact, a protector of the besieged Norwegians and to develop close ties with the Norwegian Resistance. Also, since the autumn of 1940 an active participant of the meetings of the Kreisau Circle, Steltzer informed Helmuth von Moltke, and through Moltke the Abwehr Chief, about the excesses of the Nazi authorities in Norway. Upon the arrest of Bishop Berggrav, then, Canaris and Oster decided hurriedly to dispatch two of their staff, Moltke and Bonhoeffer, to remonstrate and point out the detrimental effects on the occupation of the Nazi interference into Norwegian Church affairs.

This Norwegian mission, lasting from 10 to 18 April, was the one occasion when these two remarkable figures of the German Resistance were ever together. As a matter of fact, they found it difficult to communicate with each other. Somehow the country squire was bored in the company of the bookish patrician whose name he would not even take pains to spell properly.[141] But there was also a substantial disagreement between the two men. Bonhoeffer's friend, Eberhard Bethge, remembered the former remarking after the trip how stimulating it had been, except that he and Moltke were 'not of the same opinion'.[142] Undoubtedly he was referring to the question of tyrannicide which at that time Moltke, in contrast to Bonhoeffer, still firmly opposed. Needless to say, they did not let these differences stand in the way of their assignment which allowed them considerable latitude. The mission itself was accomplished inasmuch as it jolted the Nazi authorities in Berlin to instruct the Reich Commissar in Oslo, Josef Terboven, to release Berggrav from prison.[143] In what Moltke called the 'covert' part of the mission,[144] he took it upon himself to propose to his Norwegian friends some form of co-operation between the Norwegian Resistance movement and the German Resistance,[145] while Bonhoeffer, impressed by the corporate action of the Norwegian pastors, urged them to stand fast.[146]

It was during Bonhoeffer's next journey, which took him in May to Switzerland,[147] that he heard of Bishop Bell's visit to Sweden. He therefore cut his trip short and rushed back to Berlin where in three days, in consultation with General Beck and the Canaris people, preparations were made for his visit to Sweden. There is little likelihood that Bonhoeffer would have encountered Schönfeld in Berlin.[148] It seems fairly certain, however, that he at least knew of Schönfeld's trip since he was, as was Schönfeld earlier, briefed for his mission by Haeften on behalf of the Kreisau Circle.[149] Equipped, then, with 'Courier Pass No. 474' issued by the Auswärtiges Amt[150] Bonhoeffer departed, as instructed, on 30 May for Stockholm.

The 'riddle of the two messengers' turns out not to be much of a riddle after all. There was, as we have seen, some minimal co-ordination between the two missions, no more and no less than Resistance circles had managed to stage all along. And if Bonhoeffer was dispatched immediately after Schönfeld, it was not a matter of mere duplication. It must be explained, partly at least, by the fact that, as Bethge argues, in the conspiratorial Abwehr circles Schönfeld's reputation was, in view of his connections with Bishop Heckel, not established beyond doubt.[151] For them Bonhoeffer was the man to activate the ecumenical dialogue. Most probably Beck and Canaris sent him out, not so much in competition with his colleague, but to reassure themselves that the right message got out from the *Widerstand*.

In any event, on Sunday 31 May, the climactic encounter between Bell and the two German pastors took place in the Nordic Ecumenical Institute in Sigtuna. At that moment also, their host, Dr Harry Johansson, Assistant and soon-to-be Director of the Institute, moved into centre stage. This solicitous and modest man, a dedicated ecumenist, had in the spring of 1942 brought together a group of distinguished public figures in Sweden, the 'Sigtuna Group', for the special purpose of advising the Institute on matters pertaining to the German Resistance and on the advisability and ways in which the Institute might lend it support short of getting overtly embroiled in political action.[152] He now had the first opportunity to go into action. We can safely assume that Bonhoeffer managed to track down Schönfeld in Stockholm; but for the rest we are left with some uncertainty concerning the question whether or not the two pastors arrived together in Sigtuna.[153] Be this as it may, Bonhoeffer's agenda turned out to be quite different from that of his colleague. Impatient with Schönfeld's political exposition of resistance problems in Germany, he interrupted, saying that his 'Christian conscience' was not quite at ease with Schönfeld's ideas. And he continued:

There must be punishment by God. We would not be worthy of such a solution. We do not want to escape repentance. Our action must be understood as an act of repentance.[154]

This outburst can be read as a very personal statement. Was it his own participation in an assassination plot which now gave him pause[155] and which made him remind himself of his having to take the consequences of his deeds and commend himself to God in repentance as a sinner? By inserting the issue of repentance into the Sigtuna talks, however, Dietrich Bonhoeffer made an important statement on the general purpose of the dialogue between the German Resistance and the outside world. Already in his April Memorandum Trott had, as we have seen, acknowledged the readiness of the Resistance to accept its 'due share of responsibility and of guilt'. Now Bonhoeffer lent emphasis to this theme that far transcended the political realm. It is not that he sentimentalized, let alone depoliticized, the session with the Bishop. But he signified that discussions about frontiers and peace settlement were not enough; they were predicated upon the theological dimension of repentance which alone would give meaning to them. If Karl Barth had earlier made a case for a theology of resistance, Bonhoeffer now extended this concept, applying it to the ecumenical dialogue. The world was to understand that the coup which the German conspirators were preparing had a theological significance transcending even Schönfeld's invocation of the dimension of 'human rights'. The coup, then, had to take place as part of the 'punishment by God' and had thus to be recognized as the Germans' acceptance of guilt and repentance.[156] It was this argument of Bonhoeffer's which so much impressed the Bishop from England. While he could not get himself to overcome the reservations he harboured towards Schönfeld because of his ties with Bishop Heckel, he now was confirmed in his admiration of Bonhoeffer[157] and emerged from the meeting prepared to carry his message back to England.

One other matter was quite possibly also negotiated in Sigtuna or in Stockholm.[158] Together with William Temple (since April 1942 Archbishop of Canterbury), Bishop Bell was beginning at that time to plan for a major ecumenical conference which was to take place after cessation of hostilities and, by including representatives from the German Evangelical Church, was to pave the way for an equitable peace settlement. It can be safely assumed that this item was on Bell's agenda while he was in Sweden and that he put it before Bonhoeffer. In October of the same year, the latter travelled for the Provisional Governing Body of the Confessing Church to Freiburg to commission the 'Freiburg Council' to prepare a memorandum concerning the place that a reformed and reconsituted Germany was to take in the setting of a Christian Commonwealth.[159]

The saga of Bishop Bell's unsuccessful attempts to impress the Foreign Secretary, Anthony Eden, with the importance of the message that he had obtained from the two German pastors is common knowledge. While casting no reflection on their bona fides, Eden, in the name of the 'national interest', blocked any reply to be sent to them. Upon continued prodding by the Bishop to give some encouragement to those in Germany who repudiated the Nazi system and were filled with shame by its crimes, he merely referred him to his Edinburgh speech of 8 May in which he had appealed to those in Germany who wished to see a return to a German state based on respect for law and the rights of the individual to take active steps to rid themselves of their present regime; otherwise 'no one would believe them'.[160]

On its face value, the Foreign Secretary's argument was compelling; but, in fact, had any of the oppressed peoples of Europe at that date taken 'active steps' to oppose and overthrow the Nazi rule of terror? The German Generals had undoubtedly hesitated too long and had not taken their chances which indeed existed before the outbreak of the war. Was Anthony Eden even aware of the difficulties of staging a coup in a setting of near-total control such as existed under Nazi rule?

Be this as it may, Eden's stance in the name of the 'national interest' brought into focus the peculiarly tenuous situation in which the German Resistance found itself in the 'landscape of treason'. It was Schönfeld who invoked 'human rights' and Bonhoeffer who deepened the dialogue by introducing the religious note. In doing this, both German pastors abandoned the argument on behalf of national interest; they in fact were bound to come into conflict with it. On this score Bonhoeffer was the most candid and uncompromising, and that is why he so much impressed the Bishop. Bishop Bell in the course of years of ecumenical activity had gained considerable insight into the fabric of Nazi oppression. Thus he was able to appreciate and understand the unprecedented position in which the German resisters found themselves, prepared as they were to betray the immediate interests of their own country and to appeal to the 'solidarity and fairness', as Trott had put it in his April Memorandum, of 'responsible groups' on the other side. At the same time Bishop Bell was sufficiently tuned into that 'war behind the war', about which Visser't Hooft had written, to see it as one not between nations but rather between rival philosophies, a war in which those Germans who repudiated the Nazi system could be accepted as allies.

In his uneven duel with the Foreign Secretary, Bishop Bell was vigorously supported by Gerhard Leibholz, Bonhoeffer's brother-in-law who lived with his family in exile in Oxford. For intelligence on matters that agitated him Bell had a way of turning to friends and experts who happened to be in agreement with him. Thus, for advice on German matters, he often fell back on refugees such as Leibholz, Kurt Hahn, and Trott's friend Wilfrid Israel. Leibholz was of course deeply concerned about Bonhoeffer's well-being and during the war exchanged news about him with the Bishop whenever possible. As a political scientist, moreover, Leibholz came to assume an active part in bolstering Bishop Bell's stand on behalf of the German conspiracy. All along, in connection with his advocacy of the plight of the German refugees, Bell had argued the case of intervention as a legitimate international policy; the denial of human rights, he argued, citing Hugo Grotius' *De Iure Belli et Pacis*, justified international concern.[161] In view of the pleas of Schönfeld and Bonhoeffer in Sweden, the prerogatives of 'national interest' now seemed to recede behind those of the Church and Christianity. Historical experience has taught us that in certain situations, when religious or ideological concerns cut across established frontiers, national sovereignty and the prescription of non-intervention tend to yield pride of place to the principle of intervention. This is precisely what Leibholz argued: 'The traditional non-intervention policy of liberal Democracy belongs, at bottom, to the old world.'[162] Nevertheless, the 'old world' policy of the Foreign Secretary prevailed. Victor Mallet, the British Minister to Sweden, with whom Bishop Bell stayed while in Stockholm and who, so it seems, listened to the Bishop's tale with some sympathy, had no choice but to yield to his chief in this 'delicate matter'.[163] From John Gilbert Winant, the American Ambassador to the Court of St James, whom Bishop Bell called upon in July, came friendly noises and the promise to inform Washington; but nothing further happened.[164] Following his failure to impress British officialdom behind the scenes with the German message he brought back from Sweden, Bishop Bell decided to go public and challenge his government's policy towards the Resistance. His first opportunity to do so came on 15 October in the Upper House of the Canterbury Convocation of the Church of England when he spelled out his position of the war issues:

I could wish that the British Government would make it very much clearer than they have yet done that this is a war between rival philosophies of life, in which the United Nations welcome all the help they can receive from the anti-Nazis everywhere—in Germany as well as outside it—and would assure the anti-Nazis in Germany that they would treat a Germany which effectively repudiated Hitler and Hitlerism in a very different way from the Germany in which Hitler continued to rule.[165]

In the following months Bell also took this argument to the floor of the House of Lords in what turned out to be a duel with Lord Vansittart.[166]

The disparity between the welcoming posture on the part of the Ecumenical Movement towards the overtures from Germany and the silence from White-hall had by mid-1942 become striking; but, if anything, it encouraged the conspirators to persevere. Shortly before Schönfeld and Bonhoeffer's visit to Sweden, the Kreisau Circle had held its first major meeting at Moltke's estate,[167] with Steltzer present, who was thoroughly familiar with the Sigtuna operations. Schönfeld, upon his return from Stockholm, was met in Berlin by Trott, Haeften, Collmer, and probably also Gerstenmaier[168] for a debriefing on the mission to Sweden. Trott was the next to head north. In the talks with Bishop Bell his name had already been brought up, most probably by Schönfeld, as being a suitable intermediary if it should come to negotiations with the British.[169] So Trott took off for Sweden on 18 September. This was for him an exploratory trip, and three others that followed—in October 1943 and March and June 1944—were to constitute the ultimate test of his foreign ventures in Sweden on behalf of the Resistance. As usual, Trott had 'connections'. A German acquaintance, Heinz von Bodelschwingh, gave him an introduction to the influential Carlgren family, and the daughter of the house, Fru Inga Almström (later Fru Inga Kempe) turned out to be a charming and urbane person who was willing to open all kinds of important doors to the German visitor. Indeed she let it be known at their first meeting that she knew the British Minister Victor Mallet, but strangely Trott did not take her up on this.[170] If he had, it would perhaps have made little or no difference; but Mallet was a friend of Sir Stafford Cripps, and this connection could have helped at least to dispel some of the lingering suspicions that followed Trott everywhere. But at the luncheon given for him by Mrs Carlgren he met Bishop Björkquist and Dr Harry Johansson, and through the latter he found access to some of the members of the 'Sigtuna Group'.[171] Thus on 23 September Trott called on the influential Ivar Anderson, editor in chief of the *Svenska Dagbladet*, who was easily won over by this 'representative of the best of German culture . . . a man who, while the Second World War was raging at its height, dared to acknowledge his gratitude to Western cultural values and dissociate himself from all talk of German hegemony'.[172] Both to him and to Nils Quensel, President of the Court of Appeals, whom he called upon the following day,[173] Trott voiced his strong interest in exploring British post-war plans; but while they gave him a sympathetic hearing, they were in no position to give him much comfort. They did, however, keep the Swedish Foreign Office informed about their talks with Trott, and Anderson was able to arrange, during Trott's second Swedish visit in October of the following year, for him to see the Swedish Foreign Minister, Christian E. Günther.

For the moment, however, Trott's best bet was the bishop of Växjö, Yngve Brilioth. After the failure of Bishop Bell's efforts on behalf of the Resistance had become manifest, the Archbishop of Canterbury proceeded in July to invite a Swedish Bishop to London, and it was decided that Brilioth was to pay the return visit in November.[174] Once again it was Harry Johansson who lent a helping hand, taking 'the relatively young German diplomat who has spent long periods in England, America and East Asia, and who plays a very important part in the Opposition' to meet Bishop Brilioth in order for him to take information on the objectives of the German Opposition along on his journey to England.[175] A farewell letter which Trott wrote before leaving the country attests to his indebtedness to Dr Johansson. The latter had not only opened doors to him, but the two evidently reached a meeting of minds which, for the moment at least, gave Trott hope again and inspired him to recapture the lofty objectives of his mission:

I feel that you have fully understood that we do *not* intend to plead for support or even encouragement from friends on the other side—but that we wish to deposite [*sic*] our faith in the necessity of some such movement springing from solidaric and representative minds in the whole of Chr. Europe to make salvation possible. Personally, I leave with the conviction that a foundation for this exists and we are called upon to build on it now.—May our common effort be blessed.[176]

After Trott's visit, Johansson followed up with an elaborate brief for the Bishop about the nature, the problems, and objectives of the 'Opposition in Germany'.[177] Reminding Bishop Brilioth of the reality of the 'war behind the war', which the 'real Germany' waged on the side of those standing for the Christian tradition against the forces of the 'demonic usurper', Dr Johansson called attention specifically to that 'small and qualified' group of Protestants and Catholics engaged in deliberations concerning the spiritual and political regeneration of Germany. They were to be taken seriously, Johansson argued; their readiness for repentance should be accepted and their quest for a negotiated peace after the coup should be honoured. As for the Church and the Ecumenical Movement, they were clearly not to take part in political conspiracies; but they were entitled to recognize the new regime upon its establishment. Johansson identified the failure of the Opposition and the Anglo-Saxon powers to come to terms with each other as a vital problem. An understanding between both would certainly contribute towards eliminating the menace of the 'bolshevization of Central Europe', by which Johansson, citing Trott, meant primarily the 'inner bolshevization' that was under way in Germany itself. It was in these areas, then, that Dr Johansson expected the Bishop's help during the latter's forthcoming visit to England. From the perspective of Sweden, where bolshevization from without was of course seen as a clear and present danger, the anti-Bolshevik argument seemed more compelling than it seemed from London.

While in England between 4 and 27 November, Bishop Brilioth saw not only the Archbishop of Canterbury and the bishop of Chichester, but also called, so we are told, on the Foreign Secretary.[178] There is no written record of the encounter; the records of the British Foreign Office certainly kept their silence on an event which, from their perspective, was without consequence.

The Germans kept going to Sweden, however. Early in December Gerstenmaier and Schönfeld appeared in the Swedish capital on behalf of the Opposition[179] in order to find out what, if anything, Bishop Brilioth had accomplished in London. What he had to relate, however, was clearly not very reassuring.[180]

In March 1943 Helmuth James von Moltke himself went to Sweden. He had been on official business in Oslo where he had two secret meetings with the interned Bishop Berggrav,[181] and stopped in Stockholm for a week in order to establish a contact between Kreisau and the 'Sigtuna Group'. On the occasion of his 1942 Norwegian trip with Bonhoeffer he had already made arrangements for a visit to Dr Johansson but had had to call it off.[182] Now he wasted little time, following his arrival in Sweden on 20 March, in making his way to Sigtuna. On Sunday, 21 March the two men were together for three hours, and the following day Moltke, together with Johansson, called upon Ivar Anderson of the *Svenska Dagbladet*.[183] Both Johansson and Anderson were deeply impressed by Moltke's intelligence, integrity, and dignity. Compared with the outgoing Trott, Dr Johansson commented, Moltke appeared reserved and remotely handsome 'like a Spanish nobleman'.[184] Once again the chief topic of discussion was the 'White Rose'; Moltke was determined that information about it reach England so as to convince the British concerning the existence of resistance in Germany.[185]

Steltzer's arrival in Stockholm on the Wednesday evening added to the Kreisau representation, and on Friday he and Moltke met with members of the 'Sigtuna Group'[186] in the Stockholm City Museum. It was on this occasion that Moltke entrusted to Dr Johansson the long and moving letter which he hoped would be transmitted through ecumenical channels to his friend in England, Lionel Curtis.[187]

During the previous year, returning from his mission to Norway with Bonhoeffer, Moltke had sent off from Stockholm a long letter to Curtis. This letter was a sign of life of sorts, reassuring Curtis of his and his friends' steadfastness under the pressure of tyranny and terror and of their 'readiness for sacrifice', and even for risking the 'total collapse' of their country as a national unit, in the name of an ethical and indeed religious regeneration of Europe.[188] The letter of 25 March 1943 was more elaborate and had a distinct

political purpose. It outlined conditions in Germany including the systematic
extermination of Jews, the omnipresence of concentration camps, and the
extraordinary difficulties of resistance in Germany.[189] Moltke pleaded for the
establishment of a 'stable connection' between the German Opposition and
Great Britain and suggested that 'Michael' [Balfour][190] be attached to the
British Legation in Stockholm in order to act as liaison between Britain and
the various underground movements in Europe, especially in Germany. His
idea was to aim at a discussion involving neither possible peace terms nor a
post-war settlement but rather 'common plans'.

   Despite the fact that, for Moltke at least, the recommendations contained
in the letter were a matter of urgency, Dr Johansson did not see fit to forward
the document. Solicitous as he was of the German Resistance, he had to heed
Bishop Björkquist's instructions to keep Sigtuna clear of political involvement[191] which in this case especially might have affected Sweden's neutrality
in the war. Instead, Johansson waited until July when he was visited by Tracy
Strong, the American Executive Secretary of the World's YMCA and an old
friend of Adam von Trott,[192] who was about to return to the United States via
England. Strong then, upon Johansson's request, memorized the document to
the best of his ability in order to convey its contents, on his stop-over in
London, to Bishop Bell and William Paton for forwarding to Curtis. Since
Paton had died in 1942, Strong called on Bishop Bell on 30 August, turning
over to him a somewhat contracted Memorandum which he supplemented
with oral explanations.[193] On 14 September Bell in turn finally sent a copy of
the Memorandum to its designated destination, Lionel Curtis.[194] Bishop Bell
also sent a copy to Sir Robert Bruce Lockhart, Director of PWE (Political
Warfare Executive) and Michael Balfour's chief; and according to Balfour
the chances are that Curtis sent copies to the Foreign Office and to the British
Secret Service (MI5).[195] Also, according to Balfour, the British Legation in
Stockholm had made efforts to have him sent to Stockholm. Clearly, however,
the canons of 'absolute silence' and 'unconditional surrender' stood in the
way of this.[196]

   In this chapter on the 'ecumenical dialogue', Pater Max Josef Metzger
deserves a place.[197] Without the protection of official position which men like
Bonhoeffer, Moltke, and Trott enjoyed, this veteran of Catholic pacifism and
a sworn foe of the Third Reich, was indefatigable in his search for a formula
for a reformed Germany after the collapse of the Hitler regime. Brother
Paulus, as he called himself, had been instrumental in 1938 in the founding
of the *Una Sancta* fraternity whose dedication to ecumenism and in particular
to the reunification of the Christian Churches he envisaged as a way of
overcoming the evils of Nazism. But Brother Paulus also struck up an
acquaintance with Mrs Hanna Solf and her opposition circle.[198] Since she
took an interest in *Una Sancta*, Mrs Solf asked him to talk to the group about
his work and ideas. On this occasion he thus met Dr Richard Kuenzer, a

former Foreign Office official with close connections to the former Catholic Centre Party and also to the exiled ex-Chancellor Wirth; both men developed a mutual understanding on the need to plan ahead of time for a new government in Germany to prevent the Western Allies from imposing one by force from without.[199]

Brother Paulus was a fearless but rather careless idealist. In 1941 he composed a letter to none other than Hitler, urging him to end the war and to make way for another government that would stand a chance of concluding a tolerable peace; but upon the urging of his friends he did not send it after all.[200] Instead Brother Paulus decided to take his concerns to the outside world. He drew up a memorandum providing for a transformation of 'Nordland', an ill-disguised cover name for Germany, into a confederation of 'free states'[201] committed to a 'peace policy'[202] that was to honour human and civil rights and social justice and was furthermore to contribute to the 'United States of Europe'. The closeness of these thoughts to the aims of the Kreisau Circle has been pointed out,[203] and it may well be that he had learnt about them via the Solf Circle. Basically, however, Brother Paulus was a solitary witness who went his own way. In connection with his work for *Una Sancta* he had heard about the ecumenical work of Archbishop Erling Eidem of Uppsala, and he decided to turn to him with his memorandum that he hoped would eventually reach the British. The trouble, alas, was that he entrusted it to an acquaintance—the Swedish-born Dagmar Irmgart—who turned out to be an agent for the Gestapo. The memorandum never reached the Swedish Archbishop, and Brother Paulus was instantly arrested. The months from 29 June 1943 until his execution on 17 April 1944 he spent in Gestapo confinement. Facing the verdict of the Nazi 'People's Court' with equanimity he wrote:

I have offered to Him, the Father, my life for the sake of the peace of the world and the unity of the Church of Christ. I should be happy if by giving my life I could effectively serve the cause which on this earth I had without visible success striven to further.[204]

## 3. With Britain and the United States

For the Resistance the Swiss and Scandinavian connections were both ends in themselves and means to another end. Basically the dialogue was ecumenical. In the fury of hostilities and hatred men like Visser't Hooft and Johansson shared a singular understanding for the predicament of the beleaguered Germans with all their sincerity and courage, and they harboured a pacific Christian vision of a liberated Europe in which the Germans, with whom they were in dialogue, had a place. At the same time the ecumenists in neutral countries served as a bridge, the only possible bridge, by which the German emissaries could reach the other side of the battlefront and thus circumvent the hard fiat of 'absolute silence'.

Even in England, as we have seen, the German Resistance found one great advocate, Bishop Bell, with whom, despite enormous difficulties, a dialogue was established that was in itself a source of immense reassurance to men like Bonhoeffer and Schönfeld. The 'spirit of fellowship and of Christian brotherliness' emanating from the Bishop, which Bonhoeffer cited in his farewell letter after their meeting in Sweden,[205] left a deep impression upon Bonhoeffer, and no less so on Schönfeld; it was to carry him later through his 'darkest hours'.

Archbishop William Temple of York, though, unlike Bishop Bell, in no way emotionally engaged on behalf of the Resistance, at least maintained an active interest in the formulation of war and peace aims. In an unprecedented spirit of ecumenical unity he had published in *The Times* of 21 December 1940, along with Archbishop Cosmo Lang of Canterbury, the Roman Catholic Archbishop of Westminster Arthur Cardinal Hinsley, and the Moderator of the Free Church Federal Council Walter H. Armstrong, a ten-point letter that included the Five Peace Points enunciated by the Pope in his Christmas address of 1939 to the College of Cardinals and expanded, largely upon his initiative, to include the demand for social justice as the foundation of a future order,[206] and in January 1941 he convoked a Church of England Conference in Malvern which endorsed the Ten Points and furthermore called for 'the unification of Europe as a co-operative commonwealth' following the war.[207] The Ten Points and the Conclusions of the Malvern Conference came to form the basis for the war and peace aims debate which ensued in Britain in the course of 1941.[208] Also, in March 1941, Visser't Hooft sent to Archbishop Temple the document on post-war settlement that he had composed in Geneva with the help of Bonhoeffer and others.[209] In contrast to the official one of the British government, the Archbishop's position corresponded to the *desiderata* of the German Opposition for a formulation of equitable war and peace aims. The prince of the Anglican Church, however, stopped short of getting involved in and reacting to its peace feelers.[210]

One remove from, but not altogether outside, the ecumenical orbit were Lionel Curtis and Sir Stafford Cripps. As we have seen, both were drawn into it by virtue of their friendships with Moltke and Trott respectively. As for Curtis, he was, with his commitment to the Commonwealth idea, predisposed in any case to seek out someone like Moltke who, after the fall of the Nazi regime, might play a prominent part in a reconstructed Germany. Cripps belonged to the 'rebels' among the Labour Party[211] who, while rejecting any compromise with Nazism, favoured negotiations with the German people 'as soon as', so he wrote in the early days of the war, 'they can tell us authoritatively through reliable sources that they have asserted themselves as the free and honourable people we know them to be'. He must have had his young friend Adam von Trott in mind when he wrote this.[212] During the war both Curtis and Cripps managed, indirectly at least, as we have seen, to keep up their connection through ecumenical channels with their German friends.[213]

From the very beginning, following Trott's visit to America in the winter of 1939/40, Washington's reactions to what they learned about the German Opposition had been exceedingly reserved, if not negative; and then as the United States government was drawn into the war, Lochner's attempts to penetrate the wall of silence proved altogether futile. But in America too there existed the alternative route, the ecumenical bypass, so to speak, in the form of the Federal Council of the Churches of Christ in America. In this organization John Foster Dulles (later American Secretary of State under President Eisenhower), emerged as the chief expert on international affairs, and early in 1941 he had himself appointed by the Council to be chairman of a nineteen-member Commission to Study the Bases of a Just and Durable Peace.[214]

John Foster Dulles was a very different kind of a person from his European counterparts. Unlike Visser't Hooft in Geneva and Harry Johansson in Sigtuna, Dulles was a hard-boiled New York lawyer with a strict Presbyterian family background. He had a strong sense of religious commitment oriented towards achievement, especially in the area of foreign affairs, which he considered his family's traditional preserve.[215] As a young man he had been, with his brother Allen, a junior member of the American delegation to the Peace Conference at Versailles where he had become persuaded that the rise of Hitler was to be attributed to a large extent to the fact that the Treaty of 1919 had been 'exceedingly harsh' and its provisions 'without moral sanction'.[216] Also, through his law firm, Sullivan and Cromwell, he maintained active business contacts in Germany and in the pre-war years exhibited an ambivalent, if not tolerant, attitude towards the Third Reich. It was not love of Germany and not really a particular ecumenical concern that prompted Dulles to work with the Federal Council and to take on the assignment of the Commission. What guided him was an inherited rigid ethos of service and duty coupled with a sense of calling to contribute towards shaping a world order which, conforming to the 'moral judgment of mankind',[217] was designed to be of long duration. In a curious way the religious impulse in him blended with nakedly unsentimental ambition; he was a man of both piety and power.

Though Dulles shared none of Bonhoeffer's theological concerns or Trott's intuitive flights into religion, and most of all none of their predicament in having continually to outwit a regime of terror, somehow, even if remotely, he became linked with them by virtue of their connections with the Ecumenical Movement. Dulles was, as we have seen, a recipient of the Visser't Hooft–

Bonhoeffer memorandum of March 1941 to which he reacted, as though already in the position of a Secretary of State, with distant reserve.[218] Now, by March 1943, the Dulles Commission was ready with its report under the monumental heading of 'Six Pillars of Peace'.[219] It listed six political propositions[220] that were to guide the American nation in a world of inter-dependence requiring political mechanisms for co-operative action.

The tone of the document, which was sent out to some 60,000 Protestant ministers throughout the country with a view to getting it before 15 million lay members of their churches for discussion, was considerably less high-flown than had been any of the statements by Visser't Hooft or Paton's Peace Aims Group. Launching his report before an assembly of leaders in American public life at the Rockefeller Luncheon Club, Dulles, elaborated on the fact that the Soviet Union and decisions affecting the future of Finland, the Baltic States, and Poland were 'among the greatest post-war problems' the United States had to face.[221] In short, his 'war behind the war' was not exactly the same as was the one of the World Council in Geneva.

Nevertheless, the Dulles Commission report promised to become a major event in the ecumenical dialogue on war and peace aims. In Britain, the Peace Aims Group issued a statement, co-signed by all the senior Church leaders of all Protestant denominations, welcoming it 'unreservedly'.[222] Apparently it took months for the report to reach the World Council,[223] but from there, or possibly via Sweden, it was placed into the hands of Adam von Trott who in turn brought it for consideration before his Kreisau friends. The Whitsuntide weekend (12–14 June) meeting of the Circle held at Kreisau was devoted, among other things, to questions of foreign policy, and it was most probably on that occasion that the group discussed the 'Six Pillars of Peace'.

The upshot of this discussion was a lengthy document entitled 'Comments on the "Six Pillars of Peace" of the Federal Council of the Churches of Christ in America of March 1943 (by a Christian Study Group)', November 1943.[224] The 'Christian Study Group' undoubtedly was the Kreisau Circle, and the 'Observations' were not merely Trott's alone, as has initially been assumed.[225] Composed also in the 'we' form, these Observations reflected Kreisau's collective wisdom.[226] Much as did the British reply, the German one declared itself 'in full agreement' with the American Churches 'on many points', and for the rest it offered comments and elaborations that related the proposition of peace more closely to German conditions and in particular to the thinking among the Kreisau Circle.

For the Germans who gathered around Moltke, the Dulles document had an all too rational and business-as-usual quality. As the world around them was clearly falling apart, any planning for the future had to be contingent on a thorough rethinking of the premises of their position. This explains the somewhat high-flown tenor of their response and the reminder, in the 'Pre-liminary Remarks', that the 'transitional' or 'intermediate' regulations had to be guided by 'final Christian ends'. The Kreisau group was composed of young Germans who had come to understand that nothing short of the 'radical character' of the Christian message was necessary for regenerating Europe.

The 'Six Pillars of Peace' offered the German conspirators some distinct leads. They held out the prospect of a peace, based on equity and not retribution, that was designed to include, 'in due course', the neutral and enemy nations (Proposition 1), provide for 'autonomy for subject peoples' (Proposition 4) and the control of military establishments 'everywhere' (Proposition 5). Beyond this, however, the Kreisau response projected a radical vision of that 'European revolution', as Trott called it, that was to lead beyond the 'old ideal of a national state founded on uniformity of race and language' to a federative European order, and beyond a proletarization of the masses[227] to a 'truly Christian social order'. The Kreisau document, furthermore, raised the issue, as Trott and Bonhoeffer had earlier, of the need for repentance, calling for 'universal repentance after the terrible experiences and the chastisement of this war'.

John Foster Dulles, stringent as he may have been, had opened the door for an ecumenical dialogue, and the German response, if less down-to-earth, was circumspect and generous at the same time. It did not, however, as far as we know, reach the American shores. One wonders, of course, how far or whether at all Dulles would have been willing to follow up a path that was clearly out of tune with the policies of Washington. We do know, however, that he had at least been made aware of the existence of resistance in Germany. Upon the formation of Dulles's Commission early in 1943, a young German political exile, Fritz Ermarth,[228] engaged in the difficult task of informing the American public about the German Resistance, sounded the American out as to whether the 'eminent group' he represented 'may come out with some statement that would be encouraging to those patriotic Germans in Germany who see that Hitler is their ruin, but who also dread a new "Versailles"'.[229] Predictably cautious, Dulles's answer assured Ermarth that, while he considered it to be the task of the Commission of which he was chairman 'to seek to create public opinion which will support a reasonable peace with a de-Nazified Germany', he would not care to do it at that particular time by means of a public statement.[230] Upon further proddings by Ermarth, and after a journey to England in the summer of 1942, Dulles conceded that he had talked to persons who had had contact with 'responsible Germans' in Sweden, Switzerland, etc.,

from which there seems to be good reason to believe that Hitler and the Nazi gang could be overthrown by a revolution from within if any assurance could be given that out of this would come some decent place for the Germans who have been subjected to the tyranny which they resent and which has been almost as bad as that to which the conquered people have been subjected.[231]

In a subsequent letter Dulles lamented that no more could be done to encourage the anti-Nazi elements in Germany, adding impatiently that he wished there were stronger elements in Germany willing to bring about a change 'because they felt that this was the right thing to do and not merely that they thought that they would thereby escape the consequence of war'.[232]

Just about the time John Foster Dulles wrote this tart letter, Adam von Trott opened up contacts on an altogether different level with John Foster's younger brother Allen who had recently, in November 1942, been sent by Washington to set up a Secret Service station in Switzerland. He had so, the staff of the World Council in Geneva was convinced, been kept 'well informed' by his elder brother about ecumenical matters, and they were hopeful that this 'contact' would turn out to be 'very useful'.[233]

But, the intervention of the German exile did not help; and the 'ecumenical dialogue' with America turned out to be no dialogue after all. In America, certainly, the 'war behind the war' did not take place. There was no Visser't Hooft, no Johansson, no Bishop Bell to favour the ten righteous men of Sodom.[234]

*CHAPTER 5*

1. Carl Goerdeler as paraphrased by A. P. Young in Young, *The 'X' Documents* (London, 1974), 203.
2. See above p. 116.
3. Letter from Henry Smith Leiper to the Hon. Francis B. Sayre, 6 Apr. 1939, NA, RG 59, CDF 862.00/3842.
4. The World Council of Churches, a fellowship of Christian Churches with its seat in Geneva, grew out of two ecumenical organizations, 'The World Conference on Faith and Order' and 'The Universal Christian Council for Life and Work', both agreeing at the Conference in Utrecht, The Netherlands, of May 1938 to become part of a World Council of Churches. Willem A. Visser't Hooft became the General Secretary of what at first awkwardly was called 'World Council of Churches in Process of Formation' until after the war, in 1948, the organization was formally constituted.
5. The Nordiska Ekumeniska Institutet was founded early in 1940 by Dr Manfred Björkquist (Bishop since 1942) for the purpose of furthering close contacts between the Scandinavian Churches and the World Council of Churches. One of the driving forces in the Institute was Dr Harry Johansson, first an Assistant and since then from the autumn of 1943 Director, who was particularly active in cultivating ties with the German Resistance.
6. For the setting up of the World Council see Willem A. Visser't Hooft, 'The Genesis of the World Council of Churches' in Ruth Rouse and Stephen Charles Neill (eds.), *A History of the Ecumenical Movement 1517–1948* (2nd. edn., Philadelphia, Pa., 1968), 695–724; Visser't Hooft, *Memoirs* (London, 1973), *passim*; Hampson, 'The British Response to the Kirchenkampf', paper delivered at the Anglo-German Conference 'German Resistance to Hitler and British Attitudes towards it' held at Leeds, England, 6–9 May 1986, 312 ff.
7. Visser't Hooft, 'The Genesis', 708.
8. Letter from Bonhoeffer to Henry-Louis Henriod (World Alliance for Promoting International Friendship through the Churches), 7 Apr. 1934; WCC ipof, Bonhoeffer, quoted in Hampson, 'The British Response', 143. For the preceding passages I should also acknowledge my debt to the paper by Mrs Hampson, 'The British Response to the Kirchenkampf'.
9. See Ger van Roon, *Zwischen Neutralismus und Solidarität: Die evangelischen Niederlande und der deutsche Kirchenkampf 1933–1942* (Stuttgart, 1983), 26–7.
10. Thus the Frenchman Marc Boegner who assumed the leadership of the European Section

of the World Council; the Swiss Alphons Koechlin, a leading figure in the Swiss Protestant Federation; the Dutchman K. H. E. Gravemeijer who in April 1940 became the Secretary of the General Synod of the Dutch Reformed Church; see Peter W. Ludlow, 'The International Protestant Community in the Second World War', *Journal of Ecclesiastical History*, 29 (July 1978), 335–8.

11. 'The Ecumenical Church and the International Situation', Apr. 1940, WCC ipof XI; see also for a closer explanation of the circumstances that led to the drafting of this document and for a partial reproduction, Walter Lipgens (ed.), *Documents on the History of European Integration*, ii: *Plans for European Union in Great Britain and in Exile 1939–1945* (Berlin, 1986), 731–6.

12. Ibid.

13. Ibid.

14. See above Introduction.

15. Letter from Willem A. Visser't Hooft to Archbishop William Temple, 15 Dec. 1943, quoted in Hampson, 'The British Response', 363.

16. Thus Theo Kordt was, as we have seen, transferred immediately after the outbreak of the war to Berne as Counsellor of Legation, and in the following year Herbert Blankenhorn and Georg Federer, both in sympathy with the Opposition, were sent to the same post. To support the Consul-General in Geneva, Wolfgang Krauel, who was a determined anti-Nazi and who in 1943, when recalled to Berlin, refused to return, Weizsäcker sent as Consul in 1940 Gottfried von Nostitz and then, early in the following year, his friend Albrecht von Kessel. Also, in the summer of 1940 Hans Bernd Gisevius was appointed by the Abwehr Vice-Consul in the Zurich Consulate-General, where one of his chief concerns was to lend assistance to the activities of the Resistance in Switzerland.

17. See esp. Hans Schönfeld, 'Eidesstattliche Erklärung', Geneva, 30 Mar. 1948; Adolf Freudenberg, 'Eidesstattliche Erklärung', 17 Mar. 1948; Wolfgang Krauel, 'Eidesstattliche Erklärung', Campos do Jordao, 15 Mar. 1948; Willem A. Visser't Hooft, 'Eidesstattliche Erklärung', Geneva, 8 Mar. 1948, IfZ, Dokumentenbuch No.4, Docs. 317, 79, 132, 135; see also Armin Boyens, *Kirchenkampf und Ökumene 1939–45*: *Darstellung und Dokumentation* (Munich, 1973), 26; Visser't Hooft, *Memoirs*, 130.

18. The two had been acquainted since the late summer of 1928 when Trott, 19 years old, spent three weeks in Geneva. Visser't Hooft, then an official of the YMCA, was strongly attracted by the bright young German who was, as he later recorded, 'so keenly aware of the perilous and tragic situation of the younger generation in Germany in the spiritual confusion after the first world war' (Visser't Hooft, *Memoirs*, 155.), and Trott, in turn, saw in the Dutch clergyman, nine years his senior, a sort of father confessor to whom he revealed that, at that moment at least, he obtained his religious inspiration more from Dostoevsky than from the Bible; see also Christopher Sykes, *Troubled Loyalty*: *A Biography of Adam von Trott zu Solz* (London, 1968) 30; Henry O. Malone, *Adam von Trott zu Solz*. *Werdegang eines Verschwörers 1909–1938* (Berlin, 1986), 30.

19. Visser't Hooft composed two accounts of his talk with Trott. The 1 1/2 page 'Memorandum of a Conversation between Herr Adam von Trott and Dr W. A. Visser't Hooft in Geneva, Sept. 1940' (WCC ipof, XI, XII) succinctly summarizes Trott's main points; this document was taken along by a courier, Miss Gladys E. Bretherton, who left Geneva on 18 Sept. and reached England, travelling via Spain, Portugal, and Gibraltar, on 25 Oct. where it reached its destinees. The two-page 'Notes on the Situation' (WCC ipof, VII; see also Boyens, *Kirchenkampf*, ii. 152–4, 325–6) includes Trott's remarks together with Visser't Hooft's elaborations on them.

20. 'Notes on the Situation'.

21. 'Memorandum'.

22. Ibid.

23. Ibid.

24. Margarete Gärtner, *Botschafterin des guten Willens*: *Aussenpolitische Arbeit 1914–1950* (Bonn, 1955), 503.

25. Broadcast by Winston Churchill 30 Sept. 1940, quoted in Martin Gilbert, *Winston S. Churchill*, vi: *Finest Hour 1939–1941* (London, 1983), 778.

26. Interview with David Astor, 22 May 1980; letter David Astor to me, 27 May 1980.

27. For his part, as head of the World Council, he had to make the distinction between the Churches and the individual church members: while the Churches as such were not in a position to take the lead, the church members were to be 'in the forefront': 'they have that rock-bottom under their feet, which is needed to stand firm in the present tempest'; 'Notes on the Situation'; Boyens, *Kirchenkampf*, ii. 153.
28. 'Notes on the Situation'.
29. Visser't Hooft, *Memoirs*, 156.
30. The letter ('Dear Percy, as from Geneva, June 16th 1941' and signed 'F.Adams', WCC ipof, XI; in part reproduced in Lipgens (ed.), *Documents*, i. 391–5; see also covering letter 'Dear Visser't Hooft, Basle, Monday' and initialled 'AvT', WCC, ipof, XI) was addressed to Percy E. Corbett, professor of international law at McGill University who had belonged to the 'International Group in New York' that had convened in the winter of 1939–40 during Trott's American journey, and it was to serve as a critique of a MS by Corbett which subsequently was published, under the auspices of the Institute of Pacific Relations, in book form (P.E. Corbett, *Post-War Worlds*, New York, 1942). The letter was to be sent out by Visser't Hooft to Edward C. Carter in New York who was to forward it to its ultimate destination.
31. 'Dear Percy', 1–2.
32. Ibid. 3; as a matter of fact he argued that the whole of Europe, in the eventuality of an 'American intervention', was bound to orient itself towards Russia. Trott thought of himself as sufficiently a socialist and anti-capitalist to be on guard against the dangers of Western imperialism, whether in the British or American form. During the war, as we shall see, the thought matured in him that Germany, situated between East and West, could emerge as a proper bastion against both Western imperialism and Communism and that Russia might have to be considered a potential counterbalance against a Western predominance.
33. Ibid. 4.
34. Ibid. 5–6. Six months later, in Dec. 1941, Trott once again sought contacts with the World Council. This time he outlined the objectives of the conspiratorial group on a less grandiose scale to Mr A. Roland Elliott, the Executive Secretary, Student Division of the YMCA in New York. The striking feature of this encounter was not the nature of Trott's proposals but the fact that it was paid some attention in the British Foreign Office and the American State Department. John W. Wheeler-Bennett, Trott's old companion of the days of the Virginia Beach Conference, reported to the British Embassy in Washington that, while Trott's 'attitude to the war in general' had undergone some considerable change as a result of the German failure to defeat Russia in the summer of 1941 and the entry of the USA into the war in the following Dec., 'his ideas as to the basic principles of a peace settlement had not greatly altered, considering the course of the war between November 1939 and December 1941'; John W. Wheeler-Bennett, 'Adam von Trott and Peace Feelers', 21 Apr. 1943 and Appendix II, J. W. W-B., 'Note on the Eliot [*sic*]–Trott Conversations Geneva, December 1941', 22 Apr. 1942, FO 371/34449/C 5218/155/18. But while Trott, now as before, kept insisting that the conspiracy depended for leadership on the army, which presumably was to be decisive in the formation of a provisional government, he now (according to Appendix II) volunteered the opinion that the success of the venture was 'only possible' after the military power of Germany had been broken. Among the immediate measures towards a 'new deal' that the provisional government would enact as acts of good faith *vis à vis* the Allies he listed the following: (1) the proclamation of the restoration of the 'Rechtsstaat' (2) the rescinding of anti-Jewish legislation (3) the return of confiscated property to Jews and Gentiles alike (4) the evacuation of all occupied territory in *Western* Europe (no provision was made for the evacuation of Czechoslovakia, Poland, Austria, Greece, and Yugoslavia, and though Mr Elliott was not entirely clear on the point, it was his impression that Trott was unwilling to surrender any territory which would weaken the position of Germany against Russia) (5) A statement on the position which the new Germany sees for herself in a federated Europe which she would not seek to dominate. (Concerning this point Wheeler-Bennett noted a discrepancy with a conversation which, as he reported, Trott had in Aug. 1942 with the President of the Bank of International Settlements Thomas H.—Wheeler-Bennett identified him mistakenly as Frank—Mc-

Kittrick in which he allegedly stated that the new regime in Germany would require from the Allies recognition of a German hegemony in Europe.) (6) A proposal that, in view of the chaos which would exist in Germany after the collapse of the Nazi regime and the consequent danger of Communism, the German army in a properly reduced form should be permitted to assist and co-operate with the forces of the Allies in keeping order within the Reich. It was furthermore emphasized that, while there should be no let-up in the Allied attacks on Germany so as to encourage a movement for peace, Allied propaganda should differentiate between the German people and the Nazi Party, and no partition of Germany 'as of her former frontiers' should be envisaged. The State Department was kept abreast of the Trott–Elliott encounter by the Counsellor of the Legation in Berne J. K. Huddle (strictly confidential telegram from Berne to Secretary of State, 12 Feb. 1942, NA, RG 59, CDF 862.00/4235 and Secret Message Huddle 12 Feb. 1942, NA, R.G.226, Entry 3, Box 1.) and the intelligence about it, endorsed by Visser't Hooft, was scrutinized by Assistant Secretary of State Dean Acheson; NA, RG 59, CDF 740.00114/2164. Also German ex-Chancellor Brüning used the occasion of a trip to New York in April 1942 to call on Elliott in order to obtain a firsthand account of the meeting with Trott, but he was, as he reported to Edward C. Carter, left with the 'somewhat curious impression' that Elliott did not correctly understand 'our friend', or had deliberately refrained from spelling out details; letter from Heinrich Brüning to Edward C. Carter, Lowell House, 25 Apr. 1942, Brüning, *Briefe und Gespräche 1934–1945*, ed. Claire Nix *et al.* (Stuttgart, 1974), 394.

35. Visser't Hooft, Memoirs, 151. The first meeting between Visser't Hooft and Bonhoeffer had taken place in March 1939. Visser't Hooft was then in London and received a message from Bishop Bell that Bonhoeffer, also in London, wanted to see him. The two then arranged to meet at Paddington Station where, walking up and down the station platform, Bonhoeffer put before his companion the dilemma in which he was caught between not being able to reconcile military service with his conscience and yet possibly causing serious damage to his brethren if he made a stand on this point; ibid. 107–9.

36. Letter from Willem A. Visser't Hooft to Bishop George Bell of Chichester, Geneva, 15 Oct. 1956; Bell Papers, Box 42.

37. Visser't Hooft, *Memoirs*, 151.

38. WCC ipof XII; also reproduced in Boyens, *Kirchenkampf*, ii. 353–5; Lipgens (ed.), *Documents*, ii. 719–22. The document, composed by the General Secretary after consultation with 'almost certainly' (as Visser't Hooft later recorded) Bonhoeffer, the Swedish pastor of the WCC staff Nils Ehrenström, and 'probably' the Scotsman Denzil Patrick, was sent to Archbishop William Temple of York and to John Foster Dulles, Chairman of the recently constituted Commission to Study the Bases of a Just and Durable Peace of the Federal Council of the Churches of Christ in America.

39. See covering letter from Visser't Hooft to W.Temple, 12 Mar. 1941, WCC ipof VI; reproduced in Boyens, *Kirchenkampf*, ii. 352–3; also interpolated by Visser't Hooft in Visser't Hooft, *Memoirs*, 152.

40. Visser't Hooft, *Memoirs*, 152.

41. Ibid.

42. Letter from John Foster Dulles to Visser't Hooft, New York, 27 Mar. 1941, WCC ipof, XII.

43. 29 Aug–25 Sept.

44. See Visser't Hooft, *Memoirs*, 152–3.

45. William Paton, *The Church and the New Order* (London, July 1941). The Revd William Paton, an active ecumenist, was Secretary to the International Missionary Council and also an Associate Secretary General of the World Council of Churches.

46. The organizer and Secretary of the group was William Paton. It generally met at Balliol College, Oxford, under the chairmanship of Archbishop William Temple of York (since April 1942 of Canterbury); among its members were Bishop George Bell of Chichester, A. D. Lindsay (Master of Balliol), Arnold Toynbee, Sir Alfred Zimmern. Visser't Hooft also inspired the formation in Jan. 1941 of a parallel group under the auspices of the Federal Council of Churches of Christ in America, the Commission to Study the Bases of a Just and Durable Peace with John Foster Dulles as chairman.

47. As a matter of fact, Wheeler-Bennett, whose reports to the Foreign Office were not

distinguished by their accuracy, referred to the author of the book as Robert Paton and to the title as *The Church and the Post-War World*; Wheeler-Bennett, 'Note on the Eliot–Trott Conversations', FO 371/34449/C 5218/155/18.

48. Paton, *The Church*, esp. pp. 105–8.

49. Ibid. 75, 179; see also Eberhard Bethge, *Dietrich Bonhoeffer: Man of Vision* (New York, 1970), 643–4.

50. Bonhoeffer's draft entitled 'Gedanken zu William Paton: The Church and the New Order' and Visser't Hooft's version: 'The Church and the New Order in Europe' in Bonhoeffer, *GS* i. 355–71; the translation of the latter into German is on pp. 480–8. Visser't Hooft's version is also, in part, reproduced in Walter Lipgens (ed.), *Documents on the History of European Integration*, i: *Continental Plans for European Union 1939–1945* (Berlin, 1985), 395–7. See also Visser't Hooft, *Memoirs*, 153–5; Bethge, *Dietrich Bonhoeffer*, 643–5; Boyens, *Kirchenkampf*, ii. 175–7; Jørgen Glenthøj, 'Dietrich Bonhoeffer und die Okumene', Eberhard Bethge (ed.), *Die mündige Welt*, ii (Munich, 1956), 186–94.

51. See Bonhoeffer, *GS* i. 356 n. 1.

52. Bonhoeffer, 'Gedanken', 356.

53. Visser't Hooft, *Memoirs*, 153: ' . . . I pray for the defeat of my country, for I believe that this is the only way in which I can pay for the suffering which it has caused in this world.' See also Eberhard Bethge, 'Bericht vom Roederprozess, Heilbronn 27. Juli 1976'; Bethge now, however, tends to call in question the accuracy of Visser't Hooft's recollection. There is some confusion concerning Bonhoeffer's concrete ideas at the time about the military settlement that was to be negotiated following a coup in Germany. Towards the end of this Swiss visit he once again saw Karl Barth. According to Jørgen Glenthøj, who got his information in Feb. 1955 from Barth himself and his secretary, Bonhoeffer, supposedly speaking for 'others within the German Resistance Movement', argued that a 'generals' government' which was prepared to withdraw its troops behind the 1939 frontiers was likely to meet with a positive reaction from the Allies; Glenthøj, 'Dietrich Bonhoeffer', 185. Meanwhile, however, Barth has corrected Glenthøj's version, explicitly denying that Bonhoeffer had talked about plans to 'withdraw' the troops; instead he had proposed to 'freeze' them in the positions which they had reached at that time, leaving them momentarily in possession of the conquered and occupied territories; 'on this basis', then, he expected that negotiations with the Allies could be initiated. Also Barth remembered a 'certain amazement' on the part of Bonhoeffer when he, Barth, answered that he thought it impossible that the Allies would have anything to do with this. While Barth at no point had reason to think Bonhoeffer to be a 'nationalist', he could never quite establish to his satisfaction what had brought Bonhoeffer over to Switzerland; letter from Jørgen Glenthøj to Gerhard Ritter, 12 Sept. 1956, BA/K, Ritter 158.

54. 'Familie, Freundschaft, Heimat, Volk, Obrigkeit, Menschheit, Wissenschaft, Arbeit etc.'; Bonhoeffer, 'Gedanken', 359.

55. Ibid. 360.

56. For the active discussion in recent years among historians of the so-called German 'Sonderweg' and 'Sonderbewusstsein' (best translated as 'German way' and 'German ideology') see in particular Institut für Zeitgeschichte (ed.), *Deutscher Sonderweg: Mythos oder Realität?* (Munich, 1982).

57. Visser't Hooft, 'The Church', 362.

58. Ibid. 369–70.

59. Ibid. 363.

60. Ibid. 368.

61. See esp. Walter Lipgens, 'European Federation in the Political Thought of Resistance Movements during World War II', *Central European History*, 1 (Mar. 1968), 5–19.

62. Visser't Hooft, 'The Church', 369.

63. Ibid. 365.

64. Ibid. 369.

65. In the extant passage Bonhoeffer pointed towards 'Pan-Slavism' rather than 'Pan-Germanism' as the 'imminent danger'; Bonhoeffer, 'Gedanken', 360.

66. Visser't Hooft, 'The Church', 371.

67. The immediate recipient was Hugh Martin, Director of the SCM Press (which also had

published Paton's book) and since Sept. 1939 with the Ministry of Information, who saw to it that it reached the people connected with the Peace Aims Group and its parallel group in New York, the Commission to Study the Bases of a Just and Durable Peace.

68. Visser't Hooft, *Memoirs*, 154.

69. Writing to Leibholz: 'I entirely agree with your view on the comments from Geneva on Paton's book. . . . I am also entirely with you in what you say endorsing the comments, and have written to Paton strongly in that sense myself'; Letter from Bell to Leibholz, Hove, 30 Oct. 1941 in Eberhard Bethge and Ronald Jasper (eds.), *An der Schwelle zum gespalteten Europa. Der Briefwechsel zwischen George Bell und Gerhard Leibholz 1939–1951* (Stuttgart, 1974), 35.

70. Letter from Paton to Visser't Hooft, 6 Jan. 1942, quoted in letter from Visser't Hooft to Bethge, 31 May 1961, Bonhoeffer Archive, Ökumene; see also Bethge, *Dietrich Bonhoeffer*, 646.

71. Letter from Paton to Visser't Hooft, 6 Jan. 1942.

72. Bethge, *Dietrich Bonhoeffer*, 660. For the record: not only Bonhoeffer and Visser't Hooft but also Hans Schönfeld of the World Council's Research Department wrote a critique of Paton's book. Allowing for a basic agreement with Paton, he took issue with his pre-occupation with British and American perspectives and his corresponding neglect of the European Continent and its prerogatives; also, elaborating upon Paton's thesis that in the post-war era no return to the status quo ante was possible, he stressed the importance of adjustment to new socio-political realities of the 20th cent.; in this connection he empha-sized, not unlike Bonhoeffer, the distinctly German contribution to the 'Western tradition', resorting to an apology of the 'true Prussian tradition'. The roots of the evil were to be sought not merely in German militarism or in the moral inferiority of Germany's leadership but in the chaotic conditions everywhere; 'Gesichtspunkte und Fragen zur Diskussion über "The Church and the New Order"', attributed by Visser't Hooft to Hans Schönfeld and dated by him as of 11 Dec. 1941, WCC ipof, Peace Aims. The memorandum, designed to be the basis for ecumenical discussion, landed in the files of the World Council. In another memorandum, evidently composed the following day, Schönfeld addressed himself more concretely to the problems of a European reorganization, advocating the creation, parallel to the British Commonwealth, of a European continental commonwealth of nations informed by a distinctly Christian ethos; the settlement of boundaries according to the ethnographic principle; a general waiver on reparation claims; compensation to the Jews for the injustices perpetrated upon them by National Socialism as also by 'other states', and general co-operation in the task of 'a real solution of the Jewish problem'. The proposal furthermore stipulated the evacuation of the occupied territories, including negotiations with the British government aimed at the 'reconstruction and evacuation' of European Russia; 'Vorschläge für eine europäische Neuordnung', attributed by Visser't Hooft to Hans Schönfeld and dated by him as of 12 Dec. 1941, WCC ipof, Peace Aims.

73. For the main literature on the Bose episode see AA/PA, Info. Abt., Sonderreferat Indien; AA/PA, Büro des Staatssekretärs: Indien 1.; Affidavit by Alexander Werth, Nov. 1957, Trott Archive, Berichte; letter from Professor Dr Hans Kutscher (a German officer of the Indian Legion from Dec. 1941 to May 1945 and since Sept. 1943 Commanding Officer of its 3rd Battalion) to me, 6 Aug. 1984; letter from Heinrich von Trott (Adam von Trott's younger brother, who from 1943 also served in the Indian Legion) to me, 19 Mar. 1978; Franz Josef Furtwängler, *Männer, die ich sah und kannte* (Hamburg, 1951), 195–204; Sykes, *Troubled Loyalty*, 348–69; Mihir Bose, *The Lost Hero: A Biography of Subhas Bose* (London, 1982); Milan Hauner, *India in Axis Strategy: Germany, Japan, and Indian Nationalists in the Second World War* (Stuttgart, 1981).

74. Trott's closest fellow workers in the Section, whom he managed to have assigned to it, were Franz Josef Furtwängler and Alexander Werth, both decided foes of the regime. The former, an old Social Democrat, had worked for ten years before the Nazi seizure of power for the German Trade Unions League; the latter, after a bout in a concentration camp in 1934, had emigrated to England but returned to Germany in 1939 to join the army.

75. On the question of imperialism Trott and Moltke took very different positions. Moltke, partly due to the impact upon him by Lionel Curtis, was committed to the survival of the

British Empire whose predominant position in world affairs he considered imperative for the establishment and maintenance of a stable world order.

76. Out of an estimated 15,000 available Indian prisoners of war it did in fact recruit no more than 3,000 men organized in three battalions.

77. For pointing out to me the importance of the sporting attitude I am indebted to Professor Kutscher; letter to me, 6 Aug. 1984.

78. Sir Richard Stafford Cripps, leader of the left wing of the Labour Party and MP from 1931–50, became Ambassador to Moscow in 1940, but resigned from this position in frustration in Jan. 1942. Thereupon he was appointed to the highly prestigious office of Lord Privy Seal. Trott while a Rhodes Scholar had been close to his son John at Balliol College and had been befriended by the whole family. The Crippses, like David Astor, kept their faith in Trott, no matter what rumours circulated in London about him.

79. Telegram from von Trott to Rome, 27 Feb. 1942, AA/PA Info. Abt., Indien Bd. 4.

80. 'Störemeldungen'; von Trott to Dr [Karl] Megerle, 14 Mar. 1942, ibid.

81. This calculation also was undoubtedly behind his decision to join the Nazi Party in the spring of 1941.

82. Clarita von Trott, 'Adam von Trott', 202.

83. Interview with Freya von Moltke, 7 Mar. 1980.

84. See Sykes, *Troubled Loyalty*, 383–4.

85. As for Sir Stafford Cripps, he was most likely not kept informed by the Foreign Secretary about his India mission having been undermined by his friend (Sykes, *Troubled Loyalty*, 385); the Cripps papers will not tell the story since the bulk of them was destroyed in an air raid over London; information obtained from Dr Maurice Shock, until 1987 Vice-Chancellor of the University of Leicester.

86. Namely Hans Schönfeld and Pastor Adolf Freudenberg. The latter, a former official in the Auswärtiges Amt, had to leave the foreign service in 1935 because of his Jewish ancestry, then studied theology, spent some time as pastor in London and, at the outbreak of the war, moved to Geneva where he became head of the World Council's Secretariat concerned with relief for refugees. He was closely acquainted with Bonhoeffer who during his own wartime visits to Switzerland made a point of visiting him.

87. For the Wiskemann connection see 'Aufzeichnungen von Harry Bergholz 15.1.1950', Trott Archive, Chris Interviews; letter from Adolf Freudenberg to Ger van Roon, 7 Dec. 1966, IfZ, ZS/A 18, vol. 3; Elizabeth Wiskemann, *The Europe I Saw* (London, 1968, 156 ff., esp. 168–9.

88. In the course of their first encounter which took place sometime in Feb. or March 1942 in the room of a German refugee-friend of Miss Wiskemann, Dr Harry Bergholz, Trott outlined a programme which he thought could be accepted in London: evacuation of all occupied territories in the west including Alsace, as also of Czechoslovakia. Austria was to remain within the Reich; a 'free hand' in the east, except that Poland was to re-emerge independent; hostilities against Russia also were to be suspended. Domestically, Trott anticipated the establishment of an interim government of the Generals to yield eventually to a corporative order with a civil government of experts, since for some time to come the German people would not be politically ready for a democracy. He asked for his proposals to be forwarded to leaders of the Anglican Church. Several other meetings took place, in Geneva and subsequently in Fribourg, in which Trott allegedly modified his foreign policy terms regarding the East, and in the end alluded to the possibility of the conspirators turning, if rejected by the West, towards Russia.

89. Wiskemann, *The Europe*, 169.

90. Unidentified and undated handwritten note, and minute by G. W. Harrison, 12 June 1942, FO 371/30912/C 5428/48/18.

91. Unsigned, 'Strictly Private and Confidential' in 'Peace Moves Mr. Visser't Hooft', FO 371/30912/C 5428/48/18; reprinted in Hans Rothfels, 'Zwei aussenpolitische Memoranden der deutschen Opposition (Frühjahr 1942)', *VfZ*, 5 (Oct., 1957), 392–5 and Ger van Roon, *Neuordnung*, 572–5.

92. Originally, it appears, inspired by Pastor Hans Schönfeld in the late autumn of 1941, it was drafted in the winter of 1941–2 by Eugen Gerstenmaier and revised in the course of several evening sessions in the latter's home in Berlin-Charlottenburg with Trott and Hans-

Bernd von Haeften. It was then, at considerable risk, taken by Schönfeld across the frontier to Geneva where it was once again worked over and given final shape by Schönfeld and Albrecht von Kessel, then Consul at the German Consulate at Geneva; see Eugen Gerstenmaier, 'Der Kreisauer Kreis: Zu dem Buch Gerrit van Roons "Neuordnung im Widerstand" ', *VfZ*, 15 (July, 1967), 236–7; also Eugen Gerstenmaier, *Streit und Friede hat seine Zeit: Ein Lebensbericht* (Frankfurt/M., 1981), 140; see also van Roon, *Neuordnung*, 302–3. As for Helmuth von Moltke, he evidently was fully informed about Trott's *démarche* in Switzerland; letter from Helmuth von Moltke to Freya von Moltke, 30 June 1942, von Moltke, *Briefe an Freya*, 387.

93. Gerstenmaier, *Streit und Friede*, 140.
94. The memorandum also declared the group's readiness to co-operate 'in any international solution of the Jewish problem'.
95. Visser't Hooft, *Memoirs*, 157.
96. Ibid.
97. This is what Rothfels assumed; 'Zwei aussenpolitische Memoranden', 392.
98. Letter from Willem A. Visser't Hooft to Bishop George Bell of Chichester, 26 Apr. 1957, Bell Papers, Box 42.
99. *The Times*, 9 May 1942.
100. See 'Summary of Principal Peace Feelers, April 1941 to June 1942', PREM 4/100/8; reprinted in Lothar Kettenacker (ed.), *Das 'Andere Deutschland' im Zweiten Weltkrieg* (Stuttgart, 1977), 192. Visser't Hooft, it should be added, did not help matters by having an interview with E. N. van Kleffens, Minister for Foreign Affairs of the Dutch government-in-exile in London, in which he presented the foreign policy objectives of the German group to be considerably more ambitious than in fact they were in the Trott Memorandum, thus prejudicing the whole venture from the start; FO 371/30912/C 5099/48/18.
101. Letter from Anthony Eden to Sir Stafford Cripps, 18 June 1942, FO 371/30912/ C 5428/48/18.
102. 'Freiherr Adam von Trott' [May 1942], ibid. Henry O. Malone has established convincingly that the author of the anonymous statement was Crossman; Malone, 'Adam von Trott zu Solz: The Road to Conspiracy against Hitler', diss. (University of Texas at Austin, May 1980), 463 n. 106.
103. According to David Astor, Anthony Eden informed Sir Stafford Cripps that there was a 'formidable' dossier against Trott (David Astor, 'Von Trott's Mission: The Story of an Anti-Nazi', *Manchester Guardian*, 4 June 1956). The dossier has never surfaced. Of course there were sufficient counts that militated against Trott—such as his Cliveden connection and above all his part in the Bose affair—and it is entirely possible that the dossier was and is lodged with the Secret Service (MI5). In that case we are led to wonder why the Foreign Secretary should have seen the need to fall back on the assessment of Trott by Crossman? See also letter from Christabel Bielenberg to Hans Rothfels, 12 July 1963, BA/K, Rothfels 28, 7f.
104. Notice the vocabulary taken over from the statement by Crossman.
105. Letter from Eden to Cripps, 18 June 1942, FO 371/30912/C 5428/48/18.
106. Letter from Cripps to Eden, 20 June 1942, ibid.
107. Visser' Hooft summarizing the consensus among the group; Visser't Hooft, *Memoirs*, 157; see also Meeting of the Group on Peace Aims, Balliol College, Oxford, 15–17 July 1942, Bell Papers, Box 26.
108. Meeting of the Group on Peace Aims, Balliol College, Oxford, 15–17 July 1942, Bell Papers, Box 26.
109. Visser't Hooft, *Memoirs*, 158.
110. See ibid.
111. See G. W. Harrison's minute of 20 May 1942: 'But the point is that they must *do* something, like Belgians and Dutch, Norwegians and French, before we are prepared to believe even in their existence'; FO 371/30912/C 5099/48/18; italics in the original.
112. See Visser't Hooft, *Memoirs*, 158–9.
113. Typescript 'Notes on Conversation Visser't Hooft–von Trott December 1942 or January 1943', WCC ipof, X; meanwhile Visser't Hooft has dated the conversation Jan. 1943, Visser't Hooft, *Memoirs*, 158.

114. See above p. 248.
115. Along with the 'Notes on Conversation' there is a one-page document, unsigned but most probably also typed by Visser't Hooft, summarizing the intelligence evidently obtained from Trott, according to which Trott still expressed hope for 'trust' on the part of the Anglo-Saxon powers, envisaging retreat of the German armies in the west as soon as new governments there could take over, settlement on frontiers as of 1936 [*sic*] with a provision for later plebiscites, and, concerning the east, a proposition to the west for 'common defence'; as for Britain, it was to combine ruling its Empire with membership in a European federation. All this is rather confused and confusing, in particular if compared with the message conveyed in the 'Notes on Conversation', but at this point Trott found himself in a perplexing situation and at war with himself as much as with both East and West.
116. Visser't Hooft, *Memoirs*, 155.
117. See above pp. 270, 300 n.30.
118. Italics in the original.
119. Letter from Visser't Hooft to Allen W. Dulles, 11 Jan. 1943 in Visser't Hooft, *Memoirs*, 159. Just for the record: in mid-1942 yet another memorandum 'Deutschland und der Krieg', supposedly circulated by courtesy of 'ecclesiastic intermediaries' in London and Washington. Its author, a Swabian manufacturer, Dr Werner Plappert, belonged to a group of friends in Stuttgart to which, among others, Dr Paul Collmer and Dr Wilhelm Hoffmann, a librarian, belonged. Backed up by the industrialist Robert Bosch, the group entertained contacts with the World Council of Churches in Geneva. Both Collmer and Hoffmann also had close ties with Gerstenmaier, Schönfeld, and Trott. The memorandum, composed in the winter of 1941–2 and finished in Feb. 1942, was written in consultation with the author's friends (Collmer, Gerstenmaier, Schönfeld, Trott), and then supposedly channelled via Schönfeld to John Foster Dulles in New York and in the autumn of (*sic*; it must have been May or June) 1942 to Bishop Bell of Chichester for forwarding to the British government. Advocating the formation of a European federation, with which Britain was to be loosely connected, and the 'destruction of Bolshevism', it proposed a peace settlement on the basis of the frontiers as of 1 March 1938. To my knowledge there is no record of the memorandum actually having reached its destination in either Britain or the USA, and if it had, it would not have made any difference anyway. According to Plappert, he destroyed his copy of the document, but Collmer supposedly kept his; but the original has not surfaced so far. Anyway, Collmer related to me (interview, 8 Feb. 1978; letter from Dr Paul Collmer to me, Stuttgart, 14 Feb. 1978) that he took the 'document of friends' in Dec. 1941 (?) to Visser't Hooft in Geneva for forwarding. For the story of the origins and fate of the memorandum see letter from Dr Werner Plappert to Hans Rothfels, 15 Nov. 1957, BA/K Rothfels 28–1. The memorandum became public in a printed version in three articles 'Ein europäisches Dokument', *Basler National Zeitung*, 2, 3, 4. Nov. 1953. I am also indebted for some information on the memorandum to Peter Hoffmann (letter to me, 27 May 1988).
120. See Ludlow, 'The International Protestant Community', 321 ff.; Torleiv Austad, 'Eivind Berggrav and the Church of Norway's Resistance against Nazism, 1940–1945', *Mid-Stream: An Ecumenical Journal*, 26 (Jan. 1987), 51–61.
121. 'Furthermore Dr. Schönfeld reports that the increasing isolation of Switzerland imposes upon Sweden a special responsibility concerning the fostering of contacts'; letter from Harry Johansson to Bishop Yngve Brilioth, Sigtuna, 11 Dec. 1942, Sigtuna, Svensk Korrespondens E: I: 2, även 'Hemlig'; also Boyens, *Kirchenkampf*, ii. 164–5.
122. Bishop George Bell of Chichester, 'The Church and the Resistance Movement' (a lecture given by the Bishop in Göttingen on 15 May 1957), Bonhoeffer, *GS* i. 401, 515; see also Ronald Jasper, *George Bell: Bishop of Chichester* (London, 1967), 266. Bishop Bell was preceded in his goodwill trip by Sir Kenneth Clark, the Director of the National Gallery, and T. S. Eliot. It is not without a certain irony that the Ministry of Information should have sent out two dignitaries, Eliot and Bell, who, though of course not political people, had come out in public with a pronouncedly Christian vision of the war issues that transcended the conventional understanding of the alignment in the war. T. S. Eliot's thesis in his three lectures on *The Idea of a Christian Society* (London, 1939), minimizing the difference between 'the Idea of a Neutral Society (which is that of the society in which we

live at present)' and 'the Idea of a Pagan Society (such as the upholders of democracy abominate)' (ibid. 9) as opposed to 'the Idea of a Christian Society' was not far removed from Bishop Bell's de-emphasis of the war between rival nations as against that between the 'rival philosophies of life' in which the dictates of universal Christian brotherhood called for the transcending of all national interests. As a matter of fact, the two men had become friends in December 1930 when T. S. Eliot for the first time spent a weekend at the bishop's palace at Chichester. On the occasion of another visit by Eliot in the summer of 1934 to Bishop Bell, the Bishop commissioned the poet to write a play for the following year's Canterbury Festival, which turned out to be *Murder in the Cathedral*; see Peter Ackroyd, *T. S. Eliot: A Life* (New York, 1984), 181, 219, 225; Jasper, *George Bell*, 75, 125–6, 340. Both Bell and Eliot were united in the belief that European culture depended upon the survival of the Christian faith.

123. For Bishop Bell's Report about this leg of his trip to Sweden see *The Christian News Letter*, 24 June 1942, reprinted in Jørgen Glenthøj (ed.), 'Dokumente zur Bonhoeffer-Forschung 1928–1945', *Die Mündige Welt* (Munich, 1968), 306–9.

124. The chief sources for the meetings between Bishop Bell and the German pastors are the various accounts by Bell himself: (1) 'Memorandum of Conversation', Stockholm 1942 (presented to Anthony Eden on 30 June 1942), reprinted in Bonhoeffer, *GS* i. 372–7; (2) 'The Background of the Hitler Plot', *The Contemporary Review*, 168 (Oct. 1945), 203–8, reprinted ibid. 390–8; (3) 'The Church and the Resistance Movement' (Göttingen lecture 15 May 1957), reprinted ibid. 399–413; see also the German version of the lecture, together with the correspondence between the bishop of Chichester and Foreign Secretary Anthony Eden that ensued from the meetings in Sweden, in George K. A. Bell, Bischof von Chichester, 'Die Ökumene und die innerdeutsche Opposition', *VfZ*, 5 (Oct. 1957), 362–78.

125. From Bishop's Bell's Foreword to Bonhoeffer's *The Cost of Discipleship* (New York, 1949), 7; for the Bell–Bonhoeffer relationship see also Bethge, *Dietrich Bonhoeffer*, 283–9 and Mary Bosanquet, *The Life and Death of Dietrich Bonhoeffer* (New York, 1968), 134–5.

127. Letter from Hans Schönfeld to Nils Ehrenström, Geneva, 6 May 1942: 'Meanwhile you will most likely have heard that starting 11 May you will get a visit for three weeks ... As you will imagine, I should like then to have an exhaustive talk with George Bell ...'; Sigtuna, Utomnordisk Korrespondens E: III: 2, 1942–3. For this and much of the following information including an elaborate documentation from Swedish archives see Glenthøj, 'Dokumente', 260–355; for the most comprehensive treatment of the 'Swedish Journey' see Bethge, *Dietrich Bonhoeffer*, 661–74.

128. See Bethge, *Dietrich Bonhoeffer*, 663.

129. See van Roon, *Neuordnung*, 314.

130. The recollection of Barbara von Haeften on this matter is quite definite; interview with Barbara von Haeften, 11 Feb. 1978.

131. See Bethge, *Dietrich Bonhoeffer*, 662–3.

132. Hans Rothfels, 'Zwei aussenpolitische Memoranden', 395–7; van Roon, *Neuordnung*, 575–7.

133. Bishop Bell, 'The Church', 402.

134. See Rothfels, 'Zwei aussenpolitische Memoranden', 388.

135. Gerhard Ritter's blanket attribution (*Carl Goerdeler*, 322), however, of Schönfeld's Swedish overture to Carl Goerdeler does not stand up to the test of careful scrutiny; also Rothfels has argued convincingly that Schönfeld's proposal of a public offer on the part of the Allies to co-operate with a new German government after the overthrow of Hitler and his regime did not correspond to the position of Beck, Hassell, and Goerdeler; Rothfels, 'Zwei aussenpolitische Memoranden', 388.

136. The oral presentation: 'As to Russia, Schönfeld said that, as the German Army then held 1,000 miles of Russian territory, it was hoped that Stalin could be satisfied on the boundary question, and the German high officers were impressed by the Soviet élite and believed in the possibility of an understanding'; 'The Background' in *GS* i. 395. The 'Statement': '1. The opposition groups have no aims to conquer or to get for Germany parts of Russia as a colonial area. 2. They hope that it may be in the future possible to co-operate in a really

peaceful way with Russia, especially in the economic and cultural field ... '; 'Statement', 397.

137. See Glenthøj (ed.), 'Dokumente', 280; but Glenthøj by mistake identified Schulenburg as Chief of the Information Section (Informationsabteilung) of the Auswärtiges Amt; when at the time of the German invasion of Russia Schulenburg had to relinquish his post as Ambassador to Moscow, he was appointed Chief of the Political Division XIII (Politische Abteilung XIII) in the Auswärtiges Amt, concerned with the Soviet Union, as well as of the so-called *Russland-Gremium*, a committee which brought together some of the leading experts on Russia.

138. See entry of 9 June 1943, *Die Hassell-Tagebücher*, 368–9; also Hedwig Maier, 'Die SS und der 20. Juli 1944', *VfZ*, 14 (July 1966), 299–316.

139. Rothfels, 'Zwei aussenpolitische Memoranden', 388–9.

140. Like Bishop Bell of Chichester, Bishop Berggrav in the pre-war years and into the early months of the war was determined to seek accommodation with the Nazi regime in Germany. Still in May 1939 Berggrav cautioned Bell: 'We must not build a Maginot line of churches'; quoted in Visser't Hooft, *Memoirs*, 106; see esp. Visser't Hooft on Bell's and Berggrav's stand at the ecumenical conference in Zilven, Holland in January 1940, proposing a peace settlement between the Western governments and Hitler; ibid. 116–20; also Boyens, *Kirchenkampf*, 66 ff.

141. In one of his letters to his wife, which served him as a diary of sorts, Moltke insisted on misspelling Bonhoeffer's name ('Bonhöffer' and 'Bonhöfer') and reported with some glee that in the Oslo Hotel he was given a princely apartment in the *belle étage* whereas his 'companion' was billeted on the third floor; letter from Helmuth von Moltke to Freya von Moltke, Oslo, 15 Apr. 1942, continued on 17 April; von Moltke, *Briefe an Freya*, 362 ff.; for the spelling of Bonhoeffer's name see Moltke Papers. For the characterization of the relations between the two men I am also indebted to Freya von Moltke. As for the misspelling of Bonhoeffer's name, it should, however, be taken into account that Moltke, often relying on his ear, tended to be careless in spelling proper names; thus he never got Dohnanyi straight, nor even Gerstenmaier; letter from Beate Ruhm von Oppen to me, 30 Oct. 1988.

142. Bethge, *Dietrich Bonhoeffer*, 659.

143. He was moved to a mountain chalet where he spent the following three years under house arrest. Neither Moltke nor Bonhoeffer were able to meet Bishop Berggrav in person during this trip. Moltke was to encounter him during his subsequent missions to Norway in Sept. 1942 and March 1943; Bonhoeffer never did. Ironically the two theologians who saw fit to translate the Lutheran message into the duty of disobedience never did meet.

144. Letter from Helmuth von Moltke to Freya von Moltke, Oslo, 17 Apr. 1942, von Moltke, *Briefe an Freya*, 366.

145. See Balfour and Frisby, *Helmuth von Moltke*, 183.

146. See Bethge, *Dietrich Bonhoeffer*, 658.

147. He arrived on 11 May and left on 23 May; ibid. 660.

148. Bonhoeffer did not leave Switzerland before 24 May and Schönfeld left the German capital on 25 May, or at the latest, early on 26 May for his first meeting on that day with Bishop Bell.

149. Ibid. 663; Barbara von Haeften's recollections strongly support this version. She distinctly remembers that the two took a long walk along the Podbielskiallee, Rheinbabenallee into the Grunewald; interview with Barbara von Haeften, 11 Feb. 1978.

150. Photocopy in Bonhoeffer, *GS* i. 336.

151. It must, however, be noted here that Heckel's efforts at making his Office the sole agent of the German Evangelical Church for ecumenical work came to naught about that time. While in view of his compromising policies he found himself repudiated by the Confessing Church, he was now also attacked by the Nazis. Since 1941 Reinhard Heydrich, Chief of the Security Police, was engaged in infighting against Heckel's Kirchliches Aussenamt which, he claimed, by means of its ecumenical connections had merely served to bolster German Protestantism in its 'anti-volkish and anti-National Socialist attitude'; it was no longer fit to represent the interests of the Reich abroad, even if only in the ecclesiastical sector; copy of letter from Reinhard Heydrich to Joachim von Ribbentrop, Berlin, 2 Apr.

1942, AA, PA, Inland I-D, Deutsche Kirche 2 (1943–44). On 1 June 1942 the Foreign Minister followed up with an instruction to the Auswärtiges Amt to the effect that henceforth it was to entertain 'no relations whatsoever' with Bishop D. Theodor Heckel or his representative Dr Eugen Gerstenmaier; Secret Instruction Joachim von Ribbentrop to Ernst von Weizsäcker, 1 June 1942, ibid.; see also Glenthøj, 'Dokumente', 277–80.

152. Initially Dr Johansson had obtained his intelligence on Resistance matters from Steltzer, Schönfeld, and Gerstenmaier; as a matter of fact, Schönfeld in his letter of 6 May 1942 to Ehrenström (see above) mentioned explicitly that he wanted to get in touch with Johansson 'and his *Arbeitsgemeinschaft*'. Johansson was soon to meet Bonhoeffer (31 May 1942), Trott (Sept. 1942) and Moltke (Mar. 1943) and to direct his efforts on behalf of the *Widerstand* particularly towards the Kreisau people; interview with Dr Harry Johansson, Sigtuna, 31 May 1980; see also Henrik Lindgren, 'Adam von Trotts Reisen', 275.

153. Bishop Bell, in his accounts of the episode (Bishop Bell, 'The Background', 'The Church') insists that he was first alone with Bonhoeffer and that only afterwards Schönfeld joined them. According to Johansson, however, both Germans appeared together; he in fact elaborated on the precautions which, in expectation of their visit, he took to protect them from detection. Johansson, together with Bishop Bell, Bishop Manfred Björkquist of the Sigtuna Foundation, and Nils Ehrenström (Schönfeld's Swedish colleague in the World Council of Churches) approached the Institute from the lakeside through the back door, whereas Bonhoeffer and Schönfeld, arriving from the nearest railway station in Märsta, were to enter the building from the street; interview with Dr Harry Johansson, 4 June 1980; see also Glenthøj, 'Dokumente', 270–1.

154. 'The Background', *GS* i. 395. The corresponding passage in 'The Church' (ibid. 405) reads as follows: 'There must be punishment by God. We should not be worthy of such a solution. Our action must be such as the world will understand as an act of repentance. "Christians do not wish to escape repentance, or chaos, if it is God's will to bring it upon us. We must take this judgement as Christians".'

155. Remember also in this connection the letter by Bonhoeffer to Eberhard Bethge, 25 June 1942, in which he conceded that the entanglement in the 'worldly sector' gave him cause 'to think'.

156. See for the discussion of this particular episode also Glenthøj, 'Dokumente', 290–2.

157. Perhaps somewhat too pointedly, Eberhard Bethge, echoing the Bishop's feelings, contrasted the parts played by the two German pastors as follows: 'Sch. negotiates, B. informs; Sch. seeks a common basis, B. assumes it; Sch. threatens, with German strength, so as to get co-operation on the decisive day, B. asks. Sch. warns, B. talks of repentance. Sch. is tactical, B. fundamental. No doubt Sch. is here the more politic, but in this case and at this moment B. is the better and more effective diplomat'; Bethge, *Dietrich Bonhoeffer*, 667.

158. The meeting of 1 June in Sigtuna was followed by yet another one, arranged by Dr Johansson, in Stockholm of Bishop Bell with the German pastors on the following day. Bishop Bell himself in his various reports of the meetings in Sweden does not mention this matter; however, the case which Jørgen Glenthøj ('Dokumente', 273–4) made that it was brought up in the Sigtuna or Stockholm meetings is sufficiently convincing to accept it.

159. For the 'Freiburg Circle' or 'Bonhoeffer Circle', as the somewhat enlarged group called itself from then on, and the Memorandum see above Ch. 1, s.5.

160. The Edinburgh speech was assessed by the British press as highly significant; Fromm, *Deutschland in der öffentlichen Kriegszieldiskussion*, 163; for the epistolary exchange between Bishop Bell and Foreign Secretary Eden see Bell, 'Die Ökumene', 376–8.

161. G. K. A. Bell, 'Humanity and the Refugees' (1 Feb. 1939) in *Church and Humanity, 1939–1946* (London, 1946), 13.

162. S. H. Gerard (pseudonym for Gerhard Leibholz), 'Germany between West and East', *Fortnightly*, 158 (Oct. 1942), 256. See also an earlier memorandum by Leibholz of May 1940 which made the rounds in the World Council of Churches and which argued the case of intervention in an ideological (*weltanschaulich*) conflict determined by domestic and social alignments within the different power structures; 'Die Verantwortung der Kirchen für die internationale Ordnung' von einem früheren deutschen Professor der Rechtswissenschaften in England, WCC ipof, Life and Work D 24 Box 11. See also Max Beloff, 'Reflections on Intervention', *Journal of International Affairs*, 22 (1968), 198–207; ironically,

early on Bonhoeffer, taking an extreme stand, even rejected the label of 'intervention' for ecumenical interference on behalf of the German Church: it was 'just a demonstration to the whole world that Church and Christianity as such are at stake'; letter from Dietrich Bonhoeffer to Bishop George Bell of Chichester, London, 14 May 1934, Bell Papers, Box 42, Bonhoeffer Archive Box 41, Briefwechsel Bell.

163. Letter from Victor Mallet to Bishop George Bell of Chichester, Stockholm, 22 Sept. 1942, Bell Papers, Box 42; after the failure of the attempt against Hitler of 20 July 1944 he wrote that he considered 'the whole story' a 'nightmare', and, quite in contrast to the official line, that he thought it 'a great pity' that the plot had miscarried; letter from Sir Victor Mallet to Bishop George Bell of Chichester, Stockholm, 4 Oct. 1944, ibid.

164. Bethge and Jasper (eds.), *An der Schwelle*, 59, 66–9; Jasper, *George Bell*, 272.

165. Bell, *The Church and Humanity*, 83–4.

166. See above p. 243.

167. 22–5 May 1942.

168. See van Roon, *Neuordnung*, 314.

169. Bell, 'The Background', 396; 'The Church', 406; see also van Roon, *Neuordnung*, 314.

170. Interview with Inga Kempe, 25 Feb. 1978. The written report 'Memorandum by Mrs. Inga Kempe', Trott Archive, Berichte, sheds little light on Trott's first visit to Sweden except for relating that then she had 'no idea what was the real reason behind his visit to Stockholm'.

171. See also Lindgren, 'Adam von Trotts Reisen nach Schweden 1942–1944', *VfZ*, 18 (July 1970), 275–6.

172. Ivar Anderson, *Från det Nära Förflutna. Människor och Händelser 1940–1955* (Stockholm, 1969), 91. This passage summarized Anderson's diary entry for 23 Sept., repr. in *Der Kreisauer Kreis: Porträt einer Widerstandsgruppe*, ed. Wilhelm Ernst Winterhager (Berlin, 1985), 231.

173. Lindgren, 'Adam von Trotts Reisen', 276.

174. For much of the information on this mission I am relying on Glenthøj (ed.), 'Dokumente', 275 ff.

175. Letter from [Dr] Harry [Johansson] to 'Dear Friend' [Bishop John Cullberg], 14 Oct. 1942; Sigtuna, Svensk Korrespondens E: I: 2, även 'Hemlig'. In the course of the meeting, which took place in Nässjö, Trott pushed for information about British contingency plans for an upheaval in Germany.

176. As in the letter from Geneva of 16 June 1941 to Percy E. Corbett Trott signed 'F. Adams'; letter from Adam von Trott to Dr Harry Johansson, Hälsingborg, Saturday [26 Sept. 1942], ibid.; italics in the original. See also Lindgren, 'Adam von Trott's Reisen', 274.

177. Letter from Johansson to Bishop Brilioth, 23 Oct. 1942, Sigtuna, Svensk Korrespondens E: I: 2, även 'Hemlig'; see also Lindgren, 'Adam von Trott's Reisen', 276 (where, however, the letter is erroneously dated 24 Oct.). The letter, while referring to a 'document', evidently emanating from the Opposition itself, adds up to a running commentary by Johansson on it. I have been unable to locate and identify the 'document', but without doubt it emanated from the Kreisau group and especially reflects the thinking of Trott.

178. This is by testimony of Bishop Brilioth's wife; Glenthøj (ed.), 'Dokumente', 277.

179. There is no record in the official Archives of this mission; but Glenthøj conjectures that it was Count Friedrich Werner von der Schulenburg who, in order to enable Gerstenmaier to go on behalf of the conspiracy, staged an intricate manœuvre by convincing the suspicious Nazi Security Police that he could safely be sent abroad as an agent. If this was the case, Gerstenmaier went out, formally at least, with the sanction of the Security Police; see Glenthøj (ed.), 'Dokumente', 279–80.

180. Letter from Bishop Brilioth to Bishop Bell, 12 Jan. 1943, quoted in Bethge, *Dietrich Bonhoeffer*, 674–5.

181. During the first meeting Moltke related to Berggrav and his friend Arvid Brodersen information about the execution on 22 Feb. of Hans and Sophie Scholl and Christoph Probst, members of the 'White Rose' student group in Munich whose leaflets had called for resistance against the Nazi enslavement of Europe. It was during the second meeting on the night of 18–19 March that Moltke consulted the Bishop about the justification for a Christian to commit tyrannicide; extract from Bishop Berggrav's Diary, courtesy of Peter

Ludlow; see also *Der Kreisauer Kreis*, 232–5. On his trip home Berggrav entered into his diary: 'besides being fascinated with Moltke's personality, I was touched by the complicated and tragic situation of the Germans in opposition to Hitler. It was heartbreaking to think how they were fighting with everything against them.'

182. Interview with Dr Johansson, Sigtuna, 1 June 1980.

183. Moltke's itinerary during his Swedish visit could be reconstructed by means of the diary of Dr Johansson; interview with Dr Johansson, Sigtuna, 4 June 1980.

184. Interview with Dr Johansson, Sigtuna, 1 June 1980.

185. See Michael Balfour and Julian Frisby, *Helmuth von Moltke: A Leader Against Hitler* (London, 1972), 214. The student demonstration in Munich constituted the first manifestation of active resistance in Nazi Germany. About the same time General Beck once again sent Josef Müller to Rome to advise the Holy Father about an impending coup against the Nazi regime ('Notizen über eine Aussprache mit Dr Josef Müller am 4.1.1953', BA/K, Ritter 131; Josef Müller, *Bis zur letzten Konsequenz. Ein Leben für Frieden und Freiheit* (Munich, 1975), 158–62; Hermann Graml, 'Die deutsche Militäropposition vom Sommer 1940 bis zum Frühjahr 1943', in *Vollmacht des Gewissens*, ed. Europäische Publikation e.V. (Frankfurt/M., 1965), ii. 469–72); it was to yield to a temporary military dictatorship, and the German troops were expected to remain in the occupied territories until contacts with the resistance groups could be established that would form the nucleus for a new order. Father Leiber, who as in the winter of 1939/40 received Müller's message, voiced scepticism about the readiness of 'the Generals' to act. But in the following month, on 13 and 21 March, two attempts on Hitler's life were to be staged by three younger officers, 1st Lt. (Res.) Fabian von Schlabrendorff and Col. Henning von Tresckow and by Major Rudolf-Christoph Freiherr von Gersdorff, which, however, miscarried.

186. They included Johansson, Anderson, Quensel, and Hardy Goransson.

187. Actually, Moltke had been wrestling with the idea of himself catching a flight to England in order to inform the authorities there about the 'White Rose' and in general about the Resistance; but he had to abandon it because of insuperable difficulties; the letter then was most likely a substitute for the flight; interview with Dr Johansson, Sigtuna, 1 June 1980; see also Balfour and Frisby, *Helmuth von Moltke*, 214, 376 n. 17; also Glenthøj (ed.), 'Dokumente', 281 n. 84.

188. Stockholm, 18 Apr. 1942; Balfour and Frisby, *Helmuth von Moltke*, 184–6.

189. In this connection, apart from listing the functions of the Resistance, he also alluded to its 'many mistakes', including especially the reliance placed on the Generals; what was needed in Germany was, he argued, 'a revolution, not a *coup d'état*'; for the text of the letter see ibid. 215–24 and Lindgren, 'Adam von Trott's Reisen', 283–9.

190. Michael Balfour, Moltke's later biographer, had been befriended by him since 1936, upon an introduction from Lionel Curtis, when he and his wife visited Kreisau. During the war he served as an official of the British political-warfare establishment (from April 1942 until the end of the war he was Assistant Director of Intelligence in the Psychological Warfare Division of SHAEF). Moltke insisted that the 'stable connection' was to be free of any secret-service connection. Being himself a member of the Abwehr, he well knew about the strange interrelations between the various secret services on both sides, and had come to understand that they were secret to everybody but their opponent; their interference on behalf of the Underground would at best postpone the guillotine for three months.

191. Interview with Dr Johansson, Sigtuna, 4 June 1980.

192. Sometime in 1942 Tracy Strong, on a mission on behalf of American prisoners of war, stopped at the Trott estate in Imshausen. Adam von Trott, who was present, is said to have remarked in a somewhat euphoric mood that the future Europe was to be run by people like Strong; interview with Vera von Trott, 5 Feb. 1978.

193. 'A Memorandum Handed to the Bishop of Chichester by a Traveller from Stockholm, August 30th, 1943', Curtis Papers, Box 28, Bodleian Library, Oxford; reprinted in Ger van Roon, *German Resistance to Hitler: Count von Moltke and the Kreisau Circle* (London, 1971), 364–6.

194. Covering letter from Bishop Bell of Chichester to Lionel Curtis, Chichester, 14 Sept. 1943, Curtis Papers, Box 28, Bodleian Library in von Roon, *German Resistance*, 366–7. Meanwhile, however, Curtis, obviously unaware of Moltke's letter of 25 March, had

written a long 7-page brief on Moltke's background and political views in the form of a letter to W. E. Beckett, Second Legal Adviser at the FO and a former Fellow of All Souls College, Oxford, vouching for his trustworthiness and arguing that it was in Britain's interest to secure his safety, if possible, to enable him to make himself useful to Britain at the end of the war; letter from Lionel Curtis to W. E. Beckett, Oxford, 26 June 1943, FO 371/34450/C 8121/155/G 18. He hoped that the letter would make the rounds in the Foreign Office. Indeed D. Allen of the Central Department minuted on 17 July: 'We have still to be convinced that von Moltke is sincere and that, even if sincere, he is not being made use of to deceive us.'

195. The counterpart to the American FBI.

196. Balfour and Frisby, *Helmuth von Moltke*, 224.

197. See 'Max Josef Metzger', in Annedore Leber, *Das Gewissen steht auf. 64 Lebensbilder aus dem deutschen Widerstand 1933–1945* (Berlin, 1960), 184–6; Metzger, Memorandum an den Erzbischof von Upsala, Juni 1943 in Lipgens (ed.), *Europa-Föderationspläne*, 149–50; Marianne Möhring, *Täter des Wortes: Max Josef Metzger—Leben und Wirken* (Meitingen, 1966); Klaus Drobisch, *Wider den Krieg: Dokumentarbericht über Leben und Sterben des katholischen Geistlichen Dr. Max Josef Metzger* (East Berlin, n.d.).

198. Drobisch, *Wider*, 70–1; for the Solf Circle see above n. 62 in Ch. 4.

199. After their first encounter at the house of Frau Solf, Brother Paulus and Kuenzer met once again upon the latter's initiative and in the presence of an unidentified German businessman just returned from Switzerland. But since Brother Paulus felt uncomfortable about himself and his movement getting actively involved in conspiratorial matters, he decided to discontinue any further dealings with Kuenzer. Kuenzer himself, who had been involved in preparations of the abortive Generals' Plot of 1938 and who thereafter flew to London to urge the British to take Winston Churchill into the government and to stand up against Hitler, was murdered by the SS on 23 April 1945 when the Russians were already in Berlin; see Hugo Stehkämpfer, 'Protest, Opposition und Widerstand im Umkreis der (untergegangenen) Zentrumspartei', in Jürgen Schmädeke and Peter Steinbach (eds.), *Der Widerstand gegen den Nationalsozialismus* (Munich, 1985), 894.

200. Möhring, *Täter*, 149, 227.

201. 'Freistaaten'.

202. 'Friedenspolitik'.

203. Drobisch, *Wider*, 77.

204. Brother Paulus to Sister Gertrudis, 10 Oct. 1943, 'Abba—Vater: Gefangenschaftsbriefe 29. Juni 1943–17. April 1944' (mimeograph, Meitingen nr. Augsburg, n.d.), 17.

205. Letter from Bonhoeffer to Bell, 1 June 1942, Bonhoeffer, *GS* i. 382

206. Boyens, *Kirchenkampf*, ii. 205, 356; see also G. K. A. Bell, *The Church and Humanity*, 48–56. *The Times* in an editorial commented positively on the publication of the letter, pointing out that 'victory alone' was not enough and that it was the Churches' mission to keep alive the 'sense of wider community of mankind'; 'Foundations', *The Times*, 21 Dec. 1940.

207. Walter Lipgens (ed.), *Documents*, ii. 718–19.

208. Boyens, *Kirchenkampf*, ii. 206.

209. 'Some Considerations Concerning the Postwar Settlement'; see above Ch. 5, s. 1.

210. Remember in this respect also Archbishop Temple's extremely cautious reply to Siegmund-Schultze's peace proposal of the summer of 1941; see above Ch. 4, s. 6.

211. He was expelled from the Labour Party early in 1939 for advocating a common front with Communism against Fascism.

212. '*Tribune*', 15 Sept. 1939, quoted in T. D. Burridge, *British Labour and Hitler's War* (London, 1976), 27.

213. In this connection it should be mentioned that early in 1942 Trott's friend from Oxford, Richard Crossman, who was head of the German section of the Political Warfare Executive (PWE), composed a memorandum that recommended emphasizing in the psychological warfare against Germany, what was generally called, the 'hope theme' as against the 'intimidation theme'; it might encourage a 'true Germany' ('wahres Deutschland') movement from among the Christian conservative dissidents. This proposition was approved by the FO, although Anthony Eden hastened to minute that he did not like it 'for Russian reasons'. To be sure, Crossman himself added a note of cynicism to his scheme by arguing

that BBC reports on the 'Christian opposition' should have the effect of 'promoting' a violent attempt by the Gestapo to crush it; R. H. S. Crossman; 'Some Proposals for Political Warfare against Germany', 3 Jan. 1942 minuted by G. W. Harrison and W. Strang and 'A.E.' of the FO; draft by Crossman dated 17 Jan. 1942; approval by the FO (letter P. Scarlett, FO to D. Stephens 27 Jan. 1942); FO 371/30928/C 493/118/18.

214. The tasks assigned to the Commission were: 'First, to clarify the mind of our churches regarding the moral, political and economic foundations of an enduring peace; second, to prepare the people of our churches and of our nation for assuming their appropriate responsibility for the establishment of such a peace; third, to maintain contacts with the Study Department of the World Council of Churches (now in process of formation); fourth, to consider the feasibility of assembling a representative gathering of Christian leaders, lay and clerical, as soon as practicable after an armistice has been declared in any of the wars now being waged, for the purpose of mobilizing the support of the Christian people of all lands in the making of a peace consonant with Christian principles'; 'The Bases of a Just and Durable Peace', *Christendom: An Ecumenical Review* 6 (spring 1941), 317.

215. His grandfather, John Watson Foster, was Secretary of State under President Benjamin Harrison; his uncle, Robert M. Lansing, was Secretary of State under President Woodrow Wilson.

216. See e.g. 'Memorandum regarding Germany, February 8, 1944', John Foster Dulles Papers, Box 24, Princeton University.

217. Ibid.

218. See above Ch. 5, s.1.

219. It is reproduced in full in Lipgens (ed.), *Documents*, ii. 740–3.

220. They read as follows: '1. The peace must provide the political framework for a continuing collaboration of the United Nations and, in due course, of neutral and enemy nations. 2. The peace must make provision for bringing within the scope of international agreement those economic and financial acts of national governments which have widespread international repercussions. 3. The peace must make provision for an organization to adapt the treaty structure of the world to changing underlying conditions. 4. The peace must proclaim the goal of autonomy for subject peoples, and it must establish international organization to ensure and to supervise the realization of that end. 5. The peace must establish procedures for controlling military establishments everywhere. 6. The peace must establish in principle, and seek to achieve in practice, the right of individuals everywhere to religious and intellectual liberty.' Each one of these propositions was followed by an elaborate 'Comment'.

221. *New York Times*, 19 Mar. 1943.

222. *The Times*, 29 July 1943; see also Lipgens (ed.), *Documents*, ii. 740 ff.

223. See Boyens, *Kirchenkampf*, ii. 223.

224. The original German version was entitled 'Bemerkungen zum Friedensprogramm der amerikanischen Kirchen (November 1943)'; WCC ipof No.196/43 International Order. It has been reproduced in *VfZ*, 12 (July 1964), 318–22 and van Roon, *Neuordnung*, 578–82. The original of the English version is classified WCC ipof No.19 E/43 International Order; apart from minor omissions and additions, an added lengthy introduction and conclusion, it is a translation of the German document. A translation of the German document has appeared in van Roon, *German Resistance*, 367–72.

225. Hans Rothfels, 'Trott und die Aussenpolitik des Widerstandes', *VfZ*, 12 (July 1964), 308; Lipgens (ed.), *Documents*, i. 436 also followed Rothfels in his attribution.

226. See esp. van Roon, *Neuordnung*, 309–10.

227. The German term is *Vermassung*.

228. Fritz Ermarth, a clerk of the court ('Referendar') in Baden, was dismissed from government service for political reasons in 1933, after the Nazi seizure of power. In his American exile he dedicated much of his energy as lecturer and publicist (under the pseudonym Hans Schmidt) to the exposure of Nazism and to the advocacy of the 'other Germany'. He was in contact with many of the leading figures among the German political emigration.

229. Letter from Fritz Ermarth to John Foster Dulles, New York, 14 Mar. 1941, John Foster Dulles Papers, Box 20.

230. Letter from Dulles to Ermarth, New York, 17 Mar. 1941, Fritz Ermarth Papers.
231. Letter from Dulles to Ermarth, New York, 6 Oct. 1942, ibid.
232. Letter from Dulles to Ermarth, New York, 8 Jan. 1943, ibid.
233. Letter from Nils Ehrenström to Harry Johansson, 15 Jan. 1943, Utomnordisk Korrespondens E-III-2 1942–43, Sigtuna.
234. Addressing, however, the issue of post-war planning, the Commission on a Just and Durable Peace issued in June 1944 a 'German Statement' advocating the strengthening of the forces inside Germany committed to freedom and international co-operation; among the signatories were John W. Bennett of Union Theological Seminary (featuring as Chairman), Henry Emerson Fosdick of the Riverside Church in Manhattan, the Harvard philosopher William Ernest Hocking, the President of Smith College William Allen Neilson, Reinhold Niebuhr and Henry P. van Dusen of Union Theological Seminary, and the German exiled political scientist Arnold Wolfers teaching at Yale University. 'German Statement', in *Post War World*, 1/4, 15 June 1944, Bell Papers, Box 25.

# 6

## *The Vision and the Mirage*

### 1. The Intelligence Connection: Allen W. Dulles in Berne

All intelligence work has a way of being a game of wits and adventure as much as it is a service with assigned functions, and it has a tendency to make itself independent of the immediate political purpose it is supposed to serve. This maxim applied to the intelligence services on both sides even during the merciless Second World War. 'C', as Sir Stewart Menzies, the head of the British Secret Intelligence Service (MI6) was known in the service, Major General William J. ('Wild Bill') Donovan, the director of the American OSS, and Admiral Wilhelm Canaris, chief of the German Abwehr, were engaged in a deadly enterprise in which, however, they were peers and looked on each other with respect and curiosity. Not unlike the ecumenists, the intelligence chiefs had reason to see themselves engaged, each in his own way, in a 'war behind the war' which was somehow out of kilter with the war that was being 'officially' fought.[1] They lacked, of course, the extraterritoriality enjoyed by the Churches assembled in the World Council. While having direct access to the Prime Minister and having had countless meetings with him during the war, 'C' was not supposed to express opinions on questions of policy-making, except perhaps 'over a cigar'.[2] Donovan was at least at liberty to put before the President recommendations on issues such as 'unconditional surrender'; but these were ignored. Canaris was working under the protective umbrella of the OKW, but hawkishly watched by his rivals in the SS Security Service (RSHA). The intelligence chiefs nevertheless were eager to co-ordinate 'their war'; it is fair to say that they had a common agenda. They knew enough of each other to understand that they agreed on the advisability of overthrowing Hitler and of bringing the war to an end; after Casablanca they all agreed on their distaste for the 'unconditional surrender' policy.

Based on conjecture much nonsense has been written about the relationship between the three men.[3] There is, however, a distinct likelihood that late in 1942 both Canaris and Menzies put out feelers towards each other. Both tried, and predictably both failed. Admiral Canaris let it be known to his opposite number, most probably through Spanish connections, that he was interested in meeting him.[4] 'C' in turn seems to have thought that some arrangement with his German counterpart would be 'in Britain's long-term interests'. Considering the consistently negative policy of the British government towards any overtures from the German opponents of Hitler, however, it is not surprising that 'C' had no encouragement whatsoever from on high and no co-operation from other intelligence departments; his plan was finally thwarted 'in certain Foreign Office quarters "for fear of offending Russia".'[5]

It is of interest, in any case, that MI6 in November 1942, under Hugh Trevor-Roper's direction, prepared a position paper entitled 'Canaris and Himmler' on the Canaris problem.[6] This paper pointed out the rivalry between the Abwehr and the SS Secret Service, and that it was none other than H. A. R. ('Kim') Philby, the notorious Cambridge mole in the service of Russian Intelligence (KGB), sitting high up in the British Secret Intelligence Service, who prevented its circulation as being 'mere speculation'.[7] Then a puzzle to Trevor-Roper, Philby's intransigence is now understandable to us since we know about his double game. It is all the more understandable in view of the fact that the position paper, while not recommending any particular policy towards Germany, suggested that the split between the High Command and the SS could be exploited;[8] it was to go into circulation and furthermore to be shown to the Americans.[9] For Philby of all people it was anathema. Watching out for the interests of Soviet Russia, he was committed to preventing an understanding between any of the Western Allies and the Germans, whether Nazi or anti-Nazi, behind the backs of the Russians, and also to ensure that the break-up of the Reich should not precede the penetration of the Russian armies into Germany. When in May 1943 Trevor-Roper's Section in MI6 was dissociated from Philby's and placed directly under Sir Stewart Menzies, Trevor-Roper's first act, when set free, was to circulate the paper. He kept wondering, however, whether or not anyone read it.[10] In any case, even without Philby, in the context of the fiat of 'absolute silence', the paper would not have got anywhere in official quarters. But might it not, after all, be thought of as a manifestation, however subtle, of the British intelligence community's 'war behind the war'? Therein most likely lies its significance.

On a more restricted and local level, namely in Switzerland, a connection between Canaris's men and the American Secret Service was established late in 1942. The British intelligence station there was not willing to enter into any such adventures and therefore left the field, albeit grudgingly, to the Americans.[11] In any event, altogether new horizons seemed to open up for the scouts among the conspirators when early in November 1942 the American 'spymaster', Allen W. Dulles, arrived in the Swiss capital after a long and adventurous voyage from the United States via Portugal, Spain, and Vichy France. In retaliation for 'Operation Torch', the invasion of French North Africa by the American forces on 8 November, the Germans had just moved into unoccupied France, and only minutes before they closed the frontier to

Switzerland, Dulles managed to slip across the border. Heralded in the local press as the personal representative of President Roosevelt, he set up shop in a flat located in the old sector of town at Herrengasse 23 behind the inconspicuous sign: 'Allen W. Dulles, Special Assistant to the American Minister'.[12]

The mission assigned to Allen Dulles was to gather military, economic, political, and scientific information through nets running to Italy, Austria, Germany, Czechoslovakia, and in particular he was to penetrate Germany in order to obtain information for American policy-makers about the principal enemy; one important means to this end lay in 'the development and maintenance of contacts with Germany's anti-Nazi and underground movements'. So much for the official version of his assignment.[13] It was clearly at variance with his own understanding of his task, according to which he was commissioned 'quietly to render such support and encouragement' as he could to resistance forces working against the Nazis and Fascists in the areas adjacent to Switzerland which were under the rule of Hitler or Mussolini.[14] Here indeed lies the problem concerning Dulles's involvement in the affairs of the German Resistance. It is not that he was a man of passion; quite to the contrary, like his brother John Foster, he was a shrewd and hard-boiled realist. But it is very likely that, operating 'in the field' and 'once removed' from the centre of policy-making and being, in reality, virtually cut off from it, he had a way of making himself independent and of acting on his own. Because of his status of special emissary, Dulles was able to talk with and to support the German Resistance which neither the German Minister nor the Military Attaché of the US Legation were empowered to do.[15] He thus construed his mission as not merely the gathering of information, and his unhappiness about the official policy of 'unconditional surrender' made him all the more accessible to the agents of the German Resistance. Though without any executive powers, Dulles understood his function towards them as being 'to encourage, stimulate, support, guide'.[16] Needless to say, all his actions were predicated upon his understanding that he represented the US government to the German Resistance and not the reverse.

Since, with the German occupation of Vichy France, Switzerland was now completely surrounded by Nazi and Fascist border guards, Dulles was unable to import personnel from Washington and so had to recruit his staff from Americans who were on the scene. As his right-hand man he chose Gero von Schulze Gaevernitz, a naturalized American of German extraction whose father, an old acquaintance of Dulles from the days before the First World War, was a distinguished German political scientist who had been a delegate for the Democratic Party to the Weimar National Assembly. From his father young Gaevernitz had inherited the libertarian ethos as well as wide social connections. A dapper bachelor and an adventurer of sorts, he had sown his wild oats while travelling in Russia and working in the United States.

Subsequently, upon the outbreak of the war, he offered his services to the American authorities in Berne since, as he later explained, he had 'somehow the feeling, however hard to explain' that 'somehow and sometime' he could make himself useful there in the struggle against Hitler.[17] He was, moreover, although a complete amateur in questions of international relations, in the almost unique situation of being able, at least through the early phases of the war, to shuttle back and forth between Switzerland and Germany.[18] At first he served as liaison to the German exiles in the American Legation where he was a friend of the First Secretary and the Military Attaché; but upon the arrival of Allen Dulles they turned him over to work for the OSS.[19] Gaevernitz's strong commitment to the cause of German Resistance made him a perfect and, considering the rigid instructions that governed Dulles, perhaps too perfect, interpreter between his chief and the *Widerstand*. Indeed he went away from his first meeting with the American spymaster, which most probably took place in November 1942, with an understanding of the Dulles mission that surpassed even Dulles's own, to wit that 'U.S. policy is to help the anti-Hitler Resistance within Germany'.[20] Furthermore, from a private conversation with his chief, Gaevernitz seems to have inferred that in the last stages of the war Dulles was at least considering 'going around the Truman–Churchill–Stalin order against talking with the German high command about a secret and separate surrender'.[21]

In any case, Gaevernitz harboured views on the German situation which were by no means in concert with the directives from Washington. He identified with the emissaries of the German Resistance to such a degree that it is now virtually impossible to distinguish in his memoranda what can be attributed to them and what to him.[22] But quite clearly he was critical of the silence on the part of the American and British governments with regard to post-war plans which, he argued, had the effect of prolonging the war and militated against the one alternative to a bolshevization of Germany, namely a revolution from above. He envisaged a stalemate settlement, with the Wehrmacht remaining intact; but such an outcome was threatened by the Allied insistence on 'unconditional surrender'. Was it then altogether a formality when Allen Dulles later attested that he had 'relied heavily' on Gaevernitz for guidance 'in all matters' relating to their work directed towards Germany?[23]

There were others on Dulles's randomly chosen staff in Berne who were no less given to exceeding their brief than he himself and Gaevernitz, among them in particular Mary Bancroft, an expatriate from Boston. In Zurich she became a student and patient of the great psychologist Carl Gustav Jung with whom, after being enlisted into Dulles's services, she shared her intelligence secrets.[24] At one point, so she later recollected, the spymaster got sufficiently annoyed at her to snap: 'I wish you'd stop this nonsense. I don't want to go down in history as a footnote to a case of Jung's.'[25] But the Jungian influence upon her served no doubt to confirm her sympathies for her chief German contact, the German Vice-Consul Hans Bernd Gisevius, as also her strong distaste for 'unconditional surrender'.[26] In short, the stage was set for an intimate co-operation between the establishment in the Herrengasse and the German conspirators as well as for a thorough misunderstanding on the part of the latter of its chances of being heard in Washington. The Dulles mission thus encouraged a pattern, which increasingly was to govern the activities abroad of the German Resistance during the period after Stalingrad, of heightened expectations and of a feverish vision which, in the last analysis, was bound to be a mirage.

Neutral Switzerland was of course swarming with exiles, spies, and secret-service agents, Nazis, anti-Nazis, and sheer curiosity-seekers, and before long they converged upon Allen Dulles; the *querelles allemandes*, and not only those, one might say, were fought out in the Herrengasse. It was Gaevernitz who was in a position to separate the wheat from the chaff, and he performed this task with utmost skill, steering Dulles to the right people and warning him against the wrong ones. Of course Dulles would see exiles. While he did not have much use for *emigrés* who, according to Mary Bancroft, 'bored the hell out of him',[27] he did listen to political exiles.[28] Wilhelm Hoegner he singled out as 'an invaluable adviser' on internal German conditions.[29] Hoegner served him as a liaison to other left-wing exiled politicians, among them the former Prussian Prime Minister Otto Braun and ex-Chancellor Joseph Wirth, with whom he combined forces with the objective of exerting some influence on Allied post-war planning. The co-operation between the Socialists and Centrists in exile was no easier than it had been in the Weimar days, and it was Wirth in particular, always distrustful and all too quickly offended, and excessively under the influence of red wine, who made things difficult. Nevertheless these exiles got together in 1943 in an informal group which called itself 'Das demokratische Deutschland'.[30] For the most part the contact between Dulles and the group was maintained through Gaevernitz who put its members to work on writing reports for him.[31] Thus in November 1943 Hoegner composed a number of memoranda, one on a possible restructuring of Germany and another one on the future of Bavaria.[32] In the summer of 1943 the group emerged with a comprehensive, albeit rather high-flown, memorandum, in the name of the German people and addressed to the 'top leaders of the Anglo-Saxon family of peoples', concerning the integration of a reconstructed federal and democratic Germany into the 'European Association of States'. For one reason or another it was handed to the American Minister in Berne, Leland Harrison who, after receiving it without comment, forwarded it to Washington with comments.[33] The memorandum, however, went unanswered.[34]

As a liaison to the German Resistance the key figure turned out to be Hans Bernd Gisevius,[35] a man, at first sight, of distinctly questionable make-up and background. He was a shy, rather stiff, if not somewhat 'brutal looking',[36] Prussian of unusual height. He had a Nazi and Gestapo background but then turned his back on the Nazi fraud and became, after the Röhm purge of June 1934, an inveterate conspirator against the regime. But even in Resistance circles Gisevius was always a quite controversial figure who had strong advocates—like Schacht—as well as detractors, like, initially at least, General Beck. 'Tiny', as he was generally called in his circles, appeared in 1940 as Vice-Consul in the German Consulate-General in Zurich; in fact he was sent there as an agent of the Canaris organization with the assignment of establishing ties abroad on behalf of the *Widerstand*. His chequered career as well as his murky credentials were anything but confidence inspiring. Gaevernitz himself avoided Gisevius until a friend of the former, Eduard Waetjen on a visit from Berlin, himself in the service of the Abwehr, pointed out to him that, despite all appearances, it would be a great mistake to shun the man any further.[37] In this way contact between Dulles and the German underground was established, and Gisevius became in the OSS code world 'Luber' or number '512'.[38]

Gisevius's effectiveness as intermediary between Canaris and Dulles became jeopardized, however, when Himmler's suspicions were directed towards him in the early spring of 1943 after the discovery of an underground scheme by Dohnanyi and Bonhoeffer to assist a number of German Jews to escape across the border to Switzerland under the guise of Abwehr agents.[39] The ensuing investigations afforded Himmler the opportunity to strike against the Abwehr and led to the arrest of Bonhoeffer, Dohnanyi, and Josef Müller, and Oster himself was for the moment suspended from service. Gisevius was ordered back to Berlin to testify, but when the interrogations there came too close for his comfort, he managed to escape back to Switzerland by a devious route; he could, however, no longer risk returning to Germany.[40] To take over his function as liaison between Switzerland and Germany, however, the Abwehr early in 1944 appointed Eduard Waetjen as Vice-Consul in the Zurich Consulate-General.[41] Waetjen was a very different type from his predecessor in Zurich. A descendant of a prominent Berlin family—his father was a prosperous banker and his mother was an American—he had attended the exclusive boarding school at Salem under the direction of the great schoolmaster Kurt Hahn.[42] Early in 1931, much to the dismay of Hahn, Waetjen had joined the Nazi Party but left it again the following year. He was a close friend of Moltke and since 1940 had been in constant contact in Berlin with him and his friends. For some reason Dulles found Waetjen more congenial than Gisevius. Like Dulles, Waetjen was a lawyer, and both were socially as well as by virtue of their education on the same wavelength.[43] In any event, in January 1944 Waetjen became the OSS's 'Gorter' or number '670'. When, in April, Waetjen in turn also became suspect and could no longer return to Berlin, the shuttle services were carried on by Theodor

Strünck, who finally paid with his life for his uncompromising opposition to the Nazi regime.

It was during his visit to Switzerland in January 1943 that Trott first established contact with Allen Dulles. For reasons of security Dulles never saw Trott in person but always dealt with him through intermediaries. This time it was Visser't Hooft—incidentally OSS's number 474—who approached the American on behalf of his German protégé[44] and who managed to forward to him a statement by Trott outlining his and his fellow-conspirators' position.[45]

The message that reached Dulles expressed the 'deep disappointment' of the German Opposition over the lack of encouragement or understanding from abroad and over the insistence of the Western Allies on German military defeat 'regardless of what new regime may be created'.[46] Lashing out against the 'pharisaic condemnation and bourgeois prejudice' which he had encountered, Trott conjured up the vision of a German eastward orientation and a 'new Europe ... based on the brotherliness and experience of the oppressed common people'. This version of Trott's 'European Revolution' was hardly fit to appeal to the establishmentarian instincts of Mr Dulles; indeed all he did was to transmit to Washington the information in the Trott message for purposes of psychological warfare. At this point at least Dulles stated emphatically that he did not believe 'that there is any serious organ-ization of the opposition group in Germany and that, short of a complete military victory for the Allies, they should expect or be led to expect any encouragement from us or any dealing with us'. It can hardly be assumed that Dulles ventured this recommendation, which anticipated the proclamation of 'unconditional surrender' by ten days, only for Washington's consumption. Before long, however, he was to change his opinion on the German Resist-ance. At any rate, from early in 1943 Washington was, through its special representative in Berne, kept abreast of the fact that some sort of conspiracy against Nazism was afoot in Germany.

Starting late in August 1943 a very different kind of information reached Allen Dulles via an official of the Auswärtiges Amt by the name of Fritz Kolbe who had devised a scheme to have himself assigned as special courier to the German Legation in Switzerland and who, in the course of periodic trips across the German–Swiss border, turned over to the OSS post in Berne German documents containing vital diplomatic, strategic, and technical intel-ligence. In his book on the German Underground Allen Dulles made no mention of Fritz Kolbe, but he included the Kolbe case, which came to be coded as Operation 'Kappa'—Kolbe himself was renamed 'George Wood'—in his subsequent volume, *Great True Spy Stories*.[47] Was Kolbe, then, a spy and not a resister? The distinction between espionage and resistance, like the one between treason and resistance, is blurred; but it must be maintained. A spy is generally a professional whereas a resister is not, and the latter is impelled into action because of certain beliefs for which he is ready to stand up. Also, a spy communicates information to another, generally hostile, party, primarily in return for personal gain; a resister, by contrast, communicates information to the other party because, again, he finds himself in an extreme situation and chooses this extreme path as a last resort, but certainly not for personal gain. Hans Ritter, who took payments from Group Captain Malcolm G. Christie, was, however otherwise elevated his motives were, a German who spied for Britain. Allen Dulles, in the course of his tour of duty in Berne listened to spies, no doubt, as well as resisters. But into which category did Fritz Kolbe belong? Was he a spy, or was he after all a man of character and conscience who decided to offer resistance to the Nazi regime?

Fritz Kolbe was beyond all doubt a staunch opponent of the Nazi regime.[48] Though in a sensitive position in the Foreign Service, he avoided joining the Nazi Party. In the early stages of the war he had actually planned to escape over the Swiss border, but was dissuaded from doing so by his fatherly friend, Prelate Georg Schreiber, one of the leading Centrist politicians of the Weimar Republic and himself a declared foe of Nazism. Schreiber persuaded Kolbe that it would be more important to stay and to use his position to fight the Nazis.[49] Thus he laid the plans for his courier runs, and to do this for money was altogether out of keeping with the character of the man.[50]

Originally Kolbe had approached the British; but once again the British intelligence station, all too suspicious, refused to get involved. The case was then handled within the American intelligence community by Dulles's associate Gerald Mayer who since May 1942, under the cover title of 'Press Attaché' at the Legation, was in fact working for the Office of the Co-ordinator of Information (COI).[51] Mayer, like Gaevernitz, had a special feel for things German, and it was largely due to his judgement that the case which yielded truly spectacular results for American intelligence was pursued.[52]

Although Kolbe was close to various leading figures of the Resistance, he stayed away from involvement with any conspiratorial groups as he doubted that their elaborate planning would lead to success; and late in 1943, when during one of his escapades into Switzerland he confided to Dulles that he was finally considering joining the Underground, he was dissuaded from this plan by the spymaster who used all his talents for argument to convince Kolbe that his greatest service to the anti-Hitler cause would be to continue his courier service across the frontier.[53] This he did.

Fritz Kolbe, a rather simple but self-assured person, was one of the solitary witnesses of the German Resistance.[54] Dulles (code number 110) reported to Washington that 'Wood',

while intelligent is somewhat naïve and appears to have none of the characteristics which would qualify him to pull off doublecrossing game. So far under hours of questioning he has failed to give any clue which would raise question of his genuineness ...[55]

Kolbe was, as he described himself, 'a patriotic German with a human conscience'.[56] The service he rendered to the Americans he really rendered to his own country in order to free it from the Nazi plague. Can we not, then, conclude that he was indeed a patriot and neither a spy nor a traitor? After the war was over, however, the new German Foreign Office did not honour his application for reinstatement; he was deemed untrustworthy.[57]

All sorts of wires came together in Herrengasse 23; in order to accomplish his primary task of obtaining essential intelligence about the principal enemy, Dulles had to have traffic with all sorts of characters and not merely opponents of the Nazi regime. He once said to his sister, so the biographer of the Dulles family tells us, that he would tip his hat to the devil himself if it would help him to get a clearer picture of conditions in hell.[58] Thus he would even have to sound out adherents of the Nazi regime. In themselves such encounters would be of little consequence here, were it not for the fact that they also throw some interesting light on the German Resistance and on some of its ambiguities.

It is common knowledge that cross-connections existed between the Resistance and the SS.[59] Not only did Himmler keep himself informed about the activities of the various opposition circles, but after the winter of 1942/3, when the tides of the war in Russia turned against Germany, a situation arose in which it became apparent to some men in the SS hierarchy, as well as to some men in the Resistance, that the interests of both groups converged and that they should join forces in overthrowing Hitler. Within the Nazi hierarchy it was particularly Walter Schellenberg, from 1941 head of Amt VI concerned with foreign political intelligence in the Reich Main Security Office (RSHA), who developed a scheme to play off Himmler and the SS against Hitler to free Germany of the tyrant. But such a calculation was not confined to SS circles.

Even within the Resistance itself the possibility of an alliance, however temporary, with the SS had matured.[60] Enquiries went out to certain generals of the SS as to whether they were prepared to go along with a coup against Hitler.[61] There was also the group around Johannes Popitz, including the lawyer Carl Langbehn, which, weary of the continued unwillingness of the Generals to take action against Hitler, fell back on the proposition of staging the coup with Himmler and the SS. While in the period before the outbreak of the war the 'moderate' Göring had appeared the most likely, at least transitional, alternative to Hitler, he had lost much of his prestige through his manifest failure to protect the German cities from Allied air attacks, and now his standing was seriously compromised. Meanwhile, however, Himmler's star had risen, and it had become known that this almighty ruler over the Nazi élite guard and the secret police and, since August 1943, also of the Ministry of Interior, was grooming himself to succeed the Führer.[62] If, then, 'some of the highest leaders of the SS' had, as Langbehn reported to his fellow conspirators, come to understand the necessity of getting rid of Hitler,[63] the question remained whether 'Himmler and company' would play such a game and, of course, what effect such a procedure would have abroad.[64]

The OSS chief in Switzerland was also exposed to this strange SS–*Widerstand* connection, first through the ubiquitous Prince Max von Hohenlohe who appeared in Berne early in 1943. Since the late 1930s this international intriguer had never ceased to peddle his wares. Chiefly interested in protecting his widespread landed properties, he had obtained access to the inner councils of almost every European capital where he generally presented himself as a harbinger of peace.[65] The European high aristocracy to which he belonged knew no national boundaries, and this war in particular he viewed as destructive and fratricidal. In Germany Hohenlohe's position was also that of a trimmer: he cultivated ties with the Nazi Party and the SS as well as with the Resistance. While his initiative in Berne cannot by any stretch of the imagination be identified as either a Nazi or a Resistance venture, Hohenlohe once again saw himself called upon to use his wide and varied connections to play a decisive part in European diplomacy and now in particular to do his part in stemming the menace of Bolshevism.

The three meetings between Dulles and Hohenlohe that took place in the period between 15 January and 3 April 1943 were accompanied by elaborate provisions for security. The two men were no strangers to one another. They had met in 1916, when Allen Dulles was a junior attaché in the American Embassy in Vienna, and again after the war when Hohenlohe, on the occasion of various visits to the United States, was repeatedly a guest of the Dulles brothers on Long Island.[66] Now, in this extraordinary setting of secrecy, 'Mr Bull' and 'Herr Pauls'[67] ranged widely over the issues of war and peace, and while 'Mr Bull' did not hold back on sharp criticism of the German conduct of war and the treatment of subject populations, he in turn, so the transcripts tell us, expressed a distinct distaste for the 'bankrupt politicians, emigrants and prejudiced Jews' he had hitherto dealt with. He also voiced his preference for a federative Greater Germany in the heart of Europe to play a constructive part in staving off Bolshevism and Pan-Slavism.

In view of the obvious unauthenticity of the documentary evidence it would be a mistake to hold Allen Dulles responsible for the opinions attributed to him. He was clearly engaged, as he himself later put it, in a 'fishing expedition',[68] and he did manage to extract some intelligence from his princely friend. The news of dissension within the Nazi hierarchy alone was worth the whole venture.[69] Also, Reinhard Spitzy most probably appeared to him as a proper tool to probe further into centres of resistance. Spitzy was an Austrian SS officer who, after the *Anschluss*, had joined the Auswärtiges Amt where his work for Erich Kordt opened his eyes to the perniciousness of Ribbentrop's foreign policy. But even if subsequently he went into the services of the Abwehr 'Abteilung Z', he nevertheless managed to manœuvre skilfully in and out of the conspiracy. He identified as much with the affairs of the Abwehr rebels around Oster as he remained initiated in the affairs of the SS. He, if anyone, personified the strange convergence between the SS and the Resistance.[70]

Late in April Spitzy was drawn by Dulles into a session *à trois* with ex-Chancellor Wirth with the expectation that he might activate the 'southern connection' which in the early stages of the war had been Christie's objective.[71] There was some talk from the American that, after the defeat of Germany, southern Germany could expect a far better treatment than Prussia. Dulles also pointedly enquired after General Halder who, he had been assured by the 'Wirth Circle', was 'one of the sharpest opponents of the Hitler dictatorship'. These three men were strange bedfellows, but they could quite clearly agree on their alertness to the Russian menace and their distaste for the 'unconditional surrender' formula, and Dulles's promise to be ready at 'any time' to prevail upon Washington to enter into negotiations with a 'really serious Opposition in Germany' was likely to be music in the ears of his two partners.

We should not dispose of this chapter of the Resistance foreign policy with a moral condemnation of Wirth for taking part in the discussion 'harmoniously with an SS man'.[72] Wirth, if not wicked, was foolish as usual; somehow he liked to deal with secret services, and he got lost in that slippery terrain. Spitzy obviously enjoyed the double game he played. Dulles was on his 'fishing expedition'. And we are left to wonder what the SS officers in Berlin, who were the recipients of the report, made of it?

The German military reverses in Russia and the Allied invasion of southern Italy in July shook the myth of Hitler's invincibility and encouraged people to think of peace negotiations that would prevent a total débâcle for the German war machine. Also, the successful coup of Marshal Badoglio of 25 July 1943 against Mussolini was bound to raise new hopes among the German conspirators against Hitler; even though they were keenly aware of the fact that the Italian situation was altogether different from the one in Germany, they were now emboldened to develop plans for a palace revolt in Germany too. Such plans were initiated by Carl Langbehn in conjunction with his friends Popitz, Jens Peter Jessen, and the former State Secretary in the Reich Chancellery, Erwin Planck; Albrecht Haushofer was also in the know.[73] Langbehn was an influential Berlin lawyer of unusual independence and fearlessness. A Party member since 1933, he offered his services to defend in court victims of Nazi persecution; and while he definitely turned against the regime in 1938 when his law professor Fritz Pringsheim, a non-Aryan, was sent to a concentration camp,[74] he nevertheless continued to function as Himmler's personal lawyer. It was this special connection which allowed him to launch the scheme to engage the powerful leader of the SS in a coup against Hitler.

As a matter of fact, in December 1942 Langbehn had already approached the American OSS representative in Stockholm, Bruce Hopper, with a similar proposition,[75] and since May of the following year he had pestered Waffen SS Lieutenant-General Karl Wolff, Himmler's personal Chief of Staff, to arrange for a Popitz–Himmler meeting that might pave the way for his plan. The encounter between these two, then, took place on 26 August in the strictest secrecy in the Ministry of the Interior[76] whose direction Himmler had just recently taken over.[77] Popitz, so it seems, did most of the talking, broaching to the inscrutable Reichsführer SS the need for revamping the leadership of the Reich and identifying personalities, other than Ribbentrop and acceptable to the Western Allies, who would conduct the inevitable peace negotiations with them. This is as far as Popitz thought he could go. Actually Langbehn had hoped he would go all the way and propose a displacement of Hitler, and this is what he confided to Wolff. In any event, Himmler in the end authorized Langbehn to travel to Switzerland for the purpose of exploring the readiness of the Western Allies to enter into peace talks.

Langbehn lost no time in embarking upon his most unusual and hazardous mission, and one of his prime targets was the American OSS mission [78] where he presented his design to Gaevernitz. The latter, according to his own testimony, was quite taken by the proposition aimed at undermining the Nazi regime from within by playing the SS against the Party, and promised to take the matter up with his chief.[79]

The next we know is that after his return to Germany Langbehn had one meeting with Himmler,[80] but was soon thereafter arrested by the Gestapo, together with his wife and his secretary Marie-Luise Sarre. A coded cable from an unindentified Allied mission in Berne,[81] reporting on Langbehn's activities in Switzerland, had been intercepted by the Gestapo, and, to save his own skin, Himmler chose the path of exposing the 'treachery' of Langbehn. Popitz's attempts to intervene with Himmler on Langbehn's behalf remained unanswered.

Langbehn was a 'fanatic in the cause of justice and assistance to others'; but he was no less a 'gambler' willing to take enormous chances.[82] No doubt, his and Popitz's project was worse than amateurish. They allied with and abandoned themselves to a scoundrel on whom they had no reason to put their reliance. From their fellow conspirators, furthermore, they had only hesitant encouragement for their venture. Even Oster, a professional in deception and undercover work, was, so we are told, opposed to it, and when he informed Beck and Witzleben about it, they assented only 'with a heavy heart'.[83] Goerdeler himself had distinctly mixed feelings about the Langbehn initiative.[84] Apart from risking the ignominy of failure, Popitz and Langbehn also took it upon themselves to compromise the credibility of the German Resistance towards the outside world which, in any case, was predisposed to distrust the approaches from the *Widerstand* as being inspired by the Secret

Service.[85] On balance, then, this 'war behind the war' in the realm of the secret services, turned out to be full of pitfalls; and in this case certainly it seriously impaired the ethical stature of the German Resistance.

## 2. Kreisau Initiatives 1943–1944. Foreign Policy Statements and Explorations in Turkey, Sweden, and Switzerland

During 12–14 June 1943, which was the Whitsun weekend, the third major meeting of Moltke's Circle took place in Kreisau. One of the main points of its agenda, apart from the international economic order and the punishment of war criminals, was foreign policy, and it was Adam von Trott, by now recognized as the Kreisau foreign affairs expert, who gave the report about this area to the assembled group.

The basic outlines of a Kreisau foreign policy for the post-war era were outlined in a number of drafts and in the protocols of this third meeting of the group.[86] They are marked by a holistic vision of a European continent regenerated by the canons of Christianity[87] as well as by commitment to basic human rights, and of an international order that made possible a displacement of national sovereignties with a pervasive structure of autonomous but interdependent units from the family and the 'small community' upwards:

A just and durable peace cannot be based on force. It can only be achieved through commitment to the divine order which upholds man's inward and outward existence. Only when it is possible to make this order the measure of the relationships between men and nations will it be possible to overcome the moral and material confusion of our time and to establish a genuine peace.

and

The special responsibility and loyalty that everyone owes to his nation, his language and the spiritual and historical traditions of his people must be respected and protected. It must, however, not be abused for the benefit of the amassing of political power and for the degradation, persecution and oppression of foreign peoples. The free and peaceful development of national culture is incompatible with the retention of absolute sovereignty by each individual state.[88]

Any peace settlement, the Kreisau people insisted, was to be founded upon the internal order of the contingent powers. As far as Germany was concerned, it was to accomplish its own domestic regeneration as a result of a 'spontaneous initiative' rather than of foreign pressure.[89] But in that case Germany was to assume in a new international order the function of mediating between the 'revolutionary' East and the 'restaurative' West,[90] that is between the collective socialism of Soviet Russia and the 'outworn forms of individualistic liberalism'[91] as profiled in America. Short of pushing the proposition of a 'European revolution' as launched by Trott in his letter to Percy E. Corbett of June 1941, the Kreisau documents envisaged a special place for Germany within the co-ordinates marked by the United States, Great Britain, and Soviet Russia. The Kreisau foreign policy statements, then, outlined a strategy for a regenerated Reich to safeguard the integrity of European life.[92] They projected, especially in consideration of the outer-European interests of the major Powers of the Grand Alliance, a vision of a post-war order in which Germany was to play the part of a guarantor of European interests.[93]

A few days after his return from Kreisau, Moltke wrote to his wife from Berlin: 'I had already seen with Husen[94] that the four days had an aura of blissful transfiguration; it was the same with Adam and Eugen. Naturally I was very happy about this, for in some respects this transfiguration is more important than the concrete result. But in that respect, too, there was general satisfaction ...'.[95] They could now fall back on a broad consensus and on clearly spelled-out positions. But with the tides of war turning against their country and with the news of German war crimes multiplying, they were faced with an increasing sense of urgency. The high principles, as spelled out in Kreisau, now had to be translated into reality. An understanding with the Allies had to be reached that would stave off the deluge and salvage both a minimal territorial integrity of the Reich and the moral legitimacy for themselves who were aspiring to be recognized abroad as the spokesmen for a regenerated Germany.

If the men of the Kreisau Circle, then, took the long view of things, they did not shy away from action. Moltke in particular has all too readily been relegated to the 'ivory tower of contemplative intellectual activity by Wheeler-Bennett.[96] No doubt, the former harboured grave misgivings against political assassination, but from the summer of 1943 he, together with Trott, moved resolutely into 'the eye of the storm'[97] by taking the initiative in the hazardous undertaking of making a case abroad for the German Resistance.

Turkey was a prime target of the Kreisau group. In fact, immediately following the meeting at Kreisau, Trott, who had recently been promoted in the Foreign Office to the rank of Legation Secretary,[98] took off for Turkey.[99] There his chief objective was to persuade Franz von Papen, since 1939 German Ambassador in Ankara, to join the conspiracy. Papen had weathered many a storm during the Nazi regime, whether by virtue of his agility or his fickleness. But while official Nazi Germany still considered him something of an asset, in particular as a window to the outside world, the Resistance thought of him as a pivotal person of potential value to it. No one harboured any illusions about Papen. He was known to be weak and vacillating, but ever since he had given his famous Marburg address on 17 June 1934, in which he had severely taken the regime to task, he was thought of in opposition circles as a possible ally.[100] He had been initiated into the affairs of the

Resistance sometime early in 1943, and he liked to think of 'Herr von Trott zu Solz' as 'my contact with the German opposition group'.[101] As a matter of fact, Trott's Turkish trip took place in response to an invitation by the Ambassador in early May.[102] Now the two managed to have a 'very open discussion'; Papen, however, could not be won over to a firm commitment to the cause of resistance.[103]

Helmuth von Moltke's journey to Turkey, which took place from 5 to 10 July, was a sequel to Trott's earlier trip. Authorized by Admiral Canaris,[104] its overt purpose was for Moltke, together with his colleague from the Abwehr, Dr Wilhelm Wengler, to prevail upon the Turkish government to return to Germany a fleet of French-owned Danubian ships momentarily interned in the Sea of Marmara. But while Wengler followed up on this official assignment, Moltke went about his particular concern: the connection with the greater world.[105]

In contrast to his strangely quixotic Abwehr chief, Moltke prepared his ground in Istanbul carefully. He never bothered with Mr Earle, and a brief encounter with Papen convinced him of the fact that, as he said to Wengler, 'the man is absolutely deplorable'.[106] Moltke, however, had reliable and influential friends among the German colony in the city. In the German Embassy itself he could rely on an attaché, Gebhardt von Walther, who was always ready to pave his way.[107] But above all there was Paul Leverkühn with whom he had been in legal partnership in Berlin in 1938/9,[108] and who was now the head of the Abwehr office in Istanbul. There was also Professor Hans Wilbrandt,[109] now a German exile in the service of Atatürk, on whose friendship and help Moltke could count. Wilbrandt in turn was able to enlist his friend, the economist Alexander Rüstow who was more politically minded and willing and able to engage his connections with the American Secret Service on behalf of the German emissary.

As yet this particular visit to Turkey was of an exploratory nature. In the course of long sessions with Wilbrandt and Rüstow schemes of every kind, all of them more or less unrealistic, were explored: might not a German General Staff officer be made to parachute over England with military plans that would provide information for an opening in the German Western front for an Allied invasion? Was there perhaps a way for Moltke to be flown to Cairo in order to reach his old friend from Berlin, Alexander Kirk, now the American Ambassador to Egypt?[110] If Kirk was unavailable, might not Dorothy Thompson be reached, or else Field Marshal Smuts who was an old friend of Moltke's South African family? Since none of these schemes, of course, worked out, Moltke had to return to Berlin without any tangible results.

Along two lines, however, some headway was made. In a discussion 'under four eyes' between Moltke and Rüstow it became evident that there was strong disagreement between the two on the question of 'unconditional

surrender'. Moltke, who energetically argued the line hitherto firmly maintained by virtually all Resistance people, opposing 'unconditional
surrender',[111] encountered energetic confutation on this point from Rüstow.
Even Moltke, who even during the war had made a point of reading *The
Times*, available to him through his official work, seems, like most of his
friends in Germany, to have been unaware of the degree of determination by
the Allies to see the war through to the end. Rüstow, in turn, while not at all
unsympathetic to Moltke's position, was clearly more attuned to the Allied
grand strategy and knew what the traffic could bear. He therefore assured
Moltke that in the light of the Allied determination his position was 'utopian'
and that in any case any peace terms would by necessity be more severe under
the pressure of the threat of the Third Reich than later after its collapse. The
most favourable terms for Moltke and his friends to obtain from the other
side, advised Rüstow, were the assurance that Germany be occupied by the
Western Allies alone; any previous peace terms would have only an adverse
effect on this situation. As Rüstow finally made his further help to Moltke
dependent on the latter's acceptance of 'unconditional surrender', he finally
convinced him of the wisdom of his position. Moltke thus abandoned one of
the central arguments maintained by the emissaries who went abroad. This
change of heart certainly would weaken his position towards the Generals at
home; but would it accordingly enhance his chance of getting a hearing and
consideration abroad?[112]

Moltke's July trip to Turkey yielded another result that might possibly have
been beneficial to his cause. Through Wilbrandt and Rüstow a connection was
established with the OSS. All along Moltke had been sceptical concerning
any entanglement with the secret services, but now this connection turned
out to offer the one possibility for him to reach his targets and especially
Kirk. The OSS in Turkey was in the hands of Lanning Macfarland, a banker
from Illinois. With Archibald Frederick Coleman, a journalist connected
with the *Saturday Evening Post*, he had built up an elaborate intelligence
network called 'Cereus'.[113] One of the two branches of 'Cereus' was the
'Dogwood' chain, formally under Coleman, but in fact increasingly under
the control of its chief agent, a Czech engineer code-named 'Dogwood'. It
was unusual for the OSS to rely as heavily as did Macfarland and Coleman
on a foreigner. But by all accounts 'Dogwood' was a man of unusual drive,
self-confidence, and persuasiveness. The 'crafty agent DOGWOOD', an OSS
dispatch attested, became 'the key to any solution of the penetration of OSS
in Istanbul'.[114] He had previously worked for British Intelligence and was
subsequently turned over to the OSS in Istanbul which, to give him the
necessary cover, founded for him a company called 'Vestern Elektrik'. In fact
it had become the front for 'Cereus' and its elaborate Central European
intelligence ventures. Although 'Dogwood' made a point of staying in the
background and of not personally negotiating with Moltke,[115] he took, as

Rüstow later attested, a 'passionate interest'[116] in the negotiations.[117]

Late in October 1943 Moltke finally received the news that his contacts in Turkey had succeeded in establishing the connection with Ambassador Kirk in Cairo and that the latter was prepared to come to Turkey. Upon Coleman's insistence code-names had been assigned all around: Rüstow became 'Magnolia', Wilbrandt 'Hyacinth', and the OKW became 'Camelia'; only Moltke was spared an inclusion in the florarium: his code designation became 'Hermann' and the Kreisau Circle accordingly became the 'Hermann Group'. The stage was now all set;[115] at least the exiles turned American secret-service agents envisaged a 'far-reaching' co-operation between the anti-Nazi members of the Wehrmacht and the American civilian and military authorities, including even an assurance, 'in view of the fear of Bolshevism in German conservative circles', that 'Germany will be given an undisturbed opportunity to adopt a democratic form of Government'.[119]

On 11 December Moltke, once again with explicit sanction from Canaris, appeared in Istanbul. Contrary to expectations, however, there was no Alexander Kirk. This much we know: all kinds of alternatives were considered in the Office of the Military Attaché in Ankara to obtain special planes and the prerequisite clearings from the Turkish and British authorities either to bring Kirk over to Istanbul or to fly Moltke to Cairo.[120] A suggestion to bring Moltke and the American Ambassador to Turkey, Laurence Steinhardt together, was rejected because the security problem was considered 'dangerous'.[121]

Stranded in Turkey, Moltke wrote a long letter to Kirk[122] in which he explained why he would be unable to see anybody else before having seen him who was familiar with both the problems of living in a totalitarian state and the uncertain credentials of someone like himself. On this basis alone could military and political co-operation for the 'common cause' be outlined. In the concluding paragraph Moltke held out the prospect of his returning to Istanbul by mid-February at the earliest and at the latest in mid-April. An interview with the American Military Attaché, Brigadier General Richard G. Tindall, yielded no results. Tindall had come to Istanbul especially for the occasion, and he and Moltke met in the apartment of an Austrian merchant. But the American was a rather stiff and unimaginative fellow who thought primarily of using Moltke for espionage purposes.[123] This, obviously, was not Moltke's idea. He was no spy; he was a resister who wanted to enter into political negotiations with the other side. This subtle distinction entirely escaped General Tindall. As for Moltke's letter, it is very uncertain that it ever reached its destination; and the supposed curt answer by Kirk to the effect that he saw no purpose in meeting, since he was of the conviction that 'nothing short of unconditional surrender of the German armed forces' would terminate the war in Europe, was most probably not authentic.[124] Moltke took leave of his friend Wilbrandt with the words: 'Now all is lost.'[125]

There was a documentary sequel at least to the Moltke visit which had started under such good auspices but which, like all the other missions of this kind, failed. After his departure, his friends sat down to compose an Exposé which they hoped would find its way to the highest echelons in Washington.[126] After outlining the composition and strength of the German Opposition, greatly exaggerating the weight of the pro-Russian orientation and the 'powerful echo' evoked by the foundation of the League of German Officers in Russia, it spelled out 'Conditions of Collaboration with the Allies'. These were headed by a forthright anticipation by 'the Group' of 'unequivocal military defeat and occupation of Germany' and its acceptance of the Allied demand for unconditional surrender. These terms, however, were made contingent on German military support of an Allied landing in the west and, in turn, a consolidation of the eastern front along the line from Lemberg (Lvov) to Tilsit (Sovetsk)[127] that would prevent a Russian occupation of Germany. A western orientation of a future Germany as secured by this intricate manœuvre, however, was not to obviate a 'whole-hearted policy of collaboration with Russia' in the realm of foreign affairs.

Eugen Gerstenmaier was correct in arguing that the Exposé cannot be considered as reflecting Moltke's or his Circle's positions.[128] In fact, the exiles—especially Wilbrandt and Rüstow—had taken over and, deeply impressed by their German visitor, had for better or worse constructed a profile of him and his group that would be most acceptable in Washington.[129] Indeed on the issue of 'unconditional surrender' they had scored a breakthrough with Moltke; but while he went along with them, he by no means could hope to commit his Circle to his newly gained insight. On his journeys abroad Trott, as we shall see, continued to make a major issue of attacking the 'unconditional surrender' policy. As for the proposition that the German military would favour an invasion in the west, on the understanding that the Western Allies agree to the Germans holding the line in the east, it may well be that such an option was discussed in the Kreisau meeting in June 1943; Trott launched this possibility when on one of his missions in Sweden in March 1944.[130] It certainly did not speak for the political instinct of the drafters of the Exposé that, shortly after the conference in Tehran of November/December 1943 where the differences between the Western Allies and Russia were, for the moment at least, resolved and agreement had been reached on the Second Front, they then accentuated the Bolshevik danger and the divergent interests of the Western Powers from Soviet Russia. In short, the human understanding that the exiles shared with Moltke was not matched by their political acumen. At no point, and above all not after Tehran, was Washington prepared to accept emissaries from the German Resistance as 'allies', as 'Dogwood' had hoped.[131]

It was Brigadier General Tindall who finally put 'Dogwood' and his friends in their place; unimaginative though he was, he was also more professional and realistic. Declaring himself ready to meet with 'Dogwood', if desired, in Ankara or Istanbul, and even to fly to Cairo if that would serve any good purpose, he in effect held out no hope for success of the venture.[132] Nevertheless, he forwarded the Exposé to Cairo. With all his passion, Dogwood had tried to convince Tindall that a 'happy-go-lucky' attitude on the part of the Western Allies towards Moltke and his friends was inappropriate and urged that President Roosevelt, General Marshall, and General Donovan be fully informed about their endeavours.[133] And while it is certain that General Donovan of the OSS was kept closely abreast of the 'Hermann Group',[134] he brought the case before the President only after the plot against Hitler had failed.[135]

After the third Kreisau meeting of June 1943 Moltke was the first one to strike out for Scandinavia early in October. Travelling the first leg of this trip in an army plane, he made a stop-over in Denmark on 1 October, which turned out to be the decisive event of the journey. Since 29 August a state of emergency had been imposed upon Denmark by the Commander-in-Chief of the German occupation troops, Lt. Gen. Hermann von Hanneken, and Moltke had been informed in Berlin about the impending deportation of the Danish Jews. To begin with he had come to warn. First of all, upon hearing that German soldiers were to be involved in the round-up of Jews, he went straight to Hanneken, calling him 'mad' and reminding him that one day he would have to pay dearly for this.[136] Moreover, Moltke managed to channel this information to the Danish Foreign Office.[137] The Social Democratic as well as the trade-union leadership then did their best to mobilize all resources to warn as many Jews as possible. On the morning after the raid, on 2 October, a beaming Moltke appeared at the house of his friend Kim Bonnesen, saying: 'I congratulate you on the wonderful result. He wanted six thousand and he got only a few hundred.'[138]

For the rest, before proceeding to Oslo, Moltke transacted official business in Copenhagen where he saw as much as possible of Theodor Steltzer and 'our friends', undoubtedly discussing matters pertaining to resistance. He did not get to Sweden as planned, since he was unable to obtain the necessary visa. Instead, he returned for his last day to Copenhagen[139] there to check up once again on the tense situation in the city. But he had accomplished the main objective of his Scandinavian visit, the rescue of the Danish Jews; and that was an achievement.

From then on it was Trott who took over the connection with Sweden.[140] It is possible, as Henrik Lindgren has suggested, that he went there late in October[141] in order to ascertain whether, in response to Moltke's letter to Lionel Curtis of 25 March, the 'stable connection' in Stockholm had been arranged by the British.[142] Although, in fact, it had not, Trott had enough other connections in the Swedish capital to allow him to entertain reasonable hopes that he could follow up there one of his major concerns, namely the establishment of contact with Britain. To begin with he had been instrumental in having a trusted foreign-service friend, Karl Georg Pfleiderer, posted as Consul-General in Stockholm with the understanding that he would monitor Soviet attitudes towards Germany.[143] Also Trott knew that he could count on the Counsellor at the Legation, Werner Dankwort, as a kindred spirit. Of course, during his earlier visit to Sweden in September 1942 he had met the various members of Harry Johansson's 'Sigtuna Group', and now once again he was able to have an interview with one of them, Ivar Anderson, the influential editor in chief of the *Svenska Dagbladet*. The two men had struck it off well before as they exchanged views on the political situation. Then, mirroring 'quick changes between seriousness and joy of life', Trott had given the appearance of serenity, but this time round, troubled over the deteriorating situation at home, he could not hide a deep agitation.[144]

This second interview,[145] then, was no mere repeat performance of the earlier one. The urgency of the situation, Trott now argued, called for a departure from a 'wait and see' attitude. In Germany itself the dangers of civil war were imminent. While explicitly discounting the 'rumour' that Himmler was planning to depose the Führer to seize power himself,[146] Trott played the card of the increasing appeal of Communism in Germany itself, and moreover of the danger of the Russians winning the game and marching into Berlin. It was all the more important therefore for him to open up the connection with the Western Powers; and what were the chances, he asked his Swedish friend, of getting help from them?

With the Russian war machine turning westwards, the argument concerning the Communist and Russian menace was compelling for almost every Swede. But Anderson was level-headed enough to discourage Trott from entertaining any illusions: 'Mr. Churchill does not want a quick end of the war, and the official policy is to administer a military defeat to Germany.' He was, however, able to arrange for his German guest to meet not only with the Swedish Foreign Minister, Christian E. Günther, but also with the Deputy Director General of the British Ministry of Information, Sir Walter Monckton, who happened to be in Stockholm at the time. Furthermore, through the good offices of Fru Almström, Trott was able to see two members of the British Legation, Roger P. Hinks and James Knapp-Fisher, both in fact secret-service officers.[147] Even though all these men were greatly impressed by Trott's sincerity, they were in no position to give him any political satisfaction. Once again Trott had to taste disappointment.

As a matter of fact, the message which Trott had taken to Stockholm reached London in the form of a lengthy 'Political Memorandum', composed by Roger Hinks.[148] It was altogether a fair presentation of Trott's position. He seems to have cautioned the British against a re-education programme for the German people that would make it 'bite off a much larger piece of British liberalism than it could swallow and digest', and at the same time criticized the BBC broadcasts in German as too 'governessy'. Trott seems also to have insisted that his countrymen 'deeply resented' the suggestion that 'they alone were guilty'; a more general admission of mistakes and failure all round would make it easier for the Germans to accept unpalatable truths. As for the question of a forcible dismemberment of Germany, he seems to have predicted 'equally violent efforts at reunion' and to have argued in favour of a decentralization of German political life. But all these arguments, so it seems, were but afterthoughts to Trott's enquiry into the British and American reaction to the possible emergence of a Communist regime in Germany, and to his emphasis upon 'the growing prestige of the Soviet Union in almost all classes of German society'. He concluded with the assertion that 'Russian defeats in the field[149] were easier to bear than the indiscriminate murder of the air attacks from the west.' Following up on this theme, he is quoted as saying:

If at the end of the war the Russians had won all the battles while the British and Americans had destroyed all the cities, the political consequence of this would not be favourable to the Anglo-Saxon powers.

Trott thus spoke plainly, if somewhat acrimoniously, and surely his remarks on the bombing raids were not likely to go down well in London. The 'Political Memorandum', which was classified 'Secret' and especially urged high confidentiality upon London, reached, along with other government agencies, the Central Department of the Foreign Office. There G. W. Harrison minuted that 'our old friend v. Trott', as he put it, had skilfully propagated the 'Communist bogey' and generally mixed up fact and propaganda. F. K. Roberts entered 'very interesting'; but the document never reached the desks of the Under-Secretary or the Foreign Secretary let alone that of the Prime Minister.

When Trott returned to Berlin early in November and reported back to Moltke, however, he put a good face on his recent experience in the north; the days in Stockholm had been 'very interesting', and he thought that he had accomplished 'a few things too'.[150] Shortly after this Swedish trip Trott had his first encounter with a man with whom he was quickly to establish an intimate and decisive friendship, namely Count Claus Schenk von Stauffenberg. Although Trott, if we are to believe the SD report on this meeting, informed Stauffenberg that according to his soundings in Stockholm the readiness of England to come to an understanding '*could not be assumed*',[151] neither of the two men would leave things at that. If anything, their young friendship bolstered their determination not to give up on attempting to reach the other side.[152]

In mid-March of the following year Trott was once again in Sweden. The Kreisau friends, however, had meanwhile suffered a terrible blow when on 19 January Helmuth von Moltke was arrested by the Gestapo.[153] But the show had to go on. The work of the Kreisau Circle as such did not come to a halt. Despite the loss of their spiritual leader, they kept meeting, in Berlin, actually with increasing frequency.[154] Also, inasmuch as Moltke had been taken away, Stauffenberg now moved into the centre of resistance activity, drawing the Kreisau members, among whom was notably Trott, into his orbit.

Trott's third journey to Sweden[155] was undertaken most probably upon the initiative of the British official, Roger Hinks, with whom he had the interview during his previous trip.[156] Hinks approached Fru Almström sometime in February with the message that Trott was 'urgently' needed in Stockholm and that furthermore he was the 'only' person with whom the Allies wanted to deal in a matter of great importance. If Trott did not rush northwards to answer the call, it was because he had just recently been embroiled in difficulties with and subjected to a number of interrogations by the Gestapo over the defection to the British of two Abwehr agents in Istanbul, Erich Vermehren and his wife Elisabeth (born Countess von Plettenberg), whom he had earlier helped to get out of Germany into Turkey.[157] He therefore had to move cautiously. As before, he saw Ivar Anderson,[158] and he also conferred with Sverker Åström,[159] a former Attaché to the Swedish Legation in Moscow.

Among the British officials in Stockholm it is not altogether clear whom Trott met this time, but according to Fru Inga Kempe it was again Roger Hinks.[160] Her conjecture that behind the urgency of the call for another meeting with Trott was the British desire to find out more about the strength and power of the German Resistance before they engaged in the heavy bombings of German industrial areas, cannot be dismissed out of hand. The Ruhr area had already been the main target of Allied air attacks earlier, and the Krupp works in Essen and the ball-bearing factory at Schweinfurt had been badly crippled. Early in 1944, however, the Allied air offensive was about to be intensified, and it was precisely at this time that an intensive debate went on in Allied Supreme Headquarters (SHAEF) about the conduct and direction of air warfare over Germany.[161] The week of 20–6 February, then, turned out to mark, according to General Henry H. Arnold, the Commanding General of the US Army Air Forces, 'a decisive battle of history, one as decisive and of greater world importance than Gettysburg'.[162] Was the call for Trott to hurry to Sweden, then, connected with the Allied decision on the bombing raids? What, we must continue to ask, if Trott had actually rushed to Stockholm? It would be extravagant, to say the least, to submit that a decision of such magnitude as the bombing offensive against Germany would depend on information from a German emissary with very doubtful credentials. Nevertheless it is perfectly plausible to assume that Trott was wanted to add just one more stone to the big mosaic that formed the basis for Allied decision-making.

From a lengthy report that reached the Foreign Office[163] concerning Trott's visit to Sweden in March 1944, it becomes evident that he had, compared with his earlier visit, shifted the burden of his argumentation to the issue of the bombing raids and in particular to the British night raids which, apart from spreading terror, created bitterness against Britain. But then, changing gear, he proceeded to outline terms that would be acceptable to the Opposition, among which were three memorable items: as long as the German people would not be made to feel reduced to the position of helots, a reduction of German frontiers 'to a smaller state than that comprised by the 1918 frontiers' was acceptable; the proposition which, he claimed, he had discussed 'with the generals', to make the second front in the west a 'walkover' for the Allies; the assurance that a military coup would eventually provide for the establishment of a civilian administration.

Assuming that there was a connection between the British urgent call for Trott to come to Sweden and the broader issue of strategic bombing, the hard fact is that he came too late to make any difference. The heavy raids over Germany had already begun by the time he arrived in Stockholm. This fact may in part explain why Trott's message, as it reached the Foreign Office courtesy of the 'Swedish woman' on 30 March, was received there with the usual tired scepticism. G. W. Harrison was still wondering whether Trott was 'a conscious or unconscious agent of the German Secret Service'. This time, however, the report made its way all the way up to the Foreign Secretary. Sir Alexander Cadogan took the occasion to 'confess' that he was still hankering after some Declaration to the German People.[164] Anthony Eden minuted cryptically: 'This can certainly be examined afresh.' According to the American Minister to Stockholm, the London Foreign Office inclined to the view that Trott was 'probably [a] Gestapo agent seeking to ferret out views in Allied circles', whereas the British Legation was inclined to feel that he represented a bona fide opposition group.[165]

In any event Trott kept going. His next mission took him, in mid-April, once more to Switzerland where he had a secret meeting with Gaevernitz who in turn prepared a detailed report on it for Allen Dulles.[166] Once again Trott tried to play the Russian card, juxtaposing the Bolshevik solicitude for the Germans, especially by means of the 'Free Germany' Committee, with the passivity of the democratic countries. This time especially he presented himself as a spokesman for the German labour leaders. This stance, not at all out of tune with Trott's always latent socialist leanings, might well have reflected, as has been suggested by Hermann Graml, a certain turn within the *Widerstand* towards the Left,[167] marked by the ascendancy within it of men like Julius Leber and Wilhelm Leuschner. It might also have been adopted to counteract fears of a coup dominated by reactionary generals which, in the course of his many earlier soundings abroad, Trott had occasion to observe. The close contact between the German Communists and Russia, he now argued, should be 'balanced by an equally active contact between the German Socialist labour movement and the progressive forces in the West'.[168] The Labour leaders, he reported, therefore suggested that the bombings be concentrated as much as possible on military and industrial targets.

On this visit Trott also saw once again, and for the last time, his British friend Elizabeth Wiskemann. But this time she found him 'a shadow of his former self, grey and haggard':[169]

He was obsessed with the effects of the air-raids on Berlin and the other German towns ... He was like a broken man and said he expected to be arrested soon after his return to Germany. The usual exchange followed: 'Must you go back?' 'Yes, I absolutely must.' After he had left, he telephoned once more, of course saying it was Adam. I forgot what he had to say but I told him that he had left his gloves behind, a very fine pair. He said 'keep them as a gauge,' for his safety he meant—I think he had the sense not to say any more. In all the discussions that followed I have felt that people have not allowed enough for the condition of tremendous and mounting nervous strain in which the anti-Nazis had lived for eleven years by then.[170]

This was the voice of an understanding friend. Like Trott's, it was drowned by the fury of the war.

Soon after, in April or May, when Albrecht von Kessel met with his friend Adam in Venice, he found him 'tired and dejected ... deeply discouraged over his recent experiences in Sweden'. There he had been in touch with influential circles which were in sympathy with 'our movement' and once again sought contact with England. He had gone a fair way towards meeting what he thought to be British susceptibilities. But from England came only 'a sternly negative answer'.[171]

In the latter part of June Trott was once again in Sweden.[172] He actually had planned to go earlier, but since the Swedish press had come out in May with a dispatch about a German diplomat, formerly a Rhodes Scholar, who had recently been in touch with two British diplomats on a secret peace mission, he had to lie low for the moment.[173] Thus his friend and confidant from the Auswärtiges Amt, Alexander Werth, went in his stead.[174] In any event, on 19 June Trott himself again appeared in Sweden, with the commission from Stauffenberg, so it seems, to explore the readiness of Britain and the United States, in view of the Russian advances on the Eastern front, to negotiate with a new German government.[175] This time it was David McEwan from the British Legation with whom he had to deal.[176] Like Hinks and Knapp-Fisher, McEwan was a secret-service officer; but he was more of a seasoned professional than they were and therefore 'hard as nails'.[177] What Trott thus gained concerning security for this encounter, he lost in rapport with his partner.

McEwan did ask Trott to put information about the German Underground on paper, which indeed he did.[178] Trott was in an awkward position since, as

Fru Kempe pointed out, until the English and Americans had given some sign of their willingness to co-operate with the Resistance in Germany, he could not be sure that the information he was giving, or was about to give, would not be used against the very thing he was working for. In turn, the Allies were not willing to promise anything until they had found out exactly the strength of the Resistance.[179] Trott then worked out an answer that gave rudimentary information about the *Widerstand*, short of anything that, if used against it by the wrong hand, could be damaging to it. But on one point he was crystal clear: any mutual co-operation should depend on the rescinding by the Allies of the demand for unconditional surrender. Otherwise Trott predicted the origin of a 'stab in the back' charge against the conspirators and the rise of a new 'Hitler legend'.

We are left wondering why the British should have been so keen on information about the German Resistance? As we have seen throughout the pages of this book, they had ample opportunity to go after it. Trott himself reminded them of this fact: 'Some of these political leaders [in the Resistance] are known in England and have been carrying on intermittent contacts with the outside world through neutral countries.'[180] It is reasonable, of course, to conjecture that the British wanted to know, in view of the deteriorating conditions in the Reich, to what extent the Resistance had reduced its terms. It is no less reasonable, however, to conjecture that by virtue of 'absolute silence' and 'unconditional surrender' they had hurt their intelligence gathering and that they were now under pressure for more hard intelligence to help their decision-making process. As a matter of fact, late in May 1944, a meeting had taken place among the various Department heads of the British Foreign Office in which the question was raised as to whether there was something in the stories of 'dissident' groups in Germany, whether there was any 'organisation or co-ordination' among them, and whether it would be possible, 'by establishing contact with any group or individual', to assist military operations in Western Europe. However, the upshot of the meeting, labelled a 'periodical stock-taking' by Oliver Harvey, the Assistant Under-Secretary of State, was negative.[181] In any case, Trott's meeting with McEwan did not go at all well.

Thus Trott had all the more reason to go to great efforts to inform himself about the attitudes of the other Allies. Through the mediation of Professor Gunnar Myrdal, the well-known Swedish economist and a Member of Parliament, he had a long conference on 23 June in the latter's office in the Riksdag building with the *Life* and *Time* correspondent, John Scott, who kept the American Minister Herschel V. Johnson closely informed concerning this meeting.[182] 'With the intensity of a man who knew not only that his business was of the utmost importance but that failure might mean his life',[183] Trott pleaded for a modification of 'unconditional surrender', to encourage the Resistance in its attempt to stage a coup in Germany, and also for further

guarantees designed to allow a post-Nazi government to become effective
and to maintain at least the formality of German sovereignty. These were to
include the demobilization of the German army by the post-Nazi government,
an interval of at least several weeks between surrender and occupation,
Germany's retaining its pre-1936 borders, and the trial of war criminals in
Germany. With these terms Trott certainly had gone a long way in scaling
down the previous proposals of the Resistance emissaries, including his own,
to a level where they might have been accepted as a basis for negotiation.
Now, however, despite Myrdal's assurances to the contrary, Scott was not
able to free himself of the suspicion that Trott may after all have been a
German propaganda agent.[184] Myrdal himself had come round to convincing
himself of Trott's integrity, especially since he had learned about the latter's
connections with the Kreisau Socialists.[185] Myrdal therefore gave Trott credibility in the eyes of the American Legation, which indeed proceeded to advise
the State Department that the circumstances and nature of Trott's mission
called for 'early and careful attention' to his proposals. This recommendation,
however, fell on deaf ears in Washington.[186]

There has been much speculation about Trott's plan for a meeting with
the Russian Minister in Stockholm, Mme Alexandra M. Kollontay.[187] No
doubt, he sought her out. He had all along wanted to ascertain, as a back-
up so to speak for his approaches to the Western Powers, what the Russian
plans were for Germany in the immediate future. As a matter of fact, while
in Sweden he seems to have obtained the 'Programme of the National
Committee for a Free Germany', but seems to have come to the conclusion
that the Committee, since it merely served as a vehicle for Soviet propaganda,
was of no positive political value for the further development of Germany.[188]
The visit to Mme Kollontay had been arranged, upon Trott's initiative, by
Willy Brandt, after the war Chancellor of the Federal Republic of Germany,
but then an exile in Sweden.[189] But Trott subsequently asked Brandt to cancel
the appointment since he had obtained information that there was a German
agent in the Russian Legation.[190] In the middle of his stay in Sweden, on 25
June, after visiting Harry Johansson and Bishop Manfred Björkquist in
Sigtuna, Trott wrote to a Swedish friend acknowledging the futility, at the
moment at least, of all dialogues:[191]

At the moment one cannot bring to a standstill the terrible judgement which will
descend over all of mankind.


## 3. Goerdeler Initiatives 1943–1944. Foreign Policy Statements and Explorations in Sweden

It is striking that as late as 1943 and 1944 there should have been a minimum of co-ordination between the various resistance groups in the area of foreign affairs. On 8 January 1943 a breakthrough of sorts had taken place when, after elaborate preparations, the 'important discussion' took place in Count Peter von Yorck's house in Berlin-Lichterfelde between the Beck–Goerdeler–von Hassell group and some of the leading members of the Kreisau Circle.[192] The prime purpose of the meeting was to demonstrate to the Generals that the civilian sector of the Resistance had purpose and direction. With Beck presiding with marked restraint, the assembled conspirators addressed themselves to the chief aspects of planning: Trott spoke about foreign affairs, Yorck about administrative reforms, whereas Moltke reported on the overall condition of the Opposition. A great deal of argumentation ensued as the evening wore on between the 'excellencies', as Moltke liked to dub the elders led by the perhaps somewhat too condescending Goerdeler, and the 'youngsters' of the Kreisau group, particularly on matters pertaining to social policy. But the tone of the debate was, if occasionally heated, civil and friendly throughout, and the clandestine conclave distinctly contributed to giving a sense of common purpose to the two groups represented.

It is all the more surprising, therefore, that Goerdeler's thoughts concerning foreign affairs and his initiatives in this field should have been developed virtually in isolation from those of the Kreisau Circle. However, quite apart from the fact that there were no ground rules for the conduct of resistance foreign policy, Goerdeler was an imperious person—as was Moltke as a matter of fact. Assured of General Beck's backing, Goerdeler did not readily suffer others to interfere with his designs, and he possessed an infinite self-confidence that the righteousness of his cause would prevail. He thought that he could sway the Generals just as he thought that he could persuade even Hitler himself to resign in the interest of the German people; he was no less convinced that he had found the right channel abroad, that is in Sweden, to circumvent the 'unconditional surrender' barrier and penetrate after all to Winston Churchill.

In his letter to Lionel Curtis of 25 March 1943[193] Moltke singled out as 'the main error' committed by the Opposition the reliance on the Generals; he had all along, certainly since the outbreak of the war, been critical of their procrastination[194] and had virtually written them off. The engagement of the Generals, despite a mounting impatience with them,[195] remained for Goerdeler a prime concern. With forged papers procured from Oster, he had in August 1942 visited the Eastern front to win over the Commanders there for the conspiracy, among them Field Marshal Günther von Kluge. Likewise, after Casablanca, and after the failure of the assassination attempts on Hitler of March 1943, he kept trying to convince the military of the irresponsibility of Hitler's conduct of the war and the banefulness of his rule over Germany as well as over the Continent; he remained persuaded of the importance of their support for the coup. Thus on 26 March he composed an elaborate secret Memorandum for the *Generalität*[196] and on 17 May sent an 'urgent' appeal to General Friedrich Olbricht, Chief of the General Army Office (Allgemeines Heeresamt) in the OKH and Deputy Commander of the Reserve Army,[197] not to wait for the psychologically right moment for action: 'it must be *brought about*.'[198] Later, on 25 July, Goerdeler followed up his visit to von Kluge of the previous year with an impassioned letter to the Field Marshal,[199] pleading with him to join in making an end to the 'madness of Hitler' and thus to seize the moment, while Germany was still holding some cards to play, that might still favour the negotiation of a 'favourable peace'.[200]

The draft of Goerdeler's letter to von Kluge hardly added up, as suggested by Wheeler-Bennett, to 'an indictment of the *Generalität*'.[201] While it did give expression to the exasperation on the part of many patriotic anti-Nazi Germans over the inactivity of the Generals, and while it betrayed, in its last and over-emotional paragraph a deep anxiety as to what Kluge's decision might be, it was geared to salvage the honour and also the interests of the Generals. The Stalingrad disaster, he evidently figured, had convinced the army leaders that Hitler must be removed.[202] As a matter of fact, Goerdeler's persistent preoccupation with the *Generalität* betrays how stubbornly he, the self-avowed 'militarist',[203] continued to count on it—and this is in marked contrast to Moltke. Goerdeler's foreign policy vision accordingly remained wedded to traditional notions of German hegemonic thinking, albeit within the framework of an enlightened European order. What Moltke said during his visit to Brussels in September 1943 to General Alexander von Falken-hausen, the Military Commander of Belgium and Northern France, namely that 'the German people must first of all be for once completely broken',[204] Goerdeler would never have subscribed to. '*Even the leading position of Germany on the Continent*', so Goerdeler insisted, 'can still be negotiated.'[205] Thus he made an argument for the salvaging of the Reich within the frontiers of 1914,[206] augmented by Austria[207] and the Sudeten area. But overarching the whole Continent was to emerge a 'united Europe based upon independent European States'.[208]

Although the Goerdeler Memorandum for the *Generalität* and the two letters to the Generals were drafted before the Tehran Conference of November/December 1943, in which the Western Allies composed their differences with the Soviet Union, it is striking that Goerdeler should at this date still have banked on the long-range identity of interests between Germany, England, and the United States and accordingly on the interest of the Anglo-Saxon powers to stave off Bolshevism. He was, as he admitted, still guided in his judgement by his pre-war travels to England and America; but he felt also—unduly—encouraged by the differences between Britain and Russia that had surfaced at Casablanca. Here then is Goerdeler's overall design:

I can give assurance that a Germany which secures for itself, apart from an honourable and competent military leadership, a—plainly speaking—decent political leadership, can look forward to having the war in the air ended within 48 hours. The next steps could then be geared to a *détente* with the Western powers, which, in turn, would enable the German people to concentrate on its war effort in the East.[209]

In the hope of promoting his vision abroad, Goerdeler followed one channel, namely the powerful Wallenberg banking family in Stockholm. Through the Skandinaviska Enskilda Banken the Wallenbergs controlled a formidable empire, with interests on both sides of the war, which they skilfully nursed. Already the senior of the House, Monsieur Marcus Wallenberg as he was called, had connections with the German Chancellor Heinrich Brüning and also with Carl Goerdeler.[210] Following his death his two sons, Jacob and Marcus, divided up the representation of the bank abroad, with Jacob, the elder of the two, taking care of the German connections and Marcus the English and American ones. The two brothers, then, proved to be ideal intermediaries, so at least Goerdeler figured, between the *Widerstand* and Britain.

Between the outbreak of the war and November 1943 Jacob Wallenberg and Goerdeler met eleven times either in Stockholm or Berlin, and Marcus was kept informed about their discussions and, whenever it seemed advisable, consulted.[211] In the course of time the Swedish bankers developed a remarkable sense of intimacy and trust with Goerdeler, who, unlike in the early phases of their relationship, came not as a business partner but as a suppliant. They no doubt were greatly impressed by the pleas of the German who, hope against hope, kept feeding them with news of an impending coup in his country and who implored them to engage the British on behalf of his cause. Invoking his visit to Churchill in May 1939, he figured he might now gain a hearing from the Prime Minister. At the same time the Wallenbergs, for all the understanding they were able to marshal for Goerdeler, were shrewd men of affairs who were quite ready to advise their German friend on how to proceed in his appeal to Britain. In particular they vigorously discouraged Goerdeler from making the coup against Hitler dependent on advance assurances to the conspirators. 'You must not ask your enemies what you should do', Jacob Wallenberg argued, 'they can give you no good answer.'[212]

On the occasion of Goerdeler's visit to Stockholm in May 1943[213] Jacob Wallenberg asked him to draw up a paper on the programme of the Resistance that could be forwarded to London, and he did not fail to impress upon him the need to trim his terms, especially on the question of frontiers. The result was, by Goerdeler's standards, a concise statement of the domestic and foreign plans of the Resistance.[214] The critical passages of course pertained to the foreign realm, and they amounted to a considerably scaled-down version of his Peace Plan of mid-1941. While proposing a cessation of bombing raids against the German troops involved in insurrection and over the areas under their control, and while insisting, most probably against Wallenberg's better judgement, upon a repudiation of 'unconditional surrender', Goerdeler abandoned his earlier insistence upon the borders of 1914. The bottom line was the restitution of the independence of all European nations. The German–Polish frontier was to be determined through negotiations, and subsequently the Polish state, preferably enlarged by a union with Lithuania, was to be recognized by the new German regime.[215] Both Poland and Czechoslovakia were to be 'entirely free' to plan their political and economic future according to their own interests. In the west the frontier was to be drawn along linguistic lines. These settlements were to be subject to an overarching European community[216] among whose members there was to be no more war.

Jacob Wallenberg, who described this memorandum as a 'compromise', went so far as to send a letter containing the gist of it to London via the Swedish Foreign Office, this being the only time that he approached it on behalf of the German Opposition. In London his brother Marcus took over. The British had the highest respect for these two brothers as 'hard-headed men', and they listened to Marcus as he made a case against complete disarmament of Germany and 'unconditional surrender'. His warnings against Russia's taking advantage of an excessively rigid Western policy towards the German Opposition, moreover, did not altogether fall on deaf ears.[217] On this specific mission, however, Wallenberg penetrated to the Prime Minister's Private Secretary Desmond Morton but no further. At the end he was merely informed, through a third person, of Churchill's desire to keep this channel to the German Opposition open—but only for the purpose of obtaining more information. And that is where the matter rested.

There were other meetings between Goerdeler and Jacob Wallenberg, one early in August in Berlin,[218] and a final one, also in Berlin, late in November. Meanwhile Goerdeler persisted on his part in preparing the ground for the coveted connection with England. In the late summer or early autumn he prepared a comprehensive Peace Plan[219] in which he elaborated upon the terms of the memorandum which he had written for the Wallenbergs in May.[220] Once again this document was addressed quite explicitly to British readers. But now there was a noticeable change of emphasis in Goerdeler's argumentation. Apart from the usual implicit or explicit warning against the Russian threat, the document voiced distinct misgivings about the foreign policy objectives of the United States. Not without good reason Goerdeler expressed himself 'doubtful' that America would be ready to join in the 'securing' of Europe against Russian predominance: 'we shall have to count on the fact that America will not always assume the part of securing Europe against Russia.' This was a rather cautious and indirect statement, but it led to a vision of a truly European order independent of the two great World

Powers, Russia and the United States, whose interests, he thought, were not primarily European. He therefore designed the Peace Plan which, falling back essentially on the principle of ethnicity and self-determination, held out the prospect of a merger of the European peoples into an 'eternal League of Peace' in which neither Germany nor any other power would claim pre-dominance. This vision, which had a certain Herderian beauty, clearly shows how far Goerdeler's thinking, in the course of the war, had moved away from narrow nationalistic thinking in the direction of the whole of Europe. But it was more than just beautiful; it was also realistic in so far as it was an expression of a justified anxiety on his part, as well as on the part of the Resistance movements outside Germany, that the ideal of a renewed Europe was being taken out of their hands by the non-European great powers.[221] Still, on 21 March 1943, Winston Churchill had delivered a much-noticed live broadcast from the Prime Minister's country residence of Chequers in which he pointedly advanced a proposal for a 'Council of Europe' under an all-embracing world institution.[222] It is questionable, of course, whether Goerdeler was aware of it. Also, if, as we can assume, Churchill's speech was designed to offer a counterweight to the American abandonment, in deference to Soviet Russia, of plans for a European federation, we must of course also ask whether he was still in a position to assert himself in this crucial question against the United States; the answer is 'no'. In this light, however, Goerdeler's Peace Plan, realistic or not, remains one of the star documents among the German Resistance of the will for a united Europe.

About the same time as the Peace Plan was drafted, sometime in September, Goerdeler had a chance to present his case to the Generals.[223] Marshal von Kluge had arrived in Berlin and asked for Goedeler to come to General Olbricht's house where he, Goerdeler, found himself closeted with Kluge and Beck. In view of the deteriorating situation on all fronts, Kluge wanted to find out from Goerdeler what the prospects were for negotiating a tolerable peace, and Goerdeler then gave the desired information with, considering the conditions, inimitable self-assurance. Nothing, absolutely nothing, could disconcert him.

The territorial terms which Goerdeler outlined, according to his intelligence acceptable to the British, on the whole agreed with those contained in all his recent statements, the memorandum for the *Generalität* of March, the memorandum for the Wallenberg brothers of May, and the Peace Plan of the late summer or early autumn.[224] But in the company of the Generals nothing was said about a lofty 'eternal League of Peace'; only an economic union among the European states was mentioned, but with the exclusion of Russia. The English connection had to be presented to von Kluge *sans phrase*, by emphasizing the divergent interests of Britain and Russia and the dependence therefore of the former upon a 'sufficiently strong Germany in a strong Europe'. The question of the United States also came up in the discussions, and Goerdeler saw fit to elaborate upon the 'emergence of a deep conflict of interests between England and the USA'. Altogether he remained true to himself throughout his dealings with the different parties involved; he merely changed his emphasis here and there, hoping to achieve a commitment by both the British and the German Generals to his one objective, the overthrow of the Nazi regime.

The Moscow Conference of the foreign ministers of the United States of America, the United Kingdom, the Soviet Union, and China late in October, whose final Declaration emphasized the commitment of the Allied nations to 'united action' in the pursuit of the war,[225] could not have offered much comfort to those of the German Resistance who, like Goerdeler, banked on friction among the Allies. Nevertheless, Goerdeler soon thereafter thought himself justified in reporting to Ulrich von Hassell that he had, by way of Sweden, an 'authentic statement' from Churchill to the effect that, while he could make no binding arrangements before the Nazi government was overthrown, he believed that, if the revolt should succeed, 'a practical way would be found'.[226] Late in November, however, when Jacob Wallenberg appeared for the last time in Berlin, things did not go well. Wallenberg was edgy, asking why nothing had happened, and Goerdeler was defensive, trying to assure the visitor that, although two attempts on Hitler had failed, the preparations for the coup would continue. 'You come too late!' Wallenberg then retorted, giving air to his impatience: 'Once Germany is defeated, all is in vain. In that case even a Goerdeler–Beck Government can achieve nothing.'[227] More weighty even than these atmospheric disturbances was the news, shattering no doubt to Goerdeler, that acceptance in England of the Peace Plan 'in any form' was out of the question. Wallenberg could hold out no prospect whatsoever of assurances to the German Opposition.[228]

It should be no surprise that the visits between Jacob Wallenberg and Goerdeler now ceased. While Goerdeler kept sending messages to Stockholm,[229] there was nothing really that the Wallenbergs could accomplish by further meetings. They had tried hard to narrow the gap between Goerdeler's position and the hard-and-fast exigencies of the Allied warfare, but they had exhausted the reservoir of mutual receptiveness. Goerdeler was thus left suspended over that unbridgeable gap. It was finally only his indomitable optimism which kept him from despair.[230]

Goerdeler certainly continued to see himself as responsible for the political course of the *Widerstand*, and this kept him going. Was it pride which prevented him from joining in the ventures abroad of the Kreisau young turks? In any event, after the virtual breakdown of his Swedish connection and what he thought to be the lifeline to England, he continued to elaborate guide-lines for the conduct of German affairs after the fall of the Nazi regime. We have come to know Goerdeler as a man who believed in the power and self-evidence of reason and the word. His memoranda therefore were for him virtually a form of political action and assumed a central function in his political life.[231]

In the first months of 1944 Goerdeler, with the help of General Beck, composed an elaborate, and by normal standards tediously elaborate, memorandum 'The Way' ('Der Weg').[232] But clearly those times were anything but normal. Not only was Goerdeler, like Beck, now in a position to anticipate and plan for the collapse of the Third Reich, but, looking back, he had reason to re-examine his own premisses which were rooted in the Bismarckian Reich, that is faith in the nation state and its reliance on power politics. 'The Way', then, amounted to a grand stocktaking—Wilhelm Ritter von Schramm rightly calls it a first attempt at 'coming to terms with the past'[233]—as well as a major policy statement.

The tripartite review of the German regimes since the turn of the century— Imperial Germany, Republican Germany, and the Dictatorship—indicated the long way which Goerdeler—like Beck—had travelled during the Nazi years. The memorandum was of one piece. The survey of constitutional problems and domestic issues which constituted its core informed a re-assessment of Germany's place in European affairs. For once Goerdeler emerged with an unsparing critique of Imperial Germany. It had made the 'fatal' mistake of fighting the workers' movement, excluding it from political responsibility, and thus accentuating class warfare.[234] As for Bismarck, while having had a distinct concept, he had not attended to the instruction of public opinion or the provision for a proper succession in the province of foreign affairs, and under the Kaiser Germany had had no foreign policy course at all.[235]

From that phase of foreign policy we have to learn the lesson that its great aims must have an overall concept and that it must subject itself to one restraint: it must avoid the lust for power.[236]

Unsparing are the passages in the document, no doubt inspired by Beck, on the conduct of the First World War and on defeat in 1918. In particular since his resignation as Chief of Staff in 1938, Beck had turned to an intensive study of the great German strategist Carl von Clausewitz which opened his eyes to the detrimental effects of General Erich Ludendorff's theory of total war.[237] Unchecked by political considerations, the conduct of total war is bound to result in unsound political decisions, and the trouble in the last months of the First World War had been that weak political leadership had created a void into which Hindenburg and Ludendorff stepped—with a vengeance. The result was their precipitate demand for an armistice on 29 September 1918. But Goerdeler's memorandum, 'The Way', translated this essentially historical argument into bold political terms: it broke the shib-boleth of all German nationalists with an unequivocal rejection of the per-nicious 'stab in the back' legend which had been launched by Ludendorff himself. Whether or not the end of the 1914–18 war, that is defeat, was inevitable, it was definitely not brought about by a stab in the back.[238]

Goerdeler's critique of Imperial Germany, his measured vindication of the Weimar Republic and his devastating indictment of the Third Reich in 'Der Weg' concluded with a blueprint for the place of Germany in the European order. On the way he could not help but point out the failure of the Western Allies to prevent the Second World War. He himself had been a witness, after all, to the unwillingness of the British to respond to his repeated advice that, if Britain and France stood firm against Nazi threats and aggression, there would be no war; but he had been dismissed by official London as an alarmist. The 'unscrupulous' policies of the German dictatorship matched by the 'naïve credulousness'[239] of the Western Powers, then, was responsible for the war. Nor could Goerdeler refrain from pointing out, as he had done in his presentation to Field Marshal von Kluge, the frictions between England and Russia and between England and the United States. They were not to be exploited, however, but to be 'evaluated'[240] for the benefit of German interests and a peaceful balance of power.

The memorandum, then, concluded with the following statement:

The foreign policy of Imperial Germany has missed opportunities because it was naïve and foolish. The foreign policy of Republican Germany has missed such opportunities because of the myopia and folly of its rivals. It had to struggle for its liberation. The foreign policy of the Dictatorship has gambled away the legacy of Imperial and Republican Germany ... In the future it behoves us to aim ... at *the union of all European nation states and at the co-operation of all peoples of the world which seek peace.*[241]

It is significant that the memorandum 'The Way' was not the work of a loner. It was the result of a 'common effort' and as such an index of some minimal consensus among the different Resistance groups. It was even an effort to overcome the rift with the 'youngsters' of the Kreisau Circle.

Following the closing of the channel through the Wallenbergs, none of Goerdeler's messages reached the British whom he always had on his mind. Certainly they would no longer have been justified in branding him a 'stalking-horse for German *military* expansion'. But the hard reality was that in the course of the war the roles had been reversed. Goerdeler, beyond any doubt, had moved away from the traditional German fascination with power and the nation state in the direction of European union. The British, on the other hand, partly under American pressure, had moved away from plans for a European federation in the direction of power considerations and, as Anthony Eden had put it to the Bishop of Chichester, the 'national interest'. The Social Democrat Julius Leber himself, who since the autumn of 1943 had moved into the orbit of the Kreisau Circle and the Goerdeler Circle, characterized Goerdeler as an 'illusionist'.[242] As the German armies were about to be routed by the Allies, Goerdeler was still hoping to avert the worst: total defeat, unconditional surrender, and the occupation of his country. This was his illusion; this was his mirage.

## 4. Otto John in Madrid: Between Goerdeler and von Stauffenberg

Otto John was one of the continuities among the German Resistance. An inveterate activist, he had been with it since 1938 and thus was familiar with virtually every segment and every phase of it. He was particularly solicitous on behalf of a restoration of a Hohenzollern monarchy under Prince Louis Ferdinand who was a friend of his. But apart from running adroitly from pillar to post and keeping up his fellow conspirators' spirits, Otto John's main effort lay in the field of foreign relations. He was able to use his position as Legal Adviser to the German Lufthansa as a cover for his activities on behalf of the conspiracy, and when in March 1942 an assignment came his way to proceed to Madrid in order to reorganize the Spanish subsidiary of Lufthansa, the moment had come for him to do his part in representing abroad the interests of the *Widerstand*.[243]

The many missions which Otto John undertook under cover of his Lufthansa connection were co-ordinated with others in the Resistance concerned with foreign relations: the conspiratorial group in the Abwehr; Goerdeler and Stauffenberg; also, an old friendship tied John to Adam von Trott, and although the two did not fully see eye to eye on things—especially on the question of unconditional surrender—they were in constant touch with one another. In comparison with the other Resistance missions, however, Otto John's were not merely more of the same. By virtue of John's persistently sober assessment of the political realities on the other side, his missions take a special place in the history of the Resistance ventures abroad. He disagreed with almost everyone else on one vital point: he had no illusions about 'unconditional surrender', and his understanding of the determination that motivated the strategies of the Allied leadership protected him from chasing after mirages. All the more did John think it important for the Resistance to reach a realistic assessment of the intentions of the Allied Powers. While of course he kept nourishing hopes of some sort of recognition of the Resistance by the Western Allies, he considered it his chief responsibility to furnish the conspiracy at home with a correct intelligence picture that, however unfavourable to it, would be honest and helpful.

Initially, as soon as it became known early in 1942 that John was to fly to Madrid, he was approached by Goerdeler who, while in contact with

London—or so he thought—through the Wallenbergs, was eager also to
follow up leads to Washington. Goerdeler knew about the connection
between John and Prince Louis Ferdinand as well as about the latter's
friendship with President Roosevelt. 'Armed with Goerdeler's instructions',
then,[244] John proceeded to Madrid where, through the services of a Juan
Terrasa, formerly an Attaché at the Spanish Embassy in Washington, he
succeeded in getting together with the American Chargé d'Affaires, Willard
L. Beaulac.[245] The latter in turn brought him together in the course of time
with his Military Attaché, Colonel William Hohenthal.[246] For good measure
John also managed to establish a connection in Lisbon with a British secret-
service officer there by the name of Tony Graham-Meingott. In fact Beaulac
and Hohenthal proved more accessible to the approaches of Otto John than
any other American foreign-service officers during the war allowed themselves
to be. Beaulac, while he did not quite know how to take John, nevertheless
liked him. He had three meetings with John in his own house, two of them
over dinner. Upon his first meeting with John, Colonel Hohenthal, proud
of his German ancestry, addressed him in German and recalled common
acquaintances from his Berlin days. The British secret-service officer from
Lisbon was not at all encouraging.[247] Beaulac's reports to the State Department remained unanswered, and British Intelligence relayed warnings to him
to be cautious in seeing and talking to John.[248] Everywhere was the watchword
'unconditional surrender'.

Otto John's mission was by no means confined to winding up Goerdeler's
affairs, however. Goerdeler's original idea of using the Madrid channel as an
extension or alternative to his connection with the Wallenberg brothers
proved futile, and by the summer of 1943 he had to face up to the fact that
the memorandum which he had written for London in May had not been
answered.

By mid-1943, moreover, the whole balance within the Resistance had
changed. The centre of the conspiracy was hit by the Gestapo when, early in
April upon the discovery of the 'U7' operation,[249] it struck against the Oster
Circle, arresting Dietrich Bonhoeffer, Hans von Dohnanyi, and Josef Müller
and suspending General Oster himself from office. But just about that time
a new centre for the conspiracy arose in the person of Count Claus Schenk
von Stauffenberg. A Lieutenant Colonel with the Tenth Armoured Division
on the African front, he had been badly wounded on 7 April 1943,[250] and it
was during his convalescence in hospital that he resolved to join the plot.
Stauffenberg had no illusions concerning the tides of the war and became
determined to prevent the Führer from dragging the Fatherland down with
him. After his release from hospital he was assigned as Chief of Staff in the
command centre of the Home Army, under General Olbricht in Berlin, which
afforded him the opportunity to dedicate himself fully to the conspiracy. By
virtue of his contagious energy and persuasion, Stauffenberg soon succeeded

in committing the various groups in the Resistance to the one essential purpose, the removal of Hitler.

Stauffenberg's ascendancy, however, also provoked some tensions within the Resistance, especially with Goerdeler.[251] It may have been fundamentally a matter of the generation gap and of temperament. Goerdeler, twenty-three years Stauffenberg's senior, was rooted in a world of security and normality, and not even the shock of the First World War, the troubled Weimar years, the Nazi regime, or even another war could shake his confidence and faith in progress. His persistent optimism made him also cling to the idea that the removal of Hitler could be achieved by persuasion rather than by assassination. Stauffenberg, by contrast, was born into a world of crisis and was therefore better prepared to cope with the unforeseen and to face up to catastrophe. Both Goerdeler and Stauffenberg, moreover, were imperious persons, and Goerdeler was as determined to hold on to his position as leader of the civilian sector of the Resistance as Stauffenberg was impatient and uninhibited about trespassing into the areas Goerdeler considered his preserve. These differences between the two men were bound to build up tensions and spill over into concrete disagreements. Stauffenberg's remark to Otto John that he wanted no 'plans à la Goerdeler'[252] most probably alluded to various points of friction. He saw in Goerdeler essentially a man of the past whose commitment to the precepts of capitalism was inadequate to the needs of a changing social order. While there was no fundamental disagreement between them on foreign policy objectives, they nevertheless conceived of their immediate tasks differently. Goerdeler persisted in hoping that a political understanding could be reached with the Western Powers, notably with Britain, that would circumvent the stringency of 'unconditional surrender'. Stauffenberg was prepared to face up to the imminent military disaster, and was set on exploring ways of exacting terms in London and Washington that would minimize its effects. Also, Goerdeler kept looking towards Britain, ignoring the fact that she was no longer the dominant party in the Grand Alliance. Stauffenberg, on the other hand, was turning his attention to the Americans.

Stauffenberg no less than Goerdeler, however, was free of illusions. He took a particular interest in the John–Hohenthal connection partly because the latter, like himself, was a military man, and he felt that in this desperate situation, aiming at a direct 'soldier to soldier' relationship was preferable to the too intricate manœuvres of politicians.[253] It was Otto John who did his level best to bring Stauffenberg down to earth. In March 1944[254] he composed a memorandum for him on his mission to Spain and Portugal.[255] In no way did it give encouragement to Goerdeler's theme that tried to capitalize on potential rivalries among the Allies. Instead, it added up to a sobering reminder of the determination of the Allies to combine their plans and operations: nothing would deter them from their preparations for the invasion under the Supreme Command of General Eisenhower, and the imposition of unconditional surrender by military means was a foregone conclusion.

No other document emanating from the German Resistance ever spelled out quite so realistically the political and strategic situation. Once its premisses were accepted, what leeway, we might ask, was there left for action other than just to proceed with the coup, whatever the consequences for a new regime? Otto John nevertheless followed up with a message that his friend Terrasa promised to forward to the British representation in Lisbon in which he once again pleaded for co-operation 'either now or in the future' between the Allies and the Opposition in Germany.[256] The Report did reach London. The chances were that in any case it would not have made any difference. It is not without some interest, however, to mention that, as far as we know, it was held up at British Secret Intelligence (MI6) where it was submitted for security reasons to none other than Kim Philby who forbade its circulation as 'unreliable'.[257] Quite clearly, no intelligence was to pass to the authorities in London that might further a separate understanding between the Western Allies and the German Resistance especially since the latter was toying with the idea of making peace with the Western Allies in order to be in a position to hold the line against the Russians. Philby, of course, could console himself with the thought that the Russian and the British positions coincided in this matter. 'It would have been', so he rationalized later, 'dangerous for the Russians to think that we [*sic*] were dickering with the Germans; the air was opaque with mutual suspicions of separate peace feelers.'[258]

Quite predictably, then, Otto John did not get his message across to the British, though of course the way in which it was blocked could not have been foreseen. But the significance of John's contribution to our story rests in the fact that he got through to Stauffenberg. With his honest reporting he injected a sense of realism into Stauffenberg's assessment of the chances that were left to him to forestall the military catastrophe by means of negotiations with the Western Allies.


## 5. Contacts with Allied Resistance Movements

In a letter of 17 November 1942 to his wife Freya, Helmuth James von Moltke recorded having spent noon of the previous day with Hans Wolf von Goerschen, a businessman originally from Aachen, who had emigrated before the outbreak of the war to Holland where he acquired citizenship and had established close ties with the Dutch Resistance. The same evening Moltke went to the house of his friend Peter von Yorck in the Hortensienstrasse where he also met Steltzer, Gerstenmaier, and Trott. The topic for discussion, Moltke mentioned somewhat cryptically, was the 'translation to the European plane'.[259] This remark, the language of which was of course designed to escape the censor, most certainly circumscribed all of Moltke's group's persistent attempts to establish, as he once put it, 'the connection with the greater world'.[260] As amply demonstrated in this volume, all these approaches abroad, whether they were directed to foreign offices or secret services of the Powers or to the Churches or to friends in neutral countries, hoped to reach the Powers or merely to give witness and to say 'we are here'. Most certainly, however, Moltke had in mind yet another dimension of his and his friends' 'translation', namely their eagerness to co-ordinate their efforts with the Resistance movements, such as the one with which von Goerschen was connected, in the occupied countries.[261]

The connection with the Great Powers clearly had not worked. The German Resistance was not able to get a hearing from them, not even with the help of the few advocates it could muster abroad, men like A. P. Young, Bishop George Bell of Chichester, Lionel Curtis in Britain, Harry Johansson in Sweden, and Willem A. Visser't Hooft in Switzerland. All were manifestly men of honour and independence, but they, including even Cripps, lacked political clout and thus were unable to help in bridging the widening gap between their German friends' aspirations and the hard political and strategic requirements of the Grand Alliance. At best the Germans were drawn into the orbit of the Allies to serve as informants; but this role they were unwilling to play. They wanted to be recognized as allies of the Powers, and preferably the Western ones, in a common struggle against tyranny and in the building of a new Europe. While the Germans were increasingly ready to subscribe to such high-flown visions, however, the Powers of the Grand Alliance had in the course of the war moved away from them. They settled on the national interest, on considerations defined by power politics, and on winning the war.

For the German Resistance, then, an alternative was the road to the Resistance movements in the occupied countries. These carried the brunt in the struggle against Nazi oppression. They did not have elaborate staffs and overall strategic responsibilities. They were more or less improvised armies operating at night, exposed to constant terror, and striking from within whenever and wherever possible. Their sense of the Allies was a distant one. To set Europe ablaze they would increasingly depend on support from the Allied subversive intelligence organizations, the SOE in Britain and the OSS in the United States. To begin with, however, they were essentially autonomous units. Most of them could rely on help from governments in-exile in London, but as a rule the mutual relations remained remote, if not strained. The *Résistance* units defined themselves by the immediacy of their experience, and they furthermore held on to their own spontaneous visions of a future Europe quite apart from considerations of *Machtpolitik* or even national interest.[262] Their sense of the Germans, in turn, was an immediate one, shaped by fear, suffering, and hatred: the Germans were the oppressors and they were to be resisted at all cost.

For the *Widerstand* to build bridges to the Resistance movements in the occupied countries under these circumstances was thus all the more of a problem. However, the connections even among the latter were minimal.[263] But for any German, even if of the Opposition, to approach them he had to surmount a wall of enmity and suspicion. Of course the basic conditions under which the conservative *Widerstand* functioned were altogether singular. As its members largely worked, and indeed had to work, from within the old establishments which served them as a cover for conspiracy, they were bound to encounter even more distrust. At the same time, the emissaries of the German Opposition to the Resistance movements outside Germany were at a distinct advantage. Having the resources of their offices behind them, and being either stationed abroad or able to travel abroad, they were in a position to offer their services to help alleviate the plight of the occupied populations. The Kreisau people, moreover, had consistently and unequivocally condemned the 'degrading' oppression of foreign peoples and called for the evacuation of occupied territories. Also, Goerdeler, traditionally wedded to the idea of German hegemony in Europe, had moved away from the *Machtpolitik* of the great World Powers in the direction of a European settlement based on the principle of self-determination and independence. There was, then, enough common ground between the *Widerstand* and the other Resistance movements in their struggle against Nazi oppression, as well as in their vision of a just and lasting peace, to encourage the Germans in seeking a solidarity across the frontiers with the *Résistance* groups outside the Reich.[264]

The German opposition liaisons with the occupied countries, then, under cover of their official positions or of Church connections, had a wide-ranging agenda. This included alleviating the lot of the oppressed populations and especially warning of forthcoming hostage-taking, deportations and raids against the Jews, arrangements for an orderly transition in the occupied territories after a successful coup and, last but not least, laying the groundwork for the construction of a peaceful and federated Europe after the war. But all these agenda items were generally accompanied by the hope and expectation of obtaining, with the help of the *Résistance* groups, a hearing for the *Widerstand* with the Western Allies.

The key figure in the relationship between the *Widerstand* and the Norwegian Resistance, the *hjemmefronten*,[265] was Theodor Steltzer. A German patriot and pioneer in the embattled German Ecumenical Movement, he had, as we have seen, from the very start taken a firm stand against National Socialism.[266] His wartime service with the German Armed Forces Command in Oslo did not prevent him from getting actively involved in the struggle against the Nazi regime and becoming the centre of an elaborate Resistance network.

Before leaving for Norway he had already established a close link to Helmuth von Moltke and the Kreisau Circle, and through Moltke he also maintained a line to Admiral Canaris. His ecumenical interests led him to the Nordic Ecumenical Institute which allowed him to co-ordinate his Resistance work with the activities of Dr Harry Johansson.

In Oslo Steltzer[267] met up with Bishop Berggrav whom he had known earlier from his ecumenical work and with whom he shared thoughts on religion and of course also concerns over Nazi persecution of the Churches in Germany and Norway. Before long a close friendship developed between the German Colonel[268] and the Norwegian Bishop who, in the course of the war years, had become a prime symbol of defiance to the occupiers. Steltzer was also eager to establish ties with the secular community.[269] Here his chief contact was Professor Arvid Brodersen, a sociologist who was thoroughly familiar with Germany. Before the war Brodersen had studied in Berlin and had become friends with, among others, two men who later were to meet up in the Moltke Circle, the Social Democrat Theodor Haubach and Albrecht Haushofer. Both Bishop Berggrav and Brodersen were members of the *Kretsen*,[270] which was the general staff of the home front, and through them Steltzer gained easy access to the Norwegian Resistance.[271]

As General Staff officer, Steltzer had the privilege of taking his meals, along with a small number of other officers, with the Commander of the Armed Forces in Norway, General von Falkenhorst. Thus he became privy to all the information concerning the plans of the notorious Reich Commissar for Norway, Josef Terboven. Although Steltzer never divulged any military secrets, he saw himself justified in warning his Norwegian friends of the intended coercive measures against them. He was also in a position to curb actions against Jews and the executions of hostages and prisoners of war. He was of particular help in the case of the German raid against the university of Oslo scheduled for 30 November 1943. General von Falkenhorst had been drawn into the planning for the raid since marines under his command were needed for the operation. On the preceding day, over the lunch table, he divulged this plan to Steltzer, presumably with the idea that Steltzer would inform Brodersen which indeed he did without delay.[272] If the German raiders nevertheless managed to seize a large number of teachers and students of the University, it was not for lack of warning from Steltzer. In any case, the raid itself gave public testimomy to the fact that resistance among Norway's youth was alive.

In mid-July 1944, shortly before Stauffenberg's attempted coup, Steltzer composed, in consultation with Brodersen, a lengthy memorandum aimed at 'the highest echelons on the Allied side' which, he hoped, could be forwarded by the Norwegian Resistance to London.[273] It was a moving document, a last-minute appeal to the Allies in the name of 'our circle recruited from diverse political camps'—obviously the Kreisau Circle—to stem the threatening chaos both in Germany and the occupied territories by enlisting the help of a responsible German Opposition. For once, at the eleventh hour, this document acknowledged the reality of the Grand Alliance by proposing to send accredited emissaries to London, Washington, and Moscow in order to give more particulars about the plans of the Opposition: 'we ... feel obliged to make the attempt to reach the three Great Powers before conditions render illusory any possibility to guide the situation.' For once also the document conceded the inevitability of at least military unconditional surrender. A glimmer of hope finally was left to the author as he pleaded for a policy of co-operation rather than subjugation.

Since Brodersen knew that the head of the military branch of the Norwegian Resistance,[274] Jens Christian Hauge, was about to fly from Stockholm to London, he took the memorandum over to Hauge for forwarding. The setting for this transfer of the document, as it turned out, was not without comical moments. Both men were masked, but instantly recognized each other's voices, whereupon the meeting continued unmasked and with much laughter.[275]

Steltzer's memorandum did reach London, though not before the attempt on Hitler's life in Berlin took place. The memorandum was, according to Steltzer's directions, turned over to Moltke's friend Lionel Curtis, and then made its way to the SOE, the Foreign Office, and 'C'. But by then it was part of history and put *ad acta* as the all too familiar 'old, old story' from that 'so-called opposition group'.[276] Steltzer, meanwhile, followed an order to appear before the authorities in Berlin and was promptly arrested upon arrival at the Tempelhof airport on 1 August, but in the end escaped scheduled execution by the Nazis.[277] Immediately after the war Steltzer would be given the following tribute from Norway:

This is to certify that the former Lt. Col. Theodor Steltzer during the time when he was connected with the German Army in Norway—from 1940 until he was arrested by the Gestapo in August 1944—was in close contact with the Norwegian Resistance Movement and thereby rendered our cause invaluable services. As it is not in our power to express our profound gratitude to him by helping him in his present situation, we would greatly appreciate any help given to him by the authorities with whom he is now in contact.

The above document, dated Oslo, 3 September 1945, was signed by Paal Berg (President of the Supreme Court of Norway, leader of the Resistance movement 1940–5), Eivind Berggrav (bishop of Oslo), and Gunar Jahn (Minister of Finance).[278]

Back in Norway the connection between the German Armed Forces staff and the Norwegian home front did not break off after Steltzer's departure. Major Frithjof Hammersen took over where Steltzer had to leave off. He was the son of a Norwegian mother. Being the second in command on the

Intelligence staff of General von Falkenhorst, he was not accountable for all his moves. Thus, when at the turn of the year headquarters were moved from Oslo northward to Lillehammer, he was able to travel freely to Oslo where in the home of an elegant spinster, Ingrid Furnseth, he met Jens Christian Hauge, and warned him of Gestapo schemes against the Norwegian population.[279] While it was relatively easy for Hammersen to get to Oslo, the home front people found it difficult to reach Lillehammer whenever necessary. There was need, therefore, of a German liaison stationed in Oslo who could telephone Lillehammer with impunity. The man who took over this function was none other than Johann Wolfgang von Moltke, younger brother of Helmuth. The latter had managed, three days before his arrest on 19 January 1944, to have 'Jowo' transferred to the Norway Command where he first worked for Steltzer as courier both to the home front and the German Resistance. After Steltzer's arrest, 'Jowo' then carried on, in tandem with Major Hammersen, the hazardous task of shuttling back and forth between the inner councils of the occupier and the occupied.[280] While neither Hammersen nor the younger Moltke were or saw themselves as part of the *Widerstand*, they upheld the honour of their country by shielding the oppressed Norwegians. Moltke's particular merit, as attested by Hauge, was in the end to secure an orderly German capitulation.[281]

Particularly active was the traffic between the *Widerstand* and the Dutch Resistance movement. In this case the initiative came from ecumenical circles as well as the Kreisau people and Goerdeler. The Germans who pioneered this connection were Paul Collmer and Pastor Hans Schönfeld. It goes back to the early days of the German invasion of the Netherlands in May 1940 when Collmer was appointed adviser on social issues to the occupation forces. A deeply religious man, and anything but a Nazi, he had in the course of his association with the World Council of Churches in Geneva come into contact with Gerstenmaier and Schönfeld who now, in view of his new assignment, encouraged him to seek out representatives of the Dutch Churches.[282] Among those whom he thus met, first on his own and soon after with Schönfeld, were people like F. M. Baron van Asbeck, Hendrik Kraemer, and C. L. Patijn who eventually were to emerge as leading figures in the Dutch Resistance. The Germans, even though they had been recommended to their Dutch partners by Willem A. Visser't Hooft, of course had a wall of suspicion to overcome before they could establish relations of mutual trust. In their talks, then, both parties circled around such problems as prisoners of war, internees, and the spiritual care for Dutch forced-labourers in Germany. What was ultimately on the minds of Collmer and Schönfeld, namely the search for a common Christian response to the challenge of National Socialism, could enter only indirectly. Nevertheless, with these approaches Collmer and Schönfeld laid the groundwork for an understanding between the German *Widerstand* and the Dutch Resistance.

Actually, the architect of many of the exchanges with Holland was none other than Willem A. Visser't Hooft. In the course of the war tensions had developed between the Dutch government-in-exile in London under Prime Minister Pieter S. Gerbrandy and the leadership of the Resistance in Holland. Under the immediate oppression of the occupier the people felt that their government was too remote from their problems and all too negative in its plans for the future of Germany. The government, so it appeared, insufficiently reflected the opinions of the people at home. One of the issues causing this estrangement was that of peace aims. While in no way ready to make any concessions to the foe, Nazi Germany, the Resistance leaders were nevertheless pressing for a positive statement of peace aims that would allow them to look forward to a regenerated Europe in which a 'reborn Germany' would take its place on a basis of equality.[283] The voices which came from the homeland were, thus, reflecting the 'war behind the war' position with which Visser't Hooft, speaking for the World Council of Churches, had come to be identified.

It was Visser't Hooft who took it upon himself to resolve the differences between the home front and the government-in-exile. Upon an invitation from Gerbrandy he set off in May 1942 for London where he was received in audience by Queen Wilhelmina—'an intense and moving experience'[284] for him—and negotiated with the Prime Minister an agreement to the effect that he was to set up in Geneva a Centre for an exchange of information between the people in Holland itself and the Netherlands' government in London. The actual functions of the Centre turned out to be more than that. Visser't Hooft had, in fact, embarked upon the running of a triangular underground operation between Holland, Switzerland, and England which, with the aid of an elaborate network of couriers, co-ordinated Resistance activities and plans with the government in London. This elaborate scheme was Visser't Hooft's contribution to the so-called 'Swiss Road'[285] with which Switzerland, by virtue of its neutrality, opened itself up to a whirl of intelligence and spying activities.

However, not only did the Dutch Resistance thus benefit from Visser't Hooft's 'Swiss Road'; the German Opposition did too. In April 1940, when Visser't Hooft had defined what he understood by the 'war behind the war',[286] he had actually redefined the war as being not between nations but between the Churches and Counter-Churches. It was, in fact, a world civil war. This position had allowed him to keep channels open to the Germans of the *Widerstand* who, as he saw it, were themselves engaged in that world civil war, stemming the tide of spiritual and moral nihilism. Visser't Hooft now accordingly opened his 'Swiss Road' to the Germans with the objective of enabling them to link up with the Resistance in his home country.

In the late autumn of 1942, Visser't Hooft took the initiative in this direction by asking Schönfeld[287] to take a letter to his Dutch friend, C. L.

Patijn, requesting him to receive 'Adam von Trott zu Solz, diplomat and official of the Auswärtiges Amt in Berlin'.[288] Early in December, then, Trott took off for The Hague, and after making the obligatory official calls, as duly recorded in the local German-language press, he appeared one evening at the house of Patijn, who had made a point of gathering three associates of his: van Asbeck, J. H. van Roijen, and G. J. Scholten.[289] The four received 'Herr von Ribbentrop's official'[290] with distinct reserve; but once he had disclosed to them the existence of the conspiracy in Germany and its motivation and aims, and also explained that the reason for his coming was that the German Opposition had to depend on references from neutral and occupied territories for its approaches to the governments of the Western Allies, he won their confidence. Trott's introduction by Visser't Hooft and his own calm, serious, and matter-of-fact ways convinced them that they were confronted by a person of substance worthy of their support. In the end the group settled on Hans Wolf von Goerschen, the German-born Dutch businessman, to act as continuing liaison between the Dutch Resistance and the German *Widerstand*. He had close connections with the Dutch Underground, was an old friend of General Beck and knew both Trott and Moltke, and, having connections in the Abwehr and in the Auswärtiges Amt, was able to travel freely to and from Germany and occasionally Switzerland.[291]

Both Moltke and Trott kept up the Dutch connection. Moltke travelled to Holland and Belgium in June and again to Holland in September 1943, each time on official business and doing his level best to prevent deportations and the execution of hostages. But on the June trip, at Goerschen's office in the Alexanderstraat, he also had a talk with van Roijen that lasted one and a half hours and left him with the assurance that it should be possible to establish 'a relationship of trust' with him.[292] In September Moltke was again with Goerschen. Trott was back in The Hague in August and December 1943, progressively initiating his Dutch partners into the particulars of the conspiracy, revealing to them the names of some of the leading conspirators—Goerdeler and von Hassell—and also reading to them a Manifesto drawn up by the Kreisau people that was to be issued after the successful coup.[293]

Meanwhile still another line of communication from the German Opposition to Holland was opened up by Colonel Wilhelm Staehle.[294] Staehle, who was born in 1877 near the border with Holland, was a General Staff officer of the Imperial Army and the Republican Reichswehr, and was taken into the new Wehrmacht with the rank of a Colonel. It may well have been his Dutch mother who instilled in him a sense of independence and civic spirit, but his attitude towards National Socialism was unequivocally hostile from the start. His very appointment in 1937 to the position of military director of the Settlement for War Invalids in Berlin-Frohnau was a way for the Army Command to side-track his career on account of his manifest political views. Staehle, however, together with his wife used this assignment to stage an elaborate relief operation on behalf of persecuted Jews and political dissidents. Being a member of the Confessing Church, he regularly frequented the Sunday services conducted by Pastor Martin Niemöller in Dahlem. He also co-operated with Heinrich Grüber, the Protestant Provost, who in his vicarage in Kaulsdorf near Berlin, set up an agency, the 'Buro Grüber', dedicated to helping Christians of Jewish descent. It was also at this time that Staehle met Carl Goerdeler. This connection was most probably brought about by General Beck, a friend of Staehle's since their early common service in the Kriegsakademie.[295] Furthermore, having served in the early 1920s in the Abwehr, Staehle kept up his connections with that organization; he was well acquainted with Admiral Canaris and moreover enjoyed a particularly close relationship with the then Colonel Oster.

It was Goerdeler who was the person primarily responsible for Staehle's missions to Holland. In the early 1940s Staehle frequently travelled there, establishing and fortifying connections, but also, whenever he could, helping people who were threatened by the terror of the occupation regime or by the Dutch Nazis. At the same time he organized an elaborate network of intermediaries, in both Germany and Holland, who were to facilitate the flow of information across the border. Late in 1943, together with an old friend from his youth, Arnold Brill, Staehle finally succeeded in establishing a direct contact with the Dutch Resistance. Shortly before Christmas the two Germans met three Dutchmen, with the latter taking elaborate precautionary measures against being tricked. Among the Dutchmen was G. J. van Heuven Goedhart, one of the leading figures of the Underground and editor of the influential clandestine publication *Het Parool*,[296] operating under the pseudonym 'de Graaf'. Staehle took this occasion to inform his Dutch partners about the German Resistance and its plans for a coup. He also impressed upon them the need to explore the appropriate measures to be taken for the maintenance of law and order in the critical phase of transition. In order to establish his credibility, so it seems, Staehle also announced to them that his sponsor was in the German Foreign Office, presumably meaning Adam von Trott.[297] Furthermore he informed them that van Asbeck and Patijn, who had previously met Collmer, Schönfeld, and Trott, were threatened by arrest. We can therefore conjecture with some certainty that all the missions to Holland were somehow co-ordinated.

The Dutch delegation, while setting certain minimal conditions for a continuation of negotiations,[298] felt duty-bound to send the Memorandum outlining these conditions to London for approval. The author of the Memorandum was van Heuven Goedhart, and the connection with the Dutch government-in-exile was established via Visser't Hooft's 'Swiss Road'. On this level, too, the co-ordination of the various German efforts to come to terms with the Dutch Resistance becomes inescapable.[299] Of course Visser't Hooft obliged.[300] The Memorandum, dated 3 January 1944,[301] summarized the course of the negotiations and asked for further directions.[302] In conclusion it asked that, immediately upon receipt, Gerbrandy was to send a message to the Dutch Underground via Radio Oranje: either 'de Graaf may continue' or 'de Graaf may not continue'.

In his cover note Visser't Hooft urged the Dutch Prime Minister that 'much should be left to be decided by Holland' and that a refusal of the request should follow 'only if acceptance is impossible for international reasons'.[303] The answer from London, however, was altogether negative. No radio message could be sent, but in a written communication to Visser't Hooft, Foreign Minister E. N. van Kleffens, speaking for Gerbrandy, explained that the Dutch Prime Minister had decided to 'dissociate' himself from this action, and that it was 'not desirable' that Netherlanders should join in with it. The Dutch government had reached this decision in consultation with the British government which was of the opinion that such German initiatives, 'if not inspired by the German secret service, at least have taken place with its knowledge'; as a consequence they had been ignored by the British.[304] The Dutch government-in-exile then followed suit, much to the disappointment of the Dutch Underground which was resolved to continue the talks short of negotiating in any way with the Germans.[305]

Trott undertook a last journey to Holland early in July 1944. As usual, he met his Dutch counterparts of the Underground in Goerschen's office.[306] The main purpose of this mission was to inform the group of the impending coup. Upon their repeated question as to why he revealed this information, Trott answered that it was vital for him and his friends in Germany that the Dutch were informed so as to testify in favour of his group before the Allied governments, in case of a successful coup. Finally, upon Patijn's question as to how much of a chance he thought they had of overthrowing the regime, Trott answered: '25%'.[307]

It would be foolish to expect the connection between the Kreisau people and the Dutch Resistance to have yielded any particular results. All we know is that van Roijen, soon after escaping from Holland in October 1944 and following the instructions of van Kleffens, visited Washington. There he told former Under Secretary of State Sumner Welles and Assistant Secretary of War John J. McCloy of his and his friends' contacts with the Germans: 'in their reactions I noticed much genuine interest and no hostility.'[308] Actually, what had happened was that, in the course of the war years, the connection between the German and Dutch Underground groups had assumed a distinct reality, expressing what Patijn later called the 'historical solidarity' of the *Widerstand* with the Resistance movements in the occupied countries.[309] They shared the vision of a federated Europe and clung to it despite the fact that the policies of the Great Powers, certainly since the Tehran Conference of November 1943, pointed in another direction. They persisted in conducting their 'war behind the war'. Not only among the ecumenists who were in contact with the emissaries from the Kreisau group—van Asbeck, Kraemer, Patijn—but among most of the non-Communist Dutch Underground the prevalent view was that eventually Germany would be reintegrated into a new Europe. 'We realize only too well how easy it is for others to win popularity by proclaiming eternal vengeance on all future generations of Germans,' wrote van Heuven Goedhart in December 1942 in *Het Parool*:

Rebuilding means justice, not revenge; strength, not hatred; and above all the wisdom to realize that in history there is no such thing as a way back, but only 'full speed ahead!'[310]

The same author called for a reawakening of 'the "other" Germany' whose existence, he argued, was proved by 'the brimful German concentration camps and the fact that the Gestapo constantly have their hands full':

To bring that other Germany to maturity, to open the eyes of its young people to the profound cultural values that it is the mission of the West to defend and to promote— that is a nobler and more promising task than the repetition of Versailles. The first duty of our generation towards its successors is to win the war; the second is to win the peace.[311]

European union, so it was argued in Dutch Resistance circles, and especially in the underground journals *Het Parool* and *De Ploeg*,[312] required the inclusion of a regenerated Germany: 'for the sake of Europe' a lenient attitude towards Germany was imperative.[313] As a matter of fact, the 'solidarity' among the Resistance groups on both sides, tenuous though it was, went hand in hand with a scepticism about the objectives of the Great Powers:

We don't belong to the Americans, who think Europe has had its day and who want to divide it into an Asiatic and an American sphere of interests. For us Europe remains central—at least as far as civilization is concerned, and it is not a mere appendage to Asia . . .[314]

The alternative which Europe faced at the end of the war was perceived as one between 'annexations or European order': 'All around is vengefulness and thirst for annexation. . . . It is better to fight for our ideal of a regenerated Europe than try to slip in between the paws of the great carnivores in the hope of seizing a morsel of their prey.'[315]

But the closer the war came to its end, the more did what the Dutch Resistance called annexationism become the order of the day, and the vision of a European order by the Resistance groups on both sides become a mirage.

Of a much more remote nature were the relations between the German Resistance and the Resistance movements in other countries. In France, Moltke's contact was Carlo Schmid who since June 1940 had functioned as senior administrative officer (Militärverwaltungsrat) under the Military Commander of Belgium and Northern France, General von Falkenhausen, himself a decided foe of National Socialism. Son of a French mother, Schmid was an international lawyer and, like Moltke, guided by the ethos of his profession. Stationed in Lille, he did his level best to protect the population against the long arm of the SS and the Gestapo.[316] Moltke reported to his wife about his first meeting with Schmid that he was 'a man ... who has always supported our positions'.[317] The two men met frequently in Lille, both keenly aware of the fact that their discussions bordered on treason.[318] Schmid maintained contacts with the French Underground, and it was through him that Moltke met a member of the French *Résistance*, Marcel Pasche, pastor of the Reformed Church. But that was all.

The other contacts with the French *Résistance* were no less tenuous. Lieutenant Colonel Cäsar von Hofacker, a cousin of Stauffenberg, had since 1940 been posted to the Administrative Staff of the Military Commander of France and then, in the autumn of 1943, was taken on to the personal staff of the Military Commander, General Karl Heinrich von Stülpnagel. Initially an ingrained National Socialist, Hofacker in the course of his Parisian tour of duty developed doubts about the Nazi regime and then turned into one of the driving forces of the *Widerstand*, acting as liaison between the Paris Command and the OKW in Berlin.[319] While in France he also developed a sharply critical opinion of the objectives and oppressive measures of the German occupation policy towards France and came to advocate a German–French alliance, albeit at the price of an intensification of the naval war against Great Britain.[320]

As for Hofacker's relations with the French *Résistance*, they are shrouded in mystery. From the Communist side he has been claimed for the Communist *Résistance*.[321] Through his driver, Paul Gräfe, an old Social Democrat, so the story goes, Hofacker was brought into contact sometime late in 1943 with 'Annette' and Otto Niebergall, the head of the 'Committee "Free Germany" for the West',[322] founded in September 1943. Early in January and in mid-May of 1944, two meetings ensued between Niebergall and 'Annette' with Hofacker and 'an elderly general'.[323] The topics discussed in these meetings were: the hopeless (for Germany) situation at the fronts; the impending landing of the Allies in France; the threatening catastrophe; the continuation of the senseless war by Hitler-Fascism; and the responsibility of all patriotic forces to end the war and overthrow the Hitler regime. Hofacker also revealed that 'something' was being prepared against Hitler, without, however, giving any details about the plot.[324] On the occasion of the second meeting Hofacker supposedly declared his readiness to become a member of the KFDW.

This story about Cäsar von Hofacker, for the moment at least, cannot be verified and must therefore remain hostage to the post-war division of Germany.[325] Certainly, it does not agree with a recommendation by Hofacker of October 1943 to prevent, in view of the imminent Allied invasion, a linking of the French *Résistance* with the invading forces.[326] We are also left wondering why he should have made connection with the Communist

Underground rather than with the de Gaullist branches of the *Résistance*.[327]
A crucial question furthermore, answered in the affirmative with excessive
certainty in the literature of the German Democratic Republic, is whether
Stauffenberg in any way identified himself with the approaches of his cousin
to the French Underground.

There were still other connections with the French *Résistance*. General von
Stülpnagel is said to have commissioned a member of the German Economic
Mission in Paris, Dr Hans Buwert, to seek contact with representatives of
General Charles de Gaulle;[328] and Admiral Canaris, we are told by one of his
close aides, encouraged some of his officers to do likewise.[329] It is reasonable to
assume that, whatever connections were established by the *Widerstand* with
the *Résistance*, particularly as the war neared its end, these were designed to
persuade the latter to concentrate its attacks on Party strong-points, to look
favourably upon the forces connected with the coup, and possibly also to
envisage some sort of co-operation after the coup.

Altogether hazy is the information concerning the scene in Belgium. The
Military Commander of Belgium and Northern France, General von Falkenhausen,[330] was an officer of the old school. While himself not exactly a
member of the *Widerstand*, he was generally looked up to by all the sectors
of the conspiracy for his firmness of conviction and moral authority; in the
latter phases of the war he was, in fact, variously proposed instead of
Goerdeler for the post of the future Chancellor.[331] In his Command, Falkenhausen conducted a regime that was as humane as possible under the
circumstances.[332] He resided in the style of a *grand seigneur* in the rococo
castle Seneffe[333] where a principal figure was also his lady-friend, the Princess
Elizabeth Ruspoli. She acted as go-between with King Leopold III, interned
in Laeken Castle, and it was through her also that Falkenhausen established
ties with the Belgian population, allegedly also to the Belgian Resistance.
After the war, when he had to face a Belgian War Tribunal, he was defended
by lawyers from the Belgian Resistance.[334]

Relations between the German and the Austrian Resistance were completely *sui generis*; they were neither foreign nor domestic relations, or rather
they were both. Germans and Austrians have always been siblings with the
prerequisite familiar sentimental ties and rivalries. Since the dissolution of
the Habsburg Monarchy in 1918/19, if not earlier, the *Anschluss* movement,
favouring a union between the two, had been the order of the day. But once
the *Anschluss* had been realized under Hitler's aegis, the dream revealed itself,
to the Austrians certainly, as a nightmare. Even the most ardent apologists
of the *Anschluss* idea, among them the Austro-Marxists, had come to have
second thoughts about the *Anschluss* and to consider redefining the sibling
relationship. Perhaps Austria, even the Austria as truncated by the Paris
Treaty system of 1919, was viable after all and could exist by itself as an
independent state. Even the proposition, unthinkable in serious quarters

between the wars, that the Austrians constituted a nation separate from the Germans, gained currency after the Nazi annexation in March 1938.

The German resisters who ventured into Vienna in the early 1940s came up against this change in the Austrian climate of opinion. In most of the memoranda that emanated from the German *Widerstand*, the parts dealing with foreign affairs took for granted, as we have seen, that after Hitler Austria would remain part of Germany. At most the Austrians were to be granted the privilege of a plebiscite which, it was generally assumed, would result in an overwhelming vote for remaining part of the German Reich, purged of course of the Nazi taint.

It is symptomatic that when Goerdeler and Jakob Kaiser set off for Vienna in October 1942, their prime concern was the solidification of the coalition against the Hitler regime.[335]

Starting in October 1942 the German conspirators undertook various trips to Vienna.[336] Their objective was to draw the various dissident groups in Austria into the fold of the German *Widerstand*. They therefore made a point of conferring with the conservative Christian Socials as well as with the Socialists. The subsequent visit to Vienna in the early summer of 1943 by Wilhelm Leuschner, a leading German Socialist connected with both the Kreisau Circle and the Goerdeler Circle, was designed especially to woo the Austrian Socialists. If anything, the Christian Socials, in contrast to the Social Democrats, had throughout the years of the First Austrian Republic been sceptical of the *Anschluss* agitation. But now, much to their surprise, the Germans found resistance in various degrees among all their Austrian partners. To be sure, they were all prepared to provide special dispensation for Austria after Hitler that would prevent her from degenerating into the status of a 'province'.[337] They reasoned that the Austrians would be able to make a real contribution to a Greater Germany by counterbalancing the excessive 'Prussianization' of the Reich.[338] The Austrians were to help the Germans in coping with the shame of Nazism and to share in the act of expiation [339] before 'the world' closed in on them by military action.[340]

Lois Weinberger, however, who hosted the first meeting with Goerdeler and Kaiser, unequivocally argued the case for a free, independent Austria, independent even from Germany. [341] The Socialists were just as reluctant to oblige the German visitors.[342] If Seitz was relatively accommodating,[343] Schärf, when confronted with Leuschner, did not beat about the bush. After Leuschner had, in the course of a session lasting three hours, outlined his ideas about the Austrians joining in a 'German Revolution', Schärf interrupted, bursting out: 'Der Anschluss ist tot', adding that the Austrians had been thoroughly cured of their love for the German Reich.[344] When he had finished, he felt that it was not he, not his voice which was speaking, but another person, another voice speaking through him.[345] He left Leuschner altogether shattered. The Vienna visits gave no encouragement to the Germans of the

Resistance, and the issuance on 1 November 1943 of the Moscow Declaration by the Allies, in which they declared the occupation of Austria in March 1938 'null and void' and committed themselves to free Austria from German rule, finally buried all dreams, however well-meaning, of Goerdeler and his friends concerning the union of the two German states freed from the Nazi yoke.

On still another level, the military one, the German Resistance reached out to the Austrian orbit. Through a German military channel Goerdeler himself made an effort to get into contact with an Austrian military person, the former Colonel in the k.u.k. army, Colonel Walter Adam; but here too he ran up against doubts as to the desirability of keeping Austria within the confines of the Reich.[346] There were also German officers belonging to the military arm of the *Widerstand* who were stationed in Vienna and in turn Austrian officers and enlisted men under the command of Military Districts XVII and XVIII who were connected with the Austrian Resistance.[347] Among the former was a Bavarian nobleman, Colonel Count Rudolf von Marogna-Redwitz, chief of the Abwehr in Military District XVII and the leading figure of the German military *fronde* in Vienna; among the latter was Captain Karl Szokoll of the Organization Section in Military District XVII. Their chief function in the Resistance, however, was not political but rather the co-ordination of the military coup between Vienna and Berlin. The decision on the future relationship between Austrians and Germans had been made by the Austrians' awakening to the reality of the Nazi annexation and by the Moscow Declaration of 1 November 1943.

Moving further east, there were but the most fragmentary connections between the Kreisau Circle and the area of the *General gouvernement* in Poland. Sometime late in 1942, when the German advance into Russia had been brought to a halt, Hans-Bernd von Haeften, on a mission from Moltke to Carlo Schmid in Lille, launched the idea of arming Polish Resistance groups, albeit in order to check the Russian advance.[348] But Moltke did have a particular interest in Poland if only because of the propinquity of Kreisau to the Polish border. He therefore asked an old friend of his and member of his Circle, Fritz Christiansen-Weniger, to be his liaison to Poland.[349] Christiansen-Weniger was an agriculturist working in the experimental station at Pulawy near Lublin, and he was thus in a position to extend help to persecuted Poles and Jews. Since, however, he became too exposed in this activity and was suspected by the SS, Moltke decided early in 1943 to travel to Poland himself to confer with the Archbishop of Cracow, Prince Adam Sapieha.[350] While he actually visited his friend in Pulawy early in May,[351] he may or may not have been able to make a stop-over in Cracow.[352] In any case it is very likely that, as Ger van Roon suggests, he had a scheme in mind for deepening contacts in Poland and swaying the Polish Resistance away from an anti-German orientation towards a 'European and anti-totalitarian' course, and that he even considered, as did Haeften, providing it with arms.[353]

With the Yugoslav Partisans there were some contacts, but these ran through the Austrian Resistance.[354] With Russia there was the connection through the Communist network of the 'Red Orchestra' and through the 'National Committee for a Free Germany' and the 'League of German Officers', which have been dealt with earlier in this volume. They did not, however, link up with the conservative groups of the *Widerstand*.

It was Visser't Hooft who in 1944 made the supreme effort to rally the various European Resistance movements to a common purpose. It all started on the initiative of two Italians, Ernesto Rossi and Altiero Spinelli, who in 1943 founded the Movimento Federalista Europeo and in the autumn of 1943, after the German occupation of Italy, moved to Switzerland from where in November they sent out invitations to Resistance leaders from all over Europe to convene in order to work out a common platform for the future of Europe. Meeting up with Visser't Hooft, they had no difficulty in engaging his support since their ideas and proposals were much in line with the thinking in the Ecumenical Movement.[355]

Between March and July 1944 four meetings took place[356] 'somewhere in occupied Europe',[357] but actually in Visser't Hooft's home in Geneva. Altogether fourteen or fifteen people, chosen more or less at random,[358] participated: three or four Italians, two or three Frenchmen, two Dutchmen, and one each from Denmark, Yugoslavia, Norway, Poland, Czechoslovakia—and two Germans.[359] During the first session in March a heated debate ensued concerning the advisability of inviting members of the German Resistance, but the majority decided that Germans too should have a voice in determining the future of Europe. The two Germans who were therefore invited, and who attended, were both women from the camp of the Socialist Resistance: Hanna Bertholet, who was connected with the Militant Socialist International (Internationaler Sozialistischer Kampfbund, ISK), and Hilda Monte, an inveterate activist who was in and out of that group and who in the end paid with her life for her daring underground work. Visser't Hooft evidently did not ask Schönfeld to attend; he was never quite certain of him because of his connections with the Church Office for External Affairs. As for Trott, he had been in Switzerland just before both the April and July meetings of the international group; but committed as he was to return to Germany to take an active part there in the preparation of the coup, attendance may have been for him too much of a hazard.

Two documents emanated from the deliberations of the international group of resisters. Declaration I,[360] a general statement of principle, conjuring up the spirit of solidarity among all those fighting in the ranks of the Resistance of oppressed peoples against the common enemy, was unanimously approved. Declaration II[361] set out to translate the general consensus into more specific terms. It committed the members to the acceptance of 'the essential principles of the Atlantic Charter' and proceeded to outline the main features of a

European Federal Union; 'only a Federal Union', it argued, 'will enable the German people to join the European community without becoming a danger to other peoples.'[362] But otherwise this Declaration elicited a great deal more debate, and indeed disagreement, above all on the extent to which national sovereignty could and should be limited for the benefit of a workable Federal Union, and on the advisability of including Russia in it.[363]

Immediately following the meeting of 20 May the two Declarations were sent out to the exile groups in Switzerland and to the various Resistance movements in the countries that were represented in the Geneva meetings. But the reception which Document II was accorded was varied, and certainly not unanimously affirmative. The document called for discussion, and this it got with a vengeance. It may be that an elaborate discussion of European federation at that time was premature. In any event, the invasion of Normandy, which began soon after on 6 June, established new priorities. The Allied armies, Visser't Hooft had to acknowledge, 'carried out a policy in which there was no place for the idea of a European federation'.[364] The 'war behind the war', alas, was drowned by 'Operation Overlord'.

## 6. Germany West or East?

The one hard and irreducible reality which the German conspirators had to face up to in their relations with the outside world was the geopolitical situation of their country in the centre of the European Continent between west and east. All their secret missions abroad and all their messages were, as we have seen, aimed, directly or indirectly, towards London or Washington. At the same time, however, they were keenly aware of the Russian presence in the east, of the leverage it might lend them in their dealings with the Western Powers, and also of its impact upon their schemes to free themselves of the Nazi yoke and upon their plans for a reconstructed Germany in the heart of Europe.[365]

In their views on foreign affairs, the men of the German Resistance were, on the whole, pragmatists. The proposition, as launched in the Nazi secret-service reports, that three distinct positions had emerged among the conspirators, advocating respectively the eastern, the 'pronouncedly' western, and the mediating solutions[366] is misleading. Only the Communists had a clear commitment that pointed eastwards to Soviet Russia. Otherwise the various groups and individuals in the Resistance of course had certain geopolitical inclinations and preferences. Without question the Social Democrats, both in exile and in resistance, opted for the West; they had in the course of the Weimar years learned to face the Communists as foes. Exile had taken the Party to Prague (1933–8) and then to Paris (1938–40) and finally to London, and certain stray members to New York. The Social Democratic leadership both in London and New York withstood the temptation to form a united front with the Communists and was deeply apprehensive about a Russian sweep over Europe.[367] The Socialists in the Resistance were similarly alert to the danger lest Germany be abandoned to Soviet domination.[368]

The non-Socialist Resistance was also without question oriented towards the West. France, no doubt, featured little in its thinking. General Beck, in the spring of 1937, and Goerdeler in the spring of the following year had certainly made soundings in France, and Hans Robinsohn's Memorandum of the immediate pre-war period had stressed the need for co-operation between Germany and France. But Goerdeler in effect had, as he confided to his representative in London, 'written off' France. The insistence, furthermore, in Paris, following the opening of hostilities in September 1939, on the 'fallacy of the "two Germanies"' on which Sir Eric Phipps reported,[369] discouraged any further contacts with France. From then on ex-Chancellor Wirth and Lieutenant Colonel Cäsar von Hofacker were the only ones to persist in keeping channels open to the French. But on this score Hofacker, who in contrast to Wirth was in the centre of the German Resistance, was altogether out of line with the thinking of his fellow conspirators.

Goerdeler had his own representatives: in London—Reinhold Schairer; in New York—Gotthilf P. Bronisch; but none in Paris. Schairer, it must be added, was the one who prepared Goerdeler's Parisian trip in the spring of 1938. Subsequently, however, Goerdeler directed all his attention to a dialogue with London and Washington. Like Hassell, he thought that he spoke the same language as the Anglo-Saxons, and that he therefore had reason to persist in trying to reach them. Especially after the Nazi–Soviet Pact of 1939 both Goerdeler and Hassell banked, however erroneously, on a community of interest with Britain that might sway her to safeguard the integrity of a post-Hitlerian Reich in the interest of stemming the advance of Bolshevism into Europe.[370]

Furthermore the Kreisau people had particularly close ties, especially through Moltke and Trott, with the Anglo-Saxon world. Moltke's South African heritage was of paramount importance to him,[371] and through it he had come to know Lionel Curtis whose Commonwealth scheme became his own model for international organization; in the future Great Britain was somehow to be linked with a European federation which might enable it to assert itself *vis-à-vis* the United States.[372] Moltke's awareness of the United States was heightened through his contacts in Berlin with Alexander Kirk and George F. Kennan. With both men he developed a sense of intimacy and mutual trust, and even though in the end neither could be of any help to him in getting his message through to Washington, they greatly contributed to his realistic assessment of America's decisive part in the strategy of the war.[373] Trott of course had close ties across the Channel; since his years at Oxford he had come to think of England as his spiritual home. Moreover he was keenly aware and proud of his American ancestry. He knew that in Oxford and London as well as in New York and Washington there were many doors open to him, that is until the moment when he found out in mid-1939, and in the winter of 1939/40, that the same doors could be shut against him. It should also be remembered that Trott by no means agreed with his friend Moltke in his assessment of the function of Britain in world politics. Inasmuch as he considered himself a socialist, anti-capitalist, and anti-imperialist,[374] Trott did not share Moltke's faith in the future of the British Empire or even the Commonwealth; nor did he believe that American intervention in European affairs could ultimately redress the world balance of power. The 'European revolution' about which he had written to Professor Percy E. Corbett in June 1941, called for a much more comprehensive settlement in which some eastern orientation was inevitable and in which Russia was bound to occupy a definite place.[375]

The disposition of the German resisters to look towards the West did not of course make them oblivious to the East. The ground rules, so to speak, to the Russian problem were laid down by the professionals of the Foreign Service. In 1939, before the conclusion of the Nazi–Soviet Pact, Weizsäcker had advocated maintaining a 'tenuous balance'[376] that would have prevented Russia from concluding an agreement with either the Western Powers or with the Nazis; and Hassell fell back on the board-game metaphor of the *Mühlespiel* to indicate the need for an understanding with either side, Russia or the Anglo-Americans, while of course preferring an accommodation with the latter. The fallacy of these ground rules, however, was that they were drawn up on an assumption of the integrity of Germany as a sovereign entity in the centre of Europe with its own capacity to maintain a balance between the West and the East. It had been difficult enough for Bismarck and Stresemann to manœuvre the Reich under this kind of prescription. But how could an ill-accredited emissary from a Resistance accomplish this task which, like the German one, was so little visible and deeply distrusted abroad?

The long-range projections in Resistance circles on relations between Europe and Russia, and specifically between Germany and Russia, were strikingly uniform. In his effort to summarize the position of the Opposition, in the 'Statement by a German Pastor at Stockholm' of 31 May 1942 for Bishop Bell of Chichester, Hans Schönfeld devoted a special section to the Russian Problem. Protesting that they had 'no aims to conquer Russia or to get for Germany parts of Russia as a colonial area', Schönfeld expressed their hope 'that it may be in the future possible to co-operate in a really peaceful way with Russia, especially in the economic and cultural field'.[377] Goerdeler's earlier memorandum 'Das Ziel' was on the more sceptical side, expressing doubts concerning a 'fruitful' economic and political co-operation with Bolshevik Russia; but nevertheless it envisaged that eventually Russia would be included in a combined Europe.[378] Goerdeler, it might be added, like the architects of the Weimar foreign policy, was more preoccupied with the Polish problem than the Russian one, and persistently argued for the liquidation of the Corridor, a 'source of continuing disturbance to the justified national feelings and interests of the German people'.[379] Among the Kreisau people the views on Russia were not very different. While they abhorred Communism and its policies, they sought some formula for co-operation with Russia in the future.[380] The European federation which they sought was bound to enter into some sort of relationship with the Soviet Union. Adolf Reichwein, one of the Socialist members of the Kreisau Circle, is reported to have expressed this position most unequivocally: Russia was 'the great and powerful land of the future' without which or against which no European policy was possible.[381]

In its immediate approach to the West–East problem, however, the *Widerstand* was virtually without leverage. This being the case, it tried to create it, albeit with two almost contradictory strategies, the 'Communist bogey' and the conjuring up of the 'Riddle of the East' that might sway a post-Hitlerian Germany in an eastern direction. The 'Communist bogey'[382] was a refrain resorted to by almost all the emissaries and in almost all the memoranda of the Opposition. Both Trott and Goerdeler used this approach in trying to woo the British Foreign Office.[383] Their vision of Germany as a bulwark against Bolshevik Russia was indeed supported by their intermediaries. Visser't Hooft's 'war behind the war' recognized the threat to Christianity from both 'great counter-Churches', Communism and National Socialism. The Wallenbergs were keenly aware of the threat to Sweden from nearby Russia,[384] and the spectre of the bolshevization of Germany and Central Europe was also agitating Gaevernitz and his master in Berne. It was precisely this argument, however, which boomeranged from London against the German Resistance. Neither London nor Washington were in a mood to risk the integrity of the Grand Alliance for what was perceived to be divisive approaches from Germany.

As for the 'Riddle of the East',[385] early in the war John W. Wheeler-Bennett, in the already-quoted report from New York to the Foreign Office,[386] had set out to conjure up the 'very real danger' that a prolonged war of increasing severity and horror might result in Germany turning National Bolshevik, and thereby, in collaboration with the USSR, 'constituting an even greater threat to the fabric of European civilization'. In a covering letter to Sir Robert Vansittart he elaborated as follows:

The German people are standing at the crossroads, hesitating whether to turn to the West or the East. By tradition, culture and inclination they tend towards the West but desperation may drive them Eastwards. The very hatred of Britain which is today so violent is partly due to the fact that, in our propaganda, we have harped too much upon the note that the German people have been misled by Hitler and not enough upon what the West has to offer the German people when they have rid themselves of Hitler. I do not believe that the people themselves wish to turn towards Russia but they will certainly do so rather than surrender to a humiliating peace. The Niebellungen [*sic*] complex is still strong in Germany!

The same is true of the General Staff, and particularly of its older members, who as young colonels remember the deadly effects of Communism on the German troops and civilian population during the winter of 1918–19. These men would infinitely prefer to co-operate with the West, if the West would give evidence of something to offer, but even they may be persuaded to turn eastwards if a long war of exhaustion becomes unavoidable. They would do so because many of them have been brought up in the Seeckt tradition and because they would see in such a step a last desperate chance of getting rid of Hitler and the regime and founding upon the ruins of old Bolshevism and old National Socialism a new military Sovietism in which the army would be the ruling caste.[387]

These alarming paragraphs were no doubt inspired by Trott who at the time had Wheeler-Bennett's ear, and they temporarily at least prompted Sir Alexander Cadogan to consider exploring 'through underground channels ... what would be possible in the way of a new regime in Germany'.[388]

Neither Goerdeler nor Hassell ever resorted to this kind of argument. As the 'notables' of the conservative Resistance, they were traditionalists averse to toying with socialist experimentation of any sort, and Goerdeler in particular was firmly committed to the canons of a libertarianism conditioned by a capitalist economic and social order. The social revolutionary ideas came from the 'youngsters' in the Kreisau Circle, above all from Trott. The Wilbrandt–Rüstow 'Exposé', composed after the Moltke visit to Turkey in December 1943, pointed to the existence of a strong 'Eastern wing' of the German Opposition, represented in the Wehrmacht and above all in the Luftwaffe. In the tradition of the 'historical co-operation between Prussia and the Russian monarchy, and between the German Republic and Soviet Russia in the Rapallo period',[389] this 'Eastern wing' had worked its way towards advocating some sort of accommodation with Soviet Russia. At the same time the 'Exposé' also protested that 'the Group', for which it claimed to speak, regarded the 'bolshevization' of Germany through the rise of a 'national communism' as the 'deadliest danger to Germany and the European family of nations'. Somehow the 'Communist bogey' and the 'Riddle of the East' blended in the document. However, neither of its authors was really too well informed about the ins and outs of the Opposition in Germany, and we have reason to question how representative it was of opinion in the Kreisau Circle.[390]

In Trott's thinking, however, the eastern mystique was a persistent theme. He was as fascinated by the East as he was wedded to the West, and the more the 'uncertainties of the West' became apparent to him, the more did he seek refuge in expectations of salvation elsewhere. In contrast, the ever-resilient and hopeful Goerdeler, kept putting his bets on Britain, to the very end expecting her to respond finally to the overtures of the *Widerstand* in view of the threat of a Russian sweep over the Continent. This was Goerdeler's illusion. Sharing none of Trott's socialist and anti-imperialist tendencies, he was also on this score immune against expecting the light from the east. As for Trott, the disillusionment over the rejection of his overtures by the West, as well as the prospect of American interference in European affairs, kindled his imagination to look towards Russia as a potential counterbalance against Western preponderance. Thus Trott, the grandson of Hans Lothar von Schweinitz, Imperial Germany's Ambassador to St Petersburg, rediscovered Russia. To be sure, it was not Bolshevik Russia but a sort of timeless Russia. In any case, this was Trott's illusion.

In his two encounters with Gaevernitz in Berne of January 1943 and April 1944, Trott regaled the latter with both the 'Communist bogey' and the argument of the Germans as an 'oppressed people' tempted to turn east. Furthermore, when in Sweden in June/July 1944, he explored the possibility of approaching Mme Kollontay and sought a copy of the programme of the National Committee for a Free Germany. These moves speak of his exasperation and his determination to obtain a hearing in the East and West after all. These were not merely tactical moves; they were, however desperate, part of a broader strategy to define, as he put it, 'the condition of the German spirit between East and West' and thus to demonstrate 'the indispensability of the German element for every future European peace settlement'.[391]

Shortly before the attempt on Hitler's life, Trott composed an elaborate memorandum, 'Deutschland zwischen Ost und West',[392] which unfortunately got lost, but which by all accounts added up to an ambitious review of Germany as a mediator, diplomatic as well as cultural and social, between the two worlds, East and West.[393] It was co-authored by Trott's friend and fellow worker in the 'Sonderreferat Indien', Franz Josef Furtwängler,[394] according to whose testimony it contained a 'passionate appeal' to the Allies not to 'sink their claws' into German soil by means of occupation.[395] The more distinctive passages of the memorandum, however, evidently transcended the political realm, being engaged in speculative flights about the particular German place between the 'Realprinzip' of the East and the 'Personalprinzip' of the West.[396] Trott was particularly apprehensive lest the document get lost or be destroyed.[397] He said that he had written it 'with his heart's blood',[398] and it is thus all the more regrettable that it did disappear.[399] In any case, no degree of imagination and ingenuity could have made up for the basic weaknesses of Trott's position *vis-à-vis* the Western Allies and their refusal to give him a hearing. He had a vision of a 'European peace settlement'; but under the circumstances, due to no fault of his own, it was condemned to become only a mirage.

A most quixotic plan was hatched, probably by Henning von Tresckow, that involved one of the most hard-nosed professionals of the German diplomatic service, Count Friedrich Werner von der Schulenburg. After he had to close his Embassy in Moscow in June 1941, he took over in the Berlin Foreign Office the assignments as Chief of the Political Division XIII[400] concerned with the Soviet Union, as well as of the so-called *Russland-Gremium*, a committee which brought together some of the leading German experts on Russia.

Both positions were largely nominal, but Schulenburg used them to do his level best to persuade the German leadership of the futility of the war and the need to come to an accommodation with Soviet Russia. Like Trott, he had been informed by Peter Kleist about the Russian overtures to Germany, and he urged the pursuit of the secret negotiations. But when he found himself consistently rebuffed by the Nazi leadership, he threw in his lot, in mid-1943, with the Resistance.

If anyone among the conspirators was an 'Easterner', Schulenburg was such; but first and foremost he was a pragmatist. He offered his services in the interest of bringing an end to the war, and what particularly recommended him for this task was of course his Russian experience and his good rapport with Marshal Stalin. In the autumn of 1943, then, if we are to follow the SD Reports, Goerdeler and Tresckow discussed the possibility of smuggling Schulenburg through the German lines in the east in order to reach Stalin. Evidently Tresckow was the one who pushed the plan, whereas Goerdeler was sceptical about it; for the latter, so the SD Report about the episode correctly commented, a separate peace with Russia would have meant a change of '180 degrees' in his foreign policy concept.[401] Being Operations Officer of the Army Group Centre on the Eastern front, Tresckow was also in the best possible situation to implement his plan.

It is of interest, however, that Schulenburg was one of those Resistance figures who did not make a clean break with the Nazi establishment. Although he found the Führer adamantly opposed to any approach to Soviet Russia, he still had cause to bank on Ribbentrop, who had himself begun to develop doubts about the war and who also harboured memories of his 1939 pact with the Soviets. Some of the planning for this mad venture was actually done in Ribbentrop's Austrian summer retreat in Fuschl. But the idea was, as one of those present recorded, that the channel to Russia could eventually be used to benefit not the Foreign Minister of the Third Reich but the latter's successor.[402]

Tresckow's scheme was never implemented. One reason was that his chief, Field Marshal von Kluge, Commander-in-Chief of Army Group Centre, got cold feet and withdrew his support. In general the scheme was too adventurous. But Schulenburg was left disillusioned even with his friends in the Resistance. He had come to understand that they were no more seriously interested than the Nazis in the understanding with the Soviets which he thought indispensable for an effective German foreign policy in the centre of Europe.[403]

By the autumn of 1943, however, Schulenburg had carved out enough of a place for himself in Resistance circles to appear on the lists of members for a prospective Goerdeler Cabinet. Up to that point Hassell's name had been featured for the position of Foreign Minister,[404] but from then on it was agreed that both Hassell and Schulenburg would make themselves available and that the eventual choice would be made dependent upon the 'political situation'.[405] In case the choice fell upon Hassell, which was generally anticipated, Schulenburg was earmarked to proceed as extraordinary Ambassador to Stockholm to instigate negotiations with the enemy powers from there on behalf of the new government. In the end, Goerdeler approached Beck on 15 July 1944 with a proposal to reverse the order between the two and, 'in view of the course of the political–military situation', to nominate Schulenburg for the post of Foreign Minister.[406]

These 'decisions', which in each case depended on the tides of war from the west and east, were reached in an atmosphere of rationality and serenity. Both Hassell and Schulenburg were gentlemen and did not compete with one another; as Hassell recorded, he was 'on very good terms' with Schulenburg and 'happy and willing to have a very thorough discussion with him, not in the spirit of a "distribution of jobs", but rather in order to work out a basis for co-operation'.[407] In any event, in those last days before the fatal 20 July, Hassell sat down to write up a grand historical summary of Germany's predicament situated as it was between west and east:

It is a tragedy not only for Germany but also for the whole Continent that the thought [of Germany as the healthy and strong centre] has been so rarely understood and realized ... We had to pay a heavy price for not having succeeded in coming to terms in one or the other way with this situation.[408]

At this time the Battle of Normandy was in full swing in the west, and in the east the floodgates were opening up. These were the immediate problems that Stauffenberg and his lieutenants had to face.

## 7. 'Apparently BREAKERS are breaking': 20 July 1944

By the time Stauffenberg had moved into the centre of the plot against Hitler, other nuclei of resistance had been put out of action. General Beck had had to undergo a cancer operation in April 1943, and while he remained to the end the unchallenged authority in the *Widerstand*, his part, especially in the last phases of the conspiracy, was more advisory and symbolic than executive. With Moltke's arrest on 19 January 1944, the head of the Kreisau Circle was put out of commission. The dismissal of Oster in the previous April, the suspension from service of Canaris in February 1944, and the subsequent subordination of the Abwehr under Himmler's command, spelled for all practical purposes the end of the Abwehr as a centre of resistance. Canaris's successor as head of the Abwehr, Colonel Georg Hansen, while himself also involved in the *Widerstand*, was in no position to replace the Oster–Canaris team. The two conspiratorial centres that survived these successive blows were thus those connected with Goerdeler and Stauffenberg. Their task was to prepare for the showdown and, of course, its possible co-ordination with the foreign Powers and their armies that were threatening to engulf the Reich from both east and west.

The relations between the two, Goerdeler and Stauffenberg, were, as we have seen, not the best. Quite apart from the generation gap and temperament clashes between the two, they disagreed in particular on the question of the need for Hitler's assassination, which Goerdeler stubbornly sought to avoid. He held on to the illusion that Hitler should and could be removed by persuasion rather than violence. Concerning negotiations with the enemy powers, there was basic agreement between the two on the advisability of turning to the West and staving off Bolshevik Russia.[409] The disagreements in this area were essentially a matter of different perspectives and priorities.

Like almost all his fellow plotters, in his planning for the coming coup, Goerdeler was concerned with correlating it with the survival of the Reich and with exacting conditions from the other side that favoured the maintenance of Germany's basic territorial integrity.[410] Indeed the war against Bolshevik Russia seemed to lend him all the more reason to press the Western Powers for concessions and for rescindment of the 'unconditional surrender' policy. Even though in the course of time Goerdeler modified his terms in deference to the Western Allies and also in the light of the deteriorating position of his country, he kept insisting on patriotic priorities that should dictate any negotiations with the enemy countries. As late as May 1944 he sent over to Stauffenberg, via Captain (Res.) Hermann Kaiser, his liaison with the conspirators in Army Headquarters in the Bendlerstrasse, an eleven-point directive for such negotiations which provided for, among other stipulations, the withdrawal in the east to the Reich frontiers of 1914, the retention of Austria and the Sudetenland in the Reich, autonomy for Alsace-Lorraine, and the incorporation into the Reich of the Tyrol down to Bozen (Bolzano) and Meran (Merano).[411] Goerdeler's indomitable optimism may well have been fed by the encouragement that came from Gisevius in Switzerland concerning the readiness of the Western Allies to negotiate,[412] which also allowed him to hold on to his expectations somehow to get around 'unconditional surrender'.

Along with Stauffenberg, Gisevius correctly remarked, a 'new dynamism'[413] entered the conspiracy. Finally, there had appeared on the stage a military man whose claim to leadership was predicated upon a sense of urgency in view of the impending catastrophe. Under these circumstances, and from this perspective, the coup came to be his priority; it had to be attempted at all costs. In effect, then, Stauffenberg abandoned the linkage between the coup and the national interest that had been guiding Goerdeler.[414]

At an earlier date, sometime in 1941 or 1942, Stauffenberg's cousin, Baron Hans Christoph von Stauffenberg, upon Moltke's prodding, had enquired from Berthold, elder brother of Claus, about the latter's views, and whether he 'couldn't be useful'. A few weeks later the answer came back: 'He says that we must win the war first. While it is still going on, we cannot do anything like this, especially in a war against the Bolsheviks. When we get home, however, we can deal with the brown pest.'[415] At that moment, then, Stauffenberg's priorities were still basically the same as Goerdeler's: the survival of the Reich was his paramount concern.

By the summer of 1943, however, when Stauffenberg had recovered from his severe wounds suffered in Africa, he had changed his mind on the advisability of action against Hitler and his regime. The very fact of his own survival may have given him a particular sense of obligation and impelled him to put himself at the disposal of the conspiracy. The tides of the war, however, had changed fundamentally since the days when he had waved off Moltke and his cousin's approach to him. The likelihood that Germany could 'win the war first' had faded, and the soldier's argument against 'action' at home while the troops were fighting for their country had lost much of its weight. Earlier in the conspiracy General Halder had also been caught in the dilemma between the need for 'action' at home and his duties as warlord, and he had therefore recoiled from 'action'. Most German generals, however critical of their Supreme Commander and his policies, had been paralysed by this dilemma. As a matter of fact, in November 1943, so the story goes, Halder commissioned his intimate, Colonel Johannes Rohowsky, whom he had visited in Bavaria and who was about to return to duty on the Staff of the Reserve Army in Berlin, to take a message to Stauffenberg saying 'The aim remains the same'. But when Rohowsky delivered the message he had virtually no reaction from Stauffenberg. The latter merely leaned back in his chair for a moment and kept silent. Reporting back to Halder, Rohowsky commented: 'something is still going on there.'[416]

Stauffenberg, then, was about to resolve the dilemma for himself. The territorial integrity and indeed the survival of the Reich were now manifestly threatened, and 'action' at home was not likely to have much of an effect on it one way or another. It therefore became a matter of increasing moral necessity to stage the coup. This does not mean of course that Stauffenberg would not grasp at any straw and keep hoping and attempting to minimize, if not to avert, the impending catastrophe. On the eve of the Allied landing in Normandy, he still figured that the chances were fifty-fifty that the German troops could throw the invader into the sea, and that subsequently the British could be induced to negotiate.[417] It was not until June 1944 that Stauffenberg was ready to accept the bitter inevitability of 'unconditional surrender'. He nevertheless assumed the helmsmanship of the conspiracy with altogether different priorities from Goerdeler. In view of the severity of the crisis the latter's business-as-usual approach in his dealings with the outside world was alien to Stauffenberg. Thus he entered the scene essentially as a crisis manager, and his first objective was 'action', that is the assassination of the top Nazi leadership, and any negotiations with the British or Americans were made contingent on and subordinated to it. Even in this position, to be sure, there was plenty of room left for illusionary thinking and acting.

Goerdeler's design had been brought to a halt in Sweden late in 1943 when even his friends, the Wallenbergs, lost their patience with his insistence on assurances from Britain in lieu of, as they saw it, action. The Swiss connection with Allen W. Dulles seemed to hold out more promise for success. Goerdeler's—and General Beck's—lieutenants in the Swiss capital were Gisevius and Waetjen, and with the help of Gero von Schulze Gaevernitz, Dulles's German-born right-hand man, they managed to establish a foothold, so to speak, in the Herrengasse 23, the headquarters of the 'Special Assistant to the American Minister'. At the time when the tides of the war were mercilessly turning against Germany, Goerdeler's emissaries made a last effort to make a case for the Resistance as a viable negotiating agent and indeed spell out the 'condition' on which their group was ready to act.[418]

Even though Dulles never for a moment left the Germans in doubt that he was bound by the dictate of 'unconditional surrender' and protested that 'at all times' the 'Breakers' were 'entirely' on their own and 'at no time did they receive any encouragement or political communications',[419] he did, no doubt, informally at least and through the mediation of Gaevernitz, offer them a modicum of what he called 'quiet encouragement'.[420] The major proposition which Gisevius and Waetjen brought before the American was the possibility of the German armies somehow opening up the front to the invading armies in the west in order for the German armies then to be able to concentrate on the defence against Soviet Russia. This idea was by no means all of their own making. It had frequently been discussed previously in Resistance circles.[421] But early in 1944 Gisevius and Waetjen decided to make a case of it. Waetjen tried in March to clear it with Beck and Goerdeler in Berlin, but ran, on Beck's part in particular, into a firm refusal: 'No, I cannot do it', was the General's response. Nevertheless, back in Berne, the two hotheads forced the issue and presented their project to the American intelligence chief as though it had the approval of Beck.[422] Dulles reported the proposal repeatedly to Washington[423] which, not surprisingly, did not take the bait.

The part played by the OSS in these meetings in Berne with the two German opposition members deserves further scrutiny. The faithful accounting on the part of Dulles to the OSS in Washington was of course a matter of routine, no more and no less. But what exactly took place between him and 'Luben' (Gisevius) and 'Gorter' (Waetjen), we have no way of knowing. Was Dulles altogether ingenuous when he assured Washington that at all times the two had been 'entirely on their own' and that at no time had they received 'any encouragement or political communications'?[424] Or had he in fact offered them 'quiet encouragement'? The mutual agreement among the Allies, at the Moscow Conference of October 1943 to shun any separate peace feelers was above all designed on the part of the West to allay Russian suspicions. The State Department did send out memoranda to the British and Russian Embassies, informing them about the initiative that had come, as it had been made to understand, from Beck and Goerdeler.[425] At the same time it saw fit to 'request OSS to inform its representative in Switzerland of the position of this government with respect to such peace feelers'.[426] Had Dulles, then, overstepped his mandate after all, if only by making recommendations to Washington that were derived from his talks with the two Germans?

It can be assumed that it was not Dulles alone who was out of step with official Washington. There existed certain policy differences, not only between the OSS and State Department but also within the State Department itself. The OSS harboured a strong contingent of conservative hard-liners, some of them carry-overs from the Hoover administration, who, particularly after the formation of the 'Free Germany' movement by the Russians in July 1943, were alarmed at the menace of the Soviets' designs for the domination of Central Europe.[427] After all, General Donovan himself, having served under President Coolidge as Assistant Attorney General, had close ties with the Republican establishment which tended to chastise the Democrats over their laxity towards Soviet Russia. Also within the State Department, there existed policy differences concerning the merits of the 'unconditional surrender' formula and consequently the merits of keeping the door open to the German dissidents. Secretary of State Cordell Hull himself had his doubts on the stringency of the 'unconditional surrender' demand which, he feared, might play into the hands of the Nazi propagandists and have the effect of cementing all Germans, Nazis and anti-Nazis, into a bloc.[428] Actually, the State Department's 'request' to the OSS to straighten out its 'representative in Switzerland' went out over the strenuous objections of the very man, James W. Riddleberger, Chief of the Division of Central European Affairs, who signed it.[429] As a matter of fact, the foreign policy of the United States was shaped neither by the State Department nor by the OSS but rather in the White House, the Treasury, and by the Joint Chiefs of Staff.

In any event, Dulles forwarded to Washington the terms, which he had been given to understand had come from Beck and the other opposition generals, that would have enabled the Western Allies to enter Germany unopposed.[430] He also made distinct recommendations, such as the assignment of an American liaison officer to assist 'Gorter ... and his outfit' regarding 'Intelligence aims'.[431] Furthermore he pointedly called attention to the statement of 12 July by Prime Minister Churchill in the House of Commons in which, in answer to a question by the Labour MP Mr R. R. Stokes, he said that it would be 'a very well advised step on the part of the Germans' to overthrow their German taskmasters.[432] 'The end for Germany is in sight', Dulles advised Washington with singular self-assurance, adding an eloquent plea to lend 'encouragement' to the internal revolt that was in the making and that might 'help to save thousands of lives of Allied soldiers fighting on the various fronts'.[433]

General William J. Donovan in turn carried the message to the President, coupling the forecast of 'the end for Germany' with a plea for 'encouragement to internal revolt',[434] and he also kept up the barrage after the coup, forwarding with emphasis Dulles's 'Suggested Lines of Action'.[435] President Roosevelt, however, was clearly unmoved by the hint that the Russians were 'at the door of East Prussia';[436] he was immune to the 'Communist bogey'. In short, the OSS was out of step with the White House, and by going in to bat for the Germans, may after all not have helped them. The interplay between Dulles and Gisevius and Waetjen served in effect to nourish Goerdeler's illusionary notions about what terms he could still obtain from the other side; he kept going after the *fata Morgana* that ever eluded him in a shimmering distance. In fact, no terms whatsoever could have averted the final débâcle, and only the success of the plot against Hitler might have vindicated the German Resistance in the eyes of the Americans. As for Dulles, as late as 22 July he sent out to Washington the triumphant message:

Apparently BREAKERS are breaking[437]

But once he had convinced himself of the failure of the coup, he was found by his friend and assistant Gaevernitz in 'utter despair'.[438]

Upon entering the conspiracy Stauffenberg's style was marked by a tenacious commitment to action. Goerdeler was not so far off the mark when he referred to Stauffenberg as a 'Querkopf',[439] bent upon conducting political affairs himself. He was indeed an obstinate and determined man. 'Attentat', that is assassination of the Nazi leadership and above all of the Führer, assumed priority over all other considerations. If then his style differed markedly from that of Goerdeler who kept holding on to his illusionary notions concerning the powers of persuasion at home—the rejection of tyrannicide—and abroad—the insistence upon the territorial integrity of the Reich—Stauffenberg could rely on a team which distinguished itself from

Goerdeler's by the pragmatism and realism of its approach to the crisis. First and foremost he always had his elder brother Berthold by his side. Henning von Tresckow, with whom he had been acquainted since the summer of 1941, became a firm ally united to him by conviction and courage no less than by a sense of realism concerning the plight of the Reich. Stauffenberg had come in contact with Otto John, who was a daredevil of sorts but at the same time a man of sober judgement, through his aide Werner von Haeften, late in 1943. At about the same time, via the Haeften brothers, he had met Adam von Trott, with whom he developed a sense of mutual understanding and indeed a particularly close relationship. In the course of those last months before the coup, with all the experience behind him of dealing with the outside world, Trott became a kind of 'foreign policy adviser' to Stauffenberg.[440] Finally, there was Julius Leber, the one-time military expert of the Social Democrats, a down-to-earth man able to distinguish between what was desirable and what was possible.[441] Leber's unsparing critique of the part played by the German Social Democrats during the Weimar Republic, which he wrote about while imprisoned in 1933,[442] had its concomitant in an advocacy of a reformed democracy combined with leadership and authority. Stauffenberg in turn came to be increasingly aware of the need to better integrate the workers into a future Reich. Thus the ideas of the two men met as their personalities became attuned to each other. Stauffenberg actually came around to wishing that Leber rather than Goerdeler would become the chancellor of a renewed Germany.[443]

Berthold von Stauffenberg was, like Moltke and Trott, a student of international law. Since 1929 he had been associated with the well-known Institut für ausländisches öffentliches Recht und Völkerrecht in Berlin and served for two years between 1931 and 1933 at the International Court at The Hague; on the outbreak of the war he joined the Supreme Command of the Navy (OKM) as adviser on questions of maritime international law. In this capacity he worked closely with Helmuth von Moltke, and both men were united in their determination to subject the conduct of the war to the canons of international law.[444] In the spring of 1939 Berthold von Stauffenberg had also met Adam von Trott, and since then the two shared their concerns over the future prospects of their country.

On the whole, the part which the German Marine played in the *Widerstand* was negligible. Admiral Canaris himself can hardly be considered a representative of the navy, and Berthold von Stauffenberg was only an officer of the naval reserve. He was, however, a crucial companion for his younger brother. Whereas Claus was resolute, if not impetuous, Berthold was sensible and serene; the two brothers, then, complemented each other in their combined effort to make an end to the regime of terror. In the navy, however, Berthold was able to co-opt only one man, Lieutenant-Commander Alfred Kranzfelder, who served in Berlin as liaison between the OKM and the

Auswärtiges Amt, and who was willing to translate his detestation of
Nazidom into action. In the winter of 1943/4, presumably after Goerdeler's
last encounter with Jacob Wallenberg in November 1943, the two undertook
a trip to Stockholm with the objective of reaching the Wallenbergs and thus
establishing, so Claus von Stauffenberg hoped, a connection with Churchill.[445]
This move, even though nothing came of it, at least tells us that Stauffenberg
was informed about Goerdeler's Swedish connections and also that he, the
'Querkopf', was prepared to take over the conduct of affairs from Goerdeler.
Moreover, there is a likelihood that the connection with Churchill was
established after all, but that his reaction, predictably, was negative.[446]

As for the terms which Stauffenberg and his advisers thought of being able
to exact from the Allies in view of the imminent German military defeat, they
were considerably more realistic than the ones that Goerdeler clung to.
Propositions like holding on to the German borders of 1914 in the east, and
the granting of autonomy to Alsace-Lorraine were out of the question for
them. Goerdeler, as Leber said, was thought of as an 'illusionist'.[447] As early
as the turn of the year of 1943/4 Stauffenberg had anticipated the evacuation
of *all* occupied territories.[448] Now Leber insisted that a 'total occupation' of
Germany, whether or not a change of government had taken place, was
unavoidable; and once the Allied landings in Normandy had taken place, he
went as far as proposing 'the cession of East Prussia, Alsace-Lorraine, the
Sudeten area etc.', simply because he deemed it inevitable.[449] Surely, Leber,
a native of the Alsace, cannot have arrived at this proposal light-heartedly.
Like Otto John, he cautioned his co-conspirators, notably Adam von Trott,
against banking on a split within the Grand Alliance,[450] and he dismissed as
unrealistic Goerdeler's attempts to reach a separate settlement with the West.
Also, like Otto John, he came around, late in 1943 or early in 1944, to facing
up squarely to the inevitability of unconditional surrender.[451]

But it would be a mistake to attach fixed positions to the actors on the
stage of that tragedy. They had set out to free their country from tyranny,
pleading in vain for support, or at least understanding, from without. Now,
however, the Allied forces were closing in relentlessly from west and east.
Liberation from the Nazi yoke would come from without, and it would at
the same time bring occupation, if not partition, to a Germany freed from
the plague. The vague terrors of 'unconditional surrender', to which Winston
Churchill had alluded earlier in the year,[452] hung over all the conspirators,
and it gave them little or no encouragement that the coup, now at last within
reach, would have a tangible effect upon the Allied plans for the treatment
of Germany. The conspirators were all patriots, and while Goerdeler and
Leber represented more or less opposite positions on the strategy to be
followed in the eleventh hour of their struggle, Goerdeler himself, the incor-
rigible optimist, had his moments of dejection in which he came to face up
to the inevitability of 'unconditional surrender'. Leber in turn, the hardened

realist, had never completely abandoned hopes for an honourable peace that could salvage the core of Germany.

If anyone actually took charge of the foreign relations of the *Widerstand* in this last phase between the Allied landings and the coup of 20 July, it was Stauffenberg and Trott together. By the time they first met, young as he was, Trott had clearly emerged as the expert on foreign affairs among the conspirators. As an official of the Auswärtiges Amt, he was afforded a good overview of the international scene. He could, moreover, claim an intimate knowledge of Britain and, to a somewhat lesser extent, of the United States. During the war he had undertaken numerous trips to the neutral capitals of Switzerland, Sweden, the Low Countries, and one to Turkey in an attempt to prepare the ground for a post-Hitlerian Germany situated between East and West. Bouncy and resilient as Trott was, he had, by the time he met up with Stauffenberg, also been sobered by the repeated rebuffs and the rejection of his efforts that had come from the West. As 'foreign policy adviser' of Stauffenberg, then, his chief task was to tone down his friend's flights of imagination. Whether or not the SD Reports were correct in quoting Trott as thinking 'very little' of Stauffenberg's foreign policy skills and judgement,[453] the Colonel clearly had to make his plans in the setting of a 'panic before the deluge', as Trott put it,[454] which inevitably affected his judgement. Even granted that he was personally disposed to deal responsibly and decisively with the crisis, the objective situation itself was hardly conducive to considered political calculations. If it did not call for outright despair, it at least conjured up in front of Stauffenberg's and even Trott's vision the shimmer of *fata Morgana*.[445]

What merit was there to Stauffenberg's claim that he had a connection to Churchill? Was he referring to his brother Berthold's unsuccessful attempt in the winter of 1943/4 to communicate with the British Prime Minister? Was it a mere figment of his imagination that he had a direct channel of communication to Churchill?[456] Trott, much to the exasperation of the more sceptical Otto John, also clung to the notion that some sort of dialogue was afoot with Churchill and that the latter's address of 24 May before the House of Commons had made a deliberate distinction between Nazi Germany and Germany so as to suggest that the Allies were prepared to negotiate with a non-Nazi government.[457] Even if Trott's trip to Sweden of June/July dashed any such speculations,[458] Goerdeler seems to have persisted that late in June an enquiry 'from the highest English authority' had gone out about the conspiracy, and Stauffenberg in turn is supposed to have submitted a three-point plan to England which included a list of men who were to conduct negotiations with England, the 'desire' that Austria remain in the Reich, and the 'request' to leave the punishment of war criminals to the future German government.[459] Compared with Goerdeler's eleven-point agenda list of May, this one certainly was considerably more restrained and realistic.

All along Stauffenberg had also toyed with the idea of circumventing the politicians—with Goerdeler particularly in mind—and of establishing a 'soldier to soldier' relationship with the other side in order to bring the war to an end; but what reason did he have to assume that he could establish a direct connection with the American Generals Eisenhower and Marshall?[460] There is no reason to assume that he was aware of the Allied Supreme Command's reservations concerning 'unconditional surrender' which Generals Eisenhower and Smith voiced in April 1944.[461] In contrast to Goerdeler, Stauffenberg, as well as Colonel Hansen, seems to have been increasingly conscious of the key role played in the Grand Alliance by the United States.[462] When Colonel Hansen, in the presence of Stauffenberg, on the Saturday following the invasion of Normandy, urged Otto John to try 'at all cost' to establish a connection with Eisenhower',[463] the idea was that an armistice could be negotiated with the Allied Supreme Commander after the successful attempt on Hitler's life.

Trott may have been correct in stating that Stauffenberg acted in a vacuum on matters of foreign policy.[464] Certainly the weeks after the Normandy landings provided stern evidence to the German conspirators that the long saga of overtures abroad had failed, and that the Western Allies were now less disposed than ever to have dealings with them. Any move at that moment on Stauffenberg's part other than assassination was bound to be illusory. But inasmuch as assassination had become his one priority, he manifested a grim sense of realism after all. Come what may, the assassination had to take place. It might activate the Churchillian 'then we'll see' and, as Stauffenberg evidently hoped, lead to a recognition of a new German government by the Western Allies. But more important, he came to understand that the outward effects of the planned attempt were of secondary importance. On the evening of 4 July as he walked with his friend Rudolf Fahrner through the villa district of Wannsee on the outskirts of Berlin, the two came to agree that what mattered was 'internal purification' and the question of honour.[465] The arrest of Leber on the following day,[466] and the news leaked to Gisevius by a Gestapo connection on 17 July that an arrest warrant had been issued against Goerdeler served only to strengthen Stauffenberg's resolve to go into action.[467] When he finally staged the attempt against Hitler on the occasion of a briefing session at the Führer's headquarters in East Prussia on 20 July 1944, he followed the advice given to him by his friend Henning von Tresckow:

The assassination must be attempted at all costs. Even if it should not succeed, an attempt to seize power in Berlin must be undertaken. What matters now is no longer the practical purpose of the coup, but to prove to the world and for the records of history that the men of the resistance movement dared to take the decisive step. Compared to this objective, nothing else is of consequence.[468]

Stauffenberg's bomb, as is well known, did explode, causing four deaths and considerable damage, but it did not achieve its objective of killing Hitler. In Berlin, meanwhile, where the Plan 'Valkyrie'[469] was scheduled to unfold, the conspiracy collapsed upon news that the Führer had survived. There followed a campaign of vilification of that 'very small clique of ambitious, wicked and stupid criminal officers', as Hitler put it in his address that went out over all German radio stations about one o'clock the following morning, a bout of arrests, humiliating tirades against the accused in the 'People's Court' proceedings, brutal executions by hanging and last, but not least, the holding liable for the crime ('Sippenhaft') of the entire families, including minor children, of the accused.[470] The Third Reich thus managed to drag out its existence, and the brutal war was to take its course for almost another year.

On the morning of 21 July Henning von Tresckow, before committing suicide, said to his friend Fabian von Schlabrendorff:

Now they will all fall upon us and cover us with abuse. But I am convinced, now more than ever, that we have done the right thing. I believe Hitler to be the arch enemy, not only of Germany, but indeed of the entire world. In a few hour's time, I shall stand before God and answer for both my actions and the things I neglected to do. I think I can with a clear conscience stand by all I have done in the battle against Hitler. Just as God once promised Abraham that He would spare Sodom if only ten just men could be found in the city, I also have reason to hope that, for our sake, he will not destroy Germany. No one among us can complain about his death, for whoever joined our ranks put on the poisoned shirt of Nessus. A man's moral worth is established only at the point where he is prepared to give his life for his convictions.[471]

Even in failure the *Widerstand*, by its example, left a message to posterity. The priority which Stauffenberg had given to action, established the 'connection with the greater world', if only through the language of martyrdom, as a reminder of the existence of that 'other Germany'.


# 8. The Aftermath

Even in failure the message of the coup to the outside world, of the existence of the 'other Germany', was unmistakable. The reception of the news in the Allied capitals, however, was anything but appreciative of the conspirators. The Grand Alliance had been designed to win the war militarily, and now that victory was in sight, there was no cause to change course, even with the prospect of shortening the war and saving many lives. In addition, the many contacts which nevertheless had been established in past years with the German opposition emissaries had, if anything, served to build up rather than diminish distrust of their intentions and peace aims. Nothing now could deter the Allies from their resolve to maintain 'absolute silence' and to aim at 'unconditional surrender'.

In Washington and London especially the reaction to the coup of 20 July 1944 was chilling. The chief source of information for Washington was the OSS. Allen Dulles in Berne certainly did not fail to press for some sort of action 'short of shelving "unconditional surrender"', to maintain the momentum of the German conspiracy,[472] and his Chief in Washington fully identified with him. Donovan's chief concern was that the fatal set-back of the 'western-oriented' dissident group in and outside the army would 'still further increase the influence of Russia in Germany and somewhat decrease the influence of the West'.[473] He therefore did not hesitate to put Dulles's recommendations before the President in the form of 'Suggested Lines of Action'.[474] But the President kept his silence. The attempt on Hitler's life was, as Dulles put it, dismissed in Washington—and in London—'as of no consequence'.[475]

The American press was no less dismissive of what had happened in Berlin on 20 July. In a comment on the first show trial of the People's Court against Field Marshal Erwin von Witzleben and seven other officers, and after paying some grudging tribute to the German officers' 'fundamental virtues of discipline, honor and patriotism', the *New York Times* charged them with abandoning these and succumbing to the 'atmosphere of a gangsters' lurid underworld'. Sententiously, it saw fit to conclude that 'one does not win wars with soldiers who cheer the death of their top leaders'.[476] The *New York Herald Tribune* pontificated similarly that Americans as a whole will not feel sorry that the bomb spared Hitler: 'Let the generals kill the corporal or vice-versa, preferably both.'[477] As a matter of fact, by a directive from the President, antedating the cessation of hostilities in the European Theatre of War, there was to be no mention in print of the German Resistance,[478] and later the American occupation authorities continued to enforce the ban on such publications.[479]

The post-mortems that came from London were no more supportive. PWE set the stage with a directive on 21 July, christening the German coup, somewhat misleadingly, as 'The Revolt of the Generals',[480] and ruling out any reference to the dissidents as 'good Germans'. 'Unconditional surrender' was to remain the order of the day. On the following day *The Times* editorial concerning the events in Germany stated that it hardly needed to be said that the rivals for Hitler's power were no friends of the Allies: the generals who set themselves up as pretenders did so 'as champions not of liberty but of militarism'.[481]

The Prime Minister and Foreign Secretary were briefed by John W. Wheeler-Bennett, erstwhile friend of Trott and Goerdeler and now a confidant of Anthony Eden, who for good reasons was generally recognized in Whitehall as an authority on things German. Wheeler-Bennett composed an elaborate memorandum, dated 25 July, arguing that Britain was 'better off' with things as they were 'than if the plot of July 20th had succeeded and Hitler had been assassinated'.[482]

Not without cause he gave expression to forebodings that Weizsäcker, on behalf of 'the "Old Army" Generals', as he put it, might launch from the Vatican a peace move that would allow Germany to sue for terms other than those of unconditional surrender.[483] It was, he concluded with cold cynicism, 'to our advantage' that the purge should continue, 'since the killing of Germans by Germans will save us from future embarrassments of many kinds'.[484]

Then came the blast before the House of Commons' session of 2 August by a triumphant Winston Churchill:

Not only are those once proud German armies being beaten back on every front ... but in their homeland in Germany, tremendous events have occurred which must shake to their foundation the confidence of the people and the loyalty of the troops. The highest personalities in the Reich are murdering one another,[485] or trying to, while the avenging armies of the Allies close upon the doomed and ever-narrowing circle of their power.

The abortive uprising in Germany was, so he summarized, yet another manifestation of an 'internal disease'.[486] There was power in this speech, though for once none of the customary Churchillian chivalry. The remonstrations on the part of the Labour MP for Lambeth North, Mr George Strauss, to the effect that recent events in Germany had 'blown skyhigh' the theory that insisted upon playing down the existence of two Germanies, a good and a bad Germany,[487] were, under the circumstances, no match for the Prime Minister's rhetoric.[488]

The few advocates in wartime Britain of the German Resistance, however, and especially Bishop Bell of Chichester, remained unimpressed by the official hard-line towards the German coup. The Bishop kept pounding at the Foreign Secretary, reminding him again and again of the connection between the coup and his encounter with the two German pastors in Sweden in the spring of 1942, which he had so unsuccessfully brought to the attention of Eden.[489] Once again Bell approached the British government, this time with two requests: (1) to take steps to help the principal leaders of the revolt to escape and (2) to appeal over the heads of Himmler and Hitler to those people who had proved the reality of their hatred of Hitler by trying to take his life and destroy the regime.[490] But the Foreign Secretary remained adamant:

I am afraid that I can give you no encouragement to believe that it would be possible to act on your first suggestion. Apart from the practical difficulties, I cannot admit that we have any obligation to help those concerned in the recent plot, who had their own reasons for acting as they did and were certainly not moved primarily by a desire to help our cause. As regards your second proposal, the Government have constantly under review all means of weakening German resistance, but I am not satisfied that an appeal of the kind you envisage would in present circumstances prove an effective contribution to this end.[491]

Like Bishop Bell, Sir Stafford Cripps maintained throughout the war his positive attitude to the German Resistance. He was deeply moved upon hearing the news of the execution of Adam von Trott, a 'dear friend' of his family for whom he had the 'greatest admiration'. Moreover, Whitehall's position on the recent plot notwithstanding, he thought it 'tragic', as he wrote to Bishop Bell, that 'all these good men' were 'lost to the future of Europe'; it will 'make the task of reconstruction far more difficult'.[492]

Soon after 20 July Archbishop Temple of Canterbury sounded out the Foreign Office concerning a forthcoming visit to London by Visser't Hooft ostensibly to attend a meeting of the British Council of Churches to be held later in September. But the Foreign Office was sceptical about the prospect. While, as G. W. Harrison of the Central Department argued, Visser't Hooft himself 'in character' was 'above suspicion or reproach', the fact nevertheless remained that he was known to have been in touch with German opposition groups in the past, in particular the civilian end of the opposition. Harrison referred especially to Visser't Hooft's previous connection with Adam von Trott. He might, then supply information not only to the Archbishop himself but also perhaps to 'men like the Bishop of Chichester' about continued opposition movements in Germany, especially in Church circles. 'Find administrative and technical difficulties', Harrison minuted, to prevent the trouble-making Dutchman from coming before Germany had collapsed.[493] No doubt the abortive coup and the terrible retribution that followed it had the effect upon Visser't Hooft of causing him more than ever to identify with the conspirators whom he considered his 'comrades in a common struggle'.[494] In any case, he made his way to London via France, Belgium, and Holland and took this occasion to present an elaborate account of the German Resistance to the Peace Aims Group meeting on 7 November in London, under the chairmanship of Bishop Bell of Chichester.[495]

To begin with, he discounted Wheeler-Bennett's thesis that the 'Revolt of the Generals' wanted to save something from the ruins of their country. Leaning over in the other direction he labelled the Resistance in Germany as composed essentially of 'civil' groups and individuals who 'meant to do the right thing for Germany, Europe and the world'.[496] Visser't Hooft's exposure in recent years to men like Bonhoeffer and Trott had allowed him to perceive the ethos of the *Widerstand* and to single out its Christian, reformative, and European dimensions.

The General Secretary of the World Council was well aware of the fact that the back of the revolt in Germany had been broken, but he nevertheless saw fit to account for the causes of the failure and also to prepare the ground for a positive and constructive solution of the German problem after the inevitable military defeat. While making all the necessary allowances for the difficulties encountered by the Allies in being confronted with a resistance group in an enemy country, he took the occasion to take them to task for their lack of 'political imagination'.[497] Some assurance, he maintained, particularly from Great Britain, that the resistance once activated would have been taken seriously, could have gone a long way. Visser't Hooft was in a good position to contrast the negative policy of the Western Allies towards the German Resistance with the attitudes of the other Resistance movements throughout Europe. Although they had carried the brunt of the struggle against the German military and political machine, they had learnt, largely through their contacts with the Germans of the *Widerstand*, to insist upon the distinction between Nazis and Germans and to envisage for the Germans 'some kind of hope for the future'.[498] Stating that 'just at the moment when some of the liveliest elements are getting ready for federation', the Anglo-Saxon nations seem to have 'set their faces against it',[499] Visser't Hooft offered the services of the World Council of Churches and a possibly expanded Peace Aims Group to enter into a dialogue with the people in Germany.[500]

Before this group, of course, Visser't Hooft spoke to the converted. But politically, for the moment at least, he spoke into the wind. Admittedly he addressed himself above all to the 'spiritual dimensions' of the German problem,[501] and that in itself was of some significance. At least he spoke for the record, a record which it is up to the historian to ponder.

In contrast to the curt dismissal, in the White House and in Whitehall, of the coup in Germany, the reactions in Soviet Russia were mixed. In the foreign affairs of the Bolsheviks, propaganda objectives always went hand-in-hand with the prerogatives of the *Grosse Politik*, and, although they were designed to complement each another, they were not always in concert with one another. To judge from *Pravda*, however, the Soviets were unprepared for news of a coup in Germany. They were of course preoccupied with the outcome on the battle front. Nevertheless it is striking how poorly it informed the public about the events inside Germany. The initial Tass report relied heavily on unsubstantiated rumours from Stockholm,[502] and from then on the paper inched its way towards some sort of evaluation of the coup. Contradicting Nazi propaganda, it insisted upon stressing the 'deep roots' of the internal commotion in Germany[503] and came round to interpreting it as marking a process of internal disintegration and a cleavage within the Fascist regime. The rebels' intent, so the *Pravda* story went, was to sacrifice Hitler in order to preserve their own positions, their capital, and their lives.[504] In the end *Pravda* thus arrived at an interpretation of the event of 20 July 1944 that was roughly in line with the encompassing Marxist-Leninist theory of Fascism.

The cautious and gradualist approach of *Pravda* was not shared, however, in other quarters. To start with Radio Moscow went out on a limb, paying tribute to 'the brave men who stood up to Hitler'.[505] Then, of course, there was the 'Free Germany' movement in Russia. To be sure, there were bound to be deep cleavages within it when it came to an assessment of the events of 20 July.[506] The leaders of the German Communist exiles, such as Walter Ulbricht and Erich Weinert, obviously tended to dismiss the conspiracy against Hitler critically as a last-minute attempt to salvage the German imperialist-military order. The captive Wehrmacht officers, on the other hand, saw the deed of Stauffenberg as a confirmation of their own essentially patriotic motivation.

On 23 July the National Committee for a Free Germany issued an appeal to the German people and to the German Wehrmacht in praise of the 'brave men' who had risen against Hitler: 'Every blow against the Hitler system, *whoever* may strike it, is a blow against the mortal enemy of our nation. *Every* action *against* Hitler and his henchmen is a truly patriotic deed'.[507] Exactly one month after the events of 20 July a grand summary praised the new 'resolute leadership' of the military Opposition, singling out Colonel General Beck as an 'outstanding representative' of the best traditions of the German General Staff, and Colonel von Stauffenberg as a guarantor for the 'decent convictions' of those who took it upon themselves to spill the blood of criminals in order to spare the German people further suffering.[508]

As time went on, however, the differences within the National Committee in the assessment of the plot became more marked, and the Communist theoreticians worked their way towards what they saw as a correct Marxist-Leninist interpretation of the event. Thus, in a speech on 16 August before the National Committee, Anton Ackermann, a Communist exile, emerged with a carefully reasoned analysis of the plot as having been carried out by the traditional establishments together with disaffected Nazis, but without the people; the coup, on balance, thus amounted merely to a 'palace revolution'.[509] One step further was the position that the putsch was nothing but an attempt of the ruling classes in Germany to rid themselves of their praetorian guard; they had originally helped Hitler to power in order to prevent revolution and to salvage monopoly capitalism, and now, seeing their interests threatened by the Nazis, they turned against them with the help of the Generals. However they were not able to cope with the monster they had helped to create. Such was the version of the plot given by Rudolf Herrnstadt, an exiled Communist theoretician and now editor of the weekly paper *Free Germany*.[510]

In the Soviet Union the uprising of 20 July, then, was not ignored, as it was in official Washington; nor was it as one-sidedly dismissed as it was in official London. Dissenting voices like those of Bishop Bell of Chichester and Visser't Hooft, pleading for a reading of the legacy of the German Opposition as partners of the 'war behind the war', were for all practical purposes discounted in Britain. But in Soviet Russia some sort of dialogue ensued between the 'patriotic' and the 'Communist' interpretations of 20 July. In the last analysis, the latter was subjected to the test of Marxist-Leninist orthodoxy.

If we now compare the Nazi post-mortems concerning 20 July with those in the United States and Great Britain particularly, they were not very different. The headline for 9 August of the *Völkischer Beobachter* concerning the People's Court verdict against Field Marshal von Witzleben and company read: 'The Traitors are Brought to Justice'.[511] And indeed, in the course of the investigations of the events leading to the plot, the conspirators were heaped with insult and injury: they constituted a 'clique of traitors',[512] and Goerdeler in particular was singled out as a 'wartime spy on behalf of our enemies'.[513]

Apart from this invective, however, the SD Reports contained a great deal of sober analysis which virtually all historians of the German Resistance, including myself, have seen fit to fall back on.[514] As for the foreign activities of the *Widerstand*, I might not go along with the verdict, permeating the SD Reports, that they were naïve and unrealistic. But I have no quarrel with the statement that the 'conspiratorial clique', as the obligatory phrase went, 'hoped ... that the enemy would be prepared to negotiate with a non-National Socialist Germany on an equal footing in order to conclude an honourable peace'.[515] No such balanced assessment of the foreign-policy objectives of the Resistance came from either Washington or London, and we are left wondering what impelled the investigators of the 'crimes' of the Resistance to prepare this kind of statement for the Führer who was out for blood?

Embattled as they were and facing death, the resisters themselves made their contribution to stocktaking of the plot against Hitler. There were of course the statements these men made before the People's Court, some of them extraordinarily courageous and defiant in the face of the Court's fiendish red-robed President Roland Freisler. When Count Schwerin von Schwanenfeld and Major General Helmuth Stieff brought up the murders in Poland, and when Hans-Bernd von Haeften stood up to the Nazi judge, saying that he considered Adolf Hitler 'the executor of evil in history', they made fundamental statements about their reasons for participation in the Resistance. When Helmuth James von Moltke, in his letter to his wife Freya, triumphantly reported Freisler's tirade that in one respect Christianity and National Socialism were alike inasmuch as they demanded 'the whole man', he emphatically identified the Christian grounds for his opposition to Nazism. He, like his friends, faced death the way they had lived: the examined way. All of them bore witness to the fact that those who resisted Hitler were neither defeatists nor 'ambitious, wicked, and stupid' men, nor 'underworld' types, but that they were guided to take their stand by the highest ethical and religious ideals.

The many farewell letters and diary entries written by the conspirators during their confinement, that have been preserved, are a no less moving testimony of their motives.[516] These were of course largely personal and concerned with ultimate questions of life and death. However, a passage in one of Adam von Trott's last letters may be singled out, with relevance to our particular topic, in which this young expert on foreign affairs, writing to his wife Clarita, surveyed the mission he had set himself:

You, who like no other person have been privy to my life, its hopes and impulses and its so many inadequacies, will understand that I am most pained never again to put at the service of our country the special strengths and experiences, which I had gathered in the course of concentrating, almost too one-sidedly, on her self-assertion among the Powers. In this area I still could have made a real contribution . . .[517]

But Trott's life was brutally cut short. He was swiftly brought to 'justice'; his arrest on 25 July was relentlessly followed on 15 August by sentencing and on 26 August by execution.

There was a diplomatic postscript, so to speak, to Trott's missions on behalf of the Resistance. Shortly after his execution, an article appeared in the Swedish newspaper, *Dagens Nyheter*,[518] in the form of an interview with an unnamed 'political personality' who had taken part in conversations in Stockholm with Adam von Trott, representative of 'the most important opposition group' in Germany. The article offered a comprehensive account of the Resistance, its composition and plans. While giving due credit to Trott for having always been an anti-Nazi, it cast a less favourable light on 'the majority of the members of the opposition' as having largely been motivated by the impending defeat.

Rightly or wrongly, the American Legation in Stockholm identified Willy Brandt, a 'young anti-Nazi German' as the author of the article.[519] Of course it was noticed in Germany[520] and also made the rounds in the international press.[521] No doubt the article could be construed as a tribute to Trott; but it also stigmatized his *confrères*. Moreover, by divulging the names of people involved in the conspiracy—such as Wilhelm Leuschner—who were still alive, it played, however inadvertently, into the hands of the Nazi bloodhounds.

It is interesting that the American Legation in Stockholm should now have taken a protective stance towards the conspirators. Herschel V. Johnson, the Minister, took exception to the publication of the article; it constituted a 'grave error of judgment' inasmuch as it had served to assist the German regime in its ruthless suppression of elements of the opposition.[522]

No doubt encouraged by the *Dagens Nyheter* article, a few days later the *Life* and *Time* correspondent in Stockholm, John Scott, composed a lengthy account for *Time* magazine, based on the conversation which he had held with Trott on 23 June 1944,[523] outlining the programme and the aims of the conspiracy. However, the US Minister to Stockholm once again took exception to what he considered an ill-advised exposure of those resisters who were still alive. He was actually in a position to refuse to clear Scott's story for cabling to Washington.[524] The 'veil of secrecy' was still to be kept over Trott and the *Widerstand*, so the American Minister thought. But the veil, in their favour for once, came at a time when for all practical purposes the game was all over.

After the unsuccessful coup Goerdeler was left dangling between life and death for more than half a year. From 18 July onwards he was on the run from the authorities who had put a price of one million Marks on his head; like a hounded beast he moved from one hide-out to another and finally, making a last visit to his native West Prussia, he was detected and turned in to the authorities by a certain zealous woman. He was arrested on 12 August, but not executed until 2 February 1945. Goerdeler who, as we have seen, had always been given to trust in the power of the written word, used this particular time to set on paper, *d'outre tombe* so to speak, a whole string of elaborate memoranda, justifying his course during the past years and restating his plans for the future of his country and for the European Continent.

There has been justifiable speculation concerning the reasons for Goerdeler's protracted captivity and for his outpouring of writings.[525] Was it merely that he thought of making himself indispensable as an expert on public affairs in order to buy time until the day of liberation? Or did the Nazis keep him alive to tap his administrative expertise? Indeed he was commissioned by a high official of the Nazi Secret Police, the notorious Otto Ohlendorf,[526] to write a number of memoranda on administrative and economic topics, which he conscientiously did.[527] Late in 1944 the RSHA actually sponsored a lecture in its Wannsee guest-house on the 'Plans of the Participants of the 20th of July in the field of State and Administrative Reform' in which the contributions of Count Fritz-Dietlof von der Schulenburg—already executed on 10 August—Goerdeler, and Popitz were scrutinized.[528] Was it that the Nazi gangsters themselves, notably Ohlendorf, in view of the impending end, were thinking of saving their skins through their connection with men like Goerdeler? There is reason to believe that both Ohlendorf and Himmler had an interest in keeping Goerdeler alive.[529]

Goerdeler's writings during his flight and captivity, the last of a long line of statements emanating from the German Resistance, were as intensive as they were extensive,[530] and only an understanding of the particular circumstances in which they were composed can lend the historian the right access to them. The man who wrote them had death looking over his shoulder—and Himmler also. A passionate patriot, Goerdeler stood before his countrymen bearing the stigma of a 'cowardly traitor', and the country itself now faced the nemesis which he and his fellow conspirators had all along hoped to spare it. He had never got over the death in mid-1942 of his son Christian on the Russian front, and now the rest of his family was imprisoned and dispossessed by henchmen of the Nazis. He was a man in utter despair: 'Are there many people who have been hit equally hard by the hand of God? Those whom I love are in destitution and grief, but I have no sign of life from them', he wrote from gaol; and he continued: 'Yet God knows that I have dared everything since I wanted to spare the youth, the men and women of all peoples further suffering. Oh Lord, where is the solution to the riddle? The criminals triumph!'[531]

In his 'appeal' addressed to 'all human beings' Goerdeler insisted that he was not 'stir-crazy'.[532] But this is precisely what he was. His mood shifted from compulsive flights into the past to quixotic prophecy; and from the kind of rational analysis of the political scene, that had been the mark of his earlier writings, to fantasy and incantation. There were even moments of hope that yielded to even deeper dejection and despair.

Goerdeler was on good ground in arguing in self-defence that, while he may have been engaged in *Hochverrat*, he had certainly not committed *Landesverrat*: far from having intended to 'betray' his country, he had wanted to 'save' it. Thus he conceded *Hochverrat*; it had been justified by the crimes of Hitler.[533] From the very start he had stood up against the catastrophic terms of the Paris Peace Treaties of 1919 just as he subsequently stood up against the policies of Hitler. But he was left in the lurch by the Western Allies:

What did you do when the first cries of distress came to your ears, when the news of the murders of 30 June 1934 reached you? What did your governments do? They visited and honoured him [the Führer]! What they had denied Hitler's predecessors they conceded to Hitler.[534]

Then as now Goerdeler had defended Germany's honour, then in opposition to the injustices of Versailles and now in condemnation of Hitler's crimes. In his indictment of Hitler he kept hammering at him for having precipitated the war and condemned him for the 'bestial murder of millions of Jews' and the starving of hundreds of thousands of Russian prisoners of war.[535]

But how does all this accord with Goerdeler's undeniable connection with Himmler? According to Goerdeler's biographer, towards the end of 1944 Himmler devised a plan to commission Goerdeler to use his foreign contacts—especially with Wallenberg and the Zionist leader Chaim Weizmann— to reach Churchill with the aim of bringing about an acceptable settlement of the war.[536] This would of course have involved Goerdeler's release from confinement. According to all the evidence we have, his reaction to this proposal was not wholly negative.[537] In November he drafted a letter to Jacob Wallenberg, which his kindly warden was to turn over to the Swedish Minister in Berlin for forwarding to Stockholm, pleading with his banker friend to prevail upon Britain to take the lead in an all-out effort to make peace. 'Europe, the world, humanity and civilization', as he put it in a crescendo fashion, were to be saved lest Russian Bolshevism have the last laugh.[538] This was imperative even at the price of England 'putting up with' National Socialism. What was it that had taken the once-defiant dissenter all the way from his pre-war advice to the British to stand firm to his plea now for them to make peace even with a 'Hitler–Himmler–Schacht–Geordeler' government.[539]

We have no reason to assume that Goerdeler had gone back on his fundamental rejection of National Socialism, its policies, and its criminality. Even in these last phases of his life, he remained true to himself: a man who believed in the power of reason and persuasion. The continuities in Goerdeler's thinking were indeed striking. Now, as before, he thought he had cause to see himself as the keeper of Germany's honour; now as before he kept looking towards Britain. His projection of a 'German–Anglo-Saxon community of interest'[540] against Russia was as much his pipe-dream now as it had been earlier. Also, Goerdeler's peculiar combination of nationalism and internationalism once again manifested itself in his late compositions. If anything, he now exceeded the claims which he had made for his country in the paper which he had elaborated for Wallenberg in May 1943. He now claimed the territorial integrity of 'Greater Germany' and also the 1914 borders against Poland.[541] On the other hand, he pushed for international organization, now even proposing extravagant schemes for a 'world federation of nations',[542] indeed a 'union of unions'[543] relying on the power of reason, goodwill, and divine guidance.

Under the particular pressure of the circumstances, objective as well as personal, all these positions of Goerdeler's seem to assume a frantic, if not surrealistic, note. Neither Britain nor the United States were prepared at any time during the war to be told that they needed a strong Germany in view of the Russian danger, and the 'Communist bogey' was never a good argument in either wartime London or Washington. Goerdeler had been consistently mistaken in his assessment of the realities of power. Now, however, this argument, coupled with the proposal for an only slightly reshuffled Nazi government, cannot be viewed as other than downright absurd. Were it not for the fact of the captive's sense of urgency and despair, we would have to conclude that he, now that an Allied victory was in sight, had come all the way round to condoning a latter-day prescription for appeasement.

In this case my task cannot be to judge, but rather to understand and to accompany a man, virtually destroyed by despair, through his delirium. All that he had striven for in the past decades had now, at the threshold of a cruel death, come to naught. An outcast in his own country, he could no longer expect even to be heard abroad. From his utter loneliness he kept sending out into the void what were in effect appeals, incantations, and prophecies. In a way they were all preparations for another world; they were prayers of sorts. Ultimately he was left facing and coming to terms with his own God, and, alas, he learned in the hour of reckoning the bitter lesson that God was not, as he had always believed, the God of justice and love. Why, he now had to ask, does God abandon those who follow his commandments and let those who violate them have their way?[544] We have finally to take leave of Goerdeler in his last moments, having transcended the political realm that had all along given him his sense of mission, in the privacy of his search for a charitable God.

The protracted agony of Goerdeler accentuates the plight of the men of the German Resistance. They were all as much strangers in their own country as they were rebuffed abroad. As political men they all, beyond doubt, failed. They could not engage the 'greater world' in their struggle to overthrow Nazism, and the plot of 20 July failed. But the ethical, if not religious, motivation of the Resistance deserves all the more to be remembered.[545]

Goerdeler's invocations of God may seem at first sight all too sentimental, if not shrill and hysterical. But, again, we must remember the depth of his agony and therefore acknowledge the authenticity of his emotions. And we might want to acknowledge that they serve as an unmistakable reminder of the ethical and indeed religious dimension of resistance. Transcending his own sufferings Goerdeler, then, gave meaning to what in German is aptly called the *Galgenfrist*[546] granted him in the aftermath of 20 July.

## CHAPTER 6

1. For this 'odd brotherly game of bluff and overture' between the intelligence chiefs see also Garry Wills, 'The CIA from Beginning to End', *New York Review*, 22 Jan. 1976, 24–5.
2. For my understanding of Sir Stewart Menzies's position I am indebted to Sir Francis Harry Hinsley (interview 15 Dec. 1977); see also Richard Deacon, *A History of the British Secret Service* (London, 1969), 281.
3. According to Anthony Cave Brown 'it is evident that Canaris and Donovan did meet' during the war; Anthony Cave Brown, *Wild Bill Donovan: The Last Hero* (New York, 1982), 129. He jumps to this conclusion from a letter of 15 Nov. 1946 from Mrs Erika Canaris, widow of the Admiral, to Donovan, thanking him for helping her to re-establish herself after the war in Berlin and otherwise outlining her husband's career and attitudes; but the letter in no way so much as alludes to a wartime meeting between the two men; ibid. 129, 759. Heinz Höhne, *Canaris. Patriot im Zwielicht* (Munich, 1976), 463 goes as far as to maintain that the three intelligence chiefs met in the summer of 1943 in Santander, Spain. His source is a letter of highly questionable authenticity by a F. Justus von Einem to Dr Josef Müller of 29 Dec. 1967; Einem, addressing Müller as 'Kamerad "O"' [Ochsensepp?], claimed to have been present at the 'negotiations for a separate peace' in Santander, referring to them as 'my most exciting experience as collaborator with C.'; I owe a copy of the letter to Mr Heinz Höhne. Dr Josef Müller, upon my enquiry, was already a very sick man; in his letter to me of 28 July 1977 he did not refer to Einem at all, stated his regret at not being able to lay hands on the letter in question and added his doubts concerning the date of the alleged Santander meeting since at that time Canaris was already too much under suspicion from his rivals in the RSHA for him to take such extraordinary chances. In my interview with Dr Müller of 17 Feb. 1978 he showed no sign of recognition of von Einem's name, and in a follow-up letter to me dated 20 Feb. 1978 an assistant of Dr Müller asked me to produce the evidence on the Santander meeting

which, as he put it, 'in fact had not taken place', and I subsequently sent him a copy of the von Einem letter. Höhne himself has meanwhile come round to revising his stand on the Santander meeting. On the occasion of the International Conference on Resistance held in Berlin in July 1984 he conceded that there was no unequivocal proof that Canaris, Donovan, and Menzies actually met; Heinz Höhne, 'Canaris und die Abwehr zwischen Anpassung und Opposition', in Jürgen Schmädeke and Peter Steinbach (eds.), *Der Widerstand gegen den Nationalsozialismus: Die deutsche Gesellschaft und der Widerstand gegen Hitler* (Munich, 1985), 415.

4. See Hugh Trevor-Roper, *The Philby Affair: Espionage, Treason and Secret Services* (London, 1968), 78; Frederick William Winterbotham, *Secret and Personal* (London, 1969), 162.

5. Deacon, *A History of the British Secret Service*, 282.

6. Stuart Hampshire was chiefly, though not solely, responsible for the paper.

7. See Trevor-Roper, *The Philby Affair*, 78–9; Patrick Seale and Maureen McConville, *Philby: The Long Road to Moscow* (New York, 1973), 178. Actually, Philby had been alerted to the 'danger', as he saw it, of the Menzies–Canaris relationship. Upon learning late in 1942, via an Ultra intercept, that Canaris was planning one of his frequent visits to Spain, Philby proposed that SOE go into action to mount an assassination of the German intelligence chief. But it was Menzies, his British peer, who prevented any action 'whatsoever' against the Admiral. When subsequently questioned by Philby on this matter, he is reported to have answered, smilingly: 'I've always thought we could do something with the Admiral'; Phillip Knightley, *The Master Spy: The Story of Kim Philby* (New York, 1989), 105–6.

8. Philby's recent reconstruction of the episode states that the paper 'set out' why approaches for an accommodation with the German dissidents 'short of unconditional surrender' should be taken seriously, ibid. 107. However, as Lord Dacre (formerly Hugh Trevor-Roper) recently explained to me, any policy recommendation would have been outside the brief of MI6; letter of Lord Dacre to me, 27 Apr. 1989.

9. Knightley, *The Master Spy*, 107–8.

10. Letter from Lord Dacre to me.

11. See Leonard Mosley, *Dulles: A Biography of Eleanor, Allen and John Foster Dulles and their Family Network* (New York, 1978), 132–3; Jürgen Heideking, 'Die "Schweizer Strassen" des europäischen Widerstands', in Gerhard Schulz (ed.), *Geheimdienste und Widerstandsbewegungen im Zweiten Weltkrieg* (Göttingen, 1982), 148–9.

12. Leland Harrison. For general information on the Dulles mission see Allen Welsh Dulles, *The Secret Surrender* (New York, 1966), 12–18; *The Secret War Report of the OSS*, ed. Anthony Cave Brown (New York, 1976), 318–23; Heideking, 'Die "Schweizer Strassen"', 143–53; R. Harris Smith, *OSS: The Secret History of America's First Intelligence Agency* (New York, 1972), 204–41.

13. It is taken from a letter to me by Gene F. Wilson, CIA Information and Privacy Officer, of 6 Dec. 1976 in answer to an enquiry on my part. Mr Wilson went on to explain that 'Mr. Dulles was under strict control from Washington against any explicit or implicit political commitment. He was directed that his contacts were to be for obtaining information.'

14. Dulles, *The Secret Surrender*, 12.

15. For my understanding of Allen Dulles's singular position I am indebted to his sister (interview with Eleanor Lansing Dulles, 19 June 1976) and to one of his aides in Berne, Cordelia D. Hood (letter to me, 25 Aug. 1976).

16. These are the words of Mrs Dulles; ibid.

17. Gero von S. Gaevernitz, 'Treffen Thyssen'; Gero von S. Gaevernitz, Private Papers, Ascona; Gero von S. Gaevernitz, 'Bericht über meine Reise nach Russland im September 1923', 17 Oct. 1923, BA/MA N 524/v. 1; Leland Harrison to Secretary of State, 15 Dec. 1945, BA/MA N 524/v. 6.

18. An early instance of Gaevernitz's shuttle diplomacy was his rather quixotic effort in January 1940 on behalf of Schacht, who was eager to visit President Roosevelt in order to present a peace proposal to him (settling on the German frontiers as of 1914 except for Alsace-Lorraine which was to revert to France, and on a plebiscite in Austria), which he was confident of being able to push through in Germany 'either with Hitler, or if this

should not be possible, without Hitler'. Gaevernitz, according to his later testimony, went out of his way to arrange for Schacht to obtain safe conduct on a steamer that would take the still open Mediterranean route to the Atlantic. In order to obtain the necessary *laissez passer* for Schacht, he even met in Zurich with his friend Siegmund G. Warburg from London and an official of the British Secret Service. However the final answer from Whitehall was, predictably, 'No'; Gero von S. Gaevernitz, 'Schacht-Roosevelt', Gaevernitz, private papers.

19. Letter from Mrs Cordelia D. Hood to me, 1 Mar. 1976.

20. This statement, presumably coming from Dulles himself, appears in a filmscript based on Allen Dulles's book *The Secret Surrender* and revised by Gaevernitz; Filmscript '"The Secret Surrender". A Motion Picture Treatment based on the Book of the same Name by Allen W. Dulles' (Pictorial Research Inc., New York, NY, 1968, revised by Gero von S. Gaevernitz 1 Mar. 1968), 9; Gaevernitz, private papers. See also an earlier statement to this effect by Gaevernitz about his understanding of the Dulles mission in letter to Ger van Roon, Bad Wiessee, 1 Apr. 1964, IfZ./Ger van Roon, ZS/A-18.

21. Gaevernitz, '"The Secret Surrender"', 44. The script continued: 'They [Dulles and Gaevernitz] find themselves unwilling to say that in a situation of great opportunity they will not disobey.' Late in April 1945, it should be added, Dulles proved that he was capable of pulling off a daring venture, semi-independently from Washington, in engineering 'Operation Sunrise', the secret surrender of the German armies in northern Italy.

22. 'Vielfach ist in Deutschland die Meinung verbreitet ... ', 1942; 'Memorandum zur Kriegslage Deutschlands', June 1942; 'Members of the secret opposition in Germany ... ', Aug. 1943, BA/MA, N 524/ v. 7.

23. Letter from Allen W. Dulles to Gero von S. Gaevernitz, Berne, 5 July 1945, BA/MA, N 524/ v. 12.

24. See in particular Mary Bancroft, *Autobiography of a Spy* (New York, 1983); Mary Bancroft, 'Jung and His Circle', *Psychological Perspectives*, 6 (autumn 1975), 114–27; interviews with Mary Bancroft, 11 and 13 Jan. 1977. It is no secret that Mrs Bancroft's relation with Allen Dulles was a very intimate one.

25. Bancroft, 'Jung and His Circle', 123; also letter from Mary Bancroft to me of 5 Jan. 1976.

26. Another member of the Dulles team, perhaps less extrovert but more restrained and shrewd and, so it seems, all the more suited for effective intelligence work, was Cordelia D. Hood, who taught me a great deal about the intricacies of the Berne operation; letters from Cordelia D. Hood to me, 1 Mar., 22 July, 25 Aug. 1976.

27. Interview 11 Jan. 1977.

28. For an overall treatment of the political exiles in Switzerland see Werner Mittenzwei, *Exil in der Schweiz* (Frankfurt/M., 1979).

29. Wilhelm Hoegner (1887–1980), Social Democratic Member of the Bavarian Landtag and the Reichstag during the Weimar Republic had, as state attorney in Munich, been involved in the investigation of the Hitler Putsch of November 1923. After Hitler's seizure of power in 1933 he had to flee to Austria and the following year, after Chancellor Engelbert Dollfuss's action on 12 Feb. 1934 against the Austrian Socialists, on to Switzerland; see Dulles, *The Secret Surrender*, 17; Allen Welsh Dulles, *Germany's Underground* (New York 1947), 102; see also 'Dr. Wilhelm Hoegner', IfZ, ZS 1959; Hagen Schulze, *Otto Braun oder Preussens demokratische Sendung. Eine Biographie* (Frankfurt/M., 1977), 802 and Wilhelm Hoegner, *Der schwierige Aussenseiter: Erinnerungen eines Abgeordneten, Emigranten und Ministerpräsidenten* (Munich, 1959), 165–6.

30. Das demokratische Deutschland; the Arbeitsgemeinschaft, as it called itself, was formed partly to counteract another formation among German exiles in Switzerland, *Freies Deutschland*, which in fact was a spin-off of the Moscow 'National Committee for a Free Germany' and which attracted predominantly Communists. Das demokratische Deutschland went public in April 1945 when the rigid Swiss ordinances restricting political activities of exiles were lifted; see Hagen Schulze, 'Rückblick auf Weimar: Ein Briefwechsel zwischen Otto Braun und Joseph Wirth im Exil', *VfZ*, 26 (Jan. 1978), 150–1.

31. 'Dr. Wilhelm Hoegner', IfZ, ZS 1959.

32. 'Vorschlag für eine Neugliederung Deutschlands', 'Memorandum über die künftige Stellung des Landes Bayern', in Hoegner, *Der schwierige Aussenseiter*, 166–72.

33. 'Unsigned Memorandum presented by Dr Joseph Wirth ...', Berne, 10 Feb. 1943, NA, RG 59, CDF 862.00/4421; Leland Harrison to Secretary of State, Berne, 12 Feb. 1943, CDF 862.00/4361; also Hoegner, *Der schwierige Aussenseiter*, 175–80. Harrison, in his commentary to that 'sincere, if fumbling', attempt of the group of exiles to tackle the problem of the future Germany, pointed out the all too ready attribution in the memorandum of the German 'misfortunes' to causes beyond the German people's responsibility, the silence on the subjects of German militarism and of future German disarmament; he furthermore questioned the motives behind singling out the claim for leadership of the Anglo-Saxon peoples and the vagueness of the statement calling for adjustment 'by arbitration with understanding and justice' of future boundaries between Germany and Slavic and Latin peoples; Leland Harrison to Secretary of State, 10 Feb. 1943, NA, RG 59, CDF 862.00/4421.

34. Let it be known for the record that Dulles also had dealings with the German Communist exiles, though strictly speaking for the purpose of obtaining intelligence. His chief contact with them was Noel Field, the Harvard-educated son of an old friend, who had turned Communist and who late in 1942, like Dulles himself, had slipped across the frontier from Vichy France into Switzerland. With Freies Deutschland he kept connections to a minimum. He was willing to lend support to the conservative groups in particular and possibly also the Social Democrats, but not to go any further to the left; R. Harris Smith, *OSS*, 212, 218; Karl Hans Bergmann, *Die Bewegung 'Freies Deutschland' in der Schweiz 1943–1945* (Munich, 1974), 122–32.

35. See above Ch. 1, s. 4.

36. With these words Gaevernitz described his appearance before the two men actually got to know each other; Gaevernitz, 'Treffen Thyssen'.

37. Gero von S. Gaevernitz, ibid.; 'Gisevius: Code gebrochen', Gaevernitz, private papers.

38. Gisevius was able to prove his sincerity in the fight against the Nazis by revealing to Gaevernitz that one of the secret codes of the American Legation had been broken by the Nazis; he revealed this not for his love of the Americans, but above all in order to protect his fellow conspirators who might be mentioned in the coded dispatches of the Legation. While on one of his trips to Berlin, he had obtained from Admiral Canaris a copy of a decoded telegram that derived from the American Legation in Berne, which he rushed back to Berne to present to Gaevernitz. He, in turn, was able to put before Dulles the text of the cable that only a day before had been on the desk of Canaris: 'an unusually fast connection', so Gaevernitz later recorded, was thus brought about between the German and American intelligence chiefs; ibid. This episode which happened in Feb. 1943, shortly after Dulles's arrival in Switzerland, served to convince him of the sincerity not only of Gisevius but equally of Gaevernitz; ibid; see also Dulles, *Germany's Underground*, 130–1.

39. The codeword for the operation was 'U7'. Financial transactions were involved on behalf of the escapees to compensate them in foreign exchange for their loss of property at home which were easily interpreted by Himmler's men as irregularities.

40. See Hans Bernd Gisevius, *To the Bitter End* (Boston, 1947), 475–9; for 'U7' and the ensuing developments see Hoffmann, *History*, 293–4.

41. Waetjen was appointed to the post by Colonel Georg Hansen, also a firm anti-Nazi who, after Oster's removal and Canaris's increasing isolation, took over the direction of the remnants of the Abwehr.

42. See above p. 30.

43. Misc. OSS personnel papers; interview with Mary Bancroft, 13 Jan. 1977; see also the fine profile of Waetjen in Walter Laqueur and Richard Breitman, *Breaking the Silence* (New York, 1986), 212–14.

44. See above Ch. 5, s. 1.

45. It has been generally assumed that the statement reached Dulles through Gaevernitz (van Roon, *Neuordnung*, 311; R. Harris Smith, *OSS*, 218). It may well be that at this time Trott was already in touch with Gaevernitz; if this was the case, Visser't Hooft at least was unaware of it (Willem A. Visser't Hooft, *Memoirs*, London, 1973, 163 n. 9). However, the telegram which Dulles sent to Washington reporting on the 'views of a German' (there followed a handwritten explanation '800', the OSS code for Trott) specified that the report had been 'written by 474'; Communication 314 (CD 13033), 14 Jan. 1943, from Berne.

46. For the full text of the Trott message see ibid.; the text as it was rendered in Dulles, *Germany's Underground*, 131–2 is somewhat abbreviated.

47. Edward P. Morgan, 'The Spy the Nazis Missed', in Allen Welsh Dulles (ed.), *Great True Spy Stories* (New York, 1968), 15–29.

48. For the chief sources on 'Kappa' and 'Wood': the bulk is embedded, still awaiting systematic exploitation, in the OSS Papers RG 226 in the National Archives, Washington, DC. I have gone through all of them as far as they have been turned over to the Archives by the CIA; also State Department Special Interrogation Mission, 'Conversations of Fritz Kolbe with Harold C. Vedeler', 23–4, 26 Sept. 1945, N.A. M 679, Roll 2. Furthermore I have obtained directly from the CIA the following pieces: 'Alias George Wood'; 'Amplifications and Corrections of the Case History of Alias George Wood' (by Gerald Mayer); interview with Gerald Mayer, 28 Dec. 1976. See also Robert A. Graham, S I, 'L'uomo che tradì Ribbentrop', *La Civiltà Cattolica*, 137 (May 1986), 233–46; *The Secret War Report of the OSS*, 326–8; Morgan, 'The Spy the Nazis Missed'; Hansjakob Stehle, 'Der Mann, der den Krieg verkürzen wollte', *Die Zeit*, 2 May 1986; R. Harris Smith, *OSS*, 218–20.

49. 'Alias', 6.

50. See 'Alias', 5; 'Amplifications', 3.

51. The COI was created by President Roosevelt in June 1941 with the authority to collect, analyse and correlate all information and data which might bear upon national security. In June 1942, however, the President dissolved the agency, separating it into two newly created agencies: the OSS with the assignment of collecting and analysing strategic intelligence for the Joint Chiefs of Staff (JCS) and planning and directing such special operations as the JCS might require; and the Office of War Information (OWI) with the assignment of propagating America's image of itself to the world (see Cave Brown, *Wild Bill Donovan*, 165, 237). While in Berne, Gerald Mayer was taken over by the OWI, but, since Dulles's office was so under-staffed, he often worked in conjunction with him. In fact the two men worked together very well, as they did in the Kolbe case; 'Alias George Wood', 2; 'Amplifications and Corrections', 1.

52. The British later had reason to regret their rebuff of Kolbe, admitting that he constituted 'the prize intelligence source of the war'; 'Memorandum of Information for Joint U.S. Chiefs of Staff. Subject: OSS Operations in Switzerland 1942–1945', Donovan Papers Box 67A, No. 339. Initially Kolbe brought along 186 documents; all told he brought 1,600 (for a summary of his activities see ibid.). The 'easter eggs', as Dulles called them, mostly carried the classification *Geheime Reichssache* (top secret) and contained information about items such as Hitler's 'secret weapons' V-1 and V-2, German troop deployment along the Channel late in June 1944, and the exact location of the Führer's headquarters near Rastenburg in East Prussia. According to Mayer, a request went out to London that the headquarters be bombed; but this proved to be impossible since the range of the American planes did not permit them to make a return flight without landing and, ' "typically", the Russian "allies" refused landing rights in Russia' ('Amplifications and Corrections', p. 3). It cannot have been accidental that among the documents there was a telegram dated 13 Dec. 1943 by the German Ambassador to the Vatican (formerly State Secretary) von Weizsäcker, concerning the forthcoming Christmas message of the Pope that was to turn the Western Powers away from the formula of 'unconditional surrender'; Stehle, 'Der Mann'.

53. Allen Dulles registered this information in the form of a postscript to the Morgan chapter; Dulles, *Great True Spy Stories*, 29; also 'Alias', 18.

54. His independence did not prevent him from assembling a group of confidants whom he designated as the 'Inner Circle', drawn from industry, the military, the clergy (Prelate Schreiber) and the Youth Movement to which Kolbe had earlier belonged; 'Conversations of Fritz Kolbe'. There was also another German, the industrialist Eduard Schulte, who, putting his conscience before his patriotism like Kolbe, took information across the border to Dulles all on his own. He apprised the Allies of intelligence on the German war effort as well as on the Final Solution; Laqueur and Breitman, *Breaking the Silence*.

55. 110 to Secretary of State, 26 Apr. 1944, N.A. RG 226 Entry 121 Box 19.

56. Morgan, 'The Spy the Nazis Missed', 21.

57. 'Amplifications', 3; Stehle, 'Der Mann'.

58. Mosley, *Dulles*, 144.

59. See Hedwig Maier, 'Die SS und der 20. Juli 1944', *VfZ*, 14 (July 1966), 299–316.

60. Remember Pastor Schönfeld's projection during his visit to Bishop Bell of Chichester in Stockholm late in May 1942 of a threatening revolt within the Nazi Party by Himmler and his men against Hitler, and his proposition of a coup by Himmler and the SS as a 'first act' for an overthrow of the Nazi regime; see above Ch. 5, s. 2.

61. Thus Henning von Tresckow told Goerdeler in the autumn of 1943 that, according to his information, the SS Generals Paul Hausser and Josef (Sepp) Dietrich 'would go along'; see Ritter, *Carl Goerdeler*, 357. For the connection between Count Fritz-Dietlof von der Schulenburg and the SS see Albert Krebs, *Fritz-Dietlof Graf von der Schulenburg: Zwischen Staatsräson und Hochverrat* (Hamburg, 1964), 262.

62. See also John W. Wheeler-Bennett, *The Nemesis of Power: The German Army in Politics 1918–1945* (London, 1954), 575; Hoffmann, *History*, 295.

63. Entry of 9 June 1943, *Die Hassell-Tagebücher*, 368–9.

64. Ibid.

65. See Secret 'Summary of Principal Peace Feelers, September 1939–March 1941', FO 371/26542/C 4216/610/G; Secret 'Summary of Principal Peace Feelers, April 1941–June 1942', PREM 4/100/8; Sir Samuel Hoare to Foreign Office, 11 May 1942, PREM 4/23/2; also R. Harris Smith, *OSS*, 405 n. 26.

66. Mosley, *Dulles*, 145.

67. These were the code-names given to Dulles and Hohenlohe by the SS Security Service; Dulles's and Hohenlohe's understudies in these talks were, respectively, 'Mr Roberts', an American banker whose real name was Tyler, and 'Herr Bauer' or 'Alfonso' whose real name was Reinhard Spitzy. The documentation, coming from captured SS documents, is not altogether foolproof and does not clearly sort out the meetings and the attenders. The extant transcripts are: (1) 'Aufzeichnung über Aussprachen mit Mr. Bull und Mr. Roberts', records of the Reich Leader of the SS and Chief of the German Police, NA, Microcopy T-175, Roll 458, Frames 2 975007–15; (2) 'Sonntag, d. 21 Marz 1943 ...' ibid., Frames 2 975016–23; (3) 'Unterredung Pauls: Mr. Bull, Schweiz, Mitte Februar 1943', ibid., Frames 2 975024–30. The argument that a transcript of the talks, captured by the Russians and subsequently published in Moscow, has been tampered with, does not hold water since the text has also appeared in the material captured by the Western Allies. More weighty is the argument against the complete veracity of the transcripts since they were repeatedly doctored by the author—Reinhard Spitzy—to have the desired effect upon both Hitler and Himmler; Spitzy quoted Dulles, Tyler, and himself as saying things 'which one would not dare to say, but which, one wanted to be heard "up there"'; Reinhard Spitzy, *So haben wir das Reich verspielt: Bekenntnisse eines Illegalen* (2nd edn. Munich, 1987), 456. Transcript (1) was published in English translation with stinging commentary in the Moscow *New Times*; 'Record of Allen Dulles' Conversation with SS Intelligence Emissary Prince Max-Egon Hohenlohe', *New Times*, 27, July 1960, 12–20. See also Bernd Martin, 'Deutsche Oppositions- und Widerstandskreise und die Frage eines separaten Friedensschlusses im Zweiten Weltkrieg', in Klaus-Jürgen Müller (ed.), *Der deutsche Widerstand 1933–1945* (Paderborn, 1986), 88–9; Mosely, *Dulles*, 145–7, R. Harris Smith, *OSS*, 214–15; Spitzy, *So haben wir*, 446–56.

68. Interview with Dr Robert Wolfe of the National Archives, Modern Military Section, 11 June 1976.

69. NB The transcript, also designed for the Führer's eyes, merely quoted 'Mr Bull' as saying that, with all due respect to the historical significance of Hitler, it was inconceivable that the 'incited' public opinion among the Anglo-Saxons would put up with Hitler as undisputed ruler of Greater Germany; transcript (3). Hohenlohe had, however, made a point of spreading abroad the Himmler rumour for some time (see also 'Most Secret' Telegram Sir Samuel Hoare, Madrid, to the FO, 11 May 1942, PREM 4/23/2). He also related it to Leland Harrison, the American Minister in Berne, whom he saw after his meetings with Dulles; telegram of Leland Harrison to the State Department, 4 May 1943, intercepted by the Nazi Security Service, NA, Microcopy T-175, Roll 458, Frames 2 975043–4.

70. Spitzy, *So haben wir*, esp. ch. 'Die Fronde', 353–435; also pp. 439 ff.

71. 'Bericht des VM 144/7957 [Spitzy] über seine Begegnung mit dem Sonderbeauftragten

Roosevelts in der Schweiz, DULLES', 30 Apr. 1943, Records of the Reich Leader of the SS and Chief of the German Police, NA, Microcopy T-175, Roll 458, Frames 2 975031–6.

72. This is clearly the thrust of Bernd Martin's argument; 'Deutsche Oppositions- und Widerstandskreise', 88.

73. Irmgard Langbehn, 'Carl Langbehn', BA/K, Ritter 155.

74. Langbehn used his influence with Himmler to get him released and also to enable him to leave the country.

75. Wheeler-Bennett, *The Nemesis of Power*, 577.

76. No record of the conversation was kept; Langbehn and Wolff had to be content with waiting in an adjoining room where they engaged in a more or less parallel discussion.

77. The main source for the Langbehn–Popitz initiative is the indictment of the Nazi People's Court, dated 25 Sept., alongside comments by Marie-Luise (Puppi) Sarre, a close collaborator with Langbehn, found by Allen Dulles's people at the end of the war; Dulles, *Germany's Underground*, 147–64; SD report of 5 Sept. 1944, '*Spiegelbild*', 351; 'SS Report on July 20. From the Papers of Obersturmbannführer Dr. Georg Kiesel', 24–5, Wheeler-Bennett Papers (trans. of 'SS-Bericht über den 20. Juli: Aus den Papieren des SS-Obersturmbannführer Dr. Georg Kiesel', in *Nordwestdeutsche Hefte*, 2 1947, 5–34); Ritter, *Carl Goerdeler*, 355–6, 526 n. 40; 'Reichsführer SS Himmler auf der Gauleitertagung am 3. August 1944 in Posen', *VfZ*, 1 (Oct. 1953), 375–6; Gero S. von Gaevernitz, 'Langbehn', Gaevernitz Private Papers; Irmgard Langbehn, 'Carl Langbehn', BA/K, Ritter 155; Interview mit Herrn Hermann Schilling, 19.4.1948, BA/K, Ritter 156; Interview with Marie-Luise Sarre, Ascona, 8 Mar. 1978.

78. We do not know exactly whom else he saw. Wheeler-Bennett assumes, without giving any particular evidence, that he also saw British and other Allied Intelligence officers (*The Nemesis of Power*, 578); according to Gaevernitz he saw Carl Jakob Burckhardt, the former League of Nations High Commissioner for Danzig; Gaevernitz, 'Langbehn'.

79. Ibid.; Dulles himself, though dealing in detail in *Germany's Underground* with the Langbehn case, kept his silence over his own part in it. It is doubtful whether he reported on it to Washington. Gaevernitz himself thought that, in the interests of secrecy, it would be inopportune and premature to forward the case to Washington. Also, so far at least, neither the OSS nor the State Department files have yielded any reference to the Langbehn visit in the Herrengasse 23.

80. Dulles, *Germany's Underground*, 163.

81. Both Dulles and Gaevernitz note with emphasis that it was not American; Dulles also assures us that the cable did not originate with the British; ibid. 162; Gaevernitz, 'Langbehn'.

82. This characterization is Marie-Luise Sarre's; interview.

83. Memorandum Hermann Schilling, 13 Jan. 1948, BA/K, Pechel III, 1.

84. Ritter, *Carl Goerdeler*, 355.

85. See 'German "Dissident" Groups', 8 June 1944, FO 371/39087/C 8865; also OSS (R&A) Report 2387, 27 July 1944, NA, R.G. 226.

86. The text of Trott's report has been lost. The drafts were discovered relatively recently, in 1971, among the papers of Lothar König, S J, one of the Jesuit members of the Kreisau Circle, who between 1941 and 1944 secretly collected a dossier on the group. For the drafts see *Dossier: Dokumente aus dem Widerstand gegen den Nationalsozialismus. Aus dem Nachlass von Lothar König S.J.*, ed. Roman Bleistein (Frankfurt/M., 1987), 240–69. For the protocols see 'Grundlagen einer Aussenpolitik für die Nachkriegszeit', Kreisau, 14 June 1943, Moltke Papers, printed in van Roon, *Neuordnung*, 550–2 and in *Dossier*, 269–71 and 'Fragestellung zur Wirtschaftspolitik in ihrer Beziehung zur Aussenpolitik', Kreisau, 14 June 1943, Moltke Papers, printed in van Roon, *Neuordnung*, 552–3, *Dossier*, 274–7 and Walter Lipgens (ed.), *Europa-Föderationspläne der Widerstandsbewegungen 1940–1945* (Munich, 1968), 150–2. Both protocols trans. in van Roon, *German Resistance to Hitler: Count von Moltke and the Kreisau Circle* (London, 1971), 338–40; 'Fragestellung' trans. in Lipgens (ed.), *Documents on the History of European Integration* (Berlin, 1985), i. 425–7.

87. 'Verwirklichung christlichen Lebensgutes'.

88. Van Roon, *German Resistance*, 338–9 (with minor variations in the translation from the German in van Roon, *Neuordnung*, 550–1).
89. 'Dass die innerdeutsche Umkehr nicht als Ergebnis fremden Zwanges, sondern als spontane Willensgestaltung kommt'; 'Aussen- und Innenpolitik', in *Dossier*, 246.
90. Ibid. 243; also 'Zur Befriedung Europas', in *Dossier*, 250.
91. 'Verbrauchten Formen eines individualistischen Liberalismus', 'Aussen- und Innenpolitik', 244.
92. 'Der deutsche Ordnungsbeitrag', ibid. 248.
93. See esp. 'Zur Befriedung Europas', 249, 252. An elaborate plan for the reorganization of Europe ('Das europäische Verfassungsproblem'), supposedly handed over by Theodor Steltzer to Dr Harry Johansson in Sigtuna, Sweden in Nov. 1942 has all too readily been attributed to the Kreisau Circle. Its overall premisses, i.e. a European order founded on Christianity and a European federation based on autonomous member units, are altogether in concert with the basic thinking in the Circle around Moltke. However, the document contains other provisions which are not in tune with the Kreisau group: among the 24 autonomous units (excluding England and Russia) Bohemia and Moravia are listed separately; such a provision appears in no Kreisau document; also the stipulation for the Church (Protestant or Catholic) to be in a position of exercising a veto over the installation of the Federal President cannot be considered a position that was generally accepted in the Circle (see the correspondence between Moltke and his friend Peter Count von Yorck; van Roon, *Neuordnung*, 486–97); also the assumption of the disintegration of the British Empire is altogether in conflict with certainly Moltke's thinking (I owe a mimeographed copy of 'Das europäische Verfassungsproblem' to Ger van Roon; see also *Der Kreisauer Kreis. Porträt einer Widerstandsgruppe*, ed. Ernst Wilhelm Winterhager (Berlin, 1985), 222–8; *Dossier*, 260–9). At best the document can be characterized as a draft originating with Steltzer (see Ger van Roon, 'Der Kreisauer Kreis und das Ausland', 38); but whether it merits attribution to the Kreisau Circle (*Der Kreisauer Kreis*, 123–4; *Dossier*, 260) is another matter.
94. Paulus van Husen, connected with Moltke's Circle since 1941, was one of the participants of the recent meeting in Kreisau, for which he drafted the position papers on the punishment of war criminals. A deeply religious man of the Catholic faith, he had been dismissed by the Nazis for having used his position with the German liaison mission to the Upper Silesian Inter-Allied Mixed Commission to shield Jews from persecution. In 1940 he became Captain (Rittmeister) of the Reserve in the OKW, and was later actively involved in the preparations for the coup of 20 July 1944.
95. Letter from Helmuth von Moltke to Freya von Moltke, Berlin, 17 June 1943, von Moltke, *Briefe an Freya*, 493.
96. Wheeler-Bennett, *The Nemesis of Power*, 548.
97. Thomas Childers used this metaphor in his paper, 'The Kreisauer Kreis and the 20th of July', delivered at the Conference on 'The German Resistance Movement 1933–1945' in New York City, 24–5 Apr. 1988.
98. *Legationssekretär*; this position, though by no means elevated, afforded him more status and security; AA/PA, Personalakte Trott.
99. The journey lasted from 17 June to 3 July.
100. There were, however, some who took objection to including von Papen; among them was Ambassador Count Friedrich Werner von der Schulenburg; see van Roon, *Neuordnung*, 318, n. 8.
101. Franz von Papen, *Memoirs* (New York, 1953), 504.
102. 6 May 1943; Personalakte Trott.
103. Letter from Wolfram Eberhard to Ger van Roon, 17 Sept. 1962, IfZ/Ger van Roon, ZS/A-18; see also Christopher Sykes, *Troubled Loyalty: A Biography of Adam von Trott zu Solz* (London, 1968), 396–7.
104. Canaris himself had been in Istanbul in January to take advantage of the arrival there of an influential American, recently appointed to the position of Assistant US Naval Attaché, George H. Earle. The latter was an old friend of President Roosevelt from their Harvard years. A millionaire, he had an unusually chequered political career behind him. In 1932 he left the Republican Party in order to throw in his lot with Roosevelt. In 1933 he was

appointed Envoy Extraordinary and Minister Plenipotentiary to Vienna, but he resigned in 1934 to run for Governor of Pennsylvania. From 1935/9 he served as the state's first Democratic Governor in 44 years. From 1940/1 he served as American Minister to Bulgaria. He resigned from that position when the USA entered the war to become commander of a submarine chaser, and distinguished himself by gallantry in action. His arrival in Istanbul was accompanied by the rumour that he was sent there in the capacity of President Roosevelt's personal representative; see General Albert C. Wedemeyer, *Wedemeyer Reports!* (New York, 1958), 416–18; Franz von Papen, *Memoirs*, 499. Calling on the American out of the blue in his recently established quarters in the Park Hotel, Canaris openly introduced himself as 'Admiral Canaris, chief of the Abwehr' and proceeded to reproach him on the iniquity of the 'unconditional surrender' policy of the Allies that was an impediment for an arrangement of the German Generals with the West. As a matter of fact, Papen, inscrutable as always, through his confidant Baron Kurt von Lersner, also got involved in the Earle connection; the two, Papen and Earle, had known each other from their assignments in Vienna. However, while both Canaris and Papen encountered considerable understanding from Earle, and while later, early in 1944, an adventurous scheme was devised by Papen to have Earle flown to Berlin to give assurances to the conspirators there, Earle's reports to Washington remained unanswered. Finally a terse response came from the President to the effect that all plans pertaining to peace negotiations were to be submitted to General Eisenhower; Julius Epstein, 'Keine Antwort von Präsident Roosevelt', *Die Welt*, 19 July 1958; see also Höhne, *Canaris*, 461; 'Papen Offered to Betray Hitler, Earle Asserts in Defending Intercession', *Philadelphia Inquirer*, 30 Jan. 1949; von Papen, *Memoirs*, 499–500, 522–3; Wedemeyer, *Wedemeyer Reports!*, 416–18.

105. The basic outlines of Moltke's trips to Turkey (5–10 July and 11–18 December) have been very well presented by Michael Balfour and Julian Frisby, *Helmuth von Moltke: A Leader Against Hitler* (London, 1972), and van Roon, *Neuordnung*; I have therefore fallen back on the substance of their rendition. But by virtue of my access to OSS documents, papers from Hans Wilbrandt, and further interviews I have been able to relate the Moltke missions to Turkey more closely to the OSS Operation in Turkey. For an understanding of the latter I am particularly indebted to Walter W. Arndt (interview 29 Aug. 1977, letter 3 Sept. 1977), Hans Wilbrandt (interview 6 Feb. 1978) and 'Dogwood' (interview 24 Feb. 1978).

106. 'Er ist doch ein jämmerlicher Mann', Balfour and Frisby, *Helmuth von Moltke*, 271.

107. Thus he arranged for Moltke to meet with the Orthodox Patriarch of Constantinople; Moltke had hoped—in vain—to find access through him to the Anglican Church and thus to Churchill; letter of Ambassador Gebhardt von Walther to Ger van Roon, Ankara, 1 Mar. 1963, IfZ/Ger van Roon, ZS/A-18.

108. For a short time, in 1934/5, Trott had served as an apprentice (*Referendar*) in Leverkühn's law office.

109. See above p. 60.

110. According to Wilbrandt, a large-size American uniform had been secured for this purpose with the help of the American Embassy; interview with Hans Wilbrandt, 6 Feb. 1978.

111. Among the few exceptions to this rule was Otto John who was active for the *Widerstand* in Spain and who persistently tried to impress upon his fellow conspirators the futility of opposing 'unconditional surrender'; interview with Otto John, 18 Feb. 1978; see also Otto John, *Twice Through the Lines: The Autobiography of Otto John* (New York, 1972), 136, 317–20.

112. Letter from Alexander Rüstow to Ger van Roon, Heidelberg, 10 Dec. 1962, IfZ/Ger van Roon, ZS/A-18; also van Roon, *Neuordnung*, 319–20.

113. Named after a large cactus of the western United States and tropical America.

114. From a partly blacked-out OSS document 'From JJ1 and DH140 to DD101', 27 Feb. 1946, turned over to me by the CIA.

115. Interview with 'Dogwood', 24 Feb. 1978.

116. Letter from Alexander Rüstow to Ger van Roon, Heidelberg, 20 Dec. 1962, IfZ/Ger van Roon, ZS/A-18.

117. On balance, the 'Cereus' operation was a rather amateurish one which might explain the fact that it seems to have been infiltrated by Axis agents (see R. Harris Smith, *OSS*, 125); Macfarland was eventually replaced. 'Dogwood', alas, for all his solicitousness on behalf

of Moltke, did not escape the suspicion of having been a double agent (Cave Brown, *Wild Bill Donovan*, 406). 'Dogwood' granted me a lengthy interview in Zurich on 24 Feb. 1978, requesting me not to reveal his real name—though it is all over the OSS documents in my possession. I must honour this request. Anthony Cave Brown's assumption that 'Dogwood' perished soon after the war (ibid. 408) is obviously mistaken. Wilbrandt and Rüstow were, it must be stressed, not 'members' of 'Cereus', but highly valuable and esteemed 'resource persons'; interview with Walter W. Arndt (who was himself a member of 'Cereus'), 29 Aug. 1977 and letter from Arndt to me, 3 Sept. 1977. As for the amateurism of the 'Cereus' operation, it is borne out by the handling in Oct./Nov. 1943 by Coleman of the so-called 'Morde Incident' in the course of which Coleman mobilized his whole staff in order to bring together Papen and a bogus adventurer, Theodore A. Morde, who, once a US intelligence agent, now insisted he was on on a presidential mission. Roosevelt's alleged eagerness to negotiate, and even worse, the sweeping terms he was supposedly offering, are altogether out of keeping with his policies, just as Papen's terms cannot be considered representative of those of the *Widerstand*. If any significance is to be attributed to this episode, it might be that the Morde mission was launched by a group of right-wing Americans who were interested in torpedoing the Grand Alliance with Russia; see Archibald Frederick Coleman, 'Snapdragon: Story of a Spy', *Metro: The Magazine of Southeastern Virginia*, 7 (May 1977), 24–31, 64–9; see Cave Brown, *Wild Bill Donovan*, 366–81. The only one in official Washington willing to follow up on the Morde–von Papen escapade was—General Donovan; but the White House and State Department came down hard on him, ordering him to drop the matter; Bradley F. Smith, *The Shadow Warriors: OSS and the Origins of the CIA* (New York, 1983), 216.

118. See in particular 'Source: Cereus (13), Sub-Source: Hyacinth via Dogwood', 14 Sept. 1943; 'Source: Cereus (94), Sub-Source: Dogwood', 27 Oct. 1943; Wilbrandt Papers. According to the latter document, which mistakenly identified Moltke as a 'senior officer in the War Production Department (Wehrwirtschaftsamt) of the OKW (Camelia)', he had declared his readiness to prepare the way for 'a far-reaching development of relations between the German High Command and our [presumably the American] General Staff, provided (a) that he is informed about the principles that guide the American attitude and political intentions towards post-War Germany, (b) that he is given assurances that the fact of his collaboration with our Department [presumably the OSS] will be brought to the knowledge of the highest Allied authorities, and (c) that all possible security measures are taken and the strictest secrecy is observed'.

119. Ibid.

120. Undated 2-page listing of 'Plans Considered' on official stationery of the American Embassy. Office of the Military Attaché, Ankara, Turkey; Wilbrandt Papers.

121. 'Inclusion of S. in the plans and the presentation of H. to S. Security problem dangerous. Rejected', ibid.

122. 'Dear Mr. Kirk', Istanbul, 1943, Wilbrandt Papers; reprinted in Balfour and Frisby, *Helmuth von Moltke*, 271–3; van Roon, *Neuordnung*, 591–3.

123. Interviews with Arndt and Wilbrandt.

124. Balfour and Frisby, *Helmuth von Moltke*, 273; letter from Michael Balfour to Hans Wilbrandt, London, 14 May, 1972; Wilbrandt Papers.

125. Balfour and Frisby, *Helmuth von Moltke*, 273.

126. 'Exposé on the Readiness of a Powerful German Group to Prepare and Assist Allied Military Operations against Nazi Germany', Wilbrandt Papers; reprinted in Balfour and Frisby, *Helmuth von Moltke*, 273–7; van Roon, *German Resistance*, 372–5; German version in van Roon, *Neuordnung*, 582–6. The document was drafted by Wilbrandt, edited by Rüstow—according to Wilbrandt it was '80% Rüstow'—and translated into English by Arndt.

127. It is certainly not without irony that the authors of the Exposé chose to compare this projected 'bold act of true patriotism' with the Tauroggen Convention of 1812 when General Yorck von Wartenburg, without the authorization of his king, entered into an agreement with—the Russians.

128. Eugen Gerstenmaier, 'Der Kreisauer Kreis', 239.

129. Moltke himself never saw the document; interview with Wilbrandt.

130. See below, p. 407 n. 155.
131. See esp. copy of letters from 'Dogwood' to R. G. Tindall, 29 Dec. 1943 and 4 Jan. 1944; Wilbrandt Papers.
132. Copy of letter from Brigadier General Richard G. Tindall to 'Dogwood', Ankara, 31 Dec. 1943; Wilbrandt Papers.
133. Copy of letter from 'Dogwood' to R.G. Tindall, 29 Dec. 1943; Wilbrandt Papers.
134. See 154 and Carib (OSS, Washington) to OSS Istanbul, 10 Dec. 1943, NA, RG 226, Entry 88, Box 419. Soon after the Dec. visit of Moltke to Turkey, Donovan himself took to New York a message from the German Resistance, written on stationery of the German Embassy in Ankara, asking for an opening of negotiations with Washington. The message was signed by Paul Leverkühn with whom Donovan had been acquainted from the days before the war when Leverkühn represented Germany in the Mixed Claims Commission. While the OSS chief, after elaborate authentication of the document, allegedly recommended taking up the Germans on their offer, the President is reported to have flatly refused to negotiate with 'these East German Junkers'; Hoffmann, *History*, 226–7.
135. William J. Donovan Memorandum for the President, 29 July 1944, F.D.R. Library, PSF, 168; the wording of this memorandum suggests that this was the first time that the case of the 'Hermann Group' was brought before the President. According to Walter W. Arndt, however, the Exposé composed by Moltke's friends reached the President earlier by way of OSS headquarters in Algiers, but was met with a 'wholly negative' reception because of the canons of 'unconditional surrender'; see van Roon, *Neuordnung*, 322.
136. van Roon, *Neuordnung*, 339.
137. After completing his official business in Copenhagen, he visited his old Danish friends, the journalist Merete Bonnesen and her brother Kim who was a high official in the Ministry of Social Services; Kim then forwarded the news of the impending raid to the FO. Actually the latter had already been forewarned three days earlier by the German Attaché for Shipping, Georg Ferdinand Duckwitz, on the staff of the Reich Commissar for Denmark; the Danish Social Democrats were also alerted through Duckwitz. For the literature on Moltke's Scandinavian trip and this particular episode: letter from Merete Bonnesen to Ger van Roon, 28 June 1962, IfZ/Ger van Roon, ZS/ A-18; letters from Helmuth von Moltke to Freya von Moltke, Oslo, 4, 5, 7 Oct. 1943, in von Moltke, *Briefe an Freya*, 549–55; Balfour and Frisby, *Helmuth von Moltke*, 266–9; van Roon, *Neuordnung*, 338–40; Leni Yahil, *The Rescue of Danish Jewry: Test of a Democracy* (Philadelphia, Pa., 1969), 169, 239; Leo Goldberger (ed.), *The Rescue of the Danish Jews: Moral Courage under Stress* (New York, 1987); see also Erich Thomsen, *Deutsche Besatzungspolitik in Dänemark 1940–1945* (Düsseldorf, 1971), 180–90.
138. Yahil, *The Rescue*, 187; out of a total of about 7,800 Jews some 7,200 were saved.
139. The state of emergency had been lifted on 6 Oct.
140. On 1 Oct. Gerstenmaier and Schönfeld visited Archbishop Eidem, probably on Church matters; Jørgen Glenthøj (ed.), 'Dokumente zur Bonhoeffer-Forschung 1928–1945', in *Die Mündige Welt*, v (Munich, 1969), 282 n. 86.
141. 27 Oct. 1943.
142. Henrik Lindgren, 'Adam von Trotts Reisen nach Schweden 1942–1944', *VfZ*, 18 (July 1970) 378.
143. Interrogation of Karl Georg Pfleiderer, Jan. 1949, Berlin Document Centre, 20 July 1944 Plot Personalities; also draft (24 Mar. 1947) prepared by Pfleiderer himself for Theodor Steltzer for presentation to a de-Nazification tribunal (*Spruchkammer*), Theodor Steltzer Papers and letter from Karl Georg Pfleiderer to Theodor Steltzer, 24 Mar. 1947, BA/K, Rothfels 28, vol. 88.
144. Ivar Anderson, *Från det Nära Förflutna. Människor och Händelser 1940–1955* (Stockholm, 1969), 91.
145. Typed excerpts from Ivar Anderson's Diary, entry of 30 Oct. 1943, Trott Archive, Berichte; also IfZ/Ger van Roon, ZS/A-18; see also Anderson, *Från det Nära*, 100–1.
146. 'Herr Himmler and Herr Hitler are in the same boat.'
147. Interview with Inga Kempe, 25 Feb. 1978; Sykes, *Troubled Loyalty*, 403–4.
148. 'Political Memorandum', 5 Nov. 1943, FO 371/34462/C 13731/279/18; it was initialled

RPH (Hinks's full name was Roger Packman Hinks; see also Roger Hinks, *The Gymnasium of the Mind*, ed. John Goldsmith, Salisbury, 1984).

149. He clearly meant German defeats by Russia.

150. Letter from Helmuth James von Moltke to Freya von Moltke, Berlin, 7 Nov. 1943, von Moltke, *Briefe an Freya*, 563.

151. SD Report of 29 Nov. 1944, '*Spiegelbild*', i. 505; italics in the original of the SD Report.

152. Indeed, according to another SD Report Trott, at an unspecified but clearly later date, is reported to have said in the presence of Stauffenberg that in view of the 'extremely serious military situation ... only political negotiations could help and that on the Anglo-American side a readiness for an understanding with Germany could not be discounted'; SD Report of 26 July 1944, ibid. 56; see also Christian Müller, *Oberst i.G. Stauffenberg* (Düsseldorf, 1971), 381.

153. The Gestapo moved to arrest Moltke not because of the activities of the Kreisau Circle, but, through an informer, it had infiltrated the Solf Circle. Moltke had warned one of its members, Otto Kiep of the Auswärtiges Amt, of his impending arrest, and the Gestapo, having got wind of the warning, moved in on Moltke.

154. See Balfour and Frisby, *Helmuth von Moltke*, 299–300; Childers, 'Der Kreisauer Kreis'.

155. I must preface this particular section dealing with Trott's last visits to Sweden in mid-March and June/July 1944 with the statement that the evidence on them is blurred inasmuch as the primary sources are ambiguous; they conflate the two visits and do not clearly distinguish between which British officials Trott saw during which visit. The main source for both visits is Fru Inga Kempe (formerly Fru Almström) who after the war composed for Trott's widow what she remembered about the visits. She conceded that, since she had kept no diary, her information concerning the exact time of the different Trott visits to Stockholm might be incorrect. In fact, she telescoped them; see Inga Kempe, 'I met Adam ...', typescript, Feb. 1958, from Inga Kempe; copy also in Trott Archive, Berichte. But I have attempted to disentangle the two visits as well as possible with the help of interviews and the other documents available: interviews with Inga Kempe, 25 Feb. 1978 and with Dr Harry Johansson, 1 June 1980; 'Political Memorandum', 23 Mar. 1944, FO 371/39059/C 4118/103/18; Herschel V. Johnson (US Minister to Sweden) to the Secretary of State, Stockholm, 12 Sept. 1944, *FRUS* 1944, i. 550–1; Alexander Werth report, 'Der folgenden Aufzeichnung ...', Nov. 1957, Trott Archive, Berichte; also Ivar Anderson's diary entries for 14 and 18 March 1944, Trott Archive, Berichte. The secondary literature, no less than the documentary material, is also inconclusive about the separation of the two meetings; see Sykes, *Troubled Loyalty*, 413–15; Lindgren, 'Adam von Trotts Reisen', 279–81; also Clarita von Trott, 'Adam von Trott', 244–6.

156. This is according to Sykes. Lindgren associates the English initiative with the later visit. In both cases the initiative most probably came from the British Legation in Stockholm. Strong circumstantial evidence points in the direction that Sykes's version is correct.

157. See Sykes, *Troubled Loyalty*, 399, 411–12; Wheeler-Bennett, *The Nemesis of Power*, 595–6.

158. Ivar Anderson's Diary, entry of 14 and 18 Mar. 1944; Anderson, *Från det Nära*, 101.

159. Anderson diary entry for 18 Mar. 1944.

160. Interview with Inga Kempe. Her statement (Kempe, 'I met Adam ...') that Trott had asked for another contact 'which could handle the matter with greater responsibility' and which turned out to be Mr David McEwan, also an intelligence officer but with 'greater qualifications', definitely applies to Trott's June/July visit when he indeed saw McEwan.

161. See Forrest C. Pogue, *The Supreme Command* (*The United States in World War II: The European Theater of Operations*) (Washington, DC, 1954), 127 ff.; John Ehrman, *Grand Strategy*, v, Aug. 1943–Sept. 1944 (London, 1956), 286 ff.

162. *The War Reports of General of the Army George C. Marshall, General of the Army H. H. Arnold, Fleet Admiral Ernest J. King* (Philadelphia, Pa., 1947), 360.

163. 'Political Memorandum', 23 Mar. 1944, FO 371/39059/C 4118/103/18; the memorandum was based upon 'two conversations with a Swedish woman [undoubtedly Fru Almström] whom he [Trott] knew to be in contact with the British Legation'.

164. The project had been recently considered by the War Cabinet, but shelved.

165. Herschel V. Johnson to the Secretary of State, Stockholm, 12 Sept. 1944, *FRUS* 1944, i. 551.
166. It is not certain, as has been generally assumed, that this was Trott's last visit to Switzerland. According to a letter by Gero von S. Gaevernitz to Ger van Roon, Trott revisited Switzerland in June, discussing with Gaevernitz the forthcoming coup against Hitler and also problems of a spiritual and economic reconstruction of Central Europe after the war; van Roon, *Neuordnung*, 311–12 n. 29.
167. See Graml, 'Die aussenpolitischen Vorstellungen', in Walter Schmitthenner and Hans Buchheim (eds.), *Der deutsche Widerstand gegen Hitler* (Cologne, 1966), 137–8.
168. Dulles, *Germany's Underground*, 137–8.
169. Elizabeth Wiskemann, *The Europe I Saw* (London, 1968) 188.
170. Ibid.
171. Von Kessel, 'Verborgene Saat', 256–7.
172. From 19 June until 3 July. Meanwhile Harry Johansson had been in Berlin. He had obtained a visa from Karl Georg Pfleiderer who 'with a glint in his eyes' had made him understand that he knew all about resistance matters (interview with Dr Johansson, Sigtuna, 1 June 1980). Indeed, while in Berlin, he made the rounds in Resistance circles conferring with Gerstenmaier and Schönfeld and dining with Moltke's friend, Count Peter Yorck. Gerstenmaier then took him to Stuttgart for a meeting with Bishop Theophil Wurm, one of the few princes of the Protestant Church who firmly opposed Nazism. Upon his return to Berlin, before his return to Sweden, he met Trott and his friend Hans-Bernd von Haeften.
173. Interview with Dr Johansson, 1 June 1980; Werth, 'Der folgenden Aufzeichnung ...'. According to Dr Johansson Trott and his friends managed to get hold of the copies of the papers in the German Foreign Office which carried the dispatch and destroyed them.
174. Ibid.
175. SD Report of 8 Aug. 1944, '*Spiegelbild*', i. 175; apparently both Trott and Colonel Hansen were sceptical about this proposition since under those conditions the approach to the Allies might have been interpreted by them as weakness.
176. Dr Johansson had carefully prepared the ground by meeting with McEwan twice before, on 6 and 14 June, in Stockholm; interview with Dr Johansson, 4 June 1980.
177. Interview with Inga Kempe.
178. 5-page memorandum 'I have been asked to name ...', typed on Fru Almström's typewriter and with corrections by Trott in his handwriting; from Inga Kempe, reprinted in Lindgren, 'Adam von Trotts Reisen', 289–91; it was composed by Trott in consultation with Dr Johansson; Kempe, 'I met Adam ...'. This document undoubtedly found its way to London; it has, however, so far not been found among the FO Papers.
179. Ibid.
180. 'I have been asked ...'.
181. German 'Dissident' Groups, 8 June 1944, FO 371/39087/C 8867/180/18; see also Lothar Kettenacker (ed.), *Das 'Andere Deutschland' im Zweiten Weltkrieg* (Stuttgart, 1977), 68 (the document itself is reprinted on pp. 200–3).
182. Telegram, The Minister in Sweden (Johnson) to the Secretary of State, Stockholm, 26 June 1944, *FRUS* 1944, i. 523–5; Herschel V. Johnson, 'Views of an Anti-Nazi German', 26 June 1944, OSS No. 34872, NA, OSS, RG 226, Entry 5; see also John Scott, 'Mail Story', 17 Sept. 1944, NA, RG 59, CDF 811.91258/9—2144. In the sources there is some ambiguity about the date of the meeting between Scott and Trott. Scott himself, in his report of 17 Sept., gives the date as 26 June. The American Minister, on the other hand, in his telegram to Washington of 26 June, gives it as 23 June. It is unlikely that this latter report would have been written on the same day that the meeting between Scott and Trott took place. The diary of Gunnar Myrdal is not conclusive in this respect since it shows an entry 'Adam von Trott' for 22 June, 3 p.m.; he may on this occasion have arranged the meeting with Trott. I am inclined to accept the date given in the report of the American Minister. For a photocopy of Myrdal's diary I am indebted to Walter A. Jackson; see also Walter A. Jackson, *Gunnar Myrdal and America's Conscience: Social Engineering and Racial Liberalism, 1938–1987* (Chapel Hill, 1990).
183. John Scott, 'Mail Story'.

184. Johnson, 'Views of an Anti-Nazi German'; *FRUS* 1944, i. 525.
185. Information from Walter A. Jackson.
186. R. Taylor Cole, *The Recollections of R. Taylor Cole: Educator, Emissary, Development Planner* (Durham, NC, 1983), 81–2. R. Taylor Cole was, in 1943/4, Special Assistant to the American Minister in Stockholm in the SI of the OSS (code-name 'Creek'); he was the author of Herschel V. Johnson's telegram to Washington of 26 June 1944; the telegram as reproduced in *FRUS* 1944, i is a condensed version of the one written by Cole.
187. See in particular *FRUS* 1944, i. 524.
188. SD Report of 8 Aug. 1944, '*Spiegelbild*', i. 174.
189. Trott and Brandt had met through Steltzer.
190. Interview with Willy Brandt, 1 July 1980; also interview with Inga Kempe, 25 Feb. 1978; letter from R. Taylor Cole to me, 3 July 1984. But according to John Scott ('Mail Story') it was the Soviet Legation which sent Trott away.
191. 'Gespräche'; letter from Adam von Trott to 'Liebe gnädige Frau', Sonntag, 25/VI [1944], Trott Archive, Adam von Trotts Briefe an andere.
192. Entry of 22 Jan. 1943, *Die Hassell-Tagebücher*, 347; Letter from Helmuth von Moltke to Freya von Moltke, Berlin, 9 Jan. 1943, von Moltke, *Briefe an Freya*, 450–1; Eugen Gerstenmaier, *Streit und Friede hat seine Zeit: Ein Lebensbericht* (Frankfurt/M., 1981), 167–70; Hoffmann, *History*, 360–2.
193. See above pp. 291–2.
194. See von Moltke, *Briefe an Freya*, 37–8, 295, 490.
195. See also Marianne Meyer-Krahmer, *Carl Goerdeler und sein Weg in den Widerstand* (Freiburg i. Br., 1989), 152–3.
196. 'Geheime Denkschrift Goerdelers, für die Generalität bestimmt, über die Notwendigkeit eines Staatsstreichs, 26. Marz 1943', reprinted in Ritter, *Carl Goerdeler*, 577–95; excerpts also in transcription by Ludwig Kaiser, BA/K, Pechel III, 2.
197. Olbricht had been deeply involved since 1938 in the conspiracy against Hitler. In October 1943 Colonel Count Claus von Stauffenberg joined him as his Chief of Staff.
198. Copy of letter from Carl Goerdeler to Friedrich Olbricht, 17 May 1943, BA/K, Goerdeler 23. A facsimile of the letter is also reproduced in Ritter, *Carl Goerdeler* between pp. 352 and 353; italics in the original.
199. Reprinted as 'Goerdelers Entwurf eines Briefes an Generalfeldmarschall von Kluge 25.7.1943' in Ritter, *Carl Goerdeler*, 596–600; for the English version see Wheeler-Bennett, *The Nemesis of Power*, 570–4.
200. Actually the letter was not sent. It seems that Goerdeler's friends, after much discussion and long deliberation, dissuaded him from doing so, lest, so Olbricht argued, he damage rather than help the chances of the Opposition with the Field Marshal; Fabian von Schlabrendorff, *The Secret War against Hitler* (London, 1966), 164–5. Gerhard Ritter's conjecture that the letter from Olbricht to Kluge, in which he implored him to take charge of the conspiracy and which was delivered by Major General Helmuth Stieff on 13 Aug., took the place of the Goerdeler letter, is plausible; SD Report of 28 July 1944, '*Spiegelbild*', i. 88; Ritter, *Carl Goerdeler*, 526 n. 38.
201. Wheeler-Bennett, *The Nemesis of Power*, 574.
202. 'Summary of interview with M. Jacob Wallenberg. *Svenska Dagbladet* September 4th 1947', Wheeler-Bennett Papers.
203. 'Goerdelers Entwurf', 599.
204. Balfour and Frisby, *Helmuth von Moltke*, 264.
205. 'Geheime Denkschrift', 587; italics in the original.
206. Allowing for some adjustment of the Franco–German linguistic frontier.
207. In this connection he urged the undoing of the 'rape' of the South Tyrol of 1919, which, in turn, might be a way of reconciling the Austrians to their incorporation into the Reich.
208. Ibid. 592; as for the colonial question, Goerdeler argued that the time for acquisition of colonies by Germany was past; however, Germany was to be the beneficiary of an eventual international settlement concerning colonial claims and administration; ibid. 587–8.
209. Ibid. 590.
210. As financial adviser of the Robert Bosch firm Goerdeler was engaged in 1939, in view of the impending war, in saving Bosch holdings in prospective enemy countries by transferring

them into Swedish hands; in this transaction the Enskilda Bank had a major part; see SD Report of 17 Aug. 1944, '*Spiegelbild*', i. 246.

211. The main sources for the encounters between Goerdeler and the Wallenbergs are 'Summary of Interview with M. Jacob Wallenberg'; 'Unterredung mit Herrn Jakob Wallenberg, Samstag 26. Sept. 1953 in Stockholm, 14 Uhr 15–16 Uhr', BA/K Ritter 131; also a summary put together by Jacob Wallenberg for Allen W. Dulles, in Dulles, *Germany's Underground*, 142–6.

212. 'Unterredung mit Herrn Jakob Wallenberg ...'.

213. 9–21 May 1943.

214. Memorandum 'Das deutsche Volk muss und wird sich selbst von einem System befreien ...', presented by Carl Goerdeler to Jacob Wallenberg, 20 May 1943; BA/K, Goerdeler 23; for a photocopy of the text I am indebted to Dr. Michael Krüger-Charlé; also for a detailed commentary on the memorandum see Ritter, *Carl Goerdeler* 328–30.

215. As for the eastern borders of Poland, the memorandum insisted on those of 1938; similarly it urged the independence of Finland and declared the new regime's readiness to 'fight' for it as well as for Poland's eastern borders. In the eventuality, however, of Poland's demanding East Prussia and parts of Silesia, Goerdeler predicted dark times for 'Europe and the white peoples'.

216. 'Interessen-und Kulturgemeinschaft'.

217. Telegram from Mr Mallet to War Cabinet, 31 Mar. 1943, FO 371/34428/C3708/55/18; V. A. Mallet Conversation with Marcus Wallenberg, 17 Aug. 1943; FO 371/34435/C 9544/55/18. Wallenberg's argument on behalf of the Opposition and his reference—a few days after the foundation of the National Committee for a Free Germany—to the Russian danger got a mixed reception in the London Foreign Office; W. D. Allen minuted 'bogus', whereas Frank K. Roberts minuted 'not so far from the mark'; ibid.

218. Goerdeler, over-optimistic as usual, and being certain of an impending coup, urgently requested the Swedish banker to come to Berlin. The visit was arranged under cover of some business connected with Bosch. Once again, Goerdeler asked Wallenberg to make his brother convey to London his urgent request not to bomb the centres of the conspiracy, this time singling out Berlin and Leipzig—and subsequently Goerdeler registered with satisfaction that no raids over these cities had taken place during Sept. He also announced that the new German government would send over to Stockholm Fabian von Schla-brendorff with the assignment to negotiate an armistice. Wallenberg thought such an arrangement premature, and was also sceptical about the choice of Schlabrendorff who was not sufficiently weighty for such a mission; 'Unterredung mit Herrn Jakob Wallenberg ...'; see also Ritter, *Carl Goerdeler*, 331, 516, n. 23; Dulles, *Germany's Underground*, 144–5. At the same time, in Aug. 1943, Goerdeler also sounded out Otto John, who, in co-operation with the conspiratorial Abwehr group, had been involved since 1938 in the plotting against Hitler, about flying via Lisbon to England in order to inform the British government about his plans; but John, being one of the few among the German resisters who thought the Allied demand for unconditional surrender irrevocable, offered his services only if Goerdeler would face up to it—for which of course Goerdeler was not prepared. He and his friends persisted in what John called the 'illusion' that in case of a successful coup they could reach a peace with the Western powers by negotiation; Otto John, 'Die bedingungslose Kapitulation' (Memorandum written for John W. Wheeler-Bennett), Wheeler-Bennett Papers, St Anthony's College, Oxford; Otto John, *Twice through the Lines*, 123. In any case, the promised Sept. coup did not materialize.

219. Appendix 2 to SD Report of 17 Aug. 1944, '*Spiegelbild*', i. 249–55; also 'Friedensplan Goerdelers, vermutlich für britische Leser bestimmt. Wahrscheinlich vom Spätsommer oder Herbst 1943', Ritter, *Carl Goerdeler*, 570–6 (commented upon on pp. 332–4); reprinted in part in English translation in Lipgens (ed.), *Documents* i. 430–2.

220. In the east approximately the borders of 1914, and Poland to be compensated for a loss of West Prussia and Posen (Poznan) by union with Lithuania; in the south the borders recognized by the Conference of Munich, including Austria; also the South Tyrol down to the line Bozen (Bolzano)-Meran (Merano) to 'revert' to Germany; in the west Alsace-Lorraine either to become autonomous in the manner of Switzerland or else be divided along linguistic lines; in the north the border to be determined along similar lines.

221. For this train of thought see in particular Lipgens, 'European Federation', esp. 14–19; for the documentation see Lipgens (ed.), *Europa-Föderationspläne, passim, idem* (ed.), *Documents*, i, *passim*.
222. Lipgens, 'European Federation', 15; *idem* (ed.), *Europa-Föderationspläne*, 474–7.
223. Appendix 2 to SD Report 21 Sept. 1944, '*Spiegelbild*', i. 410–12; see also Ritter, *Carl Goerdeler*, 357–9; Hoffmann, *History*, 300, 625 n. 65.
224. Although Goerdeler added, quite categorically, one more item: 'Eupen-Malmedy [the contested area between Germany and Belgium] will remain German'.
225. For the text of the Declaration see Hans-Adolf Jacobsen and Arthur L. Smith, Jr. (eds.), *World War II: Policy and Strategy, Selected Documents with Commentary* (Santa Barbara, Calif., 1979), 277–8.
226. Entry of 13 Nov. 1943, *Die Hassell-Tagebücher*, 398.
227. 'Unterredung mit Herrn Jakob Wallenberg ...'.
228. Ibid.
229. 'Summary of Interview with M. Jacob Wallenberg'.
230. Later on at least, in the hearings before the Nazi commission charged with investigating 20 July, Goerdeler maintained he had received 'in the fall of 1943' (which, we must assume, referred to the meeting with Jacob Wallenberg in November) the message from Marcus Wallenberg to the effect that the English were prepared to follow a policy that would stop the Soviets to the east of Poland's eastern borders and would also prevent the Baltic states from falling under Soviet influence; SD Report of 17 Aug. 1944, '*Spiegelbild*', i. 247.
231. One shorter memorandum, 'Praktische Massnahmen zur Umgestaltung Europas', n.d., BA/K, Goerdeler 23 (parts reprinted in Lipgens (ed.), *Europa-Föderationspläne*, 165–7 and translated into English in Lipgens (ed.), *Documents*, i. 440–2), hard to date precisely by internal evidence, has been assigned by Walter Lipgens to the beginning of 1944 after consultation with members of the Goerdeler family and the publisher Dr Gotthold Müller, an intimate of Goerdeler's. Ritter's conjecture (Ritter, *Carl Goerdeler*, 500 n. 12), however, that it might go back to the spring of 1939 is untenable since it anticipates 'the first euphoria of peace' and also refers to 'restitution'. It certainly belongs to the wartime. I am inclined therefore to follow the judgement of Lipgens. The document constitutes an unequivocal reaffirmation of Goerdeler's commitment to the idea and reality of Europe. The existence of the great 'world structures', America, Russia, and the British Empire, he argued, made the creation of a similar formation in Europe necessary, and after the war a new European league of nations should emerge that, in co-operation with the British Empire, would transform the European Continent from a 'field covered with ruins into a garden'.
232. Actually the memorandum is without a heading. A copy is in the Bundesarchiv/Koblenz, and it has been reprinted in Wilhelm Ritter von Schramm (ed.), *Beck und Goerdeler: Gemeinschaftsdokumente für den Frieden 1941–1944* (Munich, 1965). The editor had assigned to it the title 'The Way' to set it up as a companion piece to the earlier memorandum 'The Aim' ('Das Ziel') of the end of 1941, and this designation has been generally accepted. Controversial, however, is the extent to which the document can be considered what Schramm called a 'common effort' ('Gemeinschaftsdokument'). The prologue of 'The Way' mentions somewhat cryptically that 'from another side a few ideas were furnished in outline, which we can all subscribe to without anyone sacrificing his own position' (p. 167); this certainly suggests some sort of co-operation. But concerning Beck's part, it is now generally assumed that his contribution was of a minor nature and that Goerdeler merely took over some of his ideas. Another question is the degree to which other influences fed into the document. Though Schramm's assertion that the 'initiative' ('Anstoss'; p. 60) for it came 'most probably' from the socialist side (p. 60) has to be accepted, if at all, with great caution (see Hans Mommsen, 'Gesellschaftsbild und Verfassungspläne des deutschen Widerstandes', in Schmitthenner and Buchheim (eds.), *Der deutsche Widerstand*, 266–7 n. 68; Hans Rothfels, *Die deutsche Opposition gegen Hitler: Eine Würdigung* (Neue, erweiterte Ausgabe, Frankfurt/M., 1969), 205 n. 44), the fact is inescapable that the memorandum shows distinct traces of the influence upon Goerdeler of the labour union leaders, in particular Jakob Kaiser and Wilhelm Leuschner, who since late in 1941 had joined forces with him. Also it no doubt reflects an attempt on Goerdeler's part after all to accommodate some of the thinking among the Kreisau people.

233. *Beck und Goerdeler*, 59.
234. Ibid. 171, 176.
235. Ibid. 177–8.
236. Ibid. 180.
237. See esp. Beck's talks delivered before the *Mittwochs-Gesellschaft*, 'Die Lehre vom totalen Krieg (eine kritische Auseinandersetzung)' (17 June 1942) and 'Der 29. September 1918' (25 Nov. 1942), summarized in Scholder (ed.), *Die Mittwochs-Gesellschaft*, 292–4, 307–10; see also Klaus-Jürgen Müller, 'Clausewitz, Ludendorff and Beck: Some Remarks on Clausewitz' Influence on German Military Thinking in the 1930s and 1940s', *Journal of Strategic Studies*, 9 (June–Sept. 1986), 240–66.
238. Schramm, *Beck und Goerdeler*, 183. Beck thereby also departed from the position which he had maintained in the immediate post-war period; see ibid. 63; Nicholas Reynolds, *Treason Was No Crime: Ludwig Beck, Chief of the German General Staff* (London, 1976), 29–30.
239. Schramm, *Beck und Goerdeler*, 215.
240. Ibid. 231.
241. Ibid. 231–2; italics in the original.
242. Julius Leber on 15 June 1944, SD Report of 14 Aug. 1944, '*Spiegelbild*', i. 212; Dorothea Beck, *Julius Leber: Sozialdemokrat zwischen Reform und Widerstand* (Berlin, 1983), 191.
243. The sources for Otto John's activities in Spain are Otto John, *Twice through the Lines*; Willard L. Beaulac, *Franco: Silent Ally in World War II* (Carbondale and Edwardsville, Ill., 1986); 'Beitrag zum 20. Juli' (interview with Dr Otto John, London), *Der Tagesspiegel* (Berlin), 2 Nov. 1947; Otto John, 'Die bedingungslose Kapitulation' (Memorandum written for John W. Wheeler-Bennett), Wheeler-Bennett Papers, St Anthony's College, Oxford; letter from Ambassador Willard L. Beaulac to me, Washington, DC, 7 July 1978; interviews with Otto John, 18 and 19 Feb. 1978 and with Ambassador Beaulac (via telephone) 29 June 1978; see also 'Otto John 1944', in Hoffmann, *History*, 246–8.
244. John, *Twice through the Lines*, 80.
245. The Ambassador, Alexander W. Weddell, had left for Washington for consultation early in Jan. 1942; not before May 1942 was a new Ambassador, Carlton J. Hayes, appointed.
246. Hohenthal had served earlier, when still a Major, in the capacity of Assistant Military Attaché in Berlin.
247. Most probably through him, or possibly via Beaulac, an obviously blurred, if not wild, message reached the Foreign Office in London according to which Otto John had revealed to Beaulac that a 'committee' of German generals, industrialists, and labour leaders had plans for the generals unanimously to refuse to carry on the Russian campaign and to remove Hitler; that the Crown Prince would be given executive powers for twenty-four hours only, after which he would abdicate in favour of Prince Louis Ferdinand, who would form a government to negotiate with the Allies; that the plan was scheduled to be put into effect on 20 May but might be somewhat delayed; 'Summary of Principal Peace Feelers, April 1941 to June 1942'; PREM/4/100/8.
248. Letter from Beaulac to me, Washington, DC, 7 July 1978.
249. See above pp. 320, 399 n. 39.
250. He lost one eye, his right hand, and two fingers on his left hand.
251. For detailed treatments of this subject see Hoffmann, *History*, 365–6; Joachim Kramarz, *Stauffenberg: The Architect of the Famous July 20th Conspiracy to Assassinate Hitler* (New York, 1967), 157–62; Christian Müller, *Oberst i. G. Stauffenberg*, 371 ff.
252. John, *Twice through the Lines*, 133.
253. Interview with Otto John, 18 Feb. 1978.
254. By that time the Nazis had struck yet another serious blow to the Resistance. As a result of the defection of Erich Vermehren and his wife in Istanbul (see above p. 336), Admiral Canaris was, upon Hitler's orders, suspended from service, and the Abwehr was placed under Himmler's command as 'Amt Mil' of the RSHA; its head, however, Colonel Georg Hansen, was, like Canaris, committed to the cause of the Resistance and kept directing and shielding the activities of Otto John.
255. 'Report for Graf Stauffenberg—March 1944', John, *Twice through the Lines*, 317–20.
256. 'Final Report to London from Madrid: 26 June 1944', ibid. 321.

257. Kim Philby was head of the Iberian desk in the Counter-Espionage Section V of MI6; see Trevor-Roper, *The Philby Affair*, 28–49, 78–9; Knightley, *The Master Spy*, 106–9; also interview with Otto John, 19 Feb. 1978.

258. Knightley, *The Master Spy*, 109.

259. 'Übersetzung auf das europäische Niveau'; letter from Helmuth von Moltke to Freya von Moltke, Berlin, 17 Nov. 1942, von Moltke, *Briefe an Freya*, 438–9.

260. See above p. 9.

261. I have arrived at this interpretation after a discussion with Freya von Moltke (interview 26 July 1977). Beate Ruhm von Oppen's interpretation of this passage adds yet another interesting dimension; she relates it to Moltke's persistent concern to define the relationship between the European federation, which the Kreisau group was aiming at, and Great Britain; von Moltke, *Briefe an Freya*, 430 n. 3; 439 n. 1.

262. See in this connection in particular the important contributions, cited earlier in this volume, by Walter Lipgens. But here I should refer the reader to a paper which Lipgens prepared, shortly before his death, for the International Conference of 2–6 July 1984 in Berlin on the German Resistance, 'Verbindungen zwischen dem deutschen Widerstand und dem Widerstand in den besetzten Ländern', of which I have a photostat copy. The paper was not printed in the Schmädeke and Steinbach volume, *Der Widerstand gegen den Nationalsozialismus*; see also Hoffmann, *History*, 240–2.

263. Lipgens, 'Verbindungen', 2.

264. See also Lipgens, 'Verbindungen', 3. Lipgens, in his detailed documentation of the ideas and plans of the European Resistance, has come to the conclusion that 'it was characteristic of the non-Communist resistance groups and their periodicals that they almost always distinguished between the system of Nazi domination and the German people: they recognized that Versailles was partly to blame for Nazism, and argued that after the guilty had been punished, the Germans should enjoy equal rights with other European nations'; Lipgens (ed.), *Documents*, i. 342.

265. The *hjemmefronten* was the home front in contradistinction to the *utefronten* which included all Norwegians representing or fighting for their country from abroad: the government-in-exile, the military forces fighting with the Allies, and the Merchant Marine.

266. See above Ch. 2, s. 1.

267. For Steltzer's work on behalf of the Norwegian Resistance see in particular H. O. Christophersen, 'Die Kontakte der Heimfront mit deutschen Antinazisten', translation from articles in the *Aftenposten*, 4, 5, 6. May 1970, Archive of the Nordic Ecumenical Institute, Sigtuna; 'Interview with Dr Steltzer Concerning the Activities of the Opposition in Germany' (from the *Svenska Dagbladet*, Jan. 1946), Allen W. Dulles Papers, Princeton University; interview with Arvid Brodersen, 22 Nov. 1980; see also Arvid Brodersen, *Mellom Frontene* (Between the Fronts) (n.pl. 1979), 73–126; Theodor Steltzer, *Sechzig Jahre Zeitgenosse* (Munich, 1966), 126 ff.

268. Steltzer's rank while in Norway was that of lieutenant colonel.

269. The first feelers to the Norwegian Resistance were actually put out on the occasion of Moltke's and Bonhoeffer's visit to Norway in April 1942. Together with Bonhoeffer and Steltzer, Moltke then explored whether the Norwegian Resistance could induce the King or Crown Prince to intercede with the Allies to establish ties with the German Resistance; but the idea was dropped as being premature; van Roon, *Neuordnung*, 327.

270. In German: *Kreis* (circle).

271. Brodersen was the Secretary of the *Kretsen*. The other members, apart from Bishop Berggrav were Paal Berg (President of the Supreme Court), Gunnar Jahn (later Finance Minister), Hans Halvorsen (industrialist), Einar Gerhardsen (politician), and Ferdinand Schjelderup (judge of the Supreme Court). There were other groups, partly overlapping with the *Kretsen*, with which Steltzer had contact. In the house of a German businessman, Wolfgang Geldmacher and his Norwegian wife, many sessions took place between Steltzer and some other German officers and members of the home front. Also Bishop Berggrav and Brodersen formed an informal circle along the lines of the 'Sigtuna Group' of Dr Harry Johansson which was preoccupied with outlining the relations between Germans and Norwegians after the war. They met in the villa outside Oslo named 'Smedbråten' of the industrialist Johan H. Andresen. There was some suspicion afoot, however, among the

Norwegian Resistance, that the group around Geldmacher and the so-called 'Smedbråten Circle' were chiefly serving German interests, designed to neutralize the home front; see van Roon, *Neuordnung*, 325 n. 5; *Der Kreisauer Kreis*, 166.

272. Interview with Professor Arvid Brodersen; Christophersen, 'Die Kontakte ...'; see also *Der Kreisauer Kreis*, 168.

273. 'Die deutsche Opposition gegen den Nationalsozialismus' (15 July 1944; classified 'Top Secret'), FO 371/39087/C 1096/180/18; Christophersen, 'Die Kontakte ...'; the memorandum is reprinted in Theodor Steltzer, *Von Deutscher Politik* (Frankfurt/M., 1949), 81–96 and *Sechzig Jahre*, 285–97.

274. It was called 'Milorg' (*Militærorganisasjonen*).

275. Interview with Professor Arvid Brodersen; Christophersen, 'Die Kontakte ...'.

276. Letter from Ronald Thomley (SOE) to Geoffrey Harrison (FO), 14 Aug. 1944, FO 371/39087/C 1096/180/18.

277. He was sentenced to death on 1 Feb. 1945 and scheduled to be executed on 5 Feb., but was saved by the intervention on his behalf of Himmler's Finnish masseur Felix Kersten. It was generally known that Kersten had an unusual hold over the SS chief and frequently took advantage of his powers to extract concessions from Himmler on behalf of the persecuted and doomed. Steltzer's Norwegian friends knew about this and caused Kersten to intervene with Himmler. With the remark 'one more or less does not matter' Himmler then stayed the execution at the last minute ('Interview with Dr. Steltzer ...'). After further harrowing experiences, Steltzer was finally released from captivity on 25 April.

278. Theodor Steltzer Papers.

279. Christophersen, 'Die Kontakte ...'; interview with Arvid Brodersen.

280. During his meetings with the leadership of the home front he was generally blindfolded and at the same time had floodlights turned on him; Christophersen, 'Die Kontakte ...'; interview with Johann Wolfgang von Moltke, 4 Feb. 1978.

281. Affidavit by Jens Christian Hauge, den Kgl. Norske Regjering, Forsvarsministeren, Oslo, 25 May 1946; in the possession of Johann Wolfgang von Moltke.

282. Interview with Dr Paul Collmer, 8 Feb. 1978; also Armin Boyens, *Kirchenkampf und Ökumene 1939–1945* (Munich, 1973), ii. 157–9.

283. Visser't Hooft, *Memoirs*, 136–7; Lipgens (ed.), *Documents*, i. 561–4.

284. Visser't Hooft, *Memoirs*, 139.

285. Ibid. 136–49; see also Jürgen Heideking, 'Die "Schweizer Strassen"', 143–87; Werner Warmbrunn, *The Dutch under German Occupation 1940–1945* (Stanford, Calif., 1963), 210–11.

286. See above p. 267.

287. By virtue of his position with the World Council of Churches Schönfeld was in a position to obtain visas for all continental European countries without being scrutinized by the Nazi authorities; 'Eidesstattliche Erklärung', IfZ, Dokument Buch No. 4, Ernst von Weizsäcker Dok. No. 317.

288. For this and the following episode: German translation of an article by C. L. P. (Professor C. L. Patijn) which appeared in *Wending* (The Hague), July/Aug. 1964, Trott Archive, Korrespondenz über Adam; also letter from C. L. Patijn to me, Den Haag, 18 June 1978; J. H. van Roijen 'Adam von Trott in Holland', *Encounter*, 33 (Sept. 1969), 91; van Roon, *Neuordnung*, 330–1; *Der Kreisauer Kreis*, 171; Sykes, *Troubled Loyalty*, 399–400. It is very probable that after the failure of Trott's Memorandum of April 1942, which Visser't Hooft had taken to London, to elicit any positive response, both Visser't Hooft and Trott decided to explore an approach to the Dutch Underground and through it to the Western Allies.

289. Patijn had been Director of the Department for International Affairs of the Dutch Foreign Office which was dissolved by the Reich Commissar, and van Asbeck was a Professor of International Law at the University of Leiden; both had been active in the formation of the World Council of Churches. Van Roijen had been Director of the Department for Diplomatic Affairs of the Dutch Foreign Office and had become a leading figure in the Resistance; Scholten had met Trott before at a Christian students conference. I owe these identifications to van Roon, *Neuordnung*, 330.

290. From *Wending*.

291. See also letter from J. H. van Roijen to me, Wassenaar, 12 May 1978 and letter from P. K. R. von Goerschen to me, 'S-Gravenhage, 25 Aug. 1978.

292. Letter from Helmuth von Moltke to Freya von Moltke, Brussels, 5 June 1943, von Moltke, *Briefe an Freya*, 486.

293. Van Roon, *Neuordnung*, 331.

294. For the following passages on Staehle I am fully dependent on and indebted to the work of Ger van Roon, *Wilhelm Staehle. Ein Leben auf der Grenze 1877–1945* (Munich, 1969); id., 'Oberst Wilhelm Staehle: Ein Beitrag zu den Auslandskontakten des deutschen Widerstandes', *VfZ*, 14 (Apr., 1966), 209–23.

295. Ger van Roon, *Wilhelm Staehle*, 43–4.

296. Circulation 40,000 in the autumn of 1943, 60,000 early in 1945.

297. Just about that time Staehle together with his friend Brill had called on Trott in the Auswärtiges Amt in Berlin; ibid. 54; Ger van Roon, 'Oberst Wilhelm Staehle', *VfZ* 14 (Apr. 1966) 212.

298. They were: the removal of Arthur Seyss-Inquart, the Reich Commissar for the Netherlands, and Hanns Albin Rauter, the 'Higher SS and Police Leader'; the dissolution of the Dutch Nazi organizations; the return of the deposed Dutch civil servants; the restitution of the people's liberties; the return of the Dutch labourers working in Germany; and the replacement of the Military Commander for the Netherlands, General Friedrich Christiansen, by General Alexander von Falkenhausen who as Military Commander of Belgium and Northern France had gained a general reputation of fairness; van Roon, *Wilhelm Staehle*, 53–4; van Roon, 'Oberst Wilhelm Staehle', 212.

299. However, at the time Visser't Hooft was unaware of the identity of 'the German *Oberst*' involved and of his connection with Trott; Visser't Hooft, *Memoirs*, 160, 163–4 n. 14.

300. Ibid. 160.

301. Van Roon, *Wilhelm Staehle*, 83–8; van Roon, 'Oberst Wilhelm Staehle', 220–3.

302. It is worth noting here that, according to the Memorandum, in the course of the meeting with the Dutchmen Staehle mentioned that 'negotiations with England via Sweden' were under way on plans for the removal of the Nazi regime; ibid. 87; 221. This may have been an allusion to Goerdeler's or Trott's connection or both. In any case, some co-ordination clearly had taken place.

303. Handwritten memoir by Visser't Hooft, WCC ipof, XI.

304. 'Van Ministerpresident voor Visser. Ontvangen op 2 Februari 1944', ibid.

305. On 12 June Staehle was arrested, actually over his connection with the Solf Circle and not over his Dutch connections which had remained undiscovered by the Secret Police. On 16 March 1945 the People's Court sentenced him to two years in prison and in the night of 22/3 April, as the Russian troops closed in on Berlin, he was murdered by an SS gang, together with Albrecht Haushofer and six other captives, by a shot in the back of his neck. His Dutch partner van Heuven Goedhart, summoned to England, reached London on 17 June 1944; soon afterwards he was appointed Minister of Justice in the Dutch government-in-exile.

306. Those present were Patijn, van Roijen, and H. J. Reinink, who was a leading figure in the Underground.

307. From *Wending*; letter Professor C. L. Patijn to me.

308. Letter from J. H. van Roijen to me.

309. From *Wending*.

310. G. J. van Heuven-Goedhart, 'On the coming peace', *Het Parool*, 12 Dec. 1942, in Lipgens (ed.), *Documents*, i, 572–4.

311. F. G. van Heuven Goedhart, 'For the new freedom', *Het Parool*, 28 May 1943, ibid. i. 577.

312. *De Ploeg* was a relatively small underground journal (circulation 4,000 in Aug. 1944) published by students at Groningen University.

313. From *Het Parool*, 31 Oct. 1944 in Lipgens (ed.), *Documents*, i. 602. See also the statement by a group including van Asbeck, Patijn, and van Roijen, convened in the Peace Palace at The Hague to discuss post-war problems, calling attention to the existence of 'an opposition group in Germany' and arguing the case of co-operation with these 'well-disposed elements in Germany'; 'Postwar Questions', Aug. 1944, ibid. i. 588–91.

314. From *De Ploeg*, Aug. 1944, ibid. i. 588.
315. A. J. van der Leeuw, 'Annexations or European order', *De Ploeg*, Jan. 1945 ibid. i. 603–5.
316. See Carlo Schmid, *Erinnerungen* (Berne, 1977), esp. 175–206.
317. Helmuth von Moltke to Freya von Moltke, Berlin, 10 Oct. 1941, von Moltke, *Briefe an Freya*, 299.
318. Schmid, *Erinnerungen*, 201.
319. G. Freiherr von Falkenhausen, 'In Memoriam Cäsar von Hofacker' BA/K, Ritter 155; Alfred von Hofacker, 'Der deutsche Widerstand. Cäsar von Hofacker. Ein Wegbereiter für und ein Widerstandskämpfer gegen Hitler, ein Widerspruch?', typewritten manuscript, 1981, Cäsar von Hofacker Papers.
320. Memorandum by Cäsar von Hofacker for General Karl Heinrich von Stülpnagel, 6 Jan. 1943, Cäsar von Hofacker Papers.
321. Otto Niebergall, *Résistance: Erinnerungen deutscher Antifaschisten* (Berlin, 1973), 52–5; Karlheinz Pech, *An der Seite der Résistance: Zum Kampf der Bewegung 'Freies Deutschland' für den Westen in Frankreich (1943–1945)* (East Berlin, 1974), 145–8; Kurt Finker, *Stauffenberg und der 20. Juli 1944* (East Berlin, 1977), 255–7; idem, *Graf Moltke und der Kreisauer Kreis* (East Berlin, 1978), 300 n. 107; also Allan Merson, *Communist Resistance in Nazi Germany* (London, 1985), 272.
322. Komitee 'Freies Deutschland' für den Westen (KFDW).
323. Later Niebergall conjectured that he might have been the Commandant of Greater Paris, Lieutenant General Hans Freiherr von Boineburg-Lengsfeld; Niebergall, *Résistance*, 53.
324. Pech, *An der Seite*, 146–7.
325. I am led to wonder why Otto Niebergall should have held back until 1973 with publication of the information on Hofacker's connection with the Communist Underground.
326. 'Entwurf. Geheim', Paris, 20 Oct. 1943, Cäsar von Hofacker papers.
327. A possible explanation is that Hofacker, through the mediation of his driver, was approached by the Communists; interview with Alfred von Hofacker, 20 July 1989.
328. Karl Balzer, *Der 20. Juli und der Landesverrat: Eine Dokumentation über Verratshandlungen im deutschen Widerstand* (Göttingen, 1967), 72–3; it must be noted that this book is extremely biased against the German Resistance, attributing to it a consistent record of *Landesverrat*. Also it is almost exclusively based on secondary sources. In the particular instance of Dr Hans Buwert it quotes him without, however, giving any reference.
329. Obstlt. Heinz, 'Von Wilhelm Canaris . . .', 7.
330. For access to the papers of General von Falkenhausen I am indebted to Professor Hsi-Huey Liang from Vassar College. See also Hsi-Huey Liang, *The Sino-German Connection: Alexander von Falkenhausen between China and Germany 1900–1941* (Amsterdam, 1978), 143–85; *Der Kreisauer Kreis*, 172.
331. Obstlt. Heinz, 'Von Wilhelm Canaris . . .', 87; Liang, *The Sino-German Connection*, 156.
332. When late in 1943 Colonel Staehle met the representatives of the Dutch Resistance, the latter, as we have seen, proposed General von Falkenhausen be appointed to the post of Military Commander of Holland in the place of the then Military Commander General Christiansen.
333. Two days before the coup he had to turn over his affairs to Gauleiter Joseph Grohe; he spent the rest of the war in the concentration camp at Dachau.
334. He was sentenced to 12 years forced labour but released after 16 days in consideration of his humane administration as Military Commander.
335. For the main literature on approaches to Austria: 'Aufzeichnungen nach einem Bericht von Jakob Kaiser vom 14.8.1959', BA/K, Kaiser 73; Ludwig Jedlicka, *Der 20. Juli 1944 in Österreich* (Vienna, 1965), 21–32; Nebgen, *Jakob Kaiser*, 128–60; Otto Molden, *Der Ruf des Gewissens: Der österreichische Freiheitskampf 1938–1945* (Vienna, 1958), 148–58; Ritter, *Carl Goerdeler*, 506 n. 40; Lois Weinberger, *Tatsachen, Begegnungen und Gespräche: Ein Buch um Österreich* (Vienna, 1948), 120–40; Radomír V. Luža, *The Resistance in Austria, 1938-1945* (Minneapolis, 1984), 181–2.
336. (1) In Oct. 1942 Goerdeler and Kaiser saw, among others, Lois Weinberger (a young Christian Social politician and a member of the Austrian Resistance), Felix Hurdes (a former member of the Carinthian *Land* government and active in the Catholic Resistance),

Otto Troidl (a Christian Social politician and a member of a Viennese Resistance group), Otto Ender (a Christian Social politician, Federal Chancellor, Dec. 1930–June 1931), Karl Seitz (a Social Democratic politician, Mayor of Vienna, 1923–34), Professor Heinrich von Srbik (well-known historian with pronounced Greater-Germany leanings). (2) In the early summer of 1943 Wilhelm Leuschner saw Seitz, Adolf Schärf (a Social Democratic politician and Federal President after the war, 1957–65), Weinberger, and Hurdes. (3) In June 1943 Kaiser saw Weinberger, Hurdes, Troidl. (4) The evidence of a trip by Kaiser shortly before 20 July 1944 to confer with Weinberger is contradictory (according to 'Aufzeichnungen' and Weinberger, *Tatsachen*, 144–5 the trip took place, but according to Elfriede Nebgen, *Jakob Kaiser* 158, it did not.

337. Ritter, *Carl Goerdeler*, 294–5.
338. Nebgen, *Jakob Kaiser*, 142–3.
339. 'Selbstentsühnung'.
340. Weinberger, *Tatsachen*, 131.
341. Ibid. 124, 134.
342. The only person who, predictably, gave his full support to the Germans on this issue, was Srbik, who was committed to his Greater Germany dreams. But by virtue of his initial collaboration with the Nazis, he was too compromised to feature in any plan for the regeneration of Germany.
343. 'Aufzeichnungen'.
344. Adolf Schärf, *Österreichs Erneuerung 1945–1955* (Vienna, 1955), 19–20.
345. Ibid. 20.
346. Jedlicka, *Der 20. Juli 1944*, 25–6.
347. Molden, *Ruf*, 153 ff.
348. Schmid, *Erinnerungen*, 200. Schmid's reference to 'First Lieutenant Hans-Bernd von Haeften' is confusing. Hans-Bernd had no military rank; his younger brother Werner, Stauffenberg's aide-de-camp, was the first lieutenant. But since Hans-Bernd was the one who was closest to Moltke and connected with the work of the Kreisau Circle, we can assume that it was he who called on Carlo Schmid.
349. Van Roon, *Neuordnung*, 340–1; *Der Kreisauer Kreis*, 196–7.
350. Moltke's plan to visit Cracow is documented in the correspondence with his wife; Letter of Helmuth von Moltke to Freya von Moltke, Berlin, 11 Jan. 1943, von Moltke, *Briefe an Freya*, 452.
351. Letter of Helmuth von Moltke to Freya von Moltke, Berlin, 4 May 1943, ibid. 478–9.
352. It has been generally assumed in the literature that the visit to the Archbishop did take place (Balfour and Frisby, *Helmuth von Moltke*, 258; von Roon, *Neuordnung*, 341; *Der Kreisauer Kreis*, 173). However in her edn. of the Moltke letters Beate Ruhm von Oppen has recently cast justified doubts on the fact; von Moltke, *Briefe an Freya*, 472 n. 1.
353. van Roon, *Neuordnung*, 341.
354. Luža, *The Resistance in Austria*, 161, 196.
355. The main literature on the subject is Visser't Hooft, *Memoirs*, 177–81; Lipgens (ed.), *Documents*, i. 659–96 (including documents); Klaus Voigt, 'Die Genfer Föderalistentreffen im Frühjahr 1944', *Risorgimento*, 1 (1980), 59–72.
356. 31 Mar., 29 Apr., 20 May, 7 July.
357. All the documents emanating from the meetings carried this designation. It had to be resorted to in order to evade detection by Nazi spies and also to get around the tight protection by the Swiss police of the neutrality of the country; Visser't Hooft, *Memoirs*, 177–8; Voigt, 'Die Genfer Föderalistentreffen', 62.
358. Ibid. 65, 72.
359. Lipgens (ed.), *Documents*, i. 662–3; Voigt, 'Die Genfer Föderalistentreffen', 62.
360. 'Declaration I, message of solidarity', 20 May 1944, in Lipgens (ed.), *Documents*, i. 677–8; also Voigt, 'Die Genfer Föderalistentreffen', *passim*.
361. 'Declaration II on European federation', in Lipgens (ed.), *Documents*, i. 678–82; Voigt, 'Die Genfer Föderalistentreffen', *passim*.
362. In the early months of 1944, in preparation for the conference in Geneva, Ernesto Rossi had written a position paper on the problems and needs of Europe (Ernesto Rossi, 'Tomorrow's Europe', April 1944, Lipgens (ed.), *Documents*, i. 668–72) the French edn. of

which was smuggled into France and 10,000 copies were distributed. The section on 'Germany in the European federation' opened with the statement that 'Europe needs Germany' and called attention to the 'tens of thousands of Germans who have died or are languishing in prisons and concentration camps or have gone into exile ...'. The German people should therefore be enabled to resume its place in the concert of Europe 'on the basis of complete equality of rights and obligations'.

363. Visser't Hooft, *Memoirs*, 179–80; Lipgens (ed.), *Documents*, i. 663.

364. Visser't Hooft, *Memoirs*, 180.

365. On the subject 'Germany West or East?' see also Gert Buchheit, *Soldatentum und Rebellion*, 357–61; Dulles, *Germany's Underground*, 165–74; Hoffmann, *History*, 243–5; Ritter, *Carl Goerdeler*, 368–82; Klaus Hildebrand, 'Die ostpolitischen Vorstellungen im deutschen Widerstand', *Geschichte in Wissenschaft und Unterricht*, 29 (1978), 213–41; Peter Hoffmann, 'Colonel Claus von Stauffenberg in the German Resistance to Hitler: Between East and West', *Historical Journal* 31 (Sept. 1988), 629–50; *idem*, 'War Stauffenberg "ostorientiert"?', *Die Zeit*, 29 Dec. 1978.

366. SD Report of 21 Nov. 1944, '*Spiegelbild*', i. 492–5.

367. See Anthony Glees, *Exile Politics during the Second World War* (Oxford, 1982) 216–26; *Mit dem Gesicht nach Deutschland*, 155–61.

368. See Dulles, *Germany's Underground*, 167.

369. *Dokumente zur Deutschlandpolitik*, i. 1. 38.

370. See Hildebrandt, 'Die ostpolitischen ...', 220–1.

371. See in particular von Moltke, *Briefe an Freya*, 505 n. 5.

372. See in particular ibid. 430 n. 3.

373. See in this connection Moltke's letter to his wife at the time in May 1940 when the German troops were forging into France, in which he predicted that inevitably the USA would be drawn into the conflict; letter of Helmuth von Moltke to Freya von Moltke, Berlin, 26 May 1940, ibid. 138.

374. Trott's critical stance towards the British Empire surfaced in particular in his acrimonious exchanges with his friend from Oxford, Shiela Grant Duff, about the record of Germany and of Britain in world affairs. Her reproaches to Trott and her all too ready identification of him with Germany's policies made him turn the tables on her in condemnation of the ill deeds of British imperialism; see esp. letter of Adam von Trott to Shiela Grant Duff, Peking, 20 July 1938, Klemens von Klemperer (ed.), *A Noble Combat: The Letters of Shiela Grant Duff and Adama von Trott zu Solz 1932–1939* (Oxford, 1988), 314.

375. See letter from Adam von Trott to Percy E. Corbett, Geneva, 16 June 1941, WCC ipof, XI.

376. See above p. 118.

377. Hans Rothfels, 'Zwei aussenpolitische Memoranden', 397; see above p. 284; he also added the expectation, undoubtedly inspired by Hans-Bernd von Haeften, that 'they would regard the building up of a Russian Orthodox Church by the renewal of Christian faith in Russia as a real common basis which could further more than anything else the co-operation between Russia and the European Federation'; ibid.

378. *Beck und Goerdeler*, 100.

379. 'Heads of Agreement between Great Britain and Germany' (4 Dec. 1938), FO 371/21659/C 15084/42/18; still in the autumn of 1944 Goerdeler, composing a political testament in Gestapo confinement, maintained that the Corridor should revert to Germany; 'Gedanken eines zum Tode Verurteilten über die deutsche Zukunft' (Sept. 1944), BA/K, Goerdeler 26.

380. See on this subject van Roon, *Neuordnung*, 461; van Roon, 'Der Kreisauer Kreis und das Ausland', 41–2.

381. SD Report of 21 Nov. 1944, '*Spiegelbild*', i. 492.

382. The expression was used in the British Foreign Office to identify efforts by the German Opposition and its intermediaries to play off the East against the West and to obtain a hearing in London with the anti-Communist argument; see minutes by William Strang, 11 Aug. 1943, FO 371/34415/C 8903/29/18 and G. W. Harrison, 23 Nov. 1943, FO 371/34462/C 13731/279/18.

383. See Trott's 'Strictly Private and Confidential' memorandum of the end of April 1942:

'the substance of personal human integrity, equally threatened by Nazism and anarchic Bolshevism'; FO 371/30912/C 5099/48/18; see above p. 278. See also Goerdeler's 'Friedensplan' of the late summer or early autumn 1943, Ritter, *Carl Goerdeler*, 570–7 *passim*; see above p. 344.

384. See in particular Marcus Wallenberg's conversation with the British Minister to Stockholm, V. A. Mallet of 17 Aug. 1943.
385. The term was used by Visser't Hooft in 'Notes on the European Situation', Sept. 1943 (WCC, ipof XIV); inspired by Trott, he argued that, in view of the 'uncertainties of the West', millions of Europeans and Germans in particular were beginning to look towards the East.
386. John W. Wheeler-Bennett, 'Memorandum', 28 Dec. 1939, FO 371/24363/C 1545/267/62.
387. Letter from John W. Wheeler-Bennett to Sir Robert Vansittart, 27 Dec. 1939, ibid.
388. Minutes by Sir Alexander Cadogan, 24 Jan. 1940, ibid.
389. 'Exposé', Wilbrandt Papers; it dated the Rapallo Treaty 1924 instead of 1922.
390. See above p. 332.
391. Letter from Adam von Trott to Götz von Selle (an old friend of Trott's from his student days in Göttingen), Berlin, 23 Sept. 1943, Trott Archive.
392. 'Germany between East and West', June 1944.
393. The chief sources for the memorandum are the Kaltenbrunner Reports (SD Reports of 24 July and 21 Nov. 1944, '*Spiegelbild*', 34–5 and 493). The SD Report of 24 July, to which we owe a summary of the contents of the memorandum, actually refers to a pamphlet, 'Europa zwischen Ost und West', found among the papers of Count Ulrich Wilhelm von Schwerin-Schwanenfeld. We can safely assume that it is identical with Trott's memorandum. The SD Report of 21 Nov., then, referred squarely to the pamphlet by Trott entitled 'Deutschland zwischen Ost und West'. In this connection it might be mentioned that Professor Gerhard Leibholz also wrote an article on the subject which was published in England during the war (S. H. Gerard, pseud.), 'Germany between West and East', *Fortnightly*, 158 (Oct. 1942), 255–62 and in which he urged the Anglo-Saxon countries to lend support to the 'Western-minded opposition forces' in the German army to prevent Germany from turning in defeat to Bolshevik Russia.
394. See above n. 75 in Ch. 5.
395. Franz Joseph Furtwängler, *Männer die ich sah und kannte* (Hamburg, 1951), 228; IfZ/Ger van Roon, ZS/A-18, Furtwängler. To go by the Gestapo record, it even envisaged the compensation of Poland with East Prussia and, for once, a declaration of independence for Austria.
396. This argument in the Trott memorandum was reported on by (Professor) Friedrich Lenz (a collegue of Trott's in the Auswärtiges Amt), *Wirtschaftsplanung und Planwirtschaft* (Berlin, 1948), 94; see also Hans Rothfels, *The German Opposition to Hitler: An Assessment* (London, 1970), 149.
397. Gottfried von Nostitz, 'Abschied von den Freunden. Ein Bericht', typescript, 9, Nostitz Papers; Furtwängler, *Männer*, 228.
398. Clarita von Trott, 'Adam von Trott', 263.
399. Two copies, apart from the one found by the Gestapo among the papers of Count Schwerin, can be identified: one was hidden by Trott and Nostitz under the staircase leading to the balcony of the Trott home in Rheinbabenallee 47, but got lost in the course of the war; the other one was buried in Wildpark outside Berlin in the allotment of friends of Furtwängler, but could not later be retrieved; Nostitz, 'Abschied', 10; Clarita von Trott, 'Adam von Trott', 263. Clarita von Trott also speaks of two additional copies that got lost, one of which had been handed over to Trott's friend Peter Bielenberg and the other which made its way from Trott via Dr Harry Johansson to Theodor Steltzer whose briefcase containing the document was stolen; interview with Clarita von Trott, 18 July 1989.
400. *Politische Abteilung XIII*.
401. For the main literature about this episode: SD Report of 28 Aug. 1944 in '*Spiegelbild*', i. 308–9; entry of 13 Nov. 1943, *Die Hassell-Tagebücher*, 400; letter from Hans Georg Pfleiderer to Theodor Steltzer, 24 Mar. 1947, Steltzer Papers; Ingeborg Fleischhauer, *Die Chance des Sonderfriedens: Deutsch-sowjetische Geheimgespräche 1941–1945* (Berlin, 1986), 204; also *idem*, 'Mit Todesmut gegen den Krieg. Zum 20. Juli 1944: Graf Schulenburg

wollte mit Stalin über einen Sonderfrieden verhandeln', *Die Zeit*, 22 Juli 1988; Hoffmann, *History*, 245; Ritter, *Carl Goerdeler*, 380–1.

402. Letter from Pfleiderer to Steltzer; see also Ritter, *Carl Goerdeler*, 380.

403. Interrogation by Franz von Sonnleithner (Ribbentrop's representative in Hitler's headquarters) of 8 Dec. 1947; Record Branch of the War Department, Alexandria, Va., cited in Ritter, *Carl Goerdeler*, 381; see also Hoffmann, *History*, 245.

404. 'Ministerlisten Goerdelers', Ritter, *Carl Goerdeler*, 601–3; in the list of Aug. 1943 his name appeared conditional on ex-Chancellor Brüning's unwillingness to accept the nomination.

405. SD Report of 28 Aug. 1944, '*Spiegelbild*', i. 309.

406. Ibid. See also the report written by Gisevius for Allen W. Dulles in the week of 4–11 Feb. 1945, 'The Background and Story of the 20th of July' (Bancroft Papers, 35 pp. typescript in my possession), according to which Schulenburg was scheduled to become the Foreign Minister and Hassell the State Secretary in the Foreign Office.

407. Entry of 13 Nov. 1943, *Die Hassell-Tagebücher*, 400–5.

408. Ulrich von Hassell, 'Deutschland zwischen West und Ost', 18 July 1944, BA/K, Ritter 150; Hassell struck out the last sentence after 20 July.

409. See in this connection Christian Müller, *Oberst i. G. Stauffenberg*, 377. The thesis concerning Stauffenberg's eastern orientation goes back to Gisevius. After the failed coup of 20 July 1944 Gisevius revealed to Allen W. Dulles in Berne that Stauffenberg, having gathered around him a circle of mostly young east-Elbian nobles, had toyed with the idea of a revolution of workers, peasants, and soldiers, hoping that the Red Army would support a Communist Germany organized along Russian lines (Gisevius outlined this thesis in his report for Dulles 'The Background and Story of the 20th of July', 23–4; see also Dulles, *Germany's Underground*, 170; Gisevius, *To the Bitter End*, 486–7, 509). As a matter of fact, Gisevius had not met Stauffenberg before 12 July 1944, and this encounter was marked not by a rational exchange of views but by sparring between two incompatible temperaments. Gisevius certainly brought into the discussion with Stauffenberg a marked animosity towards the Colonel; indeed he had been 'tipped off' beforehand by Goerdeler about that 'political military man' (ibid. 508). The version of Stauffenberg as a decided 'Easterner' is patently misleading. Stauffenberg may well, under the pressure of events, have toyed with the 'Eastern solution' as a contingency; such a calculation, however, would not in any way detract from his basic preference for a settlement with the West; see Hoffmann, 'Colonel Claus von Stauffenberg ...'; *idem*, 'War Stauffenberg "ostorientiert"?'; also Kramarz, *Stauffenberg*, 178–9; Winfried Heinemann, 'Aussenpolitische Illusionen des nationalkonservativen Widerstands in den Monaten vor dem Attentat', in Schmädeke and Steinbach (eds.), *Der Widerstand*, 1064. It might be added that Gisevius's profile of Trott as having in fact established relations with the National Committee for a 'Free Germany' through the Russian Legation in Stockholm with the objective of opening the Eastern front and letting the Russians march in (Gisevius, 'The Background ...', 24), is as misleading as his profile of Stauffenberg. We know that Trott neither saw Mme Kollontay nor established relations with the Committee. As a matter of fact, no one in the German Resistance even so much as considered opening the Eastern front.

410. Eugen Gerstenmaier also gave expression to this position, when as late as mid-June of 1944, in a flight of both patriotic and religious fervour, he protested that 'the Reich of course must remain intact' ('Das Reich muss natürlich bleiben'). This statement, made by Gerstenmaier to Dr Wilhelm Hoffmann on 14 June 1944 (interview with Wilhelm Hoffmann, Stuttgart, 24 Mar. 1978), clearly had a double meaning. Apart from its obvious political intent, it was meant to be an allusion to the last line of Luther's hymn 'A mighty fortress is our God': 'The kingdom yet doth ours remain', which in German reads: 'Das Reich muss uns doch bleiben'.

411. SD Report of 2 Aug. 1944, '*Spiegelbild*', i. 126–7. The 11 Points included the following propositions: (1) immediate cessation of air warfare; (2) cancellation of [Allied] invasion plans; (3) avoidance of further bloodshed; (4) preservation of defensive capability in the east; evacuation of all occupied territories in the north, west, and south(!); (5) avoidance of any occupation; (6) a free government and an independently arrived at Constitution; (7) full participation of Germany in the execution of the armistice terms and the preparation of the Peace Treaty; (8) frontier in the east as of 1914; the retention of Austria and the

Sudetenland in the Reich; autonomy for Alsace-Lorraine; the incorporation into the Reich of the Tyrol down to Bozen and Meran; (9) active reconstruction and participation in the reconstruction of Europe; (10) German responsibility for the condemnation of its own criminals(!); (11) recovery of German honour, self-respect, and reputation. The 11 point directive has mistakenly been attributed in much of the literature to the initiative of Stauffenberg; see Ritter, *Carl Goerdeler*, 609; Eberhard Zeller, *Geist der Freiheit. Der zwanzigste Juli* (Munich, 1963), 340; *20. Juli 1944*, ed. Bundeszentrale für Heimatdienst (Bonn, 1961), 94; Kramarz, *Stauffenberg*, 160, 166. The wording in the SD Report is admittedly ambiguous inasmuch as it relates that on 25 May Kaiser drew up 'for Stauffenberg' a programme for negotiations with the enemy countries. But 'for Stauffenberg' does not mean, as explicitly stated by Kramarz, 'on Stauffenberg's instructions'; it might equally mean 'for the attention of Stauffenberg'. Meanwhile Peter Hoffmann has established, based on the records of the People's Court trial against Kaiser (BA/K, EAP 105/30), the fact that 'all this was merely a copy of the letter which he [Kaiser] had handed to Count von Stauffenberg on behalf of Goerdeler'; Hoffmann, *History*, 608–9 n. 11; see also Christian Müller, *Oberst i. G. Stauffenberg*, 393, 582 n. 108.

412. See Heinemann, 'Aussenpolitische Illusionen', 1062; also Ritter, *Carl Goerdeler*, 386.

413. Gisevius, *To the Bitter End*, 479 ff.

414. Among the conspirators, it was Helmuth von Moltke, if anyone who, while no less a patriot than the others, was from the very beginning immune to this linkage. Early in the war he had already proposed to George Kennan the possibility of his homeland, Silesia, going to the Czechs or Poles, admitting that this was sad for him, 'but not important' (George Kennan, *Memoirs 1925–1950* (Boston, 1967), 121; see also for a similar statement by Moltke to Theodor Steltzer, Steltzer, *Sechzig Jahre*, 150). Europe after the war was for him less 'a problem of frontiers and soldiers' than, so he wrote to Lionel Curtis, of 'how the picture of man can be re-established in the breasts of our fellow-citizens'. (Letter from Helmuth von Moltke to Lionel Curtis, Stockholm, 18 Apr. 1942, Balfour and Frisby, *Helmuth von Moltke*, 185). Moltke was also, as we have seen, one of the first among the conspirators to abandon, however hesitantly, his objection to 'unconditional surrender'. But, while he was in support of a coup to rid his country of the Nazi regime, he, unlike Stauffenberg but like Goerdeler, rejected for ethical and religious reasons the idea of assassination; the evil of National Socialism, he persisted, could not be overcome by murder.

415. Ger van Roon, *German Resistance to Hitler: Count von Moltke and the Kreisau Circle* (London, 1971), 269; van Roon, *Neuordnung*, 286.

416. Letter from Colonel Johannes Rohowsky to General Franz Halder, Berlin, 20 Nov. 1943; commentary to the letter by Rohowsky; BA/MA, N 124/v 1, Nachlass Oberst Johannes Rohowsky. Rohowsky served as liaison officer on the staff of Colonel General Friedrich Fromm, Commander-in-Chief of the Reserve Army, and General Halder. Halder, who had been dismissed by Hitler in Sept. 1942 over his disapproval of Hitler's decision to divert troops from the other fronts to Stalingrad, lived in retirement in his native Bavaria. According to Christian Müller (*Oberst i.G. Stauffenberg*, 366), who got his information from Kramarz, the same message was conveyed by Stauffenberg to Halder through the latter's adjutant; but in view of the clear evidence presented in the Rohowsky Papers, this version of the story can be dismissed as apocryphal.

417. Otto John, 'Some Facts and Aspects of the Plot against Hitler', typescript, p. 42; IfZ, John Sammlung, Mappe 4.

418. Breakers cable 2718–22, Berne-SI, 7 Apr. 1944. 'Breakers' was Allen W. Dulles's code word for the German Resistance: 'The term "Breakers" refers to a German resistance organization which is made up of liberal and educated persons from special governmental and military circles; however, its organizational structure is loose. It is reported that they would like to see drastic social changes based on western rather than eastern orientation but that they fear that circumstances are forcing Germany toward an eastern influence'; Breakers cable 30394, OSS-USTRAVIC, London, 17 Mar. 1944. The Breakers cables were the communications which Dulles sent from Berne to keep the OSS in Washington informed about the affairs of the *Widerstand*; since Switzerland at the time was surrounded by Axis powers, there was no diplomatic pouch available to Dulles. He therefore had to send his

messages to London by commercial cables, obviously in code. The Breakers cables, originally in the custody of the CIA, have in recent years been turned over to the National Archives in Washington, DC (RG 226), where they are scattered among the various Entries and Boxes. Before their transfer to the NA, however, I succeeded in obtaining from the CIA copies of the collection of cables relating to the 'Breakers' *en bloc*. Numbered consecutively from 1–200, they include 87 cables from Berne to OSS Washington and 33 cables from OSS Washington to Berne; 24 cables from OSS London to OSS Washington and 18 cables from OSS Washington to OSS London; otherwise sundry cables pertaining to the 'Breakers' from or to other OSS posts. Four cables from OSS London to OSS Washington had at the time not been declassified on the grounds that they contained information 'received in confidence from a foreign government'.

419. Breakers cable 866–7, Berne–OSS, 26 July 1944.
420. Breakers cable 3045–3046, Berne–OSS, 19 Apr. 1944.
421. In the autumn of 1943 General Thomas had broached it to General Karl Heinrich von Stülpnagel on a visit to Paris; Georg Thomas, 'Die Opposition' (Falkenstein, 1945), typescript, p. 19, Falkenhausen Papers. About this time Admiral Canaris presented the same idea to the American Naval Attaché in Istanbul, George H. Earle; Hoffmann, *History*, 598 n. 8. Also the Wilbrandt–Rüstow Exposé composed after Moltke's visit to Turkey in December 1943 envisaged Allied—meaning Western Allied—occupation of Germany in order to forestall the overpowering threat from the east; 'Exposé', Wilbrandt Papers.
422. This information was obtained from my interview with Eduard Waetjen, 7 Mar. 1978. Over this issue too Waetjen ran into opposition from Trott: 'Adam Trott met me in April '44 in Zurich. Adam and I no longer agreed on foreign policy. He was very disturbed because of Gisevius's and my conversations with AWD about Beck's [*sic*] and Goerdeler's wish to be informed whether western allies were interested in Germany opening western front if eastern front could be held by German armies until the American and British forces had reached German eastern borders of 1920. He asked Gisevius and me to abandon our talks with Dulles and informed me that I would no longer belong to their circle if I did not do so'; Waetjen notes on a draft for Allen W. Dulles's *Germany's Underground*, Allen W. Dulles Papers, Princeton University. Shortly before the Normandy landing, Stauffenberg also put before Julius Leber the question whether it was not in the German interest to guide the invaders through the German minefields to prevent the dreaded collapse of the Eastern front; both, however, agreed that such a plan was 'unrealistic'; Julius Leber, *Ein Mann geht seinen Weg: Schriften, Reden und Briefe* (Berlin-Schöneberg, 1952), 286.
423. Breakers cables 2718–22 and 3423–31, Berne–OSS, 7 Apr. and 13 May 1944; the German Generals allegedly prepared to co-operate in this venture were, according to Dulles's dispatches, apart from 'Tucky' (Beck), Rundstedt, and Falkenhausen (mentioned by their names), 'Ladder' (Halder), 'Zeta' (Zeitzler), 'Theta' (Heusinger), and 'Eta' (Olbricht). See also Dulles, *Germany's Underground*, 135–6, 139; Memorandum by Brigadier General John Magruder, Deputy Director of Intelligence Service, Office of Strategic Services, to Mr Fletcher Warren, Executive Assistant to the Assistant Secretary of State (Berle), Washington, 17 May 1944 with Enclosure 'Overtures by German Generals and Civilian Opposition for a Separate Armistice', Washington, 16 May 1944, NA, RG 59, CDF 740.00119 EW 1939/2635, reprinted in *FRUS* 1944, i. 510–13.
424. Breakers cable 4242, Berne–OSS, 26 July 1944.
425. James W. Riddleberger, Chief, Division of Central European Affairs to Mr Warren, 22 May 1944, RG 56, CDF 740.00119 EW 1939/2635.
426. Ibid. Fletcher Warren was the liaison between the State Department and the OSS.
427. See Bradley F. Smith, *The Shadow Warriors*, esp. pp. 212–14. One of the leading right-wingers in the OSS, Dewitt C. Poole, head of the Foreign Nationalities Branch, proposed that, to rival the 'Free Germany' movement, the USA should create a similar committee composed of exiles from Central Europe. Predictably he ran into opposition from the State Department which considered this plan to be in conflict with the hard-line 'unconditional surrender' policy; R. Harris Smith, *OSS*, 217.
428. Cordell Hull, *The Memoirs of Cordell Hull* (New York, 1948), ii. 1570–82.
429. Interview with James W. Riddleberger, 27 Jan. 1977.

430. '(1) 3 Allied Parachute Divisions to land in the Berlin region with the assistance of the local Army commanders. (2) Amphibian landing operations of major proportions either at or near Bremen and Hamburg along the German coast. (3) The isolation in Ober Salzburg [*sic*] of Hitler and high Nazi officials by trustworthy German units posted in the Munich region. (4) Although the preliminary plans for landings on the French coastline will be difficult to formulate, since they cannot count on Rommel for any co-operation, the above plan will normally [be] followed by such landings'; Breakers cable 3423–31; see also Ritter, *Carl Goerdeler*, 386.

431. Breakers cable 1468, Berne–OSS, 10 Apr. 1944.

432. Breakers cable 4110–4114, Berne–OSS, 13 July 1944; *Parliamentary Debates*, 5th ser., vol. 401, House of Commons, 7th vol. of Session 1943–4 (London, 1944), col. 1734.

433. Follow-up 'flash' 175 (via radio-telephone) to Breakers cable 4110–4114, NA, among the RG 59 Papers. The phrasing of this dispatch is almost identical with Churchill's warning of 14 Aug. 1943 to the Foreign Secretary to play down 'unconditional surrender' to avoid fusing all Germans together in a solid desperate block; the break-up in Germany and the weakening of their resistance would mean 'the saving of hundreds of thousands of British and American lives'; FO 371/34450/C 9706/155/G, see also above pp. 240–1. Still, after the attempt on Hitler's life of 20 July, Dulles kept up the pressure. Immediately after the unsuccessful coup he went as far as to propose (1) Some word from the President ... (2) Air raids on the Nazi stronghold in the region of Berchtesgaden ... (3) Providing [*sic*] the rebellion gains any momentum, some announcement to the effect that any German town which sides with the opposition would not be attacked whereas Gestapo centres and Nazi strongholds would be bombed unsparingly, (4) Large-scale dissemination of pamphlets from the air; Breakers cable 4199–4200–01–02, Berne–OSS, 22 July 1944; see also Oliver Jackson Sands, Jr., Lt. Col., Acting Assistant Deputy Director, OSS Intelligence Service to Mr Fletcher Warren, State Department, 26 July 1944 (brought before the Secretary of State), NA, RG 59, CDF 103.918/7–2644. Dulles persisted in warning against 'any action which might unduly jeopardize any who might still take part in anti-Nazi action of Western oriented tendency'; Breakers cable 4305–7, Berne–OSS, undated (2 Aug. 1944). 'Some affirmative action short of shelving "unconditional surrender"', he urged, was called for 'to drive a wedge into [the] German Army ... to facilitate American and British occupation of at least Western Germany before effects of Russian successes in East create situation of complete chaos thruout [*sic*] Germany'; Breakers cable 4077, Berne–OSS, 25 Jan. 1945.

434. Memorandum for the President, 15 July 1944, FDR Papers, Hyde Park, NY, PSF 168.

435. Memorandum for the President, 22 July 1944, ibid.

436. Memorandum for the President, 15 July 1944.

437. Breakers cable 4199–4200–01–02.

438. Gaevernitz, 'The Secret Surrender', 21; also interview with Fritz Molden, 24 May 1976.

439. Goerdeler, 'Unsere Idee' (Nov. 1944), BA/K, Goerdeler 26.

440. Christian Müller, *Oberst i. G. Stauffenberg*, 379.

441. Julius Leber, *Schriften, Reden, Briefe*, ed. Dorothea Beck and Wilfried F. Schoeller (Munich, 1976); an earlier edition: Julius Leber, *Ein Mann geht seinen Weg: Schriften, Reden und Briefe* (Berlin-Schöneberg, 1952); Beck, *Julius Leber*; see also Christian Müller, *Oberst i.G. Stauffenberg*, 369 ff.; Michael Balfour, *Withstanding Hitler in Germany 1933–45* (London, 1988), 195–200.

442. 'Die Todesursachen der deutschen Sozialdemokratie: Schrift von 1933' in Leber, *Schriften, Reden, Briefe*, 179–246.

443. Nebgen, *Jakob Kaiser*, 167; Kramarz, *Stauffenberg*, 159–60; see also Leber, *Ein Mann*, 291; Beck, *Julius Leber*, 186, 370 n. 101; SD Report of 16 August 1944, '*Spiegelbild*', i. 234.

444. For Berthold Schenk Count von Stauffenberg see Zeller, *Geist der Freiheit*, 248–52; A. N. Makarov, 'Berthold Schenk Graf von Stauffenberg', *Die Friedens-Warte*, 47 (1947), 360–5; also Walter Baum, 'Marine, Nationalsozialismus und Widerstand', *VfZ*, 11(Jan. 1963), 16–48.

445. Baum, 'Marine ...', 30 n. 109.

446. According to a State Department Memorandum of a Conversation which took place between the Swedish Ambassador Erik C. Boheman, the Acting Secretary of State Robert A. Lovett, and the Chief, Division of Northern European Affairs Benjamin M. Hulley on

26 Oct. 1948, a German, identified as 'Stahremberg [*sic*], brother of the one who later plotted to assassinate Hitler' [Berthold von Stauffenberg?] came to see Boheman, then Under-Secretary of Foreign Affairs, to warn him of an impending German invasion of Sweden. Along with a similar report coming from another source, this information allegedly caused the Swedes to mobilize to deter the Germans. Also the Memorandum states that the same German returned to Sweden 'about a year later' asking Boheman, who was setting off for London, to enquire from Churchill, on what terms the British would make peace if Hitler was put out of the way and if the Germans were willing to release their grip on Norway and Sweden. The Prime Minister's answer to Boheman allegedly was that the Germans should do away with Hitler first, and 'then we'll see'. This document, apart from its garbled version of Berthold von Stauffenberg's identity [even the name Stahremberg is misspelled], is based on the erroneous assumption of a German design upon Sweden. The German General Staff did not plan an invasion of Sweden early in 1942. The Swedish mobilization in mid-Feb. was ordered in response to the German naval and artillery reinforcements along the Norwegian coast, ordered by Hitler to prevent an Allied landing. Also there is no evidence in the Swedish files that Berthold von Stauffenberg visited Sweden in Feb. 1942 and talked to Boheman. Nevertheless, the Swedish connection of Berthold von Stauffenberg, alluded to in the document in question, cannot be dismissed. There is a distinct possibility that the visit 'about a year later' was identical with the one in the winter of 1943/4; it would also follow that the connection with Churchill was established, even though the latter's reaction was negative; Department of State Memorandum of Conversation, 26 Oct. 1948, NA, RG 59, CDF 711.58/10–2648; letter Dr K.-R. Böhme (*Kungl Militärhögskolan*, Stockholm) to me, 31 Oct. 1980; letter Dr Manfred Messerschmidt (Militärgeschichtliches Forschungsamt, Freiburg/Br.) to me, 9 Dec. 1980.

447. Two meetings took place, one on 15 May (with Josef Wirmer as a host and, besides himself, Goerdeler, Leuschner, Jakob Kaiser, Leber, and Fritz-Dietlof von der Schulenburg and possibly Bernhard Letterhaus attending) and the other one on 16 June 1944 in the Hotel Esplanade (with Goerdeler, Leber, Kaiser, Wirmer, and Habermann attending) in which there was a good deal of argumentation among the participants. Leber in particular subjected Goerdeler to harsh criticism: the former Mayor of Leipzig was, he argued, '*in foreign affairs an illusionist, in his views on economics outdated* and altogether dependent on heavy industry'; SD Report of 14 August 1944, '*Spiegelbild*', i. 212; italics in the original.

448. He made only one exception, namely the Polish Corridor which was also so close to Goerdeler's heart. It was to remain within Germany; the Poles were, however, to be ensured a transit road internationally guaranteed, that was to give them access to a Polish free port; letter from Albrecht von Kessel to me, Bonn, 3 Aug. 1974.

449. SD Reports of 1, 9, 14 Aug. 1944, '*Spiegelbild*', i. 118, 179, 211–12; see also Beck, *Julius Leber*, 190–1; Christian Müller, *Oberst i.G. Stauffenberg*, 392, 405.

450. Leber, *Ein Mann*, 286; see also 'Report for Graf Stauffenberg—March 1944' in John, *Twice through the Lines*, 320.

451. This position, however, caused apprehension on the part of Stauffenberg. Early in 1944 he discussed at great length with his brother Berthold and the Counts Fritz-Dietlof von der Schulenburg and Ulrich Wilhelm Schwerin von Schwanenfeld, what position they were to take towards a government that would accede to a diktat; on that point at least they agreed, they were not able to accept the notion of a 'humiliating peace'. While agreeing among themselves that they could rely on Goerdeler in this matter, they envisaged the possibility that he would be out-manœuvred by the 'trade-unionists' like Leuschner and Leber; but there was no assurance against the new regime eventually having to yield to harsh peace terms; SD Report of 10 Aug. 1944, '*Spiegelbild*', i. 189; see also Christian Müller, *Oberst i.G. Stauffenberg*, 377.

452. See above p. 240.

453. SD Report of 29 Nov. 1944, '*Spiegelbild*', i. 507.

454. 'Toresschluss-Panik', SD Report of 31 July 1944, ibid. 111.

455. Interesting in this connection is von Hassell's commentary on the situation during the days following the Normandy landings: 15 June 1944: 'up to now we have always figured on the following alternative: either timely change of regime and tolerable peace *or* catastrophe

and "liquidation". Since the first possibility did not take place, only the last one remained. Is there perhaps yet a third possibility? I mean further delay, increasing misery, but also increasing longing for peace *everywhere*; as a result ... overthrow of the System short of the obvious catastrophe and general or partial peace through exhaustion?' But the following diary entry of 10 July retracted these speculations: 'The further events have proven every calculation of the latter sort to be a *fata Morgana* ...'; entries of 15 June, 10 July 1944, *Die Hassell-Tagebücher*, 433; italics in the original.

456. According to the SD Reports, Goerdeler mentioned having had a talk with Stauffenberg in June 1944 in which the latter claimed that the conspiracy was in contact with Churchill through Count Gottfried von Bismarck-Schönhausen, an old friend of Jacob Wallenberg's, and that he could arrange to have a message delivered to Churchill's desk within eight days. Bismarck, however, denied having sought or established a connection via Wallenberg with Churchill; SD Reports of 17 Aug. and 29 Nov. 1944, '*Spiegelbild*', i. 247–8, 505. In any case, Goerdeler was much agitated about this interference by Stauffenberg in what he considered his preserve; he even complained about it to General Beck who, however, ruled that the young 'daredevil' should not be kept on too tight a rein. Also, according to Goerdeler, Stauffenberg revealed to him during their last meeting on 18 July, that he had a direct connection with Churchill; but it is most unlikely that Stauffenberg would have pressed a 'demand' that in case of 'action' by the conspiracy all German territory should remain with or be joined to the Reich; Ritter, *Carl Goerdeler*, 537 n. 104.

457. *Parliamentary Debates*, 5th ser., vol. 400, House of Commons, 6th vol. of Session 1943–4 (London, 1944), cols. 783–4. Interview with Otto John, 18 Feb. 1978; John, *Twice through the Lines*, 141; Otto John, 'Die bedingungslose Kapitulation' typescript, Wheeler-Bennett Papers. Like Otto John, Margret Boveri, a close friend of Trott's and, as a political journalist, an astute observer of the international scene, took issue with Trott on his optimistic interpretation of the Churchill speech; Margret Boveri, 'Adam von Trott zu Solz', typescript, 6–7, Trott Archive, Berichte.

458. See above pp. 338–40.

459. SD Report of 2 Aug. 1944, '*Spiegelbild*', i. 127; see also Christian Müller, *Oberst i.G. Stauffenberg*, 415.

460. SD Reports of 8 Aug. and 29 Nov., '*Spiegelbild*', i. 174 and 507; perhaps through the Otto John–Colonel Hohenthal connection in Madrid?

461. See above p. 241.

462. Trott himself made a last-minute effort to establish a link with the USA by engaging the services of a Swiss acquaintance, M. Philippe Mottu. Mottu, until 1942 an official of the Swiss General Staff and subsequently of the Swiss Foreign Office working on post-war problems, had first met Trott in the spring of 1942 and Hans-Bernd von Haeften in November of the same year; and he was also well acquainted with Weizsäcker's men serving in Switzerland. Whenever Trott was in Switzerland, he saw Mottu, who to begin with served as a liaison between Trott and the French and Dutch Resistance movements. When in April 1944 Mottu, an ardent member of the Moral Rearmament movement, got a cable from its head, Frank Buchman, asking him to come to America, Trott, at the time in Switzerland, urged him to go, since he could thus transmit to the USA news about the state of preparedness of the *Widerstand*. The necessary travel papers for Mottu and his wife Helene having been procured through Trott and Allen W. Dulles, a final briefing of the Swiss emissary took place on 12 June in Stuttgart before his departure on the following day. At this point Trott, who was joined by Gerstenmaier, gave Mottu details about the nature and composition of the German Resistance that were to be forwarded to Washington. A Condor flight then took Mottu to Lisbon, whence a few days later he crossed the Atlantic by Clipper Service. In Washington Mottu called on, among others, Justice Felix Frankfurter, who was not interested, and Felix Morley, who was keenly interested. He had the best meeting of minds with John Foster Dulles and Vice President Henry Wallace; but the policy-makers in Washington gave him the cold shoulder. Interview with Philippe Mottu, 25 Feb. 1978; with Eugen Gerstenmaier, 11 Apr. 1978; letter from Herbert Blankenhorn to me, Badenweiler, 10 May 1978; letters of Willem A. Visser't Hooft to John Foster Dulles, Geneva, 15 May 1944, Allen W. Dulles to John Foster Dulles, Berne, 14 June 1944, Philippe Mottu to Allen W. Dulles, 12 Oct. 1944, John Foster Dulles Papers,

Box 23; Vermerk 12 June 1944, AA/PA, Inland IIg 59; see also Clarita, 'Adam von Trott', 247, 250; Henry O. Malone, 'Adam von Trott zu Solz: The Road to Conspiracy Against Hitler', diss. (University of Texas at Austin, May 1980), 570, 573.

463. The date was 10 June; undated and untitled typescript by Otto John, IfZ, Otto John Sammlung, Mappe 5.

464. '*Aussenpolitisch ins Nichts*'; SD Reports of 31 July and 11 Aug. 1944, '*Spiegelbild*', i. 111 and 198; italics in the original.

465. Zeller, *Geist der Freiheit*, 364.

466. Leber, together with his fellow Socialist Adolf Reichwein, had decided to strike up a connection with the Communist Resistance. A first meeting was staged on 22 June at Reichwein's doctor's house. Among the three Communists who appeared, one turned out to be a Nazi informer. The Gestapo struck when the group reconvened on 4 July. Reichwein and the Communists were seized upon arrival, and Leber was arrested the following day.

467. The first warning to the conspirators actually had come earlier when Colonel Staehle was arrested on 12 June.

468. Schlabrendorff, *The Secret War*, 277.

469. 'Valkyrie' was the codeword for instructions, issued on 31 July 1943 by the Commander-in-Chief of the Replacement Army, governing counter-measures in case of domestic disorders and uprisings. The conspirators in Berlin had figured on invoking 'Valkyrie' as a cover for their gaining control of the capital and the Reich; see Hoffmann, *History*, 301–11 and *passim*.

470. The figures for those arrested and executed vary greatly. According to a conservative estimate, however, approximately 7,000 people were arrested and about 200 conspirators were executed in connection with the events of 20 July 1944; see 'Zwanzigster Juli' in *Das grosse Lexikon des Dritten Reiches*, ed. Christian Zentner and Friedemann Bedürftig (Munich, 1985), 662; also Balfour, *Withstanding Hitler*, 256–9; and Ulrike Eich, 'Suizid–Volksgerichtshof—Standgerichte: Die Opfer des 20. Juli', in Lill and Oberreuter (eds.), *20. Juli. Portraits des Widerstands* (Düsseldorf, 1984), 393–409. The chief actors whom we have encountered in this book suffered the following fate: Colonel General Beck and Colonel Claus von Stauffenberg were shot on 20 July as a result of an instant court martial in the courtyard of the Bendlerstrasse on orders of Colonel General Fritz Fromm, Commander of the Replacement Army. The sequence of the other executions—by hanging—was as follows: Hans-Bernd von Haeften (15 Aug., Berlin-Plötzensee), Adam von Trott zu Solz (26 Aug., Plötzensee), Ulrich von Hassell (8 Sept., Plötzensee), Count Friedrich Werner von der Schulenburg (10 Nov., Plötzensee), Lieutenant Colonel Cäsar von Hofacker (20 Dec., Plötzensee), Julius Leber (5 Jan. 1945, Plötzensee), Helmuth James von Moltke (23 Jan., Plötzensee), Carl Goerdeler (2 Feb., Plötzensee), Colonel Hans Oster, Admiral Wilhelm Canaris, Dietrich Bonhoeffer (9 Apr., Flössenburg), Hans von Dohnanyi (9 Apr., Sachsenhausen), Ewald von Kleist-Schmenzin (9 Apr., Plötzensee). Colonel Wilhelm Staehle was, like Albrecht Haushofer, shot from behind by an SS gang on the night of 22/3 April, as the Russians approached Berlin. Among those who survived were the following: Colonel General Franz Halder, Dr Josef Müller, and First Lieutenant (Res.) Fabian von Schlabrendorff were among the consignment of notables including Lieutenant Colonel Richard Stevens, Captain S. Payne Best (see the Venlo Incident), Generals Alexander von Falkenhausen and Georg Thomas, Dr Hjalmar Schacht, the Austrian ex-Chancellor Kurt von Schuschnigg, Pastor Martin Niemöller who, in the last stages of the war, were evacuated by the SS from Dachau Concentration Camp to the South Tyrol to be eventually liquidated; but they were finally liberated by the American troops, with the help of German regular army officers. Dr Eugen Gerstenmaier was sentenced by the People's Court to 7 years in jail, but freed by the American troops; Hans Bernd Gisevius, who on 11 July 1944 had taken off from Switzerland for Berlin to take part in the coup, went underground after 20 July and managed to return secretly to Switzerland in Jan. 1945; Theo Kordt was stationed in the Legation in Berne at the time of the coup, and his brother Erich was at a far-away post in China; Otto John escaped on 24 July in a Lufthansa plane to Madrid; Ernst von Weizsäcker who, though himself not active in the Resistance, had shielded the younger conspirators in the Auswärtiges Amt, was serving at the time of

the coup as German Ambassador to the Vatican; after the war he was arrested and put on trial by the Allies as a war criminal and sentenced by an American military tribunal in the so-called 'Wilhelmstrassenprozess' to 7 years in prison. It should be noted also that the Auswärtiges Amt tried to intervene on behalf of Hassell and Schulenburg, attempting to obtain a separation of their cases from the major People's Court trials; it argued that the news abroad of the participation in the plot of these internationally known foreign-office servants would encourage a reading abroad of the seriousness of the event and encourage in the enemy camp a sense of a disintegration of Germany; AA, PA Inland IIg 59.

471. Schlabrendorff, *The Secret War*, 294–5.
472. See above Ch. 6, s. 7.
473. William J. Donovan, Director, Memorandum for the Secretary of State ('Also to FDR and Marshall'), 24 July 1944, NA, RG 226, Entry 99, Box 14.
474. William J. Donovan, Director, Memorandum for the President, 22 July 1944, FDR Library, PSF 168; see above n. 433.
475. Dulles, *Germany's Underground*, 172.
476. 'Hitler hangs his Generals', *New York Times*, 9 Aug. 1944. A much more sober and analytical account of the plot appeared early in 1946: C. L. Sulzberger, 'Full Story of Anti-Hitler Plot Shows that Allies Refused to Assist', *New York Times*, 18 March 1946.
477. 'International Swine', *New York Herald Tribune*, 9 Aug. 1944.
478. Louis P. Lochner, *Always the Unexpected: A Book of Reminiscences* (New York, 1956), 294.
479. Joachim C. Fest, *Hitler* (New York, 1973), 716; Schlabrendorff, *The Secret War*, 7. The early publications about the *Widerstand*, such as Ulrich von Hassell's diaries (Ulrich von Hassell, *Vom anderen Deutschland: Aus den nachgelassenen Tagebüchern 1938–1944*, Zurich, 1946); Hans Bernd Gisevius, *Bis zum bitteren Ende*, 2 vols., Zurich, 1946; Fabian von Schlabrendorff, *Offiziere gegen Hitler* (Zurich, 1946); Rudolf Pechel, *Deutscher Widerstand* (Erlenbach-Zurich, 1947) therefore appeared in Switzerland. Also Eugen Gerstenmaier's two articles on the Resistance, 'Zur Geschichte des Umsturzversuches vom 20. Juli 1944' appeared in the *Neue Züricher Zeitung*, 23 and 24 June 1945. In the USA the two articles in *Human Events* (Alexander P. Maley, 'The Epic of the German Underground', *Human Events*, 3 27 (Feb. 1946), 1–8; E. A. Bayne, 'Resistance in the Foreign Office', *Human Events* 3 3 (Apr. 1946), 1–8) and Allen W. Dulles, *Germany's Underground* (New York, 1947) finally broke the ice. For an excellent account of the post-war reception of Adam von Trott in Britain and America see Malone, 'Adam von Trott', diss., 16–23.
480. Michael Balfour, *Propaganda in War 1939–1945: Organisations, Policies and Publics in Britain and Germany* (London, 1979), 391; see also Lamb, *The Ghosts of Peace 1935–1945* (Wilton, 1987), 299
481. 'First Fruits', *The Times* (London), 22 July 1944.
482. FO 371/39062/C 9896; see also Martin Gilbert, *Winston Churchill*, vol. vii; *Road to Victory*, (London, 1986) 868 n. 1; Lamb, *The Ghosts of Peace*, 296–8. See also Wheeler-Bennett, *The Nemesis of Power*, 689–93, where the author reiterates his earlier reaction to the coup in Germany without, however, making mention of his memorandum for the Foreign Office.
483. It might be of interest here to mention that on 26 Aug. at the Campo Santo Teutonico Weizsäcker met General Donovan whom he had known from Berlin in 1939. The American intelligence chief enquired about with whom the Americans could work in Germany; Weizsäcker in response gave him a blast about the mistakes of the American foreign policy making the Russian advance to the Elbe a distinct possibility; Annotation of 26 Aug. 1944, *Die Weizsäcker-Papiere*, 382–3; von Weizsäcker, *Erinnerungen* (Munich, 1950), 372; Cave Brown, *Wild Bill Donovan*, 565. In October Weizsäcker took the occasion of a visit to Rome by the New York Archbishop Francis Joseph Spellman to turn over to him a memorandum outlining 'the coming Peace' that called for an occupation of Germany 'exclusively' by American and British forces; an occupation of German territories by Soviet troops would mean, instead furthering the reintegration of Germany into the European community, handing over these territories 'definitely' to the East; Letter Ernst von Weizsäcker-Archbishop Francis Joseph Spelman, 9 Oct. 1944, *Die Weizsäcker-Papiere*, 383–5; von Weizsäcker, *Erinnerungen*, 372; Konstantin Prince of Bavaria, *The Pope: A Portrait from Life*

(London, 1954), 206. The memorandum was handed by Prelate Ludwig Kaas to the Archibishop who in turn took it to the American President; and that is where it was put *ad acta.*

484. There is little doubt but that Eden went along with this analysis of the German coup and the corresponding policy recommendation; it should be noted, however, that a memorandum which he sent to the Prime Minister on the bomb plot (FO 371/30912/C5205/48/18) has been closed to public inspection until the year 2018; see also Gilbert, *Road to Victory*, 868 n. 1. Oliver Harvey, Acting Assistant Secretary of State and former private secretary of both Halifax and Eden, expressed opinions similar to those of Wheeler-Bennett: 'I am convinced that it was to our interest that the coup failed. If Hitler had died, we would have had a surge to make peace with the generals. The rot must proceed further yet. Our enemies are both the Nazis and the generals. We should make peace with neither'; Baron Oliver Harvey, *The War Diaries of Oliver Harvey 1941–1945*, ed. John Harvey (London, 1978), 368.

485. This passage clearly betrays the impact upon the Prime Minister of Wheeler-Bennett's argumentation welcoming 'the killing of Germans by Germans'.

486. *Parliamentary Debates*, 5th ser., vol. 402, House of Commons, 8th vol. of Session 1943/4 (London, 1944), col. 1487.

487. Ibid., col. 1518.

488. Another statement, very different in tone and spirit, has frequently been attributed to Churchill in which, also before the House of Commons, he allegedly paid tribute to the German opposition 'which belongs to the noblest and greatest that has ever been produced in the political history of any people'; Hans-Adolf Jacobsen (ed.), *July 20, 1944* (Bonn, 1969), 185; *20. Juli 1944*, 63–4; Lamb, *The Ghosts of Peace*, 301. No record can be found, however, of any such pronouncement of the Prime Minister. But *se non è vero è bene trovato*; long after the event and in a mellower and more chivalric mood, Churchill, upon an enquiry, conceded that he 'might quite well have used the words' as they represented his feelings on German affairs; memorandum by Mr Walter Hammer for Professor Hans Rothfels, 10 Mar. 1953 in reference to letter of Winston Churchill to Rudolf Pechel, 19 Nov. 1945, BA/K, Rothfels 28-4-2.

489. Copies of letters from Bishop Bell to Anthony Eden, 27 July and 3 Aug. 1944, Bell Papers, Box 47.

490. Ibid. Bell also sent out a similar letter to Ambassador Winant; copy of letter from Bishop Bell to John Gilbert Winant, 5 Aug. 1944, Bell Papers, Box 47.

491. Letter from Anthony Eden to Bishop Bell, 17 Aug. 1944, ibid. Winant's answer to Bishop Bell was curt, formal and noncommittal; letter from John Gilbert Winant to Bishop Bell, 9 Aug. 1944, ibid.

492. Letter from Sir Stafford Cripps to Bishop Bell, 18 Sept. 1944, ibid.

493. Letter from Archbishop of Canterbury to Alexander Cadogan, 15 Sept. 1944 with minute by G. W. Harrison (17 Sept.), FO 371/39088/C 12469/837/29.

494. Visser't Hooft, *Memoirs*, 184.

495. Ibid. 161–2, 184–5; Peace Aims Group. Notes of meeting held in London on Tuesday, 7 Nov. 1944, WCC ipof, XI. Visser't Hooft did make his way to London 'in September 1944'. I could not ascertain for certain whether he came in time to attend the meeting of the British Council of Churches.

496. Ibid. 6.

497. Ibid. 5.

498. Among those attending the meeting was Marc Boegner, President of the Protestant Federation of France, who thought himself to be in a position to report that in France there was 'complete agreement' on the establishment of new conditions 'which will not destroy Germany'; ibid. 3.

499. Ibid. 7. Visser't Hooft undoubtedly knew about the agreement signed in Quebec between President Roosevelt and Prime Minister Churchill on 15 Sept., in which they, for all practical purposes, adopted the draconic plan concerning Germany worked out by the Secretary of the Treasury Henry Morgenthau, Jr., according to which Germany was to be stripped of many of its industrial areas and converted into a country primarily agricultural and pastoral in character (Gaddis Smith, *American Diplomacy during the Second World War*

*1941–1945*, New York, 1965, 123–6); this may have given his presentation before the Peace Aims Group a particular poignancy.

500. Peace Aims Group. Notes on meeting, 8.
501. Ibid. 4.
502. N. Bodrov, 'The Events in Germany', *Pravda*. 22 July 1944. I am indebted to my friend Igor Zelljadt for his help with the translation of the *Pravda* articles.
503. N. Bodrov, 'Internal Political Struggle in Germany', *Pravda*, 23 July 1944.
504. 'International Review', *Pravda*, 23 and 30 July 1944; the article of 23 July actually used the Hitlerian epithet of a 'clique', but applied it to both the Nazi establishment and the conspirators.
505. *July 20, 1944*, 185.
506. Kurt Finker, *Stauffenberg*, 370.
507. '20. Juli: Deutsches Volk! Deutsche Wehrmacht!', *Freies Deutschland*, ii (23 July 1944), 1, italics in the original; see also Bodo Scheurig (ed.), *Verrat hinter Stacheldraht? Das Nationalkomitee 'Freies Deutschland' und der Bund Deutscher Offiziere in der Sowjetunion 1943–1945* (Munich, 1965), 230–1.
508. 'Die Wahrheit über den 20. Juli'; 'Männer des 20. Juli', *Freies Deutschland*, ii (20 Aug. 1944), 2.
509. 'Palastrevolution'; from the Notes for Ackermann's speech in Finker, *Stauffenberg*, 373.
510. Heinrich von Einsiedel, *I Joined the Russians: A Captured German Flier's Diary of the Communist Temptation* (New Haven, Conn., 1953), 159 (entry of 26 July 1944). Subsequently the Soviet historian Daniil Melnikow essentially identified himself with this position; Daniil Melnikow, *20. Juli 1944: Legende und Wirklichkeit* (Berlin, 1968) esp. pp. 187–8.
511. 'Die Verräter sind gerichtet', *Völkischer Beobachter*, Münchener Ausgabe, 9 Aug. 1944.
512. 'Verschwörerclique', '*Spiegelbild*', i. 19.
513. Ibid. 544.
514. For a judicious account on the reliability of the SD Reports as a historical source see Hans-Adolf Jacobsen's 'Vorbemerkungen zur Edition' in ibid., xi–xiv.
515. SD Report of 24 July 1944, ibid. 17.
516. See in particular Helmut Gollwitzer, Käthe Kuhn, Reinhold Schneider (eds.), '*Du hast mich heimgesucht bei Nacht': Abschiedsbriefe und Aufzeichnungen des Widerstandes 1933–1945* (Munich, 1957); Helmuth J. Graf von Moltke 1907–1945, *Letzte Briefe aus dem Gefängnis Tegel* (Berlin, 1963); Eberhard and Renate Bethge (eds.). *Letzte Briefe im Widerstand: Aus dem Kreis der Familie Bonhoeffer* (Munich, 1984); *Erkämpft das Menschenrecht: Lebensbilder und letzte Briefe antifaschistischer Widerstandskämfer*, ed. Institut für Marxismus-Leninismus (East Berlin, 1958).
517. Letter Adam von Trott to Clarita von Trott, 15 Aug. 1944, Trott Archive; the letter is reproduced fully in Clarita von Trott, 'Adam von Trott', 288–9.
518. 'Opposition Groups in Germany', *Dagens Nyheter*, 12 Sept. 1944, translated transcript, Rhodes Trust.
519. Secret Telegram from Herschel V. Johnson to Department of State, 14 Sept. 1944, NA, RG, 59, CDF 862. 01/9–1444. Brandt himself, however, later insisted that it had been based on an internal draft for his group which, to his dismay, was sent out to the newspaper; interview with Willy Brandt, 1 July 1980.
520. For the Auswärtiges Amt see AA PA Inland IIg 59.
521. For further details see Malone, 'Adam von Trott', diss., 7, 58, nn. 16–18.
522. Hershel V. Johnson to Secretary of State, Stockholm, 21 Sept. 1944, NA, RG 59, CDF 811.91258/9–2144. Also, when two months later a book appeared anonymously in Sweden on the German Resistance (*Misslyckad Revolt—Abortive Revolt*), a 'blown-up edition' of the *Dagens Nyheter* article, Herschel V. Johnson, once again suspecting Willy Brandt, took exception to it, calling it a 'major indiscretion' (NA, RG 59, CDF 862.00/11–2144). Once again Brandt later denied his authorship (Willy Brandt, *In Exile: Essays, Reflections and Letters 1933–1947*, London, 1971, 95–6).
523. See above pp. 339–40; John Scott, 'Mail Story', 17 Sept. 1944, NA, RG 59, CDF 811.91258/9–2144.
524. He did, however, allow Scott to send it by diplomatic pouch to Washington for forwarding

to the Editors of *Time* magazine as background information; see also R. Taylor Cole (a member of the OSS mission in Stockholm), *The Recollections of R. Taylor Cole, Educator, Emissary, Development Planner* (Durham, NC 1983), 82–3.

525. See in particular Ritter, *Carl Goerdeler* 417 ff.; Balfour, *Withstanding Hitler*, 171; Meyer-Krahmer, *Carl Goerdeler*, 177 ff.

526. Ohlendorf himself had a bloody record. A Party member since 1925 and an SS member since 1926, he was head of the Department III (Internal Security) of the RSHA from 1939 to 1945. From June 1941 to June 1942 he was delegated to be Commander of the Einsatzgruppe D in southern Russia, in which capacity he was responsible for exterminating some 90,000 civilians, mostly Jews. On 10 April 1948 he was sentenced by the US Military Tribunal IIA in Nuremberg to death and finally hanged, after more than three years in detention, in Landsberg prison on 8 June 1951. Ohlendorf's connection with Goerdeler was established through the former's teacher, the economics Professor Jens Peter Jessen who in turn was a protégé of Johannes Popitz.

527. The first one was in response to a questionnaire produced by a high official of the Ministry of the Interior who had been delegated to the RSHA (Carl Goerderler: 'Beantwortung von 39 Fragen über den Wiederaufbau: Datum 3.1.1945', '*Spiegelbild*', ii. 802–49); Popitz who, like Goerdeler, was kept alive until 2 Feb. 1945, was put to work on the same questionnaire to which he responded in a parallel memorandum; Ritter, *Carl Goerdeler*, 418. The other memoranda by Goerdeler dealt with Price Control ('Preisüberwachung'; see Ritter, *Carl Goerdeler*, 418, 547 n. 30) and with political and social reform based on self-administration of the Reich ('*Spiegelbild*' ii. 850–72, 873–904).

528. Ritter, *Carl Goerdeler* 419.

529. To begin with, the working relationship between Ohlendorf and Himmler was singularly poor, with the former being considered a trouble-maker by his chief, and suspected for his unsoldierly bearing and defeatism: *Trials of War Criminals before the Nuernberg Military Tribunals under Control Council Law No. 10* iv. 233 ff., 240–2. As for Himmler, since the spring of 1943 he had tried in vain to establish a contact with Jacob Wallenberg in Stockholm, and there is little doubt but that he sought thus to use Goerdeler's influence with the Swedish banker in expectation of striking a deal with the Western Allies over the head of the Führer; Ritter, *Carl Goerdeler*, 422–3.

530. The following are the main writings by Goerdeler since the arrest warrant was issued against him on 17 July 1944: 'Aufgaben deutscher Zukunft', 11 typed pages, written between 1 and 11 August 1944 in Berlin, BA/K Goerdeler 26, repr. in excerpts in Lipgens (ed.), *Europa-Föderationspläne*, 170–2 and Lipgens (ed.), *Documents*, i 444–6; 'Gedanken eines zum Tode Verurteilten über die deutsche Zukunft', 42 typed pages, written in confinement in Sept. 1944, BA/K Goerdeler 26, in part in Ritter, *Carl Goerdeler*, 553–60; 'Unsere Idee', 40 typed pages, written in Nov. 1944, BA/K Goerdeler 26; 'Mein letzter Wille', 4 typed pages, dated 4 Nov. 1944, BA/K Kaiser 135; untitled typescript starting with 'Am 11. Dezember hat der deutsche Reichsaussenminister gesprochen . . .', 3 typed pages, dated Dec. 1944, BA/K Kaiser 125; 'Im Gefängnis Weihnachten 1944', 8 typed pages, dated Jan. 1945, BA/K Kaiser 125; 'An alle Menschen' (also preface to Goerdeler's treasured 'Wirtschaftsfibel'), 15 typed pages, dated 17 Jan. 1945, BA/K Kaiser 135; 'Erfahrungen und Erkenntnisse', unfinished, 14 typed pages, written in Jan. 1945, BA/K Kaiser 125; excerpt from 'Aufruf an unser Volk und die Völker der Welt', 2 typed pages, written a 'few days before his execution', BA/K Kaiser 125.

531. Goerdeler, 'An alle Menschen', 15.

532. 'Der anliegende Aufruf an alle Menschen entspringt keiner Zellenpsychose' ibid., unnumbered prefatory page.

533. Goerdeler, 'Mein letzter Wille', 2.

534. Goerdeler, 'An alle Menschen', 4.

535. Goerdeler, 'Am 11. Dezember . . .'.

536. Ritter, *Carl Goerdeler*, 427–8.

537. Ritter's chief source for the Himmler initiative is a report available to him, written in December 1950 by Goerdeler's warden in the Gestapo prison, Wilhelm Brandenburg. Not a professional policeman, but 'drafted' for police duty because of the shortage of wardens, he was a humane person who made it his task to alleviate the lot of the prisoners under

his supervision. With Goerdeler he developed a particular relation of confidence and took it upon himself to smuggle his writings out of goal whence they eventually reached the prisoner's family; ibid. 428–9. Goerdeler prefaced his 'last will' with a tribute to Brandenburg for his 'kindness of heart and clarity' and his 'assistance and encouragement in difficult hours'; Goerdeler, 'Mein letzter Wille', 1. But Brandenburg's account of Goerdeler's reaction is not conclusive. While, according to him, Goerdeler 'rejected' Himmler's proposal, presumably because of Himmler's unwillingness to free him, Goerdeler persisted in exploring a way of implementing it, by circumventing Himmler and appealing directly to Hitler.

538. 'Der lachende Dritte wird der russische Bolschewismus'; draft of letter from Goerdeler to Jacob Wallenberg, 8 Nov. 1944, BA Kaiser 125. Also, in one of his Dec. memoranda Goerdeler alluded to a forthcoming 'official letter' from Himmler, initiated by himself but 'approved' by Himmler; Goerdeler, 'Am 11. Dezember ...', 3.

539. Goerdeler, 'Am 11. Dezember ...', 3.

540. Goerdeler, 'Gedanken', 34.

541. Goerdeler, 'Im Gefängnis Weihnachten 1944', 1, 2; also 'Gedanken ...', 32; 'Am 11. Dezember ...', 3.

542. 'Weltbund der Nationen', Goerdeler, 'Gedanken ...', 38; 'Im Gefängnis Weihnachten 1944', 2.

543. Goerdeler, 'An alle Menschen ...', 10.

544. Goerdeler, 'Anlage', 34 typed pages, undated, 29–30.

545. See in this connection my article 'Glaube, Religion, Kirche und der deutsche Widerstand gegen den Nationalsozialismus', *VfZ*, 28 (July 1980), 293–309.

546. The term is generally used as a metaphor for stay of execution.

# Conclusion

THE evidence assembled in this book has revealed a marked disproportion between the determination on the part of the members of the German Resistance to reach the 'greater world' and the result of their endeavours. In their efforts to engage the 'other side' in what they perceived to be the 'common struggle' against Nazi barbarism, they were as tenacious during the war as they were before it began. They met with no tangible success, alas. There was no 'common struggle'. Within the grid system of hard-and-fast diplomacy, the 'other Germany' found no place. It was, as Ewald von Kleist-Schmenzin lamented, left 'all alone' in the hostile environment of Nazi terror at home, while at the same time it found itself rebuffed abroad. The ventures into the field of resistance foreign policy served, in fact, to compound the failure of the plot against the regime.

The historical literature on the subject of the foreign relations of the German Resistance, with which this book has been concerned, has so far been excessively preoccupied with assigning blame, to one side or other, for the failure of communication between the German conspirators and the Allies.[1] We have every reason to eschew the temptation of being excessively judgemental. The failure of the Allies and the German Resistance to come together cannot be attributed fundamentally to faults on either side, but rather to the unorthodoxy of the operation itself and to stubborn conflicts of interest. Considering the uniqueness of the German approaches abroad, it is not surprising that London and Washington should have been puzzled by the questionable accreditation of the opposition emissaries as well as by the often uncertain credibility of many of the messages that reached them. Certainly, by all the traditional rules of diplomacy conducted between sovereign units, the odds were heavily against the success of the Resistance foreign policy. Even Willem A. Visser't Hooft, the General Secretary of the World Council of Churches, like Bishop Bell of Chichester a staunch advocate abroad of the German conspirators, had to admit that it was 'very difficult' for a government to deal with a group in an enemy country that claimed to be a resistance group, but about whose political and military power there was considerable doubt.[2] The best will for co-operation which certainly existed on the German side throughout, and on the British side intermittently under the premiership of Neville Chamberlain, was bound to yield eventually to the political realities of the war which tended to set the two sides apart from each other.

On the German side a not decisive factor was the 'Generals' to whom the conspiracy was bonded. The lack of popular backing for the German Resistance made it all the more dependent on the military, and it was to a large extent for their benefit that assurances had to be exacted from the Allies involving Germany's territorial integrity and the modification of their demand for unconditional surrender. It was not only in consideration of the army commanders, however, but also out of national pride that all the spokesmen for the *Widerstand*, with the exception of Moltke and his socialist friends in the Kreisau Circle, took positions that were unacceptable to the Allies. Goerdeler shot his bolts, so to speak, by insisting, at least until late in 1942, upon a German hegemonic position in Europe. Like Goerdeler, Trott also saw the need of ensuring for Germany a 'strong armour',[3] and still in the spring of 1942, while outlining a settlement along ethnographic lines to the British Foreign Office, he talked to Elizabeth Wiskemann about Germany's 'free hand' in the east. Neither proposition, of course, was acceptable to the British.

On the part of the British, in turn, it was their 'national interest', as Anthony Eden explained to Bishop Bell of Chichester, which did not allow Great Britain to maintain contacts with the German opposition—if only, as Eden put it tersely, 'for Russian reasons'.[4] The 'Communist bogey', as a matter of fact, so insistently invoked by the Germans and designed to appeal to the Western Allies, ironically served to antagonize them and to boomerang against the Germans. Whatever the merits of the awareness prevailing among the German conspirators of the imminent threat of Bolshevism to the European Continent, they overrated the potential for conflict between Britain and Russia. Goerdeler, in particular, wrongly banked on a potential rivalry between Britain and the United States.

At no point was the American President tempted to enter into dialogue with the German Resistance. After all, Roosevelt was the one who, at Casablanca in January of 1943, fathered the 'unconditional surrender' formula. His thinking and acting were shaped by the 'grim memories' of the Armistice in 1918[5] and by the failure of President Woodrow Wilson's 'New Diplomacy' that had so deceivingly promised a fair deal to all, victors and vanquished. This time nothing short of total victory was to be achieved.

Quite a different matter, as we have seen, was the relationship between the *Widerstand* and the Soviet Union. On the part of the conspirators, especially Trott and Schulenburg, it was most probably their council of exasperation over the failure to come to terms with the West that made them explore an Eastern solution. On the part of the Russians, their wooing of the Resistance was purely a tactical device to put pressure on London and Washington to open up the second front. The Bolshevik version of the 'New Diplomacy' so far as it survived into the years of the Second World War, was put to work to serve the interests of Stalin's Russia and nothing else.

The foreign relations of the German Resistance, however, should not be considered exclusively in relation to what I have called earlier the 'traditional rules of diplomacy' and the 'national interest'. After the Great War, the conduct of foreign policy on the part of any European power was bound to be affected by the incidence of Bolshevism in Russia and the establishment of National Socialism in Germany, both of them ideological and indeed totalitarian manifestations. And it was the Second World War that was to put the ideological features of National Socialism to the test. It was not merely a war between nations and between alliance systems but also one between what Bishop Bell called 'rival philosophies of life'. In this context the German Resistance had a distinct place. There may have been some question as to whether it was democratic and also as to whether it was really ready to sacrifice German national claims to a general 'European' settlement. The fact was, however, that there was in Germany a Resistance determined to make common cause with the Allied Powers, preferably the Western ones, and to throw off the yoke of Nazism. War or no war, it kept persisting on recognition of the 'other Germany' as opposed to the Hitler regime. The *Widerstand*, it might be argued, was engaged in what Adam von Trott called a 'world civil war' which, like an overlay, tended to redesign the contours of the basic map drawn according to the criteria of the 'national interest', and thus to affect the traditional line-up of sovereign states.

The foreign relations of the German Resistance, then, are clearly a legitimate field of enquiry into a chapter of international relations, in the age of ideologies and totalitarian regimes, in which political loyalties transcended national interests. With all the data collected, we are now in a position to state with assurance that they were not mere excursions aimed at putting on record the foreign policy objectives of a post-Hitlerian Germany, but that they were designed to serve as an integral part of the plot and thus to co-ordinate the onslaught against Hitler from within with the one from without. In the early phases of the conspiracy even Goerdeler's agonized remark as to why it should have been up to him to 'think for [the] British Empire', was not altogether out of place.[6] The gospel of firmness which he and his friends urged in vain upon the Chamberlain government in lieu of appeasement, and the prescription of *un silence menaçant* emanating from Weizsäcker, were devised to serve a common interest, namely to complement and bolster the German Opposition at home and at the same time to set the stage for the 'unwinding of appeasement' beginning in the autum of 1939. The irony here, of course, is that the new British policy of firmness eventually became directed against the Resistance itself as well as against the Nazi regime. Finally, the prescription of *un silence menaçant* was translated by Winston Churchill into the command of 'absolute silence' towards all approaches from the *Widerstand*.

Surveying the whole range of contacts between the German conspirators and the British, we can now clearly identify the period of the Twilight War as the high point of the traffic between the two parties and the Vatican Exchanges as marking the most propitious incident in their efforts to come to terms. Let us remember that they took place during wartime, albeit before the outbreak of the shooting war. The government of Neville Chamberlain had set its course on trying to win the war, short of military action, by undermining the German home front. Since military victory was not considered feasible, the government was reduced to 'hanker', as Lord Halifax put it, after a German revolution. It is not difficult to imagine how the Quai d'Orsay would have reacted to a successful conclusion of the Vatican Exchanges. Another question, of course, is whether the British would have yielded to French objections. In any case, the Vatican Exchanges were torpedoed by the Generals of the OKH in the name of the German 'national interest'. Never again did such an opportunity offer itself to the German conspirators and to the British to reach an understanding. With the German offensives in Scandinavia and in the west of April and May 1940, and with Winston Churchill's becoming Prime Minister of Great Britain on 10 May, the search in Whitehall for the 'other Germany' was over.

What followed the breakdown of the Vatican Exchanges might appear only an epilogue to the efforts of the German Resistance to negotiate terms with the other side. Certainly a resumption of negotiations, as projected in the mission of Josef Müller to Rome late in April 1940, was now out of the question. Any subsequent approach on the part of the German dissidents was bound to be discounted if not dismissed. At long last Vansittart seemed vindicated. It was he who had all along warned against what he called the 'old Adam'[7] and who came to warn so insistently against the complicity of his one-time protégé Goerdeler with the German military expansionists and the Nazis: 'the same sort of ambitions ... sponsored by a different body of men, and that is about all.'[8]

The hegemonial aspirations of the Beck–Goerdeler–von Hassell group no doubt were unacceptable in London; and Goerdeler, who for so long had advocated the restitution of the 1914 borders, did not inspire confidence on the other side of the Channel. It must be remembered, however, that even terms like these did not really reflect final and non-negotiable positions. In the course of the war, Goerdeler came round to embracing the prescription of a European federation and thus moved away from his notion of a German hegemonic position. Upon the urging of Jacob Wallenberg, furthermore, he even abandoned, temporarily at least, his insistence on the 1914 borders. Similarly since early in 1943 Trott exhibited his readiness to reduce his territorial claims.[9] It is fair to maintain that all the terms proposed by the Germans were negotiable. In the end the most unequivocal and sweeping territorial concessions to the Allies came from the Socialist Julius Leber; but they never reached the other side.

The Western Allies, in view of their commitments to their Russian ally, no doubt had reason to shun dealings with the German dissidents who made so much of the 'Communist bogey'. But is it not reasonable to argue that, in view of the cracks in the Grand Alliance and of Stalin's persistent gestures after Stalingrad towards both the Nazis and the Resistance, a warning coming from the latter concerning Russia's intentions might not have been summarily dismissed in London and Washington as a mere divisive manœuvre?

Trott's involvement with the Section for Indian Affairs of the Auswärtiges Amt, moreover, even though it may have shielded him against the Nazis at home, no doubt had the effect of deepening suspicions concerning him in Britain. This was a chance which he evidently took light-heartedly; inasmuch as, however, he considered the conduct of foreign affairs his chief mission, it might be argued that he made a mistake. But in this untried and perilous field of Resistance foreign policy, and in the particular dilemma which Trott confronted, who could have escaped making some mistakes?

Our problem here is after all not merely one of differences between the Western capitals and the conspirators on substantial territorial issues which, as we have seen, were negotiable; nor is it merely one of the integrity of the Western Alliance with Russia which, as we have seen, had some cracks anyway; nor is it one of mistakes made by the German emissaries in the course of their unorthodox approaches to the other side. Our problem here is primarily that in the Allied strategy for victory there was no place for those on the other side who, in 'gross treasonable disloyalty' against their own country, as F.K. Roberts from the Foreign Office put it, were insisting upon offering their services to the 'enemy'.

As the war went on, the Western Powers and the German resisters found themselves on completely different wavelengths. The former were relentlessly pursuing their tasks of implementing the 'national interest' and of safeguarding the Grand Alliance. On the other hand, the German conspirators were not able to escape the dilemma of having, at the same time, to seek legitimization with the Generals and in the Allied capitals. But inasmuch as they persisted with their messages and missions abroad, despite continued rebuffs from the Allies, they demonstrated that their basic purpose was more than the exaction of any specific claim, territorial or otherwise. Early on Carl Goerdeler had assured his British interlocutor, A.P. Young, that patriotism was 'not enough' and that he was committed to preserve 'the eternal moral code'.[10] Some call beyond patriotism itself had led Goerdeler and virtually all his accomplices to the verge of committing treason. 'Familiar stuff' and 'the old, old story' were the typical Foreign Office responses to the German overtures.[11] For the German conspirators, however, it was at no point 'familiar stuff' or an 'old, old story'. All of them took enormous chances; going abroad on his mission, each one left, as Ewald von Kleist-Schmenzin once put it, 'with a rope around his neck'.[12] And even though they met with virtually no response from the Allied side, they persisted in their attempts to reach the other side. Not patriotism alone and certainly not the 'national interest' would be enough to explain their perseverance. It was, then, not the 'old Adam' that motivated the men of the Resistance but altogether a new vision conditioned by the 'landscape of treason' in which they moved. They all, Goerdeler more cautiously than Trott, and Trott in turn more cautiously than Moltke and Leber, had become committed to the vision of a European solidarity transcending the front lines. But London and Washington, as well as Moscow, were not prepared to acknowledge these gestures. Determined to win the war militarily, they thus condemned to failure all the approaches of the German Resistance.

In shunning the German Resistance, the Western Allies persisted in adhering to the 'traditional rules of diplomacy' and the 'national interest'. If anything, they hardened in their position, and 'absolute silence' and 'unconditional surrender' were the markers on the road of their hardening position. The Germans, by contrast, were the ones who persisted in exploring the unorthodox ways of Resistance foreign policy and who were moving in the direction of a European commonwealth based on freedom and self-determination. Neither London nor Washington, however, were ready to bend their rules, chiefly in deference to their Russian ally. There is, of course, a special irony involved in the fact that the Russians, primarily for whose benefit the Western Powers persisted in their hard-line policy towards the German Resistance, were the ones to woo the latter. Now that all the evidence is in on the intricate manœuvres of the German Opposition, we are perhaps justified in wondering whether the 'old Adam' did not reside after all in London and Washington.

It is significant, however, that the German Resistance did find a hearing abroad after all. The exiles, who to begin with, were solicitous on behalf of the emissaries from the Resistance, were themselves too vulnerable to be effective auxiliaries. Those American foreign office servants, furthermore, like George Kennan in Berlin and Willard L. Beaulac in Madrid, who took an interest in the Germans, did not penetrate to Washington—Kennan by his own choice. As for the Intelligence community, British and American, its very line of duty of course led to the enemy side, and the shadowboxing of the heads of MI6 and OSS with their German counterpart of the Abwehr actually yielded a vision of a co-ordinated effort to facilitate the overthrow of the Nazis in Germany with a modification of the Allied demand for 'unconditional surrender'. Sir Stewart Menzies and William J. Donovan, however, lacking the necessary clout at home to push their schemes, were at best merely sleeping partners of Canaris and his fellow conspirators. As a matter of fact, in the latter phases of the war, when General Donovan went out of his way to plead with the President for support of the internal revolt in Germany, he was ignored. And the interplay of the Special Assistant to the Minister in Berne with the German resisters, well-intentioned as it was, on balance only contributed to the feeding Carl Goerdeler's illusions concerning the Western Powers' readiness to come to terms with him.

If the message of the *Widerstand* did reach a destination and was properly understood, this was among the leadership of the ecumenical movement and the *Résistance* groups, especially in Norway and Holland. Willem A. Visser't Hooft was clearly less than a professional in the world of diplomacy; and yet he was also more. Bishop George Bell of Chichester, though deeply committed to addressing himself to issues of this world, including the German Resistance, the aerial bombing of cities, and the plight of refugees, always insisted upon acting in his capacity as churchman rather than as statesman. It was their pastoral perspective that allowed these men to respond to the overtures of the dissident Germans. In the 'war behind the war', of which Visser't Hooft spoke, they were allies. Visser't Hooft and also Dr Harry Johansson from the Ecumenical Institute in Sigtuna, were always ready to mediate between the German emissaries and their British friends like Bishop Bell, Sir Stafford Cripps, and Lionel Curtis, in order after all to influence the formulation of war and peace aims in Britain. Always they appreciated, as Bishop Bell remarked, that 'the driving force' behind the German Resistance was 'a moral force'.[13] Thus they stepped into the spiritual void left by the refusal of the Powers to deal with the conspirators.

The connections, however tenuous, between the *Widerstand* and the Norwegian and Dutch Resistance movements furthermore yielded an almost complete meeting of minds. Here was a case of Resistance foreign policy in its purest form, namely a coming together of Resistance groups from opposite camps of the war. In most instances common ecumenical concerns no doubt brought them together. But there was more than a mere spiritual affinity. The 'historical solidarity' between the German and Dutch resisters, to which the Dutch *Résistance* leader C. L. Patijn pointed, actually extended beyond a sense of a common plight; both groups spoke the language of a new Europe in which a regenerated Germany was to take its place. But the war in which they had reason to see themselves as ramparts of a European order had, alas, long ceased to be a European war and, after the Tehran Conference, was inevitably heading towards a settlement dictated not by European interests but by those of the non-European superpowers, the United States and Soviet Russia. The groups of the European *Résistance*, in fact, were almost as much ignored by the Great Powers as the German *Widerstand* had been all along.

In the end, our question is not whether the Western Allies might or should have recognized the German Resistance as an 'ally'. The two parties, if we may call them such, were too far apart. Furthermore of course the West's ally was Soviet Russia. The one person in an official position in Britain who proposed to the Foreign Office that it include the dissident Germans as an 'ally', John W. Wheeler-Bennett, actually retracted once 'unconditional surrender' had become the order of the day. After the coup of 20 July 1944, in fact, he turned with a vengeance against his erstwhile friends.[14]

Our question, then, is what help, commensurate with the terms of the Atlantic Charter and the policy of 'unconditional surrender', London and Washington might have extended to the Resistance. Whatever separated the Western Allies and the Resistance, the latter was undeniably engaged in that 'war behind the war' which, as people like Visser't Hooft tried to impress upon their contacts in official London, amounted to a legitimate aspect of the war against the Third Reich.

At this point we might recall how differently the Western Allies reacted to the propositions concerning Poland that emanated from the rejected 'ally', the *Widerstand*, and from the operative ally, Russia. The chief objection in London to the proposals coming from the conspirators was their revisionist stand on the question of the Polish Corridor and Danzig. After all, the war had started over Poland, and Britain saw herself duty-bound therefore to stand up for the Polish interest. By contrast, Washington and London went out of their way, in the cause of what Eden called the 'national interest', to defer to Russia on the Polish question. Was it not the British Foreign Secretary who, when challenged in the House of Commons on the Katyn Forest massacre, responded: 'Least said, soonest mended'?[15] Subsequently, in Tehran, Stalin's Western allies assured him that they would not obstruct his freedom of action in Eastern Europe. On the all-important Polish question, President Roosevelt specifically assured the Marshal that he 'personally' agreed with him, although in consideration of the Americans of Polish extraction, whose vote he did not wish to lose, he could not 'publicly' take part in any disposition concerning Poland.[16]

For Britain and the United States the German Resistance was incomparably more peripheral than their Russian ally. But might it not be argued that the Western Allies turned their backs on those engaged in the 'war behind the war' primarily in order to favour Soviet Russia which was already setting the stage for the 'war after the war', namely the Cold War?

After the war George F. Kennan remarked about the disproportion between the abhorrence which the West felt and professed toward Hitler and the 'very low value' it placed, 'morally and politically in the willingness of other Germans to accept the enormous risks of trying to overthrow him'.[17] Surely moral encouragement to match the 'moral' force of the Resistance, about which Bishop Bell wrote, would have been in order. Surely the provision for some 'stable connection', as Helmuth von Moltke put it, would have helped.[18] Nothing of this kind was done. Surely some arrangement could have been made between the Foreign Office and the State Department, and the British and American intelligence agencies to maintain an informal liaison with the Germans that would have given encouragement to their emissaries.

There were also some steps along substantial lines which, short of detracting from the war effort, would have helped the cause of the conspirators. These could have included a firm Allied commitment to non-interference during a coup; to refrain from attacking towns siding with the Opposition; and a clear statement on the implications of 'unconditional surrender'. Even a statement on war and peace aims would have been preferable to the 'vague terrors', as Winston Churchill put it, of the calculated indefiniteness that in fact prevailed throughout the war. 'I do not know that much could have been done in those days to give them [the German resisters] real support', concluded John J. McCloy, after the war the American High Commissioner for Germany; but, he continued: 'I do not believe that either in the United States or in Great Britain enough of an effort was undertaken.'[19]

There is of course no way of knowing whether these measures would have facilitated a coup in Germany at a date earlier than 20 July 1944 and thus would have been instrumental in shortening the war. If so, it would have meant, as Winston Churchill himself envisaged, the saving of hundreds of thousands of lives. It might also have meant preventing the domination of Soviet Russia over Central Europe which became almost inevitable after the Russian armies' westward sweep in the summer of 1943. It is equally important to understand that the merest gesture of moral support on the part of the Western Allies would have meant they were living up to a universal responsibility of standing up for human rights. The determination of the German Resistance to reach the 'greater world' stands as an example for the many dissidents and freedom movements who in our own day, still plagued by oppression, are appealing to the conscience of the world. Seen from this perspective certainly, I am led to conclude, the silence of the 'greater world' towards the German *Widerstand* sent out the wrong signals to all those in the world ready to make sacrifices for the cause of liberty.

### CONCLUSION

1. On the one side the positions originally taken by Gerhard Ritter and Hans Rothfels have recently been accentuated by Richard Lamb, *The Ghosts of Peace 1935–1945* (Wilton, 1987), who launched into a comprehensive indictment of the British failure to understand the predicaments of the *Widerstand*. On the other side, Bernd Martin has emerged in recent years as one of the fiercest critics of the *Widerstand*. His piece in the Schmädeke and Steinbach volume (*Der Widerstand gegen den Nationalsozialismus* (Munich, 1985), 1037–60) has now been reprinted in Klaus-Jürgen Müller (ed.), *Der deutsche Widerstand 1933–1945* (Paderborn, 1986), 79–107. Martin maintains the thesis that the *Widerstand* was bound to fail in its foreign policy overtures, not because of the intransigence of the Western Allies, but 'because of itself' (p. 107), namely because of its far-reaching foreign policy claims as well as because of its entanglements with the Nazi regime. Meanwhile, Klaus-Jürgen Müller has persuasively taken issue with an excessively judgemental approach to our problem, inasmuch as a prima facie political-moralistic 'postulate' brought to bear on it is essentially unhistorical and tends to approach the past from the point of view of what should have happened rather than what did happen and why it happened; Klaus-Jürgen Müller, *Der deutsche Widerstand und das Ausland* (Berlin, 1986), 6–7.
2. Peace Aims Group. Notes of meeting held in London on Tuesday, 7 Nov. 1944, WCC ipof 241.172.4(42) UK.
3. 'Einen harten staatlichen Panzer', Graml, 'Die aussenpolitischen Vorstellungen', in Walter

Schmitthenner and Hans Buchheim (eds.), *Der deutsche Widerstand gegen Hitler* (Cologne, 1966), 67.

4. See above n. 213 in Ch. 5.
5. Robert E. Sherwood, *Roosevelt and Hopkins: An Intimate History* (New York, 1948), 791.
6. Letter of Carl Goerdeler to A. P. Young, 21 Sept. 1938, quoted in A. P. Young, *The 'X' Documents* (London, 1974), 101.
7. Starting in May 1930, Sir Robert Vansittart wrote a series of memoranda for the FO on the theme of the 'old Adam' in which he set out to expose the tradition of European diplomacy that led to the War of 1914. In the course of the 1930s Vansittart had come around to identify the 'old Adam' with the German menace *plus* Hitlerism; see Norman Rose, *Vansittart: Study of a Diplomat* (London, 1978), 88–102.
8. Minutes by Sir Robert Vansittart, 7 Dec. 1938, FO 371/21659/C 15084/42/18.
9. See for Goerdeler Ch. 3, s. 3; for Trott Ch. 5, s. 1; Ch. 6, s. 2.
10. Young, *The 'X' Documents*, 111, 203.
11. See FO 371/39087/C 9099/180/18 and C 1096/180/18.
12. Ian Colvin, *Vansittart in Office* (London, 1965), 226.
13. Bell, 'The Church and the Resistance Movement', in Bonhoeffer, *GS* i. 414.
14. He argued that the failure of the plot had spared Britain the 'embarrassment' of having to deal with the old Army Generals suing for peace. In any case, he registered with satisfaction that the purge following the attempt against Hitler was presumably removing from the scene numerous individuals who might have caused difficulty to the British; 'Top Secret' Memorandum by John W. Wheeler-Bennett, 25 July 1944, FO 371/39062/C 9896, quoted in Martin Gilbert, *Winston Churchill*, vii, *Road to Victory 1941–1945* (London, 1986), 868.
15. *Parliamentary Debates*, 5th ser., vol. 389, House of Commons, 5th vol. of Sessions 1942–3 (London, 1943), col. 30.
16. Minutes of Roosevelt–Stalin meeting, 1 Dec. 1943, *FRUS*: The Conferences at Cairo and Tehran, 1943 (Washington, 1961), 594; see also Voytech Mastny, 'Stalin and the Prospects of a Separate Peace in World War II', *American Historical Review*, 77 (Dec. 1972), 1388. Later on, at the Moscow Conference of Oct. 1944 between Churchill and Stalin, the British Prime Minister was the one to volunteer saying that the question of Poland was the 'most tiresome' one on the agenda and to assure the Russian dictator that the British were ready to 'bring pressure to bear' on the Polish government-in-exile; Gilbert, *Winston Churchill*, vii, 990–1.
17. Letter from George F. Kennan to Sir Ernest Llewellyn Woodward 4 Mar. 1965, Firestone Library, Princeton University, George F. Kennan File 2-B.
18. Not even the repeated suggestion that at least one person be identified to serve as inter- mediary between the two sides fell on fertile ground. On 31 May 1942 Trott's name came up in this connection in the conversation between Bishop Bell of Chichester and Schönfeld and Bonhoeffer; Bonhoeffer, *GS* i. 396. Moltke suggested in the letter to Lionel Curtis of 25 Mar. 1943 that his English friend Michael Balfour should be sent to Stockholm to keep in touch with the various underground movements in Europe, esp. Germany; Michael Balfour and Julian Frisby, *Helmuth von Moltke: A Leader Against Hitler* (London, 1972), 215. Shortly before the coup of 20 July 1944 Steltzer proposed, in his memorandum for the British, that accredited emissaries be sent by the Resistance to London, Washington and Moscow; 'Die deutsche Opposition . . .' (15 July 1944), FO 371/39087/C 1098/180/18.
19. Letter John J. McCloy to me, 3 Apr. 1979.

# BIBLIOGRAPHY

## I. INTERVIEWS

Arndt, Walter W., 29 Aug. 1977
Astor, David, 2 Apr. 1974, 22 May 1980
Balfour, Michael, 7 Apr. 1974
Bancroft, Mary, 11 and 13 Jan. 1977
Beaulac, Willard L., 29 June 1978 (via telephone)
Berlin, Sir Isaiah, 29 Apr. 1974
Bethge, Eberhard, 13 July 1975, 3 Jan., 11 Apr. 1978
Böker, Alexander, 17 Feb. 1978
Brandt, Willy, 1 July 1980
Brodersen, Arvid, 22 Nov. 1980
Bronisch, Gotthilf P., 28 Mar. 1975
Chadwick, Sir Owen, 27 Oct. 1977
Colville, Sir John, 25 Oct. 1977
Deutsch, Harold C., 11 Oct. 1975, 16 Aug. 1984
Dohnanyi, Klaus von, 14 Apr. 1978
Collmer, Paul, 8 Feb. 1978
Dulles, Eleanor Lansing, 19 June 1976
Etzdorf, Hasso von, 23 July 1975, 14 Feb. 1978
Federer, Georg, 7 Feb. 1978
Gerstenmaier, Eugen, 11 Apr. 1978
Gilbert, Felix, 9 Apr. 1976
Goerdeler, Ulrich, 1 Feb. 1978
Haeften, Barbara von, 11 Feb. 1978
Hampshire, Sir Stuart, 10 Apr. 1974
Heusinger, Adolf, 12 July 1975
Higham, Charles, 21 July 1981
Hill, Sir Christopher, 8 Nov. 1977
Hinsley, Sir Francis Harry, 24 Nov., 15 Dec. 1977
Hofacker, Alfred von, 10 Feb. 1978
Hoffmann, Wilhelm, 24 Mar. 1978
Hood, Cordelia, 25 Mar. 1975
Hopkinson, David and Diana, 4/5 Nov. 1977
Johansson, Harry, 31 May, 4 June 1980
Kempe, Inga, 25 Feb. 1978
John, Otto, 18–19 Feb. 1978
Kessel, Albrecht von, 3 July 1975
Lash, Trude, 13 Feb. 1979
Leibholz, Gerhard, spring 1980

Mayer, Gerald, 28 Dec. 1976
Meyer-Krahmer, Marianne, 21 May 1986
Molden, Fritz, 24 May 1976
Moltke, Freya von, 27 Feb. 1975, 23 Oct., 9/10 Dec. 1976, 31 Aug. 1977, 7 Mar. 1980
Moltke, Joachim Wolfgang von, 4 Feb. 1978
Mottu, Philippe, 25 Feb. 1978
Müller, Josef, 17 Feb. 1978
Nix, Claire, 27 Feb. 1975, 29 July 1977
Nostitz, Siegfried von, 8 Feb. 1978
O'Neill, Sir Con, 12 Apr. 1974
Oster, Achim, 23 June 1980
Riddleberger, James W., 27 Jan. 1977
Roskill, Stephen, 22 Nov. 1977
Rothfels, Hans, 17 July 1975
Sarre, Marie-Luise, 8 May 1978
Schlabrendorff, Fabian von, 16 July 1975
Schönfeld, Peter, 7 Apr. 1978
'Dogwood', 24 Feb. 1978
Schwerin, Gerhard Graf von, 29 May 1974
Simonis, Susanne, 10 July 1975
Sokolov Grant, Shiela, 21 Sept. 1977
Speidel, Hans, 14 July 1975
Steltzer, Werner, 11 Apr. 1978
Trott zu Solz, Clarita von, 18 Jan., 14 June 1978, 18 July 1989
Trott zu Solz, Heinrich von, 6 Feb. 1978
Trott zu Solz, Vera von, 5 Feb. 1978
Visser't Hooft, Willem A., 19 July 1975, 28 Feb. 1978
Waetjen, Eduard, 7 Mar. 1978
Warburg-Spinelli, Ingrid, 22 May, 20 Nov. 1980, 8 Oct. 1981
Wheeler-Bennett, Sir John W., 9 May 1974
Wilbrandt, Hans, 6 Feb. 1978
Wolfe, Robert, 11 June 1976
Young, A. P., 23 Mar. 1974

## 2. LETTERS TO THE AUTHOR

Arndt, Walter, 17 Sept. 1984
Åström, Sverker, 15 July 1980
Baldwin, Roger N., n.d. 1978 (?)
Beaulac, Willard L., 7 July 1978
Blankenhorn, Herbert, 10 May 1978
Böhme, K.-R., 31 Oct. 1980
Brodersen, Arvid, 4 Dec. 1980, 17 July 1981
Cole, R. Taylor, 3, 31 July 1984
Collmer, Paul, 14 Feb. 1978

Dacre, Lord, 27 Apr. 1989
Etzdorf, Hasso von, 4 July 1978, 9 Jan., 11 Sept. 1981
Haeften, Barbara von, 3 Mar. 1978, 1 Dec. 1983
Goerschen, P. K. R. von, 25 Aug. 1978
Herwarth, Hans von, 13 Oct. 1982
Higham, Charles, 7 Oct. 1981, 1 Feb. 1982
Hoffmann, Wilhelm, 9 Aug. 1978
Hood, Cornelia, 22 July, 15 Aug. 1976
John, Otto, 27 Apr. 1978
Kessel, Albrecht von, 3 Aug. 1974
McCloy, John J., 3 Apr. 1979
Messerschmidt, Manfred, 9 Dec. 1980
Nix, Claire, 21 Jan., 1 Mar., 29 July 1975
Patijn, C. L., 18 June 1978
Roijen, J. H. van, 12 May 1978
Schwerin, Graf Gerhard von, 3 Aug. 1974
Trott zu Solz, Heinrich von, 20 October 1978

## 3. PUBLIC ARCHIVES

### Britain

Public Record Office (PRO), London: FO 371 (Foreign Office Political Files), 800 (FO Private Papers); CAB 21 (Cabinet Office, Registered Files), CAB 23 (Cabinet Meeting Minutes), CAB 27 (Cabinet Committee on Foreign Policy), CAB 65 (War Cabinet Minutes); PREM (Prime Minister's Office).
University of Birmingham: Neville Chamberlain Papers.
Balliol College, Oxford: Sir Harold Nicolson, Adam von Trott zu Solz Papers.
Bodleian Library, Oxford: Lionel Curtis, Sir Walter Monckton Papers.
Cambridge University Library: Lord Templewood Papers.
Churchill College, Cambridge: Group Captain Malcolm Grahame Christie [CHRS], Admiral J.H. Godfrey, Lord Hankey, Sir Thomas Inskip, Sir Eric Phipps, Sir Robert (Lord) Vansittart Papers.
Lambeth Palace, London: Bishop George Bell of Chichester, Archbishop William Temple Papers.
Rhodes House Library: Adam von Trott zu Solz Papers.
St Anthony's College: Sir John W. Wheeler-Bennett Papers.
*The Times*, London: Geoffrey Dawson Papers.

### Germany

Auswärtiges Amt/Politisches Archiv, Bonn: Büro des Staatssekretärs: Akten betreffend Schweden, Schweiz, Indien, Vatikan; Indienarbeit; Informations-abteilung: Akten betreffend Indien; Inland ID: Deutsche Kirche, Deutschland

Kirche, Niederlande Kirche, Schweden Kirche; Inland II geh.; Handakten Keppler; Büro des Unterstaatssekretärs: Friedensbemühungen, Europareise Sumner Welles [AA/PA].

Bundesarchiv/Koblenz: Otto Gessler 62; Carl Goerdeler 9, 14, 16, 19, 23, 24, 26, 28, 29; Jakob Kaiser 44, 52, 56, 73, 125, 135, 312, 313; Rudolf Pechel I/64, 100, II/89, 120, III/1, 2, 9, 49; Gerhard Ritter 131, 137, 146, 150–2, 155–8; Hans Rothfels 28/1, 2, 4, 7, 22, 88, 128/1; Eduard Spranger/1; K1. Erw. 248, 298–2, 368–3, 469, 657; NS 6/19, 6/21, 6/22, 6/29, 6/30 [BA/K].

Bundesarchiv/Militärarchiv, Freiburg i. Br.: N28/1, 2, 4 (Colonel General Ludwig Beck Papers); N 54/22 (Field Marshal Wilhelm Keitel in captivity about Admiral Wilhelm Canaris); N 104/2 (Hasso von Etzdorf, Alfred Etscheid); N 124/1–30 (Colonel Johannes Rohowsky Papers); N 524/ 1–20 (Gero von Schulze Gaevernitz Papers); RW 4/329, 331, 764, 5/354, 355, 396–8, 639, 764 [BA/M].

Berlin Documents Centre: *varia*.

Institut für Zeitgeschichte, Munich: ED 88, 119/2, 120/4–11; Gm 07.14(a); MA 146/1, 2, 598; MS 168; Dokumentbuch Nr.4; John Sammlung; ZS A-18/1–9, A 29/1, A 29/3, 236, 240, 291, 322, 575, 603, 633, 635, 659 I–IV, 1486, 1626, 1745, 1759, 2172 [IfZ].


*United States*

Council of Foreign Relations: Carl Goerdeler.

Department of the Army, US War College, Carlisle Barracks, Pennsylvania: Major General William J. Donovan Papers.

Federal Bureau of Investigation, Washington, DC: Adam von Trott zu Solz file, vols. 1–9a (11 Oct. 1939–24 May 1956) [FBI].

Franklin Delano Roosevelt Library, Hyde Park, NY: Map Room 72, 73; Official File (OF) 10b, 198a; President's Secretary's File (PSF) 166–8, 6240, Diplomatic Correspondence 44, 70, 71; Safe File 4; Henry Morgenthau Diaries [FDR Library].

Leo Baeck Institute, New York, NY: Julie Braun-Vogelstein Papers; Diana (Hubback) Hopkinson, 'Aus Adams Briefen', typescript, 1946.

National Archives, Washington, DC: Record Group (RG) 59 (General Records of the Department of State, Central Decimal File); RG 84 (Records of the Foreign Service Posts of the Department of State); RG 226 (OSS R & A and Operational Records), Entries 88, 99, 121, 134; RG 800 (Germany—Subversive Movement) [NA].

Office of Strategic Services (OSS), via the Central Intelligence Agency (CIA): 200 'Breakers Cables' and two consignments pertaining to Gero von Schulze Gaevernitz, Eduard Waetjen, Willem A. Visser't Hooft, 'Dogwood'; file of misc. 'Kappa' documents.

University Archives: University of Delaware, Newark, Delaware: George S. Messersmith Papers; Princeton University, Princeton, NJ: Allen W. Dulles, John Foster Dulles and George F. Kennan Papers; University of Vermont, Burlington, Vt.: Edward C. Carter Papers; University of Washington, Seattle, Washington: Tracy Strong Papers; University of Wisconsin, Madison, Wis.: Louis P. Lochner Papers.

*Sweden*

Nordiska Ekumeniska Institutet: Papers pertaining to Harry Johansson, Helmuth James von Moltke, Hans Schönfeld, Adam von Trott zu Solz *et al.*


*Switzerland*

*World Council of Churches in Process of Formation* (WCC ipof): IX–XIV; 241.172.4(42); 284(43) Germany; Bonhoeffer—Long Range Peace Objectives; General Correspondence; Letters from Dietrich Bonhoeffer 1932–1937; Life and Work DA 24, Boxes 11, 12A; Occasional Correspondence; Peace Aims; Wartime Correspondence Sweden (Sigtuna); William Paton's Papers.


4. PRIVATE COLLECTIONS


*Britain*

David Astor; Shiela Sokolov Grant; A. P. Young (courtesy Sidney Aster); Geoffrey Dawson (diary, courtesy Michael Dawson).


*Germany*

Alexander Böker; Dietrich Bonhoeffer Archive (courtesy Eberhard Bethge); Hans Dohnanyi (courtesy Eberhard Bethge); Hans-Bernd von Haeften (courtesy Barbara von Haeften); Cäsar von Hofacker (courtesy Alfred von Hofacker); Albrecht von Kessel (courtesy Karl-Albrecht von Kessel); Theo and Erich Kordt (courtesy Lore Kordt; these Papers have meanwhile been moved to IfZ, ED 157); Hans Muhle (courtesy Clarita von Trott zu Solz); Gottfried von Nostitz (courtesy Mariane von Nostitz); Theodor Steltzer (courtesy A. E. Fontenay); Adam von Trott zu Solz Archive (courtesy Clarita von Trott zu Solz); Heinrich von Trott zu Solz (correspondence with Adam, 22 Feb. 1939–9 March 1943, courtesy Nancy Lukens); Hans Wilbrandt.


*Italy*

Hans Schönfeld (courtesy Peter Ludlow); Gero von Schulze Gaevernitz (courtesy Margiana Stinnes); Ingrid Warburg-Spinelli (Memoirs, typescript; correspondence with Adam von Trott zu Solz).


*Sweden*

Inga Kempe (papers pertaining to Adam von Trott zu Solz).

*Switzerland*

Gero von Schulze Gaevernitz (courtesy Margiana Stinnes).

*United States*

Mary Bancroft; Heinrich Brüning (courtesy Claire Nix); Fritz Ermarth (courtesy Michael Ermarth); General Alexander von Falkenhausen (copies of his Papers, courtesy Hsi-Huey Liang); Helmuth James von Moltke Archive (courtesy Freya von Moltke).

## 5. UNPUBLISHED MANUSCRIPTS

CONWELL-EVANS, T. P., *None So Blind: A Study of the Crisis Years, 1930–1939. Based on the Private Papers of Group-Captain M. G. Christie, Dr. Ing., formerly British Air Attaché in Washington, Berlin, Stockholm, Oslo, Copenhagen*, priv. printed (London, 1947).

HAEFTEN, BARBARA VON, *Aus unserem Leben 1944–1950*, priv. printed (Heidelberg, 1974).

—— 'Aus unseren Briefen 1931–1944', typescript (Heidelberg, 1964).

(HUBBACK) HOPKINSON, DIANA, 'Aus Adams Briefen', typescript, 1946.

KESSEL, ALBRECHT VON, 'Verborgene Saat. Das "Andere" Deutschland', bound typescript No. 40. Written in Rome late 1944–early 1945 [von Kessel, 'Verborgene Saat'].

LIPGENS, WALTER, 'Verbindungen zwischen dem deutschen Widerstand und dem Widerstand in den besetzten Ländern'; paper prepared for the International Conference on the German Resistance of 2–6 July 1984 in Berlin.

METZGER, MAX JOSEF, 'Abba-Vater: Gefangenschaftsbriefe 29. Juni 1943–17. April 1944', mimeographed copy, Meitingen nr. Augsburg, n.d.

TÖDT, HEINZ EDUARD, 'Der Bonhoeffer–Dohnanyi-Kreis in der Opposition und im Widerstand gegen das Gewaltregime Hitlers', mimeograph, 1986.

TROTT ZU SOLZ, CLARITA VON, 'Adam von Trott zu Solz. Eine erste Materialsammlung. Sichtung und Zusammenstellung', bound typescript, Reinbek near Hamburg, 1957, 1958 [Clarita von Trott, 'Adam von Trott'].

Papers delivered at the Anglo-German Conference on the German Resistance and Great Britain held at Leeds, England, 6–9 May 1986.

## 6. REFERENCE WORKS

*Biographisches Handbuch der deutschsprachigen Emigration nach 1933*, ed. Werner Röder and Herbert A. Strauss, 3 vols. (Munich, 1980–3).

*Keesing's Contemporary Archives*, London, iii (1937–40), iv (1940–3).

*Lexikon der deutschen Geschichte*, ed. Gerhard Taddey (Stuttgart, 1979).

WISTRICH, ROBERT, *Who's Who in Nazi Germany* (New York, 1982).

ZENTNER, CHRISTIAN, and BEDÜRFTIG, FRIEDEMANN (eds.), *Das Grosse Lexikon des Dritten Reiches* (Munich, 1985).


7. PRINTED SOURCES


*Documents and Document Collections*

*Akten zur deutschen auswärtigen Politik 1918–1945*, Serie D (1937–45), vi (Baden-Baden, 1956) (Bonn, 1964).
BARTH, KARL, *Theological Existence To–day*! (*A Plea for Theological Freedom* (London, 1933).
—— *The Word of God and the Word of Man* (New York, 1957).
BELL, G. K. A., and WADDAMS, H. M., *With God in the Darkness . . . and Other Papers Illustrating the Norwegian Church Conflict* (London, 1943).
BONHOEFFER, DIETRICH, *The Cost of Discipleship* (New York, 1949).
—— *Ethics*, ed. Eberhard Bethge (New York, 1965).
—— *Gesammelte Schriften*, vols. i (*Ökumene, Briefe, Aufsätze, Dokumente 1928–1942*), ii (*Kirchenkampf und Finkenwalde. Resolutionen, Aufsätze, Rundbriefe 1933–1943*), vi (*Tagebücher, Briefe, Dokumente 1923–1945*), ed. Eberhard Bethge (Munich, 1965, 1965, 1974) [Bonhoeffer, *GS*].
—— *No Rusty Swords: Letters, Lectures and Notes from the Collected Works*, ed. Edwin H. Robertson (London, 1974).
*Deutschland-Berichte der Sozialdemokratischen Partei Deutschlands (Sopade), 1934–1940*, 7 vols. (Frankfurt/M., 1980).
*Dokumente zur Deutschlandpolitik*, I. Reihe, Bd. 1: 3 Sept. 1939–31 Dec. 1941, ed. Rainer Blasius (Frankfurt/M., 1984).
*Documents on British Foreign Policy 1919–1939*, 2nd ser., vol. xvii; 3rd ser., vols. i, ii, v–vii (London, 1979, 1949, 1949, 1952, 1953) [*DBFP*].
*Documents on German Foreign Policy 1918–1945*, Series D, vols. ii, vi, vii, xi (Washington, 1949, 1956, 1956, 1964) [*DGFP*].
*Documents on International Affairs 1939–1946*, ed. Arnold J. Toynbee, i: *Mar.–Sept. 1939* (London, 1951).
*Dossier: Kreisauer Kreis. Dokumente aus dem Widerstand gegen den National-sozialismus. Aus dem Nachlass von Lothar König S.J.*, ed. Roman Bleistein (Frankfurt/M., 1987).
EADE, CHARLES (ed.), *The War Speeches by the Rt. Hon. Winston S. Churchill*, ii, iii (Boston, 1953).
*Foreign Relations of the United States: Diplomatic Papers*, 1939, vol. i; 1940, vol. i, 1944, vol. i, The Conferences at Cairo and Tehran 1943 (Washington, DC, 1956, 1959, 1966, 1961) [*FRUS*].
*Goerdelers Politisches Testament. Dokumente des anderen Deutschland*, ed. Friedrich Krause (New York, 1945).
HALDER, FRANZ, *Kriegstagebuch: tägliche Aufzeichnungen des Chefs des Generalstabes des Heeres, 1939–1942*, i, *Vom Polenfeldzug bis zum Ende der Westoffensive*

(*14.8.1939–30.6.1940*), ed., Hans-Adolf Jacobsen (Stuttgart, 1962).

HOLBORN, LOUISE (ed.), *War and Peace Aims of the United Nations*, 2 vols. (Boston, 1943, 1948).

*In der Stunde Null: Die Denkschrift des Freiburger 'Bonhoeffer–Kreises'* (Tübingen, 1979).

JACOBSEN, HANS-ADOLF, and SMITH, ARTHUR L. Jr. (eds.), *World War II: Policy and Strategy, Selected Documents with Commentary* (Santa Barbara, 1979).

KOPP, OTTO (ed.), *Widerstand und Erneuerung: Neue Berichte und Dokumente vom inneren Kampf gegen das Hitler–Regime* (Stuttgart, 1966).

*Der Kreisauer Kreis: Porträt einer Widerstandsgruppe*, ed. Ernst Wilhelm Winterhager (Berlin, 1985).

LIPGENS, WALTER (ed.), *Documents on the History of European Integration*, 2 vols. (i, *Continental Plans for European Union 1939–1945*; ii, *Plans for European Union in Great Britain and in Exile 1939–1945*) (Berlin, 1985, 1986).

—— (ed.), *Europa-Föderationspläne der Widerstandsbewegungen 1940–1945* (Munich, 1968).

MONTE, HILDA (MEISEL, HILDE), *The Unity of Europe* (London, 1943).

*Mit dem Gesicht nach Deutschland: Eine Dokumentation über die sozialdemokratische Emigration, Aus dem Nachlass von Friedrich Stampfer*, ed. Erich Matthias (Düsseldorf, 1968).

*Nazi Conspiracy and Aggression*, vii (Washington, DC, 1946).

*Parliamentary Debates*, 5th ser., House of Commons, House of Lords, 1938–1944.

*Postwar Foreign Policy Preparation 1939–1945* Department of State General Foreign Policy Series 15 (Washington, 1949).

ROTHSTEIN, ANDREW (ed.), *Soviet Foreign Policy During the Patriotic War: Documents and Materials*, i, *22 June 1941–31 December 1943* (London, 1944).

SCHRAMM, WILHELM RITTER VON (ed.), *Beck und Goerdeler: Gemeinschaftsdokumente für den Frieden 1941–1944* (Munich, 1965).

'*Spiegelbild einer Verschwörung': Die Opposition gegen Hitler und der Staatsstreich vom 20. Juli 1944 in der SD-Berichterstattung, Geheime Dokumente aus dem ehemaligen Reichssicherheitshauptamt*, ed. Hans-Adolf Jacobsen, 2 vols. (Stuttgart, 1984).

*Trial of the Major War Criminals before the International Military Tribunal, Nuremberg 14 November 1945–1 October 1946*, xii, xxvi, xxxviii, xli (Nuremberg, 1947, 1947, 1949, 1949).

*Trials of War Criminals before the Nuernberg Military Tribunals under Control Council Law No. 10*, iv, *The Einsatzgruppen Case*, xii, *The Ministries Case*, Washington, DC, n.d.

TROTT ZU SOLZ, ADAM VON, *Hegels Staatsphilosophie und das Internationale Recht* (Göttingen, 1932, 1967).

*Das Urteil im Wilhelmstrassenprozess: Der amtliche Wortlaut der Entscheidung im Fall Nr. 11 des Nürnberger Militärtribunals gegen von Weizsäcker und andere, mit abweichender Urteilsbegründung, Berichtigungsbeschlüssen, den grundlegenden Gesetzesbestimmungen, einem Verzeichnis der Gerichtspersonen und Zeugen, und Einführungen von Dr. Robert Kemper und Dr. Karl Haensel* (Schwäbisch-Gmünd, 1950).

WEBER, AUGUST, *A New Germany: A New Europe* (London, 1944).

*Die Weizsäcker-Papiere 1933–1950*, ed. Leonidas E. Hill (Frankfurt/M., 1974) [*Die Weizsäcker-Papiere*].

*Widerstand und Exil der deutschen Arbeiterbewegung 1933–1945*, ed. Friedrich-Ebert-Stiftung (Bonn, 1982).

WILLIAMS, FRANCIS, *A Prime Minister Remembers: The War- and Post-War Memoirs of the Rt. Hon. Earl Attlee, Based on his Private Papers and on a Series of Recorded Conversations* (London, 1961).

YOUNG, A. P., *Die 'X' Dokumente* (Munich, 1989).

—— *The 'X' Documents* (London, 1974).

*20. Juli 1944*, ed. Bundeszentrale für Heimatdienst (Bonn, 1961).


*Newspapers*

*Freies Deutschland* Organ des Nationalkomitees 'Freies Deutschland', 10 July 1943–1945 (microfilm, Yale University); *New York Times*; *New York Herald Tribune*; *Pravda*; *The Times*, London; *Völkischer Beobachter, Münchener Ausgabe*.


*Correspondences, Memoirs, Diaries*

ANDERSON, IVAR, *Från det Nära Förflutna: Människor och Händelser 1940–1955 (From the Near Past: People and Events)* (Stockholm, 1969).

ANDREAS-FRIEDRICH, RUTH, *Berlin Underground 1939–1945* (London, 1948).

THE EARL OF AVON, *The Reckoning: The Eden Memoirs* (London, 1965).

BANCROFT, MARY, *Autobiography of a Spy* (New York, 1983).

*George Bell–Alphons Koechlin Briefwechsel 1933–1954*, ed. Andreas Lindt (Zurich, 1969).

BELOW, NICOLAS VON, *Als Hitlers Adjutant 1937–1945* (Mainz, 1980).

BETHGE, EBERHARD and RENATE (eds.), *Letzte Briefe im Widerstand: Aus dem Kreis der Familie Bonhoeffer* (Munich, 1984).

BETHGE, EBERHARD, and JASPER, RONALD C. D. (eds.), *An der Schwelle zum gespaltenen Europa: Der Briefwechsel zwischen George Bell und Gerhard Leibholz 1939–1951* (Stuttgart, 1974).

BIELENBERG, CHRISTABEL, *The Past is Myself* (London, 1970).

BOEGNER, MARC, *The Long Road to Unity: Memoirs and Anticipations* (London, 1970).

BOHLEN, CHARLES EUSTIS, *Witness to History, 1929–1969* (New York, 1973).

BONHOEFFER, DIETRICH, *Letters and Papers from Prison*, ed. Eberhard Bethge (New York, 1972).

BOWRA, C. M., *Memories 1898–1939* (Cambridge, Mass., 1966).

BRANDT, WILLY, *In Exile: Essays, Reflections and Letters 1933–1947* (London, 1971).

BRAUN-VOGELSTEIN, JULIE, *Was niemals stirbt* (Stuttgart, 1966).

BRODERSEN, ARVID, *Mellom Frontene (Between the Fronts)* (n.pl., 1979).

BRÜNING, HEINRICH, *Briefe und Gespräche 1934–1945*, ed. Claire Nix *et al.* (Stuttgart, 1974).

BURCKHARDT, CARL, J., *Meine Danziger Mission 1937–1939* (Munich, 1960).

BUSCH, EBERHARD, *Karl Barth: His Life from Letters and Autobiographical Texts* (Philadelphia, 1976).

BUTLER, EWAN, *Amateur Agent* (London, 1962).

CADOGAN, SIR ALEXANDER, *The Diaries of Sir Alexander Cadogan O. M. 1938–1945*, ed. David Dilks (New York, 1972).

COCKBURN, CLAUD, *A Discord of Trumpets: An Autobiography* (New York, 1956).

COLE, R. TAYLOR, *The Recollections of R. Taylor Cole: Educator, Emissary, Development Planner* (Durham, NC, 1983).

DAVIGNON, VICOMTE JACQUES, *Berlin 1936–1940: Souvenirs d'une mission* (Paris, 1951).

DELP, ALFRED, S J, *Im Angesicht des Todes: Geschrieben zwischen Verhaftung und Hinrichtung 1944–1945* (Frankfurt/M., 1976).

DOUGLAS-HOME, WILLIAM, *Half-Term Report: An Autobiography* (London, 1954).

EINSIEDEL, GRAF HEINRICH VON, *I joined the Russians: A Captured German Flyer's Diary of the Communist Temptation* (New Haven, Conn., 1953).

EISENHOWER, DWIGHT D., *Crusade in Europe* (New York, 1949).

*Erkämpft das Menschenrecht: Lebensbilder und letzte Briefe antifaschistischer Widerstandskämpfer*, ed. Institut für Marxismus-Leninismus. (East Berlin, 1958).

FECHTER, PAUL, *Menschen und Zeiten: Begegnungen aus fünf Jahrzehnten* (Berlin, 1949).

FURTWÄNGLER, FRANZ JOSEF, *Männer, die ich sah und kannte* (Hamburg, 1951).

GÄRTNER, MARGARETE, *Botschafterin des guten Willens: Aussenpolitische Arbeit 1914–1950* (Bonn, 1955).

GERSTENMAIER, EUGEN, *Streit und Friede hat seine Zeit: Ein Lebensbericht* (Frankfurt/M., 1981).

GOLLWITZER, HELMUT, KUHN, KÄTHE, and SCHNEIDER, REINHOLD (eds.), *'Du hast mich heimgesucht bei Nacht': Abschiedsbriefe und Aufzeichnungen des Widerstandes 1933–1945* (Munich, 1957).

GRANT DUFF, SHIELA, *Fünf Jahre bis zum Krieg (1933–1939): Eine Engländerin im Widerstand gegen Hitler* (Munich, 1978).

—— *The Parting of Ways: A Personal Account of the Thirties* (London, 1982).

GRIMOND, JOSEPH, *Memoirs* (London, 1977).

GROSCURTH, HELMUTH, *Tagebücher eines Abwehroffiziers 1938–1940*, ed. Helmut Krausnick and Harold C. Deutsch (Stuttgart, 1970).

HALIFAX, The Earl of, *Fulness of Days* (London, 1957).

HARVEY, OLIVER, Baron, *The Diplomatic Diaries of Oliver Harvey 1937–1940*, ed. John Harvey (London, 1970).

—— *The War Diaries of Oliver Harvey 1941–1945*, ed. John Harvey (London, 1978).

HASSELL, ULRICH VON, *Vom Anderen Deutschland: Aus den nachgelassenen Tagebüchern 1938–1944* (Zurich, 1946).

—— *The Von Hassell Diaries 1938–1944: The Story of the Forces against Hitler inside Germany as Recorded by Ambassador Ulrich von Hassell, a Leader of the Movement* (New York, 1947).

—— *Die Hassell-Tagebücher 1938–1944. Aufzeichnungen vom anderen Deutschland*, ed. Friedrich Freiherr Hiller von Gaertringen (Berlin, 1988) [*Die Hassell-Tagebücher*].

HEDIN, SVEN, *Ohne Auftrag in Berlin* (Buenos Aires, 1949).

HENDERSON, Sir NEVILE, *Failure of a Mission* (New York, 1940).

HERWARTH, HANS VON, *Against Two Evils* (New York, 1981).

HINKS, ROGER, *The Gymnasium of the Mind*, ed. John Goldsmith (Salisbury, 1984).

HOARE, Rt. Hon. Sir SAMUEL (Lord Templewood), *Ambassador on Special Mission* (London, 1946).

HOEGNER, WILHELM, *Der schwierige Aussenseiter: Erinnerungen eines Abgeordneten, Emigranten und Ministerpräsidenten* (Munich, 1959).

HOPKINSON, DIANA, *The Incense Tree* (London, 1968).

HULL, CORDELL, *The Memoirs of Cordell Hull*, 2 vols. (New York, 1948).

JOHN, OTTO, *Twice Through the Lines: The Autobiography of Otto John* (New York, 1972).

JONES, THOMAS, *A Diary with Letters, 1931–1950* (London, 1954).

JORDAN, MAX, *Beyond all Fronts: A Bystander's Notes on the Thirty Years War* (Milwaukee, 1944).

KENNAN, GEORGE F., *Memoirs 1925–1950* (Boston, Mass., 1967).

KERSTEN, FELIX, *The Kersten Memoirs 1940–1945* (London, 1956).

KIRKPATRICK, Sir IVONE, *The Inner Circle: Memoirs* (London, 1959).

KLEIST, PETER, *Die europäische Tragödie* (Göttingen, 1961).

—— *Zwischen Hitler und Stalin 1939–1945: Aufzeichnungen* (Bonn, 1950).

KLEMPERER, KLEMENS VON (ed.), *A Noble Combat: The Letters of Shiela Grant Duff and Adam von Trott zu Solz 1932–1939* (Oxford, 1988).

KORDT, ERICH, *Nicht aus den Akten ... Die Wilhelmstrasse in Frieden und Krieg: Erlebnisse, Begegnungen und Eindrücke 1928–1945* (Stuttgart, 1950).

LEAHY, WILLIAM D., *I Was There* (New York, 1950).

LEBER, JULIUS, *Ein Mann geht seinen Weg: Schriften, Reden und Briefe* (Berlin-Schöneberg, 1952).

—— *Schriften, Reden, Briefe*, ed. Dorothea Beck and Wilfried F. Schoeller (Munich, 1976).

LOCHNER, LOUIS P., *Always the Unexpected: A Book of Reminiscences* (New York, 1956).

—— *Stets das Unerwartete: Erinnerungen aus Deutschland 1921–1953* (Darmstadt, 1953).

LONSDALE BRYANS, J[AMES], *Blind Victory (Secret Communications Halifax–Hassell)* (London, 1951).

LOUIS FERDINAND of Prussia, *The Rebel Prince* (Chicago, 1952).

MASTERMAN, J. C., *On the Chariot Wheel: An Autobiography* (Oxford, 1975).

MACLEAN, FITZROY, *Eastern Approaches* (London, 1949).

MEHNERT, KLAUS, *Ein Deutscher in der Welt: Erinnerungen 1906–1981* (Stuttgart, 1981).

METTERNICH, TATIANA VON, *Five Passports in a Shifting Europe* (London, 1976).

MOLTKE, HELMUTH JAMES VON, *Briefe an Freya 1939–1945*, ed. Beate Ruhm von Oppen (Munich, 1988) [von Moltke, *Briefe an Freya*].

—— *Letters to Freya 1939–1945*, ed. and trans. Beate Ruhm von Oppen (New York, 1990).

—— *Letzte Briefe aus dem Gefängnis Tegel* (Berlin, 1963).

Moravec, Frantisek, *Master of Spies: The Memoirs of General František Moravec* (London, 1975).

Müller, Dr Josef, *Bis zur letzten Konsequenz: Ein Leben für Frieden und Freiheit* (Munich, 1975).

Niebergall, Otto, *Résistance: Erinnerungen deutscher Antifaschisten* (Berlin, 1973).

Papen, Franz von, *Memoirs* (London, 1953).

Philby, Kim, *My Silent War* (London, 1968).

Ribbentrop, Joachim von, *Zwischen London und Moskau: Erinnerungen und letzte Aufzeichnungen*, ed. Annelies von Ribbentrop (Leoni am Starnbergersee, 1953).

*Roosevelt and Churchill: Their Secret Wartime Correspondence*, ed. Francis L. Loewenheim *et al.* (London, 1975).

Rowse, A. L., *A Cornishman Abroad* (London, 1976).

—— *A Man of the Thirties* (London, 1979).

—— *Poems of Delivery* (London, 1946).

Schacht, Hjalmar, *Account Settled* (London, 1948).

—— *My First Seventy-Six Years* (London, 1955).

Schellenberg, Walter, *The Schellenberg Memoirs* (London, 1956).

Schmid, Carlo, *Erinnerungen* (Berne, 1977).

Schwabe, Klaus, and Reichardt, Rolf (eds.), *Gerhard Ritter. Ein politischer Historiker in seinen Briefen* (Boppard am Rhein, 1984).

Shirer, William L., *Berlin Diary: The Journal of a Foreign Correspondent 1934–1941* (New York, 1941).

Spitzy, Reinhard, *So haben wir das Reich verspielt: Bekenntnisse eines Illegalen* (2nd edn., Munich, 1987).

Strang, Lord, *Home and Abroad* (London, 1956).

Steltzer, Theodor, *Sechzig Jahre Zeitgenosse* (Munich, 1966).

Studnitz, Hans-Georg von, *While Berlin Burns: The Diary of Hans-Georg von Studnitz 1943–1945* (Englewood Cliffs, NJ, 1965).

Templewood, Lord, *Nine Troubled Years* (London, 1954).

Thompson, Dorothy, *Listen, Hans* (Boston, Mass., 1942).

Vansittart, Lord, *Lessons of My Life* (London, 1943).

—— *The Mist Procession: The Autobiography of Lord Vansittart* (London, 1958).

Marie Vassiltchikov, *The Berlin Diaries 1940–1945 of Marie 'Missi' Vassiltchikov* (London, 1987).

Visser't Hooft, Willem A., *Memoirs* (London, 1973).

Warburg-Spinelli, Ingrid, *Die Dringlichkeit des Mitleids und die Einsamkeit, nein zu sagen: Lebenserinnerungen 1910–1989* (Hamburg, 1990).

Wedemeyer, General Albert C., *Wedemeyer Reports!* (New York, 1958).

Weinberger, Lois, *Tatsachen, Begegnungen und Gespräche: Ein Buch über Österreich* (Vienna, 1948).

Weizsäcker, Ernst von, *Erinnerungen* (Munich, 1950).

—— *Memoirs* (Chicago, 1951).

Wheeler-Bennett, Sir John, *Knaves, Fools and Heroes in Europe Between the Wars* (London, 1974).

—— *Special Relationships: America in Peace and War* (London, 1975).

Winterbotham, Frederick William, *Secret and Personal* (London, 1969).

WISKEMANN, ELIZABETH, *The Europe I Saw* (London, 1968).
YOUNG, ARTHUR PRIMROSE, *Across the Years: The Living Testament of an Engineer with a Mission* (London, 1971).

## 8. SECONDARY WORKS

### General Works

*Aufstand des Gewissens: Der militärische Widerstand gegen Hitler und das NS-Regime 1933–1945* (Herford, 1984).
ABSHAGEN, KARL HEINZ, *Canaris* (London, 1956).
ACKROYD, PETER, *T. S. Eliot: A Life* (New York, 1984).
ADAMTHWAITE, ANTHONY P., *The Making of the Second World War* (London, 1977).
AIGNER, DIETRICH, *Das Ringen um England. Das deutsch-britische Verhältnis. Die öffentliche Meinung 1933–1939. Tragödie weier Völker* (Munich, 1969).
ANDREAS-FRIEDRICH, RUTH, *Berlin Underground, 1939–1945* (London, 1948).
ANDREW, CHRISTOPHER, *Secret Service: The Making of the British Intelligence Community* (London, 1985).
—— and DILKS, DAVID (eds.), *The Missing Dimension: Governments and Intelligence Communications in the Twentieth Century* (Urbana, 1984).
ARMSTRONG, ANNE, *Unconditional Surrender: The Impact of the Casablanca Policy upon World War II* (New Brunswick, NJ, 1961).
ASTER, SIDNEY, *The Making of the Second World War* (London, 1973).
ATTLEE, C. R. *et al.*, *Labour's Aims in War and Peace* (London, 1940).
BALFOUR, MICHAEL, *Propaganda in War 1939–1945: Organisations, Policies and Publics in Britain and Germany* (London, 1979).
—— *Withstanding Hitler in Germany 1933–45* (London, 1988).
—— and FRISBY, JULIAN, *Helmuth von Moltke: A Leader Against Hitler* (London, 1972).
BALZER, KARL, *Der 20. Juli und der Landesverrat. Eine Dokumentation über Verratshandlungen im deutschen Widerstand* (Göttingen, 1967).
BEAULAC, WILLARD L., *Franco: Silent Ally in World War II* (Carbondale and Edwardsville, Ill., 1986).
*Ludwig Beck Studien*, ed. Hans Speidel (Stuttgart, 1955).
BECK, DOROTHEA, *Julius Leber: Sozialdemokrat zwischen Reform und Widerstand* (Berlin, 1983).
BELL, G. K. A., *Christianity and World Order* (Harmondsworth, 1940).
—— *The Church and Humanity, 1939–1946* (London, 1946).
—— *The Kingship of Christ* (Harmondsworth, 1954).
BERGMANN, KARL HANS, *Die Bewegung 'Freies Deutschland' in der Schweiz 1943–1945* (Munich, 1974).
BEST, PAYNE, *The Venlo Incident* (London, 1950).
BETHELL, NICHOLAS, *The Last Secret* (New York, 1974).

BETHGE, EBERHARD, *Am gegebenen Ort: Aufsätze und Reden 1970–1979* (Munich, 1979).

—— *Dietrich Bonhoeffer: Man of Vision, Man of Courage* (New York, 1970).

BIRKENHEAD, The Earl of, *Halifax: The Life of Lord Halifax* (London, 1965).

BLASIUS, RAINER A., *Für Grossdeutschland—gegen den grossen Krieg. Staatssekretär Ernst Frhr. von Weizsäcker in den Krisen um die Tschechoslowakei und Polen 1938/39* (Cologne, 1981).

BLUMENBERG-LAMPE, CHRISTINE, *Das wirtschaftspolitische Programm der 'Freiburger Kreise': Entwurf einer freiheitlich-sozialen Nachkriegswirtschaft. Nationalökonomen gegen den Nationalsozialismus* (Berlin, 1973).

BOSANQUET, MARY, *The Life and Death of Dietrich Bonhoeffer* (New York, 1968).

BOSE, MIHIR, *The Lost Hero: A Biography of Subhas Bose* (London, 1982).

BOVERI, MARGRET, *Treason in the Twentieth Century* (London, 1956).

—— *Wir lügen alle. Eine Hauptstadtzeitung unter Hitler* (Olten, 1965).

BOYENS, ARMIN, *Kirchenkampf und Ökumene 1933–1939, 1939–1945: Darstellung und Dokumentation*, 2 vols. (Munich, 1969, 1973).

BRACHER, KARL DIETRICH *et al.* (eds.), *Die moderne Demokratie und ihr Recht: Festschrift für Gerhard Leibholz zum 65. Geburtstag*, i (Tübingen, 1966).

BRANDT, WILLY, and LÖWENTHAL, RICHARD, *Ernst Reuter: Ein Leben für die Freiheit, Eine politische Biographie* (Munich, 1973).

BRISSAUD, ANDRÉ, *The Nazi Secret Service* (New York, 1942).

—— *Canaris: The Biography of Admiral Canaris, Chief of German Military Intelligence in the Second World War* (London, 1973).

BROSZAT, MARTIN *et al.* (eds.), *Bayern in der NS-Zeit*, iv, *Herrschaft und Gesellschaft im Konflikt*, pt. C (Munich, Vienna, 1981).

BROWNING, CHRISTOPHER R., *The Final Solution and the German Foreign Office: A Study of Referat D III of Abteilung Deutschland 1940–1943* (New York, 1978).

BUCHHEIT, GERT, *Soldatentum und Rebellion. Die Tragödie der deutschen Wehrmacht* (Ratstatt/Baden, 1961).

—— *Der deutsche Geheimdienst* (Munich, 1966).

BULL, HEDLEY (ed.), *The Challenge of the Third Reich* (Oxford, 1986).

BURRIDGE, T. D., *British Labour and Hitler's War* (London, 1976).

BUTLER, J. R. M., *Lord Lothian (Philip Kerr) 1882–1940* (London, 1960).

BUTLER, R. M., *Grand Strategy*, ii (London, 1957).

CAMPBELL, F. GREGORY, *Confrontation in Central Europe: Weimar Germany and Czechoslovakia* (Chicago, 1975).

CAVE BROWN, ANTHONY, *Bodyguard of Lies* (New York, 1975).

—— *Wild Bill Donovan: The Last Hero* (New York, 1982).

CHADWICK, OWEN, *Britain and the Vatican during the Second World War* (Cambridge, 1986).

CHURCHILL, WINSTON S., *The Second World War*, iv: *The Hinge of Fate* (Boston, Mass., 1950).

COLVIN, IAN, *Master Spy* (New York, 1951).

—— *Vansittart in Office* (London, 1965).

—— *The Chamberlain Cabinet* (London, 1971).

CORBETT, P. E., *Post-War Worlds* (New York, 1942).

COWLING, MAURICE, *The Impact of Hitler: British Politics and British Policies 1933–1940* (Cambridge, 1975).

CURTIS, LIONEL, *Civitas Dei*, 3 vols. (London, 1934–7).

—— *World Order (Civitas Dei)* (New York, 1939).

DAHLERUS, JOHAN BIRGER ESSEN, *The Last Attempt* (London, 1948).

DALLIN, ALEXANDER, *German Rule in Russia 1941–1945: A Study of Occupation Policies* (London, 1957).

DEACON, RICHARD, *A History of the British Secret Service* (London, 1969).

DE BEUS, JAKOBUS GISBERTUS, *Tomorrow at Dawn!* (New York, 1980).

DELFS, HERMANN (ed.), *Aktiver Friede: Gedenkschrift für Friedrich Siegmund-Schultze (1885–1969)* (Soest, 1972).

DEUTSCH, HAROLD C., *The Conspiracy against Hitler in the Twilight War* (Minneapolis, 1968) [Deutsch, The Conspiracy].

—— *Hitler and His Generals* (Minneapolis, 1974).

DIECKMANN, HILDEMARIE, *Johann Popitz* (Berlin, 1960).

DILKS, DAVID, *Retreat from Power: Studies in Britain's Foreign Policy of the Twentieth Century*, i (London, 1981).

DROBISCH, KLAUS, *Wider den Krieg: Dokumentarbericht über Leben und Sterben des katholischen Geistlichen Dr. Max Josef Metzger* (East Berlin, n.d.).

DOUGLAS-HAMILTON, JAMES, *Motive for a Mission: The Story Behind Hess's Flight to Britain* (London, 1971).

DULLES, ALLEN WELSH, *Germany's Underground* (New York, 1947).

—— *The Secret Surrender* (New York, 1966).

EDINGER, LOUIS J., *German Exile Politics: The Social Democratic Executive Committee in the Nazi Era* (Berkeley, Calif., 1956).

EHRMAN, JOHN, *Grand Strategy*, v (London, 1956).

ELIOT, T. S., *The Idea of a Christian Society* (London, 1939).

ESTERS, HELMUT, and PELGER, HANS, *Gewerkschafter im Widerstand* (Hanover, 1967).

FARNSWORTH, BEATRICE, *Aleksandra Kollontai: Socialism, Feminism and the Bolshevik Revolution* (Stanford, Calif., 1980).

FEIS, HERBERT, *Churchill, Roosevelt, Stalin: The War They Waged and the Peace They Sought* (Princeton, NJ, 1957).

FEST, JOACHIM, *Hitler* (New York, 1973).

FINKER, KURT, *Stauffenberg und der 20. Juli 1944* (East Berlin, 1977).

—— *Graf Moltke und der Kreisauer Kreis* (East Berlin, 1978).

FISCHER, ALEXANDER, *Sowjetische Deutschlandpolitik im Zweiten Weltkrieg 1941–1945* (Stuttgart, 1975).

FITZGIBBON, CONSTANTINE, *Secret Intelligence in the Twentieth Century* (New York, 1977).

FLEISCHHAUER, INGEBORG, *Die Chance des Sonderfriedens: Deutsch–sowjetische Geheimgespräche 1941–1945* (Berlin, 1986).

—— *Der Widerstand gegen den Russlandfeldzug: Beiträge zum Widerstand 1933–1945* (Berlin, 1987).

FOERSTER, WOLFGANG, *Generaloberst Ludwig Beck: Sein Kampf gegen den Krieg* (Munich, 1953).

FOITZIK, JAN, *Zwischen den Fronten: Zur Politik, Organisation und Funktion linker politischer Kleinorganisationen im Widerstand 1933 bis 1939/40 unter besonderer Berücksichtigung des Exils* (Berlin, 1986).

FOOT, M. R. D., *Resistance: An Analysis of European Resistance to Nazism 1940–1945* (London, 1976).

FORD, COREY, *Donovan of OSS* (Boston, Mass., 1970).

FRISCHAUER, WILLI, *The Man Who Came Back* (London, 1950).

FROMM, HERMANN, *Deutschland in der öffentlichen Kriegszieldiskussion Grossbritanniens 1939–1945* (Frankfurt/M., 1982).

FULLER, J. F. C., *The Second World War, 1939–1945* (New York, 1962).

GANNON, FRANKLIN REID, *The British Press and Germany 1936–1939* (Oxford, 1971).

GARLIŃSKI, JÓZEF, *The Swiss Corridor: Espionage Networks in Switzerland during World War II* (London, 1981).

GATES, ELEANOR M., *End of the Affair: The Collapse of the Anglo-French Alliance, 1939–1940* (Berkeley, Calif., 1981).

GEISS, IMANUEL, and WENDT, BERND-JÜRGEN (eds.), *Deutschland in der Weltpolitik des 19. und 20. Jahrhunderts* (Gütersloh, 1973).

GILBERT, MARTIN, *Britain and Germany Between the Wars* (London, 1964).

—— *Winston Churchill*, vi, *Finest Hour 1939–1941*; vii, *Road to Victory 1941–1945* (London, 1983, 1986).

—— and GOTT, RICHARD, *The Appeasers* (London, 1963).

GISEVIUS, HANS BERND, *Bis zum bitteren Ende*, 2 vols. (Zurich, 1946).

—— *To the Bitter End* (Boston, 1947).

—— *Bis zum bitteren Ende: Vom Reichstagsbrand bis zum 20. Juli 1944*. Vom Verfasser auf den neuesten Stand gebrachte Sonderausgabe (Hamburg, n.d. (1960?)).

—— *Bis zum Bittern Ende* (Zurich, 1954).

GJELSVIK, TORE, *Norwegian Resistance 1940–1945* (Montreal, 1977).

GLEES, ANTHONY, *Exile Politics During the Second World War: The German Social Democrats in Britain* (Oxford, 1982).

—— *The Secrets of the Service: British Intelligence and Communist Subversion 1933–1951* (London, 1987).

GLOEDE, GÜNTHER (ed.), *Ökumenische Profile*, 2 vols. (Stuttgart, 1961).

GODAL, ODD, *Eivind Berggrav: Leader of Christian Resistance* (London, 1949).

GOLDBERGER, LEO (ed.), *The Rescue of the Danish Jews: Moral Courage under Stress* (New York, 1987).

GÖRLITZ, WALTER, *Der deutsche Generalstab: Geschichte und Gestalt 1657–1945* (Frankfurt/M., 1950).

GRIFFITHS, WILLIAM, *Fellow Travellers of the Right: British Enthusiasts for Nazi Germany 1935–1939* (London, 1980).

HÆSTRUP, JØRGEN, *European Resistance Movements, 1939–1945: A Complete History* (Westport, Conn., 1981).

HAFFNER, SEBASTIAN, *Germany: Jekyll and Hyde* (London, 1940).

—— *Offensive against Germany* (London, 1941).

HAUNER, MILAN, *India in Axis Strategy: Germany, Japan, and Indian Nationalists in the Second World War* (Stuttgart, 1981).

HAUSER, OSWALD, *England und das Dritte Reich*, i, *1933–1936* (Stuttgart, 1972).

458 *Bibliography*

HAUSHOFER, ALBRECHT, *Moabit Sonnets* (London, 1978).

HECK, BRUNO (ed.), *Widerstand, Staat und Kirche: Eugen Gerstenmaier zum 70. Geburtstag* (Frankfurt/M., 1976).

HENK, EMIL, *Die Tragödie des 20. Juli 1944* (2nd. edn., Heidelberg, 1846).

HENKE, JOSEF, *England in Hitlers politischem Kalkül 1935–1939* (Boppard am Rhein, 1977).

HERLEMANN, BEATRIX, *Die Emigration als Kampfposten: Die Anleitung des kommunistischen Widerstandes in Deutschland aus Frankreich, Belgien und den Niederlanden* (Mannheim, 1983).

HESSE, FRITZ, *Hitler and the English* (Wingate, 1954).

HILDEBRANDT, RAINER, *Wir sind die Letzten: Aus dem Leben des Widerstandskämpfers Albrecht Haushofer und seiner Freunde* (Neuwied, 1949).

HILGER, GUSTAV, and MEYER, ALFRED G., *The Incompatible Allies: A Memoir-History of Soviet–German Relations 1918–1941* (New York, 1953).

HILLGRUBER, ANDREAS, *Probleme des Zweiten Weltkrieges* (Cologne, 1967).

HINSLEY, FRANCIS HARRY, et al., *British Intelligence in the Second World War: Its Influence on Strategy and Operations*, i (London, 1979).

HIRSCHFELD, GERHARD (ed.), *Exil in Grossbritannien: Zur Emigration aus dem nationalsozialistischen Deutschland* (Stuttgart, 1983).

HOARE, Sir SAMUEL (Lord Templewood), *Ambassador on Special Mission* (London, 1946).

HÖHNE, HEINZ, *Codeword: Director, The Story of the Red Orchestra* (London, 1970).

—— *Canaris: Patriot im Zwielicht* (Munich, 1976).

HOFER, WALTHER, *Die Entfesselung des Zweiten Weltkrieges* (Frankfurt/M., 1964).

HOFFMANN, PETER, *Widerstand-Staatsstreich-Attentat: Der Kampf der Opposition gegen Hitler* (2nd edn., Munich, 1970).

—— *The History of the German Resistance 1933–1945* (Cambridge, Mass., 1979) [Hoffmann, *History*].

—— *Widerstand gegen Hitler: Probleme des Umsturzes* (Munich, 1979).

—— *German Resistance to Hitler* (Cambridge, Mass., London, 1988).

HOWARD, MICHAEL, *Grand Strategy*, iv (London, 1972).

INSTITUT FÜR ZEITGESCHICHTE (ed.), *Deutscher Sonderweg: Mythos oder Realität?* (Munich, 1982).

JACKMAN, JARRELL C., and BORDEN, CARLA M. (eds.), *The Muses Flee Hitler: Cultural Transfer and Adaptation, 1930–1945* (Washington, DC, 1983).

JACKSON, WALTER A., *Gunnar Myrdal and America's Conscience: Social Engineering and Racial Liberalism, 1938–1987* (Chapel Hill, 1990).

JACOBSEN, HANS-ADOLF, *Nationalsozialistische Aussenpolitik 1933–1938* (Frankfurt/M., 1968).

—— (ed.), *July 20, 1944: The German Opposition to Hitler as viewed by Foreign Historians* (Bonn, 1969).

—— *Karl Haushofer: Leben und Werk*, 2 vols. (Boppard am Rhein, 1979).

JASPER, RONALD C. D., *George Bell: Bishop of Chichester* (London, 1967).

JEDLICKA, LUDWIG, *Der 20. Juli 1944 in Österreich* (Vienna, 1965).

KAHN, DAVID, *Hitler's Spies: German Military Intelligence in World War II* (New York, 1978).

KAUFMANN, ARTHUR, and BACKMANN, LEONHARD E., *Widerstandsrecht* (Darmstadt, 1972).

KENNAN, GEORGE F, *American Diplomacy 1900–1950* (New York, 1954).

—— *Cloud of Danger: Current Realities of American Foreign Policy* (Boston, 1977).

KETTENACKER, LOTHAR (ed.), *Das 'Andere Deutschland' im Zweiten Weltkrieg: Emigration und Widerstand in internationaler Perspektive* (Stuttgart, 1977).

KLEMPERER, KLEMENS VON, *Die 'Verbindung mit der grossen Welt': Aussenbeziehungen des deutschen Widerstands 1938–1945*, Beiträge zum Widerstand 1933–1945 (Berlin, 1990).

KLESSMANN, CHRISTOPH, and PINGEL, FALK (eds.), *Gegner des Nationalsozialismus. Wissenschaftler und Widerstandskämpfer auf der Suche nach historischer Wirklichkeit* (Frankfurt/M., 1980).

KNIGHTLEY, PHILLIP, *The Master Spy: The Story of Kim Philby* (New York, 1989).

KOEBNER, THOMAS, SAUTERMEISTER, GERT, and SCHNEIDER, SIGRID (eds.), *Deutschland nach Hitler: Zukunftspläne im Exil und aus der Besatzungszeit 1939–1949* (Opladen, 1987).

KONSTANTIN Prince of Bavaria, *The Pope: A Portrait from Life* (London, 1954).

KOSTHORST, ERICH, *Die deutsche Opposition gegen Hitler zwischen Polen- und Frankreichfeldzug* (2nd edn., Bonn, 1955).

KRAMARZ, JOACHIM, *Stauffenberg: The Architect of the Famous July 20th Conspiracy to Assassinate Hitler* (New York, 1967).

KREBS, ALBERT, *Fritz-Dietlof Graf von der Schulenburg: Zwischen Staatsräson und Hochverrat* (Hamburg, 1964).

LAACK-MICHEL, URSULA, *Albrecht Haushofer und der Nationalsozialismus* (Stuttgart, 1974).

LAMB, RICHARD, *The Ghosts of Peace 1935–1945* (Wilton, 1987).

LANGER, WILLIAM L., and GLEASON, S. EVERETT, *The Challenge to Isolation 1937–1940* (New York, 1952).

—— *The Undeclared War 1940–1941* (New York, 1953).

LANGHORNE, RICHARD (ed.), *Diplomacy and Intelligence During the Second World War* (Cambridge, 1985).

LAQUEUR, WALTER, and BREITMAN, RICHARD, *Breaking the Silence* (New York, 1986).

LEBER, ANNEDORE, *Das Gewissen steht auf: 64 Lebensbilder aus dem deutschen Widerstand 1933–1945* (Berlin, 1960).

—— *Das Gewissen entscheidet: Berichte des deutschen Widerstandes von 1933–1945 in Lebensbildern* (Berlin, 1960).

LEIBHOLZ-BONHOEFFER, SABINE, *The Bonhoeffers: Portrait of a Family* (New York, 1971).

LENZ, FRIEDRICH, *Wirtschaftsplanung und Planwirtschaft* (Berlin, 1948).

LEVERKÜHN, PAUL, *The German Military Intelligence* (London, 1954).

LIANG, HSI-HUEY, *The Sino-German Connection: Alexander von Falkenhausen between China and Germany 1900–1941* (Amsterdam, 1978).

LILL, RUDOLF, and OBERREUTER, HEINRICH (eds.), *20. Juli. Portraits des Widerstands* (Düsseldorf, 1984).

LOCHNER, LOUIS P., *What about Germany?* (New York, 1942).

LÖWENTHAL, RICHARD, *Die Widerstandsgruppe 'Neu-Beginnen'*, Beiträge zum Thema Widerstand (Berlin, 1982).

——— and MÜHLEN, PATRICK VON ZUR, *Widerstand und Verweigerung in Deutschland 1933 bis 1945* (Berlin, 1982).

LUKACS, JOHN A., *The Great Powers and Eastern Europe* (New York, 1953).

LUŽA, RADOMIR V., *The Resistance in Austria, 1938–1945* (Minneapolis, 1984).

MACDONALD, CALLUM A., *The United States, Britain and Appeasement 1936–1939* (New York, 1981).

MACDONOGH, GILES, *A Good German: Adam von Trott zu Solz* (London, 1989).

MALONE, HENRY O, *Adam von Trott zu Solz: Werdegang eines Verschwörers 1909–1938* (Berlin, 1986).

MAMMACH, KLAUS, *Widerstand 1933–1939, 1939–1945: Geschichte der deutschen antifaschistischen Widerstandsbewegung im Inland und in der Emigration*, 2 vols. (East Berlin, 1984 and 1987).

MAMATEY, VICTOR S., and LUŽA, RADOMÍR, *A History of the Czechoslovak Republic 1918–1948* (Princeton, NJ, 1973).

MANDER, JOHN, *Our German Cousins* (London, 1974).

MANN, GOLO, *Zwölf Versuche* (Frankfurt/M., 1973).

MANWELL, ROGER, and FRAENKEL, HEINRICH, *The Canaris Conspiracy: The Secret Resistance to Hitler in the German Army* (London, 1969).

MARTENS, STEFAN, *Hermann Göring: 'Erster Paladin des Führers' und 'Zweiter Mann im Reich'* (Paderborn, 1985).

MARTIN, BERND, *Friedensinitiativen und Machtpolitik im Zweiten Weltkrieg 1939–1942* (Düsseldorf, 1974).

MASTNY, VOJTECH, *Russia's Road to the Cold War: Diplomacy, Warfare and Communism 1941–1945* (New York, 1979).

MATLOFF, MAURICE, and SNELL, EDWIN M., *Strategic Planning for Coalition Warfare 1941–1942* (Washington, DC, 1953).

MATTHIAS, ERICH, *Sozialdemokratie und Nation: Zur Ideengeschichte der sozialdemokratischen Emigration 1933–1938* (Stuttgart, 1952).

MAUSBACH-BROMBERGER, BARBARA, *Arbeiterwiderstand in Frankfurt am Main gegen den Faschismus, 1933–1945* (Frankfurt/M., 1976).

MEDLICOTT, W. N., *Britain and Germany: The Search for Agreement* (London, 1969).

MELNIKOW, DANIIL, *20. Juli 1944: Legende und Wirklichkeit* (Berlin, 1968).

MERSON, ALLAN, *Communist Resistance in Nazi Germany* (London, 1985).

MEYER-KRAHMER, MARIANNE, *Carl Goerdeler und sein Weg in den Widerstand: Eine Reise in die Welt meines Vaters* (Freiburg i. Br., 1989).

MICHALKA, WOLFGANG, *Ribbentrop und die deutsche Weltpolitik, 1933–1940* (Munich, 1980).

MIDDLEMAS, KEITH, *Diplomacy of Illusion: The British Government and Germany, 1937–1939* (London, 1972).

MISGELD, KLAUS, *Die 'Internationale Gruppe demokratischer Sozialisten' in Stockholm 1932–1945* (Bonn, 1976).

MITTENZWEI, WERNER, *Exil in der Schweiz* (Frankfurt/M., 1979).

MÖHRING, MARIANNE, *Täter des Wortes: Max Josef Metzger—Leben und Wirken* (Meitingen, 1966).

MOLDEN, FRITZ, *Fires in the Night: The Sacrifices and Significance of the Austrian Resistance 1938–1945* (Boulder, 1989).

MOLDEN, OTTO, *Der Ruf des Gewissens: Der österreichische Freiheitskampf 1938–1945* (Vienna, 1958).

MOLTKE, FREYA VON, BALFOUR, MICHAEL, and FRISBY, JULIAN, *Helmuth James von Moltke 1907–1945. Anwalt der Zukunft* (Stuttgart, 1972).

MOLTMANN, GÜNTER, *Amerikas Deutschlandpolitik in Zweiten Weltkrieg: Kriegs- und Friedensziele 1941–1945* (Heidelberg, 1958).

MOMMSEN, WOLFGANG J., and KETTENACKER, LOTHAR (eds.), *The Fascist Challenge and the Policy of Appeasement* (London, 1983).

MOORE, BARRINGTON, Jr., *Injustice: The Social Bases of Obedience and Revolt* (New York, 1978).

MOORE, R. J., *Churchill, Cripps and India 1939–1945* (Oxford, 1978).

MOSLEY, LEONARD, *Dulles: A Biography of Eleanor, Allen and John Foster Dulles and their Family Network* (New York, 1978).

MÜLLER, CHRISTIAN, *Oberst i. G. Stauffenberg* (Düsseldorf, 1971).

MÜLLER, KLAUS-JÜRGEN, *Das Heer und Hitler: Armee und nationalsozialistisches Regime 1933–1940* (Stuttgart, 1969).

—— (ed.), *Der deutsche Widerstand 1933–1945* (Paderborn, 1986).

—— *Der deutsche Widerstand und das Ausland*, Beiträge zum Widerstand 1933–1945 (Berlin, 1986).

MÜSSENER, HELMUT, *Exil in Schweden* (Munich, 1977).

NAMIER, Sir LEWIS B., *In the Nazi Era* (London, 1952).

NEBGEN, ELFRIEDE, *Jakob Kaiser: Der Widerstandskämpfer* (Stuttgart, 1967).

NEUMARK, FRITZ, *Zuflucht am Bosporus: Deutsche Gelehrte, Politiker und Künstler in der Emigration 1933–1953* (Frankfurt/M., 1980).

NICOSIA, FRANCIS R., and STOKES, LAWRENCE D. (eds.), *Germans against Nazism. Nonconformity, Opposition and Resistance in the Third Reich: Essays in Honour of Peter Hoffmann* (New York, 1990).

OFFNER, ARNOLD A., *American Appeasement: United States Foreign Policy and Germany, 1933–1938* (Cambridge, Mass., 1969).

PALENZIA, ISABEL DE, *Alexandra Kollontay: Ambassadress for Russia* (New York, 1947).

PARKER, H. M. D., *Manpower: A Study of War-Time Policy and Administration* (London, 1957).

PATON, WILLIAM, *The Church and the New Order* (London, July, 1941).

PECH, KARLHEINZ, *An der Seite der Résistance: Zum Kampf der Bewegung 'Freies Deutschland' für den Westen in Frankreich (1943–1945)* (East Berlin, 1974).

PECHEL, RUDOLF, *Deutscher Widerstand* (Erlenbach-Zurich, 1947).

PENTZLIN, HEINZ, *Hjalmar Schacht: Leben und Wirken einer umstrittenen Persönlichkeit* (Berlin, 1980).

PERSICO, JOSEPH H., *Piercing the Third Reich: The Penetration of Nazi Germany by American Secret Agents During World War II* (New York, 1979).

PETERSEN, JENS, *Hitler–Mussolini: Die Entstehung der Achse Berlin—Rom 1933–1936* (Tübingen, 1973).

PINCHER, CHAPMAN, *Their Trade is Treachery* (London, 1981).

POGUE, FORREST C., *The Supreme Command (The United States in World War II: The European Theater of Operations)* (Washington, DC, 1954).

*Problems of the Pacific, 1939*, ed. Kate Mitchell and W. L. Holland (New York, 1940).

RADKAU, JOACHIM, *Die deutsche Emigration in den USA: Ihr Einfluss auf die amerikanische Europapolitik* (Düsseldorf, 1971).

REED, DOUGLAS, *The Prisoner of Ottawa: Otto Strasser* (London, 1953).

*Resistance in Europe 1939–1945* (Harmondsworth, 1976).

REYNOLDS, NICHOLAS E., *Treason Was No Crime: Ludwig Beck, Chief of the German General Staff* (London, 1976).

RIBBENTROP, ANNELIES VON, *Deutsch-englische Geheimverbindungen: Britische Dokumente der Jahre 1938 und 1939 im Lichte der Kriegsschuldfrage* (Wuppertal, 1967).

—— *Die Kriegsschuld des Widerstandes: Aus britischen Geheimdokumenten 1938/39*, ed. Rudolf von Ribbentrop (2nd edn., Leoni am Starnbergersee, 1975).

RINGS, WERNER, *Life with the Enemy: Collaboration and Resistance in Hitler's Europe 1939–1945* (New York, 1982).

RITTER, GERHARD, *Carl Goerdeler und die deutsche Widerstandsbewegung* (Stuttgart, 1955) [Ritter, *Carl Goerdeler*].

—— *The German Resistance: Carl Goerdeler's Struggle against Tyranny* (London, 1958).

RÖDER, WERNER, *Die deutschen sozialistischen Exilgruppen in Grossbritannien 1940–1945: Ein Beitrag zur Geschichte des Widerstandes gegen den Nationalsozialismus* (2nd edn., Bonn–Bad Godesberg, 1973).

ROON, GER VAN, *Neuordnung im Widerstand. Der Kreisauer Kreis innerhalb der deutschen Widerstandsbewegung* (Munich, 1967) [van Roon, *Neuordnung*].

—— *Wilhelm Stähle: Ein Leben auf der Grenze 1877–1945* (Munich, 1969).

——*German Resistance to Hitler: Count von Moltke and the Kreisau Circle* (London, 1971).

—— *Widerstand im Dritten Reich: Ein Überblick* (Munich, 1979).

—— *Zwischen Neutralismus und Solidarität: Die evangelischen Niederlande und der deutsche Kirchenkampf 1933–1942* (Stuttgart, 1983).

—— (ed.), *Helmuth James Graf von Moltke: Völkerrecht im Dienste der Menschen* (Berlin, 1986).

ROOSEVELT, ELLIOTT, *As He Saw It* (New York, 1946).

ROSE, NORMAN, *Vansittart: Study of a Diplomat* (London, 1978).

*The Rote Kapelle: The CIA's History of Soviet Intelligence and Espionage Networks in Western Europe, 1936–1945* (Washington, DC, 1979).

ROTHFELS, HANS, *The German Opposition to Hitler: An Appraisal* (Hinsdale, Ill., 1948).

—— *Die deutsche Opposition gegen Hitler: Eine Würdigung* (Frankfurt/M., 1958).

—— *Die deutsche Opposition gegen Hitler: Eine Würdigung* (rev. edn., Frankfurt/M., 1969).

—— *The German Opposition to Hitler: An Assessment* (London, 1970).

ROUSE, RUTH, and NEILL, STEVEN CHARLES (eds.), *A History of the Ecumenical Movement 1517–1948* (2nd edn., Philadelphia, 1968).

ROWSE, A. L., *All Souls and Appeasement: A Contribution to Contemporary History* (London, 1961).

SCHALL-RIAUCOUR, Gräfin HEIDEMARIE VON, *Aufstand und Gehorsam: Offizierstum und Generalstab im Umbruch: Leben und Wirken von Generaloberst Franz Halder* (Wiesbaden, 1972).

SCHÄRF, ADOLF, *Österreichs Erneuerung 1945–1955* (Vienna, 1955).

SCHEURIG, BODO, *Ewald von Kleist-Schmenzin: Ein Konservativer gegen Hitler* (Oldenburg, 1968).

—— *Free Germany: The National Committee and the League of German Officers* (Middletown, Conn., 1969).

—— (ed.), *Verrat hinter Stacheldraht? Das Nationalkomitee 'Freies Deutschland' und der Bund Deutscher Offiziere in der Sowjetunion 1943–1945* (Munich, 1965).

—— *Henning von Tresckow. Eine Biographie* (Oldenburg, 1973).

—— *Walther von Seydlitz-Kurzbach: General im Schatten Stalingrads* (Berlin, 1983).

SCHLABRENDORFF, FABIAN VON, *Offiziere gegen Hitler* (Zurich, 1946).

—— *Eugen Gerstenmaier im Dritten Reich* (Stuttgart, 1965).

—— *The Secret War against Hitler* (London, 1966).

—— *Begegnungen in fünf Jahrzehnten* (Tübingen, 1979).

SCHMÄDEKE, JÜRGEN, and STEINBACH, PETER (eds.), *Der Widerstand gegen den Nationalsozialismus: Die deutsche Gesellschaft und der Widerstand gegen Hitler* (Munich, 1985).

SCHMIDT, GUSTAV, *England in der Krise: Grundlagen und Grundzüge der britischen Appeasement-Politik (1930–1937)* (Wiesbaden, 1981).

SCHMITTHENNER, WALTER, and BUCHHEIM, HANS (eds.), *Der deutsche Widerstand gegen Hitler* (Cologne, 1966).

SCHOENHALS, KAI P. *The Free Germany Movement: A Case of Patriotism or Treason?* (New York, 1989).

SCHOLDER, KLAUS (ed.), *Die Mittwochs-Gesellschaft: Protokolle aus dem geistigen Deutschland 1932 bis 1944* (Berlin, 1982).

SCHOLL, INGE, *Die weisse Rose* (Frankfurt/M., 1955).

SCHÖLLGEN, GREGOR, *Ulrich von Hassell 1881–1944: Ein Konservativer in der Opposition* (Munich, 1990).

SCHRAMM, WILHELM RITTER VON, *Conspiracy among the Generals* (London, 1956).

SCHULTZ, HANS JÜRGEN (ed.), *Der 20. Juli. Alternative zu Hitler?* (Stuttgart, 1974).

SCHULZ, GERHARD (ed.), *Geheimdienste und Widerstandsbewegungen im Zweiten Weltkrieg* (Göttingen, 1982).

SCHULZE, HAGEN, *Otto Braun oder Preussens demokratische Sendung: Eine Biographie* (Frankfurt/M., 1977).

SCOTT, Lady DRUSILLA, A. D., *Lindsay: A Biography* (Oxford, 1971).

SEABURY, PAUL, *The Wilhelmstrasse: A Study of German Diplomats under the Nazi Regime* (Berkeley, Calif., 1954).

SEALE, PATRICK, and MCCONVILLE, MAUREEN, *Philby: The Long Road to Moscow* (New York, 1973).

*The Secret War Report of the OSS*, ed. Anthony Cave Brown (New York, 1976).

SHEEAN, VINCENT, *Dorothy and Red* (Boston, 1963).

SHEPHERD, NAOMI, *Wilfrid Israel: German Jewry's Secret Ambassador* (London, 1984).

SHERWOOD, ROBERT E., *Roosevelt and Hopkins: An Intimate History* (New York, 1948).

SIMPSON, AMOS E., *Hjalmar Schacht in Perspective* (The Hague, 1969).

464 *Bibliography*

SLACK, KENNETH, *George Bell* (London, 1971).

SMITH, ARTHUR L. Jr., *Churchill's German Army: Wartime Strategy and Cold War Politics, 1943–1944* (Beverly Hills, Calif., 1977).

SMITH, BRADLEY F., *The Shadow Warriors: OSS and the Origins of the CIA* (New York, 1983).

SMITH, GADDIS, *American Diplomacy during the Second World War 1941–1945* (New York, 1965).

SMITH, R. HARRIS, *OSS: The Secret History of America's First Intelligence Agency* (New York, 1972).

SONTAG, RAYMOND JAMES, and BEDDIE, JAMES STUART, *Nazi-Soviet Relations 1939–1941* (New York, 1948).

STAFFORD, DAVID, *Britain and European Resistance 1940–1945: A Survey of the Special Operations Executive, with Documents* (Toronto, 1980).

STAHLBERGER, PETER, *Der Züricher Verleger Emil Opitz und die deutsche politische Emigration 1933–1945* (Zurich, 1970).

STEINER, ZARA, *The Foreign Office and Foreign Policy 1898–1914* (Cambridge, 1969).

STEINERT, MARLIS, *Hitlers Krieg und die Deutschen: Stimmung und Haltung der deutschen Bevölkerung im Zweiten Weltkrieg* (Düsseldorf, 1970).

STELTZER, THEODOR, *Von deutscher Politik* (Frankfurt/M., 1949).

STEVENSON, LILIAN, *Max Josef Metzger: Priest und Martyr* (London, 1952).

STOLPE, SVEN, *Eivind Berggrav Bischof von Norwegen* (Munich, 1951).

STRAUCH, RUDI, *Sir Nevile Henderson: Britischer Botschafter in Berlin von 1937 bis 1939, Ein Beitrag zur diplomatischen Vorgeschichte des Zweiten Weltkrieges* (Bonn, 1959).

STREIT, CHRISTIAN, *Keine Kameraden: Die Wehrmacht und die sowjetischen Kriegsgefangenen 1941–1945* (Stuttgart, 1978).

STUTTERSHEIM, KURT VON, *Die Majestät des Geistes: In Memoriam Albrecht Bernstorff* (Hamburg, 1962).

SYKES, CHRISTOPHER, *Troubled Loyalty: A Biography of Adam von Trott zu Solz* (London, 1968).

TAUBER, KURT P., *Beyond Eagle and Swastica: German Nationalism since 1945*, 2 vols. (Middletown, Conn., 1967).

TAYLOR, TELFORD, *Munich: The Price of Peace* (New York, 1979).

THIELENHAUS, MARION, *Zwischen Anpassung und Widerstand: Deutsche Diplomaten 1938–1941, Die politischen Aktivitäten der Beamtengruppe um Ernst von Weizsäcker im Auswärtigen Amt* (Paderborn, 1984).

THOMPSON, NEVILLE, *The Anti-Appeasers: Conservative Opposition to Appeasement in the 30s* (Oxford, 1971).

THOMSEN, ERICH, *Deutsche Besatzungspolitik in Dänemark 1940–1945* (Düsseldorf, 1971).

THUN-HOHENSTEIN, Graf VON, *Der Verschwörer: General Oster und die Militäropposition* (Munich, 1984).

TREVOR-ROPER, HUGH, *The Philby Affair: Espionage, Treason and Secret Services* (London, 1968).

VANSITTART, Lord, *Black Record: Germans Past and Present* (London, 1941).

VOIGT, JOHANNES, *Indien im Zweiten Weltkrieg* (Stuttgart, 1978).

*Vollmacht des Gewissens*, ed. Europäische Publikation e.V., 2 vols. (Frankfurt/M., 1960, 1965).

WAGNER, WALTER, *Der Volksgerichtshof im nationalsozialistischen Staat* (Stuttgart, 1974).

WANDYCZ, PIOTR S., *France and her Eastern Allies 1919–1925: French–Czechoslovak–Polish Relations from the Paris Peace Conference to Locarno* (Minneapolis, 1962).

*The War Reports of General of the Army George C. Marshall, General of the Army H. H. Arnold, Fleet Admiral Ernest J. King* (Philadelphia, 1947).

WARK, WESLEY K., *The Ultimate Enemy: British Intelligence and Nazi Germany, 1933–1939* (Ithaca, NY, 1985).

WARNBRUNN, WERNER, *The Dutch under German Occupation 1940–1945* (Stanford, Calif., 1963).

WATT, DONALD CAMERON, *Britain looks to Germany* (London, 1965).

—— *Too Serious a Business: European Armed Forces and the Approach to the Second World War* (London, 1973).

WEINBERG, GERHARD L., *The Foreign Policy of Hitler's Germany: Starting World War II, 1937–1939* (Chicago, 1980).

WEISENBORN, GUNTHER, *Der lautlose Aufstand* (Hamburg, 1962).

WELLES, SUMNER, *The Time of Decision* (New York, 1944).

WENDT, BERND-JÜRGEN, *München 1838. England zwischen Hitler und Preussen* (Frankfurt/M., 1965).

—— *Appeasement 1938: Wirtschaftliche Rezession und Mitteleuropa* (Frankfurt/M., 1966).

—— *Economic Appeasement: Handel und Finanz in der britischen Deutschlandpolitik 1933–1939* (Düsseldorf, 1971).

WEST, NIGEL, *MI6: British Secret Intelligence Service Operations 1909–45* (New York, 1983).

WHEELER-BENNETT, JOHN W., *The Nemesis of Power: The German Army in Politics 1918–1945* (London, 1954).

—— and NICHOLLS, ANTHONY, *The Semblance of Peace: The Political Peace Settlement after the Second World War* (London, 1972).

WILMOT, CHESTER, *The Struggle for Europe* (New York, 1952).

WINKLER, ALLAN M., *The Politics of Propaganda: The Office of War Information 1942–1945* (New Haven, Conn., 1978).

WOODWARD, Sir ERNEST LLEWELLYN, *British Foreign Policy in the Second World War*, 2 vols. (London, 1970, 1971).

YAHIL, LENI, *The Rescue of Danish Jewry: Test of a Democracy* (Philadelphia, 1969).

YOUNG, ROBERT, *In Command of France: French Foreign Policy and Military Planning, 1933–1940* (Cambridge, Mass., 1978).

ZELLER, EBERHARD, *Der Geist der Freiheit: Der zwanzigste Juli* (Munich, 1963).

—— *The Flame of Freedom: The German Struggle Against Hitler* (London, 1967).

ZIMMERMANN, WOLF DIETER, and SMITH, RONALD GREGOR (eds.), *I Knew Dietrich Bonhoeffer* (London, 1966).

466                                   *Bibliography*

*Dissertations*

HAMPSON, M. DAPHNE, 'The British Response to the German Church Struggle 1933–1939' (Oxford University, 1973).

HOLLAND, CAROL SUE, 'The Foreign Contacts Made by the German Opposition to Hitler' (University of Pennsylvania, 1967).

MALONE, HENRY O., Jr., 'Adam von Trott zu Solz: The Road to Conspiracy Against Hitler' (University of Texas at Austin, May 1980).

MIRBT, KARL-WOLFGANG, 'Methoden Publizistischen Widerstandes im Dritten Reich nachgewiesen an der "Deutschen Rundschau" Rudolf Pechels' (Free University, Berlin, 1958).

THUN-HOHENSTEIN, Reichsgraf ROMEDIO VON, 'Hans Oster: Versuch einer Lebensbeschreibung' (Christian-Albrechts University, Kiel, 1980).


*Essays, Articles in Periodicals and Newspapers*

'The Appeasers of 1939', *Manchester Guardian Weekly*, 31 May 1956.

ASTOR, DAVID, 'Von Trott's Mission: The Story of an Anti-Nazi', *Manchester Guardian* , 4 June 1956.

—— 'Why the Revolt Against Hitler was Ignored', *Encounter*, 32 (June 1969), 3–13.

—— 'The Man Who Plotted Against Hitler', *New York Review*, 28 Apr. 1983, 16–21.

AUSTAD, TORLEIV, 'Eivind Berggrav and the Church of Norway's Resistance against Nazism, 1940–1945', *Mid-Stream. An Ecumenical Journal*, 26 (Jan. 1987), 51–61.

BALDWIN, HANSON, 'Churchill was Right', *Atlantic*, 194 (July 1954), 23–32.

BARTEL, WALTER, 'Die deutsche Widerstandsbewegung und die Alliierten zur Zeit des Zweiten Weltkrieges', *Zeitschrift für Geschichtswissenschaft*, 5 (1961), 993–1013.

BAUM, WALTER, 'Marine, Nationalsozialismus und Widerstand', *VfZ*, 11 (Jan. 1963), 16–48.

BAUMGART, WINFRED, 'Zur Ansprache Hitlers vor den Führern der Wehrmacht am 22. August 1939. Eine quellenkritische Untersuchung', *VfZ*, 16 (Apr. 1968), 120–49.

BAYNE, E. A., 'Resistance in the Foreign Office', *Human Events*, 3 (3 Apr. 1946), 1–8.

BECKER, JOSEF, 'Der Vatikan und die II. Weltkrieg', in Albrecht, Dieter (ed.), *Katholische Kirche im Dritten Reich* (Mainz, 1976), 171–93.

(BELL) GEORGE CICESTR (Chichester), 'The Background of the Hitler Plot', *The Contemporary Review*, 168 (Oct. 1945), 203–8.

—— 'Die Ökumene und die innerdeutsche Opposition', *VfZ*, 5 (Oct. 1957), 362–78.

BELOFF, MAX, 'Reflections on Intervention', *Journal of International Affairs*, 22 (1968), 198–207.

BENZ, WOLFGANG, 'Eine liberale Widerstandsgruppe und ihre Ziele: Hans Robinsohns Denkschrift aus dem Jahre 1939', *VfZ*, 29 (July 1981), 437–71.

BETHGE, EBERHARD, 'Adam von Trott und der deutsche Widerstand', *VfZ*, 11 (July 1963), 213–23.

—— 'Turning Points in Bonhoeffer's Life and Thought', *Union Seminary Quarterly Review*, 22 (autumn 1967), 3–21.

BORCH, HERBERT VON, 'Obrigkeit und Widerstand', *VfZ*, 3 (July 1955), 297–310.

BROWNING, CHRISTOPHER R., 'Unterstaatssekretär Martin Luther and the Ribbentrop Foreign Office', *Journal of Contemporary History*, 12 (Apr. 1977), 313–44.

BRUNNER, EMIL, 'Zum Zeugnis für Dr. Gerstenmaier', *Neue Züricher Zeitung*, 22 July 1945.

CHADWICK, OWEN, 'The English Bishops and the Nazis', Friends of Lambeth Palace Library, *Annual Report*, 1973.

CHASE, JOHN L., 'Unconditional Surrender Reconsidered', *Political Science Quarterly*, 70 (1955), 258–79.

COBB, RICHARD, 'A Personal State of War', *Times Literary Supplement*, 10 Mar. 1978.

COLEMAN, ARCHIBALD FREDERICK, 'Snapdragon: Story of a Spy', *Metro: The Magazine of Southeastern Virginia*, 7 (May 1977), 24–31, 64–9.

CROSSMAN, RICHARD H. S., 'Third Man as Hero', *Observer Review*, 24 Nov. 1968.

DAHM, KARL-WILHELM, 'German Protestantism and Politics 1918–39', *Journal of Contemporary History*, 3 (Jan. 1968), 29–49.

'Documents on Allen Dulles's Secret Negotiations with the Nazis in 1943', *New Times* (Moscow), July 1960.

DOHNANYI, KLAUS VON, 'Widerstand und Menschenrechte', *Die Zeit*, 28 July 1978.

(EARLE, GEORGE), 'Papen Offered to Betray Hitler, Earle Asserts in Defending Intercession', *Philadelphia Inquirer*, 30 Jan. 1949.

ERSIL, WILHELM, 'Das aussenpolitische Programm der militärischen Verschwörung vom 20. Juli 1944', *Deutsche Aussenpolitik*, 7 (1959), 743–58.

FIELDHOUSE, NOEL, 'The Anglo-German War of 1939–1942: Some Movements to End it by a Negotiated Peace', *Transactions of the Royal Society of Canada*, 9 (1971), 285–312.

FLEISCHHAUER, INGEBORG, 'Mit Todesmut gegen den Krieg. Zum 20. Juli 1944: Graf Schulenburg wollte mit Stalin über einen Sonderfrieden verhandeln', *Die Zeit*, 22 July 1988.

GERSTENMAIER, EUGEN, 'Zur Geschichte des Umsturzversuchs vom 20. Juli 1944', *Neue Züricher Zeitung*, 23, 24 June 1945.

—— 'Das Kirchliche Aussenamt im Reiche Hitlers', 'Zum Gedenken an Hans Schönfeld', in Gerstenmaier, Eugen, *Reden und Aufsätze* (Stuttgart, 1962), 307–18, 421–7.

—— 'Der Kreisauer Kreis. Zu dem Buch Gerrit van Roons "Neuordnung im Widerstand"', *VfZ*, 15 (July 1967), 221–46.

GLENTHØJ, JØRGEN, 'Dietrich Bonhoeffer und die Ökumene', in Eberhard Bethge (ed.), *Die Mündige Welt*, ii (Munich, 1956), 116–203.

—— 'Dietrich Bonhoeffer vor Kaltenbrunner', *Evangelische Theologie*, 26 (1966), 462–99.

—— 'Dokumate zur Bonhoeffer-Forschung 1928–1945', in Jørgen Glenthøj (ed.), *Die Mündige Welt*, v (Munich, 1969), 260–355.

GOLDMAN, AARON, 'Germans and Nazis: The Controversy over "Vansittartism" in Britain during the Second World War', *Journal of Contemporary History*, 14 (Jan. 1979), 155–91.

468 *Bibliography*

GRAHAM, ROBERT A., S I, 'L'uomo che tradì Ribbentrop', *La Civiltà Cattolica*, 137 (May 1986), 233–46.

GRAML, HERMANN, 'Der Fall Oster', *VfZ*, 14 (Jan. 1966), 26–39.

GRANTHAM, JOHN T., 'Hugh Dalton and The International Post-War Settlement: Labour Party Formulation, 1943–44', *Journal of Contemporary History*, 14 (Oct. 1979), 713–29.

HANKEY, Lord, 'Unconditional Surrender', *Contemporary Review*, 176 (Oct. 1949), 193–98.

HASSELL, ULRICH VON, 'Die Neuordnung im Südostraum', *Berliner Monatshefte* (1941), 601–11.

—— 'Ein neues europäisches Gleichgewicht?', *Auswärtige Politik*, 10 (Nov./Dec. 1943), 697–702.

HAUSER, OSWALD, 'England und der deutsche Widerstand 1938 im Spiegel britischer Akten', in Dollinger, Heinz, Gründer, Horst, and Hauschmidt, Alwin (eds.), *Weltpolitik, Europagedanke, Regionalismus* (Münster, 1982), 509–27.

HILDEBRAND, KLAUS, 'Die ostpolitischen Vorstellungen im deutschen Widerstand', *Geschichte in Wissenschaft und Unterricht*, 29 (1978), 213–41.

HILDEBRANDT, RAINER, 'Er sah die Wirklichkeit und hoffte auf die Zukunft. Zum 50. Geburtstag von Albrecht Haushofer', *Die Neue Zeitung*, 7 Jan. 1953.

HILL, LEONIDAS E., 'The Vatican Embassy of Ernst von Weizsäcker, 1943–1945', *Journal of Modern History*, 39 (June 1967), 138–59.

—— 'The Wilhelmstrasse in the Nazi Era', *Political Science Quarterly*, 82 (Dec. 1967), 546–70.

—— 'Three Crises, 1938–1939', *Journal of Contemporary History*, 3 (Jan. 1968), 113–44.

—— 'Towards a New History of the German Resistance to Hitler', *Central European History*, 14 (Dec. 1981), 369–99.

HILLGRUBER, ANDREAS, 'England in Hitlers aussenpolitischer Konzeption', *Historische Zeitschrift*, 218 (Feb. 1974), 65–84.

HOCH, ANTON, 'Das Attentat auf Hitler im Münchner Bürgerbräukeller 1939', *VfZ*, 17 (Oct. 1969), 383–413.

HOFFMANN, PETER, 'War Stauffenberg "ostorientiert"?', *Die Zeit*, 29 Dec. 1978.

—— 'Peace through Coup d'État: The Foreign Contacts of the German Resistance 1933–1944', *Central European History*, 19 (Mar. 1986), 3–44.

—— 'Colonel Claus von Stauffenberg in the German Resistance to Hitler: Between East and West', *Historical Journal*, 31 (Sept. 1988), 629–50.

HÜTTENBERGER, PETER, 'Vorüberlegungen zum "Widerstandsbegriff"', in Kocka, Jürgen (ed.), *Theorien in der Praxis des Historikers* (Göttingen, 1977), 117–34.

JONCA, KAROL, 'The Foreign Contacts of the Kreisau Circle in Contemporary Polish Opinion (1938–1944)', *Polish Western Affairs*, 1 (1988), 3–19.

KENNAN, GEORGE F., 'Noble Man: Helmuth von Moltke: A Leader against Hitler', *New York Review*, 22 Mar. 1973.

KENNEDY, PAUL, 'Approaching with Caution', *Times Literary Supplement*, 10 June 1983.

KENT, GEORGE O., 'Pope Pius XII and Germany: Some Aspects of German-Vatican Relations 1933–1943', *American Historical Review*, 70 (Oct. 1964), 59–78.

KEYSERLINGK, ROBERT, 'Die deutsche Komponente in Churchills Strategie der nationalen Erhebungen 1940–1942: Der Fall Otto Strasser', *VfZ*, 31 (Oct. 1983), 614–45.

KLEIST-RETZOW, HANS JÜRGEN VON, and SCHLABRENDORFF, FABIAN VON, 'Landesverrat?', *Deutsche Rundschau*, 84 (Oct. 1958), 927–32.

KLEMPERER, KLEMENS VON, 'A Kind of Resistance', *Times Literary Supplement*, 17 Feb. 1976.

—— 'Glaube, Religion, Kirche und der deutsche Widerstand gegen den Nationalsozialismus', *VfZ*, 28 (July 1980), 293–309.

—— 'Adam von Trott zu Solz and Resistance Foreign Policy', *Central European History*, 14 (Dec. 1981), 351–61.

KNAPP, THOMAS A., 'Heinrich Brüning im Exil: Briefe an Wilhelm Sollmann 1940–1946', *VfZ*, 22 (Jan. 1974), 93–120.

KOCH, H. W., 'The Spectre of a Separate Peace in the East: Russo-German "Peace Feelers", 1942–44', *Journal of Contemporary History*, 10 (July 1975), 531–49.

KORDT, THEO, 'Wir wollten den Frieden retten', *Stuttgarter Rundschau*, 8 (1948), 11–13.

KRAUSNICK, HELMUT, 'Deutscher Widerstand und englische Kriegserklärung', 'Aus Politik und Zeitgeschichte', B1/56, *Das Parlament*, 4 Jan. 1956.

—— and GRAML, HERMANN, 'Der deutsche Widerstand und die Alliierten', 'Aus Politik und Zeitgeschichte', *Das Parlament*, 19 July 1961.

LEIBER, ROBERT, S J, 'Pius XII', *Stimmen der Zeit*, 163 (1958–9), 81–100.

(LEIBHOLZ, GERHARD) GERARD, S. H., 'Germany between West and East', *Fortnightly*, 158 (Oct. 1942), 255–62.

LEIBHOLZ, GERHART [sic] H., 'Ideology in the Post-War Policy of Russia and the Western Powers: The Study of a Contrast', *Hibbert Journal*, 42 (1944), 116–25.

LEVINE, HERBERT S., 'The Mediator: Carl J. Burckhardt's Efforts to Avert a Second World War', *Journal of Modern History*, 45 (Sept. 1973), 439–55.

LINDGREN, HENRIK, 'Adam von Trotts Reisen nach Schweden 1942–1944: Ein Beitrag zur Frage der Auslandsverbindungen des deutschen Widerstandes', *VfZ*, 18 (July 1970), 274–91.

LIPGENS, WALTER, 'European Federation in the Political Thought of the Resistance Movements during World War II', *Central European History*, 1 (Mar. 1968), 5–19.

—— 'Das Konzept regionaler Friedensorganisation. Resistance und europäische Einigungsbewegung', *VfZ*, 16 (Apr. 1968), 150–64.

LIPPMANN, WALTER, 'The Third Alternative', *New York Herald Tribune*, 10 Oct. 1939.

LOEWENFELD, ANDREAS F., 'The Free German Committee: A Historical Study', *The Review of Politics*, 14 (July 1952), 346–66.

LONSDALE BRYANS, J[AMES], 'Zur britischen amtlichen Haltung gegenüber der deutschen Widerstandsbewegung', *VfZ*, 1 (Oct. 1953), 347–51.

LUDLOW, PETER W., 'Bischof Berggrav zum deutschen Kirchenkampf', *Arbeiten zur Geschichte des Kirchenkampfes*, 26 (Göttingen, 1971), 221–58.

—— 'Papst Pius XII., die britische Regierung und die deutsche Opposition 1939/40', *VfZ*, 22 (July 1874), 299–341.

—— 'Scandinavia Between the Great Powers. Attempts at Mediation in the First Year of the Second World War', *Sartryck ur Historisk Tidskrift* (1974), 1–58.

—— 'The International Protestant Community in the Second World War', *Journal of Ecclesiastical History*, 29 (July 1978), 311–62.

MACDONALD, CALLUM A., 'Economic Appeasement and the German "Moderates" 1937–1939', *Past and Present*, 56 (Aug. 1972), 105–35.

—— 'The Venlo Affair', *European Studies Review*, 8 (Oct. 1978), 443–64.

MACKINNON, DONALD, 'Controversial Bishop Bell', *Listener*, 21 Dec. 1967.

MAIER, HEDWIG, 'Die SS und der 20. Juli 1944', *VfZ*, 14 (July 1966), 299–316.

MAKAROV, A. N., 'Berthold Schenk Graf von Stauffenberg', *Die Friedens-Warte*, 47 (1947), 360–5.

MALEY, ALEXANDER B. (Böker, Alexander), 'The Epic of the German Underground', *Human Events*, 3 (27 Feb. 1946), 1–8.

MANN, GOLO, 'Helmuth James von Moltke', *Journal of European Studies* 4 (Dec. 1974), 368–89.

MARTENS, STEFAN, 'Hermann Göring: Der "Zweite Mann" im Dritten Reich?', in *Francia: Forschungen zur Westeuropäischen Geschichte* (Sigmaringen, 1985), 473–90.

MASTNY, VOJTECH, 'Stalin and the Prospects of a Separate Peace in World War II', *American Historical Review*, 77 (Dec. 1972), 1365–88.

METZMACHER, HELMUT, 'Deutsch-englische Ausgleichsbemühungen im Sommer 1939', *VfZ*, 14 (Oct. 1966), 369–412.

MICHALKA, WOLFGANG, 'Widerstand oder Landesverrat? Die antifaschistische Opposition als Problem der Forschung', *Militärgeschichtliche Mitteilungen*, 21 (1977), 207–14.

MINUTH, KARL-HEINZ, 'Sowjet-deutsche Friedenskontakte', *Geschichte in Wissenschaft und Unterricht*, 16 (1965), 38–45.

MOLTMANN, GÜNTHER, 'Die Genesis der Unconditional-Surrender-Foderung', in Hillgruber, Andreas (ed.), *Probleme des Zweiten Weltkrieges* (Berlin, 1967), 171–98.

MOMMSEN, HANS, 'Gesellschaftsbild und Verfassungspläne des deutschen Widerstandes', in Walter Schmitthenner and Hans Buchheim (eds.), *Der deutsche Widerstand gegen Hitler* (Cologne, 1966).

MORGAN, EDWARD P., 'The Spy the Nazis Missed' (Fritz Kolbe), in Dulles, Allen Welsh, *Great True Spy Stories* (New York, 1968), 21–9.

MÜLLER, KLAUS-JÜRGEN, 'Clausewitz, Ludendorff and Beck: Some Remarks on Clausewitz' Influence on German Military Thinking in the 1930s and 1940s', *Journal of Strategic Studies*, 9 (June-Sept. 1986), 240–66.

NAMIER, Sir LEWIS B., 'A German Diplomatist', *Times Literary Supplement*, 1 June 1951.

—— 'Resisters after the Event', *History Today*, 1 (June 1951), 13–22.

GOTTFRIED NIEDHART, 'Appeasement: die britische Antwort auf die Krise des Weltreichs und des internationalen Systems vor dem Zweiten Weltkrieg', *Historische Zeitschrift*, 226 (Feb. 1978), 67–88.

PAETEL, KARL OTTO, 'Zum Problem einer deutschen Exilregierung', *VfZ*, 4 (July 1956), 286–301.

PEZET, ERNEST, 'Contre Hitler et la guerre: Une mission secrète du chancelier Wirth à Paris (Avril 1940)', *Revue Politique et Parlementaire*, 224 (Apr. 1958), 289–305.

RITTER, GERHARD, 'The Foreign Relations of the Anti-Hitler Plot in Germany', in 'Record of General Meeting held at Chatham House' (London, 31 Oct. 1949).

—— 'Die aussenpolitischen Hoffnungen der Verschwörer des 20. Juli 1944', *Merkur*, 3 (Nov. 1949), 1121–38.

—— 'Der Gegensatz zwischen Ost und West in den aussenpolitischen Plänen der deutschen Widerstandsbewegung', 'Aus Politik und Zeitgeschichte', BL/54, *Das Parlament*, 1954, 664–7.

RÖDER, WERNER, 'Deutscher Widerstand im Ausland: Zur Geschichte des politischen Exils 1933–1945', 'Aus Politik und Zeitgeschichte', B31/80, *Das Parlament*, 2 Aug. 1980, 3–22.

ROIJEN, J. H. VAN, 'Adam von Trott in Holland', *Encounter*, 33 (Sept. 1969), 91.

ROMOSER, GEORGE K., 'The Politics of Uncertainty: The German Resistance Movement', *Social Research*, 31 (spring 1964), 73–93.

ROON, GER VAN, 'Oberst Wilhelm Staehle. Ein Beitrag zu den Auslandskontakten des deutschen Widerstandes', *VfZ*, 14 (Apr. 1966), 209–23.

—— 'Graf Moltke als Völkerrechtler im OKW', *VfZ*, 18 (Jan. 1970), 12–61.

—— 'Hermann Kaiser und der deutsche Widerstand', *VfZ*, 24 (July 1976), 259–86.

—— 'Der Kreisauer Kreis und das Ausland', 'Aus Politik und Zeitgeschichte', B 50/86, *Das Parlament*, 13 Dec. 1986.

ROTHFELS, HANS, 'Zwei aussenpolitische Memoranden der deutschen Opposition (Frühjahr 1942)', *VfZ*, 5 (Oct. 1957), 388–97.

—— 'Zur Krise des Nationalstaats', *VfZ*, 1 (Apr. 1953), 138–52.

—— 'The German Resistance in its International Aspects', in Record of General Meeting held at Chatham House (London, 14 Mar. 1958).

—— 'The German Resistance in its International Aspects', *International Affairs*, 34 (Oct. 1958), 477–89.

—— 'Adam von Trott und das State Department', *VfZ*, 7 (July 1959), 318–32.

—— 'Dokumentation. Trott und die Aussenpolitik des Widerstandes', *VfZ*, 12 (July 1964), 300–23.

SCHLABRENDORFF, FABIAN VON, 'Eugen Gerstenmaier im Dritten Reich: Eine Dokumentation', 'Aus Politik und Zeitgeschichte', B41/65, *Das Parlament*, 13 Oct. 1965.

SCHULZ, GERHARD, 'Über Johannes Popitz (1884–1945)', *Der Staat*, 24 (1985), 485–511.

SCHULZE, HAGEN, 'Rückblick auf Weimar: Ein Briefwechsel zwischen Otto Braun und Joseph Wirth im Exil', *VfZ*, 26 (Jan. 1978), 144–85.

STAFFORD, DAVID, 'Britain looks at Europe, 1940: Some Origins of SOE', *Canadian Journal of History*, 10 (Aug. 1975), 231–48.

—— 'The Detonator Concept: British Strategy, SOE and European Resistance After the Fall of France', *Journal of Contemporary History*, 10 (Apr. 1975), 185–217.

STEHLE, HANSJAKOB, 'Der Mann, der den Krieg verkürzen wollte' (Fritz Kolbe), *Die Zeit*, 2 May 1986.

STEINBACH, PETER, 'Ein Kämpfer, bereit, die Folgen auf sich zu nehmen' (Harro Schulze-Boysen), *Deutsches Allgemeines Sonntagsblatt*, 1 Sept. 1989.

STUBBE, WALTER, 'In Memoriam Albrecht Haushofer', *VfZ*, 8 (July 1960), 236–56.

SYKES, CHRISTOPHER, 'Heroes and Suspects: The German Resistance in Perspective', *Encounter*, 31 (Dec. 1938), 39–47.

THOMAS, General GEORG, 'Gedanken und Ereignisse', *Schweizer Monatshefte*, 25/9 (Dec. 1945), 537–59.

TREVOR-ROPER, HUGH, 'Admiral Canaris, the "Hamlet of Conservative Germany"', *Listener*, 12 June 1980.

VAGTS, ALFRED, 'Unconditional Surrender—vor und nach 1943', *VfZ*, 7 (July 1959), 280–309.

VANWELKENHUYZEN, JAN VAN, 'Die Niederlande und der "Alarm" im Januar 1940', *VfZ* 8 (Jan. 1960), 17–36.

VISSER'T HOOFT, WILLEM A., 'Bishop Bell's Life Work in the Ecumenical Movement', *Ecumenical Review*, 11 (Jan. 1959), 133–40.

—— 'The View from Geneva', *Encounter*, 33 (Sept. 1969), 92–4.

VOIGT, KLAUS, 'Die Genfer Föderalistentreffen im Frühjahr 1944', *Risorgimento* 1 (1980), 59–72.

WATT, D. C., 'Les Alliés et la Résistance Allemande (1939–1944)', *Revue d'Histoire de la Deuxième Guerre Mondiale (1939–1944)* (Oct. 1959), 65–86.

—— 'One Man's Opposition: Dr. Wirth's Anglo-French Contacts, 1939/40', *The Wiener Library Bulletin*, 16 (1962), 14.

WEGNER-KORFES, SIGRID, 'Der 20. Juli 1944 und das Nationalkomitee "Freies Deutschland"', *Zeitschrift für Geschichtswissenschaft*, 24 (1979), 535–44.

—— 'Graf von der Schulenburg—Mitverschwörer des 20. Juli 1944', *Zeitschrift für Geschichtswissenschaft*, 32 (1984), 681–99.

—— 'Friedrich Werner Graf von der Schulenburg: Botschafter Nazideutschlands in Moskau und Mitverschwörer des 20. Juli 1944', in Groehler, Olaf (ed.), *Alternativen* (East Berlin, 1987), 231–70.

—— 'Zu einigen Aspekten der Entwicklung des aussenpolitischen Programms der Verschwörer des 20. Juli 1944', *Bulletin des Arbeitskreises: Zweiter Weltkrieg*, ed. Zentralinstitut für Geschichte der Akademie der Wissenschaften der DDR.

WEINBERG, GERHARD L., 'Secret Hitler-Beneš Negotiations in 1936–37', *Journal of Central European Affairs*, 19 (Jan. 1960), 366–74.

WENDT, BERND-JÜRGEN, 'Konservative Honoratioren: Alternative zu Hitler? Englandkontakte des deutschen Widerstandes im Jahre 1938', in Stegemann, Dirk, Wendt, Bernd-Jürgen, and Witt, Peter Christian (eds.), *Deutscher Konservatismus im 19. und 20. Jahrhundert* (Bonn, 1983), 347–67.

WENGLER, WILHELM, 'H. J. Graf von Moltke (1906 [*sic*]–1945)', *Die Friedens-Warte*, 48 (1948), 297–305.

'Widerstand ist vaterländische Pflicht' (Aus den Akten des schwedischen Ministerium(s) des Äusseren), *Politische Studien*, 10 (July 1959), 435–9.

WILLS, GARRY, 'The CIA from Beginning to End', *New York Review*, 22 Jan. 1976.

ZERNER, RUTH, 'German Protestant Responses to Nazi Persecution of the Jews', in Braham, Randolph L. (ed.), *Perspectives on the Holocaust* (Boston, 1983), 57–68.

# INDEX

## DATE DUE

| | | | |
|---|---|---|---|
| | | | |
| | | | |
| | | | |
| | | | |
| | | | |
| | | | |
| | | | |
| | | | |
| | | | |
| | | | |
| | | | |
| | | | |
| | | | |
| | | | |
| | | | |